SAUL
BELLOW

THE MODERN JEWISH EXPERIENCE

Deborah Dash Moore and Marsha L. Rozenblit, editors

Paula Hyman, founding coeditor

SAUL BELLOW

"I Was a Jew and an American and a Writer"

—⁓—

Gerald Sorin

INDIANA UNIVERSITY PRESS

This book is a publication of

Indiana University Press
Office of Scholarly Publishing
Herman B Wells Library 350
1320 East 10th Street
Bloomington, Indiana 47405 USA

iupress.org

Manufactured in the United States of America

First Printing 2024

Library of Congress Cataloging-in-Publication Data

Names: Sorin, Gerald, author.
Title: Saul Bellow : "I was a Jew and an American and a writer" / Gerald Sorin.
Description: Bloomington, Indiana : Indiana University Press, 2024. | Series: The modern Jewish experience | Includes bibliographical references and index.
Identifiers: LCCN 2023049921 (print) | LCCN 2023049922 (ebook) | ISBN 9780253069436 (hardback) | ISBN 9780253069443 (paperback) | ISBN 9780253069450 (ebook)
Subjects: LCSH: Bellow, Saul. | Novelists, American—20th century—Biography. | Jewish authors—20th century—Biography. | Jews—Canada—Biography. | Jews—United States—Intellectual life—20th century. | LCGFT: Biographies.
Classification: LCC PS3503.E4488 Z8595 2024 (print) | LCC PS3503.E4488 (ebook) | DDC 813/.52 [B]—dc23/eng/20231026
LC record available at https://lccn.loc.gov/2023049921
LC ebook record available at https://lccn.loc.gov/2023049922

For Myra, forever

To be a Jew in the twentieth century
Is to be offered a gift. If you refuse,
Wishing to be invisible, you choose
Death of the spirit, the stone insanity.
Accepting, take full life. Full agonies. . . .
The gift is torment. Not alone the still
Torture, isolation; or torture of the flesh.
That may come also. But the accepting wish,
The whole and fertile spirit as guarantee
For every human freedom, suffering to be free,
Daring to live for the impossible.

—Muriel Rukeyser, 1944

CONTENTS

ACKNOWLEDGMENTS

I AM INDEBTED TO MANY colleagues and friends who encouraged me to stay with the Saul Bellow project even as Zachary Leader's monumental two-volume biography on the great but regrettably neglected writer was being written and published between 2015 and 2018. Deborah Dash Moore, a good friend and supporter of all my work in Jewish studies since the late seventies, was, on this project, as on all the others, a truly careful and sensitive reader and more than generous with her time. Eli Gottlieb and Larry Carr read and reread the entire manuscript and offered valuable suggestions and many enjoyable hours of conversation about Bellow's novels. Robert Polito read important sections of my drafts after years of casual but pointed conversation about Bellow and postwar American fiction in general. Lewis Brownstein, a friend and erudite partner in conversation for several decades, shared insights and ideas about Trotskyism, Stalinism, and Bellow in Jerusalem. Richard Fein read several chapters, and over the years he and I spent countless hours on the phone sharing our mutual appreciation of Saul Bellow's writing and saturation in Jewishness. Rabbi William Strongin generously supplied advice and interpretation on matters Judaic, as did Rabbi Rena Blumenthal. None of the people cited above are in any way responsible for views expressed in this book or for any misstatement of fact.

I also appreciate the good advice and guidance I received from editors at Indiana University Press, including Anna C. Francis, Allison Gudenau, and David Hulsey and his colleagues in art and design.

Myra Sorin, my spouse, devoted partner, and special friend, has been so central in all my work and life during our more than sixty-year relationship that I can't find words adequate to thank her properly. But I owe her much for allowing Saul Bellow's spirit to share our space for more than seven years. And she read every draft and every chapter of the book as it developed and applied a patient, conscientious, and keen intelligence to every sentence, as well as a fine filter that prohibited jargon and the language of literary theory from sneaking onto the pages.

SAUL
BELLOW

INTRODUCTION

I WAS WARNED THAT WRITING a biography of Saul Bellow, who lived a long and prolific life as a novelist and won the Nobel Prize in Literature in 1976, "must be like taking a test you're doomed to flunk: 'Describe the life of a great self-describer.'"[1] I remained determined, however, to write a book about Bellow that was neither a detailed description nor a comprehensive biography. Zachary Leader in *The Life of Saul Bellow: To Fame and Fortune, 1915–1964* (2015) and *The Life of Saul Bellow: Love and Strife, 1965–2005* (2018) has done an outstanding job of that. His volumes, totaling 1,500 pages, copiously documented, meticulously synthesized, and elaborately constructed, make for a wide-ranging biography and will continue to prove vital as reference tools—as they did for me. There were several avenues open to a biographer like me who chose a subject about whom good, extensive work has already been done. One option was to pretend that Leader's two-volume biography and James Atlas's earlier *Bellow* (2000) did not exist and say little or nothing about them.[2] A second possibility was to attempt to surpass the first biographers, drowning readers in a tsunami of new archival evidence. These options proved to be impossible. Both biographers have done their homework. And Leader, in particular, has dug deeply into

Bellow's papers at the University of Chicago's Regenstein Library. He makes excellent use of the materials collected there and of the interviews he conducted with more than one hundred people in five countries. I chose a third way—writing a shorter book that makes no pretense to all-inclusiveness but instead looks at Bellow from a particular and fundamental perspective: the recognition that much of his creative power was shaped and informed by the fact that he was Jewish.[3]

Leader does recognize the powerful effect on Bellow of a deeply ingrained Jewish sensibility. But sometimes what he says about Bellow's Jewishness is lost in the welter of facts about the writer's general life and work, and important Jewish material about Bellow is occasionally relegated to mere footnotes. It is only there that we learn, for example, that Bellow, through his late adolescence, obeyed kashruth—Jewish dietary laws—and was in synagogue with his father every Shabbat.

We also learn, but only in the notes, that Mitzi McClosky (a close friend of Bellow's) said, "Saul was very deeply versed in Jewish history and religion." He taught her and her husband Herb "about Judaism, and to me," Mitzi fondly recalled, "he came off as the voice of the Prophets themselves. From him I learned to be proud of my heritage."[4] By relegating significant information like this to afterthoughts, Leader's biography effectively makes secondary a vital, indeed indispensable subject that is at the heart of my book: the exquisite, complex intricacy of Saul Bellow's Jewishness and its inextricable connection to his moral vision, his writing, and his never-ending pursuit of the spiritual.

There is enough in this book about Bellow's life to make it biographical. But it doesn't look too deeply for the writer's own life in his fictional figures. Bellow clearly exploited his own personal history and appropriated other people's experiences—even experiences he had heard about secondhand. But almost none of his material is strictly autobiographical. No matter how openly he borrowed from his and his friends' lives, all was magnificently transformed by Bellow's imagination.

His first novel, *Dangling Man* (1944), depicts the intellectual and emotional ambivalence of twenty-three-year-old Joseph, an aspiring writer who is out of work and struggling to understand himself, as well as the extent of his talent and the decline in the quality of his marriage. Meanwhile, he is waiting, in the winter of 1943, to hear from his draft board—voluntary enlistment having ended in December 1942, precisely when Joseph begins his journal. These details correspond almost exactly with facts in Bellow's life during the writing of *Dangling Man*. But they hardly stand alone, bereft of an invented context, and by themselves tell us little or nothing about the writer's life.

In a much more important instance of autobiographical reference, Bellow, obsessed with his mother Liza's untimely death (and from an early age with the idea of death generally), fictionalized his mother's story in *Herzog* (1964), using many real details of her decline and passing. Just as graphically, and with as much tenderness and reimagination, he did it again when he wrote of Charlie Citrine's mother in *Humboldt's Gift* (1975). Stories and details, seemingly plucked out of real life weave their way in and out of Bellow's novels. The writing, however, is "nothing like the cutting and pasting of actual events." Saul "wielded a wand not scissors," Janis Freedman Bellow said; and with this she cautioned, "Biographers, beware."[5]

Cynthia Ozick went so far as to say—not only in regard to Bellow but with his fiction uppermost in mind—"When it comes to novels, the author's life is nobody's business. A novel, even when it is autobiographical, is not an autobiography. If the writer himself, breaks the news that such and such a character is actually so and so in real life, readers still have an obligation—fiction's enchanted obligation—to shut their ears and turn away—Fiction is subterranean, not terrestrial."[6]

Bellow was the keenest of observers and was widely acclaimed as *the* genius at making art out of life. David Mikics's *Bellow's People* does a splendid job of describing this alchemy and takes us through perfect examples of Bellow's dazzling creativity, persuasively demonstrating that his characters, even if some of their traits and experiences match his own or those of his friends and relatives, are unquestionably inventions.[7]

No matter how much is imagined, however, Bellow's fiction is replete with Jewish characters, Jewish sensibilities, and ethical concerns as well as the rhythms, nuances, and colorful idioms of the Yiddish language. It therefore reveals much about the nature, extent, and quality of his own Jewishness. Yet Bellow (along with Philip Roth, Bernard Malamud, and Cynthia Ozick, three other reigning masters of the craft) consistently resisted the label "Jewish writer."

Roth, furthest removed from the immigrant generation and Yiddishkeit, was appropriately annoyed by interviewers who insisted on asking him whether or not he was an American Jewish writer. That "epithet," he said, simply "has no meaning for me. If I'm not an American I'm nothing." Malamud, immersed in Old World Yiddish culture, when asked the same question said (also with some irritation) that he "conceived of himself as a cosmopolitan man enjoying his freedom." Ozick, whose Jewishness included some knowledge of Yiddish, religious study and ritual observance, and work on behalf of Israel, said that "gradually, it has come to me that the phrase 'Jewish writer' may be what rhetoricians call an 'oxymoron.'"[8]

Bellow tried to put the Jewish writer question to rest by claiming that "no good literature is parochial," but at the same time he insisted just as strongly that "all good literature has some color," along with some identifiable perspective, "because there is no such thing as a generalized human being."[9] Isaac Rosenfeld took Bellow's view one step further. He felt certain that his intense relationship to Jewish life gave him access to just the sort of marginal perspective to see things clearly. He denied that his views were "parochial" or any less cosmopolitan than his other concerns and interests. He argued that his intense, sometimes combative relationship to Jewish life did not hinder his understanding. Indeed, he asserted that he better understood the world because of his Jewish attachments, not despite them.[10]

Rosenfeld gave the straightest, clearest response to the Jewish writer question. But the other responses, abrupt or sly or complex and qualified, were not in any way a denial of the Jewishness in the life and work of these writers, nor were they an explicit rejection of their identity as Jews. Indeed, in a more patient moment, Roth, even as he was rejecting the "Jewish writer" tag, said, "I have always been pleased by my good fortune in being born a Jew. . . . It's [a] complicated, morally demanding, and very singular experience. I find myself in the historic predicament of being Jewish with all its implications. . . . Who could ask for anything more?"[11]

Similarly, Bellow admitted that much of his creative power came from his saturation in Jewishness at a time when he was most malleable. "That's a piece of good fortune," he reflected, "with which one doesn't quarrel." In addition, Bellow said, "to turn away from these origins, always seemed to me an utter impossibility. It would be a treason to my first consciousness."[12]

Essentially, Bellow's Jewishness, like Roth's, was "definitional without being delimiting."[13] He had "never consciously written as a Jew," he said, or tried to appeal to a particular community; he had "never thought of writing for Jews exclusively."[14] He repeatedly described himself as "an American of Jewish heritage." Adjectives characterizing or qualifying the label "writer" were an abomination to him: "When . . . people call [you] a 'Jewish Writer,'" Bellow said, "it's a way of setting you aside." He went even further, arguing persuasively that the Protestant majority, in response to the growing oeuvre of Jewish American fiction writers in the 1950s and 1960s, consciously separated Jewish writers from the universe of "real" writers—those "gatekeepers" with roots in the Old South or the WASP Northeast.[15]

Bellow also remained irritated by critics and the conventional wisdom that sewed him together with Roth and Malamud as the clothiers Hart, Schaffner, and Marx of Jewish literature. In a letter to Cynthia Ozick, he went so far as to call the "American Jewish Writer" label "repulsive." Yet he delighted in his Jewishness and was intensely interested in things Jewish; he also understood the desire or need of some American Jews to celebrate his many literary achievements, even if for them the art was secondary. But he very much wanted to be appreciated outside of the Jewish community as an unhyphenated American novelist.

And that Bellow was. Nevertheless, his Jewishness is recognizable in his multiple restatements of his ties to Jewish heritage in nonfiction essays, letters, and speeches. In his fiction, Bellow's "first consciousness" is even more radiantly reflected. As Marc Chagall said of his painting, Bellow could have said of his writing: "If I weren't a Jew . . . then I wouldn't be an artist, or at least not the one I am now." Indeed, one sees in Bellow's work the same exuberance, the same delight in the beauty of the world, as well as a sense of wonder about the world to come, as one sees in Chagall's glimmering canvases.[16]

Despite Bellow's demurs, then, and despite the secular, American quality of his work, there is no escaping the fact that his writing was profoundly rooted in his identity as a Jew—a much more important conclusion than anything one could say about the validity of calling Bellow a "Jewish writer." In the process and context of reaching that conclusion, I was especially careful not to read Jewishness into whatever Bellow or his characters say and do. This method was not without its problems. *Henderson the Rain King* (1959), for example, is about a Protestant multimillionaire pig farmer, a big man, gruff and violent. But some see Eugene Henderson as another "Bellow Jew in disguise"—hyperanimated, expressive, mournful, cerebral, and urbane.

Bellow emphatically denied Henderson's Jewishness but admitted that *The Rain King* was his favorite book and that Eugene Henderson, "the absurd seeker of higher qualities," was the character with whom he most identified.[17]

The renowned literary critic Alfred Kazin recognized the impact of Bellow's Jewishness on his writing and his power to absorb into his fiction "the modern Jewish experience." He said that even Bellow's few fictive non-Jews, such as the demonic, pathetic, yet comic Kirby Allbee in *The Victim* or the enormous, desperately unrestrained Eugene Henderson, are "wittily agonized definitions of human existence" who strongly resemble his Jewish protagonists.[18]

Whether Bellow, wittingly or not, made Henderson Jewish is of no great significance. More important by far is that one need not have been Jewish to read and resonate with what Bellow wrote in *The Rain King* or anywhere else. Bellow said he wanted to be seen as a writer who portrayed human beings some of whom happened to have "had a certain experience of life, which is in part Jewish." Here Bellow was being somewhat disingenuous, but at creating Jewish characters with powerful, universal appeal, he was strikingly successful.[19]

Even *Herzog*, arguably Bellow's most Jewish book, completed a run of forty-two weeks on the *New York Times* Best Seller list, holding the number-one spot for more than half a year. Bellow thought the book would sell fewer than 10,000 copies, but in less than a year it had sold 147,000 in hardback. *Herzog* went on to win the National Book Award in 1965 and became an international bestseller, earning many awards, including the Prix international de litterature.[20]

The commercial and critical success of *Herzog*, Bellow later believed, lay in its appeal "to the unconscious sympathies of many people." He knew, he said, from the mail he'd received that the book addressed a common predicament. It "appealed to Jewish readers," of course, but also "to those who have been divorced, to those who talk to themselves . . . to readers of paperbacks, autodidacts," and perhaps most important, to those who shared Moses Herzog's rejection of nihilism and inevitable doom, "to those who yet hope to live awhile."[21]

Born in 1915 to Russian Jewish immigrants who had arrived in Canada two years earlier, Bellow was raised in the small town—"a medieval" shtetl, he called it—of Lachine, Quebec, and then in an impoverished, predominantly Jewish, but heterogeneous section of Montreal until the age of nine.[22] He had a trilingual childhood that included Yiddish as well as English and French—and some Russian. Having memorized significant portions of the book of Genesis, Bellow also knew biblical Hebrew. But it was Yiddish and Yiddishkeit (the "stuff" of Yiddish culture) that continued to echo in Bellow's adult inner ear and permeate almost all of his writing, as did his childhood memories of the vital and vibrant Jewish life on Montreal's Napoleon and Dominique Streets, where he and his fictive Moses Herzog lived for a time.

Bellow's adolescence and young adult years were spent in the "somber, heavy, growling, lowbrow" city of Chicago. In this "colossal industrial and business center," brought to its knees by the Depression and its unusually high unemployment numbers, Bellow remembers making the "most impractical of choices": to be a writer, to be "the representative of beauty, the interpreter of the human heart, the hero of ingenuity, playfulness, personal freedom, generosity and love." This was, he wrote later, not "a bad sort of crackpot to be," even though in the 1930s the *mishigas* (craziness) of children was not encouraged or "subsidized by their families."[23]

Despite what his business-oriented, less educated brothers and father believed, Bellow was not deranged. He simply was ambitious and convinced—most of the time—that he was an enormously talented writer. He began to prove himself in the early forties with published short stories and went on to build a literary reputation with critically admired longer works of fiction.

His first novel, *Dangling Man,* influenced by the spirit of Dostoevsky and Turgenev, depicted the cerebral and spiritual vacillations of a young man trying to define "freedom" while waiting to be drafted. *The Victim* (1947), a more substantial novel, came soon after. Once again influenced by Dostoevsky, as well as Joseph Conrad, *The Victim* explores with the elegant precision of Flaubert a convoluted relationship between a Jew and a Gentile, as well as the themes of antisemitism, paranoia, and self-doubt, Jewish and otherwise, in postwar America.

Later, Saul Bellow found an altogether new and stunningly original voice with *The Adventures of Augie March* (1953). The famous first sentence reads in part, "I am an American, Chicago born . . . and go at things as I have taught myself, free-style, and will make the record in my own way: first to knock, first admitted." The novel, a picaresque story of a poor Jewish youth and his quest for self-understanding and place, is infused with brash, exuberant rhythms and idioms, not only Whitmanesque but also Yiddish. (Even as he was putting the finishing touches on *Augie March,* Bellow was helping translate Isaac Bashevis Singer's signature Yiddish story, "Gimpel the Fool," into English.)

Some have said that the widely quoted opening of *Augie* is Bellow's announcement that he is an American from the Midwest, ready to live "free-style" with no attachments to origins or heritage. But it is possible to tease out of the book's assertive announcement something different, more important and more interesting. The clenched fist is not only for knocking but also for making emphatic to wary Gentile writers what is implied here— "I'm that Jew who's been writing English as well as you and your traditional forebears, *and* 'I am an American' just as much as you are, perhaps more so."

Bellow declared himself "an American, Chicago born" but he had no desire, as he said many times, to "un-Jew" himself.[24] He would therefore be unable to escape being tagged a Jewish writer—though that alone hardly described him or any other

Jewish writer of the postwar period. With the critical and popular reception of *Augie March*, along with Norman Mailer's *The Naked and the Dead*, Bernard Malamud's *The Magic Barrel*, J. D. Salinger's *Catcher in the Rye*, and soon thereafter Philip Roth's *Goodbye, Columbus* and Grace Paley's *The Little Disturbances of Man*, Bellow represented the propulsion of Jewish writers into the world of mainstream American fiction in the 1950s.

There were some mumblings and even outright gripes about a Jewish monopoly of the "book business" by parts of the WASP literary establishment, including the well-known Truman Capote, Katherine Anne Porter, and Gore Vidal. But neither resentment nor jealousy nor antisemitism—explicit or genteel—could prevent Bellow's rise to prominence, which not only helped prepare the way for Philip Roth and many other American Jewish writers but also was part of the movement of Jews generally from the periphery to the center of American life.

In the post–World War II period, it was readily apparent that Jews had contributed mightily to the American experiment. For the children and grandchildren of Jewish immigrants from Eastern Europe, there had been an increase in prosperity and mobility—geographic and economic. Though still ethnically distinctive in their political behavior and liberal values, Jews, outside of insular orthodox religious communities, had achieved a near-complete identification as American middle class. They had proved themselves to be solid citizens in business, the labor movement, and the university, and in intellectual and aesthetic achievement as scientists, philosophers, artists, scholars, musicians, and writers. Many Jewish performers and comedians, too, along with the writers and intellectuals, were shapers of American popular culture, helping create the kind of urbanity, irony, and skepticism we take for granted in twenty-first-century America.

Jewish writers, appealing not only to Jews, were in abundant supply. I. B. Singer and his stories of the old country enjoyed an

American popularity greater than he had achieved in Eastern Europe, and authors such as Cynthia Ozick (*The Pagan Rabbi and Other Stories*), Edward Lewis Wallant (*The Pawnbroker*), and Joseph Heller (*Catch-22*) became familiar names, none more important and well known than Philip Roth and Saul Bellow. Most of the postwar American Jewish writers can be linked to one another, insofar as they use the American Jew as a "central symbolic feature" in the exploration of the American national character or soul. But without homogenizing the range of styles of these writers or flattening out the differences in the substance and meaning of their narratives, it is possible to say, as literary historian Frank McConnell does, that the Jewish writers often used the American Jew as a living test of the American dream—the outsider up against the ideal of truly universal equality and liberty.[25]

Of course, there are other outsiders represented in American literature; but the Jew, McConnell argues, most clearly Bellow's Jew, has a "special complexity," living within the heart of urban life in modernizing America, thriving but disaffected, accepting but not without a wry irony. The Jew is an "alien" but also "heir and incarnation of a moral and ethical heritage which is at the very origins of the civilization which rejects the Jew."[26]

Even as Bellow came to be seen as more mainstream, more "American," he remained distinctively Jewish, and he opened the door to a certain kind of American English sentence and Jewish prose others never really imagined possible. Philip Roth read *Augie March* in his junior year in college and said later that he had "never read anything like it before in [his] life, no one did." Who knew, he asked, that "you could write about Jews *like this*!" Just as Bellow realized that he didn't have to write like Flaubert and Dostoevsky, once he proved he could, Philip Roth discovered that "you didn't have to write like Joseph Conrad and Henry James." You could write about poor Jews, inarticulate Jews, plain Jews—"I could write about my Jews!" Roth said. Bellow had shown that "you could turn ordinary Jewish lives into literature."[27]

And you could do it with Yiddishkeit—not just Yiddish-tinged English but Yiddish itself. In Bellow's work there are untranslated Yiddish words and phrases ranging from *alehosholem* (may he or she rest in peace) to *shicker goy* (drunken Gentile) and from *hob es in drerd* (drop dead) to *mein zisse n'shamele* (my sweet little soul or gift of God); sometimes there are even whole Yiddish sentences.

The dynamic, comic, and lusty hybrid language that had become Bellow's literary signature is not only a combination of Yiddishisms and WASP speech—with idiosyncratic phrasing—but also the nuanced content and cadence of Hebrew scripture and the Christian Bible. The renowned critic James Wood calls Bellow's run-on sentences, unrestrained semantic mixtures, repetitions, gushing lyricism, and accretion of adjectives "a perfumed overflowing antique prose, all faithfully carried over from Hebrew into the King James Version, and down into Bellow's Yiddishly inflected works."[28]

We also have from Bellow, until even as late as his last published novel, *Ravelstein* (2000), large sections of explicit Jewish content as well as what the critic Irving Howe called the "characteristics" of Yiddish: "The jabbing interchange of ironies, the intimate vulgarities, the blend of sardonic and sentimental."[29] And throughout Bellow's prolific work, readers are supplied with reams of moral and philosophical speculation tied, even if at times obliquely, to Jewish tradition.

Mr. Sammler's Planet (1970), no matter how politically controversial it was at the end of the turbulent sixties, is a good example. Artur Sammler suffers the same rift in his psyche as do almost all of Bellow's Jewish protagonists, and he serves the author and his readers as a kind of literary model for the "passionate, modern conflicted self" searching for the American soul. The novel is a mirror held up to reflect the madness of the fragmented, shattered, unredeemed modern state of human existence, especially in the crisis and uncertainty of postwar America; and Sammler, a Polish-born Jewish immigrant and Holocaust survivor who occasionally feels "God adumbrations," enables us to see how deep a need there is to repair the world.[30]

Our era, Bellow said, "has been created by revolutions of all kinds—political, scientific, industrial. And now we have been freed by law from slavery in many of its historical, objective forms. The next move," Bellow insisted, "is up to us. Each of us has to find an inner law by which [to] live. Without this, objective freedom only destroys us. So, the question that really interests me is the question of *spiritual freedom in the individual*—the power to endure our own humanity."[31]

The modern world, Bellow knew, created the self, and with it the risk of filling that self with only the shallowest of interests and transactional distractions, especially the noise of commerce. In one of his many unsent letters, mulling over what he ought to tell President Eisenhower, Moses Herzog writes, "The life of every citizen is becoming a business. This it seems to me, is one of the worst interpretations of the meaning of human life history has ever seen. Man's life is not a business."[32]

The power to endure our own humanity is also undermined, Bellow argued, if modern writers and artists continue to promote alienation and nihilism, emptiness and valuelessness as the only legitimate moral and intellectual posture. Bellow repeatedly said in one form or another that in the post-Holocaust world of failed ideologies and collapsed systems, it may look as if we are at the edge of some deep and dark abyss; but he rejected the "conviction that the world is evil, that it must be destroyed" so that it will rise again in the form of a phoenix, purified.[33] Modern literature, Bellow said, would rather have "the maddest chaos" that it can summon rather than "a conception of life it has found false." But, inured against the phoenix metaphor, Bellow asked, "after this destruction what?"[34]

Humanity, Bellow contended, is not doomed to dissolution. In his interviews and essays and in his fiction, he reveals, often with great humor and delicious irony, an obligation of artists and writers like himself to defang the modernist architects of pain and suffering, of soullessness and despair. He especially named as guilty Nietzsche and Spengler, Céline and Robbe-Grillet, Eliot, Freud, Sartre, and Lawrence, all of whom questioned the idea of spiritual freedom in the individual.[35]

Bellow poured moral outrage on intellectuals for contributing to the spiritual bankruptcy of the West, but he declared that all need not be lost. While "the 'cure of souls'" isn't the business of writers, he said, it is their business to pass all the things they see and know through their own soul. In turn it is the business of readers to look more deeply into the world and into themselves. And the "writer's obligation" in this regard, "in so far as he has one, is to liberate the imagination."[36]

This he tried to do by casting his critique in witty and occasionally hilarious rhetoric. In Moses Herzog, for example, we have a confused comic figure searching for "spiritual freedom in the individual" and reaching for a "grand synthesis" of "higher values." Herzog gets into situations both poignant and funny and never fully succeeds in articulating his "grand synthesis"; but along the way he, like Bellow, makes rubbish of the nihilistic positions taken by modernist writers whose works are permeated with T. S. Eliot's gloomy "Wasteland outlook."[37]

Bellow, in the face of his many personal problems and existential crises, had no sure answers. But he and his protagonists ask the right question: In their own lives and in their relationship to society, "What can a good man do?" That question haunts *Herzog*, Bellow's sixth novel, just as it haunts *Dangling Man*, his first, and it is implicit in all of Bellow's work.

One approach to an answer, Bellow said on the eve of *Herzog*'s publication, is to struggle mightily against the idea that we live in a doomed time, to struggle against the cancerous spread of nihilism. If you abdicate to nothingness, Bellow warned, "you succumb to the . . . unenlightened, unilluminated life" and have not chosen life at all. "I have put before you life and death, blessing and curse. Choose life!" This adage, from *Deuteronomy* 30:19, could easily serve as an appropriate conclusion to nearly every Bellow book.[38]

In many of the later novels, *Humboldt's Gift* (1975) together with *The Dean's December* (1982) and *The Actual* (1997), as well as such stories as "The Old System," "Cousins," "A Silver Dish," and "Something to Remember Me By," we can find Bellow's persistently brave and stubborn quest to recover the soul for a society seemingly committed to artificial relationships and to knowledge derived from reason alone. In this struggle, Bellow, exploiting his memory and imagination, often reached back to Jewish immigrant neighborhoods and even further back to Jewish life in Eastern Europe. He had a profound unsentimental attachment to Europe's lost Yiddish culture, its moral qualities and ethical practices, and its openness to "God adumbrations" and to the reality of the soul. All of which played a central part in his enduring pursuit of the spiritual.[39]

One of Bellow's great gifts was his ability to see under the detritus of American Jewish life some connection, even if a weakening one, to Jewish life and culture in the Old World. Bellow's Yiddish heritage, as Alfred Kazin correctly points out, is Bellow's tradition. Although he is "the least ghettoized and least sentimental of 'Jewish novelists,'" Kazin said, no other talented Jewish writer in America "feels so lovingly connected with the religious and cultural tradition of his Eastern European grandfathers."[40]

ONE

IN THE BEGINNING

SAUL BELLOW IS OFTEN CONSIDERED the most learned and intellectual of modern American novelists. It thus seems appropriate that his father, Abram Belo, at age twenty in 1904, was a Yeshiva *bocher*—a student of Talmud—in Vilna, "the Jerusalem of Lithuania." Although indifferent to orthodoxy, Belo was knowledgeable enough in Talmudic matters to converse with scholarly rabbis. He was also known as an *ungekhapte*—a hot-blooded man, full of passion and fury, intense, often nervous, bursting with impatience. Some of these qualities, in one degree or another, he passed on to his youngest son, Saul.[1]

Abram Belo's anxieties doubtless derived in some measure from the growing political instability and resurgent antisemitism in Russia. The empire was marked by a long history of fierce animus toward Jews, and in the early twentieth century, beginning with a bloody pogrom in Kishinev in 1903, mass murderous violence was perpetrated against the Jewish population in all parts of the realm. This was especially true in the Pale of Settlement, a western region of Imperial Russia within which the vast majority of Jews were forced to live.

"The Jews," Saul Bellow said nearly a century later, "had a . . . one-sided connection . . . with the countries within which they were living." They could understand and even "appreciate" the various cultures around them—"a compliment," Bellow pointed out, "that was not returned by the *goyim*." Indeed, many Jews (including his parents) recognized that their Russian neighbors "never really saw [them] as human beings at all."[2]

Abram Belo and Saul's mother, Lescha (later Liza) Gordin, were raised in shtetlekh (small towns) in the Pale near the present-day border of Latvia and Belarus. After they married in 1905—a year in which nearly seven hundred mostly government-induced pogroms erupted—Belo quit studying at the seminary and fled the Pale with Lescha to settle, illegally, in St. Petersburg, an important port city on the Baltic Sea, where they managed to live by using forged papers and distributing sizable bribes.

Belo became a "produce broker," importing Spanish fruit, Turkish figs, and Egyptian onions—great delicacies in Czarist Russia.[3] Unfortunately, he wasn't a particularly good tradesman. Perhaps, like Papa in Bellow's novel *Herzog* (1964), "he lacked the cheating imagination of a successful businessman," but he worked hard and earned enough to allow the Belos to live in modest bourgeois style.[4] The family's income was supplemented significantly by the Gordins, Lescha's parents, who were well off, and by her brothers, who had once dealt in South African diamonds and owned one of very few kosher restaurants in St. Petersburg. "That was the golden time for my mother," Saul said, "when she was a young bride and there was plenty of money."[5]

The Belos kept servants, owned a cottage in the country, and hired a governess for their three children: Zelda, later Jane, born 1906; Moishe, later Maury, born 1908; and Schmuel, later Sam, born 1911. Lescha remained forever committed to Orthodox Judaism, but Abram, skeptical even as a student, believed that religious practice would impede his success in St. Petersburg, and he grew less observant. "He didn't turn his back" on Jewish rituals, Saul said, "but neither did he recommend them to his children."[6]

Abram could keep his Jewishness hidden from the authorities, but in time it became more difficult to conceal his forged papers.

St. Petersburg was awash in conspirators, double agents, terrorists, petty criminals, and informants. In 1912, when the police began to crack down, Abram Belo's documents were revealed as phony. He was arrested and put on trial. Many years after these events, Saul Bellow, along with the rest of the family, said, "I don't know . . . the whole story." [7] There was a conviction, perhaps an imprisonment, and certainly an escape from the hands of the police.

The background of systematic discrimination and conspiracy, and the commission of "necessary" crimes like bribery and forgery, may well lie behind not only Abram's and his family's attitudes to the law but also Saul Bellow's later fascination as a writer with "those who lived outside it."[8] Small-time criminals and racketeers, who are often drawn with sympathy (or at least given a degree of complexity), are featured in numerous Bellow novels, including *Augie March*, *Herzog*, *Mr. Sammler's Planet*, and *Humboldt's Gift*.

Belo held on to the Russian newspaper describing his arrest and conviction, but, as Saul said, it was all "very mysterious." His father kept the paper "locked away in his desk."[9] But every now and then, he proudly showed his children and grandchildren the tattered pages carrying the headline, "A Jew Escapes." Apparently, one of Lescha's wealthy brothers (using "the best papers he could buy," Saul liked to joke) managed to smuggle the whole family out of Russia by boat—destination, Canada.[10]

When East European Jews were on the move in the late nineteenth and early twentieth centuries, there was a Yiddish jingle that circulated among them: "*Geyt, yidelekh, in der vayter velt; in kanade vet ir ferdinen gelt*" ("Go, little Jews, into the wider world; in Canada you will earn a living"). The Belos may not have been familiar with this tune, but Abram's sister, Rosa, and her husband, Max Gameroff, had been in Canada since 1908, and they welcomed the Belo family with genuine hospitality. Two other Belo siblings and their families also lived in Canada—like the Gameroffs, in Lachine, Quebec.

A working-class village on Montreal Island, nine miles southwest of Montreal, Lachine housed some three hundred Jews, encircled by a much larger population of Ukrainians, Greeks, Italians, Hungarians, Poles, and Native Americans. Shloimo, later Solomon or Sol and finally Saul, was born on June 10, 1915, into what he called "a Jewish enclave," an urban shtetl within a heterogeneous world. Bellow vividly remembered having been surrounded in that enclave by a loving extended family; he stated that the story "you got from your parents and your uncles and aunts and their families, was that you had been brought by stormy seas and cast up on this shore and that you clung to each other.... And what happened to the family... was of utmost importance."[11]

There could be among relatives, distant or close, raging and shouting and even lifelong quarrels, but in the end, there was almost always loyalty and support, if not love. Ijah, the narrator of Bellow's story "Cousins" (1984), who has some "influence" with a judge, is asked to help a cousin soon to be sentenced for a nonviolent crime. "By sacrificing an hour at my desk I might spare Tanky a good many years of prison. Why shouldn't I do it," Ijah thinks, "for old times' sake, for the sake of his parents, whom I held in such affection. I *had* to do it.... My souvenirs would stink if I let Schana's son down. I had no space to work out whether this was a moral or a sentimental decision."[12]

The New World relatives "clung to each other," but for Bellow's mother, Canada represented a trauma of fallen circumstances. She had been the daughter of an eminent scholar who was also a wealthy merchant, and she had lived with her husband in a cosmopolitan city. When Lescha and Abram left St. Petersburg, "the trunks [they] traveled with were exotic," filled with "the taffeta petticoats, the ostrich plumes, the long gloves, the buttoned boots, and all the rest of those family treasures."[13] Liza hated the move from Russia, Bellow told an interviewer. "She had already moved too much, she thought—from Latvia to Petrograd. Then to Lachine [where] she found herself in a melting pot. . . . The mixture of languages and races was confusing to her," Bellow said, but "fascinating to me. . . . And I took it for granted—what else was I to do in childhood?—that was what life was."[14]

Everything was a wonder to young Shloimo. Looking back and reflecting on his sense of the world at three, Bellow said, "I think I had a kind of infinite excitement going through me, of being a part of this, of having appeared on this earth. I always had a feeling . . . that this is a most important thing, and delicious, ravishing, and nothing happened that was not of deepest meaning for you—a green plush sofa falling apart, or sawdust coming out of the sofa, or the carpet that it fell on. . . . Everything is yours, really."[15] Everything, including the colorful inhabitants of Lachine—his Indian nursemaid; his uncles and cousins; the storekeepers on Notre Dame, the main street of the town; a man named Ivolvsky "who owned a famous goat"; and, of course, the Lachine Canal, the town's most prominent feature. Here, still a toddler, Shloimo could stand and listen curiously to the passing bargemen as they bantered among themselves and with the people on the shore.

Even in his old age, Bellow could wax lyrical about Lachine: "I can remember Mr. Goldwater's movie house . . . on Notre-Dame . . . my uncle William in his fruit store . . . flipping open brown bags with a smart crack, or my late cousin Sam Gameroff, setting the spark of his Model T Ford. . . . This was the world as I first knew it," Bellow said. "There's nothing around that you don't possess."[16]

As Bellow's biographer Zachary Leader has pointed out, "for Bellow the child, as for the poet William Wordsworth the child, 'every common sight/To me did seem/Apparelled in celestial light.'" Wordsworth became a favorite of Bellow's, and as he puts it in the "Chicago Book" (an unpublished, unfinished work of nonfiction), "I grew up convinced of the Wordsworthian linkage of 'a life and a soul, to every mode of being.'"[17]

For this acutely observant boy, his mother's youngest (and apparently most loved), there was no missing Lescha's disappointment, nor her dreaminess and wistful yearning. Young Bellow's sensibility, emotionalism, and flights of fancy, often mocked by his father and two older brothers, were an inheritance from Lescha—a gift that fed his writerly imagination as well as his spiritual receptivity.

Throughout an extended interview in 1999, Bellow implied repeatedly that a religious feeling, some sense of the transcendent, was very strong in him when he was young and that it persisted. Three years later he said the same to Antonio Monda, author of *Do You Believe?*: "My mother was extremely religious while my father avoided the subject. I would say that he was [a] skeptical person who fluctuated continually between distress regarding the possible existence of God and the choice of agnosticism. I can tell you in all sincerity that *in the end it was my mother who had the greater influence on me.*"[18]

Lescha's greater influence in all things spiritual and emotional no doubt shaped the depiction of mothers in Bellow's fiction. Tommy Wilhelm's mother in *Seize the Day* (1956) has bequeathed her son "sensitive feelings, a soft heart, a brooding nature." Herzog's mother "often had a dreaming look" and was possessed of a "melancholy," and Charlie Citrine in *Humboldt's Gift* says that "he never lost this intense way of caring" between him and his mother. Even as an adult, Citrine "still required it," this need for mutual tenderness.[19]

Among Jewish immigrants in the early twentieth century, Bellow said, "your mother was the source of all human connectedness," which helped you deal with the uncomfortable "sense of being . . . aliens." And "it never entered your mind that you were anything but cherished, and you returned the favor."[20] The fictive Charlie Citrine said it was his connection to his mother that prompted his "utopian emotional love aura" toward women, which made them feel he was "a cherishing man."[21]

Bellow's impressions of life in Lachine blend into his years in Montreal, to which the family moved in 1918 when Shloimo, or by this time, Sol, was three. The five Bellows (Belo changed to Bellow) often visited the village of Lachine during their eight years in the big city—to see cousins and siblings, but perhaps also to get away from what Bellow called their "slum" neighborhood. They were located in an area known as the Main, on St. Dominique Street near Napoleon Street, in the heart of Montreal's Jewish section. A synagogue sat on the corner of Napoleon, a heder (Hebrew school) on Milton Street, and an open-air market stocked with kosher products was nearby on Rachel Street.

On Napoleon Street, "sometimes flogged with harsh weather," Sol and his brothers recited the ancient Hebrew prayers. "We observed Jewish customs," Bellow said, and "we recited prayers and blessings all day long."[22] This is no exaggeration. An observant Jew is obligated to pray before performing any mitzvah (commandment or sacred act), such as washing hands or lighting candles. There are prayers to recite before and after meals and upon seeing anything unusual, such as a notable person, a beautiful flower, a rainbow, or the site of a great misfortune; prayers to recite whenever some worthy deed is performed or some immoral or wicked act is perpetrated; and prayers to recite before going to bed at night and when rising in the morning.

Every day upon awakening, Sol, as instructed by the Talmud, said, "*Elohai neshamah shenatata bi tehorah*" ("My God, the soul that you have placed within me is pure"). *Neshamah,* a Hebrew word for soul, also means breath, and it reminded Sol, who was intimately familiar with Genesis, that God formed the human of dust from the earth and breathed into its nostrils the soul-breath of life.[23]

There was much ritual then, inside and outside the Bellow family apartment; but it was the fullness of life on Napoleon and

St. Dominque Streets and in the surrounding area that Bellow recalled even more fondly, because, as he has his fictive Moses Herzog say, here there "was a wider range of human feelings than he had ever again been able to find."[24] There was in the children, especially in sixteen-year-old Maury, and in their father, Abram (now Abraham), a typical zeal, even in Montreal, for what they saw as "Americanization."

America "became their paradise," Bellow said: "Equality here had some meaning. Here you could realize all the secular ambitions of the Jew, to be rich, to be happy, to be safe, and that was never real for European Jewry . . . and my father could never get over it. He would say, 'Look, I carry no papers. I can do whatever I please,'" including driving without a license![25] But Sol's mother, Lescha (now Liza), more sensitive and slow to learn English, felt more strongly that the Old World traditions that had sustained the lives of so many East European Jews for hundreds of years—some based on law, others embedded in community mores—were significantly altered in the New World, and not for the better. But all approached the process of acculturation with some ambiguity—strangers longing for a congenial, familiar setting in a strange world, they settled mostly in areas that were already densely populated by immigrants from familiar locales. In this way the immigrants retained vital parts of the past during their years as American initiates.

The move to Montreal was necessitated by a series of business failures, some of them disastrous, some shady, almost all a function of Abraham Bellow's haplessness. He had even tried his hand at farming. Using thousands of the rubles he had smuggled out of Russia, Abraham bought some land in Valleyfield, Quebec, "out in the bush somewhere," according to Saul. There were hardly any Jews—certainly not enough for a minyan—no rabbi, no kosher food, no music teachers. And the kids were forever getting lost in the woods. "My mother complained," Saul said, "so we moved back to Lachine."[26] But for Liza this was yet another step down.

"It was a very difficult time for a fine looking woman," Bellow said. "And, of course, my mother would tell [us] the story of her fall from grace" and of her hope for the children.[27]

Liza hoped that her sons would become *landonim*, learned scholars like her father. She paid special attention to Sol, her favorite and for several years the only child at home. In Montreal, at the age of four, he was put on a path to the rabbinate. "I was sent across the street . . . a slummy, European street," Bellow remembered, "full of immigrants and sailors. We were near the waterfront on a long hill, and I used to go . . . to my rabbi. . . . Shikka Stein." He "taught me the alef-beis and then we began to read *Breishis* [Genesis] and then . . . Rashi, and it was wonderful. For one thing, these [biblical figures] were all my relatives. My family was full of Abrahams and Isaacs and Chavas [Eve, more often Eva] and so forth."[28]

Bellow told the Romanian-born writer Norman Manea in a 1999 interview that "studying the Torah" felt like a "homecoming" with his parents and his cousins: "I was four years old and my head was in a spin. I would come out of [the rabbi's] apartment and sit on the curb and think it all over in the front of my house." Of course, "you memorize these things," Bellow said, and he immediately launched into a Hebrew recitation: "*Beresith bara Elohim et hashamayim ve'et Haaretz, hayta tohu vavohu . . . veruach Elohim merahefet al pney*. . . . In the beginning God created the heaven and earth. And the earth was without form and void, and . . . the spirit of God moved upon the face of it. . . . You never forget that!"[29]

Nor did Bellow ever forget life in the Jewish Main. The city's poorest neighborhood was a kind of fairyland for a boy who thought "junk yards [were] as miraculous as orange groves."[30] The district was marked by cramped, deteriorating low brick buildings, unkempt yards and alleyways, and small clothing factories and sweatshops. There were kosher butcher shops, seltzer hawkers, and pushcart vendors selling rags and eggs, clothing and scrap iron, pots and bagels, and herring right out of the barrel.

Kids played everywhere, including in Mount Royal, the city's largest park. But it was on the streets of the Main, after school and at heder, that he and his friends spent most of their time. The Romanian-born Canadian poet Irving Layton (né Izzie Lazaroff)—Bellow's exact contemporary—said that for a writer "nothing could have been better" than the streets of the Main: "Nothing. Raw, vulgar dynamic and dramatic."[31]

Most of Bellow's neighbors were Jewish, and "the only trouble we kids ever had," according to Sol's friend and neighbor Willie Greenberg, "was from a French-Canadian beat cop."[32] But Bellow remembers the French Canadian schoolboys who, perhaps having caught a look at his tzitzit—the ritual knotted fringes hanging out from under his shirt—shouted obscene insults at him and his friends. "I soon understood that I was a Zhwiff—*a muzhi (maudit) Zhwiff* at that" (Jew, damned peasant Jew).[33] But the Main was reasonably safe, like a "medieval" Jewish town, in Bellow's words, "surrounded by the others, the *goyim*."[34]

Yiddish was predominant in the Main, but the mash-up of languages, Bellow said, "was very strange. My parents spoke Russian to each other . . . Yiddish to the children and the children spoke Yiddish to them." But Bellow, his siblings, and their friends also spoke English to one another and at school. "Since it was a French-Canadian community, we also spoke French in the street." And don't forget, he reminded Manea, that his parents sent him "to learn Hebrew across the street. . . . So there was a whole mixture": Russian, Yiddish, English, French, and Hebrew.[35]

Bellow's father read Russian novels, Tolstoy for certain. He read English, too, and even spoke it, but with difficulty. Liza Bellow was also a reader of novels and would send Sol to the public library to bring home books from what she called "the Russian shelf." But she never learned English. "I often wonder how my mother lived under these circumstances," Bellow said, "because a few blocks from the house and she was lost."[36] A great treat for her, however, was an afternoon at the movies accompanied by Sol. He remembered hearing each time "a low rumbling in the theater, that of dozens of child translators, himself included, whispering Yiddish to their mothers."[37]

Both parents, Bellow said, "needed all the help they could get. They were forever asking, 'What does the man say?' and I would translate for them into heavy-footed English. That didn't help much either. The old people were as ignorant of English as they were of Canadian French."[38] It is possible that the ethnic and linguistic variety of Canada helped the Bellows preserve Yiddish and Yiddishkeit longer than if they had settled in the US directly. But it is almost certain that the mash-up of languages and the rich cultural and verbal environment in which young Bellow was saturated helped lead him to writing, writing that would inject into American English a vitality and verbal outpouring rarely heard before.[39]

As a boy, Bellow was constantly exposed to "stories." In the cold weather, Sol, who suffered various respiratory ailments, stayed indoors and helped his mother in the kitchen while he listened to her assortment of tales from the old country; later in the day, nearly every day, Abraham read aloud from the Yiddish papers, including the progressive *Der Kanada Adler* (the *Canada Eagle*) and *Der Forverts* (the *Forward*), a socialist paper with an assimilationist orientation that carried stories by Old World Yiddish writers as well as the "Bintl Briv" or "bundle of letters" section.

This section, which would play a legendary role in the history of American Jewish assimilation, began in 1906, when the *Forward* commenced publishing letters from readers about poverty and sickness, love and divorce, unemployment, intermarriage, socialism, generational conflict, and declining religious observance. Responses written by the venerable editor Abraham Cahan and his staff tried to suggest that the immigrants should not make excessive demands on themselves and should even enjoy life a little. The editors did not advise immigrants to give up their religious and ideological commitments entirely, but they did encourage the newcomers to make the needs of everyday life in the New World primary. Bellow's brothers, Maury and Sam (who changed their names to Bellows), took this advice seriously, each in his own way, as did Sol—though quite differently, as we shall see.

Sol's favorite evening entertainment was listening to his father read aloud from the stories of Sholom Aleichem. The ironic genius that Saul Bellow later displayed in his own writing was influenced by this great Yiddish author, who showed him how "the profoundly sad, bitter spirit of the ghetto"—more precisely, the shtetl—"laughed at itself and thereby transcended itself."[40] The humor in Bellow's work also "comes directly from [other] Yiddish stories," which he said are "characteristically Jewish. In them, laughter and trembling are so curiously mingled that it is not easy to determine relations of the two." Writers Sholom Aleichem, I. L. Peretz, and Mendele Mokher Seforim, for all their pathos and darkness, are, Bellow insisted, "full of humor." Comedy, he added, is good; "jokes are good—indeed essential. Groaning is monotonous."[41]

This mingling of humor and high matters, Bellow said, is "a family thing among Jews. . . . I think it has its origin in feelings of ineffable beauty and wonder. You know . . . when things couldn't have been worse, my father would have a laughing attack." No money for rent or to pay the grocer, and the kids are sick. "And yet suddenly something would strike my father as funny, and we all responded in the same way. . . . I . . . see this sort of thing," Bellow concluded, "as a Jewish moment, you know?"[42] After all, Bellow went on, "there's no coming between a Jew and his jokes—a sort of permanent love of paradox and funny occasions."[43]

Bellow was influenced not only by his father's sense of humor; he also credited his father with his own sense that everything was a story. Without a doubt, Jewish daily life, from the old country to the New World, would have been inconceivable without stories. "My father," Bellow remembered, "would say, whenever I asked him to explain any matter, 'The thing is like this: There was a man who lived . . .' 'There once was a widow with a son . . .' 'A teamster was driving on a lonely road. . . .'"[44] Montreal neighbor Willie Greenberg also knew Abraham Bellow as an entertaining storyteller. He knew, too, that there was no keeping secrets around Abraham or his son, because everything Sol Bellow saw or heard he'd use in some reimagined or exaggerated way to tell a story. After Sol's visits with her son, Greenberg's mother would shake her head and say, "*Oy, is dos kind a bluffer!*" ("Oh boy, is this kid a bullshitter!").[45] Seventy years later, Bellow summed up his paternal literary inheritance with a Yiddish adage: "*Meshugena genz, meshugena gribenes*" ("Crazy geese, crazy giblets").[46]

Abraham considered his son's later pursuit of the writing life *narishkayt*—foolishness or worse. "*Was meinst du 'a writer'?*" ("What does it mean, 'a writer'?"), he asked: "You write, and then you erase. You call that a profession?" Still, it is undeniable that the father unwittingly contributed style, substance, and energy to his son's quest.[47]

In his own pursuit of a "profession," Abraham was a serial failure and was responsible for the family's need to move from Montreal. Sometime in the winter of 1923–24, the Bellow family's last in Canada, Abraham and a partner borrowed the necessary cash from moneylenders and took a brief shot at bootlegging. While making a late-night run on the road between Montreal and the US, the partners were hijacked. Everything they had was taken, including their truck, and they were beaten badly—Abraham more so because he was an *ungekhapte*, a passionate man, and fought back.

Maury, the oldest of the Bellow boys, went to search for their father and found him in a ditch, weeping, soaked in blood, his clothes in tatters—but not entirely without fight left in him. When Maury asked what had happened, his father "beat the shit" out of him.[48] Abraham's temper and, of course, the shame he had experienced in front of Maury had gotten the best of him.

All the Bellow boys, over time and more than once, had felt their father's wrath, no uncommon thing between immigrant fathers and first-generation American sons. Saul said that, although as the youngest and "the plaything of everyone," he was spared the worst of Abraham's violence, he had had his share. He described his father as "tyrannical" but also loving.[49] As a child, Saul saw his father in a biblical frame: "My childhood lay under the radiance (or gloom) of the archaic family, the family of which God is the ultimate father and your own father is representative of divinity."[50]

The young son's veneration for his father remained with Bellow and carried over into his fiction. In a scene in *Herzog*, for example, in a feat of reimagination, Bellow depicts the father's return from a hijacking in the most loving terms:

> Father Herzog, with a gap in his teeth, his coat torn, and his shirt bloodstained, entered the dark kitchen on Napoleon Street. We were all there.... "Sarah!" he said. "Children!" He showed his cut face.... Then he turned his pockets inside out—empty.
>
> As he did this he began to cry, and the children standing about him all cried. It was more than I could bear that anyone should lay violent hands on him—a father, a sacred being, a king. Yes, he was a king to us. My heart was suffocated by this horror. I thought I would die of it. Whom did I ever love as I loved them?[51]

And much later, in the novella-length story "Something to Remember Me By" (1990), the fictive eighteen-year-old Louis is late coming home after a harrowing but absurdly comic experience. He ends up with a swift and hard paternal blow to the head. Yet he thinks of his father's "blind Old Testament rage" not "as cruelty but as archaic right everlasting."[52]

The hijacking was bad enough, but an even more critical problem befell the Bellows in the same winter of 1923–24. Sol, eight years old, suffered an attack of appendicitis, and after an emergency operation (possibly botched), he developed serious complications including peritonitis and pneumonia. Multiple surgeries followed, including four abdominal operations. And for a time the doctors at Royal Victoria Hospital thought Sol had also contracted tuberculosis. "It was not TB," Bellow remembered; "it was something called empyema—an infection of the respiratory system that fills the lung cavity with fluid" and causes shortness of breath.[53] He ran a fever every afternoon and had to be "tapped." Anesthetized and drifting in and out of consciousness, Sol had to be "haggled open. It was draining, I stank."[54]

Bellow was dangerously ill. Indeed, he and nearly all the other boys in Ward H were close to death. During the night, "there was a lot of fuss in the darkness."[55] The nurses, Bellow remembered only too well, "were running, a light would go on, a screen would be set up along somebody's bed. In the morning it was an empty bed—and you knew the kid had died."[56] And "by noon there was another kid in the empty bed, and that was how it went." All the boys understood, "although nobody talked about it. The beds were a little too far apart for the kids to have discussions and there was nobody to talk to about any of these things." When boys disappeared in the night, "you had to make your own record of them."[57] Strong enough occasionally to climb out of bed, Sol read his chart: "It was very unpromising." He knew he was in serious trouble, but he was not resigned to dying. He "would hunker down in . . . bed," Bellow confessed, "and make [himself] as small as possible so that death could not find [him]."[58]

His parents could be with him only once a week and only one at a time. Liza and Abraham took turns visiting during a winter Bellow remembered as especially bitter, with "heavy snow, fantastic icicles at the windows, streetcars frosted over."[59] After his parents left and the ward grew dark, "he could not call out in the night" for them, or anybody, "because nobody [was] going to come."[60]

The trauma of separation from his parents, watching children die and bodies disappear, and thoughts of his own demise at eight years old made the hospital experience frightening enough to remain forever embedded in Bellow's imagination. Death was not a stranger to young Bellow. At four, he and his older brother Sam, from their upstairs window, stared down at St. Dominique Street, where there were endless black-clad funeral processions carrying victims of the 1918–19 influenza epidemic; and at seventeen, Sol was witness to the "long, drawn-out cancer death" of his mother. Liza's agony, Bellow said, was "the greatest challenge to my imagination . . . because I couldn't imagine existence without her."[61]

The attempt to understand death—the experience, the aftermath, the meaning—marked almost all of Bellow's fiction. It echoes throughout his work as his protagonists yearn to recover loved ones and fail to do so: Eugene Henderson in *The Rain King*, who believes that "the biggest problem of all" is how "to encounter death," frantically plays the violin in order to make contact with his deceased parents. Charlie Citrine in *Humboldt's Gift* says, "I cannot accept the view of death taken by most of us . . . I am obliged to deny that so extraordinary a thing as a human soul can be wiped out forever."[62]

In "The Old System," the reflective Isaac Braun thinks, "One after another you gave over your dying. One by one they went. You went. Childhood, family, friendship, love were stifled in the grave. And these tears! When you wept them from the heart, you felt you justified something, understood something. But what did you understand? Again, *nothing*! It was only an imitation of understanding. A promise that mankind might—*might* mind you—eventually through its gift which might—*might* again!—be a divine gift, comprehend why it lived. Why life, why death."[63]

And in Bellow's last novel, *Ravelstein*, the eponymous Abe adjusted himself "long ago to dying a natural death, like everybody else. I've seen plenty of dying in my time, and I'm prepared for it. Maybe I've been a little too imaginative about the grave—the dampness and the cold. I've pictured it in too much detail and maybe feel a little too much—feel abnormally—for the dead."[64]

Sol, directly facing his own death, was genuinely frightened, and the limited visits from his parents and the general inattention, insensitivity, and even anti-Jewish bias of the overworked nurses meant that he was increasingly isolated. "I had nobody to depend on but myself," Bellow said, so "I began to make all kinds of arrangements," like holding on to things, "secrets"—such as the antisemitism of the nurses—that you "couldn't tell the parents." The "lies," even if only by omission, engendered a kind of guilt, which, in combination with secrets, may have been, Bellow thought, the start of a "career" in literature.[65]

The prejudice of the nurses was particularly pronounced at Christmas, when a tree was placed in the ward and stockings for gifts were hung at the foot of each bed. "You were a little Jewish kid," and the nurses "kept reminding you of it." Sol was angry. "I was mad enough to kill," he said. "But I was also very puny. . . . I weighed forty pounds or something like that."[66]

Antisemitism, about which Sol "learned a great deal," was only "one of hundreds of things you couldn't tell [your parents]." He also stayed mum about the "horrible food" the hospital served, food he ate but with great distaste—"diced pork on a tin plate." He felt guilty for eating *treyf*, "but I knew enough about Jewish tradition," Bellow said, "to know that this was permitted—anything is permitted that keeps you alive." All the food was horrible, but the diced pork, Bellow repeated, was "especially awful." Although by the time he was sixteen he had gotten used to eating food that was not strictly kosher, Bellow was "really quite old" before he was "ready to eat pork."[67]

While an adolescent in Chicago, Bellow met "many cosmopolitan Jews" from Warsaw and Moscow in and around Humboldt Park. He was "astonished at the ease with which they ate *treyf*." They thought nothing, he said, of "putting butter on bread and a piece of meat on top of it." This kind of thing, Bellow said, was "absolutely unheard of" in his more familiar circles. These cosmopolitan Jews who ate *treyf*, he thought at the time, must have been close to starvation—perhaps during wartime. "They were speaking Yiddish," Bellow told an interviewer nearly seven decades later, and "they were very Jewish in all their ways" except in their violation of kashruth, especially by eating pork. When asked whether this had made him uncomfortable, Bellow said, "I was." And at eighty-four, "I still am."[68]

In the hospital, isolated from his parents by separation and secrets and from the other boys on the ward by the distance between the beds, young Bellow became more dependent on reading. There were "funny papers . . . stacked beside the kids' beds," but they would also "come around with a cart. . . . And you would pick some books . . . mostly . . . foolish fairy tales, but occasionally there was a real book," like *Uncle Tom's Cabin* or *Black Beauty*. Bellow remembered feeling "very receptive" to what he was reading "about life in America, pioneers, farmers, immigrants, hunters, Indians."[69]

From his parents, however, Sol kept his most significant reading: the New Testament. "There was nobody to talk to," Bellow said, "except the ladies from the Bible Society, the Christian ladies, we used to call them."[70] A "solemn, grim, middle-aged" woman, "dressed with many layers of clothing, long skirts, boots, a big hat," brought a copy of the Christian Bible.[71] She read passages aloud and had Sol do the same, and then she left the book behind. And Bellow, who "read everything [he] could get [his] hands on," immediately continued reading "the entire book by himself."[72]

Jesus "overwhelmed" him. The New Testament, the words and deeds of Jesus, Bellow said later, "moved [him] beyond all bounds." They were "a big hit with [him]." He had heard only "marginal information" about Jesus, all "unfriendly." "Why should it have been friendly?" Bellow later asked. The Gospels were filled with vile accusations against the Jews, who were named "the enemy race, universally to be hated by the rest of mankind." But, more than six decades later, Bellow, while deriding the Gospels as horridly antisemitic, could still write, "I was moved out of myself by Jesus."[73]

This, of course, was another thing he kept to himself. "It was not *their* Bible," Bellow said of his mother and father, and "Jesus was not discussable with them." His parents, he told biblical scholar Stephen Mitchell, had to "live, as all Jews must, under a curse" of deicide, and Abraham and Liza were "not prepared to interpret this" to a confused eight-year-old, a boy who was moved by Jesus and horrified by the crucifixion and the assertion that the Jews were responsible.[74]

Sol himself began to feel responsible, but he thought, "How could it be my fault? I am in the hospital." He reasoned that he "didn't have it all quite straight."[75] How, suffering so badly, could he have made sense of Jesus telling his followers to yield to harsh treatments and demands (Matthew 5:39–48)? And what sense could he possibly have made of Jesus's instruction to "hate" his beloved family (Luke 14:26), after having read in the Hebrew scriptures that "each of you must respect your mother and father" (Leviticus 19)? So, Bellow said, "I made a fairy tale of it for myself." The crucifixion "was something that happened a very long time ago, to Jesus, who was a Jew, and that counted heavily."[76]

If the Gospel was a fairy tale for Sol, the Pentateuch (the first five books of the Jewish Bible) had for him a different kind of substance; it "was not a fairy tale. It was a holy book, in Hebrew, and you knew it had to be true, because it said God created the world—and here was the world! Here's the proof. Right outside the window," the window of your hospital or your apartment, here "was your proof." The biblical Abraham, the father of his people, "our first Jew, so designated by God himself," and Abraham Bellow were somehow the same for Sol. "It was a continuing thing. It was impossible for a child of eight to make all the necessary distinctions, and I didn't even try to make any distinctions, because

I was enchanted with the whole thing; it was a straight line from the top, where God was, to the bottom, where I was!"[77]

He "felt very cozy with God, the primal parent," and since the time he read about the Patriarchs, at the age of five, Bellow said, "I felt they were very much like members of my family. I couldn't really distinguish between a parent and the heroic ancestors—Abraham, Isaac, and Jacob, and the sons of Jacob, especially Joseph"—the name of the protagonist (with no surname) of Bellow's first novel, *Dangling Man*.[78]

In the hospital he had been "so sick" and had suffered so powerful a "nightmare" that he had become, Bellow said later, "spiritually earnest." The "whole thing made a deep impression" on him, he remembered, an impression reinforced by the mildness and kindness of his rabbi. So, while Sol may have brought home with him a "secret" Jesus, the home to which he was bringing his new hero was that of the *real* Bible, the Hebrew Bible, filled with Sol's Hebrew ancestors.

Over time, Bellow's powerful imagination, immersed in Yiddish stories and the world's greatest literary classics as well as the mythologies, parables, and human truths of the Bible—both testaments—would produce the most significant body of literary work by any postwar American novelist.

TWO

ADAPTING TO AMERICA

WHILE SOL WAS STILL IN the hospital in Montreal, Abraham, looking for new employment, came to the United States six months ahead of the rest of the family. As soon as the youngest Bellow was well enough to travel, his parents (aided by his father's bootlegging associates) smuggled him and his sister and two brothers past the unobserving eyes of the border patrol to immigrant-packed Chicago.

When the Bellows arrived in the Northwest Side of the city in 1924, there were close to three hundred thousand Jews, mostly from Eastern Europe, living in this polyglot cosmopolis of slightly over three million people. Chicago, a hub of manufacturing, mining, meatpacking, and marketing, was not only America's second-largest city by 1930—six years after the Bellows arrived—it also housed America's second-largest American Jewish community, by then grown to 350,000.

Jews were a highly visible presence in Humboldt Park, the Bellow family's new neighborhood. All along North Avenue, there were Hebrew relief associations, free loan societies, congregations large and small, and landsmanshaften (Jews from the same town or region in the old country who got together for poker, pinochle, and the pleasure of each other's company). Abraham continued the tradition of attending shul on Shabbat and made sure his boys had a Jewish education.

Sol attended Sunday school at the Jewish People's Institute, where he continued to study Talmud and Torah. If passages in *Herzog* about learning Hebrew approximate anything like reality, it was not always a joyous experience. "The pages of the Pentateuch smelled of mildew. . . . The rabbi, short-bearded, his soft big nose violently pitted with black," scolded the boys almost as if he took pleasure in it: "You watch your step, Herzog, Moses. Your mother thinks you'll be a great *lamden*—a rabbi. But I know you, how lazy you are. Mothers' hearts are broken by *mamzerim* [bastards] like you! Eh! Do I know you, Herzog? Through and through."[1] But Sol paid close attention, learned a great deal, and forgot almost nothing. And until late adolescence, he was at synagogue every week, sitting downstairs with his father and the other men, while his mother and sister sat upstairs in the women's section.

During their uprooting from Canada and their transplantation in the US, the family was aided by Abraham's younger cousins Louis Dworkin and his sister Flora, who had fled Russia and come to the US in 1912 and 1913. They were generous to the Bellows, helping the family as their family had been helped earlier. Abraham, now forty-three, was put to work on the night shift in Louis Dworkin's Imperial Bakery, where the two cousins grew close; they worked hard but enjoyed each other, often laughing and joking in Yiddish.[2]

Still, adjustment to Chicago was difficult for Sol's parents, especially for Liza, who saw the move to the US as one more defeat in the struggle to regain status and wealth. Nor did she ever feel at home in America. "She was thinking of her family in Riga all the time," Bellow said. "And this was just a sort of exile, purgatory as far she was concerned. It was very hard to bring up four children in so strange a place."[3] The Humboldt Park neighborhood was indeed "strange" in the eyes of the Bellows. In addition to some six thousand Jews—about 25 percent of the population of Humboldt Park—there were also many Poles, Ukrainians, Scandinavians, Italians, Greeks, Irish, and African Americans, too, up from Alabama and Mississippi.

Sol's own initiation into Chicago street life was not easy. At first the other kids, even Jewish kids, made him "feel like a foreigner, an outsider," calling him a "Canuck." He felt like both a participant and a marginal observer of his new life in the streets. These feelings persisted, Bellow recalled, "even though I went to . . . school and college in Chicago, lived in the streets and knew it so well. I felt there was a kind of exoticism about the place." He thought that his mother's sense of displacement, to which he was especially sensitive, contributed to his own feelings of "strangeness."[4]

Adapting to America, "making it" in this country, Bellow wrote in the 1970s, could be baffling and bruising, painful for every immigrant group, and the Jews were no exception. He excluded neither his family nor himself from what he called "that mixture of imagination and stupidity with which people met the American Experience, that murky, heavy, burdensome, chaotic thing." The hunger of immigrants and their children for "true Americanism," Bellow thought, had yet to be adequately described.[5]

In Bellow's short story "Cousins," narrator Ijah Brodsky declares that "being an American had always been something of an abstract project. You came as an immigrant. You were offered a most reasonable proposition and you said yes to it."[6] Bellow, of course, had said "yes to it," but he agreed that the new democracy with its new abstractions could be cruelly disheartening. Americanization could "be made to sound like fun," he said, but "it is hard to think of anyone who underwent the process with joy."[7]

No, perhaps not joy—but for tens of thousands, there was at least a sense of achievement. In an early unpublished Bellow manuscript, "Memoirs of a Bootlegger's Son," a fictive Uncle Jomin says, "It is a strange country. But you have to keep your head. That's the main thing about strangeness." Aunt Julia, however, wonders how Jomin "could be so weak-minded, so forgetful, so ignorant as to talk loosely about the strangeness here. She showed you how the old country was sealed up in doom and death. She spoke strongly, and as though it was a credit to her to have come here. Escape? No, it was more like a triumph."[8]

The father in *Herzog* (1964) is not so "weak-minded" as to forget that the old country was sealed up in doom and death. He recalls that in Russia, he was put out at four years old to study, away from home: "Eaten by lice. Half-starved in the Yeshivah as a boy.... He worked in Krcmenchug for his aunt as a young man He had a fool's paradise in Petersburg for ten years, on forged papers. Then he sat in prison with common criminals."[9]

Escaping to America did not at first improve his situation: "Starved. Cleaned stables. Begged. Lived in fear. A *baal-chov*—always a debtor.... Taking in drunken boarders. His wife a servant." But after a time, there was upward mobility. Abraham, like the fictive father in *Herzog*, soon felt no significant strangeness in America. He could walk around with no documents. "Look," he repeated many times, "I carry no papers. I can do whatever I please."[10] *Feh!* on the old country.

Whatever strangeness or pain Bellow met in the process of becoming an American, he was keenly attuned to his surroundings. Chicago, for him as a boy, was "a sprawling network of immigrant villages, smelling of sauerkraut and home brewed beer, of meat processing and soap manufacture." Despite the crooked politicians and mobsters, life in the big city, at least to Sol and his friends, seemed calm, predictable: "A seven-cent streetcar fare took us to the Loop," the commercial center of the city that reached down to Lake Michigan. On Randolph Street, filled with jazz bands and city hall sorts, Bellow remembered, "we found free entertainment at Bessinger's billiard saloon and at Trayfon's gymnasium where boxers sparred."[11]

If Sol and his friends overspent, they "came back from the Loop on foot—some five miles of freightyards and factories." They passed Klee Brothers, "where you got a baseball bat with the purchase of a two-pant suit; Polish sausage shops; the Crown Theater" with its posters of Lon Chaney and Joan Crawford, and "its popcorn machine crackling; then the United Cigar Store; then Brown and Koppel's restaurant, with the nonstop poker game upstairs."[12]

Along with his friends, Sol "grasped the tacit Chicago assumption that this was a rough place, a city of labor and business, gangs and corruption, ball games and prizefights. We were the children of groping baffled immigrants," old country Jews "who were trying to figure out what had become of them in America." And Chicago, like the rest of modernizing America, was a place where physical matter ruled, "a place where stone was value and value stone. If you were drawn toward a higher life—and you might well be, even in the city of stockyards, steel and gangsters—you had to make your own way towards it."[13]

Yes, but young Bellow knew, too, that Chicago was something of an artistic hub in the early part of the twentieth century with a reputation for nurturing literary and intellectual talent. Chicago-based writers whom Bellow, even as a schoolboy, knew and would read hungrily included Sherwood Anderson, Theodore Dreiser, James Farrell, Sinclair Lewis, and Earnest Hemingway.

Meanwhile, the boy who had survived a six-month bout in the hospital with peritonitis and pneumonia and had had a long flirtation with death in Montreal was determined to be out in the world, healthy and strong. He believed that he "was ahead of the game," or as the Chicago gamblers used to say, the rest is "playing on velvet." A "kind of book-keeping took place," Bellow remembered: "*I owed something* to some entity for the privilege of surviving. I've kept such a feeling of being overjoyed, being full of a welling vitality."[14]

Everything fascinated Sol, including the "crudity, disappointment, sickness, heartbreak, money, power, happiness, and love" at the heart of the city. The workings of the bakery where his father was employed captivated him as well.[15] Everyone, he recalled, was dusted with flour, their boots and protective clothing clotted with dough. And "the bakers worked in undershirts, big muscled men . . . scooping the loaves up with quivering long handled peels."[16] Abraham's job was also heavy work, stacking boxes, lugging sacks, and harnessing horses. Bellow's fictive "Pa" in "Memoirs of a Bootleggers Son" felt demeaned, like Abraham, if he had to work for someone else, and he saw himself as no better than a *bettler* (beggar).[17] Encouraged by Liza, who also thought this kind of toil, working with his hands, beneath him, Abraham went into business for himself. She supplied the necessary capital from her *knipl,* the money a Jewish wife saves out of the household allowance and squirrels away for future use.

Abraham sold wood to the Jewish bakeries in Chicago for fuel. This involved going to lumber mills in Michigan and Wisconsin, buying up scrap wood, bringing it back to Chicago in freight cars, and then selling it to the baker shops. And "we knew all the Jewish bakeries," Bellow recalled. "That was a great privilege for me," Sol said, because, with Abraham he could come into the rear of the shop where the baking was done. Working with his father also meant that Sol "was in the railroad district of the city" seeing things that "very few kids of [his] background ever got close to."[18]

When gas ovens were brought into the bakeries, coal replaced wood, and Abraham wisely got into the coal business, an atypical enterprise for Jews. But the Carroll Coal Company, with the help of the older Bellow sons, Maury and Sam, and occasionally from Sol on weekends, was a success. By himself, Bellow knew, his "father couldn't have made it." But Maury and Sam did all the difficult work and "became very wealthy at this."[19]

Sol said he had his own "engagements," and his participation in the coal business was minimal; when there was little coal to weigh, he sat in the office and read. He recalls one occasion when his reading of Marx's *Value, Price and Profit* was interrupted by a raid on a brothel across the street, most likely for failure to pay protection money. From the window of the small company office, Sol could see cops throwing furniture, including beds and bedding, onto the street.[20] Occasionally Sol also went along on deliveries. "This brought me into the slums," Bellow said, "in a way I had never had access before—those were tough people, and fighting and guns were common; the unions were present and there was a lot of strife." Actually, Bellow said, working at the Carroll Coal Company was "a better education for me than the university."[21]

By his own "engagements," Sol most likely meant his exploration of the streets of Chicago, reading at the Humboldt Park public library, and keeping up with his formidably intelligent friends. As a young adolescent, he preferred the streets with their sandlots and the poolroom over playing the violin or going to Hebrew school.[22] The streets meant talk about baseball and prizefights, speakeasies, jazz, and graft, and language that was in Bellow's words "rough cheerful energetic clanging largely good natured Philistine," American.[23] The streets "won out," Bellow said; he then quickly added, "together with the public library," where he read Gogol's *Dead Souls*, *The Iliad* in prose translation, Dreiser, and Dostoevsky—and not, as Bellow himself pointed out, the Talmud or the Torah.[24]

But none of this was disavowal of his Jewish identity. "I think a human being has to be faithful to his unique history," Bellow famously said much later. "If we dismiss the life that is waiting for us at birth, we will find ourselves in a void. . . . The only life I can love or hate . . . is this American life of the twentieth century, the life of Americans who are also Jews. Which of these sources, the American or the Jewish should elicit the greater piety?

Are the two exclusive? Must a choice be made?" He confessed that he "never felt it necessary to sacrifice one identification for another" and that he retained his mother's deep religious feeling, her sense of the transcendent, and faith in his history, a "reverence for the source of one's being."[25]

On the Chicago streets, as Sol grew to high-school age, this source was manifest. The Humboldt Park area was attractive to political and religious radicals and was known for promoting Yiddish culture. "On Division Street you could find anything," Bellow remembered. "Yiddish . . . Marxism, anarchism," and a *glezel tei* (a glass of tea). "On Friday night you could hear speeches on everything from national tax plans to breathing right."[26] Right way or not, Sol was breathing it all in, including soapbox speeches on a wide spectrum of subjects, from abstract art to Zionism, from the "false consciousness" of the bourgeoisie to vegetarianism. Speakers, with their tea, often spilled over into Humboldt Park itself, where garment workers "read their Yiddish poems to one another."[27]

Men carrying typewriters could be hired for two bits to write letters to family and friends in the old country. And at Ceshinsky's bookstore on Division Street, clusters of old country intelligentsia could be found, Polish-Russian-Yiddish-speaking Jews, who wore pince-nez and argued about socialism, capitalism, antisemitism, and Darwin.[28] Chicago's Jewish neighborhood was an ideal environment, a petri dish, for a budding writer. As in the Main in Montreal, so in Humboldt Park, "idiomatic English enriched by Yiddish, Hebrew and Russian" could be heard, all in an atmosphere of scholarly rabbinical tradition, secularized.[29]

When Bellow entered Chicago's Tuley High School in 1930, it was modern in look and methodology, and it had the reputation of being "academic." But it was generally undemanding. No matter—the students, as Bellow remembered, made their own demands on themselves and their friends. "The children of Chicago bakers, tailors, peddlers, insurance agents, pressers, cutters, grocers, the sons of families on relief," Bellow wrote later, "were reading Buckram-bound books from the public library and were in a state of enthusiasm, having found themselves on the shore of a novelistic land to which they really belonged, discovering their birthright, hearing incredible news from the great world of culture, talking to one another about the mind, society, art, religion . . . and doing all this in Chicago."[30]

Decades later, in a talk at the Chicago Public Library, Bellow recalled the atmosphere of the North Avenue Branch:

> Like a church or a school, [it] offered a privileged environment. The books were bound in brown buckram. The pages were stained with soup, or cocoa or tomato ketchup or by tears or by nosebleeds, and they were also fiercely annotated by borrowers. Readers denounced writers or praised them, argued with other readers around the margins—self-made prophets, poets in their own right, patriots, subversives, philosophers, neighborhood historians arguing the Civil War or the Russian Revolution. One could learn a lot about the mental life of a democracy from these annotations. Strange forms of originality sometimes appeared, special kinds of intelligence, passion and madness.[31]

Before Bellow attended high school, he had already done considerable reading—Dreiser, Tolstoy, Gogol, Sherwood Anderson, Edith Wharton, Sinclair Lewis, Dostoevsky. But so had many other students. Cynthia Ozick has it right: "Tuley was where the excitations of intellectual ambition first encountered their kin in the formidably intelligent children of mostly working-class immigrant Jews, boys and girls drenched in ferocious bookishness and utopian politics, unselfconsciously asserting ownership of American culture at a time when it was most vigorously dominated by WASPs."[32]

Bellow and friends started a Russian Literary Society and a Socialist Society, as well as a debating club, a bibliophile club, and a scribblers club. On Friday nights the literati came together at a local hot dog stand to read what they had written and to argue about politics, religion, art, and literature. The debating club was a particularly competitive group. "Someone was ahead of you on Nietzsche," Bellow said, "but you were up on something else"[33]—Spengler, for example, or Marx, or Freud.

Sol also belonged to a three-member study group that met on a bench in Humboldt Park to analyze Oswald Spengler's *The Decline of the West.* Bellow was joined by the ubiquitous Isaac Rosenfeld, his closest friend and later sometimes bitter rival, and by Joe Polowsky, who, unlike so many of the other Jewish boys from Tuley High School, remained in the working class and grew up to drive a cab. But as Bellow told an interviewer some five decades later, Joe didn't forget his "Jewish- American-populist-liberal democrat[ic]" roots and went on to wage a long, often lonely campaign for improved US-Soviet relations.[34]

These classmates not only rejected Spengler's Teutonic pessimism; they tore apart his antisemitism. Spengler had assigned the Jews as a race to the "Magian" phase of world history, a backward phase allegedly superseded by a modern "Faustian" stage, for which Jews would never have an affinity. This notion angered Bellow and Rosenfeld, both aspiring to be modern writers, but it did nothing to deflate their ambition.

The emotional intensity of all the groups to which Bellow belonged is captured by his memories of the debating club and of one meeting at which Rosenfeld rose and asked for the floor. Despite his round face, thick glasses, and short pants, Isaac, with some solemnity, announced his subject to be Schopenhauer's *The World as Will and Idea,* a difficult book at any age, no less at fourteen. Isaac "spoke with perfect authority," Bellow recalled. "He is very serious. He has *read* Schopenhauer."[35]

Sol, popular, a track runner, an ambitious boy, and strikingly good looking, loved Isaac and enjoyed intense intellectual and philosophical stimulation in his company. Wanting to spend as much time as he could with him, Sol introduced the socially awkward Isaac to a lively group of talented Jewish students, witty and smart about literature, worldly wise, and more comfortable in the company of girls.[36] Rosenfeld went on to lead a brilliant but at times tortuous life as a writer—a life and career cut short by a heart attack at the age of thirty-eight.

In the meantime, Rosenfeld, according to his biographer, Steven Zipperstein, had so intimate a relationship with Jewishness that in Isaac's view there was no need to identify himself as a "Jewish Writer." He had about him, as Irving Howe put it, "an air of Yeshiva purity." Such purity Bellow did not exude. He had put some distance between himself and Orthodox Judaism, but he, too, in goals and ethical values as well as in his attachment to Rosenfeld, felt no need to use the adjective *Jewish* to describe the kind of writer he would become.[37]

Vital to both Bellow and Rosenfeld, "perhaps their dearest and most loyal friend," was Oscar Tarcov.[38] Like Sol and Isaac, Oscar was the son of Russian Jewish immigrants. He also shared their ambition for a literary career, and decades later he wrote his first and only novel, *Bravo, My Monster* (1953), in the same year that Bellow published his blockbuster *The Adventures of Augie March*. A short, horrific parable of the Holocaust, *Bravo* was, according to poet and critic Alan Tate, "a brilliant . . . exploration of a realm of experience opened up by Kafka."[39] Bellow, too, associated Kafka with the Holocaust, calling *The Metamorphosis* "the most impressive story I know in that line." And of the many writers Rosenfeld talked about, Kafka, along with Freud and Marx, Jews all, topped the list.[40]

Marx, however, despite his rabbinic ancestors, did not identify as a Jew; on the contrary, he was an antisemite and a racist. Trotskyist students at Tuley could talk the talk about "surplus value," the "fetishism of commodities," and what Marx "really" meant. There is no evidence however, that they faced until much later the antisemitism in Marx's writings, which defined "*the emancipation of the Jews*" as "the emancipation of mankind *from Judaism*." If Tuley boys and girls had read Marx's "On the Jewish

Question," they don't seem to have talked about it.[41] For they were Trotskyists, communists all—with a small *c*, perhaps—who were technically neither socialists nor, in the 1930s and 1940s, intensely committed communist "fellow travelers." Stalin was the enemy, not Marx. Most, including Sol Bellow, did not join the "capital C" Communist Party or the Young People's Communist League, both organizations saturated in Stalinism.

Among the Tuley boys, Bellow, Rosenfeld, and Tarcov formed a kind of triumvirate. Almost as close to Sol was Dave Peltz, who remained a lifelong friend. He had to drop out of high school after a year because his family ran into financial difficulties. But he kept his Tuley friendships. He scraped along at odd jobs, including one at the Carroll Coal Company, but he earned little. Apparently trying for better luck, Peltz found himself at the card table, playing poker with the likes of novelist Nelson Algren and journalist Studs Terkel. Afterward, he ran afoul of a crime syndicate because of a supposed gambling debt and so became familiar with Chicago street types, including "the low-life . . . the tough guys . . . the boys training to be hoodlums."[42] Bellow got to know some of the "gangsters" circuitously through Peltz, and he delighted in observing them from the outside. In *Humboldt's Gift* (1975), Peltz is recreated as George Swiebel, who keeps the protagonist, Charlie Citrine, informed "about criminals, whores, racing, the rackets, narcotics, politics and Syndicate operations."[43] Sol also had indirect entrée to this world through his older, tougher, and much more aggressive brother Maury, a nonpracticing lawyer who served for a while as a "bagman" for an assemblyman and may have had ties to organized crime.[44]

Bellow's other Tuley friends included Sam Freifeld, whose father owned a pool hall, at which Sol saw and mixed with other "vulgar company." But the Freifeld family was warm, welcoming, and more affluent than most. Sam had an enviable library, through which he introduced Bellow to the works of Havelock Ellis, Max Eastman, and Edmund Wilson. Sam also had records and a record player. Bellow preferred books over instruments like the violin, which he played moderately well but had given up; nevertheless, he absorbed a considerable amount of music at the Freifeld home. Sol was grateful to Sam for the opportunity and even more so to his own piano-playing sister Jane, who introduced him to Mozart, an artist for whom he kept "odd corners of [his] existence reserved." Handel lived in these corners too, as did the Ballet Russe de Monte Carlo and the San Carlo Opera, whose performances Sol attended as an unpaid usher at the Auditorium Theatre, one of Chicago's great cultural institutions.[45]

But it was mainly in the Freifeld household that Bellow and the other Tuley boys had the opportunity to expand their aesthetic and artistic horizons—and Sam's mother cooked hamburgers! What better place could there be for high school intellectuals to gather and talk about Shakespeare, the nineteenth-century poets, Marx and philosophy, Freud and sex—which mostly meant talk about girls they ran after on Division Street and in the hallways of Tuley High. Peltz remembered that "we didn't have sex" in high school: "That all happened later. We talked about it, but we didn't do it. Petting was as far as it went."[46]

Bellow had several female friends at Tuley. His great love was Eleanor Fox, more beautiful than smart or well read, a condition that Sol (to her annoyance) tried to fix. An older Eleanor is captured by Bellow in *Humboldt's Gift*. During a sentimental visit to his old girlfriend, the fictive Charlie Citrine is still talking about the big ideas, such as feudalism and "the history of human suffering." Eleanor tells him he was thrilling in high school but reminds Charlie that "when you used to lecture me[,] I couldn't follow you at all . . . with your Swinburne and your Baudelaire and Oscar Wilde. . . . Boy, you certainly did carry on."[47]

But it was an open relationship, and Sol could be seen some evenings climbing the porch to Zita Cogen's second-floor apartment. Sol was also smitten, indeed overwhelmed, by Yetta Barshevsky—class orator of 1932, delicately built, good looking, fearless, and a vital, insistent member of the Young People's Socialist League. Sol got to know most of her family, including her grandfather, "whom I would often see at the synagogue when I came to say Kaddish for my mother. He was an extremely orthodox short bent man with a beard that seemed to rush out of him and muffled his face." The grandfathers were the pious ones, Bellow remembered. "The old women, it seems were wildly radical Communist sympathizers," and hence not often in shul.[48]

Yetta, rumored to have been a member of the Young Communist League before becoming a socialist, was, as Bellow put it at the time of her death in 1996, "one of those persons who draw you into their lives and install themselves into yours."[49] At Tuley, Yetta "introduced [Sol], after a fashion, to world politics. . . . [he] was even then 'literary,' while she was political." Crossing Humboldt Park together after school or sitting in the Rose Garden, Yetta lectured Bellow "on Leninism . . . on democratic centralism . . . on the sins of Stalin and his inferiority to Trotsky," including Stalin's disastrous insistence on building a new society and a "new man" in one country—the USSR—as against Trotsky's "politically correct" advocacy of worldwide revolution. Sol listened, all the while paying as much or more attention to what he called Yetta's "Jewish beauty."[50]

Trotsky's appeal to the anti-Stalinist group of radicals at Tuley in Chicago and to the Trotskyists in archive 2 at City College in New York (CCNY) was rooted in several sources, including their Jewishness. Trotsky (or Lev Davidovich Bronstein), Jewish at birth, was thoroughly persecuted by the Stalinists whom the Tuley group and the CCNY students despised. And like Jews everywhere, Trotsky carried the definitive mark of the "outsider"—exclusion and exile. In addition to their ideological affinity with Trotsky, there was some hidden delight for the Tuley boys and girls in knowing that they were part of an elite. In the 1930s, Trotskyists in the US numbered fewer than one thousand.[51]

Bellow, although ostensibly a Trotskyist, was less interested in overthrowing the American government than in the candidacy of Franklin Delano Roosevelt, nominated at the Democratic Convention in Chicago in 1932. Sol remembered listening on the radio to a "portly sonorous Mr. Sugarman, the *schochet* (kosher slaughterer) on Division Street, sing out the names of the states during the Democratic roll call. . . . He did this in cantorial Jewish style, as though he were standing at the prayer desk, proud of knowing the correct order from A to W, an American patriot who wore a black rabbinical beard"[52]—a perfect Jewish American moment.

Still, mild as it was, Sol's Trotskyism caused perennial conflict in the Bellow household. Abraham was visibly distressed that his youngest son was reading revolutionary materials. "He was very shrewd about these things," Bellow said of his father, "and he knew a lot about the Soviet Union . . . much more than I did." Bellow could have saved himself a lot of trouble, he admitted, if he had listened to his father, who had seen the authoritarianism and absolutism inherent in Soviet Communism straight from the beginning. Abraham, like so many immigrants who had made it in America, was proud of his adopted country. After all, he asked, "What had Lenin done for the Jews?"[53] Here in the US, Abraham believed, Jews were at least—and at last—free.

He gave Sol's Trotskyist friends a hard time. "He was right," Bellow said, "but I felt ashamed that he should be such a reactionary."[54] A decade later—perhaps even as early as 1940, when Trotsky justified the Soviet invasion of Finland—Bellow was fully on his father's side. In a 1974 story, "Zetland: By a Character Witness" (apparently based on his close friend Isaac Rosenfeld), Bellow could lampoon radical politics with a mix of respect and irony: "Zet was identified with the avant-garde . . . and with radical politics. When the Russians invaded Finland, radical politics became absurd. Marxists debated whether the workers' state could be imperialistic. This was too nonsensical for Zetland. Then there was the Nazi Soviet Pact, there was the war."[55]

Even as early as 1944, Joseph in *Dangling Man* (presumably speaking for Bellow) says he "never enjoyed being a revolutionary" and had quit the party. He is enraged when a former comrade refuses to speak with him: "Forbid one man to talk to another . . . and you've forbidden him to think." Sounding much like his father, Bellow wrote, "When a man obeys an order like that, he's helping to abolish freedom and begin tyranny."[56]

Bellow's mother had also had a taste of tyranny in the Old World, and she was even more unfamiliar than Abraham was with America. She was especially "frightened by my excess," Bellow said: "I was a bohemian and a left-winger . . . and she was worried."[57] Liza had been diagnosed with breast cancer in 1929, and by 1932–33, with Sol preparing to graduate from Tuley, she knew she was dying and wouldn't be around to take care of her wayward son. Both parents were very suspicious of Sol's outside contacts. They thought they were wild, which they were, Bellow agreed, "but they were wild high-school intellectuals."[58] His family saw them as meshuggah (mad, crazy), and some were, Bellow said; but others went on to become successful and important people in the community, like Sydney J. Harris, Bellow's closest friend in young adolescence, who later had a thirty-year career as a journalist with the *Chicago Daily News.*

Without the perspective of the long run, Liza and Abraham feared Sol's Trotskyist high-school friends as "alienating influences."[59] Alienating they were, but not necessarily from Jewishness. All Sol's associates, Trotskyist or otherwise, were Jews with varying degrees of attachment to Jewish tradition, culture, and identity. Isaac Rosenfeld was more saturated in Jewishness than most, but neither Bellow nor any of his Trotskyist friends were involved in explicit disavowals of their Jewish identities. Bellow and his closest friends—Rosenfeld, Tarcov, and Peltz, for example—were interested in politics, but it is good to be reminded that they, like Sol, who put literature first, were no revolutionaries, ready like Robespierre to say "*Détruis tout*" (destroy everything).

The "Chicago boys"—Bellow, Rosenfeld, and Tarcov—"were sophisticated about politics," wrote Irving Kristol, "but literature was their passion." Unlike at CCNY, at Chicago "you didn't *have* to be political to lead a vigorous intellectual life and be a member of an authentic intellectual community."[60] The quest for spiritual enlightenment and the love of literature remained paramount and permanent for Bellow, who could say (as Trotsky himself did) that compared to politics, literature was "a world that was more attractive than any other."[61]

"My closest friends and I were not activists," Bellow said; "we were writers" and readers: "Through 'revolutionary politics' we met the demands for action. But what really mattered to us was the vital personal nourishment we took from Herman Melville, from Dreiser and John Dos Passos and Faulkner."[62] The American writers Bellow most valued were linked in their resistance to what he called "the material weight of American society." Edith Wharton, Sherwood Anderson, Sinclair Lewis, and Dreiser in particular proved what was not immediately obvious: that "we live in an age in which the impact of material forces is well-nigh irresistible; *the spiritual nature is overwhelmed by the shock*."[63]

The overweening force of materialism is nowhere better expressed in Bellow's fiction than in his novel *Humboldt's Gift*. Humboldt, as a widely recognized and critically admired poet (partly drawn, Bellow admits, from the life of Delmore Schwartz), is on his way to the very pinnacle of the artistic world when he becomes obsessed with the American definition of success. Money hungry and desperate for fame in the world of machers (worldly operators with power), Humboldt becomes merely "the figure of the poet" rather than a real writer.[64]

The political implication in what he was reading and later writing, if not always direct, was always clear to Bellow: "The world is too much with us." Wordsworth, whom Bellow singles out among his favorite poets as a lasting influence, made what the novelist took to be a powerful "point about emotion recollected in tranquility." Nor did Bellow miss the poet's "emphasis on the supreme importance of a state of attention or aesthetic concentration that would put the world of profit and loss in its place."[65]

In an interview in 1980, when asked to describe his life in the 1930s, Bellow began with his deep and varied reading, spoke of his intellectual friends, and finally proudly revealed his knowledge of the Chicago streets.[66] Less was said about politics. Whatever their proportionate emphasis, however, Bellow's activities and goals continued to bother his parents. His politics, over which there was more than one shouting match that nearly turned physical, frightened them; they attributed his writing to adolescent foolishness and worse.

To his business-minded father and brothers, Sol was thought little more than an "idiot . . . a moon-faced ideologist," who, despite odd jobs delivering flowers, working in a shoe store, and caddying, contributed little to the family's needs.[67] His sister Jane, nine years Bellow's senior, graduated from high school but, her ambitions ignored, went no further in her education. She took a secretarial job in the Loop to help support the household. His brothers, on the other hand, Saul said, were "hustlers." They "sold papers on the street, and peddled chocolate bars on the commuter trains," and later went on to build Carroll Coal Company and other businesses, Sam's often more legitimate than Maury's.[68]

Both brothers were ambitious: Sam wanted to go to medical school, "but there wasn't a chance we could afford it."[69] Maury went "to some cheap Law school in downtown Chicago" for "city boys from the immigrant neighborhoods." To pay his tuition, he earned money ferrying bribes to an Illinois state representative—skimming off a portion for himself, of course, half of which he gave to Liza. Soon Maury was "branching out into haberdashery and women." He never got caught with his little Gladstone bag or dipping into its contents. "That's lucky," Bellow told Philip Roth in an interview, "because they would have broken his hands."[70]

Maury was loud, wore expensive clothes, and boasted about "syndicate" friends. He was proud of his connections, his insider status, his cynicism. Unlike Sam, who married an Orthodox woman, daughter of a rabbi, Maury was full of contempt for Jewish observance and even "family feeling." He felt these were chains binding him to his father's will. His oldest brother, Bellow said, "was determined to become a world-beater. . . . From the first he would say to me" that he had had "enough of this old crap about being Jewish."[71] To achieve full Americanization, Maury, like the fictive Philip in Bellow's story "Him with His Foot in His Mouth" (1984), paid "the price of his soul. But then he may never have been absolutely certain that there is any such thing as a soul. What he resented about me," the narrator goes on, "was that I wouldn't stop hinting that souls existed. What was I a Reform rabbi or something?"[72]

In *Humboldt's Gift*, Maury is a model for Julius, refashioned, but not entirely. And when Charlie Citrine, the narrator of the novel and a seeker of spiritual truth, is in a particularly nervous state about money, not having it, or worrying about not having enough, he knows that

> only one man in all the world could help me, my practical brother Julius a real estate operator in . . . Texas. I loved my stout and now elderly brother. Perhaps he loved me too.
>
> In principle he was not in favor of strong family bonds. Possibly he saw brotherly love as an opening for exploitation. . . . He wished to be a man entirely of today, and had long forgotten the past. . . . He thought me some kind of idiot. He himself a wizard with money, built shopping centers, condominiums, hotels.[73]

In the days when Citrine still argued with his brother, he would say, "'You've given your Russian Jewish brains away out of patriotism. You're a self-made ignoramus and a true American.' But I long ago stopped saying such things. I knew that he shut himself in his office with a box of white raisins and read Arnold Toynbee . . . or Cecil Roth and Salo Baron on Jewish history. When any of this reading popped up in conversation, [Julius] made sure to mispronounce key words."[74]

When the real Maury visited Saul, he would play the dumb clown, pull a book off a shelf, and demand, "Who's this guy Prowst?" Once when Saul was struggling to pay their bills, Maury visited and tossed a pile of his old shirts at his brother. Having become a virtual tycoon, with three hundred suits and a hundred pairs of shoes, he cut a substantial figure in Chicago; he loved to lord it over people, partly because he was a bully but also because he needed to show just how successful a businessman he was.

Saul's middle brother, Sam, who owned a chain of nursing homes, was also a successful businessman. But, as Bellow put it, he was of the Old World, Orthodox, "with his wife and children, and granddaughters who had to be married off." There were no such compromises for Maury, "the entirely American brother." Sam and Maury could unite in belittling Sol's dreamy literary ambitions, but Maury and Sol "were united in . . . disapproval of brother Sam," who had chosen to be imprisoned in formal Orthodoxy.[75]

Sol did not reject Jewishness as "crap" but was persistently suspicious about Orthodoxy. When Sam and his wife Nina's family, including her father, the Orthodox rabbi Moses Wolf Kahn, got together with the Bellow family to celebrate Jewish holidays, Maury was generally absent; but Saul would spar with the rabbi—in Yiddish—over Talmudic matters. Rabbi Kahn would quote from the Bible, and Bellow would quote from Shakespeare.[76]

Maury also introduced Sol to "the idea of chasing women drinking . . . wild parties—I didn't have much taste for this," Bellow said, "but it was interesting to see how life was shaping up," and "I became conscious that my oldest brother [despite everything] was doing me good. That is to say, he couldn't Americanize himself fast enough," and "I was very happy to be Americanized" in turn by him, at least insofar as it came to dressing, speaking, and imagining an open future.[77] Of course, as far as Maury and Sam were concerned, "there was only one future and one career, and that was business, and nothing else mattered, and you were made of disagreeably soft stuff if you went in for 'that'"—meaning writing.

Maury was disdainful of Sol's nonremunerative choice of career, which he considered *luftmenschlich*—impractical, frivolous. Choosing writing, Bellow said, meant "you were not a *mensch*, you'd never amount to anything."[78] But as he said much later, "there was not a chance in the world that Chicago, with the agreement of my eagerly Americanizing extended family, would make me in its own image. Before I was capable of thinking clearly, my resistance to its material weight took the form of obstinacy. I couldn't say why I would not allow myself to become the product of an environment. But gainfulness, utility, prudence, business had no hold on me."[79]

In "Something to Remember Me By," set in 1933, the narrator's elder brother, Albert (who often behaves and speaks like Maury), is described as "a night-school law student clerking for Rowland the racketeer congressman . . . who hired him not to read law but to make collections." Toward the narrator, with his lack of business sense and profound naiveté, "Albert is scornful. He says, 'You don't understand fuck-all. You never will.'"[80]

Bellow's feelings about businessmen were not entirely negative. He said of his brother Maury, for example, "He was made for Chicago. He adopted the style of a racketeer and put himself over as a wheeler-dealer." Maury was aggressive and of "an underworld coloration," which made even his "legitimate business seem or sound crooked." He epitomized the cult of power and material success that both fascinated and repelled Bellow. But in Maury, Sol "recognized . . . the day-to-day genius of the U.S.A."[81] A less forceful commercial astuteness is also celebrated in Bellow's fiction, with the depiction of Cousin Isaac in "The Old System" (1968). Isaac "had put his stake together penny by penny, old style, starting with rags and bottles as a boy; then fire-salvaged goods, then used cars; then learning the building trades. Earth moving, foundations, concrete, sewage, wiring, roofing, heating systems. He got his money the hard way."[82]

Bellow himself valued money and joined Maury as a speculator or investor in a number of business ventures. When Sam and Maury talked of possible deals, Saul would ask, "*Vu bin ich*?" (Where am I in this?), which apparently became a Bellow catchphrase. His eagerness to participate suggests not only Bellow's desire to make money but also a longing to amount to something in his brothers' eyes.[83]

But Bellow burned to write, he "knew what was necessary to [be] a writer," and he "wasn't going to let anything interfere with it."[84] Much later, he said, "Chicago is not a city that produces sophisticated people, but it was in Chicago where this child of Jewish immigrants got the idee fixe of becoming an American author."[85] It is not as if Chicago failed to produce prodigious writers—there were, after all, Sherwood Anderson, Gwendolyn Brooks, Ernest Hemingway, James T. Farrell, and Carl Sandburg—but none of them was Jewish. To be a great author was an ambition shared by many of Bellow's Jewish high-school friends, but Sol, as Dave Peltz put it, "was focused, he was dedicated"—fiercely—to becoming a writer, and "from the beginning . . . he never veered"; he could make his mark anywhere.[86]

During his last year at Tuley, Sol's mother had grown increasingly ill with cancer, and Sol came home from his after-school jobs to be with her. Near the end, at Liza's bedside or just outside her door, he kept a solitary vigil. Thirty years later, in *Herzog*, Bellow presents a fictionalized version of his mother's final days: Moses sits at the oilcloth-covered kitchen table enraged by reading Spengler, who dismissed Jews as historical relics, incapable of grasping the Christian "world idea," powerless to function productively in Western civilization:

> When I looked away from the dense print and its insidious pedantry, my heart infected with ambition, and the bacteria of vengeance, Mama was entering the kitchen. . . . Her hair had to be cut during her illness, and this made those eyes hard to recognize. Or no, the shortness of her hair merely made their message simpler: *My son, this is death*. I chose not to read this text. "I saw the light," she said, "What are you doing up so late?" But the dying for themselves, have given up hours. She only pitied me, her orphan, understood, I was a gesture-maker, ambitious, a fool; thought I would need my eyesight and my strength on a certain day of reckoning.

A few days later, when his mother had lost the power to speak, Moses entered her room,

> holding his school books, and began to say something to her. But she lifted up her hands and showed him her fingernails. They were blue. As he stared, she slowly began to nod her head up and down as if to say, "That's right, Moses, I am dying now." He sat by the bed. Apparently still "trying to comfort Moses," Mama Herzog began to stroke his hand. She did this as well as she could; her fingers had lost their flexibility. Under the nails they seemed to him to be turning already into the blue loam of graves. She had begun to change into earth! He did not dare to look but listened to the runners of children's sleds in the street, and the grating of peddlers' wheels on the knotted ice, the hoarse call of the apple peddler and the rattle of his steel scale. The steam whispered in the vent. The curtain was drawn.[87]

Bellow tried to hide his distress over Liza's illness and death from his friends. "It was a very shattering experience for him," Dave Peltz recalled. "He did talk about it," but not much and not to many people. Fred Glotzer, another Tuley friend, recalled that Bellow at this time in his life was a "kind of lonely guy who needed approval from his friends."[88] To get away from his frantic father and the gloom and doom of his apartment, he often slept nights on a couch at Sydney Harris's family's apartment. "I was turned loose," he recalled decades later, "freed in a sense; free but also stunned." Even in his eighties, he struggled for words to convey the immense and devastating importance of his loss.

One could be forgiven for speculating that Bellow—in Herzog's words—was "mother-bound" and that this had something to do with his profound attachment to his childhood past and to his having been married five times. Was he subconsciously trying to replace her? To his biographer James Atlas, Bellow said simply, "I was grieving. . . . My life was never the same after my mother died."[89] An undertow of grief, an attention to the inevitability of death and its meaning, would mark almost all of Bellow's future work, along with a yearning for the original world of pure feeling and family closeness, which, if not entirely vanished for him, faded some with his mother gone.

THREE

THE EDUCATION OF SAUL BELLOW

IN THE FALL OF 1933, months after his mother's death in February and after a semester at Crane Junior College, Sol Bellow, following Isaac Rosenfeld's lead, enrolled at the University of Chicago. The Great Depression was at its peak, and unemployment in Carl Sandberg's "City of Big Shoulders" was especially steep. Men and boys waited in line for soup, sold apples, and slept in parks. Carroll Coal, bucking the trend, experienced an improvement in its financial fortunes, but Abraham Bellow, still frantic about the loss of Liza and permanently dismayed about Sol's choice to pursue writing as a career, had to be bullied into paying his son's first-year fee of $300.

It had been difficult for youngsters to find steady work, and many of the brightest boys, especially Jewish boys, had registered for college. Jews made up less than 10 percent of Chicago's population in 1933 but constituted a third of the University of Chicago's entering class. Abraham, however, couldn't comfortably explain to his friends, several of whom also had sons in college, "just what [Sol] was doing at the university."[1] He was not pursuing a premed course like many of his Tuley classmates, nor did he study law or economics. His father "resented the embarrassment [Sol] caused him," Bellow said, by not doing something "practical," by failing to understand "what sacrifices . . . families were making."[2]

But Bellow, as his friend Oscar Tarcov had said, "never veered." Sol himself made clear that his "unshakeable purpose in life . . . was to be a writer," and he admitted that he "never seriously considered giving it up." Like his father, Sol "was an *akshn* (obstinate person) as Jews like to say. A very stubborn creature." When anyone referred to his aspirations as ephemeral or questioned whether it was really possible to make a full-time career of writing, Bellow would get his dander up. Insisting he had no ambition to be a personality, only "an ambition to write well," he confessed to being "bull-headed" about the whole thing "and just threw away alternatives."[3]

In his first year, in addition to registering for required courses, Bellow studied drama, poetry, and Shakespeare. He wasn't happy with the size of the university and its concomitant need for multiple-choice exams. He felt lonely in its vast lecture halls, where he understood almost nothing of what guest speakers like Thornton Wilder or Gertrude Stein had to say. But he liked the spirit of Robert Hutchins, "in which the place was saturated." As president of the university, Hutchins had earlier introduced a novel pedagogical system built on the "Great Books," Socratic dialogue, and comprehensive examinations. The idea, Bellow said, was that if you lasted four years and met all the requirements, "you would know everything there was to know . . . Everything." "In all this," Bellow remembered, there was a "kind of crazy, cockeyed arrogance . . . which really appealed to young Jews from [Chicago's] West Side."[4]

But Bellow did not last the four years; in the middle of his second year (during which he took elective courses in anthropology and economics), he had to abruptly withdraw from school. A truck driver for Carroll Coal had been killed while unloading a shipment, and Sol's older brother Sam had forgotten to renew the company's insurance policy. Presented with a huge bill, Abraham could no longer afford the fees for his younger son's education. For years, Bellow recalled, all the brothers worked to pay off that debt.[5] But Sol, with his eye on the prize, was not to be deterred. By adding odd jobs on top of his primary work at the coal yard, he earned enough money to attend the University of Minnesota in the summer of 1935 and transfer to Northwestern as a junior in the fall; in neither school were there very many Jews, students or faculty, unlike at the University of Chicago.[6]

In addition to English literature, Bellow studied anthropology under Melville J. Herskovits, one of the most influential social scientists of the day. Professor and student, notwithstanding some minor personal irritations on both sides, took to each other easily. Like Bellow, Herskovits came from immigrant Jewish parents, went to Hebrew school, and for a time thought he'd be studying for the rabbinate. Herskovits, who was working on his breakthrough study, *The Myth of the Negro Past* (1941), which explored cultural continuities from Africa to African American communities, had been drawn to anthropology (as were many of its Jewish pioneers, including Emile Durkheim, Franz Boas, and Ruth Leah Bunzel) by something quite special at the discipline's core.[7]

As Bellow put it, "a very democratic idea" lay at the heart of anthropology: cultural relativity. The African Dahomey people, for example, "have their culture and we have ours," Bellow said, and "we should not get carried away by our own ethnocentrism."[8] It was encouraging for Jews, "outsiders," like himself, Bellow thought, to learn that there were so many variations in cultural behaviors that what seemed right among the African Maasai, for example, could be seen as wrong among the Eskimos, and vice versa. Anthropology gave Jewish students a greater sense of independence and immunity from Anglo-Saxon custom—a degree of freedom from worrying about being accepted or excluded by "a society of Christian gentlemen."[9]

For his senior thesis, Bellow had been studying a tribe of Eskimos who reportedly had preferred to starve rather than eat accessible food that was taboo. Would Bellow have been reminded of his hospital experience, when he, all of eight years old and critically ill, had overcome his revulsion and guilt over eating pork—a Jewish taboo—by remembering that in Jewish tradition, eating "anything is permitted that keeps you alive"?[10] In any case, he would later come to see "right for one, wrong for the other" as a "treacherous doctrine," as too permissive. Morality, he came to determine, "should be made of sterner stuff," and in the 1960s he, along with several other older, white male intellectuals, moved closer to a position of social conservatism. But in his early twenties, Bellow was a cultural relativist.[11]

"Why are Jews such avid anthropologists?" asks Ijah Brodsky in Bellow's story "Cousins." Jews pursuing anthropology, Ijah said, "believed that they were demystifiers, that science was their motive and that their ultimate aim was to increase universalism." A truer explanation, Ijah thinks, is the "nearness of ghettoes to the sphere of Revelation, an easy move for the mind from rotting streets and rancid dishes, a direct ascent into transcendence." Jews may have thought they were "going out to do science upon exotics," but in the end Brodsky concludes "it all came out in Rabbinic-German or Cartesian-Talmudic forms."[12]

As many as fifty years before Bellow's "Cousins," his confidence in anthropology as a social science—and in social science generally—began to wane, and he grew absorbed by "spiritual investigation" as the only true methodology. "To me," Bellow said, anthropologists "were suspect because they had no literary abilities. . . . They brought what they called 'science' to human matters, matters of human judgment, but their science could never replace a trained sensibility." Ijah, too, as Bellow draws him, believes that a trained sensibility "releases you back again" to "that original self or soul." Only in this way, Ijah thinks, are you "free to look under the debris of modern ideas, and . . . with a lucidity altogether different from the lucidity of *approved* types of knowledge."[13]

Even under the tutelage of Herskovits, Bellow brought what he called "a radical Jewish skepticism" to most claims made by anthropologists. Many years after graduating, Saul told an interviewer that "there was a kind of buried arrogance in the whole idea" of anthropology—by studying "simple peoples," it was thought depths could be plumbed, allowing social scientists to "nail down the meaning of life." But after all your reading and even your observations, Bellow said, "what you knew was the version of an educated . . . European."[14] Bellow, who had never been to Africa, admitted that his portrayal of the continent in *Henderson the Rain King* (1959) suffered the same shortcoming. But serious scholars have demonstrated the novel's indebtedness to the kind of research Bellow had done in anthropology.[15]

There are hints throughout Bellow's letters and interviews implying that anthropology at Northwestern absorbed less of his time than creative writing. He began to sign his many essays for the *Daily Northwestern* "Saul Bellow," and he apparently wrote a good number of short stories. But only one piece from that period survives: "The Hell It Can't." The title echoes Arthur Koestler's ironic name for his 1935 novel *It Can't Happen Here,* and the story neatly dovetails with Trotsky's notion that in any coming world war, there will be little to choose from between the great powers. The battle will signify not a conflict between Western democracy and Axis fascism but a struggle between two imperialisms. In 1944, however, Joseph in *Dangling Man* qualifies the rawness of the Trotsky-Bellow perspective by saying, "As between their imperialism and ours, if a full choice were possible, I would take ours."[16] Bellow's acceptance of Trotsky's myopic view is easier to credit in 1936—even in 1944—than it would have been in the postwar world, because the radical evil of Nazism had not yet made itself fully manifest.

Having lost interest in becoming an anthropologist, the twenty-one-year-old Bellow could more heavily invest in his most powerful and enduring ambition—writing as a career. But how to support himself—or postpone supporting himself—in the meantime? One answer was to try for a postgraduate scholarship in English. When Saul approached William Frank Bryan, the chair of Northwestern's English Department, for guidance and support, Bryan, a specialist in Old and Middle English, told Bellow, "You've got a very good record, but I wouldn't recommend that you study English." Saul may have looked surprised, because Bryan, "an elegant, courtly, Southern gentleman," added a seemingly discreet but nonetheless offensive antisemitic remark: "You weren't born to it."[17]

Trying to walk his own bias back a bit, Bryan said that Saul would face several hurdles as a professor of English: gaining acceptance from students, for example, or finding any kind of remunerative writing job in the first place. There were no Jews in the English Department at Northwestern and only two Jewish faculty members in the entire university. Bryan, an Episcopalian, dedicated golfer, and member of the prestigious University Club, suggested Bellow consider staying with anthropology—a field already resembling a sort of Jewish club. Bellow described the moment with Bryan as one of his earliest encounters with the view that having been born to a family that spoke no English, he "had no business" writing or teaching literature: "I was told that!" This drew a reaction, sotto voce, from Bellow as he walked out of the chair's office: "Well, the hell with you."[18]

It is good to remember that when Bellow was growing up, Lionel Trilling, an instructor in English at Columbia in 1932—a first—was discouraged from pursuing tenure at the university because as a Jew he could not really understand the nuances and idioms of English literature and would not by "happy" as a tenured professor at Columbia.[19] And when Bellow began to write, the most celebrated American novelists were Fitzgerald, Faulkner,

Hemingway, and Thomas Wolfe—a markedly non-Jewish group who often conveyed a genteel but clear antisemitism. And from T. S. Eliot and Ezra Pound, antisemitism was explicit and ugly.

Despite his fading interest in anthropology, Bellow, not yet ready for the "starving artist" role, accepted a fellowship at the University of Wisconsin in the Department of Sociology and Anthropology. Madison, Wisconsin, was close to Chicago, where Bellow had family ties and a growing love interest. In addition, his friend Isaac Rosenfeld, a transfer student from the University of Chicago, would be waiting for him there. At Wisconsin, the two grew ever closer, glad, both, to be out from under the often-oppressive atmosphere of proverbial Jewish parental care and resistance to the idea of literature as real work.[20]

Just before leaving Chicago for Madison, Bellow had had a ferocious fight with his father, "an awful blowout." Bothered by lingering feelings of anger and guilt, Saul wrote to Oscar Tarcov telling him that Abraham had damned "all the things I stood for, which was the equivalent of damning me also." Through his brother Sam, Saul discovered that Abraham was heartbroken over the battle they had had, the insults, "the shouts and imprecations." When advised by his brother Sam to get in touch with his father, Bellow asked Tarcov, "But what have I to say to him?" He saw his youngest son as "a perverse child growing into manhood with no prospects of bourgeois ambitions, utterly unequipped to meet the world (he is wrong, not unequipped, but unwilling)." Bellow calmed down later in the letter, at least enough to describe his family as "good folk, when they are not neurotic." But "what, after all, can we expect," he asked Tarcov. "Such conflicts must come if we are to honestly follow out the concepts we learn or teach ourselves."[21]

In the following weeks, Saul told Tarcov, "Just now I am deeply in love, and I think I shall continue in love because it is my salvation." He also encouraged Tarcov, in a highly qualified way, to stick with anthropology, a discipline he himself could no longer fully abide, Bellow abandoned graduate study soon thereafter, confessing that "every time I worked on my thesis, it turned out to be a story."[22] Presumably his adviser agreed. Bellow returned to Chicago to marry Anita Goshkin, of Lafayette, Indiana, a daughter of Jewish immigrants from Crimea and an erstwhile Trotskyist who had been prominent in radical circles at Northwestern.

In his short time in Wisconsin, Bellow was with Rosenfeld often. They talked neither politics nor anthropology, but literature. They went from Shakespeare to Kafka, Tolstoy to Babel, and Balzac to Proust. They also had the pleasure of reading Delmore Schwartz's newly published short story, "In Dreams Begin Responsibilities," which Bellow "considered . . . a masterpiece." The story, originally appearing in *Partisan Review,* was widely anthologized, and over time it became—and remains—a classic piece of American Jewish literature.[23]

Together they wrote one-act plays and poems, including "Dissertation on Beet Borscht," an improvised dialogue performed at a Young People's Socialist League social; "Twin Bananas" (with Tarcov); and the best-known and most enduring work by Bellow and Rosenfeld—"Der shir hashirim fun Mendl Pumshtok" or "The Song of Songs of Mendl Pumshtok"—a shrewd and hilarious parody of T. S. Eliot's "The Love Song of J. Alfred Prufrock." The most famous lines mimic and mock the best-known lines of the original: "I grow old, / I shall wear my trousers rolled" becomes "*Ikh ver alt, Ikh ver alt / Un der pupik vert mir kalt*"—"I grow old, I grow old / And my belly button grows cold."

Unlike Philip Roth, who, a generation later, with little (if any) knowledge of Yiddish, would use the word *pipik* (belly button) as a nod to the immigrant past, Bellow and Rosenfeld had an intimate acquaintance with Yiddish. So, they entered American literature with the language that drew upon the cumulative experience of Jews in Eastern Europe, and they valued the gift they had inherited for the way it enhanced their cultural options.

Other memorable Yiddish lines the two Chicago boys wrote in their Prufrock parody include the transformation of Eliot's "In the room the women come and go / talking of Michelangelo" into *"In tsimer vu di vaybere zenen, / Redt men fun Karl Marx un Lenin"* ("In the room where the wives are / They talk of Marx and Lenin"). Bellow's title is a direct allusion to "The Song of Solomon," which is most often read on the Sabbath during Passover and is interpreted by many as a celebration of sexual love, rare in the scriptures.

Pumshtok's song is racier than Prufrock's in other ways as well. "Do I dare eat a peach?" becomes *"Meg ikh oyfesen a floym?"* or "May I eat a prune?" Eliot's distance from and dread of the corporeal is disparaged and ridiculed throughout. The poem, as Rosenfeld's biographer, Steven Zipperstein, shrewdly points out, "is packed with wet socks and dirty bedding; its women are 'wives' not the desiccated seductresses of Eliot's imagination."[24] The Chicago boys continue their spoof of the cleverly intellectualized despair of the Eliot poem with this passage:

Oyf dem vant	On the wall
Funem Yiddishe restoran	Of the Jewish restaurant
Hengt a shmutizke betgevant	Dirty linens are hanging
Un vantzn tantzn karahot	And bedbugs dance in circles

A classic of twentieth-century modernism, Eliot's poem, with a hero whose erotic fire is deadened by urban routine, is actually ridiculing the love song of earlier English and European literature. Prufrock, inhabiting a world that lacks the passion of Dante or Shakespeare, is no longer able to pursue romance, let alone sing about it. Bellow and Rosenfeld, by restoring robustness and grit, chose life over Eliot's begrudging vision.

The chutzpah and irony employed by Rosenfeld and Bellow in their mockery of Eliot mark it as a dark and humorous tease, but the two writers were also composing an implicit veneration of a great poet. At the same time, they were denouncing "their own exclusion as Jews" from the English literary world, proclaiming, in their inimitably brilliant fashion, what verve and excitement they could bring to English if only the WASP gatekeepers stopped marginalizing them.[25]

Ruth Wisse, an eminent professor of Yiddish at Harvard, said that "if asked at what point American Jewish letters gave notice of its independence from Anglo-American Modernism, I would cite the day Isaac Rosenfeld, with the help of Saul Bellow, composed [their] parody of Eliot's 'The Love Song of J. Alfred Prufrock,'" a tour de force that friends could still recite by memory after more than fifty years. T. S. Eliot, the giant among poets "who could not be ignored," believed Jews to be corrupters of his culture. What better way, Professor Wisse asked, was there to credit Eliot as an artist and "discredit him as an anti-Semite than by Yiddishizing the poet who so feared the Yid?"[26]

It is good to be reminded that Eliot was not above lines replete with representations of Jews as loathsome, subhuman creatures whom the world would be well rid of:

> The rats are underneath the piles
> The jew is underneath the lot.
> (from "Burbank with a Baedeker: Bleisten with a Cigar")
>
> Rachel née Rabinovitch
> Tears at grapes with murderous paws.
> (from "Sweeney among the Nightingales")
>
> My house is a decayed house,
> And the jew squats on the windowsill, the owner
> Spawned in some estaminet of Antwerp
> Blistered in Brussels, patched and peeled in London.
> (from "Gerontion")[27]

Eliot's antisemitism was not limited to his poetry. In a series of lectures delivered at the University of Virginia in 1933, in the year Hitler was appointed chancellor of Germany, the poet said, "What is still more important [than cultural homogeneity] is unity of religious background, and reasons of race and religion combine to make any large number of free-thinking Jews undesirable."[28]

Eliot repeated this defamation in *The Idea of a Christian Society* (1939), further convincing Bellow that there would be no place for him as a Jew in that kind of Christian civilization; and he "rejected all of that." Bellow saw Eliot's literary Christian "traditionalism" as a further "descent into the nihilistic pit." Traditionalists, he believed, had actually "gone deeper into the night with their fascism and anti-Semitism."[29]

In an eloquent, deeply moving and revealing talk, Bellow said in 1988 that Jews in Europe "might be welcomed in almost every field of knowledge but as artists they would inevitably come up against a national or racial barrier." Wagnerism in one form or another would reject them. Even Goethe, who Bellow admitted was much more sensible than Wagner, wrote in *Wilhelm Meister*, "'We do not tolerate any Jew among us; for how we could grant him a share in the highest culture, the origin and tradition of which he denies?'"[30]

Bellow was not surprised by any of this rhetorical nonsense, and in his lecture he said that it is not so much the Jew but rather the traditional Christian culture that by silencing the "outsider" does the denying. He made a classic defense not only of Jews but of the outsider—in general and everywhere—against the charge of lacking respect for the advanced rules and genius of English idiom and grammar. If we are to regard Poles and Irishmen—Joseph Conrad and James Joyce, for example—as aliens, there are grounds, Bellow argued, for supposing that outsiders have contributed more richness to English in the twentieth century "than any of the pure-blooded men of letters who stick to the finer rules."

To Joyce and Conrad, Bellow said, "we can easily add . . . Apollinaire in French . . . Babel, Mandelstam, and Pasternak in Russian, Kafka in German." Certainly, Bellow concluded, "it is not easy in this cosmopolitan age to remove the *métèques* [French, for resident aliens] from modern literature without leaving it very thin."[31]

In America, a land of immigrants and their acculturated children, a term like *métèque* or *alien* is—or was—inapplicable and inappropriate. All the greater, therefore, was Bellow's "enthusiasm for embracing the American democracy with all its crudities." The US, he said, "granted me an equality which I felt was mine by right. I wasn't going to be ruled off the grounds by . . . WASP hotshots" or by the likes of T. S. Eliot.[32]

Some, if not most, young Jewish intellectuals fell "crazily in love" with Eliot—more for the rhythms and music of his verse than for the meaning. They told themselves that the poet's reactionary politics was muted some by his insights into the decadence of middle-class society. The passages about Jews, however, in Eliot (and in Pound, too) caused pain, embarrassment, and the discomforts of cognitive dissonance, which in turn required tortuous explanations. While Bellow thought Eliot a great poet, he left it at that, concluding he "is not for me"—not the nihilism of *The Wasteland* nor the fascistic antisemitism appearing in much of the poet's oeuvre: "No . . . I much prefer more strengthening of the soul—the soul of a Jew, I should add."[33]

In the first days of 1938, several months after Saul and Isaac composed their Eliot send-up, Bellow and Anita Goshkin were married. Saul first encountered Anita in Hyde Park in 1936, the summer before his senior year at Northwestern. In *Herzog*, Bellow fictionalizes the moment. Moses spots Daisy, a pretty young woman with slant green eyes, clear skin, and bare legs, wearing a simple seersucker dress, her hair held at the top by a barrette. Daisy's presentation, Moses thought, expressed character: "stability, symmetry, order, containment"—the ability to organize daily life, something the dreamy and ambitious Bellow had little talent for.[34]

Joseph in Bellow's first novel, *Dangling Man*, also sought some way to bring stability into his daily existence. In the very conclusion of the book, the protagonist, when finally drafted in 1943, says, "I am no longer to be held accountable for myself. . . . Huray for regular hours! And for the supervision of the spirit! Long live regimentation!"[35] Welcoming regimentation may appear strange coming from Bellow, a man who invested so much in "the freedom in the individual." But neither Bellow nor his characters desired to be controlled, as some critics seem to imply.[36] Classic authoritarian personality traits, or eagerness to serve an outside power blindly, are rarely or ever on display in Bellow's writing. About the various forms of absolutism evident in the 1930s, Bellow said, "Every ideology at that age presented itself to me as an orthodoxy; and there was something about radical orthodoxy" that resembled religious orthodoxy "in that it was enforced by people who insisted rigidly on the legitimacy of their political position."[37]

Bellow was not a man or a writer enthralled with imposing order; on the contrary, his call for "stability" is more like the call for an unwavering, quiet context within which one could use the imagination in search of spiritual guiding principles. The noise of the material world with all its myriad distraction was always the great enemy.

For Bellow, Anita, like the fictive Daisy in *Herzog*, represented quietude and (despite her political activism) an orderliness disconnected from dissonance. And like Daisy, she also appeared to exude, in addition to "the fragrance of summer apples," a "laundry purity" and the characteristics of a "conventional Jewish woman."[38] Anita herself was far from conventional. In school, she had regularly spoken at political meetings and was active on the ground as well. She had, for example, helped organize steelworkers in Gary, Indiana, where she was arrested and spent a night in jail, along with Bellow's friend Oscar Tarcov.[39] Something of a risk taker, Anita was also practical. Eight months before her marriage to Saul, she enrolled in a two-year MA program at Chicago's School of Social Service Administration.

Abraham Bellow had no negative opinion of Anita, but he disapproved of the marriage; he thought his youngest son, with no head for business, could not support himself, no less a wife and family. But he failed to consider the generosity of Anita and her family's household. The Goshkins—Anita's mother, Sophie, a suffragette and socialist in the old country, and Anita's four older siblings—took Bellow into their Ravenswood apartment, insisting that he "must be given a chance to write something."[40] Anything? Bellow, the "crazy scribbler," as his relatives called him, would not publish any fiction for three years into his marriage, and that came more than five years after he had determined to lead a life of the mind and of a full-time writer.

In Eastern Europe, the life of the mind for men who studied Torah was possible only because women made it so. In the New World, as the novelist Dara Horn puts it, "if one substitutes Torah study for an intellectual life of a different sort, one finds that Rosenfeld and Bellow during their early careers, despite their deliberate distance from traditional Jewish culture, were in an important sense actually leading the traditional Ashkenazi [Eastern European] lifestyle—with their intellectual gifts entirely subsidized, both financially and personally, by their wives. Bellow's case was at one point traditional in the extreme. During his first marriage he actually lived as a kind of literary *kestler* [boarder] in his wife's parents' home, writing the great American novel while his mother-in-law prepared his meals."[41]

Anita left the Goshkins' crowded household weekday mornings for the university, where she was working toward a degree in social work, and her siblings were off early to their jobs. Bellow camped out at a card table in a back bedroom and wrote.

Words did not come easily. What he was putting on paper, Bellow claimed he could not remember, but he guessed "it must have been terrible." Indeed, if he had "been a dog," Bellow said of his attempt to write, "I would have howled."[42]

On his daily, post lunch walks in the nearly empty sun-drenched sidewalks of Chicago's Ravenswood district, Bellow, though frustrated, felt certain still that he had been "born to be a performing and interpretive creature" and that he was meant "to take part in a peculiar, exalted game." But by his own admission, at twenty-three, he was also "extremely proud, ornery and stupid."[43] Ornery he would remain.

After about a year at the Goshkins' home, Anita left graduate school and found a job as a social worker for twenty-five dollars a week, mostly delivering welfare checks. With her salary (and perhaps some help from her family), she and Saul moved from the crowded apartment to "rooms of their own" in Hyde Park. Bellow continued to insist that nothing of worth was coming from his pen, and he returned to the less-than-serious life of a University of Chicago grad student, a life he found difficulty justifying. Bellow's need to become a great novelist, according to Edward Shils (a longtime friend and sagacious Chicago colleague), was the same as wanting to be "a saint, an 'unacknowledged legislator of mankind,' one who was consecrated to the highest function of which any human being is capable, namely, to be an artist."[44]

In the meantime, Bellow, like Joseph in *Dangling Man*, idled by the Depression, was oppressed by the "narcotic dullness" of his existence.[45] By 1938, however, Bellow found a job at Pestalozzi-Froebel Teachers College on South Michigan Avenue, teaching anthropology and English—including a course on American minority groups, an interest carried over from studying with Herskovits at Northwestern about African and African American cultures. And in his English classes, he was thrust back into the familiar world of his most admired novelists—Flaubert and

Dostoyevsky, for example, as well as Dos Passos, Dreiser, and Sherwood Anderson.

Bellow also worked briefly for the New Deal's Works Progress Administration (WPA), composing short biographies of writers from the Midwest. The seasoned writer Nelson Algren did similar work for the WPA, as did Isaac Rosenfeld and Richard Wright—both, like Bellow, future novelists. "I never had it so good," Bellow said. Being among writers, writing about writers, and earning twenty-four dollars a week allowed him to "justify the idea" that *he* "was a writer."[46] But it wasn't enough.

Bellow's ineluctable drive to be a novelist dominated all else. His ambition was intensified by his need to prove his worthiness to his father and brothers, who remained contemptuous of Bellow's literary fantasies. His frustration sometimes expressed itself as obstinacy and impulsive bursts of foolishness. "I was peculiarly touchy, vulnerable, hard to deal with," Bellow admitted.[47] With his closest Hyde Park friends—Oscar Tarcov; Sydney Harris, his coeditor and founder of the Northwestern University left-wing monthly, *The Beacon*; Harold "Kappy" Kaplan, a Francophile and student of Proust's work; Isaac Rosenfeld; and Herb Passin, with whom he had adventurously ridden the freight rails after graduating from Tuley (apparently a Depression-era rite of passage)—Bellow's interactions were often troubling and disruptive. There was also fractiousness in his marriage. Bellow told Tarcov in 1940 that he and Anita were "in numerous ways disagreeable to one another" and on the verge of separating.[48]

Also imminent was separation from an already fractured Trotskyist Socialist Workers Party, to which Bellow and Tarcov were attached—though tenuously, ever since the Nazi-Soviet Pact in 1939. "I was alienated before the factional fight," Bellow wrote in the same letter, "but now the whole affair has become nauseous."[49] What with the rise of Nazism, the civil war in Spain, and the persistence of the Great Depression, engagement in politics for Bellow and his Jewish associates could hardly be avoided.

But as Bellow's son Greg said in retrospect, "literature was Saul's life, not politics."[50] Consequently, it wasn't all that difficult for Bellow, very much like his friends, to grow weary of and distant from the increasingly intense sectarianism at the core of Trotskyism.

By the spring of 1940, he was done with the movement—to which he never fully belonged—but he remained committed to a fierce anti-Stalinism. Much later he told a correspondent in a crumbling Soviet Union that "Jewish adolescents in Chicago in the Thirties . . . drew the line at Stalin and by the time the war began we understood how wrong we had been about 1917. Marxism Leninism fell away completely during and after World War II."[51]

In the summer of 1940, Bellow was the recipient of a windfall; his mother's life insurance policy, seven years after her death, finally paid its $500 premium. Abraham, in need of the cash, insisted the funds were his, but Saul was named beneficiary and refused to hand over the money. A passionate, forceful argument ensued, Abraham trying yet again to exert what he saw as his archaic rightful tyranny over his rebellious son.

"My father," Bellow told Philip Roth years later, "was a tyrant, with a perfectly good claim to his place in the all-time gallery of great tyrants."[52] He wrote the same to Irving Halperin, a professor of the humanities at San Francisco State University. "Russian Jewish fathers were naturally tyrannical," Bellow said, particularly if they were immigrants. For the fathers "knew as their children did not, how different from the Russian life of their own boyhood our lives in America were. . . . Our lives seemed to them a paradise which we had done nothing to deserve."[53] Abraham, and Russian Jewish immigrant fathers like him, tried to navigate in an alien terrain in a foreign language, even as they watched their children, upon whom they were forced to rely for interpretation and explanation, steer through the strangeness with comparative ease.

The injured pride of the fathers was most often displayed when the sons resisted; and for Saul, the devotion to writing rather than to success in business or a profession was itself a form of defiance. Bellow's first published story, "9 a.m. without Work" (1941), features a young man, a champion of art, whose chosen role is to observe and contemplate but whose enraged father, apparently disdainful of writing as a profession, forces him out of the house each morning to look for a real job. Abraham's own frustration with what he considered Saul's unemployment would sometimes morph into tyrannical rage.

"Yes, my father was tyrannical," Bellow said in the same letter to Halperin, but "our fathers lacked the support of a tyrannical society, and we were not in awe of their authority." A much younger Bellow had been enchanted with the idea that his father Abraham was the Abraham of the Bible and that his thunder represented the thunder of God. But as an adult, Bellow recognized that in America, "without an authoritarian society to support them," fathers, even as they turned up the heat, "seemed quite weak . . . and their storming did not impress us."[54]

Bellow had defied his father by getting married in 1938 during the Depression's second great slump, and now three years later by refusing to give any of his mother's life insurance premium to Abraham; instead, he and Anita used the money for a trip to Mexico. Having spent most of his life in "weary, stale, flat . . . Chicago," Bellow said he needed "color," "glamour," and even what he and his immigrant parents and their generation saw as distinctly un-Jewish: "barbarism" and "risk." Bellow had been reading D. H. Lawrence, about whom he had great reservations, but was especially moved by *Mornings in Mexico,* with its positive take on the instinctual sensuality of Mexican culture. Saul and Anita quit their jobs, left Chicago in June, and took the bus to New York.[55]

Apparently, "there was some compelling reason to go to New York" on the way to Mexico instead of taking the Greyhound directly to Texas. In the initial decision to make Mexico his target destination, Bellow, looking back, admitted there was "more agony than boldness." An older and more mature Bellow said he went to New York as part of a serpentine trip to Mexico, to seek a kind of implicit support for his defiance of his father from his Uncle Willie, Abraham's brother. A brush maker, Willie Bellow was "unemployed and brooding his life away in Brownsville, Brooklyn," his fate partly the result of his own rebellion as a youngster.[56]

When Willie, as an adolescent and against his father's wishes, joined the Bund—the General Jewish Workers Union, a socialist group in the old country—he was punished by being apprenticed to a brush maker. The Russian Bellows in the Old World, Saul told Roth, "did not work with their hands," and it was clear that Willie, coerced into such a degrading job, was meant to be chastened and disgraced for defying his authoritarian father. His humiliation was designed to be especially demeaning and punitive because he would be working with the bristles of hogs—*treyfidikhe khayes*—unkosher animals. "Willie in Brownsville," Saul said, "illustrated what might happen to a Bellow who rebels." Saul later confessed that he "ought to have shared the five hundred bucks" with Willie, but "[he] was . . . headed for Mexico."[57]

Never having been in the Deep South before, Bellow was genuinely upset at what he saw when his bus was briefly held up by a chain gang doing roadwork. Sitting in "a window seat holding a copy of Stendhal's *The Red and the Black*," Bellow witnessed firsthand the exploitation and suffering of Black men and was stunned by the spectacle of naked brutality. Later he wrote sympathetically, elegantly, and colorfully about the scene: "Outside, a green landscape; the freshly turned soil was a deep red. The shackled convicts were black, the stripes they wore were black and yellow."[58]

Another stop was made, far less stunning, Saul recalled, in Augusta, Georgia, where his "Uncle Max was selling *schmattes*"—literally rags, but more likely inexpensive used clothing—"on the installment [plan] to black field hands."[59] Although southern Jews for the most part embraced Dixie and were silent on civil rights, Eastern European Jewish merchants in the South, like their German Jewish predecessors, were more interested in customers than they were in the local custom of racial discrimination. They sold on credit and cultivated a Black clientele, who could try on clothing before deciding to purchase—an eyebrow-raising practice rarely if ever allowed by white southern storeowners. As one Jewish merchant put it, "Selling on credit to the Negro was called 'having a book on the *shvartzers*.' Do not misunderstand me," he said, "*Schvartzers* was not a sign of disrespect. . . . We were probably the first white people in the South who paid the Negro people any respect at all."[60]

From Georgia, Saul and Anita continued to New Orleans and El Paso before crossing into Mexico near the end of June. They were joined a few days later by Bellow's friend and fellow anthropology student Herb Passin and his wife, Cora, who had come south by car. From Mexico City, the two couples continued south, first to Cuernavaca and then on to Taxco. The foursome rented a villa overlooking the town, with its coarsely patched cobbled streets, tiled rooftops—blood red—and silver-tinted iron-grilled balconies overflowing with jasmine.

Afternoons were spent horseback riding, evenings generally at Paco's, the local cantina filled with expats. Mornings were for writing. What survives from this period are about one hundred handwritten pages of "Acatla," a projected novel, which unfolds in Taxco-like settings. Events center around the consequences of an interracial couple's attempt to book a hotel room, and the story reimagines the actual experience of publisher Joseph Hilton and Black cabaret singer Hazel Scott, whom Bellow met at Paco's. The manuscript is notable for its focus on racial injustice, the same theme that saturates *The Very Dark Trees*, a novel Bellow finished in 1941 but did not get to publish.

His interest in race and racial justice was long-standing, fostered not only by his studies with Herskovits at Northwestern but also by the University of Chicago, which had a history of supporting research into "Negro-White relations." And for most of the twentieth century, despite significant frictions and mutual bias—much of it manifest in the late 1960s—there had been in the US an affinity, even a sense of kinship, between Blacks and Jews. Both groups had had a rich history as people apart. Though Black people faced a racism more endemic, more virulent, more deeply institutionalized, and more disabling, both groups had suffered discrimination from the majority white Christian society.[61]

As a resident of Chicago, a notoriously segregated city, Bellow was sharply attuned to the problems of racial inequalities. The masses of Black people who migrated from the south to the Midwestern city during the Great Migration of the first half of the twentieth century settled in what became known as the "Black Belt"—a string of neighborhoods that ran thirty blocks along State Street on Chicago's South Side. Three-quarters of the city's African American population, suffering all the attendant ills of poverty, lived in the Black Belt in aging, dilapidated, overcrowded, and underserved buildings. Bellow's awareness of the enduring systemic nature of racism was sharpened during his travels by bus through the Deep South and in Mexico itself. From the social pain and immorality of racism there was no escape.

There was also no escape from politics. When the Bellows arrived in New York in June 1940 on their way to Mexico, they heard the news that German troops had entered Paris and were parading down the Champs-Elysées. Realizing that after seven years of preparation, Hitler was about to lay siege to Europe, Bellow understood that the continent faced "a devastating event"; and knowing the history of the pogroms in the East, he saw, in addition, an existential threat to European Jewry.[62]

Although he had drifted away from the Trotskyist movement, Bellow was still in awe of Trotsky himself, and he continued to hang on to an image of the revolutionary as an ideal figure, born Jewish, and informed by great literature and ideas even as he made history. It was no surprise then that Bellow, upon hearing in late August of an attempt on Trotsky's life, decided to visit Stalin's wounded archenemy at his Coyocan retreat near Mexico City. Trotsky was the grand Old Man who had, in the minds of many of his acolytes, especially after the Bolshevik revolution had degenerated into mass terror, managed to preserve its original ideals—and he remained a charismatic romantic revolutionary vindicated even in defeat by what was seen as a triumph of the intellectual over the inexorable express train of history. Bellow couldn't possibly have argued with Trotsky about imperialism or about his having put his imprimatur on the Soviet invasion of Finland—"theoretical questions," Bellow said, "that he understood a thousand times better than I."[63]

Acutely aware that even in exile, Jews and Jewishness persisted, just as the exiled Trotsky and Trotskyism persisted, Bellow, like his Jewish friends at Tuley High School, had admired Trotsky not only for his ideas and literary bent but also as one who carried the definitive mark of the outsider—banishment and exile. In *The Adventures of Augie March*, though he has strong reservations about Trotsky's politics, Augie is in awe of the Old Man's "exiled greatness, because the exile was a sign to me of persistence at the highest things. So I was wild with enthusiasm." As he drifted away from Marxism, Bellow still admired Trotsky, the great creator of the Red Army who had read French novels at the front while defeating the Russian lieutenant general Denikin.[64]

Posing as newspapermen, Bellow and Herb Passin took themselves to Mexico City in the hope of hearing a few words from Trotsky. But they arrived only in time to see a bloodied Lev Davidovich Bronstein, dead or dying from an attack by a Stalinist assassin wielding an ice axe.

Bellow's need for "barbarism, color," and even "glamor" may have been satisfied at this point in his Mexican sojourn; but his need for "risk" apparently was still roiling within. He decided to spend a week sleeping with another woman, identified by neither of his biographers. Furious recriminations followed, as did Anita's involvement in a very public retaliatory affair. Bellow then sent his "wife off to Acapulco" because, as he confessed to Philip Roth, he had a "strong desire to go it alone." But given his recent faithlessness (and hers), it is difficult to credit his circumspect claim that "it never occurred to [him]" that there might be danger in having Anita "shipped off." The Bellows returned home together and continued the marriage for another twelve years, but their stay in D. H. Lawrence's instinctually sensual Mexico seriously increased the difficulties in their relationship.[65]

FOUR

DANGLING MEN

SAUL AND ANITA'S ADVENTURES IN Mexico brought to the surface and deepened the tensions in their marriage. Back in Chicago the couple settled into their old routine; Anita returned to social work, and Saul resumed teaching at Pestalozzi-Froebel. But the Mexican experience, filled with adventure and mutual infidelity, increased Bellow's desire to go his own way. Despite ostensibly sharing bed and board with his wife (who was working full-time), Saul, excited by his connections with the *Partisan Review* crowd and the freedom of New York, began to make regular visits to the city.[1] The surprise is that the Bellows' relationship survived another dozen years—through innumerable infidelities and twenty-two changes of address. In the meantime, the war and the possibility of conscription, rather than his marriage, figure prominently in Bellow's correspondence during this period. Not yet a citizen, having been smuggled into the US from Canada when he was nine, Bellow believed himself exempt from the draft.

He didn't feel "exactly comfortable and secure," but unlike the dithering Joseph in *Dangling Man,* he thought it "reasonably permissible" for him to begin some serious writing.[2] But what to write and how? As opposed to Jewish American novels, filled with traditional ethnic themes, like Abraham Cahan's *Yekl* (1896) and *The Rise of David Levinsky* (1917), Anzia Yezierska's *The Bread Givers* (1925), and even Henry Roth's brilliant major work, *Call It Sleep* (1934), American novels written by Jews were rare.[3] As valuable as they were to an author like the young Bellow, the early Jewish novelists never fully escaped the limits of a narrative method whose mix of local color and realistic technique restrained their imaginations.

Bellow, influenced by Dreiser, Sherwood Anderson, Fitzgerald, and Faulkner, among the American greats, was determined to write an "American novel"—and he would. *Dangling Man*, Bellow's first novel, is an American novel, with only hints that Joseph is Jewish. But that novel was more than three years away. In the meantime, he sent short stories to magazines, including large-circulation periodicals like the *Saturday Evening Post* and smaller journals like *Kenyon Review*. They were rejected with depressing regularity.

But the magazine that really mattered was *Partisan Review (PR)* a Communist journal, founded in 1934 and located on Sixth Avenue between Tenth and Eleventh Streets, very near Cooper Union in the East Village. The magazine, however, had a short life; the editors of the journal, shocked and alienated by the murderous brutality of the Stalin regime and Soviet duplicity in the Spanish Civil War, shut *PR* down in 1936. It was reborn in 1937 as a thoroughly de-Stalinized Marxist periodical and relocated to the Tenth Street townhouse of political activist and culture critic Dwight Macdonald. *PR*, needing more space, moved again in 1942 to a nearby building on Astor Place, but the offices remained cluttered with books, magazines, and work in progress.[4]

Publishing in *PR* was taken to mean that you had made it in New York, the hub of the literary world, the place where one's credibility as a writer could be witnessed and promoted. The city was host to dozens of brilliant exiles and émigrés, including W. H. Auden, Bertolt Brecht, and Hannah Arendt, and had become the capital of international modernism after the fall of France to the

Nazis in 1940. The circulation of the magazine, chiefly edited by Ukrainian-born Philip Rahv (né Fevel Greenberg) and William Phillips (né Litvinsky), the son of Ukrainian Jewish immigrants, was only about three thousand in 1937 but would grow to fifteen thousand in the postwar period.

At the start, its readers were mostly its own contributors but included nearly every writer or critic of consequence: John Dos Passos, T. S. Eliot, and James T. Farrell appeared alongside Arthur Koestler, Delmore Schwartz, Lionel Trilling, and even Kafka—introduced to Americans for the first time with "In the Penal Colony," a chilling posthumous work. Trotsky, briefly an exile in New York City, was discussed often in the magazine, and he himself contributed an essay, "Art and Politics" (1938), a stirring statement, a manifesto really, on behalf of artistic autonomy, however limited by his instruction to serve the revolution. A second generation of *Partisan Review* writers who regularly made memorable contributions included Nathan Glazer, Alfred Kazin, Elizabeth Hardwick, Irving Howe, Isaac Rosenfeld, and Saul Bellow.

In the May/June 1941 issue of *Partisan Review,* along with a long poem by T. S. Eliot, appeared "Two Morning Monologues," a story by Saul Bellow identified only as "a young Chicago writer." The first monologue, "9 a.m. without Work," deals with the precarious situation of Mandelbaum, a young man who, like Joseph in *Dangling Man,* is unemployed and impatiently waiting for a notice from his draft board. His father, with classic Yiddish inflection and irony, hounds him to look for work—"You're a teacher aren't you? Five years in college. The best." The second monologue, "11:30 a.m. The Gambler," features penny-ante mobsters and confidence men resembling the Chicago lowlife types Bellow had observed hanging out at the pool parlor owned by his friend Sam Freifeld's father.

Over the next year, Bellow published two more stories, including "The Mexican General," which appeared in *Partisan Review* as the lead item in the May/June 1942 issue. Here was Saul, the self-described "young hick" from the Midwest, now in New York and associated with the widely admired "*PR* crowd" of mostly Jewish intelligentsia—or the New York intellectuals, as they came to be known.[5] Bellow became friends with several in the group, including art historian Meyer Schapiro, art critic Clement Greenberg, and writers Delmore Schwartz and James T. Farrell.

The New York intellectuals weren't a community. They did not, for example, despite their preoccupation with one another, read one another's works in progress, nor did they refrain from attacking one another in reviews. To some—Irving Howe, for instance—neglect and insolence were seen as both Jewish and a matter of principle: "Rudeness was not only the weapon of cultural underdogs, but also a sign that intellectual Jews had become sufficiently self-assured to stop playing by Gentile rules. At the least, this rudeness was to be preferred to the frigid 'civility' with which English intellectuals cloak their murderous impulses, or the politeness that in American academic life could mask a cold indifference."[6]

Bellow had friends among them, but as he confessed, "They weren't always friendly friends." They were, however, "always stimulating friends." And he enjoyed the open fraternization that enriched ongoing discussions among these children of Jewish immigrants, including Schwartz, Kazin, and Rosenfeld—all of them marked by conscious and unconscious confirmation of Jewishness as well as by "fantasies of universalism," which bordered on denial of Jewishness.[7]

Some denials, however, as literary historian Sanford Pinsker has shown, have a way of exposing or turning into varieties of confirmation. Delmore Schwartz's "In Dreams Begin Responsibilities," for example, a story that appeared in the very first issue of the new *Partisan Review* in autumn 1937 and brought the twenty-four-year-old Schwartz instant attention, "still stands as one of the richest, most artistically achieved renditions" of the contradictory impulses that characterized the New York intellectuals' attraction and repulsion toward the Jewish immigrant world within which they grew up.[8]

Here in Schwartz's story, and in much of *Partisan Review* going forward, were a distinctly urban tone and a string of Jewish cultural allusions that made young Jewish intellectuals hear a voice that seemed their own—though as Irving Howe said, "it had never really existed until Schwartz invented it."[9] Others who heard that voice included Leslie Fiedler, Isaac Rosenfeld, and Saul Bellow. This cluster of young men, all studying in the Midwest, all influenced by Marxism, all products of Yiddish-speaking households—who unabashedly proclaimed their Jewishness—gravitated in the late 1930s to *PR* and the New York group.

Fiedler said that in dealing with *Partisan Review,* he had the sense of beginning his own "autobiography"—that is, "my life as an urban American Jew, who came of age intellectually during the depression; who discovered Europe for the imagination before America; who was influenced by Marxist ideas . . . who wanted desperately to feel that the struggle for revolutionary politics and the highest literary standards was a single struggle; whose political certainty unraveled during the Second World War."[10]

Saul Bellow could easily have said the same thing. He made clear what the periodical meant to him by distinguishing it from other journals of arts and opinion. *Partisan Review,* he wrote in his preface to a 1996 anthology, unlike the *Southern,* the *Hudson,* or the *Kenyon Review,* gave us "what we longed for" as Jewish intellectuals: "deep relevance, contemporary high culture, left-wing politics, avant-garde painting, Freudian mining of the unconscious or Marxist views of past and future revolutions," and a way of staying Jewish even as observant Judaism for the most part faded.[11] And the Jewish writers, in turn, gave *PR* a tone of "eager restlessness, a moral anxiety, an openness to novelty, a hunger for dialectic, a refusal of contentment, an ironic criticism of all fixed opinions."[12]

Not all the members of the *Partisan Review* gang were New Yorkers. Fiedler and Bellow thought of themselves as Chicagoans who had grown up in ethnically mixed districts of Poles, Germans, Irishmen, Italians, and Jews—unlike the New York writers, who came from predominantly Jewish communities. The New Yorkers, Bellow said, were "emotionally thinner, or one-dimensional." The Chicagoans had "fuller or, if you prefer richer emotions."[13] Bellow never wanted to become part of the New York *Partisan Review* gang, but like many of its members, he was, as he put it, "an emancipated Jew who refused to deny his Jewishness."[14]

Wherever they were from, several members at the very core of the group were not Jewish: Dwight Macdonald, Mary McCarthy, and William Barrett, for example, as well as F. W. Dupee, James Baldwin, and Elizabeth Hardwick. At the periphery of the group, too, there were Gentiles, including Robert Lowell, James Agee, John Berryman, and Ralph Ellison. You didn't have to be Jewish, then, to be a New York intellectual, but it helped. The Kentucky-born writer Elizabeth Hardwick claims that she came to New York to be a "Jewish intellectual," and William Barrett describes an atmosphere so "pervasively Jewish" around *Partisan Review* and its associated circles that he often forgot that he was "not a Jew after all."[15]

The "Jewishness" that Barrett, Hardwick, and others experienced vicariously and the Jewishness that the *PR* crowd lived (sometimes unwittingly) consisted of shared experiences growing up in urban, Yiddish-speaking immigrant communities, the style and rhythm of language that were products of that milieu, a sharp method of argumentation laced with skepticism and irony, and an emphasis on rationalism but also a set of moral priorities having to do with social justice as well as freedom of the individual.

For the first generation of New York intellectuals—Lionel Trilling, Philip Rahv, Meyer Schapiro, Paul Goodman, and others—Jewishness as sentiment and cultural source had played only a modest role in their conscious experience. As late as 1944, Trilling, for example, could still say that "the Jewish community as it now exists" gives no nourishment to American writers or intellectuals born Jewish. Indeed, Trilling said, it had never done so before. "Have any Jewish writers in English," he wanted to know, "ever added even a small amount to his reputation by 'realizing his Jewishness.'"[16]

Trilling and many of the other first-generation New York Jewish intellectuals, including Sidney Hook, Harold Rosenberg, Clement Greenberg, and Lionel Abel, only a few years removed from immigrant neighborhoods in the Bronx and Brooklyn, proclaimed themselves, in the late 1930s and early 1940s, "radical internationalists, spokesmen for cultural modernism, men of letters transcending 'mere' ethnic loyalties." Although Saul Bellow would reject for himself the label of "Jewish writer," he, unlike the others, also rejected transcending ethnic loyalties. "To turn away from [my] origins," Bellow said many times in one way or another, "has always seemed to me an utter impossibility. It would be a treason to my first consciousness to un-Jew myself. One may be tempted to go behind the given and invent something better, to attempt to reenter life at a more advantageous point. In America this is common, we have all seen it done, and done in many instances with great ingenuity. But the thought of such an attempt never entered my mind."[17]

Meyer Schapiro, Paul Goodman, Lionel Trilling, and Philip Rahv, former socialists and Communists, now Marxist universalist writers for *Partisan Review,* may have avoided a pronounced Jewish identification or resisted outright assertions of Jewishness, but they shared a Jewish heritage (at least at the level of personal understanding and intellectual sympathies) that helped draw many of them together. This was especially true when they experienced the genteel antisemitism of literature's gatekeepers. When they encountered the presumption of universal Protestant culture and identity, the "Jewish universalists," Irving Howe remembered, "would aggressively proclaim our 'difference,' as if to raise Jewishness to higher cosmopolitan power." And if one were to go through the first twenty years of *Partisan Review,* one would see, Howe said, just "how frequently Jewish references, motifs, and inside jokes break past the surface of cosmopolitanism."[18]

Bellow did not identify with the *PR* crowd to the degree they had anticipated. Indeed, the Chicagoan in him was both engrossed and irritated by the arguments over highbrow culture that distinguished the New York intellectuals. He relished but was somewhat amused by their interminable discourse about Marx and Freud, as well as their convoluted struggle to make a synthesis of modernism and Marxism. Bellow was well aware of the celebratory side of modernism and appreciated the many rhapsodic moments in the work of the great modernists, like Joyce and Proust. But he recognized that the political implications in much of modernism could be reactionary and subjective, sometimes mystical, and frequently marked by nihilism. Rahv and Macdonald, modernists and Marxists, were hardly nihilists, but Bellow leaned toward a Marxism with a more positive emphasis on historical victory and a future less dark.

He also shared the New Yorkers' stated conviction that the significance of literature was outside the arena of ideological debate, and so he quite disliked the sporadically recurring insistence at *Partisan Review* that intellectuals who believed in cultural freedom had to ally themselves with radical movements, Trotskyist or otherwise. Having come of age in Marxist Depression-era Chicago and gone east to make his mark—and perhaps his fortune—in the literary world, Bellow found himself in an even more magnified intellectualized and politicized milieu.

Within the *Partisan Review* crowd in its prime, in a century of all-devouring ideas and ideologies, Bellow distrusted the big theory, the blanket explanation. He, unlike Rahv, Macdonald, and the art critic Clement Greenberg, favored Chekhov's injunction that "major writers and artists should engage in politics only enough to protect themselves from it."[19] Better to shun all ideologies and go it alone, Bellow thought, as he moved among the *PR* crowd but kept a wary distance.

Years later Bellow told Kazin that "neither Isaac [Rosenfeld] nor I could think of ourselves as provincials in New York" or in any way inferior to the city's intellectuals. The "pride" of having had a superb R. M. Hutchins education at the University of Chicago "shielded" them. "The U.C. didn't have to compete with the Ivy League," Bellow said, "it was obviously superior. It never entered our minds that we had lost anything in being deprived of Eastern advantages. So we came armored in self-confidence and came to conquer. Ridiculous boys!"[20]

Not so ridiculous, really. Gertrude Himmelfarb, an American historian who wrote extensively on intellectual history as well as on contemporary society and culture, watched Bellow and Rosenfeld, the two "Chicago Dostoyevskians," in operation. Her judgment: "The Chicagoans were more cultivated, more literary, more musical, more philosophical. . . . It was the New York group that was parochial."[21]

To William Phillips and several others at the magazine, Bellow's "strong sense of being set apart" was apparent from the beginning.[22] When Bellow questioned the opinion of other writers toward his work, he could get feisty, even openly angry—sometimes so much so, Bellow told his friend Mel Tumin in 1942, that he bit "people's heads off."[23] Even after he had become a well-known author, Bellow occasionally pointed out that hidden in his Jewish immigrant blood were signs of hesitation as to whether he had the ability, and more so the right, to practice the writer's craft. He was more infuriated than intimidated by the WASP gatekeepers; but Bellow at times, at least subconsciously, could feel that he was an imposter, especially when challenged, even in the mildest way, by friends and family.[24]

Bellow also could be extremely suspicious, Phillips said, but his manner was "self-assured . . . and when he felt at home . . . even his egocentricity added to his charms." Phillips and his circle remember Bellow as "extremely handsome, with soft, large eyes and long lashes, giving focus to a soft, quizzical look that was not entirely lost on women."[25]

Whichever way the editors and writers saw Bellow, he did not develop into the kind of novelist that *Partisan Review* apparently wanted to endorse. Some in the *PR* crowd had placed a great deal of faith in his talents as a writer best qualified to counter antisemitism in American literary and academic circles. Others thought he might just be the "highbrow with muscles" they were looking for "to tell the story of the Jewish romance with America."[26] Bellow, however, was not prepared then or ever to be only a distinctively Jewish novelist.

There was nothing directly Jewish about *The Very Dark Trees*, a novel Bellow wrote in 1941 about an English professor, "an enlightened Southerner," who teaches at a Midwestern university. On his way home after class, the professor suddenly feels as if he's been struck by lightning and—in a bit of premature magical realism on Bellow's part—finds himself turned into a Black man. At home the professor startles his wife, and she locks her husband in the basement so as not to alarm the neighbors.[27]

Bellow's friend Nathan Gould remembers the novel as a humorous but "caustic tale of a liberal Southerner confronted by the reality of prejudice." Other readers said the manuscript was not only about prejudice but also a Kafkaesque fable about the flimsy nature of identity, one in which any personal transformation or metamorphosis—say, from Russian Jewish to American—could be penalized by disaffection from one's family, and even, as in Gregor Samsa's case, by confinement or forced isolation. And because such a fate seemed to come upon the English professor without input from him, the story suggests that change in the New World "just happens" like a bolt of lightning out of the blue.[28]

The manuscript made the rounds and came to be known among publishers as "that Negro book." It was met with mixed reviews from editors ranging from provocative and absorbing to unbelievable and unmarketable and was returned several times. But Bellow, who may now have had his own doubts about the worth of the book and even about his abilities as a writer, was nevertheless "determined [the book] must be published, for it is to give me the right . . . to continue as a writer."[29]

The book finally found a publisher in 1942 with William Roth at Colt Press. *Very Dark Trees,* however, was affected, sadly, by a very dark war. Roth was drafted, stationed in Alaska, and forced to suspend operations at Colt Press. Bellow received a fifty-dollar kill fee, and after reading *Very Dark Trees* through again, he determined that "it wasn't good enough." He didn't want "this albatross hung around my neck," he said, so he "just threw it into the furnace."[30] Even as his first novel was going up in smoke, Bellow told the editors of *Partisan Review* that his agent—acquired after the publication of his stories—was sending along a story called "Juif!" (Jew!), which never materialized. He also informed them that he was at work on a new novel: *Notes of a Dangling Man,* which did materialize later, albeit under an abbreviated title.

While writing, Bellow would go to New York for intellectual nourishment on a regular basis. It was a forty-eight-hour ride from Chicago by bus, but for an ambitious midwesterner, New York was an inevitable destination, even if he had to "live in some room with bedbugs in Greenwich Village." Bellow usually stayed with Isaac Rosenfeld and his wife, Vasiliki, in a cramped apartment in the West Seventies, where sometimes cockroaches sprang "from the toaster with the slices of bread," and then in 1942 in the Village on Christopher Street in an apartment—with bed bugs.[31] The arrangement didn't last. Isaac's boldness and imagination appealed to Saul, but Saul was congenitally averse to Isaac's unmanageable bohemianism. "Isaac preferred to have things about him in a mess," Bellow said. "I have an idea he found good middle-class order devitalizing—a sign of meanness, stinginess, malice and anality."[32]

When in New York, Bellow also spent time with Alfred Kazin, an editor at the *New Republic* and a literary critic, who, when the two men first met in 1942, had just published *On Native Grounds*, an encapsulating and exultant story of modern American literature, including essays on Edith Wharton, Willa Cather, Fitzgerald, Hemingway, and Faulkner and an exquisite, captivating essay on Lincoln. In over five hundred pages, Kazin explored how the calamitous social and moral disruptions of industrial capitalism in the late nineteenth century shaped modern American writing.[33]

With this book, Kazin, only twenty-seven, accomplished what Bellow would do later even more dramatically. Kazin had broken through the WASP gatekeepers, revealing to the surprise of the New England and southern literati that a Jew from Brownsville, in the bowels of Brooklyn, the son of a dressmaker and a housepainter from the Old World, could master over fifty years' worth of American literary, social, and political history with elegance and wisdom.[34]

Bellow and Kazin, both sons of Jewish immigrants, born only days apart in June 1915, got along well for several years. Both had been suspicious of political doctrine from the beginning, and both invested more faith in the human imagination and saw the possibilities for art—not the class struggle—as the catalyst for social and cultural renewal.

Kazin remembered Bellow as "friendly, unpretentious, and funny" but also "ambitious and dedicated in a style I had never seen in an urban Jewish intellectual." It seemed to Kazin when he talked with Bellow that although the Chicago writer had published little and was virtually unknown, he "carried around with him a sense of his destiny as a novelist that excited everyone around him." He spoke of D. H. Lawrence, Hemingway, Joyce, and Fitzgerald "not as books in the library, but as fellow operators in the same business." Kazin sensed that Bellow's determination was so great that the Chicagoan, with no novel yet published, could say with Lawrence, "I am a man and alive. . . . For this reason I am a novelist. And being a novelist, I consider myself superior to the saint, the scientist, the philosopher, and the poet, who are all great masters of different bits of man alive, but never get the whole hog."[35]

Kazin shared Bellow's faith in himself as a novelist because, "like his strength in being a Jew, *this* was a sealed treasure undamaged by his many anxieties." Bellow was clearly a man of natural ability, Kazin said, "like those Jewish virtuosos—Heifetz, Rubenstein, Milstein, Horowitz—who had been shaped into . . . elegant men of the world by talent." And it was refreshing to be with a man like Bellow, who "disposed of so many pedantic distinctions"—an ability that seemed to Kazin "to have something to do with his love of Yiddish and Jewish jokes, his affection for big-city low life, his sense of himself as a *creative* Jew." To be in Bellow's presence made Kazin—and later so many other readers and writers—"intellectually happy."

Kazin the literary critic and Bellow the writer of short stories took walks across the mile-long Brooklyn Bridge with its granite towers, steel cables, and cathedral arches linking the boroughs of Brooklyn and Manhattan. They also walked in and around Kazin's favorite streets in Brooklyn Heights. Saul looked upon Alfred's New York with "great detachment." And without warning, after "a séance of brooding Jewish introspection," Bellow would make Kazin see significance in "the most microscopic event in the street because *he* happened to be seeing it." Bellow was "a nimble adept of the University of Chicago style," Kazin thought, "full of the great books and jokes from Aristophanes," but also an unembarrassed Yiddishist, at ease with his Jewishness. "He was proud in a laconic way," Kazin added, "like a Jew who feels himself closer to God than everybody else."

New York was not a permanent residence for Bellow, and by the summer of 1943 he was back in Chicago with Anita, waiting, like Joseph in his novel, for a call from his draft board. Volunteer enlistment for service having ended in late 1942, Saul could avoid significant discomfort over his being seen as a healthy young man walking around in the city not in uniform. While waiting to be called, Saul was finishing revisions to *Dangling Man*, as the novel was now titled—the Dostoevskian *Notes* having been dropped. Earlier that summer, he had submitted the manuscript to James Henle, the publisher of Vanguard Press, who had rejected *The Very Dark Trees* but remained interested in Bellow's work.

In late July there was a contract. Bellow was ecstatic. By November the book was in proofs, and he indulged in the luxury of arguing over trifles. Henle was concerned that the word *nooky* would offend readers; Bellow, pointing to the profanity in *Ulysses*, thought not. More important was Bellow's use of the word *darky*. It was vernacular, Bellow argued, and he insisted the word had nothing to do with his position on the "Negro question"—as his abandoned manuscripts, including *Very Dark Trees*, and *Atacla*, too, ought to have made clear. "I can't make the changes," Bellow said, and he did not.[36]

Lionel Trilling declared after World War II that "the great work of our time [will be] the restoration and reconstitution of . . . the great former will of humanism."[37] But writers in the mid- to late 1940s (including Bellow), in the aftermath of depression and war, focused not on recovery, national self-esteem, and a brighter future but on alienation, disorientation, and guilt. Articles about Kafka or Dostoevsky or French existentialism and on the "crisis of reason" or the "failure of nerve" filled the pages of *Partisan Review*, *Commentary*, and the *Nation*. Even the titles of relatively well-known authors announced a mood of darkness, depression, and distress. Robert Lowell's *Lord Weary's Castle* (1946) was a portrait of alienation of "modern man," as were Arthur Miller's *Death of a Salesman* (1949), David Reisman's *The Lonely Crowd* (1950), and Carson McCullers' *Ballad of a Sad Café* (1951).[38]

This is not to say that these works were painted dark for the simple sake of underwriting despair, or that they were without subtle social critique, or courage, or hope, altogether. Although Bellow's *Dangling Man* (1944) and *The Victim* (1947) were also portraits of men in various stages of confusion, fear, and detachment, Bellow refused to join in any consensus about an intractable alienation, which he would later describe in *Herzog* as "the Wasteland outlook . . . the cant and rant of pipsqueaks about Inauthenticity and Forlornness."[39] Despite all the darkness and anguish over failed hopes, the American future, capitalism, and the juggernaut of modernization, Bellow, while consciously resisting accommodation to the new and decidedly bourgeois status, resisted forlornness and alienation and rejected nihilism.

Dangling Man, Bellow's first novel, deals with many of Bellow's lifelong concerns and those of his future protagonists. The shadow of war and its horrors darken *Dangling Man* throughout. But as in almost every other book Bellow went on to write—*The Adventures of Augie March* and *Henderson the Rain King* being the clearest examples—the dominant theme in *Dangling Man* is choosing life, by which Bellow means, in the main, choosing freedom. Just as *Dangling Man* was being published, however, Bellow told David Bazelon (a fellow writer and a friend from his Greenwich Village days) he was speaking "of wretchedness" and saying that "no man by his own effort finds his way out of it" into freedom. "To some extent, the artist does," Bellow said. "But the moral man, the citizen, doesn't. He can't."[40] At the same time, Bellow wrote to Kazin saying that *Dangling Man* was meant to show "the impossibility of working out one's destiny in such a world."[41] It is difficult to know here whether Bellow, by saying "such a world," meant the contemporary world of war or the generally pessimistic world of modern man.

Nearly twenty years later, however, Bellow made things a little clearer by saying that each of us, not exclusively artists, must "find an inner law by which he can live," implying that the working out of one's destiny is not, after all, an "impossibility." To Mel Tumin, Bellow wrote that "freedom has proved . . . burdensome to modern man." Its misfortune, he argued, is the anxiety and loneliness it imposes on the individual—"unless he can reunite himself with [freedom] on a higher level," meaning spiritually, beyond the materially quantifiable.[42]

Dangling Man portrays the intellectual and emotional equivocations and consternations of Joseph, who seeks freedom "on a higher level." He is an unemployed twenty-three-year-old struggling to understand himself, his fears, his limits, and the nature and quality of his marriage—and to define "freedom" and work his way out of depression—all while waiting, between December 1942 and April 1943, to be drafted.

Inspired by writerly ambition, Joseph keeps a journal filled with literary references to Marx, Thoreau, Hobbes, and Mozart, among others, in which he demonstrates his central challenge—to find that elusive "inner law by which he can live." His search leads him to make reference to Goethe very early in his journal, then again midway, and finally within its last pages.[43] It is no coincidence that the nineteenth-century German Romantic poet, the author of *Faust,* is mentioned prominently in *Dangling Man*; published in 1944, Bellow's novel was written when much of Christian Europe had sold itself to the devil. The Goethe allusions articulate Bellow's long-standing and long-lasting interest in modern Romanticism as a progenitor of Nazism.

The word *Jew* never appears in the novel—there is only one reference to antisemitism, and another to Joseph's "people," who have inherited a penchant for argument. But Joseph's Talmudic questions reverberate throughout.[44] Behaving like an Old World rabbinical student, relentlessly arguing with himself on the page as well as in his head, Joseph deliberately asks himself, "How can a good man live; what ought he to do?"[45] Bellow himself, from early on, never stopped trying to expose our most deeply hidden questions about the purpose of living as humans in a world that outlasts us.

In his very first journal entry, in an oblique takedown of Hemingway, Joseph rejects "hardboiledness"—a code that insists on the strangulation of feelings, the disparagement of life, and the love of nothingness—all contrary to the teachings of Judaism. Joseph recognizes the vacuousness and harm of strangled feelings, and though he keeps his demoralization and difficulties confined to his journal, he is enamored by the life of the imagination. Believing that the only worthwhile sort of work was "that of the imagination," Bellow, from *Dangling Man* forward, insisted that "the imagination has to provide something that explicit statements of belief can never provide satisfactorily." Ethically, "none of us have the strength," Bellow said, "to set things right" without "the power provided by the imagination."[46]

Joseph fears that he hasn't the imagination, the inventiveness, or the talent of an artist who can turn personal troubles into universal concerns, and the novel starts out like one by Kafka or Beckett with a man alone in a room. But in the course of the narrative, Joseph goes from loneliness, distraction, and self-denigration to the realization that redemption of his self-esteem, indeed his selfhood, is dependent not on a "hardboiled" code à la Hemingway but instead, finally, on its very opposite, a "goodness . . . achieved not in a vacuum but in the company of other men, attended by love."[47]

Through most of the novel, Joseph remains edgy and bitter, unable to endure the company of his friends or family—nor they his—and he suffers the shrinkage and debasement of his humanity. Joseph's despondency appears to be part of his personality. But he blames the times for his vexation. Like later Bellow protagonists who wrestle with the tensions and reduction of inner spirit, Joseph in his post-Marxist life seems to nourish melancholy as a substitute for activism. He feels "harried, pushed, badgered," not only by external forces but by "the world internalized"[48]—not unlike some other disappointed wartime radicals who made depression the intellectual's illness of choice. His public statements and journal jottings throughout the war years echo the artists of despair, including contributors to *Partisan Review,* and the writers they valued: Dostoyevsky, Kafka, Nietzsche, and Camus.

Joseph's mood is matched by the idleness and sterility, the vast emptiness of the streets, "the intense cold," and the general yearning for warmth. And then, even here in Bellow's first and most tightly knit novel, the true Bellovian note bursts through for a moment. While Joseph is polishing his shoes, he recalls doing the same as a child in Montreal and thinks,

> I have never found another street that resembled St. Dominique.... Little since then has worked upon me with such force as, say, the sight of a driver trying to raise his fallen horse, of a funeral passing through the snow, or of a cripple who taunted his brother. And the pungency and staleness of its stores and cellars, the dogs, the boys, the French and immigrant women.... The very breezes in the narrow course of that street, have remained so clear to me that I sometimes think it is the only place where I was ever allowed to experience reality.[49]

And now in New York, perhaps on the strength of that memory, Joseph says, "In the middle of winter, isolating a wall with sunlight on it, I have been able to persuade myself despite the surrounding ice, that the month was July not February." His "windows with their glowing shades, set two orange rectangles, trademarks of warmth and comfort, against the downpour and the dark... the armor of ice on the street" and against thoughts about the war.[50]

But the war—a world in crisis—weighs heavily on Bellow's writing of *Dangling Man* and generates oblique references to the Holocaust, as well as explicit references to antisemitism, German antisemitism most directly. Joseph recounts a scene from his adolescence during a visit to the home of a schoolmate whose parents are German. The father remarks that Joseph is handsome, to which the mother replies, *"Mephisto war auch schön"*—"Mephistopheles was also good-looking."[51]

Joseph knew the significance of what was said, and "stood frozen." He never saw the parents again, avoided his friend at school, and "spent sleepless hours" uneasy about what had transpired. Here, in the only truly clear reference to Joseph's Jewishness in the entire novel, Bellow is alluding to centuries of Christian characterization of Jews as agents of the devil, associated with darkness, and named as the murderers of Jesus and the children of Satan.[52]

It is not difficult to link Joseph's anxious sleepless nights as a teenager to the description of his adult bedtime:

> It was good to lie in bed, not dreaming. . . . I sleep badly. I have never known dreamless sleep. In the past my dreams annoyed me. . . . But now my dreams are barer and more ominous. Some of them are fearful. A few nights ago I found myself in a low chamber with rows of large cribs of wicker bassinets in which the dead of a massacre were lying. I am sure they were victims of a massacre, because my mission was to reclaim one for a particular family. My guide picked up a tag, and said, "This one was found near. . . ." I do not remember the name; it ended in Tanza. It must have been Costanza. It was either there or in Bucharest that those slain by the Iron Guard were hung from hooks in a slaughterhouse. I have seen the pictures. I looked at the reclining face and murmured that I was not personally acquainted with the deceased. I had merely been asked as an outsider. . . . my guide turned smiling, and I guessed that he meant. . . . "It's well to put oneself in the clear in something like this." This was a warning to me. He approved of my neutrality. . . . Could I be such a hypocrite? . . . The bodies as I have said, were lying in cribs, and looked remarkably infantile, their faces pinched and wounded. I do not remember much more. I can picture only the low-pitched, long room . . . the childlike bodies with pierced hands and limbs [and] an atmosphere of terror such as my father many years ago could conjure for me, describing Gehenna [Hell] and the damned until I shrieked and begged him to stop.[53]

The passage, with its references to the Iron Guard, Bucharest, massacre, and hell, needs no deconstruction to see its relevance to the Holocaust. And the sentence "It's well to put oneself in the clear in something like this" also has resonance, especially in regard to the charge of American inattention to the Nazi genocide.

American novelists such as Bellow were faced with a troubling circumstance: during the Second World War, in the very years during which European Jewry was being "cleansed" from the face of the earth, American Jews were successfully acculturating if not fully assimilating. Jewish writers of Bellow's generation had grown up in materially impoverished immigrant communities and entered adulthood during the Great Depression. In the 1940s and '50s, these writers were getting a sample of America's abundance, as they collected honors and earned readers. How could they evenhandedly deal with both their own bright, positive, and promising experience as Americans and the darkness of the central Jewish experience of their time? Despite what Bellow wrote to Cynthia Ozick nearly a half century later about not truly confronting the Holocaust, the reality is that Bellow strained to answer that question several times in his long and prolific career, beginning with *Dangling Man*.

Joseph's dreams and his broken sleep make him cranky and even more disputatious. Outside of his room he almost inevitably tangles with his relatives and associates. He roughs up his landlord and shouts at an employee of the bank. Why he's "been creating agitation," he's not sure: "Perhaps eager for consequences. Trouble like physical pain makes us physically aware that we are living."[54]

"Disgraced myself at my brother's house last night," reads an entry in Joseph's journal, testifying to his inability, as he puts it, "to stay out of trouble."[55] And so, he retreats. But despite his attempts to maintain a hermetic moroseness, Joseph's encounters with his family and friends, and his unrelenting Talmudic-like debates with himself, bring him along a tortuous path to seeing that he is indissolubly bound in interdependence with humanity. "Whether I like it or not," he declares, "they were my generation, my society, my world. We were figures in the same plot eternally fixed together. I was aware also, that their existence, just as it was, made mine possible." He "was not so full of pride," he says, "that I could not accept the existence of something greater than myself."[56] Joseph is endowed, obviously, with intellectual awareness and a prophetic sense of larger purpose. Despite his lack of confidence in his ability to do so, these resources help him transform his preoccupations into questions of universal significance.[57]

Sounding much like the God of the Hebrew scriptures, who in the very beginning of Genesis says, "It was good," six times (and ending with the declaration, "God saw everything he had made and behold it was very good"), Joseph says, "In a sense everything is good because it exists. Or good or not good, it exists, it is ineffable"—undefinable, overwhelming—"and for that reason marvelous."[58]

When Joseph is finally drafted, he says, "I am no longer to be held accountable for myself. . . . I am in other hands, relieved of self-determination, freedom canceled. Hurray for regular hours! And for supervision of the spirit! Long live regimentation!"[59] These lines, the last in the book, puzzled many readers and critics. In that ending, Bellow told David Bazelon, he was only "making an ironic statement about the plight of the Josephs." He wasn't advising "others to follow the *Dangling Man* into regimentation. . . . I don't encourage surrender."[60] And earlier, Bellow had admitted to Mel Tumin that *Dangling Man* would "end with questions not answers."[61]

The questions remain. But Bellow's many protagonists, including Joseph, are social creatures, most of whom ultimately consider solitude anathema. Consequently, most of Bellow's novels conclude with some kind of reintegration, an escape not from freedom but from the tyranny of structurelessness.

It is possible, given Joseph's apparent awareness of biblical verse, that his reentry into society was accompanied, even prompted, by a veiled memory of *Proverbs* 18:1: "Whoever isolates himself... he breaks out against all judgment." Or perhaps he has recalled the injunction in *Hebrews* 10:25: "Do not neglect to meet together, but encourage one another and all the more as you see the day drawing near." Joseph goes from having said earlier that alienation is a feeling of "fundamental discontent," to declaring "that we should not make a doctrine of our feeling," to finally acknowledging alienation as "a fool's plea."[62] He seems to have returned to a proposition he may have believed in from the start: better to dangle, attached to *something,* than to remain entirely apart.

FIVE

IN THE SHADOW OF THE HOLOCAUST

BELLOW HAD BEEN WRITING *DANGLING MAN* from early 1942 through the beginning of 1944, during which time he was also going through the process of naturalization. He became a US citizen in August 1943 and was classified 1A, making it more likely he'd be drafted. He could not go back to teaching, he said, because of the "uncertainty"—which also affected his writing, rendering it "impossible," he told Dwight Macdonald, "to make the best of [his] capacities."[1] News of the brutal fighting in Europe and Asia didn't help. There were enormous losses everywhere. And even as the Nazis retreated from the East, the wholesale murder of Jews continued. In Poland, for example, Jewish ghettoes were being systematically liquidated. Thinking about the war, even as it turned in favor of the Allies, was unavoidable.

After three deferments, two related to a hernia and a botched surgery, Bellow said that he found "the prospects of enjoying the benefits of a peace without having contributed to [that] peace . . . intensely disagreeable," and he later told his publisher, "I don't want to dodge."[2] And in 1945 he enlisted in the merchant marine. Stationed in New York, out of the way of real danger, and within commuting distance of Manhattan, Bellow was virtually exempt from participation in an "imperialist war"—which is how some of his estranged Trotskyist friends and a small, lingering, but rapidly fading part of himself still characterized the conflict. By the time he left his Trotskyist friends behind, Bellow had become disenchanted by abstractions that prioritized ideology, that chose the good of mankind over flesh-and-blood individuals. He, like Joseph in *Dangling Man*, finally "realized that any hospital nurse did more with one bedpan for *le genre humain* than the [Trotskyists] did with their entire organization."[3]

Bellow thought he "knew most of the story" of what came to be called the Holocaust. He was mistaken; but he knew enough to say later, "Not only did I feel my Jewish Marxist friends were wrong in theory" about the Second World War, "I was horrified by the positions they—we—had taken" on the nature of the war as a struggle between two imperialisms, instead of what it was—a battle to defeat Hitler and fascism.[4]

As early as 1942, well before much credible news of genocidal attacks on Jews had reached American shores, Bellow, in the course of one of his New York City walks with Alfred Kazin, made some "startling observations on the future of the war, the pain of Nazism," and "the lasting effects of Hitler." Yet he later thought that it was not until 1945 that he and many other intellectuals on the left had fully "recognized Hitler for 'what he was.'"[5]

Such recognition occurred at various times for Saul's contemporaries. Kazin came to see the radical evil in Europe for "what it was" in 1943—much earlier than most. Lionel Abel, an eminent playwright, essayist, and theater critic and member of the *PR* circle, had no such revelation until "sometime in 1946."[6] After Kazin learned that the Warsaw Ghetto had been destroyed in May 1943 during the largest single revolt by Jews during World War II, and after he read that Szmuel Zygelbaym (a member of the National Council of the Polish government-in-exile) had committed suicide in London in order to draw attention to the Nazis' murder of three million Polish Jews, Kazin published Zygelbaym's suicide note and his own powerful and moving response in the *New Republic.*

Zygelbaym's note read, "By my death, I wish to give expression to my most profound protest against the inaction in which the world watches and permits the destruction of the Jewish people. . . . The responsibility for the crime of the murder of the whole Jewish nationality in Poland rests first of all on those who are carrying it out, but indirectly it falls also upon the whole of humanity, on the peoples of the Allied nations and on their governments, who up to this day have not taken any real steps to halt this crime." The piece did not get anything like the attention it deserved—neither from Bellow, who was busy revising *Dangling Man,* nor from the New York intellectuals or anyone else.[7]

Later, Bellow would be very hard on himself for pursuing his burning ambition to be a novelist at the expense of paying more direct attention to the plight of the Jews. In the aftermath of the Warsaw Ghetto uprising, in the last months of 1943, unlike Kazin, Bellow wrote nothing about the event. He was still working on *Dangling Man,* a chapter of which appeared in *Partisan Review*'s September/October 1943 issue, with the Dostoevskian title "Notes of a Dangling Man." But it was not as if Bellow was indifferent to the tragic fate of European Jewry or failed to see that the Nazi regime was something qualitatively new in the history of evil. The Holocaust haunted his first novel in 1944 and would cast dark shadows over *The Victim,* his second, in 1947.

In the meantime, Bellow told Kazin that *Dangling Man* was giving him *veytig*—pain or woe. The "writing is sound," Bellow said; "the idea is a good one. The rest is a mishmash for which I deserve to be mercilessly handled."[8] More than once over the years, beginning in high school, Bellow stated with blunt confidence that he expected to become an important writer; but he also said that while it took courage "to assert that a world without art was unacceptable," the simple truth was that "the hero of art was himself unstable, stubborn, nervous, ignorant."[9] And in a nod to his disdainful brothers Sam and Maury, successful businessmen both, and to his angry, condescending father, Saul said in an unpublished note, "Those you love . . . didn't know what you were up to. You yourself didn't know what you were up to."[10]

His admitted vulnerability showed publicly only in occasional sniping and stormy outbursts over criticism of his work. When Diana Trilling assessed *Dangling Man* in the *Nation* on April 15, 1944, as small, sterile, and nondimensional, without heft or breadth, Bellow was furious.[11] Sitting with his friend Mel Tumin in the dining hall of the University of Chicago, he complained bitterly of Trilling's antipathy. Tumin, with whom Bellow had had correspondence and conversation about *Dangling Man* while it was in progress, advised Bellow not to take the review seriously—indeed, to ignore it altogether. Saul flew into a rage and ordered his friend from the table. Nearly a year passed before they spoke to one another again. Bellow's volatility, like the "mad fear of being slighted or scorned" felt by Joseph in *Dangling Man*, was a product of his older brothers' scorn of his literary ambitions and an inheritance from the paternal side of his family—"a people of tantrums," to use Joseph's phrase.[12]

The very next day, Bellow's *veytig* turned to tsuris—a much more serious trouble. Anita, pregnant since August, went through a difficult labor and finally had to deliver Greg by an emergency cesarean section. After the doctor told Bellow he doubted he could save either Anita or Gregory, Saul, up all night, walked the hospital corridors in agony for hours. Both mother and son nearly died, but fortuitously Anita pulled through, and Gregory, after spending the first five days of his life in an oxygen tent, did too. Bellow wired his publisher: "DANGER PASSED EVERYONE SAFE."[13]

For weeks following this traumatic experience, Bellow exulted in Anita's return to good health and in the survival of Gregory, who came to be known in the family as Hirsch, a diminutive for Herschel, "a fine old Yiddish name," which Saul celebrated.[14] Only months later, however, when Bellow was called up by his draft board for a physical, he was again deferred, having been diagnosed with an inguinal hernia. "Immediately I went into the hospital to have surgery," he said, "but the operation was not successful."[15] It took many weeks for him to recover. This painful experience and the life-threatening ordeal his wife and child had suffered so recently likely prompted Bellow's memory of his own childhood pain, hospitalization, and near-death experience that would be reimagined and described powerfully in *Herzog* and *Humboldt's Gift*.

Whatever the case, the dangers he and his family had faced surely recharged Bellow's preoccupation with death, and so, also, with the fundamental value of life—both in his daily existence and in his future fictional narratives. His protagonists, the beleaguered and possibly mad Moses Herzog, the bitter and alienated Holocaust survivor Artur Sammler, and the self-destructive Humboldt Van Fleisher, as well as any number of other Bellow characters, are men in spiritual crisis. Challenged and nearly overcome by the immense scale of the insanities of the twentieth century, they are unnerved and frightened by the inevitability of death—and the future of their souls.[16]

Soon after the Japanese surrender in August 1945, Bellow, who had begun writing *The Victim* while in service, was released from the merchant marine and returned to civilian life. A film studio executive, having seen in the *Chicago Sun* a photograph of Saul, the "beautiful young Jewish intellectual incarnate," offered to make him a movie star—an incident that found its way into Bellow's 1956 novel, *Seize the Day*, but only incidentally into his life. He was told he could play the guy "who has lost the girl to the Errol Flynn . . . type."[17] Bellow decided to stick with literature but unsurprisingly found it difficult to make a living. He needed help from his brothers, who were generous but also patronizing toward that dreamy-eyed Saul.[18]

Bellow did find paid work with the *Encyclopedia Britannica* as an indexer of "ideas," but he complained that the job took precious time away from writing. He hoped to quit if *Dangling Man* sold well enough. But John Henle, his publisher, cautioned prudence. He sounded very much like Bellow's father, who had asked more than once, in one form or another, with full Yiddish resonance, "From writing you can make a living?" As to surviving "on what you earn as a writer," Henle said, "I have to warn you . . . there are very few human beings in this world who are able to do this IF THEY WANT TO DO HONEST WORK." This turned out to be sound advice. The first edition of *Dangling Man* sold only 1,506 copies.[19]

Bellow, determined to succeed, grew impatient with the Chicago to which he returned in the fall of 1945. The city "grows more like Siberia all the time," he told James T. Farrell in a letter that included an allusion to an essay by Edmund Wilson. Writing about Jane Addams's Hull House, Wilson had said, he was "amazed, desolated, stunned," by Chicago, one of the bleakest of the great cities, with its warehouses, stockyards, skyscrapers, "black factories and long streets . . . that stretch away into darkness."[20]

Grim and ominous and far from the center of literary and intellectual activity, Chicago could not contain Bellow's ambition. Saul was determined to "move East" and told his friend Sam Freifeld he would make his way "Rosenfeld-style as a freelance."[21] He simply "had the obligation of going to the Big Town and taking it on, the immemorial pattern of young hicks."[22]

At the end of September, he packed up his family, stored his furniture in a hotel owned by his brother Maury, boarded the train to New York, and, like his own adventurous Augie March and Twain's Huckleberry Finn, "lit out for the Territory." New York had already become a mecca for artists and authors from all over the United States, and from the mid-1930s forward the city sheltered an unparalleled influx of refugees as well from Europe—writers, scholars, and intellectuals, including many

Jews, such as Erwin Panofsky, Claude Lévi-Strauss, Ernst Cassirer, Max Ascoli, Marc Chagall, Henry Kissinger, and Hannah Arendt.

Arriving in New York with nowhere to stay, the Bellow crew ended up on the doorstep of Arthur Lidov, a commercial artist who nursed loftier goals and, like Bellow, a University of Chicago Jewish alum, who had fled the city for New York. On the walls of Lidov's fifth-floor walk-up studio apartment were his paintings of "emaciated rabbis standing behind barbed wire in Nazi camps.... Jewish children with eyes like black marbles waiting their turn for the gas chambers."[23] Alfred Kazin, a tenant soon after Lidov left, said the paintings "threatened" him, even in the dark. "They surrounded me," he admitted, "with such an air of judgment," saying, "'Kazin had done nothing, *we* had done nothing.'"[24]

Bellow did not have to put up with the alleged insinuations of the art. The family did not get to share the apartment with Arthur Lidov and his wife, Victoria; the pair were leaving for a rented farmhouse in Patterson, New York. Fortunately for the Bellows, and apparently on a whim, the Lidovs invited Saul, Anita, and Greg to come along. Arthur painted in the attic. On the floor below, Bellow wrote unsigned reviews for the *Nation*, the *New York Times Book Review*, and the *New Republic*, as well as readers' reports for a British publisher. He "was trying to write *The Victim*," he told a friend, and "did all kinds of jobs to feed my sheep and stay alive myself."[25] He earned barely enough to support the family.

Sharing the rent was convenient, but the advantages of communal living apparently paled for the Bellows in a house with only one bathroom and a coal furnace that went out every night in the winter. Saul found another farmhouse near Holmes, New York. But very soon after the Bellows moved in, Anita had to return home to Chicago to attend to her brother Jack, ill with terminal cancer.

Bellow found himself lonely for Anita and six-month-old Greg. He complained to Henle that he was "holding down this eight-room house, a servitor to the pipes and heaters."[26] Domestic life, as Anita had early discovered, wasn't exactly Saul's métier. He always had a rationale for avoiding mundane tasks near at hand. After all, Bellow was keeping up a Jewish tradition, just as he had done in his mother-in-law's home in the Ravenswood section of Chicago—studying and writing while the women did the household chores and the child nurturing—though Saul at times could be a doting father.

"There hasn't been an honest workingman on either side of the family as far back as can be known," Bellow confessed to Henle. "Most of my forefathers were Talmudists. My maternal grandfather," Saul seemed to brag, "had twelve children and never worked a day in his life."[27] Resembling the *talmidei khokhemim*, those students and sages revered for their scholarship in his family's shtetl past, Bellow spent his days bent over his notes and manuscripts.

Saul told his publisher that his work on *The Victim* was going very well and that he was in "a state of high excitement." But living in the country soon wore on him, and when a second application for a Guggenheim Fellowship was unsuccessful, Bellow grew ever hungrier for New York City. It had become impossible to meet expenses, however, and the family had to retreat to Anita's mother's apartment in Chicago. Soon thereafter, luckily, a friend of the Lidovs offered the Bellows a free flat near Columbia University. Here they spent the summer of 1946 until Bellow at long last found steady employment as an instructor of English at the University of Minnesota in its newly founded humanities department. Herb McClosky, a professor of political science at the university, who had met Bellow through Sam Freifeld, helped him procure the invitation to teach in Minneapolis for the then-considerable sum of $2,500.[28]

Bellow's father was not impressed. When Abraham visited the university in the fall, he found his son living in a Quonset hut, a lightweight prefabricated structure of corrugated steel, on the

Agricultural School campus. There was no running water in the Bellow family quarters and no dividing walls, and a kerosene stove provided the only heat. Abe stayed with the McCloskys but could not eat in their nonkosher home. He did, however, join Herb and Mitzi McClosky for morning coffee, all the while lamenting the low depths to which his son had fallen. His father asked himself, What was Saul doing in Minneapolis, anyway? What were any Jews, including Herb and Mitzi, doing in Minneapolis? And what, after all, was wrong with the family coal business, where Bellow could earn a real living? Abraham, according to his granddaughter Lesha Bellows Greengus, could talk for hours about "Saul's foolish choice of working for such a small salary when he could have joined [his father] in the coal business."[29]

This kind of eternal and apparently universal pattern of conflict between father and son in an immigrant Jewish family was made explicit by Isaac Rosenfeld in his first and only novel, *Passage from Home*.[30] Published in 1946, when Abraham and Saul were entangled in yet another episode of their classic confrontation, the novel could easily have been inspired by their troubled relationship. Bellow in his life and work demonstrated a loving attachment to family and, especially after his mother's death, a need to be embraced and admired by his father. At the same time, there was a deep yearning on Saul's part to be free of the oppressive quality of life with Abraham.

In Rosenfeld's novel, Bernard (the narrator and chief protagonist) has, like Saul, lost his mother while still in his teens, and he is pulled between saturation in the affectionate company of his relatives and the deep need for liberation. Soon after Bernard returns from a temporary escape from home, there is a memorable scene involving father and son. The elder Rosenfeld gets up from sitting on his son's bed and walks "around the room, stopping before the bookcase and looking at my books. He always seemed to regard them as strange and remote objects, symbols of myself, and thus related to him—it was with his money that I had bought them—and yet [they were] as alien and as hostile as I myself had become."[31]

As Irving Howe wrote in his review of *Passage from Home,* "Nobody who has been brought up in an immigrant Jewish family and experienced the helpless conflict between the father, who sees in his son the fulfillment of his own uninformed intellectuality, and the son for whom that very fulfillment becomes the brand of alienation . . . can read this passage without feeling that here is a true and accurate perception."[32] Only two months later, Howe himself, in what was largely a personal essay, wrote "The Lost Young Intellectual: Marginal Man, Twice Alienated" for *Commentary* magazine: "Usually born into an immigrant Jewish family, he teeters between an origin he can no longer accept and a desired status he cannot attain. He has largely lost his sense of Jewishness, of belonging to a people with a meaningful tradition, and he has not succeeded in finding a place for himself in the American scene or the American tradition."[33]

Decades earlier, Franz Kafka made an uncannily similar observation. Most young Czech Jews, who in the early twentieth century began to write in German, "wanted to leave Jewishness behind them," Kafka said. "But with their hind legs they were still glued to their fathers' Jewishness and they found no ground for their front legs." Despite Howe's handwringing about "alienation," one senses that his "legs were still glued" to Jewishness and that he was never fully uprooted from a "people with a meaningful tradition." Later, in his intellectual autobiography, *A Margin of Hope,* he said so himself. Indeed, the 1946 essay was the beginning of his engagement with questions about Jewish identity that he would continue to explore for nearly fifty years. Again, like Kafka, who said of the young Jewish Czech writers, "Their despair became their inspiration," Howe ended his essay by writing that the "lost young intellectual" can "find consolation and dignity . . . in the consciousness of his vision, in the awareness of his complexity, and the rejection of self-pity. To each age its own burdens."[34]

Here again we see that some denials have a way of revealing, or becoming, varieties of confirmation. For Howe, as with Isaac Rosenfeld, who knew he was Jewish in his bones and in his every thought, there was no real loss of a "sense of Jewishness," nor for Bellow (despite his annoyance at being asked whether or not he was a Jewish writer) would there be any sense of loss of "belonging to a people with a meaningful tradition." Yet, Bellow, whose early years resembled in many ways the fictive Bernard's life and author Rosenfeld's experience, found *Passage from Home* overly sentimental and generally disappointing, and this put a great strain on the Bellow-Rosenfeld friendship. That *Dangling Man* and soon *The Victim* received more critical admiration than *Passage* only made things worse between the two men.

The greater strain, however, was in the relationship between Abraham and Saul Bellow. According to the McCloskys, Abe, assessing the material situation of his thirty-one-year-old son, "really thought Saul was a failure."[35] But the younger Bellow, though he complained about the condition of his residence and about having to teach Advanced Composition, was delighted with his new post. He was, however, intimidated at first by the "well-bred WASPS" in the English Department, including Joseph Warren Beach, a poet and Hardy scholar; Samuel Holt Monk, author of *The Sublime,* a breakthrough study in the humanities; and Henry Nash Smith, a renowned Twain specialist.

Bellow, according to Mitzi McClosky, Herb's wife, "was always bristling after he got the job, always bristling with imagined insults and possible insults."[36] Saul was not necessarily obsessed with mistrust. Minneapolis in 1946 had been labeled with some justice by Carey McWilliams, the future editor of the *Nation,* as the "Capital of Anti-Semitism" in America. In his book *A Mask for Privilege,* McWilliams described the widespread discrimination against Jews, who constituted about 3 percent of the population in the city, as an "Iron Wall" separating "Hebrews" from almost every part of Gentile life—including the Automobile Club of America.[37]

More troubling was the disproportionate number of antisemitic preachers in Minneapolis and the presence in the city of America's largest chapter of the Nazi-wannabe, fascist-hate group, the Silver Shirts.[38] In the English Department, of course, prejudice against Jews was not nearly so vulgar; it was expressed mostly by acidic condescension and "innocent" or "unwitting" antisemitism. When Joseph Warren Beach, for example, finished reading *Dangling Man,* he told Herb McClosky (who had urged the book on him) that he found it "very interesting. Your friend has a wonderful Jewish mind."[39] This remark may not have been as antisemitic as it sounds. Beach later did well by Bellow.

And Bellow had an ally and paternal mentor in Robert Penn Warren, more a writer than an academic, who, though busily working on *All the King's Men,* lunched with Bellow occasionally, and he read *The Victim* in manuscript. The two were soon close friends. Bellow also befriended Leonard Unger. Born into a Yiddish-speaking family in Corona, New York, Unger was raised in Nashville, Tennessee, and had been a student of Warren's at Louisiana State University. Saul later told Warren that "Leonard and I have sized each other up as people from the same layer of the upper air (or lower depths, whichever you like)."[40] Upper or lower, Bellow and Unger often entertained each other with humorous Yiddish chatter in the sober corridors of the English Department.[41]

The extent to which the scholars in the department looked down on Jews is hard to measure. Beach, for example, who thought Bellow had a "wonderful Jewish mind," nonetheless soon promoted him from instructor to assistant professor, with a $1,000 raise attached. Bellow also had good relations with Alburey Castell, the cofounder of the humanities program, and with Sam Holt Monk, Beach's successor as department chair. "Monk is wonderful," Bellow reported to Warren, and in a letter to his friend David Bazelon, he called his colleague "a very decent, generous and intelligent guy."[42]

Still, Bellow "always felt like he was on display," Mitzi recalled. "Not paranoia," she said, "because he was justified" in seeing that decorous antisemitism did indeed exist in the English Department. Bellow was attentive to this disagreeable predilection among some of his colleagues while he was completing *The Victim*. The increasing paranoia and growing prejudice in the novel, as Bellow's biographer Zachary Leader speculates, "may have been exacerbated by comparable feelings in Bellow."[43] Or the paranoia in the novel may have helped reinforce that impression in Bellow as he interacted with the scholarly gentlemen in the English Department.

The Victim concerns an ordinary middle-aged New Yorker, Asa Leventhal, nominally Jewish and an associate editor at a trade journal, who is pursued and haunted by Kirby Allbee, a man he scarcely knows. Allbee accuses Leventhal of having been responsible, through a puzzling sequence of events, for the loss of his job. The ensuing interactions between Allbee, a down-and-out, classic antisemite, and Leventhal, who is habitually anxious, impassive, and muddled, border on the Kafkaesque in their feeling of mysterious inevitability.

Allbee, a widower and heavy drinker, arrives in a near-derelict state at Asa Leventhal's apartment house. He follows Leventhal into a crowded park, confronts him about the loss of his job, and then, whining, insulting, and demanding, continues pursuing his confused and shaken prey for days. Evicted from his boardinghouse, Allbee persuades Asa (whose wife, Mary, is away) to take him in. The more an increasingly paranoid and guilt-driven Leventhal acquiesces to Allbee's belligerencies, the more persistent and aggressive Allbee becomes. He progressively violates Leventhal's personal security and privacy by pervading his apartment, wearing Asa's clothes, reading his mail, and eating his food. That

Asa doesn't just tell Allbee to get lost is Bellow's way of suggesting that assimilation for a modern, urban Jew can produce neurosis, or at the very least a negative self-consciousness.

Writer Sarah Blacher Cohen asks if Leventhal, so taken advantage of, isn't a schlemiel, transplanted from the shtetl, and whether Allbee isn't a version of the schnorrer, the "professional beggar" who in Jewish Eastern Europe felt no shame living off the wealth of others because giving charity to the impoverished was considered a mitzvah, a sacred duty. Stories and anecdotes familiar to Bellow, from the old country, often featured paupers who felt they were doing their benefactors a favor by accepting their kopecks. There is the added factor in Allbee's case of seeking recompense from perceived injustice, but it looks like Allbee and Leventhal are ensnared in a familiar piece of shtetl theater.[44]

The Victim does have an old country dimension, but at its center it is a New World story of conflict between antisemite and Jew, spinning out within a larger moral discourse about the modern "conditions of life," which, as Bellow put it, "make the humanity of others difficult to discern."[45] Asa's reactions to Kirby's accusations go from resistance, dismissal, and denial to ambivalence about his responsibility for Allbee's unemployment and deteriorating condition—ambivalence, too, about his responsibility toward humankind, symbolized in Allbee's name.

In the face of Allbee's spurious, sometimes funny, but almost always absurd antisemitic "lectures" and allusions, Asa must confront yet another responsibility—the quality of his Jewish identity, which has no obvious connection to the ethical, cultural, or religious tradition of Judaism. The two men met briefly at a party during which Allbee, an aristocrat manqué, exposed his clumsy and perhaps whiskey-fueled antisemitism by interrupting two Jewish guests who were singing spirituals and old American ballads. Allbee says, "Why do you sing such songs. . . . It isn't right for you to sing them." Virtually mimicking the adviser at Northwestern who tried to steer Bellow away from studying English by saying, "You weren't born to it," Albee blurts out, "You have to be born to them." Sing a psalm, Allbee insists, or any "Jewish song. Something you've really got feeling for."[46]

Allbee thinks Leventhal intentionally caused him to lose his job as revenge for these demeaning remarks. His insistence forces Asa to ask himself, "Had he unknowingly" or "unconsciously wanted to get back at Allbee? He was sure he hadn't."[47] But Leventhal lives with uncertainty. As he continues to suffer Allbee's unrelenting accusations and antisemitic insults, Leventhal grows wary, and his feeling as a Jew of not quite belonging increases. Is he trespassing? Has he been malicious and manipulative by usurping a place in the world that rightfully belonged to Allbee?

The feeling of not belonging, of not possessing the ground one stands on, is the malaise of the modern urban world, which Bellow brilliantly captures in his portrait of the city with its immense challenge to everything human. It is also familiarly Jewish. The fundamental involvement of Jews in the modern city makes them not only the target of malevolent reactionaries epitomized here by Allbee but representatives of the human situation and modern fate. Leventhal may be a stand-in for Everyman, but he is mostly a Jew, an alien in a non-Jewish environment, an outsider full of self-doubt. This allows him to slip unconsciously into becoming what Jean-Paul Sartre had called an "inauthentic" Jew, permitting himself "to be poisoned by the stereotype that others have" of him.[48]

As Allbee ramps up his demands that Leventhal make good for his alleged treachery, Leventhal becomes increasingly caught up in Allbee's delusions and comes to absorb Allbee's antisemitism as a projection of his own self-repugnance. Consequently, he tends to see his fellow Jews, including his father, in formulaic fashion. He recalls a verse his father enjoyed repeating:

Ruf mir Yoshke, ruf mir Moshke,
Aber gib mir die groeschke

Call me Ikey, Call me Moe,
But give me the dough.[49]

Asa knew that his father aimed "to be freed by . . . money from the power of his enemies." But he thinks, unfairly, that his father's enemies were imaginary.

Leventhal had already heard his own boss at the magazine, Mr. Beard, accuse him unjustly "of taking unfair advantage. Like the rest of his brethren." Beard even went on to say he'd never known a Jew who wouldn't take advantage. They "always please themselves first."[50] This kind of random, spontaneous antisemitism, prevalent in America in the 1940s, warps the social context in which Bellow's characters like Mr. Beard and Leventhal's father must perform.

Asa is bothered but doesn't dwell on what he's overheard. Allbee, however, really piles it on. "You people," he tells Leventhal—setting the Jews outside of Christian society and the universe of moral obligation—are trying to take over the country.[51] Look, he says, "how many Jewish dishes are in the cafeterias, how much of the stage—how many Jewish comedians and jokes, and stories, and so on, and Jews in public life, and so on."[52] Allbee is equally distressed at seeing a book in the library "about Thoreau and Emerson, by a man named Lipschitz. . . . A name like that?" It seems to Allbee that "people of such background couldn't understand," a prejudicial point of view Bellow had encountered when he was in college, which continued to pursue him right on through to his Nobel Prize and beyond.[53]

Unlike Bellow, Leventhal lacks the internal resources, the confidence, the self-esteem, to defend himself, and he tries desperately to maintain his innocence in the face of Allbee's allegations. He asks his friend Williston, who knows both men, what he thinks had transpired between them. "Maybe you aimed to hurt him," Williston says, "and maybe you didn't. My opinion is that you didn't. But the effect was the same. You lost him his job."[54]

Bellow takes the position through Williston that individuals are responsible for all their actions, conscious or unconscious. Although he illustrates this point using lines from a tale in *One Thousand and One Nights* as an epigram, the roots of his view may also be found in Hebrew scripture and classical Talmudic literature, which emphasize responsibility for all deeds, intentional or not.[55] Asa comes to regard being responsible as the most important quality of being human. He "liked to think human meant 'accountable'" and, despite weaknesses, in the end "tough enough to hold."[56] Is Leventhal thinking about Allbee's failure to own up to his personal mistakes, or is he obsessed about his own part in contributing to Allbee's misfortunes?

Bellow insisted on promoting this question in *The Victim* by including a scene that his publisher John Henle thought unnecessary. It involved Schlossberg, a kibitzer, a cafeteria philosopher who writes random pieces, mostly about theater, for the Yiddish newspapers. At lunch with a small group of men, including Leventhal, Schlossberg gives his opinion on what constitutes good stage-acting and, by implication, good living.

"It's bad to be less than human," Schlossberg says, "and it's bad to be more than human. . . . So here is the whole thing then. . . . I have a high opinion of what is human. This is my whole idea. More than human, can you have any use for life? Less than human, you don't either. . . . Have dignity, you understand me? Choose dignity."[57] Bellow argued that Schlossberg's fervent sermon on what it meant to be human—neither self-righteously and judgmentally dismissive of man's inherent frailty nor stubbornly dismissive of one's own moral accountability—pointed up the meaning of his book. He explained that "the moral act is the human one and implies humanity on all sides, but the conditions of life make the humanity of others difficult to discern."[58] The Schlossberg passage stayed in.

Throughout the novel, Allbee and Leventhal do a surreal dance about responsibility and accountability in which the partners occasionally change positions. It is apparent that in his troubled life, Allbee has often acted deplorably, for which Leventhal holds him responsible. But Leventhal is also conscious of general injustice and suffering. "There was great unfairness," he thinks, "in one man's having all the comforts of life while another had nothing. . . . Admittedly there was a wrong, a general wrong."[59]

Leventhal doesn't quite mean that Allbee's behavior and personal accusations are justified. But he occasionally said to his wife Mary, "revealing his deepest feelings, 'I was lucky. I got away with it.'" He meant "his bad start"—the details of which are never revealed—"might have wrecked him." He himself might have "fallen in with that part of humanity of which he was frequently mindful . . . the part that did not get away with it—the lost, outcast, the overcome, the effaced, the ruined."[60]

Allbee displays an even more explicit contradiction than Leventhal's. On the one hand, he implies that it is the weakness of the Jews to sympathize with the unfortunate, but then, "mystifyingly off-center," he says that Jews as a people are without compassion and give no thought to human frailty. "It's necessary for you to believe that I deserve what I get," Allbee tells Leventhal. "It doesn't enter your mind, does it—that a man might not be able to help being hammered down?" But "take it from me . . . there's no denying that evil is real as sunshine." If a man suffers, Allbee says, "a man like me," you think, "it's his fault," that "I deserve what I get." It's a "Jewish point of view," Allbee says, upping the temperature, and "that leaves your hands clean." Leventhal is horrified. How can Allbee talk this way? "Millions of us have been killed," Leventhal blurts out. "What about that?" he asks, not expecting an answer from someone so hateful.[61]

Leventhal recognizes that Allbee has moments of "genuineness," saying things that are "clear, familiar, and truthful," indicating remorse for his own failings. But then Kirby switches to wildly inconsistent charges, blaming Asa for everything that has recently gone wrong in his life. It becomes clear that Allbee assumes a determinism in regard to himself that precludes his own moral accountability, but he projects a free will in regard to Leventhal, which holds the Jew responsible.

Despite the fierce verbal dueling, or more likely because of it, Leventhal, in a dream, has a crucial illumination—one he desperately wants to hang on to when he wakes in the morning. Sounding very much like Joseph in *Dangling Man,* who said, "We were figures in the same plot eternally fixed together," and the existence of others, "just as it was, made mine possible," Asa says on waking, "It was supremely plain to him that everything, everything without exception, took place within a single soul." And he realizes, in connection with this, that "truth must be something we understand at once, without an introduction or explanation, but so common and familiar that we don't always realize it's around us."[62]

Without reducing Leventhal, a creatively imagined character, to a direct reflection of Bellow's own spiritual struggles, we can say that Leventhal's statements about "the truth" echo Bellow's Jewishly embedded conviction that rationality is not the only path to illumination, that science doesn't have all the answers, that the soul exists.

Bellow has invented his two protagonists as "unwitting but not unwilling doubles" bound together by the surfacing of antisemitism, "the longest hatred."[63] Bound doubles or not, the tangled relationship moves quickly to an explosive conclusion. Coming home one day to find his front door locked and chained, an outraged Leventhal breaks it down only to find Allbee in bed with a woman. Asa has had it. "'Enough!' he decides, 'Enough, Enough!'" Kirby is banished. Leventhal tells himself he will be less passive in responding to Allbee's egregious violations and his ugly prejudices. He will no longer run away from his Jewish identity, which he finally understands amounts to a rejection of himself. Casting out Allbee for good, along with his own yetzer hara or "bad impulse" to internalize stereotypes of Jews, Leventhal becomes responsible; he will start "taking care of things by himself" and become accountable for his obligations as a Jew and a man.[64]

In a climactic transgression, however, Allbee intrudes one final time. He enters the apartment while Asa is asleep, puts his head in the oven, and tries, by turning on the gas, to kill himself and most likely Leventhal, too. Asa awakes from a fitful dream into foul and acrid air, rushes "from bed, dragging the sheets into which his foot had caught," and finds it hard to breathe: "Gas was pouring from the oven."[65]

A symbolic enactment of the Final Solution? Allbee may be committing suicide, but he is also murdering Asa, the Jew. The Holocaust is alluded to directly only once in the novel, but, among other powerful things, *The Victim* is also about the Shoah, even if some of its many allusions—to railway stations, crowds, heat, and blackness—are less literal than when an exasperated Leventhal shouts out his question about the murder of millions of Jews.[66]

Nearly all of Bellow's books, in prose and symbol, reflect a deep Jewish cultural inheritance. But in *The Victim,* we are offered a more direct, unmediated glance into the social weight of that Jewish inheritance—which among other profound episodes in Jewish life and history includes antisemitism and the Holocaust. It is quite correct to state that *Mr. Sammler's Planet* was Bellow's first book about a Holocaust survivor, but as *The Victim* and even *Dangling Man* make clear, *Sammler* was not his first book about the Holocaust itself, either in abstract concept or in graphic reality, nor would it be his last.

SIX

IN THE LAND OF THE HOLOCAUST

AT THE END OF THE 1947 spring semester, not knowing whether he'd be reappointed at the university or where his family would live, Bellow, with the help of "Benzedrine tablets," had been relentlessly revising *The Victim*, and for months, according to Anita, he had become unbearable to live with. When she complained about Saul to the McCloskys, Herb told her, "Don't worry, it's what you get with genius." Anita shot back, "Genius, shmenius, his father's the same way."[1]

In June, Bellow not only received a new contract but also was invited by the dean of science, literature, and the arts to accompany a small group of Minneapolis undergraduates to Spain for a summer seminar. This was just what he needed, he wrote to David Bazelon, "a marvelous break." The galleys for *The Victim* in hand, Bellow sailed to the continent in early summer with the ten students he was to oversee. Because his means of transportation, a converted cargo vessel, was not safe for small children, Gregory and Anita were forced to stay behind. She resigned herself to "vacationing" for two weeks with Gregory and her in-laws in a kosher hotel in Wisconsin before returning to the Goshkin household in Chicago for the remainder of the summer.[2]

The ship, no luxury liner, had to withstand a rough nine days at sea, as did Bellow. He was queasy much of the time and spent most days in a deck chair trying to read galleys—a task that made him "weary to the bone" and bored him so that he muttered something to the McCloskys (who were accompanying students to England) about throwing the pages overboard.[3] He didn't, but the proofs were much neglected.

For Bellow, crossing the Atlantic by boat was a way of reliving his father's voyage to Halifax in 1913. He felt as if he were "reversing his parents' journey." In his mind, he was going home.[4] "My parents," Bellow said later, "were European through and through. . . . I grew up under this influence myself."[5] Europe! Bellow anticipated that the Old World would be as marvelous as he had pictured it from his father's stories and his own devoted reading of nineteenth-century European and Russian classics.

Spain in particular seemed "ancestral" to Bellow. He felt as if he were "returning to some kind of . . . homeland" and "even had notions that in an earlier incarnation I might have been in the Mediterranean."[6] People, Saul thought, "had Tolstoyan-style households with a feudal servant class. Even their gestures, the way they smoked, reminded me of my father." He added, "And the heavy white table linen was like the table linen my parents brought over from St. Petersburg."[7]

Bellow was not too put off by the decrepit condition of Madrid, a city still suffering from the physical and psychological effects of the Spanish Civil War. But he was distressed by the ominous character of Franco's police state—especially the ubiquitous presence of the Guardia Civil. "Police come first to your notice in Spain," Bellow wrote, "taking precedence over people, the streets, and the landscape." In the context of Europe's more promising qualities, however, he was not driven away.[8]

On the ship, Bellow met Francisco Garcia Lorca, the younger brother of Federico Garcia Lorca, the great Spanish poet who was murdered by the fascists. Francisco introduced Bellow to a group of journalists, poets, and novelists, including the pro-Fascist writer Gimenez Caballero. Through Lorca, Bellow also became acquainted with members of the anti-Franco underground who came together in a café near his pension in the Puerta del Sol. It was odd that members of the resistance should meet in the same square that housed the Direccion General de Seguridad, Franco's security police. It was stranger still that fascists like the "literary man" Gimenez Caballero and members of the anti-Franco underground should be in the same circle. But Caballero, with whom Bellow "had a few dinners," was an unusual supporter of Franco—being anti-Nazi and philosemitic.[9]

Another favorite watering hole in Madrid that attracted the German community was Restaurante Horcher. Here Bellow met several important figures and "a blonde buxom lady" who had been secretary to the head of the Spanish Secret Police. Bellow coyly confessed to Robert Johnson, one of the older students on the trip and a great admirer of Bellow, that he and the blonde, "a charming German lady, still quite young," were having an affair. One supposes that "*had been* secretary" was the operative phrase for Bellow regarding the charming lady's fascism. But maybe not. These kinds of complications at the cafés and gathering places, together with the simple fact of Bellow's being in Europe with so much to absorb and synthesize, may have temporarily blunted the novelist's readiness to question.[10]

That Spain was destitute and unthreatening to outsiders like Saul helped him make the most of his contacts while storing up impressions. Bellow later told an interviewer, "Madrid was a great eye opener for me. . . . I met a great many Spaniards; it was my first prolonged contact with Europeans and the European intellectual." So isolated had these Spaniards been that even "a trifling instructor from Minnesota," as Bellow modestly categorized himself, "was eagerly taken up by them."[11] In turn, the proximity of the writers, artists, and intellectuals was intoxicating and energizing for Bellow.

His academic obligations were light. The class met only once weekly in a café; mostly he was on his own. Determined to make a side trip to Paris, Bellow invited an eager Robert Johnson to be his traveling companion. Saul felt quite close to Johnson, a Gentile farm boy from Minnesota. Indeed, they described themselves as "soul mates." For Saul, a soul mate had to be a man, but not necessarily a Jew. He only had to possess what Bellow considered Jewish sensitivities: emotional intensity, a near reverence for Russian literature, and a ready willingness to engage in intellectual gossip. Johnson, who fit the bill, described himself in a way Bellow likely saw him—"a *goy* with a *Yiddisher kopf*," a Gentile with a Jewish head or mind.[12]

In Paris, Bellow spent time with the McCloskys and with Herb Kaplan and his wife, Celia. A member of the old Hyde Park gang, "Kappy" was serving as an adviser to the newly established UNESCO (the United Nations Economic and Social Council) in France. Saul had long seen Kappy as the most talented writer among his early friends, surpassing even Rosenfeld, and therefore as a rival of sorts. But if Kappy made Bellow vaguely anxious, his wife, Celia, was a font of solace, mainly because she was an excellent Yiddishist—always a positive credential in Saul's mind, a source of comfort, and a spur to positive memories of his *Yiddishe* childhood in Montreal.

Bellow's complex attitude toward Kappy, who had given up writing as a trade, shows up in a letter to Mel Tumin. The trouble, Bellow wrote, was that "Kappy has made himself after his own image, has chosen to be the Parisian Kappy and has put behind him that part of his history that doesn't fit the image," the old Jewish neighborhood: "Why should he be the Kaplan his mother bore and Newarkstamped when he has the power to be the Kaplan of his choice? You have felt that, I have, [Herb] Passin has. Only some of us have had the sense to realize that the man we bring forth has no richness compared with the man who really exists, thickened, fed and fattened by *all* the facts about him, all of his history. Besides, the image can never be *reyn* [pure, in Yiddish] and it is especially impure when money and power are part of its outfit."[13]

Bellow seems to be suggesting that Kappy was hankering to have access to wealth and influence over everything else. But in his next sentence, Bellow implies something else more important, his belief that Kappy was betraying his Jewish past and his gifts as a writer: "It's the best, the strongest, most talented whose lives miscarry in this way. I deeply hope, for Kappy that he recovers before the damage to his power to feel goes any further."[14]

On the ship home from Spain, Bellow's spirits, according to Mitzi McClosky, were low, held down by worries about his neglected galleys for *The Victim* and even more by doubts about his marriage. Bellow, now thirty-two, told Mitzi that he was a champion of monogamy as the foundation of social stability. Yet Saul did not avoid women who chased him, and he continued to initiate infidelities, including an affair on the return voyage with a nineteen-year-old Wisconsin undergraduate.[15]

If a third-hand account can be believed, Bellow, much later and after a second divorce, told one of his several lovers that he seemed "to have a bad character—a character that demands a test, and then after a struggle fails." He is alleged to have gone on to say that he had a "disorder. . . . Do you think I want to *be* like this?" Bellow may very well have said that the quality of his character often came up short—this admission appears sporadically in his letters—and he often thought of himself as a "jerk," as distinct from a mensch. And if he sounds here a lot like Herzog, Bellow also has Herzog say, "I hate the victim bit." That the author of *The Victim,* a book abounding with questions about blame, freedom in the individual, and the need to choose, should have played this kind of "victim card," while hardly impossible, is in this undocumented case difficult to credit.[16]

On his way back to Anita, Saul reiterated his qualms about his marriage, admitting to his friends that he had never experienced real passion. He told the McCloskys he felt "burdened" and "deadened" at home. He acknowledged his debt to Anita for providing the order, stability, and income that made it possible for him to write *Dangling Man*; but like his fictive protagonist Joseph, Saul saw order and stability as impeding his quest for greater spiritual insight, his search for freedom.

When Bellow got to New York harbor en route to Chicago, Anita was waiting at the dock. She was tan and slim, and to Saul she looked ten years younger. But it was a troubled reunion. Anita was angry that her husband had gone off for three months, leaving her alone with three-year-old Gregory—and with proofreading and publishing arrangements to attend to.[17]

The Bellows returned to Minneapolis in September and moved into a large house in a suburb populated by other professors. To meet the rent, Saul and Anita had to take in boarders, one of whom was Max Kampelman. An instructor in political science who went on to do significant diplomatic work for the US government, Kampelman also later served on the board of the Jewish Institute for National Security Affairs, a think tank.

While living with the Bellows, Kampelman was astonished to learn that Jews could not be members of a variety of organizations in Minneapolis, including the Automobile Club. He had lots of talks with Saul and Herb McClosky about this kind of thing, an education, really, in anti-Jewish discrimination. Bellow and McClosky, however, were two very different kinds of Jews. "Herb was a 'culinary' and Jewish joke-telling Jew," his wife Mitzi explained, "whereas Saul was very deeply versed in Jewish history and religion. He taught us about Judaism, and to me, he came off as the voice of the Prophets themselves. From him I learned to be proud of my heritage."[18]

McClosky was not only about food and fun. He took his Jewish identity seriously enough to become part of the brain trust that Minneapolis Mayor Hubert Humphrey's administration had assembled in its efforts to combat antisemitism and racism in Minnesota. Bellow, though not active politically or involved directly with any Jewish organizations, on or off campus, was acutely aware of antisemitism—part of the reason he liked Humphrey "a lot." In what the mayor was trying to do, Bellow said, Humphrey "wasn't faking it."[19]

When *The Victim* came out in November 1947, it was described by *Time* in a benighted and faintly antisemitic review as "a competent little story about a touchy Jew and a fantastic Gentile who accuses him of ruining his life." And two weeks later in its annual fiction review, the magazine gave praise but reduced Bellow's complex, multilayered novel to "the year's most intelligent study of the Jew in US society."[20] There were, however, other more sophisticated, largely positive reviews in the *Nation* and the *New York Times*. In *Partisan Review*, Bellow was celebrated as fiction's "great hope." *The Victim* was "marked by thorough and exquisite honesty," Elizabeth Hardwick wrote, and "it would be hard to think of any writer who has a better chance than Bellow to become the redeeming novelist of his period."[21]

An equally clairvoyant essay by Martin Greenberg appeared in *Commentary*. It was almost as if Greenberg had seen that Jewish novelists would be preeminent in the long postwar period from the 1940s to the 1980s. *The Victim*, he declared, was "the first attempt to consider Jewishness not in its singularity, not as constitutive of a special world of experience, but as a quality that informs all modern life, as the quality of modernity itself."[22]

Indeed, beginning with *Dangling Man* and now with *The Victim*, Bellow laid claim to a considerably larger public—less parochial and less ethnic than the Jewish audience for Abraham Cahan, Anzia Yezierska, or Daniel Fuchs. His Jewishness, Bellow said often—and throughout his entire career—was "a gift, a piece of good fortune," and a "source of inspiration."[23]

Yet he would continue to repudiate the idea that he was a "Jewish" writer. He was "an American," he said, and "a Jew, a writer by trade."[24] In pursuit of that trade, Bellow had written two "proper" books. He felt, he said, that "I as the child of Russian Jews, must establish my authority, my credentials, my fitness to write books in English."[25]

No matter what the Harvard-trained professors thought of it, *The Victim* was admired by a broad range of the literati, including Alfred Kazin, Robert Penn Warren, Elizabeth Hardwick, and even Diana Trilling, who had panned *Dangling Man*. Bellow's second novel was a critical success, but when all the figures were tallied, Saul, who had had an advance of $500, owed his publisher John Henle $170. Henle had warned him more than once that there was no money in literature. And when Bellow's accountant learned that *The Victim* left its author with a debt, he recommended that Saul find another line of work. It was too late for that. Bellow, like many in his family line of *schreibers* and *talmidei khokhemim* (writers, sages, scholars, and lifelong students of Talmud), never thought about doing anything else. "What else could I have done," he asked. "I'm not fully myself unless I'm writing something. If I stop writing, I might as well stop breathing."[26]

Relying mostly on royalties and Anita's insufficient pay, Bellow had intermittent trouble paying his rent. This, while his brothers regularly appeared in the Chicago newspapers reporting on their real-estate empires—Sam's nursing homes and Maury's hotels and landfill operations. The brothers, together with Abraham, who had finally, at the age of forty, become a prosperous businessman, constituted a triumvirate whose material success stood as a persistent rebuke of Bellow's penury. On occasion, however, items in the papers about Saul's brothers were less than celebratory, detailing kickbacks, strong-arming, and bribery. But it was the bad boys who were seen as having made good; Saul was considered the failure.

The glowing reviews of his son's latest novel left Bellow's father unimpressed. "The fact that I was a celebrity last week," Bellow wrote to Bazelon, "made no difference to him." He didn't even "read my reviews"; he "only look[ed] at them" before he dismissed them. To save him from a life of impecuniousness and what he saw as Saul's continuing pursuit of *narishkayt* (foolishness), Abraham offered to make his youngest son "a mine superintendent at ten thousand. . . . A mine's a mine," Bellow wrote, but reviews to Abraham were "mere stirring with wind."[27]

Perhaps. But reviews and supporting letters are what finally earned Bellow a Guggenheim on his third try. Again, Abraham remained indifferent. In his letter to Mel Tumin, Bellow wrote that when he told his father of the award, "he looked . . . as he had looked, at the gold star in my third-grade copybook." The expression on his father's face, Bellow thought, had said clearly, "Yes, very fine, but there's still life with its markers, alleyways and bedrooms where such as you are conceived between a glass of schnapps and a dish of cucumbers and cream."[28] The Polish name for this dish, *mizeria*—derived from the poverty of the peasants—means "misery," which Bellow no doubt continued to experience in his relationship with Abraham, a Russian Jewish immigrant father who was perfectly capable of mixing love with irony and cruelty.

In his proposal to the Guggenheim committee, Bellow had written that "the scope of the mind has, through science been immensely extended while that of personality has shrunk." For this "devaluation of man," Bellow held all sources of cultural authority "suspect," including all the social sciences. These, he said, neglect the soul and give us only an environmentally constructed human being, turning modern "Man" into "an object of slender importance."[29] "The sociologists are the greater offenders," Bellow argued in his letter to Tumin: "I listen to them . . . with every effort to be fair and understanding but I can't make out their Man. Surely that's not *homo sapiens, mon semblable*! [not my fellow man]. The creature the theologians write about is far closer to me."[30] No doubt. Bellow had always insisted on the infinite value of the soul—its individual uniqueness, its power, and its supreme importance to human understanding.

In his correspondence, Bellow insisted that unlike the social scientist, the novelist "labors in character" and imagination to produce a complex vision of a person—a person with consciousness who makes choices and possesses a soul.[31] He was unyielding in his defense of meaning and responsibility and about the great worth of human existence in both his real and fictive worlds. And his view was strengthened by the positive reception of *The Victim,* a book replete with questions about culpability and the need to choose.[32]

Bellow told close friends that he was working on something new—a projected "novelette"—called *The Crab and the Butterfly,* which would, like his first two novels, deal with choice and moral accountability. Before leaving for Paris with his Guggenheim, Bellow told Tumin and Bazelon that the story centered on "a man who is rotting to death in a hospital room. His stink offends the other patients. The hero of the story defends him because nothing is for him, more valuable than life or more sacred than the struggle to remain alive."[33]

In the manuscript, however, the hero, in many of his assertions, gives the impression of once having been a nihilist, impatient with the idea of value. By the time Bellow was working in Paris, he had become "terribly downcast" over his writing about a claustrophobic hospital room, and he vacillated about employing the kind of trendy negativism pronounced by his protagonist. "There was something in me," he said, "perhaps of Jewish origin which had nothing to do with negativism." His hero, in the end, like Bellow himself, rejects nihilism and continues to coax "a dying man to assert himself and claim his share of life."[34] Once more, then, for Bellow, it was "choose life"—a commandment, a sacred injunction, that remained the most tenacious theme in his work.

With these ideas and convictions, a work in progress, a $3,000 advance from Viking (his newly acquired publisher), a fellowship from Guggenheim worth $2,500, and a year's leave from the University of Minnesota, Bellow, family along, left for Europe. When they arrived in the City of Light, there was a deep chill in the air, and Paris "gloom" lay heavy everywhere, darkening everything, including the general mood. The despair, Bellow said, was "not simply climatic, it [was] a spiritual force that act[ed] not only on building materials . . . but also on character, opinion, and judgment."[35] The French were still suffering the humiliation of defeat and four years of German occupation. Having had to concede weakness, they were forced to descend from the high perch of arrogance to ground-level cynicism—a variety of self-contempt now turned outward toward their American liberators.

Bellow quickly recognized a ubiquitous and powerful anti-Americanism, especially in Paris. "I had a Jewish explanation for this," he told Philip Roth years later: "bad conscience." Not only had the French been overrun by the Germans in a matter of weeks; many on the left, especially after the Molotov-Ribbentrop Pact (Nazi-Soviet Pact, August 1939) and before the German invasion of the Soviet Union (June 1941), had actively undermined the French war effort. And throughout the occupation, a sizable part of the population collaborated with the Nazis, sometimes with eagerness. The ready capitulation and passive acceptance of the Vichy government, Bellow thought, had made the French people sour and cynical. Throughout the war they pretended that there was an immense underground doing irreparable damage to the German effort; but resistance to Vichy and Nazi occupation was negligible, Jean-Paul Sartre's claims notwithstanding.[36]

Whenever he was exposed to anti-American prejudice, which pushed him slightly rightward politically, Bellow thought about the shameful behavior of the wartime French, not only in regard to the Germans but especially in regard to the Jews. Particularly galling to him was the memory of the *Rafle*, a roundup, in the summer of 1942, of more than thirteen thousand Jewish men, women, and children. The operation was carried out entirely by the French police, who were reported "to have worked with an enthusiasm that surprised [even] the German occupiers who had commanded them." Those caught in the *Rafle*, along with some sixty thousand other Jews, were transported to concentration camps. The survival rate was 3 percent.[37] It must have been doubly distressing for Bellow to find himself in Europe as an American Jew, beset by antisemitism—which was to be expected—and virulent anti-Americanism, which seemed to originate in some of the same sources as hostility to Jews.

Distressed or not, Bellow settled into a studio on rue des Saint-Péres to work on his new novel, while Anita found a job with the American Jewish Joint Distribution Committee (JDC). The JDC, or the "Joint," as it was affectionately dubbed, was privately funded by American Jews in an effort to relocate and repair the broken lives of Holocaust survivors. After ministering to children in orphanages, Anita was promoted to the Jewish Medical Department, where she conducted "a survey of the chronically sick [Jews] in France who are receiving aid from J.D.C." In this way, Anita told the McCloskys, she was brought "into contact with all the Jewish clinics in Paris" and was immersed daily in the accumulating and appalling revelations about the death camps.[38] And because it was so common, she may also have experienced irritating interactions with French Jews who, like the French generally, didn't like Americans.

In all likelihood, she shared with her husband much of what she witnessed and learned, day after day. Bellow himself, by speaking directly with survivors and deportees, was also learning a great deal about "what life had been like under the Nazis, about roundups and deportation."[39] He told Oscar Tarcov, near the end of 1949, that after six months of discussions with Holocaust survivors, he was staggered—shockingly reminded that "there's nothing in my private existence that justifies complaint or melancholy for myself."[40]

Angry enough already, Bellow was further outraged when in Paris he read Louis-Ferdinand Céline's *Les Beaux Draps*, a collection of "crazy, murderous harangues, seething with Jew-hatred."[41]

Céline had supported the Axis powers during the war, and his book was published in France in 1941, like the plays of Jean-Paul Sartre, under Nazi occupation. How could Céline, "a superb writer," Bellow wondered, "have taken the line . . . he took on the Jews during the Holocaust?" It was "an unpleasant puzzle for us," he said in an interview many years later. He "couldn't understand why so many Jews joined the army of [Céline's] supporters." Did they justify their support for Céline because he "was a great artist and therefore everything must be forgiven?" Bellow had "heard this argument used on behalf of Wagner"—and Eliot, too—"until it was coming out of [his] ears," and he "wasn't going to have it again."[42]

He regarded Jewish attraction to Céline with skepticism and similarly was suspicious of the Paris infatuation of some of his Jewish friends. The glamour of "Paris between the wars" had faded radically for Bellow—the Paris of Proust, Rilke, Joyce, Brancusi, Modigliani, and Zola was gone. But in the late forties, Bellow wrote, Céline's Paris "was still there, more *there* than Sainte-Chapelle or the Louvre."[43] His experiences in Paris in 1948 and 1949 made Bellow keenly aware of how recently the Nazis had departed. And "I knew," he said, "that when I took a deep breath, I was inhaling the crematorium gases still circulating in the air."[44]

Yet forty years later, in 1987, in a long letter to Cynthia Ozick, Bellow indicted himself for his "unspeakable evasion" of the "terrible events in Poland." He was "too busy becoming a novelist," he said, too busy with art and literature and advancing "recognition of [his] talent" to "have reckoned more fully" with the Holocaust. But he also told Ozick that he had been, for over four decades, "brooding about [this] crime so vast."[45]

Despite what he seemed anxious to confess, then, Bellow's almost half century of brooding about the Shoah indicates no "evasion" of the horror. Nor did his becoming a novelist entail an escape from confronting the genocidal murder of the Jews.

Indeed, his first two novels include several allusions to existential antisemitism and representations of the Holocaust, not yet so labeled until 1961. This "crime so vast" is signified obliquely in *Dangling Man* (1944) and more directly, even if still implicitly, in *The Victim* (1947).

These books suggest that Bellow was too critical of himself for what he felt was his "Holocaust avoidance." Even Ozick expressed genuine skepticism about the truth of his explanation. It may be true that Bellow, like many other American Jews, believed that "we knew what happened to the Jews of Europe," and yet "we didn't know." He told writer Jonathan Rosen in 1990 that in Paris in the 1940s, Holocaust survivors were everywhere, and that as a Yiddish speaker, he had access to the terrible truths they harbored. But Bellow, dressed for the interview with Rosen in "a brown fedora, a silk suit threaded with red and blue, a red and white bow tie, a pink shirt and pink socks," said, "I wanted my American seven-layer cake," and he did not want to burden his writing so early in his career with the encumbering weight of Jewish history.[46]

As late as 1999, when he was eighty-four, he told an interviewer that somehow the Holocaust "didn't come through, as it would have for a European, because we had no immediate contact with it."[47] Perhaps suffering a prolonged bout of survivor's guilt, Bellow, in his letter to Ozick and in the interviews he gave in 1991 and 1999, failed to mention the "immediate contact" Anita had experienced while working at the JDC and forgot his own contact and interaction with survivors. Whatever the case, Bellow, in the mid to late forties, earlier than many, had become acutely cognizant of the terrible events in Poland. And his experience in Paris made him even more mindful of the Holocaust, its perpetrators, its victims, and its incalculable moral costs.

"Wie Gott in Frankreich"—like God in France—was an expression used by the Jews of Eastern Europe to describe perfect happiness. For Bellow, France clearly failed to meet that mark. But despite the anti-Americanism, the sharp reminders of French collaboration in German war crimes, and the haunting presence of Holocaust survivors, Paris had its bright moments. The proximity of American friends and acquaintances helped. Bellow interacted more or less regularly with Mary McCarthy, a novelist and political activist; Lionel Abel, an eminent American Jewish playwright and critic; James Baldwin, an African American novelist, poet, and activist; William Phillips, coeditor of *Partisan Review*; and Herbert Gold, a young acolyte with whom he took a long, talk-filled journey to Spain, in the course of which Bellow consumed "a fine dinner of seafood—to the horror of my ancestors, probably"—and apparently (as with pork) not without some revulsion on his part: "All these nasty little creatures scraped up from the sea-mud."[48]

When not writing, Bellow spent the most time with his Chicago buddy, Harold Kaplan. It was at Kappy's lavish upscale house parties in Montparnasse that Bellow met Miles Davis, who was at the very beginning of his rise to eminence as the most influential figure in the history of jazz; Albert Camus, the author of the classic novel *The Stranger*, who, at the young age of forty-four, won the Nobel Prize in Literature; Hungarian-born Arthur Koestler, a disillusioned Communist, already famous for his novel *Darkness at Noon*; Nicola Chiaramonte, an Italian émigré, author, and antifascist activist; and Czeslaw Milosz, Polish poet and future Nobel laureate. Milosz, like Bellow, was intensely interested in "the question of spiritual freedom in the individual" and recognized the reality of the soul and the impossibility of communicating "to people who have not experienced it, the undeniable menace of total rationalism."[49]

Bellow was traveling in elite cultural circles and appears to have been accepted as an equal among these cosmopolitan European writers, poets, and artists—none of them French except for Camus, who was born and raised in Algeria. The Bellows were also invited for drinks, dinner, and other entertainments at the home of Americans Eileen and Stanley Geist. Eileen worked for the Paris office of the Marshall Plan (detested by many leftists in France as an expansion of American hegemony and a threat to French sovereignty); Stanley, who had been a junior fellow at Harvard, had come to Paris to write.

The Geists had some family money and threw crowded, peppery parties for the literati—marked by many instances of flirtation, which is what Herb Gold remembers best. Guests at the frequent gatherings hosted by the Geists and the Kaplans, later interviewed by Zachary Leader, reminisced about Bellow—good looking, full of funny anecdotes, and unsafe around women.[50] Richard Wright, whom Gold ranked, right alongside Bellow, as "the most esteemed American writer in Paris" in the late forties, was occasionally in attendance. He had already written *Native Son* (1940) and his autobiography, *Black Boy* (1945).[51]

Two afternoons a week, Bellow also met Jesse Reichek, his exact contemporary, an American painter who devoted his retirement years to exploring ancient works like kabbalah, the Song of Songs, and ancient myths about mortality and death. They would meet in a café on rue du Bac in the nasty winter of 1949–50 to drink cocoa together while discussing art and culture. The café was in the heart of the Marais district, which was heavily populated by Old World Jews, very many (if not most) speaking Yiddish without hesitation. So, Jesse and Saul themselves turned to Yiddish, enjoying the opportunity to "regress . . . shamelessly to childhood" by conversing mostly in their beloved first language.[52]

There were also good times to be had away from Paris—"pleasant holiday[s]" with the family on the Riviera, at Nice, and in San Remo, Italy. In Rome, Bellow met with antifascist novelists Ignazio Silone, Alberto Moravia, and Elsa Morante, Moravia's Jewish wife and also an important writer in her own right.[53] Here, Bellow spent evenings at the Antico Caffè Greco, the oldest and most ornate bar in Rome, where Byron, Keats, Ibsen, Stendhal, and other notables had also enjoyed coffee.

These nights in cafés or at soirees hosted by the Kaplans and the Geists were cheerful and entertaining enough, but they were in no way comparable to the epiphany Bellow experienced on a Paris street during the day. On a spring morning in 1949, walking slowly to his writing studio, Bellow was "terribly depressed" by a loss of interest in *The Crab and the Butterfly* and "down in the dumps" over his disintegrating marriage. Anita was furious about Bellow's multiple infidelities—including a short but apparently serious interlude in London—and frantic that these betrayals were public knowledge. The weight of these personal problems lifted, however, when Bellow gave his attention to the street sweepers who had opened the hydrant taps to hose down the grimy boulevards—flushing away "cigarette butts, dogs' caca, shredded letters, orange skins, candy wrappers, into the large-mouthed sewers."[54]

Watching the flow, Bellow said, freed him "from the caked burden of depression that had formed in my soul." There was a touch of sun, Bellow told Philip Roth a half century later, which made an "iridescence" in the water and transformed the gutters into a larger, more embracing vision of beauty: "Just the sort of thing that makes us loonies cheerful." Bellow supposed that "a psychiatrist would say this was some form of hydrotherapy." He knew now, he confessed to Roth, that he "must get rid of the hospital novel—it was poisoning my life." There had been enough darkness in *Dangling Man* and *The Victim*, both of which reprise the bleak accursed gravity of the midcentury mood:

> I recognized that this was not what being a novelist was supposed to have meant. This bitterness of mine was intolerable, it was disgraceful, a symptom of slavery. I think I've always been inclined to accept the depressions that overtook me and I felt just now that I had allowed myself to be dominated by the atmosphere of misery and surliness, that I had agreed somehow to be shut in or bottled up. I seem then to have gone back to childhood in my thoughts and remembered a pal of mine whose surname was August—a handsome, freewheeling kid who used to yell out when we were playing checkers, "I've got a scheme!"[55]

Bellow felt liberated from the dreary cargo of death and decay that was turning his novel into an inexorable grave. It was time again to "choose life," to write a different kind of narrative, one not nearly so grim. He thought a fictional biography of an intelligent, spirited, indeed impulsive Jewish boy seeking meaning and place would surely be worth tackling. "Augie," the boy Bellow had in mind, may have been a composite of some of the young Chicago neighbors Bellow had not seen since they were teenagers, or it may have been only Charlie August, who shouted things like "I've got a scheme."

Either way, one or more of the Chicago Jewish street boys introduced Bellow to the American language, and it was in this crowd that he "had unwittingly learned to go at things free-style, making the record in my own way—first to knock, first admitted." His projected story, unlike the now-discarded hospital novel, would incorporate that American language, both philosophic and pragmatic—which, in Bellow's hands, became a fusion of "colloquialism and elegance."[56]

The writing excited Bellow. He was "stirred to the depths," he said, and the words, with "magical suddenness," just "rushed out of [him]." The language, Bellow remembered, was "immediately present." All he had to do was "be there with buckets to catch it."[57] The buckets had to be huge. The printed pages of *Augie March* came to just over six hundred, which, as Bellow admitted later, was about two hundred pages too long. And even though Saul took to writing the book "in all places, all postures, at all times of day and night," it took a full four years to complete.[58]

In the meantime, there were reviews, stories, and essays to write for *Harper's Bazaar* and *Partisan Review*; and for *Commentary* he contributed a short piece to a symposium on antisemitism in response to Leslie Fiedler's celebrated 1949 article, "What Can We Do about Fagin?"[59] In addition to Bellow, respondents included top-tier critics such as Harold Rosenberg, Philip Rahv, Irving Howe, Alfred Kazin, and Lionel Trilling.

Fiedler had encouraged writers to counter depraved images of "the Jew" in English-language literature by fashioning new, more confident images of Jewishness. Bellow argued that it was irrelevant to squabble over stereotypes, because "great things always give pain; they can never be taken smoothly." We cannot read Lear or Job, for example, without pain. But these troubles, Bellow said, are not the same for everyone: "For us the pain of Shylock may be greater than for others because we are Jews." *The Merchant of Venice* shocks us. But this punishment is the "primitive work of literature," and "it doesn't drive us from own nature."

Fiedler is correct, Bellow wrote, when he says that the Jew has been represented in classical literature as malevolent: "Evil stimulant, heartless rationalist . . . clever man of the industrial city, stupid financier blowing his cigar smoke over Venice. But is this characterization of us true? And in the great writing of the past is there something that rejects us such as we are now?"

The answer is obvious, Bellow said, because "'modern reality' had made the lies inherent in historic antisemitism 'plainer.'" But what is to be done, Bellow asked, "about modern Jew-despising writers? . . . Should we continue to wrangle with the 'heirs' of antisemitism for whom these lies are a very valuable part of the estate" of their great past? "History has given us the means to act more wisely." The modern "heirs" of antisemitism have a single great advantage over the past: they know more history. "This knowledge makes their dislike of the Jew . . . stupendously horrible. . . . Modern reality, with the gases of Auschwitz still circulating in the air of Europe, gives us an excellent opportunity to judge" modern writers who employ malevolent images of Jews as despicable.[60]

Beginning in the spring of 1950, there were more essays and reviews to write as well as invited lectures to deliver at the Salzburg Seminars in American Studies. And there was more traveling—visits to Venice, Florence, and Rome—before returning to America in September. Soon after the Bellows settled into new quarters in Queens, New York, Saul accepted another invitation from Salzburg to facilitate a month-long seminar in the winter of 1951. As he had his first time, Bellow enjoyed the experience in Salzburg overall. He described his students as "overjoyed and enthusiastic." But sightseeing in Vienna he "didn't like . . . much"—perhaps because, as Alfred Kazin, who also taught at Salzburg, put it, Austrians were still "the most enthusiastic Nazis in German-speaking Europe."[61]

The Bellows took advantage of their time on the Continent by touring Florence again and revisiting Rome, where Saul wrote every morning for six weeks at an outdoor café in the Borghese Gardens for the full time he was in the city. On most days, so absorbed was Bellow in Augie's adventures that he failed even to notice the fierce Roman heat. But he soon took up his writing pattern in cooler Positano, a small fishing village near Sorrento, off the coast of Salerno, recommended by Paolo Milano.

The family spent many days in Rome with Milano, an intellectual and a very good friend in the forties and fifties, to whom Bellow had dedicated *The Victim*.[62] Jewish, Milano had emigrated from Italy to France in 1939, a year after Mussolini adopted the Manifesto della razza, the Charter of Race, which culminated in antisemitic laws similar to those adopted earlier in Nazi Germany. When the Germans conquered France, Milano fled to the US, where he soon became a contributor to a number of literary and political magazines, including *Partisan Review*.

Back in New York in the summer of 1951, Bellow, after visiting with family and friends in Chicago, looked at nine different colleges for teaching work or fellowships. Finding no new post, he retained his part-time position at New York University[63]—more time for Augie, but no steady income. Anita remedied that some by taking a job in Far Rockaway, Queens, with Planned Parenthood, helping manage a birth-control clinic, while seven-year-old Greg for a "few miserable weeks" attended the local grade school.[64]

He was soon moved to the Queens School, a private establishment presumed to be progressive—teachers and students were on a first-name basis, and Black people were admitted, such as the sons of Brooklyn Dodger greats Jackie Robinson and Roy Campanella. But, Greg says, "no one taught me how to read or write." Nevertheless, Anita was delighted that they had "after-school day care." In practice, the program meant letting kids with working parents have the run of the school and the playground until Mom or Dad picked them up. Yet, this arrangement, "allowing her to work," was vital for Anita, because after the prolonged dissolution of their marriage, Saul moved out permanently in 1952.[65]

Bellow's freedom to write and to foster relationships with male friends had increased as his relationship with Anita deteriorated. In the early fifties, he and Isaac Rosenfeld were colleagues at New York University, where they continued to deepen their friendship, with the same sporadic strains that had begun when they were schoolboys. During these same years, while Bellow worked steadily on *Augie March,* he developed what would become another nearly lifelong friendship—with Ralph Ellison, who was writing his classic novel *Invisible Man*. The relationship between the Jewish man and the Black man grew increasingly close as they recognized how strikingly they resembled each other, both as men and as writers. While Ellison was writing what would become his signature book and Bellow was writing his breakthrough novel, they fed each other's creative imagination and productivity and together made a brilliant contribution to modern literature.

SEVEN

THE ADVENTURES OF SAUL BELLOW

ALTHOUGH IT TOOK UNTIL 1954 for an official separation and until 1956 for a divorce, the Bellows' marriage had really ended years earlier. In 1937, Saul told his friend Oscar Tarcov that he was "deeply in love" with Anita, and for many years thereafter he seemed to have remained so. But as we have seen, there were problems early, including infidelities on both sides—even if at the start Anita's affairs were largely retaliatory. And from at least as early as 1947, Saul had complained to Herb and Mitzi McClosky about being constrained at home, burdened by the stable, conventional, middle-class life he said Anita preferred.[1]

Joseph in *Dangling Man* and Tommy Wilhelm in *Seize the Day* take leave of their wives to escape such stifling atmospheres. Saul, on the other hand, stayed with Anita for more than thirteen years; but in 1950 he installed another presence in their Queens apartment: an "orgone energy accumulator," a device invented by Wilhelm Reich, a Jewish refugee from Nazi-occupied Europe. By sitting in a five-foot-tall box insulated with steel wool, an entirely nude patient, Reich promised, would collect orgone—"sexual energy"—in concentrated form. In the process, which included "full and repeated sexual satisfaction," the patient would become capable of discarding "artificial sociality, artificial masks," or character "armor"—those multiple levels of cultural overlay that Bellow's post-1950 fictional protagonists (Herzog, for example, or Charlie Citrine in *Humboldt's Gift*) strove to jettison, without orgone boxes.[2]

Although Bellow owned and used an orgone box, he labeled men with whom the box was popular "extreme eccentrics."[3] But as Alfred Kazin said (though clearly exaggerating), nearly "everybody of [his] generation," including an exceptional number of Jews who were once "old-fashioned moralists," had an orgone box and had been through Reichian analysis searching for "fulfillment" by way of sexual liberation.[4] Norman Mailer, Allen Ginsberg, Paul Goodman, and J. D. Salinger had orgone boxes. Jack Kerouac and William Burroughs, Gentiles both, also had them, but it is tempting to ask whether it wasn't mostly Jewish boys who participated in what Bellow later called, somewhat disingenuously, a game—young men trying to free themselves from all those parental repressions and "thou shalt nots."[5]

Bellow himself insisted that he was simply determined to throw off the inhibitions of Protestant literary culture. More often, however, he claimed that he had engaged in Reichianism, including analysis with a Reichian-trained therapist, because Isaac Rosenfeld was doing it and had asked Bellow to do it too. He told his biographer James Atlas and his close friends Philip Roth and Norman Manea that in the 1990s "he went through the analysis . . . just to stay close" to Isaac. He did not want to lose his intimate, decades-long link with Rosenfeld, who, with his own literary star fading, grew increasingly jealous of Bellow's continuing success.[6]

There were other clearer and even more convincing motives for Bellow to have engaged with Reichian therapy, motives closely connected to his own personal and sexual complications—about which he complained repeatedly to Herb and Mitzi McClosky on the return voyage from Spain in 1947. Bellow knew that he was an anxious man, competitive, thin-skinned, and promiscuous—carrying on with women with little satisfaction; and he was self-aware enough to recognize his own rigidity. Nevertheless, he felt constrained and crowded in what he saw as a bourgeois marriage. Anita, he grumbled, "kept him on a short leash."[7] He whined that he had married too young and so had never had—despite his Mexico adventures and his European journeys—the youthful escapades he yearned for. Above all, he confessed, he had never experienced real passion.[8]

Saul believed that Anita had inherited her mother Sonia Goshkin's obsessive fear of disorder. He saw Sonia as a strong-willed woman who had command "in all things." Each object in the Goshkin household—its plants, for example, or the ashtrays, the doilies, the chairs—had an assigned "military place." The effect of this mastery, Bellow said, referring to both his mother-in-law and his wife, was "to paralyze the spirit."[9]

Reichian therapy, with its emphasis on breaking down inhibitions to maximize the power of emotion and the body, held out the possibility of releasing the spirit from paralysis—and by extension seemed to assure men who felt bound, imprisoned in marriage, that by separation or divorce they had nothing to lose but their chains. In the hope of saving her marriage, Anita tried to use the orgone box herself and several times visited Saul's Reichian therapist, Dr. Charles Raphael, who in the end assessed her character as too rigid—"confirming" Bellow's long-held opinion that his wife was a controlling figure.[10]

More than twenty years later, Bellow claimed that "Reichian therapy broke up his first marriage."[11] In reality, the therapy merely buttressed his long-repressed feeling of entrapment in an unsuitable relationship. For some time, he thought correctly that he had found in Anita the kind of wife who in Eastern European Jewish tradition would take care of the domestic end of things and who would even work to put him through lean times while he wrote. But he told the McCloskys that, while unable "to resist safety"—the kind of safety his early years with Anita provided—he "[had]n't been able to rest in it."[12]

Years later, Bellow admitted that by living more instinctively he might have thrown off too much social armature. He was feeling, he told an interviewer, "the excitement of discovery" through Reichian therapy. "I had . . . increased my freedom," Bellow said, "and like any emancipated plebian I abused it at once"—in part by writing what he later thought an overly long and diffuse *Augie March*.[13]

He confessed to having given up his resistance in his writing and his life, saying "you learn to give in" to your emotions, to your temper, as well as to your body. But, as he told Norman Manea, "you find you can't control it." Bellow remembered that "there were these bad scenes on subway platforms. I was ready to fight at any minute." It was "absolute nonsense," as was "this nude therapy on the couch being my animal self. Which was a ridiculous thing for me to have done." But as his worried and overprotective Jewish mother had feared, he was "always attracted," he said, "by these ridiculous things."[14]

Bellow hadn't needed Reichian therapy to pursue other women during his marriage, but he apparently felt "freer" to do so afterward. Despite their frequency, however, Bellow's adultery and promiscuity continued to make him "uncomfortable." He sustained a dependable host of sexual partners, but as he told Mitzi McClosky, this practice "was not a happy thing."[15]

Vi zol a gut mentsh leben? "How should a good man live?" is a question raised in nearly all of Bellow's novels written over a period of more than half a century. His protagonists ache for an answer and crave the qualities that represent goodness; but, as Bellow told an interviewer ten years after his divorce from Anita, his fictional characters, often frail and comic figures, "seem unable" to satisfactorily define (no less achieve) these qualities "on any significant scale. I criticize this in myself," he said; "I find this a limitation."[16] Later Saul ceded the moral high ground to Anita, comparing his own love, "tainted by chronic sexual and personal selfishness," to the "unselfish love" his first wife offered.[17]

The truly "happy thing" for Bellow was that he threw off the restraints that, even after two novels, kept him bound to the "incredible effrontery" of having announced himself to the WASP world as a writer. In creating *Dangling Man* and *The Victim,* Bellow was forced, he said, "to touch a great many bases, demonstrate my abilities, pay my respects to formal requirements." In short, he admitted to an interviewer, "I was afraid to let myself go."[18]

When he began to write *Augie March* in 1950, Bellow "took off many of these restraints," too many, perhaps; yet he had discipline enough to produce a steady flow of tightly constructed stories and reviews for *Penguin New Writing, Harper's Bazaar, Partisan Review,* and the *New York Times Book Review.*[19] And for *Commentary* he wrote "Man Underground," a concise and perceptive review of Ralph Ellison's *Invisible Man* (1952).[20]

By the time Bellow was writing his review, he and Ellison had developed a close friendship. *Invisible Man,* Ellison's first and only completed novel, had a dynamic resonance for Bellow. "I was keenly aware of a very significant kind of independence," Bellow wrote, "for there is a way for Negro novelists to go at their problems, just as there are Jewish ways." But Ellison, like Bellow in his own fiction, does not adopt a "minority tone." If he had, Bellow argued, he would have failed to establish a universal, true "middle-of-consciousness for everyone."[21]

Invisible Man, Bellow thought, displayed an ingenious, imaginative synthesis of the particular and the universal, and it exhibited a sophisticated intermingling of the white perception of Black people as primitive, even joyful, and the reality of an oppressed but dignified people who are kept under—literally under in this fabulist novel—where at the start we find the protagonist in a warm hole in the ground and at the end in a dark tunnel In these spots, the central character notes that he is invisible, but more notably, he says, "I am invisible, understand, simply because people refuse to see me."[22]

Some critics like Irving Howe, mightily impressed with *Invisible Man* overall, nevertheless found unpersuasive the hero's final discovery that "my world has become one of infinite possibilities."[23] To try to define one's individuality, Howe wrote, meant stumbling over social forces that do not allow one "infinite possibilities." Bellow clearly understood that Black people (and, to a much lesser extent, other minorities) were severely burdened by race prejudice and subject to grave abuses by white privilege, power, and authority. But he believed that Ellison—later cruelly criticized by more militant Black people as an "Uncle Tom" and by white leftists as "reactionary"—proved that "the single soul of an individual" could achieve a spiritual strength mightier than social and economic forces ranged against it.[24]

In the end, Bellow found this kind of romanticism—which emphasized the separation of the individual from society entirely—a sure road to nihilism; but here in his response to Ellison's *Invisible Man* he seemed to be channeling Emerson and Thoreau, and even Rousseau, the philosopher he later held guilty for contributing to the thinning (if not the breaking) of the social contract. "In our society," Bellow wrote, "Man Himself is idolized and publicly worshipped, but the single individual must hide himself underground and try to save his desires, his thoughts, his soul, in invisibility," before he can return to his true self.[25]

Of course, as Howe suggested, "*Invisible Man* is a Negro novel—what white man," he asked, "could have written it?"[26] At the same time, however, the novel could and did speak to millions of white people who also recognized the great but not altogether impossible task of resisting "those powers which attack and cripple modern mankind"—including Black and Jewish people.[27] As Ellison saw it, Black and Jewish people shared "traits" especially crucial for minorities, including a discerning, prudent, and practical sense of the world and a culturally and experientially ingrained wariness about the arrogant, condescending, and fatally flawed perception of themselves by others.

Ralph Ellison and Saul Bellow not only shared traits; their friendship continued to grow. Greg Bellow remembers that in 1951, when *Invisible Man* was nearing completion and *Augie March* was not far behind, Ralph and his wife Fanny "spent a good deal of time at our apartment" in Queens. The two families vacationed together on Long Island in the summer and shared in a general conviviality.[28] The comfort and familiarity Ellison felt with Jewish Americans, so obvious in his relationship with Bellow and family, were partly a product of his perception of Jews as "different" from other American white people. He thought Jews, like Black people, knew and lived something more; indeed, to Ellison, Jews didn't seem white at all, and he thought that the positive distinction ought to be maintained.[29]

Ellison felt at home with liberal Jews, many of whom, like Bellow, had moved (as he had himself) far from their Communist-Trotskyist pasts. The two writers often conversed in Yiddish when they accompanied each other in New York City for walks and talks in Riverside Park. Ellison is likely to have "picked up the language when, as a boy, he worked at Lewisohn's Department Store in Oklahoma City," his hometown. Later, at the writer's New England summer home, a neighbor reported that Ellison and her "husband would sit on the porch and converse very easily in Yiddish." Ellison apparently had no trouble speaking or understanding Bellow's first language and lifelong love.[30]

It early became clear to Bellow that Ellison was not merely a Black writer "but also an American writer who was black." And "I was a Jew and an American and a writer," Bellow said, announcing once again his resistance to being labeled simply a Jewish writer, which in his mind meant "being shunted to a siding." This "taxonomy business," he said, "I saw as an exclusionary device; Ellison had similar objections to classifications." Both writers saw the Negro and the Jew as authentic "creators of American history and culture. . . . We found each other sympathetic," Bellow said, and "we got along splendidly."[31]

Just as Bellow wanted to go beyond describing or "documenting" Jewish ethnic life, Ellison wanted to go beyond talking and writing about "authentic" Blackness. Both men were after something more subtle and encompassing, whole ways of being, more varied and complex, even as they reshaped themselves and took on some of the cultural characteristics of the larger American society. "Why is it," Ellison asked, "that so many of those who would tell us the meaning of Negro life never bother to learn how varied it really is?"[32]

It was during this time, too, that Bellow wrote "Looking for Mr. Green," a short story with no Jewish protagonists, set in Chicago's Black ghetto during the Depression when the economic, social, and physical underpinnings of society were deteriorating. Ingredients of social protest literature of the 1930s mark these pages, surely, but for Bellow the story is not an exercise in moralism or a simple attack on economic and racial injustice. It is instead an artistically rendered portrait of the complexities of racial attitudes and class differences and concludes in ambivalence for the main protagonist. The story is set in the Depression, but it speaks in a timeless way to the social and economic conditions of minority enclaves in America's inner cities.

George Grebe, an "educated" white man aiming to be a teacher but whose "luck had not been good," finds himself delivering relief checks in Black South Side Chicago to people too feeble to come to the welfare agency. Grebe's search for Mr. Green borders on the Kafkaesque, but it illuminates a "parallel universe" of Chicago slums unseen by most middle-class white people.

Grebe is shocked by the suffering he witnesses and by the crumbling physical world he temporarily inhabits: "Factories boarded up, buildings, deserted or fallen, gaps of prairie between"[33]—omens of human futility. He is surprised, therefore, that more often than not, he is greeted with great wariness, even hostility, from people who desperately need the checks. Perhaps Grebe is a process server, a bill collector, or some other source of trouble coming from the white world. This ironic suspicion, central to the story, helps illustrate the degree to which Black people mistrusted white people even as the Depression, by some measures, had narrowed the gulf between them.

Grebe wants to accomplish something, anything, to help relieve the misery he sees all around him. But the intractable conditions of the South Side and the recalcitrance of its Black inhabitants defeat him. Mr. Green remains an invisible man. There is no way of knowing for certain whether this empathetic story was related to the close relationship between the two writers; but it was written in 1951 when Bellow and Ellison were in each other's company a good deal of the time.

Whatever the case, "Looking for Mr. Green" demonstrated that Bellow, the Jew, could more easily avoid becoming a spokesman for his group than Ellison the Black man could for his. As early as 1950 in an essay for *Commentary* on antisemitism in literature, Bellow made it clear that he had no interest in playing a role in correcting the image of the Jew in fiction or in life, nor did he think it necessary to. It was virtually inevitable, however, that Ellison would have pressed upon him the task of combating the Negro stereotype, which in a 1953 essay he described as "an image of the unorganized, irrational forces of American life."[34]

Even after his "struggle to stare down the deadly hypnotic temptation to interpret the world and all its devices in terms of race," there was no escape for Ellison. "Being black in America," as David Mikics wrote, "was not and is not like being Jewish in America."[35] Still, both writers shared the goal of exposing and ridiculing deep prejudice. Just as Ellison targeted "Negrophobia," Bellow, in much of his work, eviscerated antisemitism, real or perceived—most directly in *The Victim* and almost twenty-five years later in his sixth novel, *Humboldt's Gift* (1975).

In the academic year 1952–53, Bellow, after enjoying his first residency at Yaddo (the artists' colony in Saratoga Springs), was teaching at Princeton. The barely disguised antisemitism he experienced at the university was featured in *Humboldt's Gift*. Charlie Citrine (the narrator and protagonist, descended from Russian Jews) and Von Humboldt Fleisher (the son of Hungarian Jewish immigrants) expect that at Princeton, as elsewhere in WASP territory, Jewish writers will be seen as trespassers on the American cultural scene. Although Humboldt is initially warmly welcomed by the likes of T. S. Eliot, Charlie fears that his friend's "syntax would be unacceptable to fastidious goy critics on guard for the establishment and the Genteel Tradition."[36] Humboldt knows very well that his situation at Princeton is precarious. "You and I are expendable here," he tells Charlie. "Why? I'll tell you why. We're Jews, shonickers, kikes," he says, and advises Charlie to try thinking of himself as Sheeny Solomon Levi: "In Princeton you and I are Moe and Joe, a Yid vaudeville act. We're a joke—Abi Kabibble and Company. Unthinkable as members of the [university] community."[37]

Before Bellow arrived at Princeton, he was a "Visiting Writer" in the spring of 1952 at Reed College in Portland, the University of Oregon in Eugene, and the University of Washington in Seattle. In Portland, Bellow at thirty-seven had a brief sexual interlude with Alice Adams, an aspiring writer, twenty-six, whom he encouraged throughout her successful career as a novelist and writer for the *New Yorker*.[38]

But the most important contact Bellow made was with Bernard Malamud, an instructor at Oregon State whose first novel, *The Natural*, was about to be published. Bellow, who was very likely to have read the half dozen or so short stories published by Malamud in the late forties and early fifties (two of which appeared in the *Partisan Review* and *Commentary*), was pleased to find Malamud, so obvious a "New York type," in Corvallis, Oregon. It did the inland university "great credit," Bellow wrote later, "to have imported such an exotic," though he was "not an exotic to me. We were cats of the same breed," Jewish to the core.[39]

At Princeton, Bellow found "some" of the faculty "likeable," but he told interviewer Keith Botsford that he "wasn't overwhelmed by the Ivy League," whose schools he saw as "compounds for class and privilege." He did not, however, "assume a posture of slum-bound" alienation at Princeton.[40] Instead, as Leon Edel (a Henry James scholar) remembers it, Bellow, when he wasn't cutting and polishing *Augie March,* was often visible and genial. He showed up for most, if not all, of the widely admired Christian Gauss Seminars at Princeton, where he displayed a "quick wit that bounced and bounded as if he were playing a fast game of tennis." Delmore Schwartz also attended the Gauss lectures and, according to Edel, asked many "tangential questions," which "nearly always seemed a fireworks display."[41]

One can easily picture two Jews, New York types, trying to dazzle the WASP Ivy Leaguers. Carlos Baker, chair of the English Department and biographer of Ernest Hemingway, also remembered Bellow's energy. He was "brilliant, lively, and effervescent," Baker said, and he was "able to narrate sidesplitting Yiddish yarns by the hour."[42]

Dozens of brilliant people were attracted to the gathering of writers and intellectuals at Princeton in 1952. Edmund Wilson and the poet John Berryman were fixtures on the scene, as were Allen Tate, Randall Jarrell, and the historian R. W. B. Lewis. Ralph Ellison, soon to win the National Book Award for *Invisible Man,* "came down regularly to attend . . . parties" with Bellow and the others.[43]

Not directly related to the university but having lived in Princeton, Irving Howe reflected years later about his association with Schwartz, Berryman, and Bellow. He described the triumvirate as "hangers on at Princeton," hankering for full-time jobs, and called himself a "hanger-on of hangers on." Observant and discerning, Howe saw Bellow as resolute—more resilient than Berryman and Schwartz, and very discerning, even crafty in "the arts of self-conservation."[44] Nonetheless he designated all three men as a "haughty aristocracy of letters, devoted to the stress of their temperaments, bound together by a fraternity of troubles."[45]

Schwartz, already depleted by inner demons and the drugs and alcohol he used to repel them, died broken and alone outside his dreary hotel room in 1966. At Princeton, however, he was hardly exceptional in his instability. The poet Theodore Roethke, an occasional visitor at the Princeton home of Edmund Wilson, had been in and out of psychiatric clinics and, according to the writer Eileen Simpson, was clearly "not in his right mind." Simpson's husband, John Berryman, scholar and brilliant multi-award-winning poet, was, according to his wife, the least stable of the Princeton crowd. In 1972, after being dissuaded by Schwartz years earlier, Berryman committed suicide by throwing himself off the Washington Avenue Bridge in Minneapolis.[46]

Bellow certainly had his troubles, but he was neither tormented by mental illness nor attracted to the irrational, and he avoided the tragic, self-destructive course followed by the two poets. In virtually all of the stories and novels Bellow went on to write, from *The Adventures of Augie March*—nearly completed at Princeton—through *Humboldt's Gift,* he demonstrated an irrepressible faith in a Jewish moral ethic suffused with the idea that life is a great gift not to be renounced.

Soon to become a regular at Princeton gatherings was Sondra Tschacbasov, a young, very attractive, self-possessed graduate of Bennington College, who, four years later, would become Bellow's second wife. They'd met at the offices of *Partisan Review,* where Sasha, as Bellow called her, worked as a secretary. She was clever and well-read but had no secretarial skills at all. It wasn't difficult, however, for her to find a job. She was "stunning beyond words, with pale skin and china-blue eyes," the poet Stanley Burnshaw remembered, and "extremely pretty," according to one of Bellow's female friends, with "incredible sex appeal. The very thought of her made [*PR* editor] Philip Rahv drool."[47]

Bellow was persistent, but it took some time before the couple slept together. "It was a fairly commonplace thing," Sasha wrote in a memoir, "to sleep with one of your students or a recently graduated editorial assistant."[48] She knew it would happen soon, because she "had a 'look' and he was hot for the Russian mystique." One impediment to a consummation of their relationship was Sasha's earlier conversion to Catholicism, which, of course, marked adultery as gravely sinful.

Her conversion, she explained later, was part of an effort to reverse the bohemian chaos of her upbringing by absorbing into her life, however illusory, a sense of order and tradition. When Sondra was a child, her father, a Chicago businessman turned artist, unexpectedly pulled up stakes and moved the family to Paris and back again. By the 1950s and '60s, he was a painter living a wildly unconventional life on West Twenty-Third Street in the Chelsea Hotel, where he was seducing his art students. Sasha herself claimed that she had been subject to the horror—regularly—of sexual abuse by her father.

One of the most appealing things about Bellow, Sasha said, was his earnest attitude toward writing. It did not fit the bohemian stereotype and distinguished Bellow from Berryman, Schwartz, and Rosenfeld.[49] "What was most seductive," Sasha wrote, "was the very workmanlike way he viewed himself in his craft. . . . He 'went to work' so to speak, like it was a regular job [to which] he was . . . seriously committed." Bellow, who liked to write with Mozart blaring, emerged from his study each day, soaked in perspiration from hours of intense concentration. After lunch he was ready to edit the morning's work. It was in the strictness of his routine that Sasha saw Bellow as "part middle-class Jewish businessman"—with headquarters at home—"part contemplative, scholarly rabbi."[50]

Unlike Berryman and Schwartz, Bellow felt an ardent and consistent obligation to live and to live meaningfully—a commitment internalized by him as a youngster growing up in the Jewish milieu of Chicago and reinforced during his long, drawn out, life-threatening illness as a boy, and not least by his saturation in Tanakh (a contraction derived from the first letters of the Hebrew names for the Torah, the *Prophets,* and the *Writings*), passages of which Bellow had memorized as a child and could recite even as an adult.

The fictive Augie March's upbringing and young adulthood were dramatically different from the saturation in Yiddishkeit experienced by his creator. This may have prompted some critics to say that Augie was Bellow's "least Jewish protagonist." But this is off the mark. Augie was as Jewish as most of Bellow's featured characters. In a talk Bellow delivered in 1988, he discussed what he was trying to do in *Augie March*:

> The condition I [was] looking into is that of a young American who in the late Thirties finds that he is something like a writer and begins to think what to do about it, how to position himself, and how to combine being a Jew with being an American and a writer. Not everyone thinks well of such a project. The young man is challenged from all sides. Representatives of the Protestant majority want to see his credentials. . . . The Jews too try to place him. Is he too Jewish? Is he Jewish enough? Is he good or bad for the Jews? Jews in business or politics ask, "Must we forever be reading about his damn Jews?" Jewish critics examine him with a certain sharpness—they have their own axes to grind. As the sons of Jewish immigrants, descendants of the people whose cackling and shrieking set Henry James's teeth on edge when he visited the East Side, they accuse themselves secretly of presumption when they write of Emerson, Walt Whitman, or Matthew Arnold. . . . On the other hand, one can't always be heroic, and there were times when shades of Brownsville and Delancey Street surrounded Jewish lovers of American literature and they were unhappily wondering what T.S. Eliot or Edmund Wilson would be thinking of them. Among my Jewish contemporaries, more than one . . . came up with different evasions, dodges, ruses, and disguises. I had little patience with that kind of thing. If the WASP aristocrats wanted to think of me as a Jewish poacher on their precious cultural estates then let them. It was in this defiant spirit that I wrote *The Adventures of Augie March*.[51]

Twenty years earlier, in speaking about *Augie March*, Bellow told an interviewer that he could not with the Flaubertian style he had developed in his first two books "express a variety of things I knew intimately," including the swoop, the noise, the smells, the *narishkayt* (foolishness) and *menschlikhkayt* (humaneness) of Jewish immigrant life. The Flaubertian standard "was not so bad," Bellow admitted, but it was "constraining to a son of Jewish immigrants raised in Chicago."[52]

Augie March, like Bellow, the son of Jewish immigrants raised in Chicago in the 1930s, also feels "constrained." He is a happy, frisky youngster with preternatural energy and intelligence, and so he refuses to live a life of "quiet desperation" or even "to lead a disappointed life."[53] He educates himself with thoughts of becoming a writer and, like Bellow, tries to find a way "to position himself, and combine being a Jew with being an American and a writer."[54]

It is true that Augie, like Bellow, plays down his ethnicity. He doesn't, for example, take to heart the antisemitism of his Polish neighbors: "Sometimes we were chased, stoned . . . and beat up for Christ-killers, all of us. . . . But I never had any special grief from it, or brooded, being by and large too larky and boisterous."[55] Nor does Augie encounter, or more precisely see, antisemitism as an adult. And like Joseph in *Dangling Man*, he enters World War II with no evident feeling that he is fighting against fascism. At the conclusion of the war, Augie on the Continent says nothing about the near-total destruction of European Jewry.

Augie March is an American novel with universal appeal, just as Bellow had hoped; but just as clearly, it is an American Jewish novel. Qualities of Jewishness, even if not directly articulated, are recognizable in nearly everything Augie does. As the poet Karl Shapiro put it, "It is the poetry of the Jew," the Yiddish-inflected speech, the search for a better world, and a healthy dose of ambition, "that makes [this] hero what he is, in Chicago, in Mexico, wherever Augie happens to be."[56]

It is evident that Augie is a Jew among Jews in Humboldt Park, which is populated by the Kleins, Finebergs, Einhorns, Weintraubs, and Condlins—and many others of Eastern European origin—including some "superior" men and "fine" old ladies, along with a gallery of schlemiels, schnorrers, and *ganifs* (thieves). There is no effort by Bellow to make these Jews more noble. Many, if not most, were low-level operators, doing deals just to get by. He felt no need to protect them.

These Jews speak the language of Jewish immigrants with the rhythms and convolutions of Bellow's foreign-born parents: "I could not find myself in love, without it should have some peculiarity," or "I don't want you should have anything against me," or "try out what of human you can live with."[57] Yiddishkeit, including English spoken with Yiddish cadence and expression, is one of the more important influences shaping Augie's personality and character, as is his devotion to family and to the idea of family. At a typical Friday night at his brother Simon's house, the extended family gathers with "tumultuousness and family heat, melding yells at the pinochle table, the racing of the kids, pitchers of cocoa and tea and masses of coffee cake carried in, political booming . . . and all this grand vital discord." Bellow's biographer James Atlas writes, "If there is such a thing as Jewish atmosphere, this is it"—the grand vital discord of the extended Jewish family.[58]

A young Jewish American like Bellow, aspiring to become a writer by calling on his Jewish experience, would have had to ask themselves, Where would the Jews, "people rooted in home and family, fit into American fiction with its outward-bound loners?"—homeless, motherless, and fatherless figures like Natty Bomppo in *The Last of the Mohicans,* Twain's Huck Finn, Melville's Ishmael, and Hemingway's Nick Adams.[59] In "Strangers," a 1977 essay on Jewish immigrants, Irving Howe asked about these heroes, "Didn't they know where life came from and returned to?"[60] Many Jewish boys and girls, children of immigrant parents, like Howe and Bellow, knew or came to know the answer to Howe's question.

They grew up speaking Yiddish at home, reading and writing English in school, and talking "American" in the streets. Many of the more talented children, like those filling the classrooms at Tuley High School in Chicago in the thirties—Bellow, Isaac Rosenfeld, and Oscar Tarcov, for example—used their rapidly growing English to saturate themselves in the great American novels.[61] Could they avoid comparing the stranded and lonely individuals they were reading about to their own lives, crowded with several generations of family? These boys and girls were certainly not alone. They were brought up in families full of love along with emotionally painful arguments. There were moans and groans as well as embraces, even if those embraces were sometimes so tight that they chafed.

American declarations of individualism, elevated to a principle of life, from Emerson to Hemingway, promised something larger than family—the precious benefits of isolation, including silence, solitude, and time for unmediated and uninterrupted reflection; but Bellow and other aspiring Jewish writers doubted that isolation was a true gift. Accepting it would come at the price of rejecting mishpocha—the entire family network—and the neighborhood with its heritage of communal affections and responsibilities, and the love, with all its chaos that family provided. *The Adventures of Augie March* was, among many other things, Bellow's answer to the question of how the lone traveler and the family man could mix, even if in unusual ways.

Adventurous and self-reliant, Augie is nonetheless a family man, part of the vitality—the discourse and discord of a large and growing Jewish circle. At home, he is knit together with an adopted Grandma Lausch, a boarder and caregiver to Augie's abandoned, simple-minded, and nearly blind mother, and his developmentally disabled brother Georgie. When Grandma Lausch places Georgie in an institution—"He had to learn to do *something* . . . basketry or brush-making"—Augie is troubled by the "diminished family life, as though it were care of Georgie that had been the main basis of household union and now everything was disturbed."[62] During one of his countless adventures, with their various disappointments, Augie says, "I was a sucker for it . . . family love."[63]

This does not prevent Augie from seeing himself as the genuine individual against the world. With the opening paragraph, Bellow develops a protagonist and omniscient narrator who is boldly daring, confident, and independent—emotionally prepared for a new history but steeped in the old. "I am an American, Chicago born—Chicago, that somber city—and go at things as I have taught myself, free-style, and will make the record in my own way: first to knock, first admitted; sometimes an innocent knock, sometimes a not so innocent. But a man's character is his fate, says Heraclitus, and in the end there isn't any way to disguise the nature of the knocks by acoustical work on the door or gloving the knuckles."[64]

In the first phrase of that famous opening sentence, "I am an American, Chicago born," is a direct translation from the Yiddish—Chicago *geboren*; and the last phrase, "sometimes a not so innocent," has an unembarrassed *Yiddishe tam* (Yiddish flavor). Yiddish, Bellow's first language, may even have been the idiom he dreamed in. And at the same time that he was busily revising *Augie*, he was working with the help of Irving Howe and Yiddishist Eliezer Greenburg to translate "Gimpel the Fool," a stunning Yiddish short story by Isaac Bashevis Singer about a simple but saintly man. Singer was utterly unknown outside the world of Yiddish speakers, but after his story was published in *Partisan Review*, he found an abundance of readers. Bellow had sat at the typewriter occasionally asking about refinements of meaning, while Howe watched "in a state of enchantment." After four hours of translating and fine-tuning, Bellow read aloud the version of "Gimpel" that has since become famous. "It was a feat of virtuosity," Howe recalled, "and we drank a schnapps to celebrate."[65]

Bellow's translation retained only six Yiddish words—*golem, mezuzah, challah, kreplach, schnorrer,* and *dybbuk*; but his sentences sometimes sound more Yiddish than the original. David Mikics gives us a fine example: Singer wrote, "*Az Got git pleytzes muz men shlepn dem pak*"—"Since God gives shoulders, you have to carry the pack." Bellow turned this into, "Shoulders are from God, and burdens too"[66]—the Yiddish comma of hesitation. Things are good . . . but also bad.

As important, Bellow's translation tells us something about Augie, whose speech has all the patois of Chicago but also bounces around with a decidedly Yiddish rhythm and style of conversation. Bellow was well aware of the link he was creating between Yiddish and Augie March. In "Laughter in the Ghetto" (an appraisal of Sholem Aleichem's unpublished Yiddish novel for the *Saturday Review* in May 1953, only months before the release of *Augie March*), Bellow wrote, almost as if it were a preview of his own forthcoming novel, that Motl, the main character of Aleichem's Yiddish novel, is always happy: "Almost nothing can take place which he is unable to make into an occasion of happiness: with boundless resilience he tells, after his father's death, how quickly he learns the prayer for the dead, how well everyone treats him now that he is an orphan." Motl has "an inexhaustible power of enjoyment and cannot be affected. . . . He declines to suffer the penalties the world imposes on him."[67] This portion of Bellow's review could have come, almost verbatim, directly from *Augie March,* as when Clem Tambo (a friend of Augie's) tells him, "A train could hit you, and you'd think it was just swell and get up with smiles, like knee deep in June."[68]

Bellow pointed to yet another link to Augie. "The most ordinary Yiddish conversation," Bellow said, "is full of the grandest historical, mythological and religious allusions. The Creation, the Fall, the Flood, Egypt, Alexander, Titus, Napoleon, the

Rothschilds, the sages, the Laws, [may lead] into a discussion of an egg, a clothes-line, or a pair of pants." This manner of talk, including historical greatness combined with the utterly mundane, exposed the powerlessness of the so-called Chosen People and the East European shtetl's "sense of the ridiculous."[69]

In the second sentence of the celebrated opening of *Augie March*, the name Heraclitus is only a small sample of Augie's Yiddish habit of peppering his descriptions of machers, ward healers, pool sharks, whores, and merchants with references to classical literature and historical figures—Prometheus, Plutarch, and the Pentateuch; Bolingbroke, Brutus, and Bolsheviks. These allusions to the Western canon came from the weighty books that Augie, like Bellow in his adolescence, could not afford and had to filch.

Bellow goes on in "Laughter in the Ghetto" to write that the Jews of the shtetl "found themselves involved in an immense joke. They were divinely designated to be great and yet"—anticipating Art Spiegelman—"they were like mice. History was something that happened to them; they did not make it." But when history happened it belonged to the Jews, inasmuch as it was another step toward "the coming of the Messiah—their Messiah—that would give it meaning. Every male child was potentially the Messiah."[70]

Augie is no Messiah, nor does he want to be, but he sees himself as an innocent youth untouched by the vulgarity and corruption of Chicago. He commits himself to remaining an independent self, undetermined by others, and searches for a new Eden—a community of interactive, independent selves, not separate from society à la Rousseau, who, according to Augie, was "a sheer horse's ass . . . who couldn't get on with a single human."[71]

Augie yearns for a better society, but he is constantly challenged by "Reality Instructors" who seek to deflate his affability and his apparent immunity from pessimism.[72] In the early chapters of the novel, we get an example in Grandma Lausch. She makes the March family "take a long swig of her mixture of reality," which preaches cynicism and heartlessness as the only way to survive, and discredits Augie's type of sanguinity and goodness. At the same time, however, Grandma softens her hard-heartedness and unkindness by saying, "Nobody tells you to love the whole world," only to be *ehrlich*—honest and dutiful. "And that's respect," she adds.[73]

Grandma Lausch practices what Augie labels a "kitchen religion" that has nothing to do with the God of creation. She eats bread during Passover and loves pork and canned lobster. Lausch never goes to synagogue but does light a yahrzeit or memorial candle every year and says prayers. They are more like incantations over baby teeth or against the "evil eye," for example, but Augie thinks "it was on the side of religion at that."[74] Grandma commands Augie, in tentative English, to "Remember me when I am in my grave . . . when I will be dead!" and then repeats it in Yiddish: "*Gedenk, Augie, wenn ich bin todt.*"[75]

Augie engages in no rituals and is unconcerned about the "right way" to approach God; but he seems to have read the Hebrew prophets, who reinforce his natural inclination to defend the poor, the widows, and the handicapped, starting with his family—his weak and increasingly blind mother and his "feeble-minded" brother, Georgie.

Another kind of reality instructor is Augie's orthodox cousin Anna Coblin, who one summer takes Augie into her household to help with her husband Hyman's business—managing newspaper delivery routes. Augie discovers that Anna "wouldn't touch money on holy days. She observed them all. . . . She thought it was her duty while I was in her house to give me some religious instruction, and it was a queer account I got from her in a spout of Hebrew, Yiddish, and English, powered by piety and anger"[76]

At one of his steadier jobs, few and far between, Augie tries to cobble together an identity for himself, a way to be in the world—he works as an errand boy for William Einhorn, a handicapped, small-time businessman and landlord who runs a billiard parlor and many other operations, some of them shady.[77] At first, Einhorn, who becomes a mentor, reinforces Augie's natural inclinations and optimism. The stock market crash, however, shatters Einhorn's positive outlook, and he becomes just another reality instructor. His new advice? "One should gain strength from disadvantages and make progress by having enemies, [and by] being wrathful or terrible."[78] Augie, hearing an echo of Grandma Lausch at her worst, objects, and Einhorn soon recognizes that Augie has "*opposition*" in him. Augie agrees: "I did have opposition in me, and great desire to offer resistance and to say '*No!*'"[79]

Augie thinks that "all the influences were lined up waiting for me. I was born and there they were to form me."[80] That thought may appear to contradict the first two sentences of the novel—"I . . . go at things as I have taught myself, free-style, and will make the record in my own way"; and "a man's character is his fate, says Heraclitus"; but instead Augie's "opposition" helps him resist effects external to his character and allows him to believe that his character, "free-style," will determine his own fate. He "had to struggle," Augie says, but he "managed."[81]

He even remains positive and resilient in the face of his brother Simon's bullying. Always a kind of reality instructor, Simon, very much like Maury Bellows, loves his younger brother but from early on persists in advising Augie to make himself "hard" and cynical, a posture and an attitude that Augie, like Bellow, "didn't fundamentally believe" in.[82] Maury may very well have been creatively reimagined as Simon. If so, Bellow toned down Maury's toxic masculinity and ominous aggression, turning his older brother into a rough and tough but vital lover of life rather than a violent, nervously turbulent man.

As Augie matures, he experiences a series of devastating occurrences, mistakes, misunderstandings—and bad luck. Case in point—Mimi Villars, a waitress, friend, and neighbor, is pregnant and needs an abortion. She almost dies at the hands of an incompetent doctor. When Augie helps Mimi out, he is mistaken for the father, and his fiancée, Lucy Magnus, breaks off their engagement. Augie goes through the heartbreak of love—more than once. He also experiences the dissolution of family ties when both Georgie and his finally blind mother are institutionalized. He suffers through the Great Depression, becomes a union organizer, gets caught in a squabble between the AFL and CIO, is beaten by agitators, and has to hide out to avoid being killed.

Having lost much but not all of his youthful suppleness, Augie continues to seek paradise, which he envisions as an escape from his dilemma—forces and people who want to coach him in the fundamentals of the darker side. Mimi, like his other reality instructors, berates Augie; he was not "mad enough about abominations or aware enough of them, didn't know how many graves were underneath [his] feet, was lacking in disgust, wasn't hard enough against horrors or wrathful about swindles."[83] Mimi tries to drag Augie down, not only into cynicism but into the mire of nihilism. She fails, as do all the other instructors. "I wouldn't want to become," Augie thinks, "what other people wanted to make of me."[84] He remains optimistic, unbeaten by life; he is simply unable to believe that "all was so poured in concrete . . . that there weren't occasions for happiness."[85]

In the main, Augie successfully defies his reality instructors without surrendering entirely; but he realizes that after all the trauma he's experienced, he "was no child now, neither in age or in protectedness," and he "was thrown for fair on the free-spinning of the world."[86] Like Joseph in *Dangling Man,* Augie comes to see that living in society exerts too much control over him but is still preferable to self-imposed alienation. Bellow admitted to Edith Tarcov an inability to accept "so much control" in his own life and that he had "passed this inability on to Augie."[87]

Bellow, responding to Bernard Malamud's critique of the novel, explains that Augie "isn't to me an Olympian," but he (like Bellow?) "is engaged in a war of Independence and the odds are vastly against him. It is the devaluation of the person that he fights with."[88] Augie continues that fight and search for a new Eden in which he can hide, at least for a time, and retrieve the innocence he has lost. He tries Mexico, but his experience there, including a fair number of memorable and dangerous episodes, is far from paradise. Indeed, it is a trip to hell.

Back in the US and late into his ongoing adventures, Augie encounters Mintouchian, "another of those persons who persistently arise before [him] with life counsels and illumination throughout [his] entire earthly pilgrimage."[89] An Armenian lawyer, his language laced with Hebrew and Yiddish phrases, Mintouchian befriends Augie and hires him to manage his black-market operations in Europe. Mintouchian is convinced that man is duplicitous by nature, fraudulent and shifty. But Augie, wary of the negativism, says that he himself "had looked all [his] life for the right thing to do, for a fate good enough." And you will understand, he tells Mintouchian, "that I had always tried to become what I am. But it's a frightening thing. Because what if what I am isn't good enough?"[90]

Augie, near tears, answers his own question: "I suppose I better anyway give in" and be who he is. "I will never force the hand of God to create a better Augie March nor change the time to an age of gold." Mintouchian agrees. "That's exactly right," he says. "You must take your chance on what you are. . . . You will not invent better than God or nature. . . . This is not given to us."[91]

Augie, nearing the end of his kaleidoscopic story and despite Mintouchian's advice, holds on to much of his natural optimism; but after the many hard knocks he has had, he realizes that all along he has been trying to hide from the complexity of life—"from this mighty free-running terror and wild cold of chaos."[92] So, Augie, like Huck Finn, remains suspended between naive idealism and hard-earned knowledge, ready for the next adventure, though it promises neither great insight nor peace or happiness. The dream of finding some unknown land that will be fertile ground for his imagination, however, continues to hover in Augie's consciousness.

His more sober hope is to buy property, settle down on it, get married, have children, and start a school in a green Walden-like setting for people like his brother Georgie.[93] Augie badly wants to give Georgie a chance at beating "life at its greatest complication and *meshuggah* power" by starting "lower down, and simpler."[94] By implication, Augie, though still a dreamer, is admitting that his own expectations may have been exceedingly romantic. And finally, he is smiling again. "That's the *animal ridens* [animal laughing] in me, the . . . creature, forever rising up," who laughs at nature which thinks it can win over our power of hope. Not a chance, says Augie. "I am a sort of Columbus," not of distant continents but "of those near-at-hand and believe you can come to them in this immediate *terra incognita* that spreads out in every gaze."[95]

Bellow associated optimism with the United States, but he knew that this feeling could be merely reflexive, without real content. It was hope more than optimism that was truly American for Bellow, as both substance and symbol. In the last sentences of the novel, Augie thinks that as a "Columbus of those near-at-hand," he may well be a failure. But, he adds, "Columbus too thought he was a flop, probably, when they sent him back in chains. Which didn't prove there was no America."[96] In the first decades of the twenty-first century, more than sixty-five years after Augie's last adventures, Bellow's hope may "seem merely a symbol. Which doesn't mean there's no hope."[97] Hope connects the essential Jewishness of the novel and Bellow's determination to live an ethical life, grateful for the gift of existence. The book had an ecstatic critical reception; but as lauded as it was, *Augie March* was merely a *farshpayz*—a small taste of the major creations that lay ahead.

EIGHT

FATHERS AND SONS

RALPH ELLISON'S HERO IN *INVISIBLE MAN* concludes that his "world has become one of infinite possibilities." Elsewhere, Ellison praised *Augie March,* whose peripatetic hero was anything but invisible, for the novel's "big conception of human possibility."[1] But for some critics, Augie's story, with its emphasis on hope and human possibility, seemed too optimistic, too accommodating for an era in which America had seen so much turmoil. Race riots erupted regularly as the Great Migration of Black people from the South to northern cities continued through the 1950s. In the same period, less than five years after World War II ended, we were at war again—in Korea. The nation was inextricably caught up in a nuclear arms race with the Soviet Union, and schoolchildren were being drilled to shelter under their desks in the possibility, however remote, of a direct strike on the US. Meanwhile, gruesome, credible information about the Holocaust was slowly finding its way to public attention. And at the same time, under the sway of the Red Scare and the trampling of American civil liberties by anti-Communist crusaders and congressional investigatory committees, many Americans breathed a chilling, oppressive climate of anxiety.

There is no denying that, along with Augie-quality optimism, there was a dark undertow to life in postwar America. Opposing this, however, was the emergence of nonconformist cultural phenomena, such as the Beat poets, film noir, comic books, and early stirrings of rock 'n' roll. There were important rumblings, too, in nascent movements for gender and racial equality. And for a significant swath of Americans—though far less dramatically in numbers and visibility for women and Black people—the fifties were an age of measurable economic and social mobility.

With the intensification of the Cold War, and with the historic economic recovery of the US still underway in the wake of World War II, even some dissenting writers, artists, and intellectuals (including Saul Bellow) came to see America as increasingly attractive compared with the Soviet Union. Many could begin to think about steady jobs, reasonable standards of living, and even prosperity. All of this made it easier for some writers and critics to give up their radicalism and their sense of alienation—though for many of them, "post-Marxist deconversion" was gradual and sometimes tortured. Bellow, who had been steadily moving away from Trotskyism, had no such difficulty. In any case, there was a growing tolerance, if not downright appreciation, for liberal democracy among the intelligentsia and literati.[2]

Augie March is full of the aforementioned vitality, cheer, and hopeful energies. But this "bright side" is partly Bellow's "corrective" reaction to the grim view of the human condition taken by European modernists, existentialists, and nihilists, as well as by some American writers: Carson McCullers, Arthur Miller, Robert Lowell, and dozens of others who homed in on the darker side of the American experience. Its celebrations of postwar America apart, however, *Augie March* is also a product of what Bellow witnessed firsthand in Europe, the touted heart of Western civilization: the destruction, exhaustion, and despair—along with the haunting evidence of an enduring antisemitism widespread across the continent.

"I really knew much more about darkness than I let on," Bellow told an interviewer. He "knew perfectly well what nihilism was" but wanted to create a certain type of 1930s American character—"naive, easy-going, tolerant . . . youthfully affectionate." Bellow continued to embrace the openness and general liberalism of the US, especially after his European sojourns. But he consciously resisted accommodation to the bourgeois status quo and was committed to living life without pronouncing an adherence to an intellectually fashionable alienation, even in the face of continuing social and cultural conflicts and collisions in American society.

He told an interviewer that he had created Augie as a near-perfect naïf partly to say that a "kind of blindness to the greatest of evils [was] an important by-product or result of Americanization." As a nation, Bellow said, "we prefer the mild or the vaguer view."[3] At the same time, but with an entirely different target, Bellow had also striven to celebrate Augie's ability to love and be loved, counterpoised against the sense of pointlessness and futility, the surrender to nihilism, by many in his generation.[4]

Lionel Trilling, who had originally praised *Augie March* in manuscript, later voiced serious reservations about the book and the hero's failure to learn little if anything from his adventures—no "function" or fixed definitive sense of himself. Bellow reacted sharply, saying "that to love one another, genuinely to love, is the inception of function."[5] Partly to defend himself against Trilling's assertion "that Augie is wrong, i.e., unprincipled," Bellow wrote to a friend, admitting that Augie has "opposition" in him and that he does become a kind of "outlaw" with "a bent to the illicit"—but only because "he misses the love, the harmony and safety that compensate our obedience."[6]

In a letter to his Tuley classmate and longtime friend Sam Freifeld, Bellow agreed that he, like Augie, was an outlaw: "But in outlaw bravado," Saul had "no interest. I only meant that I wished to obey better laws."[7] For Bellow, Augie was the Jewish "embodiment of willingness to serve, who says, 'For God's sake, make use of me, only do not use me to no purpose.'"[8] Historian Judd Teller, closely echoing Bellow's assessment of Augie's motives, wrote that Jews have been forever characterized by a "craving to be used," to be of service not only to God but also to themselves and others. Without forfeiting experience or pleasure, Teller argues persuasively, Jews have committed themselves to moral and social concerns and have eternally searched "for some transcendental meaning . . . for a 'piece of the action' in a greater universal scheme."[9]

Augie March received only a handful of negative reviews, which were nearly lost in the overwhelmingly positive responses from critics, writers, and readers. In manuscript or proofs, *Augie* had been read by close friends as well as editors. Bellow expected unreserved praise and was as usual exasperated and enraged by even the slightest criticism, but he often expressed regret for "having blown [his] top." From the start Bellow was, as he has Augie say, "the type that comes down as fast as he boils up." In like manner, Bellow described his father as well as Joseph, the protagonist in *Dangling Man,* who thinks his explosiveness is an inheritance from his Jewish family—"a people of tantrums."[10]

The novel was greeted with all the acclaim Bellow had sought and been denied (unfairly, he believed) for his first two books. There were admiring reviews from Robert Penn Warren and John Berryman and a glowing essay by Delmore Schwartz in *Partisan Review,* a front-page review in the *New York Times Book Review,* and a notice in the *Saturday Review* comparing the novel to Joyce's *Ulysses. Augie March* won the National Book Award for fiction in 1954, made the bestseller list, and was declared "one of the hundred best novels in the English language" by *Time* magazine and the Modern Library Board.

Decades after its publication, Philip Roth, who had read the novel in college in the early fifties, said that *Augie* was the first American narrative "that gave voice to the language you spoke and the stuff you heard"[11]—an exhilarating new voice in a Jewish urban style, exclusively Bellow's. Many others also recognized Bellow's enduring gift—a new language, a magnificent bricolage, uniquely Jewish, which within a paragraph, even a single sentence, fused the vernacular of streetwise machers, con-men, Jews living prosaic lives, with the grandiose, often condescending vocabulary of Harvard University.

Roth was literally astonished. "Here was this guy" observing Jews and Jewish families and then "making literature of them," Roth said, "and that was a revelation to me." He "had never read anything like this before in [his] life," Roth continued. "Nor had anybody else." That Bellow had written so creatively, darkly, and comically about Jews, poor and prosperous Jews, cunning and conscientious Jews, gruff and gregarious Jews, gave Roth the sanction to shout out, "I could write about my Jews!"[12] *Augie*, Christopher Hitchens wrote much later, was "the first time in American literature that an immigrant, would act and think like a rightful Discoverer, or a pioneer." Bellow had indeed "normalized" Jewish culture. His novel took "*Yiddishkeit* out of the 'torture rooms' and out of the ghetto and helped make it an indissoluble and inseparable element in the great American tongue."[13]

The patrician Trilling made little sense of this, nor did he have much understanding of Bellow's sense of himself as a Jew. As late as 1944 and right on through to the 1980s, Trilling could say, for example, "The Jewish community . . . can give no sustenance to the American artist or intellectual who was born a Jew. And . . . it had not done so in the past." He knew "of no Jewish writer in English who has added a micromillimeter to his stature by 'realizing his Jewishness.'"[14]

In the late forties, Trilling, learning that Irving Howe was translating Sholem Aleichem and I. J. Peretz, told him rather bluntly, "I suspect Yiddish literature." Howe, who treated the Yiddish writers with the same passionate intensity he directed toward Dostoevsky, Conrad, and Faulkner, never forgave Trilling, who didn't know "a damn thing about Yiddish."[15] The remnant of Jewishness Trilling maintained was trivial—a "feeling that I would not . . . deny or escape being Jewish." And he suggested with astounding blindness or denial that this was "the position of most American writers of Jewish birth."[16]

In an ongoing conversation and exchange of letters with Bellow in the 1990s, Roth said, "There was a way of being a Jew that was Trilling's way"—never denying but assimilated, presenting himself as Western, tweedy, inaccessible. And there was Bellow's way, which Roth characterized as "a strange way . . . because it was both a way out and a way in." It wasn't "just that you were finding a way out" of being only, or primarily, a Jewish writer; "you were *finding a way as a writer into being a Jew* without doing what Malamud did." Bellow admired Malamud, a friend ever since they had met as visiting professors in Oregon, but in the exchange with Roth, Bellow cruelly characterized Malamud's way as "shtetl shtick adapted to the U. S. A."

"That's right," Roth chimed in, "with all the sentimental baggage that comes with it." But Bellow jettisoned that baggage and "plugged into Jewish aggression and Jews as businessmen [which accounted for] Jewish success in America." After all, the "real thing the Jews did in America, their great, their real genius and success, was in business," Roth said: "That's what's at the heart of [*Augie*], which is the small-time lawyers, the owners of the middle-sized businesses, the conniving and the cheating. You were not ashamed of Jewish aggression because you saw it as American aggression. . . . It was Chicago aggression."[17]

"My eldest brother," Bellow said, "was a lesson to me in this respect." When he was an adolescent, Saul was in awe of Maury, overwhelmed by his aggressive, confident brother, who, like Simon in *Augie March*, Julius in *Humboldt's Gift*, and a dozen other characters in Bellow's novels and stories, was a large, often brutal man who amassed his Chicago fortune "somewhere between business and politics . . . connected with the underworld although without being a part of it."[18] Maury wore flashy, expensive clothing and bragged about syndicate friends and about how much worldly knowledge he possessed. He was "very proud of his extraordinary group connections, his cynicism, his insiderhood."[19] Bellow, like Augie March, may have had "a bent to the illicit," but his attitude toward Maury's "outlaw" behavior was like his attitude to American materialism—against which he turned away but to which he was mightily attracted.

At home, Maury—so unlike Saul, who had "an instinct for clinging to affection and the family"—rejected family sentiment and religion. He was "full of contempt" for "kashruth and Jewish observance." Americanization was his goal. He had had enough of the "old crap about being Jewish and so forth."[20] For Bellow, "being Jewish" was hardly crap. But he retained little in the way of formal ritual, and he had fled Orthodox Judaism—the mode of Jewish identity chosen by the middle brother, Sam. Saul shared with Maury this disdain of Sam's way of being Jewish, but little else.

One of the important differences between the eldest and youngest brothers was that Saul wore his Jewish identity on his sleeves, which were rolled up periodically to defend his work against the Brahmin gatekeepers of the literary world. "I began to understand what I had done with *Augie March* that had upset so many people," Bellow told an interviewer in 1997. "I had unintentionally turned over a good many WASP applecarts. I had introduced a note in American fiction that was dangerous. It was undisciplined, it was awkward, it was jazzy and it reflected immigrant—and particularly Jewish—points of view that were unwelcome to the WASP establishment." Bellow went on to say (tongue in cheek, presumably), "It had never occurred to me before that I might be treading on the toes of the Brahmins or the heirs of the Brahmins with an interest in controlling their undisciplined and disciplined unfortunate Jews who had not been sent to Harvard."[21]

Bellow told Roth that somewhere in his blood, his "Jewish and immigrant blood," there had been traces of uncertainty about whether he had "the right to practice the writer's trade."[22] Doubt had crept in, he said, because "our own Wasp establishment represented by Harvard-trained professors" considered a son of immigrant Jews unfit to write books in English.[23] Should Bellow, then, have made the opening line of *Augie March*, "I am a Jew, the son of immigrants"? No, Roth said. The words "I am an American" are better—they give a son of immigrant Jews the right to crash through the gates of the Ivy League professors by flatly announcing, without apology or hyphenation, "I am an American, Chicago born."[24]

It was not a declaration Bellow made because he rejected Jewishness but an announcement, with an appropriate fury at WASPs in the academy, that he, a Jew and the son of immigrants, was as good as or better than any or all of them. "I am an American"—no hyphens. In any case, these guardians of the culture, Bellow told Roth, constitute "our own establishment," but by the late 1940s they no longer intimidated him; instead, as Roth later commented, "these guys infuriated him."[25]

The freedom Augie seeks is the same freedom sought by Joseph in *Dangling Man* and by Asa Leventhal in *The Victim*, freedom from the danger of becoming trapped in other people's definition of you, freedom from reality instructors, a freedom Bellow himself sought. He, too, might have said, "Look at me, going everywhere"; by which he meant, going where his upper-crust, degree-bearing "betters" wouldn't "have believed he had any right to go with the American language." Saul Bellow was indeed Columbus for people like Philip Roth, the grandchild of Jewish immigrants, who now, after Bellow, felt confident enough to "set out as American writers."[26]

The critical and commercial success of Bellow's *Augie* made it more likely that Jewish writers of fiction, poetry, and essays, including Bernard Malamud, followed by Herbert Gold, Grace

Paley, Stanley Elkins, and more than a dozen others, would find their way to the American literary scene and nearly dominate it in the postwar era and into the late 1960s.[27] Having been through a war and having earned college degrees, these writers could appreciate being "at once alien *and* American," so that they harbored fewer doubts than Bellow had had at the start about belonging in "the literary mainstream."[28]

But as the critic and essayist Leslie Fiedler said, it was Bellow's emergence and "breakthrough" that made him "the first Jewish-American writer to stand at the center of American literature." He is "flanked by a host of matching successes on other levels of culture . . . what Bellow is for highbrow literature, [J. D.] Salinger is for upper-middle brow, and Herman Wouk for lower middle-brow." On all of the nation's cultural levels, Fiedler went on to say, "the Jew is in the process of being mythicized into the representative American."[29]

Bellow may have aimed—consciously or otherwise—to draw the Jew as Everyman, but either way, he never considered himself a writer for highbrows; he did not want to become a writer with a "small public," like James Joyce or Marcel Proust, for example. "My real desire," Bellow said, "was to reach 'everybody.'" He wanted to have a "large public" without compromising his art, and at this he succeeded; he produced more than a dozen novels, several of which sold quite well, and at the same time garnered prestigious literary awards.[30]

Augie March impressed even Saul's father, Abraham—or, as Bellow put it in a letter to Freifeld, "He's impressed by my new fame and even more so by the sales of the book" and now "feels uneasy and wants, too late, to go on record as a good parent." Bellow, thirty-eight and not yet emotionally reconciled with his father, tried "to make [Abraham] feel that there [was] plenty of time" for Saul to grant forgiveness.[31] Only weeks after *Augie March* went on sale, Saul received a letter from his father, along with money for more copies. Abraham wrote that he had had a "slight" heart attack earlier and now was out of the hospital and "fine." The letter ends with, "Wright me. A Ledder, Still I am the The Head of all of U," signed, "Pa A. Bellow."[32]

In September 1953, just as *Augie March* was making its way to the bookshops, Bellow accepted a job at Bard College teaching Studies in American Literature. The small classes, with no more than ten students, compensated for the inadequate pay—$4,500. But he said it was the roughest teaching job he ever had, "progressive for the students, reactionary for the enslaved faculty." Nonetheless, Bellow did enjoy the attractive countryside setting and pleasant air in Avondale-on-Hudson, and he thought it a good place to entertain ten-year-old Greg—"take him out of the city, keep him with me on holidays and long weekends. Much nicer than dragging him around to museums and zoos in New York. Nothing is more killing. To the divorced, the zoo can be a Via Crucis."[33]

Most of the faculty were conservative, many of them graduates of the Ivy League. But Bellow did find like-minded colleagues in his department. He met twenty-five-year-old Keith Botsford, whose family had been expelled from Italy at the start of World War II. They became lifelong friends. Bellow also warmed to poets Andrews Wanning and Anthony Hecht, who remembers "gracious friendly Saturday night dinners—very genial, full of fun," at Saul and Sasha's place in Barrytown about three miles from the campus. Jack Ludwig, an aspiring novelist, also became a close associate.

At a department dinner party the weekend before the start of the fall semester, Botsford, who had just purchased and read much of *Augie* on his way to Bard from New York City, recognized Bellow, now famous thanks to the positive reviews of the novel accompanied by photographs. He wanted to join him, but there was an "obstacle"—Ludwig, a "bulky Winnipeg hockey body, a heft arm leaning against the wall," with a "mass of hair that bristled, resilient and thick . . . and a flow of Yiddish, of back-slapping laughter."

Botsford thought he was witnessing "an attempted possession" by Ludwig, a young, ambitious man, newly hired, who found "himself face to face with [Saul Bellow], the Real Thing, the man he always wanted to be." Part of Ludwig's "possession" grew into a later affair with Sasha, which Bellow, along with a strong dose of self-deprecation, fictionalized vengefully ten years later in *Herzog*. Finally needing a drink, Ludwig limped away on his permanently damaged foot, clearing a path for Botsford. "A very needy man," Saul told Keith. "Thank God you rescued me from that butcher boy Yiddish. Let's go get some fresh air."[34]

Bellow soon befriended the "butcher boy," forgiving his mangled Yiddish—which he later parodied, mercilessly. But at Bard, Bellow was drawn to Ludwig because he was a fervent devotee; because Bellow found him stoic, never complaining about his troublesome handicap; and last but hardly least, because he was "Jewish where there were not many Jews and none quite like him."[35]

In New York on many weekends, Bellow attended parties with well-established literary figures, including Lillian Hellman, Arthur Miller, and Nobel laureate John Steinbeck. He could see ten-year-old Greg every other weekend and a month in the summer, but little else was settled with Anita, who suffered serious depression when Bellow left her and Greg. For many years she had been the primary breadwinner, and now after *Augie* was published and selling well, she rightly felt entitled to a share of the income.

Royalty checks continued to arrive, but Bellow, perhaps for the purpose of influencing the divorce proceedings, said he was hard-pressed. He told John Berryman that Anita had "not let up in her campaign to get [him] crucified." But he had enough money saved, he wrote Oscar Tarcov, to leave Bard, a "pretty shaky" place right now; he needed stability, he said, and in June 1954 he resigned his post and dedicated himself to writing full-time.

Overall, he had enjoyed his college experience, and he would miss Jack Ludwig, Andrews Wanning, and philosopher Hans Blucher (husband of Hannah Arendt, who rarely appeared on campus). He would also miss "fiddling" together with violinist Emil Hauser and their many walks filled with "excellent conversation." But Bellow never really felt comfortable in an academic setting and "couldn't survive meetings" or abide the college president—"an Ivy League *shlimazel* [an inept loser]." In any case, he was hungry for a career as a writer. Uncertain, however, that he'd be able to produce another bestseller, he knew he was taking a risk in leaving Bard with its small but steady income.[36]

He needed "to have stability *somewhere*," he told the poet Ted Weiss: "It would do Gregory good too; he loves to be with me, and it makes him happy to come to me in a stable place." Sam Freifeld had apparently offered Bellow a sizable loan after he complained, "Anita keeps me fairly strapped. She always took," he wrote unfairly, "far more than she gave. I don't reproach her with anything; her nature is its own reproach. I am genuinely sorry for her but I can feel more compassion as an ex-husband."[37]

Bellow the writer could see malice, injustice, projection, and comic egocentricity in his protagonists while at the same time lauding their determination to live freely and honorably. Bellow the man believed that he was making the effort to live nobly, but he admitted that his periodic choice of freedom over nobility, as in the case of abandoning Anita and Greg, was a significant personal limitation, and in many of those instances he apologized or at least expressed regret—sooner or later.[38]

In the summer of 1954, Bellow took a pass on an opportunity to travel to Europe and turned down an invitation to visit Leslie Fiedler in Montana. He told Ted Weiss and Herb McClosky that he had to be with Greg on Cape Cod for the summer and in New York City every other weekend. Saul said his son "can't do without my help this year. *It is also somewhat the other way around*. He's starting at another school [and] I am beginning another book."[39]

In his memoir, *Saul Bellow's Heart,* Greg attests to these feelings of love and mutual need. His father, Greg writes, "was the parent who understood me best," and when he left, "I felt like a deep-sea diver cut off from my oxygen."[40]

Saul and Greg spent the summer at Wellfleet, Sasha coming out on weekends from New York. Regulars at the beach, which had come to be known as *la plage des intellectueles,* were Alfred Kazin and his wife, Ann Birstein, an author in her own right; Mary McCarthy, whose novel *The Group* had just been published; and historian Arthur Schlesinger Jr. On any given day, one could run into Harry Levin, a scholar of modernism, or Daniel Aaron, a writer and literary historian. Their beach might easily have been called *la plage des Juifs*!

Rumor had it that there was so much important writing going on in Wellfleet that one critic's wife, trying to keep down the noise of the neighborhood children, put her head out the window and pleaded with the kids to be quiet. She said, "The professor is writing a book review. I'm sure all your mothers and fathers have reviews to write, too." Bellow was working on a novel, the draft notebooks of which were labeled with the pithy title, "Jews." Together, the notes, over 170 typed pages, became "Memoirs of a Bootlegger's Son," a manuscript featuring a fictionalized, overbearing Abraham Bellow, who had been robbed and beaten—omitted in *Augie March*—in a story that was drawn very closely to Bellow's life. Pa Lurie, the father, and Joshua, the fictive son and Bellow's alter ego, were mutually sensitive and affectionate but also captious and judgmental. Abraham was not likely to read "Memoirs," but as with *Augie,* if he learned how his family had been reimagined, he would not have been happy.

Comfortably well off, Abraham, living in retirement with Fannie, his second wife, on the North Side of Chicago, was actively engaged with the local synagogue—president for a time—but was in poor health. He continued to complain about his heart, but he was an inveterate smoker, and like the father of Moses in

Herzog, he grew "stormier and more hotheaded and fractious as he aged."[41] He died May 2, 1955. There is no indication that Bellow sat shiva, the weeklong mourning period for immediate family, or that he said Kaddish, the prayer praising God during the period of bereavement, eleven Hebrew months in the case of a parent. Apparently, these were practices that no longer spoke to him. But that does not mean that Bellow didn't mourn.

"When my father died," Bellow wrote several years later to Mark Harris, the future author of *Saul Bellow: Drumlin Woodchuck,* "I was for a long time sunk. I hope you're a wiser sufferer. My business is survival with pain unavoidable."[42] And when Ruth Miller, another prospective biographer and Saul's former student, visited Bellow in 1955 at his New York apartment, he was listening to Mozart's cheerless *Requiem* and weeping when he opened the door.[43]

Bellow had wept at the funeral, too, but Maury, his eldest brother, "ashamed of all this open emotionalism," the demonstrative display of "weakness" in front of his golfing and business associates, scolded him: "Don't carry on like an immigrant!"[44] Bellow later included this scene in *Herzog.* After being admonished by his older brother Shura, Moses Herzog thinks, "I still carry European pollution, am infected by the Old World with feelings like Love—Filial Emotion, Old stuporous dreams."[45]

Bellow's ardent expression of feeling was an inheritance from Abraham very like his tendency to rise too quickly to anger. Decades later, he wrote a letter of comfort to novelist Martin Amis, who had lost his father, Kingsley Amis, renowned author of *Lucky Jim* (1954). Bellow said that "losing a parent is something like driving through a plate-glass window. You didn't know it was there until it shatters, and then for years to come you're picking up the pieces—down to the last glassy pieces. . . . I understand your saying that you are your dad. . . . I can see this in my own father. He and I never *seemed* to be in rapport: Our basic assumptions were *very* different. But that now looks superficial. I treat my sons"—by this time, three of them—"much as he treated me, out of breath with impatience, and then a long inhalation of affection."[46]

His father's death may have brought a halt to Saul's work on "Memoirs," in which he dealt severely with Pa Lurie, the fictive stand-in for Abraham. That Bellow never returned to the manuscript may have had something to do with his uneasiness about going over the details of his youth so soon after his father died. But ten years later, many of those details did find their way into his fiction in the background of Moses Herzog. At least until the early sixties, then, Bellow could not rid himself of his feeling of failure in the eyes of his father. Even after winning the National Book Award for *Augie* in 1954, Bellow believed he "never could do much to please his father." Abraham was "a severe critic" of his son.[47] As pleased as he was with Saul's literary renown, Abraham wondered how successful his youngest son could be if he was perpetually without money. In 1955, Bellow, nearing forty, was still receiving checks from his father. Nor in the minds of his brothers Maury and Sam, now partners in the family coal business, did Saul's accomplishments amount to substantial success.

"My writer brother is famous," Maury said, "but I have money and he doesn't." Sam, too, spoke disparagingly of his "kid brother" whose name "you could look up in the library" but who still had to come to his siblings for money. Bellow valued wealth, possessing it even more than spending it; but he didn't know much about money and never went to the trouble of learning how to make it. Sam saw Saul as "a perverse child growing into manhood with no prospects or bourgeois ambitions, utterly unequipped to meet his world." Bellow told Oscar Tarcov that Sam "is wrong, [I] am not unequipped but unwilling."[48]

The disdain and dismissal from Sam and Maury, in whose eyes Bellow still wished "to count," along with his own mixed feelings about his father, with whom reconciliation was no longer possible, moved Saul to put away "Memoirs" and turn to completing

Seize the Day, a much darker but less directly autobiographical novel. About forty years after the publication of *Seize,* Philip Roth asked Bellow why "he'd moved from the euphoric openness of Augie" to what Bellow himself called "the full catalog of repressions" that define Wilhelm ("Tommy") Adler, the central character of *Seize.*[49]

But it wasn't as if Bellow went straight from Augie's almost feverish need to express joy to Wilhelm's wallowing in self-pity. In the three years that followed the publication of *The Adventures of Augie March,* Bellow had been working on "Memoirs," which centered on the complex and frustrating relationships of his Jewish family, especially between immigrant father and American-born son. Bellow's reluctance to complete a novel that drew more directly from his own life than anything he'd ever written seems to have stemmed from a fear of revealing what he implied was forbidden material. While working on "Memoirs," Bellow told John Berryman that as he crept "near the deepest secrets of [his] life," he "drop[ped] off like a lotos-eater."[50] "Memoirs" remained unpublished but served as a bridge leading away from *Augie* and toward *Seize the Day.*

Seize explores, over the course of one day, the mournful life of forty-four-year-old Wilhelm Adler (a.k.a. Tommy Wilhelm), who has fallen from a modest but respectable job as a traveling salesman into unemployment and a separation from his two boys and from his wife, Margaret, to whom he has been unfaithful but who refuses him a divorce. The novella follows the hapless and pathetically gullible Wilhelm in his search for mercy, or at least a lucky break, and finally, like all of Bellow's key figures, some kind of meaning in what is depicted as the chaotic and unforgiving materialistic world of the 1950s.

A large, shambling sort of man, Wilhelm likes to wear nice clothes, but they don't fit quite right—perhaps a metaphor for himself—and he fills the pockets of his jacket with crushed cigarette butts, packets of pills, and strips of cellophane. He lives on the Upper West Side of Manhattan in the Gloriana, a fictive stand-in for the Ansonia, a residential hotel on Broadway inhabited mainly by elderly Jews. Bellow gives us a picture, lyrical and gritty, that captures upper Broadway with its old cathedral-size hotels on their way down and its benches filled with aging retirees, the unemployed, and the homeless.

The tenants of the Gloriana include Dr. Adler, Wilhelm's father, who reluctantly and resentfully pays his son's rent. There are few familial relationships more fraught with psychological complexity than that of father and son—even more so if the father is of the immigrant generation. And there is nothing extraordinary about a second-generation Jewish writer like Bellow reflecting on that relationship in his novels no matter how creatively he reconstructs his strained connection to his father. Think of Henry Roth (known best for his classic immigrant novel, *Call It Sleep*), Isaac Rosenfeld, and third-generation Philip Roth producing first novels featuring the sons of Jewish immigrant fathers.[51]

Although these writers, including Saul Bellow, recognized and paid homage to the struggles of their parents, they wanted to declare independence from what they saw as their constricting lives at home. *Seize the Day* belongs in this category of generational struggle. But in *Seize*, Bellow's key protagonists play their roles in what has been called a "reverse immigrant novel," where the conventional account of hustling New World sons, made uncomfortable by the vulgar, uncivilized behavior of their Old World fathers, is inverted. It is the father here who is materially successful and fully assimilated and the son who is confused, flailing, and desperate to make his ragged life meaningful.[52]

Dr. Adler is a "master of social behavior," of New World decorum and protocol. He has "made himself sound gentlemanly, low voiced, tasteful."[53] And he is disgusted by what he takes to be his son's lack of control, his emotional eruptions, and his failure to acculturate, adjust, and achieve. Dr. Adler is well aware that second-generation Jewish Americans, through hard work and sacrifice and with eyes trained by history and discrimination to see opportunity—and to seize it—had achieved economic security with remarkable speed. Wilky—the name his father calls him—was not part of this success. Like Augie March, Wilhelm wants to be "freed from the anxious and narrow life of the average," freed from a business culture that measures the self only by style and money. But he lacks Augie's gumption, perseverance, and irrepressible optimism, and he is riddled with self-pity.[54]

Wilhelm doesn't need or want a lot money, he says, but he is desperate for funds just to get by; in a key scene, he begins to choke himself in order to dramatize for his father his general feelings of vulnerability, dependency, and despondency and to illustrate just how tight a stranglehold his greedy and vengeful wife has on him. "Stop that—stop it!" Adler commands. Bewildered by his father's unwillingness or incapacity to listen, Wilhelm "struggle[s] for breath and frown[s] with effort into his father's face."[55] "There's no need," his father says, "to carry on like an opera, Wilky." Though wealthy enough to give Wilky money, Dr. Adler fears the draining of his retirement funds by his son's repeated need for financial bailout. He "behaved toward his son," Wilhelm thinks, "as he had formerly done toward his patients"—without much feeling or warmth—and this is "a great grief to Wilhelm. . . . almost too much to bear. 'Couldn't he see—couldn't he feel?'" Had his father "lost his family sense?"[56] Perhaps. It was, after all, from his long-lost mother that Wilhelm "had gotten sensitive feelings, a brooding nature, a tendency to be confused under pressure."[57]

Wilhelm's name change from Wilhelm Adler to Tommy Wilhelm was as much a way of distinguishing himself from his utterly distant father as it was to adopt a stage name in his futile and reckless pursuit of stardom in Hollywood. When asked by his neighbors about the different names, Dr. Adler says, "My son and I use different monikers. I uphold tradition . . . He's for the new."[58] But at the level of emotional style and the Jewishness of Wilhelm's heart and soul, it is very much the opposite.

Wilhelm's histrionic behavior reflects what Bellow has called, with some fondness, "the immigrant Jewish opera." Indeed, the strangulation scene harks back to what Bellow saw as "the Old System" of Jewish emotions, affections, and family loyalty. In *Seize,* as in almost all of his writings, Bellow reveals a fierce attachment to the immigrant generation and its passions. The civility displayed by Dr. Adler, in Bellow's reckoning, is a function of repression, the denial of "our need to connect at the level of raw, unmediated feelings, unencumbered by layers of education and acculturation—as feeling human beings, like our forebears, linked to others through bonds of human solidarity and identification." In short, civility disguises what Bellow calls our individual souls, "the characteristic signature of a person."[59]

Wilhelm suffers fatherly rejection and defeat in the marketplace, but he comes across as the most truly human character in the entire narrative. There is no getting away from the fact that he is a schlemiel who, just as his father bitterly remarks, invariably takes some course of action he has already rejected innumerable times. Nor does Wilhelm, unemployed and without funds, act with much forethought; he just waits for financial and emotional support and encouragement from his father, who stubbornly, with few exceptions, refuses him. People like him, the doctor tells his impecunious son, who just wait for help—"They have got to stop waiting." Wilhelm's retort, though banal, carries some power: "It isn't all a question of money—there are other things a father can give to a son." But this bromide only turns his father more deeply against him. "Get away from me now," the doctor cries. "It's torture for me to look at you, you slob."[60]

That he is a schlemiel and a slovenly one at that certainly helps account for Wilhelm's lack of success, but it is his human concern and sensitivity that effectively doom him in a world of rational function. He demonstrates sympathy for individuals even though several are initially repellent to him. A part of him finds hideous Mr. Perls, for example, one of his father's tablemates, with his wrinkles and pointed crowns. He doesn't understand how Perls could have become so ugly. But he backs off, thinking, "Each of those crowns represented a tooth ground to the quick," and together they epitomize Perls's accumulation of grief. When adding in the old man's flight from Germany and guessing at the origin of his wrinkles, Wilhelm, in this allusion to the Holocaust, understands that Perls carries in his life "a sizable load."[61]

Wilhelm can also respond sympathetically to people in general, even if he sometimes maintains that sympathy only temporarily. Going through a subway corridor beneath Times Square, he experiences an epiphany:

> In the dark tunnel, in the haste, heat, and darkness which disfigure and make freaks and fragments of nose and eyes and teeth, all of a sudden, unsought, a general love for all these imperfect and lurid-looking people burst out in Wilhelm's breast. He loved them. One and all, he passionately loved them. They were his brothers and his sisters. He was imperfect and disfigured himself, but what difference did that make if he was united with them by this blaze of love? And as he walked he began to say, "Oh my brothers—my brothers and my sisters," blessing them all as well as himself.[62]

Freud would have understood Wilhelm's experience as a manifestation of "oceanic feeling"—an impression of eternity, a feeling of being one with the whole outside world. But Freud also implied that the oceanic feeling is rooted in a sense of powerlessness and helplessness against fate. The subway scene, however, appears from its content and passion to show that Wilhelm is not simply surrendering but relying on his better memories to induce a feeling of self-empowerment. On this "day of reckoning," Wilhelm "consulted his memory again and thought, I must go back to that. That's the right clue and may do me the most good. Something very big. Truth, like."[63]

Irving Howe put it neatly: "Tommy is a slob who feels, a schlemiel who struggles to understand his failure."[64] He desperately needs two things, money and (even more importantly) sympathetic attention. Both needs are connected to masculinity in American and Jewish culture. The failure to earn a living, the need to borrow money, as Bellow himself had to do at times, carries a threat to male self-image. Early in his career, Saul's dependence on his materially successful brothers, Maury and Sam, and on his father carried some shame—exacerbated by the family's contempt for writing as a career. Even after becoming well known and admired in American letters, Bellow needed the attention and the respect of these critically important male figures in his life.

Wilhelm's matching needs are not met by his father. But Dr. Tamkin, also a resident of the Gloriana and thought to be a psychologist, attempts to help by providing attention and economic guidance. Tamkin (Potemkin? Or Tam, Yiddish for fool?) is a liar and manipulator whose credentials as a therapist are suspect; he's also an unreliable financial adviser. But he is not so easily dismissed by alert readers. He is stuffed with intellectual rubbish and inconsistencies, but he has something no one else in the story has—vitality. He is a shyster, a clown, and when it comes to speculating in commodities, he is unmitigated trouble for Wilhelm. Tamkin sucks him into a "partnership" for buying and selling futures, a zero-sum game. in which nothing of real value is produced. Bellow signifies here the soullessness of the free market, a subtle slap at capitalism.

Tamkin goes on to tell Wilhelm, "Every public figure had a character neurosis. Maddest of all were the businessmen, the heartless, flaunting, boisterous business class who ruled this country with their hard manners and their bold lies . . . They were crazier than anyone. They spread the plague." Wilhelm, inclined to agree, supposes that Tamkin, "for all his peculiarities, spoke a kind of truth and did some people a sort of good." Businessmen, on the other hand, "steal everything, they're cynical right to the bones."[65] This exchange between a small-time operator and a nonachiever, more pointed and not too far from Bellow's own view, pictures a materialistic society gone berserk, a capitalism powerful enough to undermine traditional morality.

Unsurprisingly, Wilhelm, following Tamkin's advice, loses $700, the last of his money. He had been warned not to trust Tamkin, but after his usual dithering, Wilhelm writes him a check. He regrets it immediately and then deeply thereafter. Despite the fact that Tamkin's conduct often clashes with his vision, Wilhelm thinks that the psychologist, unlike his father, "at least sympathizes with me and tries to give me a hand." Kindness and mercy are what Wilhelm craves desperately, "that someone should care about him, wish him well."[66] That he can find this only in a hustler like Tamkin says something about Bellow's take on the misdirection of modern society. Though a cheat and a fraud, Tamkin makes Wilhelm laugh; more significantly, he is a source of authentic ideas about regeneration for those downtrodden in spirit or divested of energy—he is something of a healer.

Bellow wrote more than once, in one form or another, that the moral function of the novelist is "to order experience, to give value, to make perspective," and, alluding to Deuteronomy, to "carry us toward sources of life, toward life-giving things." Tamkin, though hardly a novelist, represents a position that Bellow assiduously defended—a position that combines an acute recognition of human spiritual anguish with a resolute belief that the misery suffered is a result of the disaffection of individuals from their souls, their innermost selves, their life-giving qualities.[67]

Tamkin defines salvation and redemption of the self in terms of escape from a "pretender soul," a product of the socially constructed ego, and a growing consciousness of the "true soul." This recognition directs the individual toward the experience of love through which genuine selfhood is attained—leading "toward a consummation of the heart's ultimate need."[68] It is this "description of the two souls" that awes Wilhelm. In Tommy, Wilhelm "saw the pretender. And even Wilky might not be himself. Might the name of his true soul be the one by which his old grandfather called him—Velvel?"—a Yiddish equivalent of Wilhelm and another way Bellow links Wilhelm to the "Old System."[69]

Wilhelm benefits spiritually and psychologically, if not materially, by reflecting often on what Tamkin says, and he is particularly taken by the concept of the "true soul." As Leon Wieseltier, literary editor and Bellow's friend, wrote, "Saul's notion was that there could be nothing wan about the truth, or about the quest for it, or about the language in which the quest was depicted. His novels and his stories, for this reason, often place wisdom in the mouths of charlatans . . . hustlers" and schlemiels: "Accept the truth from whoever speaks it, the Talmud advises."[70]

Charlatans like Tamkin and losers and schlemiels like Wilhelm became ubiquitous figures in Bellow's postwar work. Other Jewish novelists, too, went from lamenting the social and economic victims of capitalism so prevalent in the literature of the 1930s and '40s to near-celebration in the 1950s and '60s of the schlemiel, the antihero, the ineffectual man in the marketplace, even the *ganif*—character types, creatively borrowed by Bellow as well as by Malamud, with subtlety, irony, and humor from Old World Yiddish writers.[71]

The Jewish dimensions of *Seize*, then, were clear, at least to readers of Bellow's generation. But in the 1990s, a group of Israeli students in a class on ethnic literature at the Hebrew University in Jerusalem were puzzled by the novel's inclusion in the course. They were looking for what the anthropologist Clifford Geertz has called "thick description" when evoking a cultural group—its languages, for example, or group self-images, traditions, diet, and the tastes and aromas of ethnic kitchens.[72]

In *Seize*, Tommy Wilhelm is described in some detail, but without reference to so-called Jewish features or language patterns—no mingling of grandiose intellectual bluster with street talk so often associated with Bellow's characters. Nor does Wilhelm eat Jewish food or speak or understand Yiddish or Hebrew, which becomes obvious when he visits his mother's grave and has to pay a man to chant *El molai rachamim* (God full of mercy), a Jewish prayer for the soul of the departed. He "occasionally perform[s] certain devotions, according to his feelings," but never attends synagogue.[73] And he named his children, perhaps unwittingly, after Christian saints, Peter and Thomas Jr., this last being a violation of a European Jewish practice carried to the New World—naming a son for a living father. And when well into the story, Tamkin asks whether out on the road, "dealing with narrow-minded people," Wilhelm ever experienced anti-semitism, he answers, "I can't afford to notice."[74]

Wilhelm also has a Catholic girlfriend, and he forgets or would have disregarded Yom Kippur, had he not been reminded by one of his father's tablemates to reserve a seat at the synagogue he has never attended. And at the funeral of a stranger, Wilhelm cries out silently, "Oh, Father, what do I ask of you?"—an oblique reference to the last words of a dying Jesus.[75] Although death is a major theme in *Seize,* there is only one indirect and fleeting allusion to the Holocaust, and Israel is never mentioned.

It is not surprising, then, that the students in a class on ethnic literature would be puzzled by the inclusion of *Seize the Day,* which they had not found particularly Jewish. The visiting American professor, explaining his choice, read several passages aloud from his 1956 edition of the novella, including a scene in which Wilhelm is more or less pushed into a funeral parlor, where he sees "the white of the stained glass [which] was like mother-of-pearl, the blue of the Star of David like velvet ribbon." The students, however, had been using a more recent edition of *Seize,* which now read, "with the blue of a great star like velvet ribbon."[76]

Was this significant change—the erasure of the Star of David, the most familiar and preeminent badge of Jewish identity in modern history—Bellow's way of escaping, consciously or not, the label "American Jewish writer," a label he considered "an implied put down" by the WASP establishment?[77] Was Bellow trying to make a not overtly Jewish story—at least on the surface—less deeply ethnic? Not likely, given the palpable, unmistakable Jewish content of Bellow's post-*Seize* books and stories including *Herzog*, "Cousins," *Mr. Sammler's Planet*, "The Old System," and *Humboldt's Gift*. And Jewishness makes its way throughout *Seize* itself, which if not evident to the Israeli students was evident to many readers, particularly the literary critics—Kazin, Fiedler, Howe, and most if not all of the writers for *Partisan Review* (where *Seize* was first published as a long story before it was taken up as a novella by Viking Press). Kazin went so far as to say, ten years after the publication of *Seize*, that the book was "probably the most successful rendering of the place, the time, the style of life of Bellow's representative Jew. The protagonist is the city man who feels that the sky is constantly coming down on him."[78]

Brendan Gill, a literary critic for the *New Yorker*, also recognized the Jewishness of Bellow's Upper West Side and its inhabitants, but he described *Seize* as filled with "gross, talkative, ill-dressed nonentities, offensive to look at, offensive to listen to, offensive to touch." Gill's revulsion, shocking but hardly unprecedented, undoubtedly reminded Bellow of Henry James's distaste for the abrasive, urban tenors of immigrant voices when he visited the Jewish Lower East Side a half century earlier. Whatever the case, Bellow was already unhappy with Gill and others at the *New Yorker*, which had rejected several of his stories, including *Seize*, as too long. "Strange people," Bellow said of the *New Yorker* editors: "But I tell you this, I have no desire to understand them."[79]

Gill's obnoxious review was the least of Bellow's troubles. While writing *Seize* and just before finishing it, Bellow had had a number of hard knocks Not only had his father, Abraham, died in 1955, a year before the book was published; Saul, after years of bitter arguments about money, which continued into January

1956, was still involved in his protracted divorce from Anita Goshkin; and only months later, Isaac Rosenfeld, Saul's best friend for many years and a partial model for Wilhelm, died at the age of thirty-eight, never having quite fulfilled the promise of his genius.[80] Bellow's personal losses no doubt contributed to the tightly crafted noir style in which the book is cast. Wilhelm's sense of defeat in New York also derives in part from Bellow's own less-than-happy experience in the city. Not long after the publication of *Seize*, Bellow, musing with Ralph Ellison about where he might settle down, said, "NYC is out. Too rough. Too choking. It wins by a decision over me. No knockout, but I'll never be the same."[81] An atmosphere of constriction, defeat, and death suffuses the novel—culminating in the book's classic, enigmatic, and cathartic ending.

Wilhelm, still separated from his job, his wife, his two sons, and the last of his money, is swept by a crowd of mourners into a funeral parlor, where, knowing nothing about the dead man in the coffin, he breaks down and weeps long and hard. Has Wilhelm begun to sense "from some remote element in his thoughts" that death is indeed the ultimate reality?[82] How else to explain the newly sharpened memories of his mother and her untimely passing, his unbidden thoughts about his own inevitable demise, and his mixed feelings around the foreseeable death of his eighty-year-old father?

Has the stranger in the coffin, gray but not old, reminded Wilhelm that he will likely amount to nothing other than what he already is? Is his conspicuous release of emotion yet another scene from a cryptic Jewish opera—one in which Wilhelm, in a "happy oblivion of tears," expresses pure Jewish feeling about death, just as Saul Bellow himself did with unquelled tears as his father was being buried only a year before the publication of *Seize*? Will the passionate rush of outgoing emotion from Wilhelm also open up a Jewish pathway leading inward to *nefesh*, the spirit of the living, the "true soul?" Perhaps, for even at the very end, "feel[ing] shame and impotence" for having lost everything, Wilhelm, like Bellow himself, suspects that when facing the truth about oneself, "the business of life, the real business . . . the only important business, the highest business was being done."[83]

Now bereft of his monetary hopes, has Wilhelm, in facing the truth about himself, found the strength to free himself from the past, in which he had had so few good moments after his mother died? Will he find the will to commit to the present—to seize the day—and choose a different mode of existence based neither on the pursuit of material success nor on the respectability demanded by his father, but on love—love of his girlfriend, or love for humanity as expressed in the subway scene? And finally, has Wilhelm, in this defining moment, found and embraced his own humanity in his sensitivity, his unwillingness to be hard and distant?

Readers and critics, including Bellow's close friend John Berryman, said they felt the power of the conclusion of *Seize*, even while admitting an inability to understand it. Responding to Berryman, Bellow confessed that the ending "is pitched high, but I am especially fond of it. That the last pages bewilder you I do not wonder for I am not ready to swear that I know what I meant. Quite."[84]

In the same letter, however, Bellow suggested a tentative meaning: "In a city like NY a man," not necessarily a Jewish man, "must adopt an occasion or convert it to the needs of his heart when those needs become irrepressible. . . . And perhaps something like this: suffering is not a way of life but must have a culmination, and its highest culmination is in the passionate understanding. This sort of understanding belongs to the heart," not to an intellectual construction, theological doctrine, or an adopted ideology.[85]

In saying "suffering is not a way of life," Bellow was not suggesting that pain—physical, psychological, or spiritual—could be avoided. He knew that deep sadness and mental anguish were inevitable, but he was quite convinced that they were not to be embraced. No question about it, Tamkin tells Wilhelm, there are many people "dedicated to suffering," but "I'm trying to help you, don't marry suffering."[86] Steeped in Torah since his very early years, Bellow knew well the Jewish commandments to experience joy, but he also knew from personal experience and his reading in the Jewish wisdom books—Job, Ecclesiastes, and the Prophets—that there was no wholesale escape from profound sorrow.

NINE

HUSBANDS AND WIVES

IN *SEIZE THE DAY*, BELLOW pitted survival and spiritual renewal against the dark disposition of death and despair. The same tense dialectic was reflected in Bellow's personal life. "I congratulated myself with being able to deal with New York," Bellow told Philip Roth near the end of his life, "but I never won any of my struggles there, and I never responded with full human warmth to anything that happened there."[1]

The troubles Bellow had had in New York had much to do with the incessant noise, by which he meant the myriad distractions of modern life and commerce. But there was trouble, too, with the *New Yorker* editors, who not only rejected several of Bellow's submissions, including *Seize the Day*, as too long for a short story, but chose Brendan Gill, with whom Bellow shared a personal animus, to review the book after it was published as a novella. Gill's take on the book was, as we saw in chapter 8, distinctly ugly. There were even troubles with Viking, whose editors Bellow believed did not really like *Seize*. He felt depleted by it all.[2] But even before he left the city, he found potential for renewal. Bellow would "never be the same" after New York, he said, but he had avoided a "knockout." Indeed, he not only survived but would thrive—"with pain unavoidable"—for another five decades after he successfully oversaw the publication of *Seize* in November 1956.

In 1955, several months after his father died, Bellow received a second Guggenheim Fellowship, which buoyed him. The plan to use the award money for a writing trip to Rome was scrapped when Bellow and Sasha decided to go west together instead—Saul to Pyramid Lake, forty miles outside of Reno, Nevada, where he anxiously awaited official divorce papers from Anita, and Sasha to Malibu, California, to stay with friends for a few months.

The drive west, Sasha admitted, was among the best times she and Bellow ever had together—talking, laughing, and snuggling at night in rustic motels for what she called "hot sex." Upon her return from Malibu, however, Sasha learned that Saul had also helped himself to a short stint of "hot sex" with a local woman. More shocked than angry, Sasha confronted her soon-to-be husband. Sounding like some of his protagonists, Bellow characterized his wayward behavior as "a moment of weakness" arising from his "need for comfort." Saul seemed authentically contrite, Sasha said, and when he insisted that "all he ever wanted was her," she just "had to forgive him."[3]

The couple did very well together afterward, taking walks, sightseeing, and discussing what they were reading—Hardy and Lawrence, mostly. And Saul was "going great guns" on the "Africa book" he had been working on for almost two years. In this harmonious mood and creative state, Bellow proposed. In February 1956 Saul married Sondra—not yet widely known as Sasha—and was ready for a new start. To Ruth Miller, his former student and future biographer, he sent a wedding announcement along with a letter saying he was "beside [him]self" and "shall let a Yiddish word speak for [him]: *glucklikh* [lucky]."[4]

Sasha found a rabbi in Reno who was well acquainted with Bellow's novels and was eager to talk with him about Jewish American fiction and *Commentary* magazine. At the wedding, along with the rabbi and some new local friends, who "came respectfully to the synagogue and then rollicking to the house," there was Pat Covici, Bellow's editor and publisher at Viking Press. Covici was the sort of Jew, Bellow said, "who made and lost fortunes," adding with the same obvious appreciation he had for his older brother, Maury, that Pat dressed elegantly and lived ostentatiously. He "knew head waiters . . . how to order a fine dinner . . . how to cherish a pretty woman."[5]

Other guests were Leyla and Jack Ludwig, Bellow's Yiddish-speaking friend and fawning admirer since his days at Bard. "I guess," Sasha said, "it was important" for Saul to have an approving father (Covici) and an approving brother (Ludwig) present. "And of course, he couldn't wait to unveil Henderson," his novel in progress, mostly set in Africa—a place he'd never been, but with desert landscapes much like those of Pyramid Lake.

In June, after nine months in Nevada for Bellow and six for Sasha, the couple drove back to the East Coast. They stopped in Chicago, where page proofs of *Seize the Day* awaited Saul. It was here that Sasha met the Bellow clan for the first time. She was not exactly impressed, especially by Maury, whom she described as "a big fat pig of a vulgar man." All the family members, other than Sam, the middle brother, were "heavy-set, gross people" who were so full of themselves that "they ignored [her] completely." And the brothers treated Saul like a "little *pisherkeh* [bedwetter or squirt]." Sasha's reaction was terse: "Lose my number," she said, "I don't need these people."[6]

By the fall of 1956, the Bellows were back in New York state looking for a place to live. Sasha preferred the excitement of New York City, but Bellow said he needed a quiet place, preferably in the Hudson Valley, to write undistracted by the "great noise" of the city. It didn't take long for Bellow, with the help of Jack Ludwig, to find a house—located in the town of Tivoli just north of Bard College, where Ludwig was still teaching. Using his father's inheritance money and funds from the sale of his shares of the

Carrol Coal Company to his brother Sam, Bellow purchased a ramshackle Hudson River mansion with three floors and fourteen rooms, including what had once been a ballroom, for what seemed a bargain price of $16,000.

Only after the sale was complete did Saul and Sasha discover how much work the place needed. There was no working kitchen and no heating system. A new well had to be drilled, the roof badly needed repair, and the plumbing, in critical condition, had to be entirely replaced. The renovations, many undertaken by Bellow himself, were ruefully remembered in *Herzog* (1964). Herzog "learned masonry, glazing, plumbing. He sat up nights studying the *Do-It-Yourself Encyclopedia,* and with hysterical passion he painted, patched, tarred gutters, plastered holes."[7]

Bellow, not sure he'd have enough money to keep the place running, had to take an advance of $10,000 from Viking on *Henderson the Rain King,* a book already rewritten several times. At the Tivoli house amid the noise and confusion of the constant repairs, Bellow was again frantically revising. Covici was in something of a hurry to get the book out. Bellow fled to Yaddo for the first three weeks of September, while Sasha helped get the house in order.

Saul, however, was not pleased by Sasha's extravagance. She had installed all new kitchen appliances, bought expensive utensils and glassware, and filled the kitchen shelves with fancy goods—marmalade, biscuits, tea bags, canned soups—from the gourmet shop S. S. Pierce. Some of Sasha's indulgences are reimagined—only slightly—in *Herzog*: "Madeline had come back from Sloane's Bath Shop with luxurious fixtures, scallop-shell silver soap dishes and bars of Ecusson soap, thick Turkish towels. As she laid everything out, Herzog worked in the rusty slime of the toilet tank, trying to get the cock and ball to work. At night he heard the trickle that was exhausting the well."[8]

Despite problems, however—even rutted roads and awful winter weather that made acquiring basic supplies challenging—Sasha had become more proficient in the kitchen. By Thanksgiving she managed to cook a turkey dinner for Bard friends and several freshly arrived émigrés, refugees from the Soviet Union's invasion of Hungary, now at the college to learn English.[9]

At Yaddo, Bellow believed he was "doing more and better work" on *Henderson*. And back at Tivoli the nonstop writing went on, Bellow countenancing few interruptions. Nevertheless, he responded positively to an invitation from the *New York Times*. Asked to participate in a committee of writers and publishers established in October 1956 by President Eisenhower to counter Soviet propaganda and promote American values abroad, Bellow wired back that he was "WILLING TO RISE TO EMERGENCY."

When Bellow arrived for a committee meeting, William Faulkner, the chairman, was inebriated (to no one's surprise). And in a discussion about Hungarian refugees (the sort that Sasha and Bellow would share a Thanksgiving turkey with at Tivoli in November), Faulkner so annoyed Bellow that he left in disgust. In so doing, he missed Faulkner's argument in support of a campaign to free the fascist poet Ezra Pound. The renowned writer of the *Pisan Cantos* was being held at St. Elizabeth's Hospital in Washington, DC, after a trial for treason in which he was found insane. When Bellow later learned of the petition circulated by Faulkner, he wrote to him: "If sane [Pound] should be tried again as a traitor; if insane he ought not to be released merely because he is a poet." After all, Bellow explained,

> Pound advocated in his poems and in his broadcasts enmity to the Jews and preached hatred and murder. Do you mean to ask me to join you in honoring a man who called for the destruction of my kinsmen? I can take no part in such a thing even if it makes for effective propaganda abroad, which I doubt. . . . Free him because he is a poet? Why better poets than him were exterminated perhaps. Shall we say nothing in their behalf? . . . What staggers me is that you . . . who [has] dealt for so many years in words should fail to understand the full import of Ezra Pound's plain and brutal statements about

the "kikes" leading the "goy" to slaughter. Is this—from the *Pisan Cantos*—the stuff of poetry?[10]

It is not poetry, Bellow concluded; "It is a call to murder." Very soon after Bellow had castigated Faulkner's thoughtlessness, Sasha, after a difficult and protracted pregnancy, gave birth to a boy in February 1957—three weeks overdue and weighing less than six pounds. He survived to everyone's delight, but a struggle ensued over what to name their child. Sasha vetoed Abraham—after Saul's father, dead less than a year. "I don't want an Abie," she said. "How will he bear it growing up in Dutchess County with such a name, not a Jew in sight?" And Bellow wouldn't have one of Sasha's "Catholic names," like Timothy or John. They finally agreed on Adam Abraham.[11]

In May, at the end of the spring semester, Bellow wrote to Ralph Ellison, telling him that the "new kid," Adam, was "beginning to sit up and take notice. He seems to have a sense of humor. Having survived the birth trauma, [Adam] finds life a laughing matter."[12] This pleased Saul to no end. He himself had continued from childhood forward to believe that laughter and comedy were essential, "our only relief from the long prevalent mood of pessimism [and] discouragement."[13]

Laughter, Bellow wrote, though often mixed with trembling, had helped Old World Jews transcend, at least partly, the many tribulations of shtetl life. Jewish humor was mysterious, he thought; it eluded efforts at analysis. But he would often point to a story written by Hyman Slate, an old Tuley High School buddy and lifelong friend, to repeat his argument that "laughter, the comic sense of life, may be offered as proof of the existence of God." Existence, Slate implied, is "too *funny* to be uncaused." Bellow agreed; he thought Jews had an enduring love affair with absurd and humorous circumstances.[14] The real secret, he argued, "the ultimate mystery" around comedy, "may never reveal itself to the earnest thought of a Spinoza, but when we laugh (the idea is remotely Hasidic) our minds refer us to God's existence. Chaos is *exposed*."[15]

In a second letter to Ellison, Bellow wrote, "Adam is walking.... Life is just one long country fair for this kid." Saul could easily have been thinking about his own sense of the world as a child. Everything had been a wonder to him. He told an interviewer that he had had "a kind of infinite excitement going through me, of being part of this, of having appeared on this earth." He had always had, since childhood, "a feeling . . . that this [existence] is a most important thing, and delicious . . . that everything [in sight] is yours, really."[16]

In June, when Sasha, Saul, and Adam returned to Tivoli, the couple seemed to be getting along well; Saul growing zucchini and tomatoes and doing push-ups to keep himself in shape, Sasha baking bread, making jam, canning peaches, and doing lots of typing—mostly for Saul. But Sasha had little patience with Saul's literary friends, who were often at Tivoli for dinner. And in late March 1958, back after a ten-week teaching stint in Chicago at Northampton, Saul was hard on Sasha. He was exhausted. He had been working almost nonstop on *Henderson*, sometimes as many as fourteen hours per day. He was increasingly moody, impatient with the inevitable need to take breaks.

They argued hard and long about money and about Saul's "other women." Bellow "lost his temper over the house," Sasha wrote, "grabbing me by the shoulder like an unruly child, marching me to the scene of my latest failing"—a pot left unclean, socks in the sink, dust on the floor, too much attention "wasted" on her graduate studies in medieval Russian history and Slavonic languages. The fictive Madeline in *Herzog* "built a wall of Russian books around herself. Vladimir of Kiev, Tikhon Zadonsky. In my bed!" Moses Herzog declaims. "It's not enough they persecuted my ancestors. Now they're in bed with my wife."[17]

Bellow wasn't completely insensible to the idea of women as independent thinking beings. Many of his fictive women were strong and intelligent, as were all five of his wives. But like so many men facing even the moderate feminism of the 1950s, it was his custom to pursue younger women, valuing their physical endowments much more than their intellects. If Bellow, with his innumerable conquests, infidelities, and betrayals, seemed extreme in this regard, he was. His behavior went even beyond the far end of the "normal" range of male sexism for his time. There were exceptions for him, but females in his life were mostly secondary figures who served his conceits about women as providers of domestic comforts, entrappers, and even vampires. His most well-known protagonist, Moses Herzog, channeling Freud, writes in regard to Madeline, the fictive stand-in for Sasha, "[I] *will never understand what women want. What do they want?*" Moses adds his own distinctly nasty observation: "*They eat green salad, and drink human blood.*"[18]

Sasha, however, cared less and less about Saul the more she learned about his many sexual escapades as he traveled between Yaddo and New York. She complained about him to Leyla and Jack Ludwig, who were having marriage difficulties of their own, telling Jack that Saul was constantly finding fault with her, in bed and out. Ludwig in turn was feeding Sasha stories about Saul's various infidelities, including one with a student in their bed at Tivoli. At the same time, Saul was completely in the dark about Jack's lust for Sasha and was confiding in his closest friend, telling him that she was selfish, "immature, spoiled, a sexual flop."[19]

Sasha seemed oblivious to Jack's motives when he came—alone—to comfort her in Saul's absences. She was surprised but ultimately not unhappy when Jack confessed his feelings for her in May. Ludwig had wanted to be Saul Bellow from the moment he'd met him at Bard in 1953. Theodore Weiss, a poet and chair of the literary division at the college, aptly nailed Ludwig's motive in pursuing Sasha: "If he couldn't go to bed with Saul, he'd go to bed with his wife."[20] In June 1958, Jack and Sasha became lovers. In the same month, the Bellows had an angry, prolonged, and ultimately fatal argument, which had nothing to do with Sasha's duplicity—of which Saul was still unaware. Sasha now had had enough of complaints and ferocious rows, and she left Tivoli with Adam to stay with friends in Brooklyn in order "to think." In July, during Greg's summer visit to Tivoli, Bellow asked Sasha to return from Brooklyn to help him care for his older son, along with the children of Edith and Oscar Tarcov, whom Saul had agreed to take in after Oscar suffered a heart attack. She agreed to come back to Tivoli, but no mention was made of a return to Bellow.[21]

In the midst of the quarrels and his looming breakup with Sasha, Saul learned to his devastation that his nephew Larry Kaufman, his sister Jane's older son, had committed suicide in his jail cell the night before he was to be released. Although in a rush to finish *Henderson*, Bellow, with no hesitation and in keeping with his commitment to family loyalty, drove directly to Chicago. On his mind, too, was his growing awareness that he'd sunk his legacy into a Hudson Valley mansion in need of continual repair and renovation.[22] Running short of money and anticipating the proposition of a teaching position at the University of Minnesota for the 1958 fall semester, Bellow urged Ralph Ellison to apply for a post at Bard. He offered his old friend and his wife Fanny free residence at Tivoli in exchange for looking after the place. He hoped that Ralph, who had considerable "handyman" skills, would help sustain and patch up the disintegrating house.[23]

Bellow accepted the offer to teach again in Minnesota, beginning in September, but only if Jack Ludwig (who, unbeknownst to Bellow, was about to be let go at Bard) was also appointed. It appears as if Sasha, perhaps manipulated by Ludwig, made this request of Bellow. Ralph Ross, the head of the Humanities Division at the University of Minnesota, was certain that Saul had been "conned into this arrangement."[24]

In any case, during the fall semester, Bellow finally completed *Henderson*, and his spirits began to recover. Sasha, too, seems to have relaxed and, pursuant to her interest in Catholicism, continued taking courses in medieval history at the graduate school. They were both in therapy, which was Sasha's condition for remaining in the marriage. Unfortunately, they were both seeing the same doctor, not only as clients but also when socializing. This extraordinary and unprofessional arrangement was riddled with complexities on all sides. Needless to say, none of this helped anyone in the long run, and Sasha was still sleeping with Ludwig when the Bellows returned to Tivoli in June 1959, four months after the publication of *Henderson.*

February had been a significant month for Bellow. Only days after he was awarded a Ford Foundation Fellowship worth $16,000 early in the month, *Henderson the Rain King* was published. Reviews were mixed but were filtered for Bellow by Sasha. Referring to Isaac Rosenfeld's death in July 1958, Saul said that Sasha was protecting him. She "felt that I shouldn't have to lick any more wounds than I received last summer, and I suppose she's right."[25] Bellow, of course, knew that many reviews were not favorable and that sales would suffer as a consequence.[26]

He was much criticized, he told Philip Roth, for surrendering to mad, zany impulses in writing *Henderson* and for deserting urban and Jewish themes. But *Henderson* doesn't stray all that far. The novel recaptures something of the resilience, optimism, and boisterousness of a Jewish Augie March, and its mixture of riotous comedy and misery points the way to Bellow's next work: *Herzog,* his most Jewish book and character. But Bellow himself agreed with some critics that Henderson—a giant of a man, an alcoholic, a brawler, and a multimillionaire pig farmer—is not Jewish.[27] Bellow continued to insist "that [his] subject was ultimately America."[28] Henderson is surely an American—in size (six feet four) and in attitude (aggressive). His ancestors stole land from the Indians, and the founder of the family fortune became "the most unscrupulous capitalist" in the US.[29]

Still, Bellow admitted that *Henderson the Rain King* was his favorite novel and that Eugene Henderson "was the character with whom he most identified."[30] Henderson does have some stereotypical Jewish features—a large nose and dark, curly hair—but far more important in measuring degrees of his putative Jewishness is the intensity of his desires. Among the more famous sentences in the novel is Henderson's description of the throbbing at the center of his inner turmoil: "Now I have already mentioned that there was a disturbance in my heart, a voice that spoke there and said, *I want, I want, I want!* It happened every afternoon, and when I tried to suppress it got even stronger. It only said one thing, *I want, I want!* And I would ask, 'What do you want?' But this is all it would ever tell me. It never said a thing, except, *I want, I want, I want*!"[31] Though not intellectualized by him or smothered in theoretical constructs, his "wants" resemble the yearnings of Bellow's Jewish protagonists, including, later, Herzog and Humboldt, those "absurd seeker[s] of higher qualities."[32]

Alfred Kazin saw the greatly uninhibited Henderson as one of Bellow's most "wittily agonized definitions of human existence," a character who resembles Bellow, at least in his quest for meaning, and who strongly resembles Bellow's other fictional Jews.[33] Bellow himself placed Henderson right alongside Moses Herzog and alongside Charlie Citrine, too.[34] It was Herzog and Citrine, the central character in *Humboldt's Gift*, who together created what critic Adam Kirsch calls the classic Bellow hero: "hyperarticulate, rueful, sentimental, urban, intellectual, Jewish."[35] Henderson is not an intellectual or even a Jew in disguise, but he fits enough of Bellow's qualifying characteristics to be a near-typical Jewish central actor.

The intensity of Henderson's desire for significance and worth makes it impossible for him to live at peace with anyone near him, including his wife, kids, and neighbors. He is tempestuous, rude, and aggressive, makes odd sounds, picks fights, drinks too much, rants wildly, and consequently faces a mountain of problems: "My parents, my wives, my girls, my children, my farm, my animals, my habits, my money, my music lessons, my drunkenness, my prejudices, my brutality, my teeth, my face," and last but far from least, "my soul!"[36]

He is obsessed by death and has in the past failed to react to the loss of loved ones with composure or dignity. At fifty-six, he plays the violin compulsively in the hope of communicating with his dead parents. One of the songs he plays for them, "Man of Sorrow," includes a line from the Hebrew Bible, Isaiah 53:3—"He was despised and ejected, a man of sorrows, acquainted with grief." It seems to be an attempt by Henderson to elicit sympathy and, through the power of art, to rise above or even deny the finality of death.[37] It is also the first, but not the last, of his references to Hebrew scripture.

The strength and durability of his yearning are a curse to Henderson, but the same yearning also embraces the potential for his redemption; it keeps him from falling into a state of sleep, an ailment he (and Bellow, too) thinks lethal. A phrase that reverberates through the novel comes from Shelley's poem "The Revolt of Islam" (1818): "I do remember well the hour that burst/My spirit's sleep." These words, underlining the need to stay awake and act, preoccupy Henderson, who describes himself as a man "who had to burst the spirit's sleep, or else."[38] The dissatisfaction he feels, even if he cannot analyze it or articulate it, is deep enough to drive him away from wife, family, and country.

He may have stared for a time into the abyss, but unlike some characters in Kafka and Beckett, Henderson is not immobilized. His search is the opposite of nihilism; he seeks authenticity and value, self-understanding, and inner peace. Henderson's quest takes him by chance to Africa and then portentously into the remote interior of the continent. He leaves behind a photographer companion, equipped with state-of-the-art gear. After all, part of "my object in coming here," Henderson explains, "was to leave certain things behind," including modern technology. He also wants to leave behind what the modern world takes for reality—which Henderson sees as sordid, confusing, and purposeless, blinded by its emphasis on materialism.[39]

When he encounters his first Africans—the Arnewi and later the Wariri—he is reminded of the Hebrew Bible's patriarchs. "How old is this place, anyway?" he asks Romilayu, his hired guide and translator. "Hell, it looks like the original place," Henderson thinks; "It must be older than the city of Ur," the presumed birthplace of Abraham, a home of ancient, sacred wisdom.[40]

Despite what Henderson might have been thinking at first, the Arnewi and the Wariri are not inhabitants of a pristine, innocent past, nor, except for the eloquent, well-educated King Dahfu, are they in possession of any particularly special spiritual wealth or wisdom. They are dynamic tribes, blessed—or cursed—by complexity, partly constructed out of Bellow's anthropology studies at Wisconsin and Northwestern.[41]

Henderson's Africa was not drawn by Bellow to be authentic. It was created as the landscape of Henderson's quest, a place where Westerners like him, in the throes of romanticism and alienated from their own chaotic and corrupt world, hope to burst the spirit's sleep, to finally find wakefulness and true reality. Some critics and readers from a postcolonial perspective see imperialism in Bellow's projection of Africa and find the book culturally retrograde. The faithful Romilayu mostly prays and fasts and says almost nothing on his own initiative. Henderson makes repeated references to "savages" and "amazons" and uses what was thought to be pidgin English for African speech; others, however, feel that Bellow, implicitly alluding to Huck and Jim in Mark Twain's novel and to Crusoe and Friday in Defoe's *Robinson Crusoe,* was, with heavily ironized passages, effectively mocking colonialism and the white man's perception of Blackness.[42]

The intention of Bellow's fourth novel does not appear to be racist. There is mutual respect, admiration, and wonder among Black and white characters. And Henderson is repeatedly struck by the beauty of Africa's natural environment, a landscape painted superbly by Bellow: Henderson "came into a region like a floor surrounded by mountains. It was hot, clear, and arid. . . . The mountains were naked, and often snakelike in their forms, without trees, and you could see the clouds being born on the slopes. From this rock came vapor, but it was not like ordinary vapor, it cast a brilliant shadow."[43] "The moon itself was yellow, an African moon in its peaceful blue forest, not only beautiful but hungering or craving to become even more beautiful. New ideas as to its beauty were coming back continually from the white heads of the mountain."[44]

Henderson's ideas about Africans are formed and transformed as he, along with Romilayu, lives among the Arnewi and later the Wariri. The Arnewi are a peaceful and hospitable people. But they have an enormous, intractable problem: their water supply has been contaminated by an invasion of frogs, and they are in the midst of an interminable drought. Milk drinkers exclusively, the Arnewi must water their cattle in order to sustain themselves. But it is taboo among them to allow their cows to drink water infested with other animals. Nor are they permitted by custom to touch the creatures in the reservoir.[45]

Henderson, challenged by this dilemma, "realized that I would never rest until I had dealt with these creatures and lifted the plague." He tells Prince Itelo that the "last plague of frogs I ever heard about was in Egypt," just before the Hebrews made their exodus. This connection, Henderson says, "reinforced the feeling of antiquity the place had given me from the very first."[46]

Still puzzled by the fatalism inherent in Arnewi logic, Henderson points out that rain isn't likely, and then with obvious impatience, he says, "You've got this reserve of [water]." Why not use it? Lowering his voice, Henderson says, "Look here, I'm kind of an irrational person myself, but survival is survival."[47]

The intractability of the Arnewi was likely based on an example of similar behavior that Bellow had come upon in his anthropology courses at Northwestern—a tribe of Inuit who reportedly had preferred to die of starvation rather than eat accessible food that was prohibited by custom. If Henderson were Jewish, perhaps he would have told the prince that the Hebrews also had taboos, especially around food and particularly on pork, but that the God they worshipped insisted on survival. Bellow himself, at the age of eight, in the hospital on the edge of death, ate the pork the staff served, knowing that it was allowed, indeed commanded, under the circumstances: "Survival is survival." Using such an example, however, would likely have been seen by readers as paternalistic on Bellow's part, as if saying, "My people are superior to your people. Take a page from our book."

But Jewish history provides Henderson with another example: "Do you know why the Jews were defeated by the Romans? Because they wouldn't fight back on Saturday. And that's how it is with your water situation. Should you preserve yourself, or your cows, or preserve the custom? I would say yourself."[48] Survive, choose life, a Bellow perennial.

Having won a "welcoming" wrestling match against Prince Itelo and given his history of winning fights by mere force, Henderson assumes that he can simply apply force to get rid of the frogs. But in using a makeshift bomb, he not only blasts the frogs out of the reservoir but also blows up the retaining wall, leaving the Arnewi high and dry. Before the disaster, Henderson had entertained the royal family with "Man of Sorrow," his favorite song. When the queen first heard the line, "He was despised and rejected," she said, "Man want to live."[49] But now he is no longer welcome among these gentle people who had never meant to harm animals.

What comes to mind here, and what Bellow seems to have intended, is an image of a Jew who meanders in and blunders his way among Gentiles. Henderson did want to help, and he does seek higher qualities, but whatever else he did, with the Arnewi he has acted like a schlemiel, a calamitous bumbler.

He next comes upon the Wariri, "the children of darkness." Although they are a tribe prone to hostility and violence, Henderson establishes an intimate relationship with their king, Dahfu, a sensitive, hospitable man who has spent some time in his youth studying medicine at American University in Beirut. Full of psychological insight (much of it suspect), Dahfu recognizes that Henderson has problems—he is an "avoider" and has a neurotic preoccupation with death; impermanence terrorizes him. Dahfu, very much like Einhorn in *Augie March* and Tamkin in *Seize the Day,* is a bit of a lunatic, but he is also a healer who wants to help Henderson transcend his anxiety. Henderson himself tries to lessen his dread of death by bolstering his long-held conviction that "the dead are not utterly dead. I admire rational people and envy their clear heads" when they say, "Dead is dead." On the other hand, Henderson says, "what's the use of kidding" ourselves?[50]

Intimations of immortality appear throughout the story. Bellow, late in his life, admitted that he himself had "a kind of perennial attachment" to his own family and wished to see the people he loved again, his "mother first and foremost." He guessed that "we probably all have such feelings. . . . Of course, it's easy to say [it's just] childish fantasy, but all the same it's hard to get rid of these feelings." Charlie Citrine in *Humboldt's Gift* explains, "There were the dead to think of. Unless I had utterly lost interest in them, unless I were satisfied to feel only a secular melancholy about my mother and my father or . . . I was obliged to investigate, to satisfy myself that death was final, that the dead were dead. Either I conceded the finality of death and refused to have any further intimations, condemned my childish sentimentality and hankering, or I conducted a full and proper investigation. Because I simply didn't see how I could refuse to investigate."[51]

Judaism is famously ambiguous about an afterlife. The resurrection of the dead, the "world to come," and the immortality of the soul—all feature prominently in postbiblical Jewish tradition. But exactly what these concepts mean and how they relate to each other has always been imprecise. In answer to an interviewer who asked, "What's your intuition: oblivion or immortality?" Bellow said, "My intuition is immortality. No argument can be made for it, but it's just as likely as oblivion."[52]

Time and again Bellow demonstrated that his "natural skepticism [was] directed against science, not religion."[53] And much if not all of his fiction is hospitable to imagination and the nonrational. Bellow has a deep-rooted Jewish consciousness and agonizes over American culture's worship of the new, the scientific, the strictly logical, the exclusively rational. Like Bellow, Henderson remains open to ways of thinking about life that are exasperating to modern science. If the tyranny of science and reason has made the world difficult to live in, then there is a need, Bellow consistently argues, to look for the transcendent, to explore the nonrational and even the irrational, if we are to be at peace and in possession of our souls and self-understanding.

In Africa, far from home, Henderson muses about what the world calls reality and confirms his earlier assessment: it is empty and meaningless, noisy, nasty, and polluted. And if modern civilization rejects things the world once found real and beautiful—purpose, justice, soul, love, God—then perhaps what moderns see as unreal is exactly what Henderson is seeking. What he wants, he says, is something like what "I saw when I was still innocent and have longed for ever since, for all my life. . . . My spirit was not sleeping then, I can tell you."[54]

Bellow said repeatedly that "you can go back at will to the earliest years of your life," when you were still innocent and in touch with your soul, "before 'education' had enclosed you in its patterns and representations." Henderson, like Bellow, looks for calm and truth "in what he was before he accumulated this mass of 'learning.'"[55]

In what amounts to a series of psychotherapeutic sessions, Dahfu tries to help Henderson get back to a kind of innocence, back to what Bellow calls "something ultimately unteachable, native to the soul."[56] The king tries to persuade Henderson that imagination has the power to do this and the power also to help him conquer his fear of death. "Imagination is a force of nature," Dahfu insists. "Is this not enough to make a person full of ecstasy. Imagination, imagination, imagination, imagination! It converts to actual. It sustains, it alters, it redeems!" The king means to say that imagination is not only a remedy for the fearful. He is making the improbable claim that imagination can fully transform the world—the way we think, live, and behave toward one another. Dahfu is convinced that "what Homo Sapiens imagines, he may slowly convert himself to."[57]

Henderson is happy to swim in this river but recognizes when the water gets too deep. He spots delusions in the king's approach to reality and does not follow him upstream to the radical conclusion that imagination has the power to completely remake humanity and the nature of the world. Bellow's Henderson is in pursuit of reintegration and regeneration, not an unrealizable total reinvention. He pleads for a sense of the self that is given rather than developed, the self that is vital. Bellow's protagonists, nearly all of them, speak in terms of realizing themselves rather than inventing themselves; they all withdraw from the world temporarily to simplify their lives, and each, for all their cognizance of material reality, experiences hints at least of that self that contains some portion of spiritual autonomy. Augie, who realizes that "it is better to die what you are than to live as a stranger forever," implies a "you" that is definitive; Henderson seeks such a "you" when he says, "I should move from the states that I myself make, into the states which are of themselves."[58]

Dahfu has yet another way, beyond talk, that he hopes will help Henderson rise above his anxieties about impermanence. For complex personal and political reasons of his own, he tries to coax (trick?) Henderson into the lion's den to "meet" Atti, the most fearsome beast in the land of the Wariri. Henderson asks what the lion can do for him. You will become more lionlike, the king answers; you will absorb her qualities, strengthen your character: "She will make [your] consciousness to shine. She will burnish you. She will force the present on you."[59]

In the lion's den, over a period of several days, Henderson is instructed to crawl and to roar with great ferocity along with the lion. This makes for a petrifying, powerful sequence of scenes, too rich to unpack here. It is clear, however, that no matter how much Bellow condemned the search for symbols in literature, Atti represents the primal beast Henderson must confront and purge from his essential self if he is to find peace.[60]

Like the king's promotion of the absolute transformative power of the imagination, the roaring is a nod to the psychoanalyst Wilhelm Reich and a respectful parody of his radical therapeutic practices. Bellow, in Reichian therapy for several years in the 1950s, had done some primal roaring of his own and some "nude therapy on the couch, being my animal self," which, he said, "was a ridiculous thing for me to have done." His animal self, Bellow thought, brought more trouble than liberation.[61] He celebrated emotion and imagination, but his rational side could never fully accept Reich's notion that emotion was all, that it was the only unadulterated expression of what is essentially human and the only path to liberation. Henderson, however, having faced Atti, touched her, and roared with her, does achieve a sense of liberation—most likely because he got out the lion's den alive.

Overall, Henderson has a kind of sardonic Jewish response to the Atti experience: "This is all mankind needed," he says, "to be conditioned in the image of a ferocious animal." When the king asks him how he feels having been with Atti, adding, "Not many persons have touched a lion," Henderson thinks, "I could have lived without it."[62]

In the lion's den, Henderson, fighting against his fear that life might after all be merely "a sick and hasty ride, helpless, through a dream into oblivion," offered up a prayer: "Oh, you . . . Something," Henderson said, "you Something because of whom there is not Nothing. Help me to do Thy will. Take off my stupid sins. Untrammel me. . . . Open up my dumb heart and . . . preserve me from unreal things"—which by this time means purposelessness, materialism, and even ego. "Oh, Thou who tookest me from pigs, let me not be killed over lions. And forgive my crimes and nonsense and let me return to Lily and the kids."[63]

Henderson, post roaring, moves from personal chaos to spiritual regeneration and a more integrated worldview. He recognizes that "the world of facts is real, all right, and not to be altered . . . it belongs to science." Like his creator, Henderson always understood that life was full of hard facts; as Bellow's brilliant friend Allan Bloom put it, "Even if you are on your way from Becoming to Being, you still have to catch the train at Randolph Street."[64]

Still, there is the imagination department, "and there we create and create and create."[65] Unlike Marlow in Joseph Conrad's *Heart of Darkness*, who journeys into the African interior only to be exposed to the human potential for degradation, Henderson grasps the human possibility of universal nobility. Bellow's hero may have found what he "wants," and it resides in what America is missing—a place for the spiritual, for the nonrational heart and soul. No longer in anarchic despair, Henderson returns to America, bursting back into the world with fresh eyes—with a stop, aptly enough, in Newfoundland. "I believe he comes out sane," Bellow says of Henderson, "though he goes in mad. And that's news."[66]

By the time *Henderson* arrived in the bookstores in February 1959, Bellow's marital troubles were well known to relatives and friends, but the difficulties, sometimes public, were also an item for readers of citywide newspapers. It was more than a year since Sasha and Ludwig had initiated their affair, and Saul still had no idea. Sasha claimed that it was "awful" for her to be "running an affair and a marriage at the same time." It was the marriage she gave up, announcing in October 1959 that she wanted a divorce. In a series of letters to the Ellisons, Botsford, Richard Stern, and Covici, Saul, while admitting to recent difficulties, claimed to have been baffled by Sasha's announcement.[67] He did acknowledge, however, "the talent for self-candor which . . . I have been able to invest only in the language I've written. I should be able to do better than that. People are waiting. My soul is waiting."[68]

Before 1959 ended, Sondra and Saul separated after four years of marriage. Bellow had no teaching position in the fall and limited access to his three-year-old son, Adam, and for a stretch he lived in a hotel. So, when he received an offer from the State Department to travel to Eastern Europe as a cultural ambassador on a lecture tour, Bellow accepted, and he took with him the $16,000 awarded by the Ford Foundation.

He would never have consented, Bellow said, "without the need to wear myself out so I could bear the misery of divorce."[69] His travels not only distracted him from his marital difficulties—lots of lectures, lots of women—but deepened his understanding of the world his parents had come from and amplified his horror at the atrocities of World War II. From Frankfurt, Bellow wrote to Oscar Tarcov, his old friend and Tuley High School classmate, to say that in Poland he had visited Auschwitz "and understood that concern with my private life was childish. Before that I had forty nights of insomnia over Sondra. Now I'm losing sleep over the camps and ghettoes of Warsaw and Cracow."[70]

"Wander[ing] through the totally empty ghetto" in Cracow, Bellow was so shaken that he remembered his experience in some detail almost forty years later. He was immediately reminded of Saint Dominique Street—"the synagogues, the ritual baths, the gloomy yards, the muddy streets":

> My parents often spoke about mud in the old country. I had never really understood why it should have been described in such extraordinary terms. The mud was like a thick, old gray soup, cold of course and pouring into your shoes when you crossed the street. There was nothing in the shops except pages torn from Hebrew and Yiddish books. For the first time in my life I understood why Eastern European Jews drank tea with lemon. They needed it for warmth, and a slice of lemon was important not only for its flavor but also because it resembled the sun they never saw. Lemon played a figurative role here, something like a reminder of the absent cosmic radiance.[71]

Many years later Bellow remained astonished at what he saw at Auschwitz. He told Norman Manea that even with everything he knew before his first visit in 1960, he found Auschwitz "inconceivable": this "deliberate plan to cast out a part of the human race, to declare it dead and gone, stinking and harmful. And there was a terrible grim joke connected with the whole thing. . . . When you saw these mountains of eyeglasses, mountains of toothbrushes, mountains of combs, what were they for? They were not meant for redistribution." The whole thing was "meant to strike a chord of triviality," to show these dead Jews as the "lousy bourgeois with their property," who had been living out a "form of bourgeois existence [that] the Nazis intended to eliminate forever in the name of a heroic age."[72]

Images of the ghettoes and the camps stayed with Below for the rest of his trip and well beyond. Mary McCarthy, who was also on the State Department lecture tour, attested to this obliquely in a letter to Hannah Arendt. Saul "was in better shape than when he was in Poland, yet I felt sorry for him when I saw him go off on his own to Italy, like Augie with a cocky sad smile disappearing into the distance."[73] In the spring of 1960, after a short stay in Italy, Bellow was off to Israel.

Coming to Israel after Eastern Europe led Bellow to reflect even more deeply about his identity—Jewish and American. Several of his European cousins had immigrated to Israel when World War II ended; among them were Baruch and Lisa Westreich from Riga, who had survived the German occupation of Latvia. Bellow visited their family in Holon, near Tel Aviv. The Westreichs knew quite a bit about Bellow's family through correspondence with Abraham, who from time to time urged the couple to come to the United States—even offering to pay their airfare.

Abraham in his letters described Saul as a worry to the family because he was the only son "not working, only writing." Before Abraham died, Bellow had already published three novels, including the National Book Award–winning *Augie March*, and he was nearly finished writing *Seize the Day*. His father's description of Saul may have been good for a smile, but it was not an obstacle to conversation and comradery among the cousins.

The Westreichs owned a small grocery store "no bigger than a pantry," and they lived a challenging life, on their feet many hours a day. Having encountered slave labor, "arrest, deportation, massacre and war," Bellow's cousins accepted what he called "ordinary" lives. "They have," he wrote later, "more rest in their souls than the American side of the family; they are less secure but also less fretful." After a number of return visits to his Israeli family, and having observed "their temper and their ways," Bellow wondered about "the effects of limitless expectation on the American sense of reality."[74]

More thinking about national and cultural identity was prompted by an "amusing and enlightening conversation" Bellow had with S. Y. Agnon, "the dean of Hebrew writers." Agnon chatted with Bellow as they sat together drinking tea. In Yiddish, Agnon asked Bellow whether he had been translated into Hebrew. He had not. Disappointed, Agnon said, with what Bellow called "lovable slyness," that this was most unfortunate, because "the language of the Diaspora will not last," and Bellow's books "would survive only" if translated into "the Holy Tongue." Despite his irritation, Saul wanted the conversation to continue. He asked, "What will become of poets like poor Heinrich Heine . . . who did quite well with German?" Agnon told Bellow not to worry; Heine "has been beautifully translated into Hebrew and his survival is assured."[75]

The Israeli was making the Zionist argument that the appropriate language, the *only* appropriate language, for a Jewish writer was Hebrew. "The spare old man . . . feels secure in his ancient tradition," Bellow said, and "I didn't care to argue the matter." He thought (but didn't say) that "Jews have been writing in languages other than Hebrew for more than two thousand years." Bellow knew that Agnon, although half serious, was also half joking. He hoped Bellow's works would be translated into Hebrew but was not expecting him to dismantle his life and start over by learning the language of modern Israel.[76]

Still, Bellow was irked by the chauvinistic strain in Israeli attitudes toward Jewish writers in the diaspora. By insisting on Hebrew, Agnon overlooked Jews who wrote "characteristically Jewish stories" in other languages—French (Andre Schwarz-Bart), Italian (Italo Svevo), German (Heinrich Heine), and Russian (Isaac Babel). Babel knew no Hebrew but knew very well how to write in a Jewish language, Yiddish. Before being swept up in one of Stalin's purges and executed, Babel had been put in charge of translating and publishing the works of the Yiddish writer Sholem Aleichem into Russian. Although Babel chose to write his own stories in Russian, the language of his oppressors, there is no surprise here. Like Ze'ev Jabotinsky, the Russian revolutionary Zionist revisionist (who among other things wrote the novels *Samson* and *The Five*), Babel had Russian as his primary language, and Russian was *the* language of Odessa.

It is clear, however, that in his 1960 conversation with Agnon, reconstructed and analyzed in his introduction to *Great Jewish Short Stories* (1963), Bellow recognized the phenomenon "Jewish writer"; he just didn't want what he thought was a reductionist label applied to himself, and he resisted the Malamud-Bellow-Roth concoction, which he saw as a commodification of Jewish writing invented by critics and scholars. Bellow avoided labels generally, but he made clear in an irate letter to Leslie Fiedler what he thought being Jewish for a writer *didn't* mean.

In a review of Karl Shapiro's *Poems of a Jew* (1958) in *Poetry* magazine in its spring issue (1960), Fiedler contended that Jewish writers had discovered their identities as Jews to be "an eminently marketable commodity." He accused Shapiro of trying to "ride beside [Herman] Wouk and Salinger, Bellow and Malamud, Philip Roth and [Leon] Uris—the bandwagon which travels our streets, its calliope playing *Hatikvah*," the national anthem of Israel. Bellow demanded to know "what is this 'marketable' Jewishness you talk about? And who are these strange companions on the bandwagon that plays *Hatikvah*? It's amusing. It's utterly wrong. . . . What you think you see clearly is not to be seen. It isn't there. No big situation, no connivances, no Jewish scheme produced by Jewish minds. Nothing. What an incredible *tsimis* [meaning literally a dish of stewed fruits but implying an imbroglio] you make of nothing!"[77]

From Israel, there were journeys to Naples, Rome, Paris, Edinburgh, and Manchester. As early as the end of January, Bellow was worn out, but after he recovered some from the frisson he experienced in Auschwitz and Cracow and got over what he called a "trifling infection," he was sleeping and sexually active again. Wherever he traveled—in Paris, London, Poland, and Yugoslavia—Bellow continued his energetic womanizing. Letters from nine different European women awaited him at home. About three weeks before he was due back, he told Pat Covici that he had "had too much of sights and flights, and girls" and "was ready to go back to [his] business, which [was] to . . . write books."[78] There had been some expression of distress from a Ford Foundation executive over how much time Bellow was spending traveling rather than writing. Bellow told his editor at Viking that he *was* writing—revising a play and working on what may have been the beginning of *Herzog*.

He defended his travel itinerary as critical, saying he hadn't been on a "gay lark"—far from it: "I have been dutifully suffering my way from country to country," including Poland, Yugoslavia, and Israel, "thinking about Fate and Death," and "what I saw between Auschwitz and Jerusalem made a change in me. To say the least."[79]

A likely outcome of this change in Saul was his production of *Great Jewish Short Stories* (1963), an anthology of texts from Biblical apocrypha and the Haggadah to Nachman of Bratslav and Isaac Bashevis Singer to Philip Roth and Grace Paley. Bellow's introductory essay masterfully and neatly points to the heart of what he was doing in collecting these stories written in Hebrew, German, Yiddish, Russian, and English. "We do not make up history and culture," Bellow wrote, "We simply appear, not by our own choice. We make what we can of our condition with the means available. We must accept the mixture as we find it—the impurity of it, the tragedy of it, the hope of it."[80]

Bellow's European journey ended in March 1960 in London, where it had started, but it wasn't yet the end of Bellow's curiosity about new people and new ideas. Before heading home to the US, Bellow was entertained by George Weidenfeld, his new British publisher and editor. Convivial and Jewish, Weidenfeld connected easily with Bellow. When he told him that he had escaped from Vienna in 1939 and had a strong interest in Israel, Saul's memories of Auschwitz and Jerusalem were stirred. It was a good beginning and encouraged a friendly relationship. It helped, too, that the two men belonged to what Weidenfeld described as "the NCL, the Non-Communist Left," and were comfortable with each other's politics.

Unlike Bellow, however, Weidenfeld was a committed Zionist. It was a surprise to Bellow that he could be outspoken and passionate in his support of Israel and at the same time circulate among and maintain friendships with "pedigreed" non-Jews. "I didn't have hang-ups," Weidenfeld told an interviewer. "We are better than them. . . . Who are [they]? Robbers! Fourteenth century? My family," Weidenfeld claimed, "are rabbis who came from Barcelona. Who the hell are [they]?"[81]

Weidenfeld's "mentality toward the English aristocracy" bore a strong resemblance to Bellow's attitude toward the American literary gatekeepers—members of the WASP establishment who were trying desperately to preserve the "purity" of the English language.[82] *The Adventures of Augie March* and *Henderson the Rain King* had been serious body blows suffered by the gatekeepers in their fight for purity. But it was in his next and most Jewish novel that Bellow would find the fullest form of his own literary language. And it was a knockout.

Abraham Bellow's passport (more than likely forged). Photo, 1913. *Courtesy of Daniel Bellow.*

Lisa and the children in Lachine, 1918. From left to right, Saul, Lisa, Maury, Sam, and Jane. *Courtesy of Daniel Bellow.*

Saul and his sister, Jane, c. 1926. *Courtesy of Daniel Bellow.*

Saul and his first wife, Anita Goshkin, 1937, Hyde Park. *Courtesy of Daniel Bellow.*

Saul and one-year-old Adam, son of Sasha, Saul's second wife, 1957. *Courtesy of Daniel Bellow.*

Saul, Adam, and Daniel Bellow, son of Susan (née Glassman), Saul's third wife, at Martha's Vineyard, 1965. *Courtesy of Daniel Bellow.*

Saul, Susan, and Daniel Bellow, 1965. By 1966, Saul was no longer in the picture. *Courtesy of Daniel Bellow.*

Saul and Daniel at the National Book Award ceremony for Saul's *Mr. Sammler's Planet*, 1970. *Courtesy of Daniel Bellow.*

Saul Bellow at a book signing in 1975 for *Humboldt's Gift*, winner of the Pulitzer Prize. *Courtesy Hanna Holborn Gray Special Collections Research Center, University of Chicago Library.*

Saul Bellow with Alexandra Ionescu (Bellow's fourth wife) with President Jimmy Carter at the White House, marking the peace treaty signed between Israel and Egypt, 1979. *Courtesy Hanna Holborn Gray Special Collections Research Center, University of Chicago Library.*

Saul Bellow at the wedding of Adam Bellow and Rachel Newton, 1986. *Courtesy of Daniel Bellow.*

Saul Bellow accepts the National Medal of the Arts from President Ronald Reagan, 1988. *Courtesy Hanna Holborn Gray Special Collections Research Center, University of Chicago Library.*

Saul and Janis Freedman Bellow, Saul's fifth wife, in Brattleboro, Vermont, 1991. *Courtesy of Daniel Bellow.*

TEN

FRIENDSHIPS AND BETRAYALS

BELLOW'S RETURN TO MINNEAPOLIS WAS disastrous. Apart from seeing Adam, it "was a nightmare," he told Ralph Ross: "Sandra threatened to call the cops if I came near the house, and I repressed the impulse to kill her."[1] There were also seemingly intractable legal wrangles over the couple's divorce agreements. Bellow fled to Chicago for three weeks, where he used the university office of his friend Edward Shils, a sociologist, who was abroad.

Once back at Tivoli in May 1960, Bellow entered therapy with Albert Ellis, the grandson of Russian Jewish immigrants, author of *Sex without Guilt* (1958), and an early proponent of cognitive behavioral therapies. The doctor said the "goal" of the therapy was to get Bellow "unangry." It "was pool-room grad work," Saul told James Atlas. Ellis spoke about "what to do, how to lay a girl"—as distinct from getting a "girl" into bed—which suggests talk of sexual dysfunction or dissatisfaction in the therapeutic sessions as well as anger. Bellow quit the therapy after three or four months.[2]

The summer of 1960 was pitched toward recuperation. Ralph Ellison, who was teaching at Bard, accepted Bellow's invitation to move into the Tillson house. "I always believed," Bellow said years later, "this was an act of charity" on Ralph's part. In any case, "the . . . house was no longer empty—no longer gloomy."[3] All day long, Bellow said, "I heard the humming of [Ralph's] electric typewriter. Its long rhythm made me feel that we were on a cruise ship moving slowly through the woods."[4]

Ralph's wife, Fannie Ellison, the founder of the Negro People's Theater in Chicago, was working in New York City and stayed over on weekends. Other visitors to Tivoli included Greg, now sixteen, and Bard faculty and associated writers and critics. But Ralph was Saul's most important company. They ate simple meals together in the flagstone-paved kitchen, which became their habitual meeting place for breakfast and again at cocktail time.

Ellison, always nattily dressed, came down for breakfast wearing a heavy "striped Moroccan garment" and Turkish-style slippers. Bellow, usually a snappy dresser himself, consistently amused Ellison with his comparative "slovenliness," purposefully wearing "the same blue jeans and chambray shirt" for several consecutive days. At breakfast, Bellow learned from his "tenant" how to brew drip coffee properly—with a Chemex, a manual glass coffee maker. He kept a vegetable garden and at the kitchen door planted herbs; Ellison taught him how to care for houseplants. Ellison had set himself up in the sunny second-floor former ballroom, which ran the entire length of the house; he kept African violets there, watering them with a turkey baster. "Ralph and I," Bellow felt, "brought the house under civilized control."[5]

Ellison was also able to service his own car with the well-organized cache of tools he kept in the trunk. The repair of radio and hi-fi equipment was another of his talents. Although Bellow was passably handy himself, he envied Ralph his "esoteric technical skills." Where Bellow saw "a frightening jumble of tubes, dials, and condensers (I can't even name the parts)," Ellison saw order. Bellow, for whom "there was no coming between a Jew and his jokes," was playing with the stereotype of a Jew's relative inability to do methodical hands-on work, an image that still serves as the core of various self-deprecating but funny Jewish anecdotes.[6]

As writers understandably drawn to solitude, Ralph and Saul "did not seek each other out during the day." A nod in passing was enough. But after a day's work, the two would have drinks and chat about their writing. "Ralph mixed very strong martinis," Bellow attested, "but nobody got drunk." There were long talks about literature and their personal histories. Often "they rambled together about Malraux, about Marxism or about painting"—or, no surprise, about writing novels.[7]

There were also long discussions of US history and slavery, which they saw as the "poison pill" America had swallowed at the beginning of its history; they spent many hours talking about the Civil War. Bellow said Ellison was better at history than he could ever be, "but it gradually became apparent that [Ralph] was not merely talking about history, but really the story of his life, tying it into American history." Ellison saw African Americans as major contributors to American history and culture. Bellow was also convinced of that, just as he was that Jews, too, had been influential in that ongoing process of cultural creation.[8]

Bellow and Ellison did have other literary company in Dutchess County. Richard Rovere, an important political journalist, editor, Jewish author, and former Communist, had written four books up to that time; his most recent was *Senator Joe McCarthy* (1959), published the same year as Bellow's *Henderson*. He lived in Rhinebeck, twelve miles from Tivoli, and in Bellow's view was "the only genuine democrat"—and Jew—"in our literary set."[9] Fred Dupee, a distinguished American literary critic, essayist for *Partisan Review* and the *New York Review of Books*, and professor of English at Columbia University, like Rovere, had been a radical Marxist. Gore Vidal, a public intellectual, well known for his many critically hailed novels and sharply pointed political and cultural essays, had a patrician manner and what Bellow understatedly called "a fine house" on the riverbank.

"Ralph and I, in our slummy mansion," Bellow wrote later, "could not entertain these far more prosperous literary country squires." The Dupees and the Roveres invited the Tivoli pair for dinner occasionally, but "Gore Vidal viewed us with a certain ironic pity; socially we didn't exist for him." Saul and Ralph, however, were as amused by this "campy patrician," as Ellison called him, as Gore was amused by them.

"No one in our Dutchess County group," Bellow said, "was altogether free from pride." Even Ralph had "an aristocratic demeanor," but these others, Vidal and Dupee particularly, were markedly wealthier and had literary connections at higher levels. Vidal also made genealogical claims and had real money. "The presence of a Jew or a Negro" in such a group, indeed, "in any group," Bellow thought, "is apt to promote a sense of superiority in those who—whatever else—are neither Jews nor Negroes."

Ralph Ellison "had the bearing of a distinguished man," Bellow said, "an appropriate kind of avowal." And why not? A young Black man from Oklahoma City and educated at Tuskegee University, he had aimed high; "he had learned from Malraux as well as from Richard Wright, and with *Invisible Man* he had earned the right to be taken seriously." Bellow could think the same of himself: a young Jew from a poor immigrant family, educated at the Universities of Chicago, Wisconsin, and Northwestern, he had set his sights high, and with *The Adventures of Augie March* and *Seize the Day* he had earned the right to considerable respect.

One other visitor to Tivoli that "recuperative" summer of 1960 was Susan Glassman, daughter of a prominent Jewish surgeon, with whom Bellow was having an affair. And she had come to stay a while. They may have met for the first time in the fall of 1957 at the University of Chicago when Bellow delivered a lecture at Hillel Hall, the nationally connected Jewish organization on the campus. Glassman was at the university doing graduate work in English and was in the audience the day of Bellow's address as

Philip Roth's date. When Bellow finished his talk, which Roth remembers "as very engaging, tremendously exciting," and full of "self-delight," Glassman, "believing" she may have met Bellow at Bard, headed for the podium to say hello. Roth saw the lively engagement between her and Saul and thought, that's "the best thing that ever happened to me and the worst thing that ever happened to Saul." It was "the beginning of Saul's tsuris"—Yiddish for "real troubles," plural. Yiddishists say that "*tsuris* does not really exist in the singular, because Jews don't do trouble in the singular. It has to be in the plural," as Bellow was soon to find out—again.[10]

In the fall, Susan left the Hudson River mansion and returned to Chicago for the start of classes; soon thereafter, Bellow, trekking back and forth regularly from Tivoli to Manhattan, slept with four different women—and in a convoluted way learned of the affair between his good friend Jack Ludwig and Sasha, with whom he was now tied up in divorce proceedings. That same night he hurried over to Ralph Ross's house and threatened "to catch that son-of-a-bitch Ludwig and beat him to a pulp." Ross actually had to restrain Bellow physically, later advising him, "Be a mensch—have an ulcer" instead. Saul may have developed an ulcer, but he also "talked wildly about getting a gun."[11]

In the meantime, in an exchange of letters among Bellow, Ludwig, and Botsford, who together had been editing an experimental literary magazine, the *Noble Savage*—an excellent but short-lived periodical—there were only harsh complaints about Ludwig's editing work, nothing about his betrayal.[12]

But in a letter from the University of Puerto Rico at Rio Piedras, where Bellow was teaching for the spring 1961 semester, Saul, after paragraphs of scathing criticism of Ludwig's editorial failures, got more personal and sarcastic—"since we're not only colleagues but 'friends'": "In all this there is some ugliness, something I don't want explained, though I'm sure that as a disciple of Hasidism and . . . enthusiast for [Abraham Joshua] Heschel. . . .

You have a clear and truthful explanation. And all the worse for you if you are not hypocritical. The amount of internal garbage you have not taken cognizance of must be, since you never do things on a small scale, colossal."

Bellow said he wanted no explanation, because even "with the sharpest eyes in the world I'd see nothing but the stinking fog of falsehood."[13] But how could so many of his friends and colleagues notice what was going on, while the forty-six-year-old Bellow, "the great noticer, noticed nothing?"—even when Sasha was desperately sad, even when she got pregnant and had an abortion in the spring of 1959?[14] Simply put, he wasn't paying attention. He was writing, and he needed Sasha to be okay and Ludwig to be a true friend. Years later in a letter to Ross, he attributed his failure to notice the double betrayal to his determination "not to understand whatever was deeply threatening—allowed myself to know only what conformed to my objectives."[15]

Bellow, in his letter to Ludwig, frankly admitted his culpability. In "the whole Sondra-Jack Ludwig business . . . I leave infinities on every side to be desired. But love her as my wife? Love you as my friend? I might as well have gone to work for Ringling Brothers and been shot out of a cannon twice a day. At least they would have let me wear a costume."[16] When Bellow wrote this letter, he was well into writing *Herzog*, a book in which he would exact eviscerating revenge. He was also four years into his third marriage and was a new father for the third time.

It was apparently easy to fall in love with Susan Glassman; by all accounts she was a stunningly beautiful woman. She was also smart and had intellectual aspirations. After Wellesley, she did graduate work in English at Harvard and at the University of Chicago, and she did serious reading, plowing through novels from Dostoyevsky to Yukio Mishima. Her file drawer, stuffed with unpublished stories, attested to her writerly ambition. Still, Bellow's moves toward a third marriage puzzled many who knew him. For one thing, he hadn't yet fully extricated himself from the second marriage and was still paying alimony and child support to his first wife, Anita.

Several friends, including novelist Richard Stern, wanted to know why Saul was attracted to an institution for which he was apparently unsuited. As Bellow told Mitzi McClosky a decade and a half earlier, when his marriage to Anita was on increasingly shaky grounds, the "idea" of marriage appealed to him. In it were possibilities for stability, companionship, and traditional family life. The problem arose in Bellow's having to play a central role in that family life, which meant sharing himself, his inner thoughts and feelings, with another person, the kind of intimacy Bellow shied away from. Years later, Saul's son Adam had it right when he said, "My father needed to be taken care of."[17]

In jettisoning his wives and seeking new ones, Bellow was acting like many of his cohort. A common behavior pattern of middle-aged men raised in the 1930s and 1940s was to marry—and, if divorced, to remarry. This pattern appears to have been relatively widespread, especially among Jewish writers and critics.[18] Bellow would in the end have been married five times, which sounds extraordinary, but Kazin, Howe, and Budd Schulberg each had four wives, and Norman Mailer, six.

"I shrink from marriage still," Bellow told Stern, "but not from Susan."[19] Partly because Bellow did indeed still "shrink from marriage," his relationship with Susan had problems from the beginning. The first sign of trouble came after Bellow had accepted an offer from the University of Puerto Rico to teach in the spring. The very public scandal surrounding his breakup with Sasha eliminated the possibility of an offer from Minnesota, even though the students made a strong play to bring Bellow back.[20] He needed the money—badly. He still owed Viking between $10,000 and $15,000 and was short of funds for his yearly payments of alimony to Anita and Sasha. That there was no talk of Susan accompanying Saul to Puerto Rico was a sign on his part of a hesitancy to commit.

He was also involved with Rosette Lamont, a strikingly attractive professor of French and comparative literature at Queens College, who knew about Susan and considered her a rival. In the long spring and summer of 1960, Bellow was also sleeping with at least two other women. Lamont, who broke with Bellow close to the very moment he was leaving for Puerto Rico in January 1961, concluded that "Saul wanted women to go after him and make up his mind for him."[21]

In the correspondence between Susan and Saul, even before he left for Puerto Rico, there were, along with expressions of love, signs of trouble. In late August, Susan, depressed about having to live with her parents in Chicago, had written Saul two accusatory letters. In the first, she admitted to worrying about Bellow's feelings. "You never speak your mind on a subject, do you?" she said, and she went on to complain in the second letter about his volatility: "That grim voice of yours that starts those announcements with 'Now look'. . . ." After Susan returned from a March visit with Bellow in Puerto Rico, she wrote to him about her experience on the island. Upset with Saul's "getting irritable, my getting resentful," Susan said, "You only spoke your mind in rages . . . and then I was angry, and worse, withdrew."[22]

When Bellow returned to the mainland in May 1961, he wanted to be at Tivoli, where it would be quiet and he would have more time to work on *Herzog*, which had "grown big and fat" in Puerto Rico; Susan preferred New York, where she was teaching at the Dalton School, a fashionable private preparatory school on the Upper East Side. Tivoli it was, and then it would be off to Chicago.[23] But first, Bellow, still in need of money, agreed to be a "tutor" in fiction at the annual Wagner College (Staten Island) writing conference. He was in good company; Robert Lowell was there for poetry, and Edward Albee for drama.

There were more than a dozen students in Bellow's fiction class, some of them quite talented, including Donald Barthelme; Arlo Karlen, an already published author; Susan Dworkin, who went on to write a fair number of bestsellers; and Bette Howland, who published three critically admired books in the 1970s and 1980s, including *Blue in Chicago,* a largely autobiographical story of a working-class Jewish family. Although Bellow was formal and wary with his female students, he took to Howland from the start, "Since," as she put it, "I'm from Chicago and probably reminded him of his relatives"—and, "Actually," she said, "I can write."[24]

Bellow agreed. "I want to see you do well," he wrote her in August 1961. "I believe in fact that you can go as far as you like in writing."[25] Later, they met up again after a reading Bellow did at the University of Iowa, where Bette was studying for her MFA. "It did start out," Howland remembered, "as it usually started out with women," but "I soon found out there was no percentage in this, it was quite senseless, and we just became friends." That friendship, though there would be some trouble in years to come, became lifelong, supportive, and fruitful for both Bellow and Howland as they read and commented on each other's writing over a fifty-year period.[26]

In addition to teaching in the writing seminar, Bellow agreed to deliver an endowed lecture at the University of Michigan. In "Where Do We Go from Here: The Future of Fiction," Bellow proposed a question and a theme that he used in many of his essays. He claimed that if there were any truth to the fashionable assertion that the novel was dead, it derived from the disappearance of "the person, the character, as we knew him in the plays of Sophocles or Shakespeare, Cervantes, Fielding and Balzac."

Another culprit in the alleged death of the novel, Bellow said, was the passing of drama "from external action to internal movement." Modern novelists believe humankind faces the universe "without the comforts of community . . . surrounded by dubious realities and discovering dubious selves." Much of this is true. But there are novelists, Bellow argued, whose "books have attempted . . . to create scale, to order experience, to give value, to make perspective and to carry us toward sources of life, toward life-giving things." Choose life, make meaning—a relentless Bellow theme, rooted in Jewish tradition. In the end, he reiterated his belief that "the novel, in order to recover and flourish, required new ideas about humankind." And we must see ideas, he said, "in flesh and blood," which means the restoration in fiction of "character, action, and language."[27]

In his talk Bellow had obliquely set the stage for *Herzog*, in which the protagonist "knows very well that habit, custom, tendency, temperament, inheritance, and the power to recognize real and human facts have equal weight with ideas."[28] More directly, the way was prepared for Bellow's forthcoming novel by the publication of an early version of the first chapter in the July issue of *Esquire* magazine.[29] The reaction was uniformly positive. Alfred Kazin and Robert Lowell, with hardly any qualifications, thought very highly of the chapter, as did Elizabeth Hardwick, who had not liked *Henderson the Rain King*. This was the beginning of a constant flow of critical acclaim, honors, medals, awards, and calls to speak or to serve on literary panels that accompanied Bellow over the next four decades of writing.

Lowell and Hardwick, husband and wife, wrote individual letters at the beginning of 1962 inviting Bellow to be a contributor to the first issue of the *New York Review of Books*, because of his "absolute leadership" in "the field of fiction."[30] He was also invited, along with two hundred other leading American writers and cultural figures, to a dinner at the White House in honor of Andre Malraux in the spring of 1962 and was awarded an honorary doctorate by Northwestern at its June commencement. And when he responded affirmatively to one of the many job offers, even before the *Herzog* excerpt was published, Bellow, in the winter quarter of 1962, became a "Celebrity in Residence" in the English Department at the University of Chicago—something concocted by the public relations office.

Although Susan Glassman and Saul were married in November 1961, she was hesitant to leave her recently acquired job at the

Dalton School and so stayed in New York when Saul went off to Chicago in January.[31] During his first week in Chicago, Bellow visited his son Adam, now three and living with Sasha; he was "simply wonderful," Saul wrote to Susan. "I'm taking [him] to Lesha's [Saul's niece] little girl's birthday party," Bellow told Susan:

> That made him happier. He sounded slightly tearful. *Oy*, we with our tears oiling the wheels of the universe. If we [Jews] had no tears we wouldn't be ourselves, but the mind still finds them an oddity. . . . [Maury] gave me a handsome Irish tweed coat . . . which seems to fit, But apparently I insulted him bitterly [after] he said he couldn't read any of my books, except a few chapters in Augie; the rest was nonsense to him and he failed to understand how they could be published profitably. I said after all he was not a trained reader, but devoted himself to business and love. He was offended and said I didn't *respect* him, and that I was a terrible snob. I thought I was being angelically mild, and put my arms about him and said I was his loving brother, wasn't that better than heaping up grievances? Finally I melted him from his touchiness. He freezes when he's offended, and if you think *I'm* vulnerable. I recommend you study him.

Bellow also revealed that when Edward Shils, his Jewish friend and colleague at the university, heard about the tension between the Bellow brothers, he gave Saul "a long lecture on the touchiness of Jews."[32]

Susan resented having to move to Chicago on any long-term basis. But after Saul was reappointed to the English Department at the university, followed by a five-year contract as a professor in the prestigious Committee on Social Thought, there was little choice about where they would live.

Bellow's colleagues on the committee included a historian of religious thought, Mircea Eliade; classicists David Grene and James Redfield; economist Frederick Hayek; John U. Nef, a historian and founder and chair of the committee; and sociologist Edward Shils, who was the most influential force behind Bellow's appointment. Nef hoped to bring together not only scholars but people "in other creative walks of life than the academic."[33] No such individual was on the committee, and Shils, a friend of Bellow's since the 1930s, thought Saul was a perfect candidate.

Many people thought that Shils, a short, stocky man with red hair going gray, who carried a cudgel-like walking stick, had come from England. He did teach there half the year and sported something of a British accent. But Shils, like Bellow, was a descendant of *ostjuden*, Jews of East European descent, and his parents were working-class. And, like Bellow, Shils was openly Jewish and loved Yiddish. One of his favorite Yiddish words was *chachem* or *chachema*, meaning a wise and erudite man or woman. According to his friend, writer Joseph Epstein, Shils, himself brilliant and greatly learned, "always said [*chachem*] sarcastically," except when applied to Bellow. Shils, despite his merciless belittling of Bellow's "immigrant ways," became Bellow's closest colleague at the university, and for nearly ten years Shils played an important and supportive role in Bellow's life. As Epstein put it, Shils was fierce in his allegiances.[34]

Bellow had fierce allegiances of his own, some of which Susan felt bitter about. She begrudged Bellow's attachment to Chicago, the city of their youth, and referred to him—apparently contemptuously—as her "ghetto lover." Was she alluding to the East European roots of Bellow's extended family, to which he was also unwaveringly attached and to which he returned so often in his writing? Or was Susan referring to the Black citizens in Hyde Park, several million of whom surrounded the university on three sides? It is a curiosity, often noted by other writers, that this Black neighborhood was called a ghetto, while the beleaguered, much smaller encampment of mostly white academics in its midst was not so labeled.[35]

"Hyde Park is now an enclave in Black Chicago where gangs roam the streets," Bellow wrote sadly to Ruth Miller. But then he wrote something perplexing, or perhaps just sardonic: "One ghetto more. Maybe that's among the attractions that drew me back."[36] Still, it is more likely that in using the term *ghetto lover* Susan had been thinking not about Blacks but about Jews, and in particular Bellow's Jews.

Susan was of German descent, and her father belonged to the Standard Club, a German Jewish association, as distinct from the Covenant Club, Maury's gathering place for *ostjuden*. She had little patience with Bellow's devotion to his East European family and their history, and even less with his actual relatives. On one occasion at Tivoli, a carful of Saul's kin from Montreal had come for dinner. Susan found them "crude." She was offended by their voices, their behavior, and the bottles of Pepsi-Cola, rather than glasses of wine, that found their way to her expensive antique dining room table. When the relatives began to sing Yiddish songs, Susan had about had it, and she complained bitterly afterward. Another time, Bellow, indulging in one of his favorite amusements, took out photographs from the family album; Susan wanted no part of it.[37]

Nor did she want any part of Bellow's attachment to his old Humboldt Park Division Street friends and the culture of the 1930s and '40s which she associated with the higgledy-piggledy Yiddishkeit of Bellow's youth. The attachment for Saul was deep and enduring. Sharing memories in 1990 with Albert Glotzer, his lifelong Chicago friend, Bellow wrote, "On gloomy days these recollections cheer me up."[38] Saul "wonder[ed] what it is that fascinates us about the old city. I suppose we had instinctively understood that it filled our need for poetry." Whatever the case, it seemed to Bellow that on the streets of Chicago, Jews made "excellent use of the liberty we enjoyed as schoolboys."[39]

It was Bellow's permanent connection to his past among his Jewish friends, as well as his fiction, and his distinction as a writer that enabled those friends, as Mel Tumin put it, to put their identities together. "We learned from him," Tumin said, "the importance of applying to the world the force of one's own being; of harnessing one's powers and pressing down with them on the refractory materials of experience and imposing on that experience, a shape and a vision that one could call one's own."[40]

Dave Peltz, Bellow's lifelong Tuley High School and Division Street pal, visited the Bellows occasionally and attested to Susan's distance from the old neighborhood. Dave, according to Barbara Wiesenfeld, one of Susan's friends, was earthy; Susan was not. Bellow and Peltz "had a lot of Yiddishkeit; she didn't have enough," though she was connected to her own brand of Jewishness.[41] As Dave put it, Susan "was an upper-middle-class Jewish lady whose father came from the West Side of Chicago" and fought his way out and into becoming one of the more distinguished bone surgeons in the city. For the less-than-glamorous past, hers or Bellow's, Susan had no nostalgia.[42]

She had no use either for Bellow's academic colleagues. In a letter to a Tivoli friend, Susan complained that these scholars were less interesting than the porpoises in the aquarium. She complained, too, of how hard it was to be a writer's wife. "I'm just Mrs. Bellow," she said, even though, earlier in their relationship, Susan had liked to introduce herself as Bellow's date or girlfriend. "Life here in this gray, gloomy city," she seems to have decided, "is somewhat less than amusing."[43]

Even though, according to one friend, "Susie was angry from day one of the marriage," there were occasional expressions of happiness. Two years into the marriage, almost to the day, Susan thought everything was "simply splendid. I've never felt better or looked better if I am to believe my uxorious husband."[44] But some of the couple's incompatibilities, obvious from the start, made it nearly inevitable that the relationship would unspool when seriously challenged.

The spring of 1964 was a chaotic time for the Bellows. Susan was up at night with a new baby, Daniel Oscar, born March 17. Saul, still haunted by the death in October 1963 of Oscar Tarcov, for whom Daniel was middle-named, and feeling miserably guilty for not having worked up the courage to attend Tarcov's funeral, was also up at night—writing, and thinking about the thinning of his contemporaries. First Isaac Rosenfeld at thirty-eight, and now Oscar, carried off by a heart attack, at forty-eight. Two-thirds of the Tuley High School triumvirate of budding novelists, gone. "I'd rather die myself," Bellow wrote to Berryman, "than endure these deaths one after another of my dearest friends. It wears out the heart."[45]

A few days after the funeral, Saul did show up at the home of Edith Tarcov, Oscar's widow, a friend with whom he had talked often about literature before and after Oscar's death. The literary critic Ted Solataroff recalled that Bellow, even though distraught, was "very tender" that day at the Tarcov home. In what seemed like self-criticism, Bellow told Solataroff that Oscar, with only one published novel, may not have had a successful life as a writer, but he had had a truly successful life as a man.[46] Similarly, he wrote to Nathan, Oscar's young son, telling him that his father's "sort of human being is very rare." Anticipating the conclusion of *Herzog*, his sixth novel soon to be published, Bellow told Nathan that Oscar had "invested his life in relationships. In making such a choice a man sooner or later realizes that to love others is his answer to inevitable death."[47] No doubt, Bellow, making these observations, was thinking about his substantial responsibility in making a mess of his personal life—twice divorced and for the most part separated from his boys.

Whatever he was thinking, Bellow now dedicated himself more than ever to achievement in the world of letters. Through the spring and summer nights, he worked hard and long on the last thirty pages of *Herzog*. He was also continually revising his play *The Last Analysis*, a parody of reductive Freudian personality myths, which he thought was headed for Broadway. What new difficulties there were between Saul and Susan in this period after the birth of Daniel in March is not clear, but that there was serious trouble roiling beneath the surface of the marriage became evident in August on Martha's Vineyard.

There was a steady stream of guests and visitors to the standard A-frame house on Menemsha Pond that the Bellows had rented again that summer. Directors, actors, and drama critics, mostly Jewish, including Robert Brustein, stopped in or stayed for a time, as did publishers, lawyers, and the novelists William Styron and Lillian Hellman. According to Barbara Hanson, a recent graduate of Radcliff and the family's au pair, Hellman "came over all the time. She wanted to be in Bellow's orbit."[48] But Saul, Hanson thought, wasn't interested in celebrity. It was Susan who "just sort of swanned around; she *loved* being Mrs. Bellow. It was her career," Hanson wrote in her journal: "Susan just wanted to go out to dinner all the time and play tennis with the swells." Saul, on the other hand, made it clear that he just wanted to work; he would not tolerate being disturbed during his writing time—every day from nine to one.

Outwardly, life seemed calm. Bellow was "cheerful" much of the time and was playful with seven-year-old Adam, who visited for nearly a month. Hanson recognized that Saul felt genuine affection for his children; but "it's all very sad," she said, "the divorces and all." She was "sure" that Bellow loved Susan, but she could "sense Mr. Bellow's intense feeling of aloneness." There's Gregory and Adam, and now Daniel, Hanson wrote, "but it's oddly enough still not a whole family." Saul, she noted, "is the only connecting link between his three sons, and his family life will always be a bit incomplete."

There were other worrisome signs, in addition to those observed by Barbara Hanson, that the Bellows' marriage was in distress. Susan, downplaying the deterioration of the relationship, wrote to a friend that her life with Saul had "the usual storm of our domestic life."[49] But arguments seemed to occur with increasing frequency; Susan, trying to dismiss them, told the au pair that altercations were a normal part of marriage. "People fight," she said; "it's a fact of life."[50]

When Saul's lawyer and Jewish friend Marshall Holleb and his wife, Doris, visited, they were greeted at the ferry by Susan wearing curlers in her hair and in a foul mood. At the house, Bellow, fuming, let Susan, and presumably the Hollebs, know that he was embarrassed by her appearance. "It was one of the more unpleasant times," Holleb remembered. After ten days the Hollebs departed, convinced that the Bellow marriage was in deep trouble.[51]

It was clear to Barbara Hanson and to most visitors and guests at Martha's Vineyard that Bellow felt lovingly toward his kids and seemed to like having them around. Visitors weren't likely to know, however, that it was the everyday tasks of raising children, the dreary monotony of caring for them, that he found insufferable. The immediacy of a child also meant that Bellow himself was no longer the most important person in the family whose needs required attention. That moment of recognition for him came in each of Saul's marriages at different times. He left Anita when Greg was eight, left Sasha when Adam was two, and would leave Susan around the time Daniel turned two. It is hard to argue with any conviction that Bellow, a serial philanderer, who expected his wives to do all (or nearly all) the work of child-raising, did no serious wrong in these relationships. But it is also relatively easy to show that Bellow's women (Anita less so) played their own major role in chasing him away. The Hollebs, witnesses to the turmoil on Martha's Vineyard, predicted that Saul and Susan would soon divorce.[52] It took two more years. In the meantime, there was the phenomenon of *Herzog*.

"If I am out of my mind, it's all right with me, thought Moses Herzog." So reads the familiar first line of the novel, but it could just as easily have been the last line. Indeed, it does turn up again near the very close of the book. It is an indication that Herzog, having been badly shaken by tumultuous divorce proceedings and other untoward experiences, is back to strength and relative confidence following a moving, byzantine, often comically picaresque quest for insight and revelation.

At heart, *Herzog* is a droll portrait of the psychological drowning and then relative resuscitation of an educated man, a struggling professor of history trying to write a sequel to his successful first book on Christianity and Romanticism. But his roughly drafted manuscript remains mostly untouched, while he spends much of the weeklong time span of the novel in his dilapidated country house in the Berkshires compulsively writing letters—never sent—to relatives and friends, famous men dead and alive, "everyone under the sun."[53]

Herzog has withdrawn from the hustle and bustle of the city in order to get a grip on himself and the world because he fears his sanity is failing him. The artifice of unsent letters allows Bellow in *Herzog* more than in any other of his novels to address more directly the questions that bedeviled a postwar liberal conscience. The letters are summoned up by reminiscences, anger, and love. They are heavy with intellectual and philosophical questions; but, often laden, too, with sarcasm, humor, and twisted aphorisms, they acknowledge the parody of his dilemma. He writes, for example, to Martin Heidegger, the German philosopher and seminal thinker—during the war a supporter of the Nazi Party—asking a question both serious and ironic: "*Dear Doktor Professor Heidegger, I should like to know what you mean by the expression "the fall into the quotidian." When did this fall occur? Where were we standing when it happened?*"[54]

Herzog complains that Heidegger and the contemporary society he inhabits love "*apocalypses too much,*" and as for the adoration of "*crisis ethics and florid extremism with its thrilling language,*" Moses is having none of it: "*Excuse me, no.*" Referring to the disasters of modernization, with emphasis on the Holocaust, when souls flew "*out in smoke from the extermination chimneys,*" Herzog writes, "*I've had all the monstrosity I want.*"[55] By the time Bellow had started writing *Herzog*, and possibly much earlier, he knew that three of his father's sisters, his mother's brother, and other relatives who had remained in the Pale had been lost to the anti-semitism of the Nazis and their willing executioners.[56]

Herzog desires to be a good man. Whether or not there has been, as Heidegger argues, a "fall" from grace or from some other near-perfect state, Moses wants to avoid evil and "do the right thing." But in the crisis of his life—a twofold betrayal by his best friend, Valentine Gersbach, and his wife, Madeleine—Herzog looks to his classical education to furnish him a way forward. Soon enough, of course, he discovers the limitations of his formal education in regard to his struggle with life's true calamities.

It was through his own frightful marital experience that Bellow had come to see "the inapplicability of . . . higher learning" in dealing with personal problems. Indeed, he told Keith Botsford that when put to the test, his "higher education" blocked any insight into his own mess. "It didn't work," Bellow said: "I began to understand the irrelevancy of it, to recoil in disappointment from it." But he also saw the comedy of it. He has Herzog asking himself, "What are you proposing to do when your wife takes a lover? Pull Spinoza from the shelf and look into what he says about adultery? About human bondage?" Where was Spinoza, Moses wants to know, when his wife's lover snaked his way into his confidence?[57]

Bellow was not against "higher education"; he did, after all, enter the field himself. He had contempt for education strictly geared to the practical, to the merely instructive, or to an over-emphasis on "knowing the facts," even the facts about Spinoza or Aristotle. This kind of education led to mere "head-culture," Bellow argued, the kind found among journalists, the "professoriate," or the chattering, opinionated classes generally.

Bellow, trying to "explain" *Herzog* to yet another interviewer, said that Moses "looks for repose in what he had been before he accumulated this mass of 'learning.'" He, like Henderson before him and like Bellow himself, "returns to Square One" and asks "the essential question, 'What was it that I ought to have been doing? Or, what was my created soul? And, where is it now?'"[58]

"In our greatest confusion," Bellow wrote elsewhere, "there is still an open channel to the soul. It may be difficult to find because by midlife it is overgrown, and some of the wildest thickets that surround it grow out of what we describe as our education. But the channel is always there and it is our business"—as it is Herzog's—"to keep it open, to have access to the deepest part of ourselves."[59]

Much of what happens in *Herzog* is a reconstruction of the life Bellow lived with Sasha while he was writing *Henderson* and starting on his new novel. Anyone who knew Saul and Sasha knew that the protagonists Moses and Madeleine Herzog were faithful recreations of the Bellows' own marital roller coaster of accusation and counteraccusation. But tens of thousands of readers who knew little or nothing about Bellow's second marriage came away from *Herzog* with wonder and admiration for the writer's masterful autopsy of a matrimony on the rocks. And even those who knew that Moses and Madeleine were the creatively reimagined Mr. and Mrs. Bellow recognized that *Herzog* was an example of Bellow's remarkable ability to transform personal experience into art.[60]

Madeleine, her behavior, indulgences and tastes, her moony adopted Catholicism, and her treachery, was inspired by Sasha, but she is not Sasha, as critics and Sasha herself knew. Bellow as the creator of the characters in *Herzog*, however, had the upper hand and used it vengefully. His peculiar portrayal of the proverbial battle between the sexes opens with serious questions about being and becoming and ways of knowing. "One of the things that bothers Herzog, that eats at him," Bellow explained to an interviewer, "is the fact that his extensive education doesn't work for him. . . . But the [real] question in *Herzog* is whether it works for anyone." Higher education can't "teach" you how to be good. Or, really, why you ought to be good. Herzog learns that "you can't apply the lessons of high culture to the facts of ordinary life." That, Bellow said "is where the comedy comes from."[61]

It took Bellow more than three years and more than fifteen drafts to write the novel because he found himself being drawn too strongly to seriousness, to writing a kind of manual about the consequences of bad behavior.[62] He knew the book had to be funny as well as illuminating and provocative; he was "especially unhappy," even years later, that critics, especially those in academia, had often "missed the humor of *Herzog*."[63] Still, as late as 1999, he told Norman Manea, that *Herzog* "raises questions that to this day [he hasn't] got the answers for."[64]

There is comedy in Madeleine, but she is mostly drawn with "pure venom," a caricature of the ruthless emasculating woman, and her portrait is a classic example of male retaliation. Figuratively, she does "eat green salad, and drink human blood," but she barely resembles a conceivable person. No matter. Moses Herzog evokes "troubles" that stand well outside the ruins of the author's marriage.[65]

In his self-examination, Herzog admits that he had "mismanaged everything—everything. His life was as the phrase goes ruined."[66] He had been "a bad husband—twice. Daisy, his first wife, he had treated miserably. Madeleine, his second, had tried to do him in. To his son and his daughter he was a loving but bad father. To his own parents he had been an ungrateful child. To his country, an indifferent citizen. To his brothers and his sister, affectionate but remote. With his friends, an egotist. With love, lazy. With brightness, dull. With power, passive. With his own soul, evasive."

He positively enjoys "the hardness and factual rigor of his judgment," but the evasion of his soul continues to trouble him as he faces the precariousness of his disintegrated family life.[67] He has multiple wives and children, but they are apart and adrift. Herzog knows that neither his "higher learning" nor his high-minded thinking—which only adds "a second realm of confusion"—will save him from emotional turmoil.[68] But he can help himself, he thinks, by searching through some of "the wildest thickets" of midlife for that "open channel to the soul," the source of his true feelings. Herzog believes he can find that source in memories of his early family life in Jewish immigrant Montreal and Chicago. In some of the most luminous, lyric writing of his entire oeuvre, Bellow imports readers back to the "ancient time . . . remoter than Egypt" in Herzog's childhood on Napoleon Street, where he and his brothers put on their skullcaps and prayed together, "Ma tovu ohaleha Yaakov . . ." / "How goodly are thy tents, O Israel."[69] Repeatedly, in his novels and stories, Bellow's protagonist dreams back to the days of his childhood on Saint Dominique Street in Montreal or to the later years just east of Humboldt Park in Chicago, neighborhoods riddled with Yiddishkeit.

The portrait of Herzog's mother, though drawn with immense fondness and nuance, is finally that of an Orthodox woman of her day: doting, devoted, and self-sacrificing; she "did the wash, and mourned" for her old life in St. Petersburg. Bellow, like Herzog, was loved by his mother unconditionally. He may have been, in his fictional portraits as well as in his real-life lovers, trying to retrieve or recapture her. Herzog recalls, for example, the motherly devotion of his Polish mistress, Wanda. What made her "kindness even more significant," Herzog felt, "was the radiant . . . buxom beauty of the woman." Herzog is also deeply moved by the firm breasts of Ramona, another mistress. "He might think himself a moralist," Herzog thought, "but the shape of a woman's breasts matters greatly."[70] These illustrations, and there are countless more in his other novels, strongly suggest that Bellow has a fixation with the mother figure.

Herzog's father, Jonah, a former student of Talmud, was frightened enough by financial instability to take a chance at the risky business of bootlegging. His older brother Shura, "with staring disingenuous eyes was plotting to master the world, to become a millionaire." Herzog also remembers well and with some reverence his brother Willie struggling bravely with his asthmatic fits and "his soft prim" sister Helen playing the piano. On summer nights she played with the window open, and the clear notes of Haydn and Mozart floated out into the street. "Oh, the music! thought Herzog."[71]

Crazy Napoleon Street, "flogged with harsh weather—the bootlegger's boys reciting ancient prayers. To this Moses's heart was attached with great power." Here, Herzog thought, was "a wider range of human feeling than he had ever again been able to find. . . . What was wrong with Napoleon Street? thought Herzog. All he ever wanted was there."[72]

Well, not quite. Bellow's vast pictographic gifts shouldn't distract us from the gulf that exists between yearning for a place and the possibly idealized place itself. A long way from his old, poor Jewish neighborhood, the adult Herzog knows he has wronged many people and has committed sins "of some kind against his own heart," all while searching for a grand synthesis "of higher values"—courage, goodness, love, duty—virtues thought to have disappeared but that Bellow thinks "are just hiding everywhere."[73] He sends Herzog out to find them and to internalize them at a deeper level of understanding.[74]

In this pursuit, Herzog, the intellectual wanderer, falls into situations both poignant and humorous, involving lovers and lawyers, cars and courtrooms, cops and guns and jail cells, imaginary conversations, and friends and enemies. Yet even in his state of "wild internal disorder," Herzog reflects on his difficulties with droll self-deprecation: "I fall upon the thorns of life, I bleed. And what next? I get laid, I take a short holiday, but very soon after I fall upon those same thorns with gratification in pain, or suffering in joy—who knows what the mixture is! What good, what lasting good is there in me? Is there nothing else between birth and death but what I can get out of this perversity—only a favorable balance of disorderly emotions? No freedom? Only impulses? And what about all the good I have in my heart—doesn't it mean anything?"[75]

He doesn't find perfect answers to his questions; but along the way, Moses, like Bellow himself, tries to establish a peaceful coexistence with the world of the modern city, which threatens the absorption or destruction of the self. He has a "country home" in the Berkshires, which allows him respite from urban excesses—"*his* Chicago: massive, clumsy, amorphous, smelling of mud and decay, dog turds; sooty facades, slabs of structural *nothing*."[76] Herzog promises himself that he is "not going to be a victim" of his environment or his emotional confusion—"I hate the victim bit," he insists.[77]

Attempting to preserve his stability and integrity and protect the spirit of freedom in himself, he resists getting caught up in whatever he sees as socially dangerous or evil. He is fierce in his denunciation, for example, of the nihilistic positions taken by modernist intellectuals and writers whose output is imbued with T. S. Eliot's pessimistic "Wasteland outlook."[78] This generation, he fumes, "thinks—and this is its thought of thoughts—that nothing faithful, vulnerable, fragile can be durable or have any true power."[79]

Toward his ambitious goal of eviscerating nihilism by recovering value and meaning in life, Herzog reluctantly agrees to review an overly long monograph by history professor Egbert Shapiro. He is dumbfounded by and rejects the pessimistic postures taken by Shapiro in his masterwork. It irritates Herzog that the professor is comfortable with the views of Spengler and Freud, Nietzsche and Eliot. He writes,

> Are all the traditions used up, the beliefs done for. . . . Has the filthy moment come when moral feeling dies, conscience disintegrates, and respect for liberty, law, public decency, all the rest, collapses in cowardice, decadence, blood? . . . Visions of darkness and evil can't be passed over. But . . . visions of genius [quickly] become the canned goods of the intellectuals . . . the cheap mental stimulants of Alienation, the cant and rant of pipsqueaks about Inauthenticity and Forlornness. I can't accept this foolish dreariness. We are talking

> about the whole life of mankind. . . . It torments me to insanity that you should be so misled. A merely aesthetic critique of modern history! After the wars and mass killings!

And then in marvelous, darting Jewish shorthand, Herzog writes, "You are too intelligent for this. You inherited rich blood. Your father peddled apples."[80]

Herzog stakes out a very different position in his own "work-in-progress," in which he attempts to destroy the philosophy of nihilism. The concepts of Christianity and Romanticism, he argues, comprise the foundation of twentieth-century thought, and they are positively antithetical to humanism. The excesses of romantic individualism, the exaggerated glorification of the Self, produced—as Herzog recognized and Bellow wrote elsewhere—"a disgust and hatred for the Self" and a concomitant "admiration for . . . hardness, even . . . brutality."[81]

Not satisfied "simply to dismiss a romantic outmoded corruption of the self, the dominant strain of modern literature," Bellow maintained, "curses the self. It hates it. It rends it, it annihilates it."[82] Conversely, Christianity and Romanticism are essentially detrimental because they encourage secession on individual terms from the collective life; they encourage transcendence *of* the human rather than *within* the human realm, as called for by the Hebrew prophets. These prophets, Herzog knew, had an unshakable faith in human moral improvement even while predicting doom and destruction. Christianity and Romanticism, on the other hand, he wrote, regarded the world as a dreary place on the edge of apocalypse and sought refuge in one kind of utopia or another.[83] Moses Herzog reflects, "I a Jew . . . no matter how hard I tried . . . would never grasp the Christian . . . world idea, forever alien to me."[84]

His study, he says, is about "a new angle on the modern condition, showing how life can be lived by *renewing universal connections,* overturning the last of the Romantic errors about the uniqueness of the Self; revising the old Western Faustian ideology; investigating the social meaning of nothingness."[85] He rejects without reservation the key conviction of nothingness that "the world is evil" and "must be destroyed" so that it will emerge again reborn, cleansed.[86]

Destroy the world? No, but that it must be cleansed is something Herzog learns or relearns several times in the course of his trip from self-proclaimed madness to stability and calm. In a city courtroom, Herzog, dealing with his own existential pain, witnesses the trial of two defendants, a man and a woman, themselves victims of disease, abuse, and murderous poverty, who have killed their small boy after years of neglect and beatings. Medical witnesses attest to unusually heavy bruises everywhere on the kid—back and legs, shins, and the belly in the region of the genitals. In the end, the woman had hurled the boy against a wall, killing him, while the man, her lover, looked on apathetically from bed.

"I fail to understand," thinks Herzog. "This is the difficulty with people who spend their lives in humane studies and therefore imagine [that] once cruelty has been described in books it is ended." For the first time, Herzog must recognize human suffering for what it is—"the monstrousness of life." When, near the end of the trial, the last witness stands up, Moses also stands. Reaching the corridor, he says, to himself, "Oh my God!" and in "trying to speak discover[s] an acrid fluid in his mouth that ha[s] to be swallowed." He feels stifled and sick, with a "repulsive headache, piercing and ugly." He concentrates "with all his might—mind and heart," trying to "obtain something for the murdered child. But how?" Cry, pray? Is there anything "in modern, post . . . post-Christian America to pray for? Justice—justice and mercy?"[87]

At the center of this courtroom episode, almost too much for Herzog to bear, is the deepest kind of sadness over blatant injustice in modern civilization, which produces victims who suffer, who in turn produce yet other victims. And what redeeming meaning can there be, Herzog thinks, in a mother's mortal beating of her child? Here is an outrageous evil that cannot be explained by any conceivable intellectual paradigm or theological notion of redemption or sanctification. Moses comes to recognize, partly through the trial he has witnessed, that he himself has been selfish. So absorbed in emotional turbulence and intellectual pain, and so overly attentive to theoretical abstractions, he has neglected his own daughter, June. Guilt is added to his burden of unsolicited suffering.

One of the more prominent phenomena experienced by Bellow's Jewish protagonists is suffering; but in no way does this assertion support the argument made by literary historian John Clayton that "anguish is particularly Jewish." Clayton goes completely astray by his wrongheaded reading of Bellow and Jewish literature generally, claiming that Jewish writing, in whatever language—Yiddish, Hebrew, Russian, or English—reveals a tradition of "Jewish despair, Jewish guilt, and self-hatred." Clayton sees Bellow's male figures as well within this tradition and proclaims that Asa Leventhal (*The Victim*), Tommy Wilhelm (*Seize the Day*), Eugene Henderson, and Moses Herzog are "pathological social masochists, filled with guilt . . . *needing to suffer* and fail."[88]

On the contrary, as biblical scholar and professor of comparative literature Robert Alter has persuasively demonstrated in his masterworks, "Jews by and large, did not revel in suffering." Rather than favoring "fashionably modern views of *Angst*" or existential hopelessness, Jews generally rejected suffering as a means of individual fulfillment.[89] Herzog, like Tamkin in *Seize the Day*, sees that excessive or persistent suffering ought not to be embraced or adopted as a form of identity. Bellow's view is that "suffering breaks people" more often than it wakes them up or "bursts the spirit's sleep." Instead, it "crushes them, and is simply unilluminating."[90] Like many romantics in the eighteenth and early nineteenth centuries, Bellow in the twentieth believed that some suffering could make one more maturely human, but he did not ignore or minimize the pain of suffering and was well aware that "an excess of suffering does not foster character but destroys it."[91] In another unsent letter, this to a scholarly rival, Moses goes on to argue that "the advocacy and praise of suffering," particularly by dogmatic and apocalyptic Christians and modernists, "takes us in the wrong direction, and those of us," he continues, "who remain loyal to civilization must not go for it."[92] This insight, articulated by Herzog, is a profound ingredient of Bellow's understanding of the human condition and is not in any way the fruit of Jewish masochism or self-hatred; it is a product of the convergence of several humanist traditions, including secular Judaism, that support the fundamental importance of the ordinary individual and everyday life with all its joys and sorrows.[93]

After observing the soul-stunning murder trial, Herzog, with an increase in moral clarity, feels ready to confront his disloyal friend and unfaithful wife and to rescue his daughter from what he sees as an unhealthy situation. When trying to get back at his enemies, Moses from time to time intuitively shouts out scriptural phrases: "*Yemach sh'mo!* Let their names be blotted out. They prepared a net for my steps. They digged a pit before me. Break their teeth, O God, in their mouth."[94] Not leaving it to God, however, Moses returns to his family home, finds his father's antique gun, and sets out to murder his former friend Valentine Gersbach. But while hiding outside their house and seeing Gersbach through a window gently giving June a bath, he thinks, "To shoot him—an absurd thought"; indeed, it was an impulse indicative of the nihilism Bellow detested.[95]

Not long before this realization, Herzog had said to himself, "I dislike having a face, a nose, lips, because he [Gersbach] has them."[96] Now, witnessing the love and care implicit in Gersbach's behavior, "an actual person giving an actual bath, the reality of it, the tenderness of such a buffoon to a little child," Herzog sees his enemy as a fellow creature and sees "his intended violence turned into *theater*, into something ludicrous."[97] He "congratulated himself on his luck. His breath came back to him; and how good it felt to breathe!"[98] Understanding that good and evil are inextricably linked, Moses acknowledges that life is far more complex, more subtle, than any theory about it; he recognizes, too, that none of the intellectuals he is addressing can answer his most important question—What does it mean to be a good man?

In conversation with his friend Luke, a zoologist at the University of Chicago, Herzog tries to explain, in biblical cadence, what being a good man means to him: "Let's stick to what matters. I really believe that brotherhood is what makes a man human. If I owe god a human life, this is where I fall down. 'Man liveth not by himself alone but in his brother's face. . . . Each shall behold the Eternal Father and love and joy abound.' When the preachers of dread tell you that others only distract you from metaphysical freedom then you must turn away from them. The real and essential question is one of our employment by other human beings and their employment by us."[99]

Man is vulnerable, Moses feels. His capacity for evil is eternal, but so is his capacity for good.[100] Freud, for whom neither Bellow nor Herzog had much use, wrote that a moral man is one who reacts to temptation without yielding to it, as in Moses's decision not to murder Gersbach.[101] For Herzog and Bellow, however, and by implication for Jews generally, man is moral not only or primarily when he suppresses the bad but when he aspires to do right.

There is a maddening moment when Herzog, in deep trouble and emotionally confused, experiences a desperation that summons an inner voice saying, "You think history is the history of loving hearts? You fool! Look at these millions of dead, can you pity them, feel for them. You can nothing! There were too many. We burned them to ashes, we buried them with bulldozers. History is the history of cruelty, not love. . . . If the old God exists he must be a murderer." But Herzog shuts up that inner voice, thinking, "It's easier not to exist altogether than accuse God. Far more simple. Cleaner. But no more of that!"[102]

"I continue to believe in God." Moses thinks, "though never admitting it." Our attraction to the good in our souls, as well as our ability to transcend evil in a hellish world of our own making, is what Herzog seems to mean by "God." And to this God he jots several lines: "How my mind has struggled to make coherent sense. I have not been too good at it. But have desired to do your knowable will, taking it, and you, without symbols. Everything of intensest significance. Especially if divested of me."[103]

It appears that for Herzog, God is authentic illumination of experience, not diluted by fear of death, ego, institutions, rituals, or theoretical constructs. He confesses that in the conduct of his life he had "willfully misread my contract." His thoughts still not completely straight about the meaning of life and death, he decides he must choose life—Bellow's unwavering leitmotif—"He must live. Complete his assignment whatever that was."[104] Is this the end of an obsession with the need to explain and its replacement by a perspective of contemplative approximation? Perhaps.

Very near the conclusion of the novel, Moses writes to a former therapist, saying he "is much better now at ambiguities. I think I can say, however, that I have been spared the chief ambiguity that afflicts intellectuals, and this is that civilized individuals hate and resent the civilization that makes their lives possible. What they love is an imaginary human situation invented by their own genius and which they believe is the only true and the only human reality. How odd! But the best-treated, most favored and intelligent part of any society is often the most ungrateful. Ingratitude, however, is its social function. Now there's an ambiguity for you!"[105]

As Bellow says elsewhere, there are "human characteristics or qualities that have no need of justification" or explanation. "Existence, quite apart from our judgments, has value," and

"Herzog wants to live!"[106] When Moses returns to his country home, musty, messy, and in much need of repair, he puts away thoughts of hammers, paints, and putty—and soon, even letter writing. "Enough of that," he says as he contemplates the natural beauty of the area.[107]

Herzog's brother Will, worried about Moses's mental state, visits the Berkshire house for the first time and looks around, well-intentioned, tender, but with eyes "quietly and firmly shrewd." Herzog easily sees what Will is thinking about his country home, silently expressing it in Yiddish: "*In drerd aufn deck.* The edge of nowhere. Out on the lid of Hell."[108] True, Moses admits, but he is truly hopeful and excited to be back. "I am willing without further exercise in pain to open my heart," Herzog says. "And this needs no doctrine or theology of suffering."[109] Quoting his biblical forebear, Moses calls out, "Here I am. *Hineni*!" Here I am, and ready. In the Torah, the word *Hineni* is spoken eight times, each time signifying a turning point, a readiness, a "potentially life-changing moment," requiring decision, resolution, and action.[110] Rediscovering brotherhood, solidarity, and compassion—virtues he associates with his Jewish heritage—Herzog commits himself to community as "a child of this mass and a brother to all the rest" and acknowledges his moral responsibilities.[111]

"'How I wish it!'" he says, "'How I wish it were so!' How Moses prayed for this!"[112] To make "steady progress from disorder to harmony," so "that the conquest of chaos need not begin anew every day." The road forward he sees clearly now is "to share with other human beings as much as possible and not destroy my remaining years in the same way." Whether or not his commitment will stand the test of time, Moses feels "a deep dizzy eagerness to *begin*."[113]

ELEVEN

WEALTH, FAME, AND JEWISH IDENTITY IN 1960S AMERICA

HERZOG CONCLUDES WITH NEITHER A bang nor a whimper but, as Bellow explained later, "with that very first step . . . the first *real* step" toward the conquest of emotional and intellectual chaos. This is no small victory. "Any man who has rid himself of superfluous ideas in order to take that first step," Bellow maintained, "has done something significant."[1] He has acted. He will judge himself now the way many Jews following an ancient tradition have generally judged themselves and others—not so much by the intellectual content of their beliefs or their ideas or even the faith they hold but by the way they live—by how much they contribute to the overall goodness of the world.

Herzog is often referred to as a comic novel. Indeed, Bellow himself said the book would be "ruined by seriousness." But the writer's effort, drafted ten to fifteen times, is as much a somber meditation, a compelling quarrel with modernism, a case for transcendence, as it is a comedy. Discussing the book, Bellow told a class of university students that life, his life, at "its most serious [is] some kind of religious enterprise, not one that has to do with the hurly-burly of existence."[2] Later, he reinforced this idea by telling an interviewer that he had earned a degree in anthropology and had read thinkers from Aristotle to Adorno, from Freud to Foucault, and from Machiavelli to Marx; but, like *Herzog*, he had over the years "become aware of the conflict between the modern university education I received and those things that I felt in my soul most deeply."[3]

According to educated modern man, Bellow went on, "I'm not even supposed to have a soul"; for most intellectuals, "the soul is out of bounds." But life has "a much larger meaning that [he] had been ignoring—a transcendent meaning." There are, he concluded, "persistent ideas," hopes, and beliefs, the truth of which cannot be "proven" but "which we recognize when we meet them in literature."[4] Readers might meet these ideas in *Herzog*, but Bellow did not expect the book to be a bestseller. After all, how many people would read, no less buy, a novel about a professor of little prominence who writes letters to dead people?

Bellow thought the book would sell fewer than 10,000 copies, but in less than a year it had sold 142,000 in hardcover.[5] Arguably Bellow's best and most Jewish book, *Herzog* completed a run of forty-two weeks on the *New York Times* Best Seller list, holding the number-one spot in fiction for more than half a year just ahead of John le Carré's *The Spy Who Came in from the Cold*. The novel went on to win the National Book Award in 1965, Bellow's second, and became an international triumph, earning many awards, including the prestigious Prix International de Litterature.[6] The commercial and critical success of *Herzog*, Bellow later believed, lay in its appeal "to the unconscious sympathies of many people."[7]

The publication of *Herzog* was a breakthrough moment in the phenomenal rise of Jewish American fiction. "Over the past ten or 15 years," the literary critic Julian Moynihan proclaimed in the *New York Times*, "Jewish writers—Bernard Malamud, J.D. Salinger, Norman Mailer, Philip Roth, inter alia—have emerged as a dominant movement in our literature. *Herzog*, in several senses, is the great pay-off book of that movement. It is a masterpiece, the first the movement has produced."[8]

In the wake of *Herzog*'s success, Bellow told an interviewer that when he wrote, he had "in mind another human being who will understand me. I count on this. Not on perfect understanding, which is Cartesian, but on approximate understanding, which is Jewish. And on a meeting of sympathies which is human."[9] He knew, he said, from the mail he had received that the book addressed a common predicament. It "appealed to Jewish readers," of course, but also "to those who have been divorced, to those who talk to themselves . . . to readers of paperbacks, autodidacts," and perhaps most important, to those who shared Moses Herzog's rejection of nihilism and inevitable doom, "to those who yet hope to live awhile."[10]

Suddenly, Saul Bellow was a wealthy man. "Guys I'm rich," he told his old Chicago buddies, and if the shouting got too loud, he said, "I can always stuff my ears with money."[11] But Bellow's joy was diminished by the death of Pat Covici, his friend and editor at Viking, who had suffered a heart attack on October 14, 1964, the month after *Herzog* was published and only days before the book went to the top of the bestseller list. "I loathe funerals and wasn't planning to attend," Bellow wrote to the novelist Norman Rosten, "but I did love the old man dearly and at the last minute I found I was unable to sit it out in Chicago."[12]

Bellow was also unhappy over the mortifying flop of his play *The Last Analysis,* mostly judged a long-winded monologue. He wanted more rhetoric in theatrical productions but got more than he bargained for. The rhetoric in his play was too long—"Eight hours too long," he said only half-jokingly.[13] More deflating for Saul was the reaction of his brothers to his substantial earnings. Although Maury remarked that "the kid finally did it," Bellow's status in the family remained inferior—mostly because Maury and middle brother Sam had long been involved in ever-expanding enterprises raking in far more money.[14]

Feeling the everlasting need to prove himself to his brothers and even more so to his father, Bellow, who had written vividly in his fiction about the forcefulness of family bonds, the "immigrant loving" that energized his feelings toward his siblings, complained disconsolately that he was still looked down on by his relatives. Not making the "truckloads of money" his brothers did, Bellow described himself, in the eyes of certain members of his family, as just "some schmuck with a pen."[15] Neither Maury nor Sam nor any of the relatives seemed to understand that the critical and commercial success of *Herzog* had thrust Bellow to the center stage of American literature and turned "the tormented Jewish male" into a cultural prototype, a new literary hero, the very symbol of man's alienation in the modern world.

With the royalties Bellow received from the strong sales of *Herzog*, he and Susan purchased a co-op apartment in an imposing building on South Shore Drive in Chicago overlooking Jackson Park bordering Lake Michigan—a grand neighborhood far from declining Humboldt Park where Bellow had grown up. Aspiring to create a writer's salon, Susan, resuming her compulsion to shop and decorate, filled the apartment with loads of expensive furniture and, as Bellow put it, "more mirrors than Versailles." He found the new environment stifling and thought his wife was trying "to spend him into the ground." He was especially distressed by the study Susan had designed for him, more like a woman's private dressing room than a place for creative work.[16]

The marriage, doomed even before *Herzog* reached the bookstores, took another hit in arguments over the apartment. Bellow was desperate for a real home, but he found Susan's bourgeois version of it oppressive. Dave Peltz, Saul's old Division Street friend, never warmly welcomed by Susan when he visited Bellow's apartment, sat with Saul on a bench in Jackson Park across the way. Dave, recognizing that Bellow was "nearly hyperventilating," said, "Saul, you can't breathe; get the fuck out of that relationship. It's smothering you."[17] George Swiebel, a Bellovian elaboration of Peltz in *Humboldt's Gift*, warns Charlie Citrine that he's "not getting enough air with that woman. You look as if you're suffocating. Your tissues aren't getting any oxygen. She'll give you cancer." "Oh," Citrine says, "she may think she's offering me the blessings of an American marriage. Real Americans are supposed to suffer with their wives, and wives with husbands. Like Mr. and Mrs. Abraham Lincoln. It's the classic US grief, and a child of immigrants like me ought to be grateful. For a Jew it's a step up."[18]

Susan did damage, but Saul had equally significant responsibility for the destruction of his third marriage. There was infidelity on his part as early as 1962, barely a year after his wedding; it continued until he separated from Susan in 1966.

In the meantime, *Herzog*'s many months on the bestseller list made Saul Bellow a household name. A poll conducted by the *Chicago Sun-Times* found that Bellow by an impressive margin was thought to have written "the most distinguished fiction of the post-war period." Just below Bellow were Nabokov, Faulkner, Malamud, Salinger, Ellison, Mailer, and Hemingway, a stunningly impressive list. In the same poll, three of Bellow's books, *Seize the Day*, *Henderson the Rain King*, and *Herzog*, were ranked among the best American novels written between 1945 and 1965. Convinced as far back as Tuley High School (albeit with an occasional doubt) that he was destined for greatness, Bellow took great satisfaction in his new role, but he began to think it possible that celebrity might eclipse the artist and transform him into a "literary figure," a writer of books known even to people who don't read books.

Still, he rarely turned down a request for an interview. In 1965, he did a "walking tour talk" with Gloria Steinem, no doubt prior to the kerfuffle Bellow got himself into later for his alleged sexism.[19] Steinem, a very attractive former Playboy Bunny, a columnist for *New York* magazine, and later cofounder of *MS.*, a leading feminist periodical, was shepherded by Bellow around Chicago. He was anxious to show off the city that played so powerful a role in shaping him, but given his lascivious history, might Bellow also have been on the make that day?

Whatever the case, he was harmless that afternoon. The tour started with Maxwell Street, where the array of shops, Bellow explained, constituted "an old-style European market." He stopped to chat with a pushcart peddler. "*A gutn tog, fraynt*" (good day or hello friend), he said in Yiddish, followed in English by, "Remember me? I'm the Quotation Man." The vendor nodded in recognition and immediately began to quote Hebrew scripture. Bellow responded in kind.

Further along the way, a shop owner stepped out of his doorway to say hello; he and Bellow shook hands and bantered in Yiddish. Saul told Gloria that he had asked the storekeeper "if he was praying," and the merchant had come back at the novelist with a friendly, impeccable Old World quip: "God is an old man who sleeps all day; why should I disturb him?" Did Bellow pray? He would tell people, sounding much like the old shopkeeper, "I pray but my requirements are trivial; I don't bug God." Prayer was not usually petitionary for Bellow but "above all an act of gratitude for existence . . . an intimate checkup with the headquarters of the universe." He prayed as well, he said, through meditative reading of the Pentateuch in Hebrew.[20] Moving along Maxwell Street, Bellow traded quotations from the Talmud with yet another vendor, who for a few moments turned away from his display of tchotchkes to offer, after what must have been some good-humored but weighty exchanges, a parting remark: "Death awaits us all."[21]

Exiting the market district, Saul and Gloria began discussing Richard Poirier's negative review of *Herzog* in *Partisan Review*. Poirier was an old friend of Jack Ludwig, and his review was not only biased and cranky; it was a hatchet job. Poirier had some positive things to say, especially about the Napoleon Street portions of Bellow's novel, but he mostly complained about the very nature and meaning of the book. Moses Herzog's "pseudo-philosophical" bouts of theory, Poirier contended, were mere "sophomoric taglines" that "don't deserve the status of 'ideas.'"[22]

Bellow explained that he was "fair game now; I am on top and must be cut down."[23] Steinem asked where Poirier taught. "Harvard, of course," Bellow responded with swift disdain. Harvard professors and alumni were a special target for Bellow, and their Jewishness did not protect them. Bellow referred to the literary critic Harry Levin with the unfortunate term "Harvard kike." Indeed, any Ivy League affiliation was for Bellow an abomination; it meant a Jew who very likely had become a de facto WASP—another gatekeeper.

By "gatekeeper," Bellow meant mostly writers with roots in the Old South and the WASP northeast, those members of the native intellectual elite who found the success of Jewish writers insufferable and, as Irving Howe put it, fought to preserve American "purities of speech" from the "usurpers, those Bronx and Brooklyn [and Chicago] wise guys" on the make.[24] Saul, as we have seen, had encountered an early gatekeeper and "reality instructor" in William Frank Bryan, chair of the English Department at Northwestern, who recommended that Bellow not study English in graduate school because of his Jewish immigrant background.[25] There would be many more in Bellow's lifetime who would take to the barricades against Jewish literary influence.

Truman Capote, Katherine Anne Porter, and Gore Vidal, for example, were displeased with the "sudden" appearance of a "Jewish Literary Establishment." Capote, in particular, lamented the rise of what he called "the Jewish Mafia in American letters": a "clique of New York-centered writers," he said, meaning Bellow et al., and critics—Kazin, Howe, Leslie Fiedler, Harold Bloom—"who control much of the literary scene through the influence of the quarterlies and intellectual magazines. All these publications are Jewish-dominated," Capote complained, "and this particular coterie employs them to make or break writers by advancing or withholding attention. They are determined that only members of their particular clique rise to the top."[26]

Backing up a little, Capote without much conviction added that he didn't think there was a "sinister conspiracy" on the part of Jewish writers, and he was generous enough to admit that Malamud, Bellow, Roth, I. B. Singer, and Mailer "are all fine writers." He quickly slipped back, however, into his paranoia about cabals and syndicates, saying, "But they are not the only writers in the country, as the Jewish mafia would have us believe."[27]

What Bellow thought of Capote, none of it positive, was revealed in an interview in 1968. In one of his stories, Capote had written that "Jews ought to be stuffed and put in museums." Bellow laughed and told the interviewer that Capote more rightly belonged there. Actually, Bellow thought Capote "really belong[ed] in Auschwitz on the general's staff . . . in the barracks with a swagger stick."[28] He felt that many writers during the 1950s and '60s "treated their Jewish colleagues with unpardonable shabbiness, and anti-Semitism after the Holocaust," he said, is "absolutely unforgivable."[29]

While Porter and Vidal also used the label "Mafia," they dropped the tag after some blowback and instead focused on what they called the "corruption" of American prose in Jewish fiction. Many years after *The Adventures of Augie March* won the National Book Award in 1954, Porter, still seething with resentment, warned the country that granting Bellow such attention and prestige posed a danger to the English language. By his use of Yiddish words and inflections, Porter said, Bellow was "bastardizing" American writing. Her "people," she claimed, came to Virginia in 1648, and it is "the South and the West" that are the true makers of American literature: "We are in the direct, legitimate line; we are people based in English as our mother tongue, and we do not abuse it or misuse it, and when we speak a word, we know what it means."[30]

But these Jews, Porter said, "these others have fallen into a curious kind of argot, more or less originating in New York." Their idiom, in contrast to that of true Americans, is "a deadly mixture of academic, guttersnipe, gangster, fake-Yiddish"—how would she know?—"and dull odd worn out dirty words." Their writings expose "an appalling bankruptcy in language." And in an apparent state of hysteria, Porter continued, "They hate English and are trying to destroy it along with all other living things they touch."[31]

Only five years after Porter's ranting, Vidal, in *Commentary* of all places, attacked those he labeled "literary gangsters," most of whom were Jewish. In line with Porter, he complained that "confused thinking, poor education, and the incomplete assimilation of immigrant English" promoted with each generation "the degeneration of American prose."[32]

That similar xenophobic grumbles had been articulated in earlier decades by such leading literary figures as Henry James, Dreiser, Fitzgerald, Hemingway, Willa Cather, and e. e. cummings made them no less offensive in the postwar years. Such malicious comments had always bothered Bellow, especially after the torrent of critical and popular acclaim for *Augie*. He "began to discover," he later recalled, "that while I thought I was simply laying an offering on the altar like a faithful petitioner, other people thought I was trying to take over the church. It came at a strange point when I think the WASP establishment was losing confidence in itself, and it felt it was being challenged by Jews, blacks and [other] ethnics." They saw us as "an unwelcome eruption." There was a "pathetic absurdity" to the whole thing: "All we wanted was to add ourselves to the thriving enterprise we loved; no one wanted to take over."[33]

Life magazine had no such trouble with the "new boys" on the block. Indeed, the editors wanted Bellow connected to the magazine and asked him to do a profile of the recently bereft Robert F. Kennedy, who was still mourning his brother Jack, assassinated in 1963. By the time Bellow interviewed RFK's sister-in-law, Jackie Kennedy, she had read *Herzog*. "I felt sorry for the author," she said, apparently without embarrassment. In any case, she thought

Bellow would be "out of his depth" writing about the Kennedy family. "Meaning," Bellow said, "What do you Chicago Jew boys know about an Irish Catholic who would buy the Presidency for his son?" After shadowing Kennedy for some weeks in June 1966, Bellow abandoned the assignment, saying he liked the former attorney general too much to write about him.[34]

The late sixties were illustrious years for Bellow, and he earned substantial amounts of money; but much of what he received went to alimony and the child support he owed his first two wives, Anita and Sasha, and their children, Greg and Adam. And Susan, in what would become a rancorous ten-year ordeal, dragged Saul through the courts in pursuit of larger and larger cuts of his new income.

Almost immediately before their separation, new hostilities erupted in the marriage; Susan found a number unknown to her on the telephone bill. It belonged to Maggie Staats, twenty-seven years younger than Bellow, who had been raised in an abusive, "hell-fire and brimstone" household. She had escaped as soon as she could, leaving behind the New Testament and Nancy Drew. Staats took a handful of graduate courses in literature at Northwestern and Yale and ended up working at the *New Yorker.* She would slip in and out of Bellow's life for years to come, often turbulently. He and Maggie were even engaged for a time. She could be insecure and vulnerable, and Bellow for his part could be brutal and imperious; his vanity, jealousy, and occasional paranoia brought, on rare occasions, physical violence to their relationship. There were also many other women; Bellow cheated on his girlfriends as well as his wives. Still, his impulsive love of Staats was compassionate and all-consuming. His many letters to her are conventional love letters, tenderhearted but needy and vulnerable, and somehow connected to his feelings about the significance of his childhood memories.[35]

Bellow kept no notebooks or journals, but among his papers were random notes addressing his own emotional conflicts, his attempts to understand, to explain himself to himself. One set of remarks, undated but from some time in 1966, was connected to the penetrating impact of his earliest fundamental experiences:

> Unwillingness, reluctance to recognize the reality of the present moment because of attachment to something in childhood.
> Therefore a brother rather than a father to the children.
> And the great fatigue of a struggle of 50 years. Feel it in my arms, in my very *fists*.
> Locate the Old System with passion—not so other things.
> Maggie is part of this. Has the purity of earliest connections.
> Miraculous to have accomplished so much in the world while in such bondage.
> But they heard my childish voice—and their own childhood in it.
> Nadine [another girlfriend] said *T'es un bebé* [You are a baby].[36]

The *bebé*, it appears, was still identifying himself as a son, one who lost his mother when he was only seventeen and thereafter spoke often of "a failure to properly mourn."[37] If the attachment and bondage he mentions allude to his intimate connection with the past, it is indicative of the intensity of Bellow's emotional conflict in the late sixties. For surely it was his fidelity—not his bondage—to the memories of his early life that inspired him to write the most moving and genuine passages in his fiction.

The use of the phrase "the Old System," the title of a story Bellow was working on in 1966, strongly suggests the same fidelity, the same powerful (and for him necessary) connection to memories of his intertwined primordial family relationships.[38] Isaac, the protagonist in the story, a committed Jew and successful entrepreneur, treasures deep memories of the Jewish family forces and "the Old Testament, the Talmud, and Polish Ashkenazi Orthodoxy" that shaped him; he lives the "Jewish way," not what he calls the Gentile silent way. Dr. Braun, a sensitive, introspective teller of the story who watched Isaac grow up, knows that the Jewish way can be easily sentimentalized, but he knows, too, from his own observations and experiences that the Jewish way is "real" and that it consists of profound "family feeling" demonstratively expressed—not as silent contact but the open articulation of annoyance, aggravation, and anger as well as love.[39]

Dr. Braun, near the end of the story, is thinking about Isaac and his estranged sister Tina, whose approaching death creates emotion so strong that it becomes "a situation of opera, which at the same time was a situation of parody." He is "bitterly moved" remembering these emotions but finds them inexplicable: "What good were they. . . . Perhaps the cold eye was better. On life, on death." But no, he realizes that it is precisely at these times when crises generate such powerful feelings that "humankind . . . grasped its own idea, that it was human and human through such passions."[40]

The story spoke to Bellow's own awareness, at once bitter and sweet, that his childhood affections had influenced him powerfully and ineradicably and that there was nothing that could replace the reciprocated love he experienced in his Jewish family. This was true for his father and his siblings but for his mother most of all, which may help explain his inability to sustain relationships with women. In Jewish immigrant families in the early twentieth century, Bellow said elsewhere that "your mother was the source of all human connectedness." And "it never entered your mind that you were anything but—cherished, and you returned the favor."[41] Adam Bellow, Saul's second son, said that his father "kept making and breaking families, but his only family was the original family. . . . He just loved them all."[42]

The "original family" was, of course, the most important source of Saul Bellow's Jewish identity, his Yiddish and Yiddishkeit, his love of stories, his wit and irony and consciousness of history, his nomadic spirit attached tenuously and restlessly to a need for stability. Together these various core elements constituted Bellow's Jewish sensibility and were second nature to him from childhood on, topping any other identity, including a temporary Trotskyism, an even shorter Reichian period, and later for a time an attraction to the spiritual philosophy of Rudolf Steiner. It was not surprising then that in spring 1967, Saul, who had already made several trips to Israel, answered a reporter's questions about the forthcoming trip by saying "It would be very strange and unnatural for a Jew," with Israel threatened by war, "not to want to know what is happening [there]."[43]

About five days before the Six-Day War broke out, Bellow wrote to biographer Ruth Miller, "I may be gone in a day or two. . . . I have made myself available" to cover what looked like a war in the Middle East: "I could not explain why. I have never been a Zionist. . . . But something about that particular occasion—the fact that for the second time in a quarter of a century the Jews were having a gun pressed to their heads—led me to ask *Newsday*," published by Bill Moyers, "to send me as a correspondent."[44] Moyers, who knew Bellow's reputation as a writer, as an openly self-identified Jew, and as a keen observer of contemporary events, commissioned him to report on the coming war.

Once in Jerusalem, Bellow didn't just hang back at the King David Hotel, observing the fighting from a distance; he walked the streets of Old Jerusalem, where losses were great, and he lit out as well to the battlefield in the Sinai, where he saw bloated corpses "black and stinking in the sun." Bellow witnessed suffering in Gaza, too, and after leaving the region he "saw no live Egyptians except for a group of captured snipers lying bound and blindfolded in a truck." He ventured into the North, where "day and night the armored columns came down the main street of Tiberias, turned left at the Lake of Galilee and continued northward past the Mount of the Beatitudes, where Jesus preached. . . . One could see the fields blazing, set afire by artillery, and hear the deep growling of bombs. Tiberias was blacked out. People sat by the water and listened to the news, exchanging rumors and predictions."[45]

On June 10, after visiting a Palestinian settlement in Nablus in the Jordan Valley, territory taken by the Israelis the previous week, Bellow submitted a final report. Although openly pro-Israel, Bellow records the pain, anguish, and injustice visited on the Palestinians: "No one can reasonably claim that right is entirely on the Israeli side, and though some Arab leaders exploited the misery of the refugees to intensify hatred of Israel, the Israelis might have done more for the Arabs. It should have been possible, for instance, to set aside money for indemnity and reconstruction. Part of the money paid to Israel by West Germany might have been used for this purpose."

Bellow thought that if the older ways continued, "the UN will be supporting more dozens of rotting slums in which demoralized, idle young men can concentrate on 'politics.'" He thought, too, that the intensifying nationalism of the Arabs could only lead to more destruction, and in his report, he was openly hostile to the world powers who had abandoned the region, and particularly Israel, to its fate.[46] "What you do know," Bellow concluded in *To Jerusalem and Back* (1976) after two more trips to Israel in the seventies, "is that there is one fact of Jewish life unchanged by the creation of a Jewish state: you cannot take your right to live for granted. Others can, you cannot. This is not to say that everyone is living pleasantly and well under a decent regime. No, it means only that the Jews, because they are Jews, have never been able to take the right to live as a natural right."[47]

Gregory Bellow, Saul's oldest son, now twenty-three, was angry with his father for having flown to Israel without letting him know he was going; he was also genuinely concerned that his father might have put himself in great danger. Bellow's response to Greg's worry was simple: "I had to go." After Israel, Bellow flew off to London to lecture at the American Embassy. He continued on from there to Poland to do research for a work in progress—ultimately *Mr. Sammler's Planet*—centering on a Polish Jew and his experiences in World War II. Moses Herzog has a similar trip to Poland where he thinks, "The stones still smell of war-time murders."[48]

The following year proved rich in honors. B'nai B'rith presented Bellow with its Jewish Heritage Award acknowledging his discerning coverage of the war in the Middle East; a number of universities granted him honorary doctorates, and the French government awarded him the order of the Chevalier des Artes et des Lettres in recognition of his work. The year was capped with the publication of *Mosby's Memoirs and Other Stories*, a collection of Bellow's short fiction, which included the title story and his consummate tale, "The Old System."

These honors and accomplishments did not erase Saul's haunting visions of death in Israel and the Levant. But the emotional arguments aroused by the Six-Day War had been eclipsed by the turbulence surrounding US involvement in Vietnam. Saul had made it plain from the beginning of the conflict in Southeast Asia that he was opposed to the war. He was also supportive of SANE (the National Committee for a Sane Nuclear Policy), CORE (the Congress of Racial Equality), and the teach-ins and rallies against the war in Vietnam that appeared on campuses all over the US; but he objected strongly to unruly demonstrations and even to civil disobedience, especially when it shut down colleges.[49] And as the student movements grew increasingly countercultural and unrestrained in activity and style, Bellow grew even more critical.

He still thought of himself as "some kind of liberal," though he would never accept the label, and like his Jewish friend and colleague Edward Shils, he was intensely resistant to what he called "antinomianism" in the developing behavior and thought of the students. Bellow thought that at its center antinomianism—literally the rejection of a socially established morality—tempted the young to believe that they were born unencumbered by a past and could simply coax freedom from traditional authority into existence.[50]

Bellow's outlook and the Jewishness to which it was inextricably intertwined made him impatient, even anxious, about the growing counterculture of the students, who he believed were contemptuous of rationality and tired of nuance and the habit of reflection. Either they seemed to want, as Irving Howe put it, the "narcotic of certainty as unarguable as orgasm and as delicious as a lollipop"—or they embraced the nihilism inherent in modernism, against which modernist masters like Kafka, Joyce, and Proust had always struggled.

It may seem paradoxical that Bellow regarded with increasing consternation the so-called sexual revolution, fulminating against the unfettered carnality of the 1960s while passing up no opportunity to participate in it himself. Bellow was hardly an abstemious man, and premarital sex and infidelity were quite familiar to him well before 1960. Yet something about the unconstrained, let-it-all-hang-out spirit of the sixties activated a deeply antagonistic and frightened response in him; it was almost as if he believed that his tenacious hectoring, his rabbinic chastising of the hedonism of the young people, could somehow nullify or at least restrain his own libertine impulses.

Later, looking back, Bellow blamed his compulsive sexual behavior on a combination of his Reichian experiments in the fifties and the sexual revolution, the zeitgeist of the sixties. "What a woman filled life I always led," Charlie says in *Humboldt's Gift*, and then chalks it off to "this sexually disturbed century."[51] Arlette Landes, in a temporary but troubled and anxious relationship with Bellow, brushed aside his rationalization, saying that he "had a biblical Old World morality, but his fly was entirely unzipped at all times."[52]

Whatever contradictions or inconsistencies Bellow harbored, he had begun to feel that the civilized university, indeed the stability of society, was being threatened by the unruliness of the students and their never-to-be-fulfilled pursuit of "instant gratification." Though the exact concept hardly existed in the ancient Hebrew world, warnings against putting off important long-term pursuits are legion in Hebrew scripture and were part of the biblical literature in which Bellow was saturated. Perhaps the most well-known warning against paying obsessive attention to immediate concerns to the neglect of more spiritual or social long-term possibilities is the aphorism proffered by Rabbi Tarfon: "It is not your duty to finish the work, but neither are you at liberty to neglect it."[53]

Bellow's increasingly conservative views were well known; yet in 1968 he was invited to San Francisco State University (SFSU), a major center of radical student demonstrations that had recently experienced a prolonged student-led strike. Why he was invited to lecture at an overheated campus about to blow up again is unclear except that his talk had been scheduled as part of a five-day, five-college tour ending with SFSU. Why Bellow accepted is even more confusing, but he did have friends there, including Herb and Mitzi McClosky, long-term buddies from Minnesota.[54]

Whatever his reasons for agreeing to the visit, it turned into a nasty "encounter," reimagined later at some length in *Mr. Sammler's Planet.* Saul's lecture on "The Writer in the University" went well; students described Bellow as "an exciting speaker—witty, entertaining and definitely cynical." But things went very badly during the Q and A when Bellow was mocked and insulted.[55] The verbal battering he suffered in the postlecture exchanges was mostly delivered by Floyd Salas, a faculty member. A teacher of creative writing and a former boxer, Salas, who knew Bellow's books well, admitted later that he had gone berserk and had accused Bellow of "trying to make the university into a genteel old maid's school" and that he had finally shouted, "You're a fucking square."[56]

Bellow, though he had answered some questions briskly and without "courtesy or an[y] attitude of sympathetic understanding," took these invectives and fully out-of-order verbal abuse by saying smoothly, "I don't mind answering questions, but it's not hospitable to insult your speakers, so let's call it off." Bellow picked up his notes and left.[57]

Bellow's disdain for student radicals, whom he believed were out to overturn the culture in lecture halls, "on the streets, and in bed, beaches, or the back seats of cars," and who wanted to tear down the university rather than open it up to new possibilities, made it less likely that he would see potential value in student behavior or much validity in their complaints.[58] Still irritated five months after the SFSU debacle, Bellow, upset by not only the rudeness he had experienced but also what he saw as the students' contempt for thought itself, wrote to potential biographer Mark Harris, "The thing at S.F. State was very bad . . . So, I left the platform in defeat. Undefended by the bullied elders of the faculty. . . . No, it was very poor stuff, I assure you. You don't found universities to destroy culture. For that you want a Nazi party."[59]

Floyd Salas and a handful of students had been vulgar and abrasive, but they were neither Nazis nor barbarians at the border aiming to annihilate the university or overwhelm Western civilization. Bellow's conservativism seemed to be turning him into another kind of gatekeeper, not quite like but resembling the neoconservatives, the disenchanted progressive Jewish intellectuals such as Norman Podhoretz, Irving Kristol, Nathan Glazer, and Daniel Bell.

Though long finished with his Trotskyist phase, Bellow, unlike the neocons, remained deeply marked by his engagement with left-wing politics, traces of which surface in his novels—*Seize the Day* and *Herzog*, for example. And as late as 1968, in the midst of Bellow's consternation with the student radicals, he could write a story like "Mosby's Memoirs" featuring a sympathetic Jewish socialist named Lustgarten. Dr. Mosby, the chronicler of the tale, a successful, erudite Fundamentalist Christian out of Missouri, is writing his memoirs in Mexico after the Second World War. He makes the acquaintance of Lustgarten, whom Mosby thinks is politically naive in the extreme for believing that Tito can redeem Marxism from the sins of Stalinism. With his internationalist belief in the Trotskyist theory of permanent revolution, Lustgarten sets off for Yugoslavia for what he assumes is an invitation to observe Titoism in action. He returns bitterly disappointed after being punished for his political errors in what has turned out to be forced work in a labor brigade.

But Mosby, who represents the political right, comes off worse than Lustgarten. For all his clever political pronouncements and his negative assessments of Marxism, Mosby has "disposed of all things human." Unmarried, friendless, childless, he has no connection whatsoever to society, unlike Lustgarten, the loving father and loyal husband. These doubles, one conservative, one socialist, allowed Bellow to parody both left and right, with the socialist looking rather better in the comparison. "What you invest your energy and enthusiasm in when you are young," Bellow said later, "you can never bring yourself to give up altogether."[60]

Given Bellow's history of left politics, including his three-year-old stance against the war in Southeast Asia, poised alongside his opposition to the student "revolution," one might have thought that his new novel, *Mr. Sammler's Planet* (1970), would contain within it the preeminent political issue of the 1960s, the war in Vietnam. But unlike other major novels of the time that dealt with politics, including Norman Mailer's *The Armies of the Night* (1968), Kurt Vonnegut's *Slaughterhouse-Five* (1969), and John Updike's *Rabbit Redux* (1971), which feature the war's continuing stormy impact on the American scene, *Mr. Sammler's Planet* mentions Vietnam only twice, both in the same sentence—a sentence that does not address student behavior. It is a serious weakness in the novel, which nonetheless went on to win the National Book Award, Bellow's third, and along with that an avalanche of controversy over political regression, misogyny, and racism.

As literary historian Joseph F. McCadden notes, "Sammler does not perceive, nor is it pointed out in the novel," that the central cause of political disruption in America "was not [the] protesting college students but government prosecution of a disastrous war in Asia."[61] This omission on Bellow's part makes the student radicals involved in political protest and disruption of colleges and universities look like demented young people running around in a frenzy about some huge mystery.

In Bellow's earlier books, the fictionalized lives of first- and second-generation Jewish immigrants in one stage or another of assimilation are on display. In *Mr. Sammler's Planet*, Bellow chose a painful "other" for the Americanizing Jewish community—a survivor of the Holocaust. Artur Sammler, nearly blinded in one eye after being struck with an SS officer's rifle butt, crawled out of a mass grave from under dozens of murdered prisoners, including his wife. A man literally returned from the dead, Sammler was rescued from a displaced persons camp in 1947 by an American nephew. He was removed from the madness of Nazi Germany only to find himself in the incomprehensible world of modern urban America in the 1960s.

In 1966, Bellow had been in Poland to conduct research for what would become *Mr. Sammler's Planet*. He talked with survivors of experiences similar to what he had in mind for Sammler, adding to the picture he had developed from speaking with the survivors in Paris during his Guggenheim trip in 1948. He talked with several men who had escaped from the Lodz ghetto, and he interviewed Marek Edelman, the last survivor among the leaders of the Warsaw Ghetto Uprising. Back in New York, he met with yet more Polish survivors.[62]

Mr. Sammler's Planet was the first novel in which Bellow directly confronted the fate of Jews in World War II. In *Dangling Man*, Bellow's first book, there is no mention of Jews, but the Holocaust is evoked obliquely in Joseph's dreams. In *The Victim*, the presence of the genocide is implicit and serves as the fundamental source of Leventhal's defensiveness about antisemitism. In the only reference to the Holocaust in the novel, Leventhal heatedly reminds the Jew-baiting Kirby Allbee that "millions of us have been killed."[63] In *Herzog* there are many more references to the extermination of the Jews, but the Holocaust is not central and is only one among other horrors of the modern world mentioned as "part of the program of destruction into which the human spirit had poured itself with energy, even with joy."[64]

Because *Mr. Sammler's Planet* deals more directly than these earlier novels with twentieth-century Jewish history—the Holocaust, Israel, and the American Jewish community's reaction to both—it is seen by some as an even more Jewish book than *Herzog.* This opinion is sustained by the fact that many of the values that thread their way through the novel are fundamental propositions (though not exclusively) of the Jewish world: a love of life and the rejection of despair; a belief in human survival under almost any circumstances; a powerful stress on rationality and intellect, part of a centuries-long tradition of scriptural exegesis; a decided preference for mitzvot—good deeds and right action—over faith or rumination; and a rejection of alienation, madness, or suffering as in any way enlightening, redemptive, or meaningful.

These Jewish values are embodied in Artur Sammler, although subject to his periodic doubt. He occasionally even violates these values, but they are deep and consistent enough to transform him in the eyes of his friends and family into a symbol, a spiritual leader, or a judge—even if audacious and often without empathy. By picturing him so, Bellow successfully avoids the potential sentimentality in this transformation of Sammler by his close associates. Instead, his protagonist and his ethical predicaments become the means by which the writer makes one of his most potent arguments in defense of humanism and in renunciation of the nihilism he sees invading the traditional culture.

Sammler is a "ghost" with a damaged eye but is alive on the Upper West Side of Manhattan. This second-generation Jewish neighborhood is similar to Bellow's West Side of Chicago. Together, these two Bellow-inhabited vicinities became his own created regional locale, much as Yoknapatawpha County belonged to Faulkner and Westchester, New York, to Cheever. The streets are populated by bag ladies, including Sammler's own daughter Shula, machers (hotshots who get things done), political and academic opportunists, and cranks. Madmen, common criminals, and sexual perverts are also plentiful. But the neighborhood is populated as well by German Jewish refugees, liberal reformers, Holocaust survivors, literary types, and a multiplicity of ethnic groups, some stuck, some eager to rise. West Side streets and campuses are also peppered with the racial turmoil and angry voices of various liberation movements that helped define the 1960s.

Mr. Sammler is disgusted with all the "movements" he encounters—a disgust reinforced in an episode based on Bellow's experience at SFSU. Artur, charmed by Lionel Feffer, "an ingenious operator, less student than promoter," agrees to deliver a lecture at Columbia University in 1969 after a student-led strike.[65] Sammler, delivering his lecture about England in the 1930s, is boorishly interrupted by a faculty member who screams offensive, scatological epithets at him and then asks the audience, "Why do you listen to this effete old shit? What has he got to tell you? His balls are dry. He's dead. He can't come."[66]

Bellow's fictional version makes the audience's behavior more rambunctious and portrays the verbal attack on Sammler as more malignant and portentous than what had actually happened, which was bad enough. Some thought Bellow's revision of the actual events mean-spirited—an authorial indulgence of indignation. But just as in the 1950s when Bellow had refused to fall in with the labeled radicalism of the *Partisan Review* writers, so during the controversy that ensued over *Mr. Sammler's Planet* he identified with neither right nor left, amplifying his growing reputation for irascibility.

In any case, Bellow's Artur Sammler is shocked into silence by the ad hominem attack he suffers. He, and doubtless Bellow himself, is critical of the young people. In their "revulsion from authority," Sammler thinks, youth generally "would respect no persons. Not even their own persons." This, he thinks, is especially true of women. His sexism here grows out of his traditional notions of women and their physicality. "Some of the poor girls had a bad smell," Sammler muses; "Bohemian protest did them the most harm." It was basic among the responsibilities and problems of civilization, thinks Artur, "that some parts of nature demanded more control than others. Females were naturally more prone to grossness, had more smells, needed more washing, clipping, binding, pruning, grooming, perfuming, and training." These "poor kids may have resolved to stink together in defiance of a corrupt tradition built on neurosis and falsehood," but an unanticipated result of their way of life, Sammler thinks, was a loss of femininity for the women and a loss of self-esteem for all.[67]

Bellow did not share Sammler's notion that women were more prone to grossness than men, but he was opposed to what he saw as the radical dimensions of the feminist movement, perhaps to feminism altogether. Feminism had been roiling under the surface of middle-class American society for some time, but it emerged into the open in the mid to late sixties. In that context, a female graduate student in Bellow's Joyce seminar thought it was important enough to interrupt the class with a message for the other students. But Bellow was outraged when she "swept into class in the midst of the national student strike [in 1970] with a list of non-negotiable demands." He shouted, "You women liberationists! All you're going to have to show for your movement ten years from now are *sagging breasts*!"[68]

With his failing eyesight, Artur had earlier hired some students to read to him. Now, he no longer wants the protesters in his room. He is tired of the youngsters with their "big dirty boots and the helpless vital pathos of young dogs with their first red erections, and pimples sprung to the cheeks from foaming beards, laboring . . . with hard words and thoughts," that forever have to be explained.[69]

Almost immediately following his disaster at Columbia, Sammler, on a bus carrying mostly middle-class white passengers, is witness to the handiwork of an elegantly dressed, confident Black pickpocket. Aware that he has been seen, the thief, cool, unafraid, leaves the bus with Sammler and follows him into an apartment house lobby, backs him against a wall, and exposes his formidable, tumescent penis to the old Jew. No contest here, the pickpocket, without a word, seems to say—"I am (perhaps "*We* are") in control. Just give it up."

Bellow often used carnal imagery, mostly in association with something Eastern or African, rarely if ever Jewish. Unfortunately, and notoriously, here in *Mr. Sammler's Planet*, Bellow links lewdness with African Americans and in the telling uses the ill-fated and loathsome term "sexual niggerhood"—a poor choice of words easily misunderstood. What Bellow seems to be saying is that from "the Black side strong currents were sweeping over *everyone*." But Bellow also said that millions of white people, before reading *Mr. Sammler's Planet*, had been deceiving themselves about the meanings of racial difference and "wanted the oceanic, boundless, primitive," and romanticized outlaw status they mistakenly associated with Blackness.[70]

Bellow made clear his opposition to this primitivism trope in regard to Black people as early as 1952 in his review of Ralph Ellison's *Invisible Man* (discussed in chapter 7). "It is thought," Bellow wrote, "that Negroes and other minority people, kept under in the great status battle, are in the instinct cellar of dark enjoyment." This idea, Bellow declares, is not only false; it is dangerous, in that it "provokes envious rage" over sensual pleasure.[71] Nonetheless, in Bellow's seventh novel, Sammler's use of disparaging, racially charged language echoes, as Adam Kirsch points out, Nazi talk of instinctive Jewish licentiousness and summons the term "sexual Jewhood."[72]

Yet Bellow's use of a Black man as sexual force and as "other" in contrast to Sammler's intellectual nature is not necessarily a reaffirmation of an ugly racial stereotype. Sammler, after all, feels a certain admiration for the Black man because he has class, mastery, dexterity, and elegance. The old man seems certain, too, that the thief has been (is still?) on some level a victim. Nonetheless, he feels "the breath of wartime Poland passing over the damaged tissues" of his nervous system.[73] He is frightened by the silent irrational display of phallic supremacy by the "other." Residing at the center of these two episodes, on a campus and in a hallway, sits raw sexuality, much on the mind of Bellow, who, like Sammler, felt anxious and threatened by the fervid sixties.

Sammler wanders the uptown streets feeling like a tiny island trapped in a tidal wave of compulsive pursuits, a "revolution of things colliding" in the noise and despair of the contemporary city. He is appalled at what he sees, perhaps figuratively with his bad eye only, as the "collapse of civilization."[74] But, as with so many of Bellow's heroes, Mr. Sammler is systematically reflective about these troubling scenes, incidents, and episodes, and in the end he sees, as if with both eyes now, that the end of civilization is not inevitable or nearly as catastrophic or apocalyptic as the Holocaust. Doomsday is not emerging on 84th Street and Amsterdam Avenue or on the Columbia University campus at Broadway and 116th Street. Sammler sees that even within this cauldron of the Upper West Side, people live. This is what Bellow's oeuvre continually brings to our attention—people live!

Sammler, too, lives. Through most of the novel, he cannot forgive the world—why would he after what he has been through? He resembles for a time an austere misanthrope, a bitter moralist. But his hope for human community and moral accountability is eventually reborn in New York, not because of his experience of suffering at the hands of the Nazis but despite it. Bellow argues even more clearly here than he did in *Herzog* that continual suffering is more likely to be crippling than ennobling.

Sammler had earlier learned, in the Holocaust years, not only about the human capacity to commit previously unthinkable atrocities but also how harsh realities can damage or destroy a person whose belief system is settled in the world of humane ideals and ideas. In the forest to which he had escaped, Sammler shot and killed an unarmed German soldier who had pleaded for his life. He took the man's clothing and food; he also took pleasure—indeed joy—in the experience: "When he had fired his gun, Sammler, himself nearly a corpse burst into life. . . . His heart felt lined with brilliant, rapturous satin. To kill the man and to kill him without pity . . . There was a flash, a blot of fiery white. When he shot again it was . . . to try again for that bliss. To drink more flames."[75]

Occasionally after his rescue, Sammler turns to the memory of violence-generated bliss "for reference." But he also reviews the time "when he himself was nearly beaten to death. Had to lift dead bodies from himself. Desperate! Crawling out. Oh heart-bursting! Oh vile! Then he himself knew how it felt to take a life. Found it could be an ecstasy."[76] These events have left him woefully damaged. They haunt Sammler and make him more cynical, even contemptuous at times. But despite the atrocious violations he has suffered and the physical and psychological impairment he has sustained, Sammler searches for spaces within which the moral spirit can be renourished and extended. Such places are not easily found on Mr. Sammler's modern, materialistic, and almost exclusively rational planet, whose broken mechanisms of social life need to be fixed—whose souls, much like the vessels of divine light broken at the beginning of creation, need to be repaired in order to redeem the world, which has fallen into chaos.[77]

Sammler is distressed but always in a kind of Talmudic disputation with himself—sometimes ponderous, sometimes profound—about what he sees, including what he thinks is the representative behavior of Angela, the daughter of his nephew, rescuer, and benefactor, Dr. Arnold Elya Gruner. She is sexually provocative, promiscuous, and full only of herself. Bellow often had trouble writing sympathetically about women, and with Angela as with Shula, Sammler's loony but amiable daughter, now divorced from an even loonier and dangerous Israeli, and with his obsessive, overly talkative, but well-intentioned and social-justice-oriented niece Margotte, he continues with some exception to shortchange women. He is dismissive, but he is brilliant in using Angela (as well as Gruner's son Wallace) as a symbol of the incoherence of modernity, the degeneration of shared norms, and the unrelenting gratification of base impulses.

It is with niece Margotte, who flirts with the idea of granting Christian forgiveness to the Nazis, that Sammler has a long exchange about Hannah Arendt's *Eichmann in Jerusalem: The Banality of Evil* (1963). Bellow thought Arendt's views about the routine nature of malevolence and her notion about Jews cooperating in their own demise were not only wrong but shameful. It may very well have been Arendt's book that spurred him to think seriously about writing a novel in which the Holocaust is dealt with directly.[78] *Mr. Sammler's Planet* is that novel. And Bellow includes the discussion about *Eichmann in Jerusalem* to make several important points.

For one thing, we see that for all of his attraction to Jesus's message of love and brotherhood, Bellow had little tolerance for the Christian notion of "forgive them for they know not what they do." Instead, Bellow and Sammler propose something momentously different—and Jewish. Artur asks, "Do you think the Nazis didn't know what murder was? Everybody . . . knows what murder is. That is very old human knowledge. The best and purest human beings, from the beginning of time, have understood that life is sacred. To defy that old understanding is not banality. There was a conspiracy against the sacredness of life. Banality is the adopted disguise of a very powerful will to abolish conscience."[79]

The phrase "old understanding" again calls to mind the title of Bellow's story "The Old System," written about the same time as the novel. The story sheds interesting light on Mr. Sammler as well as on the complexity of ideas and feelings Bellow was grappling with in the 1960s. The narrator of "The Old System," Dr. Samuel Braun, is a scientist and profound intellectual, for whom detachment is distinctive, critical to his success as a professional chemist. Recently, however, "self-observation and objectivity" have begun for Braun to seem a misdirection, a threat to the values of the Old System. In lamenting the "great traditions" displaced by modernity, Braun, sounding much like Sammler in the opening paragraph of *Mr. Sammler's Planet,* questions ideas and practices like detachment and neutrality.[80]

For Sammler, as for Braun, the knowledge that comes to matter is not "head-culture," as Bellow had named it elsewhere, but the result of profound feeling: "The soul wanted what it wanted. It had its own natural knowledge. It sat unhappily on superstructures of explanation, poor bird, not knowing which way to fly."[81]

Bellow knows about the soul and about the direction it ought to fly, but he also knows "that human nature is full of many kinds of wickedness which must be fought" and that not everyone knows absolutely "in their hearts what's right and wrong."[82] He also argues, however, that when not burdened by cultural or ideological overlay, we know what evil is when we see it; we know right from wrong. These ideas are central to his worldview and run through most of his work. In an interview after the publication of *Mr. Sammler's Planet,* Bellow said that he did not believe in

> shifting the blame from the murderers to those of us who, perhaps in our minds have done . . . terrible things, but who have in fact done nothing of the kind. In my own mind this is the difference between the Jewish and Christian outlook: Jesus said that if you lusted after a woman in your heart, you might as well have committed the adultery. The Jewish outlook is that unless you have committed the crime, you are not guilty of it, no matter what you have thought. The mental capacity to do the thing we mustn't forget, but neither must we think that the evil happens in a dream: it happens in fact, and those who commit evil in fact are in fact evil.[83]

And "evil imagination was very great" in Nazi Germany. Anyone, Bellow added, who describes evil as "a function of banality," as does Arendt, is herself banal. Bellow also detests, as Sammler does, the "image of evil in the eyes of the sentimental" or in the eyes of intellectuals who get their notions about these matters from literature.[84] Herzog, too, came to recognize that intellectuals who "spend their lives in humane studies" imagine that once cruelty or suffering has been described in books, it is over, or stranger still, that "there is no true evil anymore."[85] Bellow's Jews say no. Cruelty must be seen for what it is—"the monstrousness of life."[86] Doesn't Margotte see, Sammler wants to know, that if it is possible to make evil look ordinary, banal, merely bureaucratic, it is easier to recruit ordinary people to do the job? The mind that invented bureaucratic banality was not banal, Sammler insists. It was diabolically creative.

Bellow is much concerned with the conduct of his Jewish protagonists, who, like Sammler, are important not for their outward Jewish trappings and rituals, which range from minimal to nonexistent, but for what Bellow perceives to be their "Jewishness:" a moral obligation to this world, an acknowledgment of what we owe one another. Bellow's own Jewish identity is never clearer than when he writes about or alludes to contract and obligation. The question, "What do we in fact owe one another?" is not new to Sammler, but it confronts him most immediately and dramatically on his way to visit his dying nephew Elya in the hospital. His driver pulls over so that Sammler, who is in a hurry, can get a closer look at what is holding up traffic.

A crowd is watching a violent tussle between a Black man—yes, the notorious and ubiquitous pickpocket—and none other than Feffer, the radical student opportunist who had charmed Sammler into lecturing at Columbia. About twenty people are crowded around the bus on which the pair were traveling. More are beginning to gather, but "no one [is] about to interfere."[87] Feffer, who is holding on to the Minox camera with which he captured the thief in action, is overmatched by the size of the pickpocket. In his fawn-colored suit and blue-tinted Dior shades, red tie, and matching crimson belt, the Black man is crushing Feffer against the bus much as he held Sammler with his forearm against the lobby wall.

"Some of you," Sammler calls out, "Help! Help him." But the "some of you [do] not exist." No one will do anything. Sammler spots his son-in-law, Eisen, newly arrived from Israel, and asks him to help Feffer, now in the chokehold of the Black man. To the pickpocket Sammler says, "Let him go," and to Feffer, "Give him the camera. . . . Hand it over." Finally, Sammler, desperate to rescue Feffer, turns to Eisen, again saying, "Do something." Sammler stares hard at the crowd, thinking, "Wouldn't anybody help?" Wasn't it true that "where people were help might be?" Wasn't it an instinct and a reflex? No one moves. "How strange a quality their inaction had," Sammler thinks; "they are here and not here. They are present while absent":[88]

> But there was something worse here than this event itself, namely, the feeling that stole over Sammler. It was a feeling of horror and grew in strength, grew and grew. What was it? How was it to be put? *He was a man who had come back. He had rejoined life. He was near to others.* But in some essential way he was also companionless. He was old. He lacked physical force. He knew what to do but had no power to execute it. He had to turn to someone else—to an Eisen! a man himself very far out on another track, orbiting a very different foreign center.[89]

"Eisen," Sammler pleads, "separate them. . . . Just take the camera. . . . That will stop this." Eisen holds a bag full of his large metal sculptures, a variety of objects. With a wide, swinging blow, Eisen, the powerful iron foundry worker, strikes the pickpocket: "He had the strength not only of his trade but also madness. . . . Everything went into that blow, discipline, murderousness, everything." Artur is shocked; he never meant for Eisen to hit the Black man. He thinks, "This is the worst thing yet."[90]

The pickpocket is stunned, his cheek bleeding and swelling. Before Sammler can stop him, Eisen, even more heavily than before, slams the face and head of the pickpocket, who has sunk to the street. He prepares to hit him again and would certainly have killed him if Sammler, horrified, weren't able to seize Eisen's arm. Still wearing the silly but ominous smile he wore throughout the ordeal, Eisen says, though now winded, "You can't hit a man like this just once. When you hit him you must really hit him. Otherwise he'll kill you. You know. We both fought in the war. You were a Partisan. You had a gun. So don't you know?"[91]

Sammler is no doubt reminded of his own second shot at the German soldier, a shot taken not for self-defense but for the "bliss" it brought. Is what Artur did in the war the moral equivalent of what Eisen has done on a New York street? Perhaps. Sammler has no answer, but his arms and legs are trembling, and he is sick with rage at Eisen. And the Black man? He "was a megalomaniac": "But there was a certain—a certain princeliness. The clothing, the shades, the sumptuous colors, the barbarous-majestical manner. He was probably a mad spirit. But mad with an idea of noblesse. And how much Sammler sympathized with him—how much he would have done to prevent such atrocious blows! How red the blood was, and how thick—and how terrible those crusted, spiny lumps of metal were! And Eisen? He counted as a war victim, even though he might anyhow have been mad. But he belonged in the mental hospital. A homicidal maniac."[92]

Sammler tells Eisen to "get away from here. You're in trouble." To Feffer he speaks in the disgusted tones of accusation: "What have you to say now?" The Black man "was picking the purse, I swear," says Feffer, oblivious to the pickpocket, whose head is still dripping blood. "I caught him in the act," Feffer says proudly, "and I got two shots of him."[93] By constructing this embroiled triangle—the unnamed Black pickpocket; Feffer, the Jewish macher; and Eisen, the lunatic Israeli—Bellow produces a sharply sculpted metaphor for the near impenetrability of race relations in the 1960s.

Stanley Crouch, a poet, culture critic, and syndicated columnist and a Black man whose early intellectual development was shaped in part by the Watts, Los Angeles, race riots in 1965, wrote an introduction to a later edition of *Mr. Sammler's Planet* and makes Bellow's metaphor more explicit. Crouch sees in the "machinations of Feffer" and his camera "a merciless criticism of the Jewish opportunists who sold real and imagined black pathology under the banner of 'serious discussion'"; with the pickpocket, Crouch sees "the kind of black 'leaders' who made their money ripping off or intimidating middle-class whites," especially Jews.[94]

Crouch also touches on the dissolution in this era of the important but always "uneasy alliance" between Blacks and Jews. The 1960s witnessed newly emerging anticolonial states in Africa and an inherently separatist Black Power on the one side, and the Israeli victory in the Six-Day War and the intensification of Zionism, with its own implications of separatism, on the other. Bellow was keenly interested in these issues.

His oldest son, Gregory, attested to his father's strong "support . . . of the civil rights movement." He "was all for the Freedom Rides," Gregory said, and very supportive of "the voting rights legislation." But he was fearful of "black political empowerment," especially in the way it manifested itself in Chicago, where there was a huge dose of antisemitism in the Black Power movement. According to his youngest son, Daniel, Saul "was always talking about African Americans . . . the Holocaust, Zionism, and Black-Jewish relations in the cities. . . . He was never boring . . . and he wasn't always predictable," as evident in the conclusion of *Mr. Sammler's Planet*.[95]

Eisen has smashed the head of the Black pickpocket—twice—with that bag holding, among other things, a welded-iron Star of David. With this he nearly kills the Black man in "broad daylight on a city block in sophisticated Manhattan." Bellow may have meant Eisen (*ayzn* means "iron" in Yiddish) to be a stand-in for Israel—an Israel whose military actions are sometimes, like Eisen's, disproportionate.[96]

And Sammler in all of this? Pushing himself closer and closer to the crowd, which is there but not there, he appears to learn anew, through frank memories of his shortcomings in human feeling, the brave sense of compassion. The Black pickpocket lying wounded and bleeding thick red blood in the street makes Sammler more fully realize that the thief is a man. Artur relives yet again the butt of the German's rifle against his own head and realizes that it had blinded him to the humanity of others. He realizes how important it is that humans see the humanity of others if we are to turn away from believing that we are trapped forever in these dark repetitions of brutality.

Once again in the hospital waiting room with Angela, Sammler, who is usually disgusted at the fleshliness and promiscuity of his niece and always saw her as a kind of skank, begins to feel some empathy; he recognizes Angela now as a woman trapped—trapped inside the splendor of her own sexuality and inside a generation that hides itself in lifeless definitions of freedom, compulsively gratifying the senses while avoiding the needs of the soul. Being "trapped" sounds like fatalism. But Artur's musings and meditations begin to point to a tentative faith in the values of mutual respect, commitment, and universally shared principles.

Sammler means "collector" in Yiddish. And Artur has spent his life collecting—materials from books, personal observations, ideas. In the end he tries another form of collecting. He makes a valiant effort to bring together Gruner's family—Angela, and Elya's money-hungry, irresponsible son Wallace—to convince them to give their dying father some comfort, some reconciliation. They are unwilling. "What do you want," Angela asks with bitter sarcasm, "an old time deathbed scene?"[97] Sammler reminds her that Elya was a good man. Though flawed like everyone else—his fortune came in part from having performed illegal abortions for Mafia friends he'd grown up with—he was "a dependable man—a man who took thought for others," a man whose feelings of moral accountability make him truly "human."[98] Angela responds, "I thought everybody was born human." Sammler's retort is pregnant with meaning: "It's not a natural gift at all. Only the capacity is natural."[99] In an especially astute rabbinic commentary, it is suggested that God did not say "And it was good" after creating man because man's nature was not determined. Bellow and the poets of Genesis knew what Freud did not, the pull of moral indeterminacy.

Sammler's ability to look past Elya's questionable connections derives from an Old World attitude toward the law, an attitude Artur may have had in the end toward the Black pickpocket—seeing him as someone who out of necessity was committing "permissible" nonviolent crimes.[100] In Eastern Europe, striving and struggling Jews broke or bent the law out of necessity, with no injury to their Jewish self-respect. Bellow's own father, Abram, in the Old World, in an effort to avoid antisemitism and systematic discrimination, had committed "necessary" crimes like bribery and forgery. He was exposed and arrested and had to flee.

This may help explain Saul Bellow's own later attitude toward the law and his attraction as a writer to "those who lived outside it."[101] Petty gangsters, criminals, and pickpockets, who are often sympathetically portrayed or given a degree of dignity and complexity, appear in many Bellow novels, including *Augie March*, *Herzog*, and *Humboldt's Gift*, as well as here in *Mr. Sammler's Planet*.

Artur fails with Gruner's family, but not in his own responsibility. Elya is dying, an ordinary, imperfect man, but a man with the moral strength and resources necessary for sustaining human community, a man who was good and quite generous to Artur and his daughter. Sammler returns again and again to Gruner's hospital room and, by his words, thoughts, and actions, insists that no matter how darkly desperate our time, we can still find value in life, in "swimming and boating in that cloudy, contaminated, confusing, surging medium of human feelings," and most of all in our obligations.[102]

Sammler thinks Elya at his very best was much kinder "than I have ever been or could ever be."[103] But speaking on the very last page of the novel, Sammler articulates his recognition of that iron law of commitment that our humanity imposes on us: "He was aware that he must meet, and he did meet the terms of his contract," his personal covenant. "The terms which in his inmost heart, each man knows. As I know mine. As all know. For that is the truth of it—that we all know, God, that we know, that we know, we know, we know, we know," a kind of post-Holocaust declaration of moral responsibility as durable as the end of Molly Bloom's "yes I will" soliloquy.[104]

Nine "knows," six in the concluding sentence! But what do we in fact know? Bellow has made evident, even if at times only obliquely, what he thinks we know, not only in Mr. *Sammler's Planet* but in most of his work. Artur Sammler, like Eugene Henderson, Moses Herzog, and Bellow himself, realizes or intuits that the business of life is essentially a "religious enterprise." We know, Bellow argues persistently, that on some level there is a spiritual charge stored up inside every person and that it passes from one human being to another. We long for a human community in which "we all know" that ethical behavior within a framework of traditional morality is at least conceivable.[105] Sammler himself says directly that he would not count out the idea "that there is the same truth in the heart of every human being or a splash of God's own spirit, and that this is the richest thing we share in common."[106]

There is an element, whether conscious or not, of Hasidism in this view. Classical rabbinic Jewry sees the scholar, one who has studied the Law in all its implications and complications, as the moral leader of the community. Hasidism, on the other hand, holds that the spiritual leader, who may or may not be learned, exemplifies the Law in his conduct, his deeds. The natural knowledge that guides Mr. Sammler and that Henderson, Herzog, and Citrine in *Humboldt's Gift* attain at the end of their fictional journeys is consistent with Hasidic belief. These Bellow protagonists reach their knowledge of good and evil without extensive study; it is as if they discover something they knew all along.[107]

Like Moses Herzog, Sammler sees that he has "misread [his] contract," but he now knows what Herzog learned in the end: the road forward is "to share with other human beings as much as possible and not destroy my remaining years in the same way."[108] Like Sammler, who, even after suffering the horrors of the Holocaust, came to believe again in humanity, Bellow still believed in the possibility of being truly human even in modern society, and he therefore argued that the individual self was still worth writing about. With *Mr. Sammler's Planet* as with *Herzog, Henderson the Rain King, Seize the Day,* and *The Adventures of Augie March,* Bellow masterfully demonstrated that alongside his celebration of community and rationalism, he would continue to stand for feelings and emotion and against the contemporary literary theme of "annihilation of the Self."[109]

TWELVE

LOVE AND DEATH

QUESTIONS ABOUT SAUL BELLOW'S ATTITUDE toward women and female physicality, raised early in his career, reached their apotheosis with the publication of his provocative new novel, *Mr. Sammler's Planet* (1970); those questions continued to spark debate well after Bellow had become a venerated veteran of the literary wars of the1960s. Were expressions of disgust at the organs and odors of women in *Sammler* a reflection of Artur's traditional Old World values about sexuality, or were they signs of distaste and revulsion on Bellow's part?

If Bellow suffered from dealing with the body parts and aromas of his female sexual partners, that suffering, if any, appears more than matched by his feelings of attraction. And without being overly apologetic or reductive, it still bears mentioning that any indicators of negativism toward women by Bellow in the late sixties may have been due in part to the troubles he was having with his former wives while working on *Sammler.*

Beginning in 1968, Sasha was badgering Bellow about money, and Susan was in messy, exhausting divorce negotiations with him. At the same time, he was having affairs with a rotating chorus line of women. Bellow's most intense and long-lasting sexual liaison was with Maggie Staats, whom he saw frequently in

New York. Apparently, Staats was the only woman, other than his three former wives, whom Bellow had actually loved. "I didn't believe it possible," he wrote to her on April 7, 1966: "I thought I was damaged, or self-damaged, too badly for this." Five days later, Bellow told her that he was in love with "everything I can remember of you."[1] He spent two summers at the Hamptons with Staats in the late sixties. After having read Betty Friedan's *The Feminine Mystique*, Staats became "a convert," yet she still acted as Bellow's "handmaiden . . . because that's what you were supposed to do."[2] Whatever understanding they reached did not preclude Bellow's relationships with other women.

In Chicago there was his "companion, Bonne Amie" Bette Howland, along with his cleaning lady—an African American woman "about twice as tall as he was, and well built, striking," according to his friend Richard Stern, the novelist. It is difficult to imagine that this was, for Bellow, anything other than a predatory, exploitative circumstance. He was also chasing and sometimes catching Arlette Landes, twenty-five, the same age as Staats and less than half Bellow's age. Apparently undeterred by her organs and odors, Bellow saw Arlette as "a sex goddess."[3]

Bellow's womanizing was common knowledge. His friend and fellow novelist Norman Rosten, for example, wrote saying, "Saul, I think of you juggling all those oranges—girls, wives, children—and I think, Is God nice to him or just fattening him up for some fearful retribution?"[4] Retribution or not, Bellow continued to think his serial philandering "not a happy thing," or so he said.[5] But his relationship with Staats, the longest lasting and most turbulent, was based on more than sex. Maggie valued the talks they had, most particularly while Bellow was writing *Sammler*. They discussed the Second World War and spoke often about the Holocaust survivors Bellow had interviewed in Poland in 1966 and twenty years earlier in France.

The metaphysical questions raised in *Sammler* and in "The Old System" engaged the two of them, because Maggie shared

Bellow's feeling that the life they lived in the present could not have been their beginning, nor could inevitable death possibly be their final end. Bellow's reflections about death were part of his consciousness and essence from the time he was hospitalized long-term at the age of eight, and they were sustained throughout his life by many losses, the heaviest of which was the death of his mother when he was seventeen (chap. 2). The loss of his mother, whom he felt he had never properly mourned, was traumatic and affected his future decisions, most often about women. An undercurrent of anguish and an attention to the inexorableness of death and its meaning would mark nearly all of Bellow's writing, along with a hunger for the "original world" of unadulterated feeling and family intimacy, which, though hardly erased, faded with his mother gone.

And now in the 1960s and early '70s, there was a new string of deaths. One of his dearest Tuley High School friends, Oscar Tarcov, another aspiring novelist, died in 1964 at the age of forty-eight. Delmore Schwartz, a Jewish wunderkind and a literary comet whose flame fizzled early, died in 1966 at the age of fifty-four after years of ragged decline. His passing preceded the death in 1968 of Saul's close friend since high school Louis Sidran. Nobel laureate John Steinbeck died in the same year, and the novelist Josephine Herbst, who had become a close friend and correspondent in the 1950s, died in 1969.

Herbst and Bellow were something of an odd couple. Before she wrote her novels, she was a radical journalist with American Communist Party associations strong enough to elicit the charge of Stalinism from some critics. But Herbst possessed original and independent views, and as Bellow discovered from reading parts of her unpublished memoirs, she was an unusually talented writer. He initially praised her work as "going along at first in a plain, truthful fashion and suddenly, without effort or engineering, becomes beautiful," which as he said would have been enough.[6] But after reading another long section of her work in

1959, Bellow, twenty-three years younger than Herbst, was inspired to tell her that like *Daiyenu,* a Jewish hymn of praise, "It would have been enough, Lord if you had only created the earth, but there is more. And the whole catalogue of gifts and miracles, which ends in *Daiyenu*—Had you done no more. Well, now Josie, I'd love you whether you wrote or not. But there's more. The piece is wonderful."[7]

Herbst was indeed a remarkably gifted writer who nevertheless had difficulty getting published after 1941, ostensibly for political reasons. By the late fifties, she was effectively impoverished and dependent on the generosity of her friends. Bellow, partly by publishing extracts of Herbst's manuscripts in the *Noble Savage,* became the mainstay of her literary existence, so much so that "without his contribution," according to Herbst's biographer, "it is not certain that any of her memoirs would ever have appeared."[8]

Bellow also tried to help Delmore Schwartz during his battle with mental illness, but Schwartz continued to spiral downward. He landed in Bellevue hospital in 1957 like the fictive Van Humboldt Fleisher after having been "rushed off dingdong in a paddy wagon like a mad dog, arriving foul, and locked up raging."[9] Bellow created a fund to pay for Schwartz's therapy at the Payne Whitney Clinic in New York City. But intervention and treatment provided no benefit. Schwartz actually pocketed the money Bellow had collected and signed himself out—or, as Bellow put it, "he broke loose and I can be of no other use to him now."[10]

Extremely paranoid, Schwartz got it in his mind that Bellow was "one of his ill-wishers" and began telephoning him at all hours of the early morning, "using techniques the GPU [Directorate of State Security in the USSR] might have envied." He was "threatening to sue me for slander," Bellow said, and he was "frightening my poor wife."[11] According to James Atlas's superbly rendered biography of Schwartz, "No great significance can be attached to Delmore's choice of Bellow as a prominent figure in the conspiracies he perceived, for he had become indiscriminate in his suspicions."[12] But it was clearly Bellow's success and his many awards that Schwartz envied, and he continued over the years to mock and belittle his old friend Saul and his accomplishments. Hard and strong-willed as he was, Bellow could not be anything but affected in his heart and consciousness by the pain of losing Schwartz as a friend and then losing him altogether.

In the years that followed Schwartz's hospitalization, Bellow put aside Delmore's harassment and tried to help him, principally to find teaching jobs.[13] And then in June 1966, after almost ten years of not having heard from or seen him, Bellow, at the height of his success and with the beautiful Maggie Staats on his arm, spotted a battered and decrepit-looking Schwartz—and he hid. He later owned up to the sin he had committed, but he had never actually stopped loving Schwartz. He substantiated that love (and possibly exorcised some of his guilt, irrational or not, for having succeeded where Schwartz had failed) by writing *Humboldt's Gift*, a novel that, among other things, served as an homage to Delmore.

Bellow also tried to help his friend John Berryman, one of the leading poets of the postwar period, by providing moral support while Berryman was in the process of divorce from Eileen Simpson in the mid-fifties. And in the sixties, when Bellow was away and between marriages, he invited Berryman to stay at the Tivoli house, telling him that "there is coal in the grate, great whiskey on the shelf, and feathers in the bed." Berryman, however, as he had throughout much of his life, continued to abuse alcohol and struggle with depression. In the first week of January 1972, he killed himself by jumping from the Washington Avenue Bridge in Minneapolis. Harvey Swados died the same year, as did the esteemed critic Edmund Wilson and Bellow's longtime literary agent Henry Volkening. Philip Rahv perished in 1973.

The poet Anne Sexton, forty-six, committed suicide in 1974. She treasured Bellow's writing, especially his novel *Henderson the Rain King*, whose motifs inspired several of her poems. The two pursued a lively and touching correspondence, in which, according to her biographer Diane Wood Middlebrook, Bellow seems to encourage the unhappy, desperate Sexton to cling to life. The biblical injunction, "I have set before you life and death, blessings, and curses. Now choose life, so that you and your children may live," is Bellow's recurrent Deuteronomic adage, a basso continuo.[14]

Bellow wrote to Ralph Ross from Aspen, saying he didn't "know what we survivors should do with this slaughter-legacy our old friends have made us." Bellow was thinking of Isaac Rosenfeld and Schwartz, and John Berryman, who had said "that he'd never drink again, that he wanted more love affairs. At the same time, he knew he was a goner. . . . There's something culturally gratifying, apparently, about such heroic self-destruction."[15] This notion resurfaces sporadically in Bellow's letters and appears in *Humboldt's Gift*.

Over a seven-year period, there were ten untimely deaths of people in Bellow's life, part of a world and generation supremely important to him, his heart, and his soul. In 1968 he also came very close to losing Bette Howland, yet another valued, indeed cherished friend. She had been Bellow's student in a creative writing class in 1961, in which she started writing stories based on her Jewish working-class family in Chicago. From about the mid-1960s, Bellow also became her erstwhile and perhaps recurring lover, and she continued over the course of her lifetime to remain among the first readers of his written drafts. Doing secretarial and editorial work for Bellow in his apartment in the summer of 1968 while he was in the Hamptons with Maggie Staats, Howland attempted suicide by swallowing a lethal dose of sleeping pills.

Howland's relationship to Bellow was, to say the least, complicated. From the Rockefeller Foundation retreat at Lake Como, Italy, Bellow had written to her as late as September 1968: "I think about you several times a day. My silly mind seems to be finishing out the last stages of some apprenticeship, and you are one of the topics of a maturer interest." In the same month, Howland told Bellow that when she answered his phone, it was "agony" for her to be reminded of his many girlfriends. But if Bellow played a part in Howland's suicide attempt, it was as much because of his temporary neglect of Howland as a friend, "a colleague, an ally," as his neglect of her as a woman—a view attested to by Dave Peltz and by Howland's later correspondence.[16]

Irving Howe, who knew Bellow, Schwartz, and Berryman in Princeton in the early sixties, saw Bellow as "very strong-willed"—hardier than Berryman and Schwartz, and "very shrewd in the arts of self-conservation."[17] Bellow's letters in the 1960s and beyond show a man capable of summoning high spirits from low and keeping himself out of the clutches of "the newest wrinkle in anguish." In a letter to art critic Meyer Schapiro about Delmore Schwartz, dead now two years, Bellow, in one of his many moving life affirmations, remarked that he could "see why these self-destructive lives are led. But I can't convince myself that it is a good tradition."[18]

Bellow's concerns about death reappear later in Charlie Citrine, who says in *Humboldt's Gift*, "I am obliged to deny that so extraordinary a thing as a human soul can be wiped out forever."[19] For Staats, however, feelings about death were a foundation for anxiety: Her father was what she called a "Bible Belt" type, and she and her siblings were instilled with a deep conviction of hellfire and brimstone. "My whole life," she confessed, "was wrapped up with the question of whether I was going to go to hell." Surprisingly, Bellow had never run into this question before, but he took it seriously.[20]

He saw Staats's fear of damnation as "a real problem." She, like Clara Velde in *A Theft* (1987) and Demmie Vonghel in *Humboldt's Gift*, had dreadful nightmares. For Staats, the terror of perdition was extreme in the late sixties. Clearly, what connected her to Bellow "wasn't just the sex," she said; it was the question of death that "joined [them] from day one." Bellow's concern with the soul, Maggie believed, was his one "true" connection to the world of thought, and he pursued it "without bias for the rest of his life." This assessment of hers held true in Bellow's life and in his writing, beginning most plainly in *Herzog,* continuing more obviously in *Humboldt's Gift,* and from there evinced clearly in *The Dean's December* (1982); it lasted until he wrote his last novel, *Ravelstein* (2000), at age eighty-five.[21]

After his difficult experience at SFSU in 1968, it would be reasonable to think that Bellow might shy away from speaking engagements on college campuses. But when Robert Penn Warren, Bellow's friend and former colleague at Princeton University, asked him to speak at Yale to a handpicked group of English majors, he agreed. He faced a torpid and oddly unresponsive group. One student who had apparently failed to read *Mr. Sammler's Planet,* or was trying to set Bellow up, asked his opinion of the campus "revolutionaries" of the late 1960s. Bellow answered by saying, "The trouble with the destroyers is that they're just as phony as what they've come to destroy. Maybe civilization is dying, but it still exists, and meanwhile we have our choice: we can either rain more blows on it, or try to redeem it." Bellow's answer was met by an eerie stillness. "I see I've reduced you all to silence," Bellow quipped, only to be met again with no response. Well, he said, "It's late" (it wasn't), "and I have an early train to catch" (he didn't). He left, telling Warren in an ironic understatement that he and the students "[did]n't talk the same language."[22]

Bellow told this story to Jane Howard, who was interviewing him in the spring of 1970 in his large five-room South Side Chicago apartment. In response to a question about *Mr. Sammler's Planet,* Bellow said, "I had a high degree of excitement writing it . . . and finished it in record time. It's my first thoroughly nonapologetic venture into ideas." In *Herzog* and *Henderson the Rain King,* Bellow said, "I was kidding my way to Jesus, but here I'm baring myself nakedly," again signifying Bellow's belief that life, and in particular his own life, was a "religious enterprise."[23]

Bellow showed Howard around the apartment and had her flip through his treasured family photo album. "Three divorces notwithstanding," Howard wrote, "Bellow genuinely cares about his family and tries to keep in touch with all its generations and branches." She pointed out that the rye bread he served was baked in his father's cousin's bakery, where Bellow's father had worked years earlier. And the bread was layered with "chicken liver chopped by a niece." Other traditional Jewish food favored by Bellow included black bread, pickled herring, and smoked whitefish.[24] After their snack he offered to guide Howard around the city. The tour began with the obligatory view of the skyline panorama and proceeded to "the open markets of Maxwell Street, whose proprietors, uncoaxed, conversed with Bellow in . . . Yiddish."[25]

Three months later in the summer of 1970, Bellow traveled to Israel again. At the invitation of Hebrew University's English Department, he participated in a panel discussion with Israeli writers including the poet Yehuda Amichai and novelist A. B. Yehoshua. It appears that Bellow, the guest, did most of the talking. He focused on the experiences of his generation of American Jews, caught between the hardships of their own upbringings and the seemingly unregulated freedom they had bequeathed to their children—who he thought were currently dragging America into a state of siege.

What he described as "the strong Jewish element" in his personality was genuine. But at the same time, he was very much an American, even more so in Israel, where Hebrew writers were eager to make him part of their tradition. Bellow had promoted their interest, consciously or otherwise, after he said he identified more with Isaac Babel, I. L. Peretz, and S. Y. Agnon than with the writers of his own generation. But for Bellow, while the painful history of the Jews was inscribed in his soul, so was a Yiddish skepticism and a spirit of American independence.[26] He said that "the Jewish community in America was delighted when Jewish writers appeared on the scene because they felt it would be good for the Jews in America. This put us in a rather awkward position of doing public relations, unwillingly, for the American Jews, and we were also expected to refrain from any sharp criticism of persons who were Jews."[27]

Bellow understood why American Jews took pride in the literary success of their sons (and daughters, too), but many writers found this pressure to refrain from criticism "extremely disagreeable." It was an imposition on truth, he thought, "to have to make things come out nicely . . . and give the people a pleasing impression." Most Jewish writers, he said, reacted negatively to such expectations. The pressure put on them, Bellow ventured, may have made some bend over backward into contrariness and become "quite nasty in their portrayal of Jews." This is "an accusation that has been brought against Philip Roth, who has gone much further in this direction," Bellow said, "than I ever dreamed of going."[28]

Roth's brilliant but wicked novel *Portnoy's Complaint* had arrived in US bookstores near the end of 1969, only months before Bellow made this trip to Israel. A significant number of American rabbis and community leaders, beginning as early as 1959, accused Roth of "cultural treason." But Bellow counseled his friend "to ignore pious critics who would have him write the Jewish equivalent of 'socialist realism'" and encouraged him to "continue on his current course."[29]

Bellow's summer stay in Israel coincided with the twenty-fifth anniversary of the liberation of the Bergen-Belsen concentration camp, and he was invited to Jerusalem for a banquet commemorating the historic event. The main speaker was Elie Wiesel. Critic and memoirist Alfred Kazin, also in attendance, described Wiesel's speech as "a survivor's soliloquy, a litany, a hymn, a *Kaddish*," but like Bellow sitting on the other side of his table, he grew mostly bored as Wiesel "teetered on the edge of incommunicable profundities." Bellow (according to Kazin) was much more interested in Golda Meier, the energetic Israeli prime minister, who got up to speak surrounded by soldiers armed with Uzis. In Yiddish, she declared, "No matter what they do to us, we'll beat them." She paid sincere homage to the Belsen survivors and brusquely ended, "Believe me, friends, we shall overcome."[30]

Sitting with Bellow was Fran Gendlin, an American woman he had known since the spring of 1969. She described herself as "this nice Jewish housewife," apparently just what Bellow seemed to need, a bright enough woman who could deal with his personal and domestic chaos, but one, as he said, whom "he could only love . . . so far." Bellow referred to her as "my *Yidineh*," Yiddish for a shallow, uncultivated, gossipy woman. Gendlin told Zachary Leader that Bellow could from time to time treat her "like crap," but she confessed that she was "addicted to him" nonetheless. The relationship ended after five years.[31]

Fran Gendlin may have inspired Bellow's creation years later of Katrina (Trina) in his long story "What Kind of Day Did You Have?" (1984). Victor Wulpy, the central male figure in the story, is a loosely attached paramour of Katrina, a divorced matron with two kids. She sees Victor—who resembles the New York intellectual Harold Rosenberg—as "the man in her life"; he sees her as "pretty enough," a bit on the plump side but pleasantly so. Katrina is noticeably clumsy, but clumsiness Victor thought "might come out as girlishness if it was well managed." There "were few things," however, "which Trina managed well [and] her options were increasingly limited by Wulpy," who had "his own special difficulties to deal with"—his advanced age, the state of his health, and his prominence.[32]

When Bellow was asked by a *Washington Post* interviewer about his unflattering portrayal of a female character in his story, a woman who is "old-fashioned and sexually enslaved without a mind of her own," Bellow responded, "Well, I'm sorry girls—but many of you are like that, very much so. It's going to take a lot more than a few books by Germaine Greer or whatshername Betty Friedan to root out completely the Sleeping Beauty syndrome."[33]

This kind of defensive remark, made after being charged, even surreptitiously, with sexism, was not atypical for Bellow. Many if not most of his fictive women were indeed bitter, emasculating, or avaricious. They were also "sexy." But they were also very strong and intelligent, as were the women Bellow chose to marry. Anita Goshkin, his first wife, was a graduate of Northwestern, a politically astute activist, and a social worker; his second wife, Sondra Tschacbasov, graduated from Bennington, wrote poetry, and felt comfortable in the company of writers and artists; Susan Glassman, Bellow's third wife, was a University of Chicago graduate, a vivid and literate letter writer, a serious reader, and an aspiring author with a drawer full of unpublished stories. She also read and critiqued *Herzog*. Alexandra Ionescu Tulcea was an internationally renowned mathematician. Later there would be Janis Freedman, who graduated from the University of Chicago and earned a degree in literature and philosophy in the university's Committee on Social Thought program. Bellow characterized her as a person of considerable intellectual force and independence. Eventually, she earned a PhD and went on to teach at the university level.

In 1969, five years after the publication of *Herzog*, Bellow continued to be honored by the literary world and the American Jewish community and endured a hectic schedule of travel. He was elected a Fellow of the American Academy of Arts and Science in Boston, was granted an honorary degree by New York University, and received the Jewish Heritage Award in Washington, DC. And in August, after attending twenty-five-year-old Gregory's wedding in San Francisco, Bellow returned to Nantucket, spending part of the month with thirteen-year-old Adam.

None of this required intellectual focus or a writer's energy, but when William Maxwell asked Bellow to deliver an annual lecture to the American Academy and National Institute of Arts and Letters, Saul, though "greatly honored," turned down the invitation, saying he was in no state of mind to compose such an address. By the mid-1960s and continuing well into the 1970s, Bellow said he was in a "period of turmoil" and undergoing extremes of jealousy, mistrust, and belligerence. The chopped, bitter tone in sections of *Mr. Sammler's Planet* was partly a product of this psychological chaos. Bellow himself told the writer Daniel Fuchs that "Sammler isn't even a novel; it's a dramatic essay of some sort, wrung from me by the crazy '60s."[34] And Alfred Kazin, recognizing something like this in his mixed review of *Sammler,* called the novel a "*cri du coeur* that does not disguise the punitive moral outrage behind it."[35]

Bellow never forgave Kazin, even though his old friend remained cordial and generous. Despite a chill in their relationship, it was still possible for them to come together at a conference in Washington, DC, and join Arthur Miller and Norman Podhoretz in petitioning the Soviet Union to end the persecution of the Russian writer Alexander Solzhenitsyn.

In Bellow's correspondence during this period, he frequently refers to his "bad behavior" in regard to women, editors, colleagues, and friends as a product of character, a "part of the package," as well as a response to external aggravations. At the very end of the sixties and through the seventies, Bellow was looking to become more of a mensch, to be a "better man," something like the well-intentioned but fragile men he was trying to create in his literature.[36]

In the spring of 1969, Bellow entered therapy for the fourth and final try, this time with the distinguished psychoanalyst Heinz Kohut. The Austrian-born Jewish doctor, an admirer of art and literature, was not narrowly focused on psychoanalysis, emphasizing instead the role played by environment, culture, and conscious thought and decision-making in the development of character. Kohut's not particularly profound conclusion appears to have been that Saul's eagerness for women "was motivated not by libidinal but by narcissistic needs."[37]

The doctor's conclusion might have had merit, but the patient described in Kohut's published book as "Mr. I," a university professor who suffers from "Don Juan syndrome," may not in fact have been Bellow. The doctor's records were confidential, of course, but armed with Kohut's diagnosis that the unnamed analysand was attempting to "provide an insecurely established self with a continuous flow of self-esteem," James Atlas merely guessed that the patient was Bellow. Perhaps more important, few if any people who knew Bellow would think he was suffering from a clinical narcissistic personality disorder. His emphasis on the individual in no way precluded his recognition of the supreme importance of community. Bellow did not believe that the self was the only thing that mattered or that it could live in a social vacuum.

Known by many as a "great observer," Bellow, though acerbic at times, was also remarkably curious, open, and sympathetic to other people. With *Augie March, Henderson the Rain King, Herzog*, and *Humboldt's Gift,* and in nearly all the writing that followed, Bellow demonstrated not only that special curiosity and sympathy but also a rich grasp of the sights, smells, and textures of the corporeal world outside of the self and was attuned to the strange and often rough quality of that world as well as to its melodiousness and sweetness.

If not a full-blown narcissist, Bellow's eagerness for women—libidinal to be sure—was also egotistical. While at the Rockefeller Foundation retreat at Lake Como, in 1969, Bellow was attracted to the poet Louise Gluck (later a Nobel laureate) because, as she put it, she was "nubile." But as Gluck told Atlas, Bellow's seduction technique was more "literary than physical." In bed, he read to Louise from his drafts of *Humboldt's Gift,* and she read him poetry.[38] Maggie, and Sasha and Susan, too, before they were Bellow's wives, became his audience from time to time; reading his writing aloud, Bellow could sometimes go on through the night.

In his quest for *menschlikhkayt,* although still juggling women, Bellow tried to do more for his broken families. When Sasha moved from Long Island to the Upper West Side of Manhattan, she enrolled Adam in the Dalton School, and Bellow willingly paid the fees. In addition, in March 1970 he paid for Adam's bar mitzvah ceremony and reception, something that his oldest son, Greg, had been permitted to forgo. Bellow also paid for Adam's post–bar mitzvah Hebrew lessons, which the boy had been pursuing since he was nine.

Sasha estimated that as many as a thousand people, almost the entire congregation of the Park Avenue synagogue, turned out for the bar mitzvah ceremony. *Sammler* had been published only five weeks earlier, and everyone, Sasha said, wanted a look at the famous author and his son.[39] And famous he was and continued to be. *Sammler* had garnered mixed reviews, but it won the National Book Award, Bellow's third. Many, if not most, critics agreed with Joseph Epstein's assessment of Bellow's standing in American letters: He "is the best writer we have in the literary form that has been dominant in . . . the past hundred years."[40]

Two months after the bar mitzvah, it was Bellow's turn to chair the Committee on Social Thought. In his courses at the university, he taught what he liked in small classes. He talked about his own life as an artist. According to Arlette Landes, Bellow "figured that was what people came to hear—and he was enchanting." He called his courses, she said, "episodes in the history of the soul in modern times."[41]

Bellow was glad to teach these courses, which, along with his eight-year position as chair of the committee and his steady writing, kept him busy, distracting him from personal difficulties. He was also able to escape some of the freneticism of the legal process in which he was caught—the demands of lawyers, wives, editors, and publishers—by serving as writer-in-residence and Guest Fellow at the American Institute for the Humanities in Aspen, Colorado, during the summers of 1971 to 1975. For five years running, Bellow relaxed at this western retreat—so much so that during several summers he occasionally invited visitors, including close friends, such as Edward Shils, David Peltz, and his sons Adam and Daniel.

Bellow also developed a friendship at Aspen with the novelist James Salter (originally Horowitz). The two writers, over sour mash whiskey, exchanged ideas and remembered mutual friends and relationships, spending a good deal of time talking about John Berryman's 1972 suicide. At Princeton in their younger days, two decades earlier, Berryman and Bellow had shared an enthusiasm for each other's work that sustained them both. Now he felt Berryman's absence.

Salter admired Bellow as a writer but did not envy him as a man: "I felt he was harried" and "beset by problems of guilt and behavior." Bellow enumerated the exasperations he suffered in a letter to Shils: "Law suits, taxes . . . the gnawing volume of daily mendacity, obstinate stupidities of the educated in intellectual professions, and my own persistent wicked habits of soul."[42] When Fran Gendlin visited Bellow at the Aspen retreat in 1972, her "take on the whole thing [was] that [Bellow] was beginning to fear his mortality. His friends were dying." He talked about John Berryman and Isaac Rosenfeld "all the time and [a lot] about Delmore Schwartz." She thought that in the face of all this, she helped make Bellow "feel younger." Perhaps having her around, she said, was his "way of avoiding the Angel of Death."[43]

In May 1973, more than a year after Berryman's death, Bellow, still haunted, wrote an elegy for his poet friend in the *New York Times*:

> He was a husband, a citizen, father, a householder, he went on the wagon, he fell off, he joined A.A. [Alcoholics Anonymous]. He knocked himself out to be like everybody else—he liked, he loved, he cared, but he was aware that there was something peculiarly comical in all this. And at last it must have seemed that he had used up all his resources. Faith against despair, love versus nihilism had been the themes of his struggles and his poems. What he needed for his art had been supplied by his own person, by his mind, his wit. He

> drew it out of his vital organs, out of his very skin. At last there was no more. Reinforcements failed to arrive.[44]

Bellow, who, like Berryman, made "faith against despair, love versus nihilism," the themes of his life and work, was at the time well into writing *Humboldt's Gift,* a novel infused with the spirits of John Berryman, Isaac Rosenfeld, and especially Delmore Schwartz. Indeed, a good part of the novel is a protracted elegy, with Charlie Citrine weeping for Von Humboldt Fleisher and cursing materialistic America for driving the brilliant poet to ruin.

Bellow's days in the early seventies were not all gloomy. A revised version of his play *The Last Analysis* was restaged in June 1971, off Broadway, at the Circle in the Square on New York City's Bleeker Street. The play was reviewed positively by *New York Times* critic Clive Barnes as "a peculiar mix . . . of wild humor and cheerfully careless craftsmanship . . . one of the funniest comedies written in the last few years." Enjoying himself immensely, Bellow wrote to his friend and neighbor Constance Perrin, a cultural anthropologist, about the play's reception. Referring to the existence of a "stony professional prejudice against novelists in the theater," Bellow told Perrin that the success of the play and its critical reception "are the victories that gratify my litigious character and my vengeful Jewish heart." And he sent a note congratulating the cast for "redeeming [the play] from the butchers."[45]

Bellow also had a stint in Japan in 1972 as an International Exchange Fellow. He was expected to offer talks, seminars, and interviews and to attend receptions. The number and pace of events was staggering; there were "no small gatherings," Saul wrote to Fran Gendlin, "only mobs." Two weeks passed before things slackened enough for Bellow to get out of Tokyo. He rented a tranquil old-style guesthouse in Kyoto. "Sleeping on the straw mat and lying on the floor . . . half the day admiring the little moss garden," he told Gendlin, "was childhood again and childhood," Bellow affirmed, as was his wont, "is still the most pleasant part of life." This, he said, was not just a paean to youth but "a confession of adult behavior."

As it is, Bellow told her, "the world seems to expect that I will do all kinds of good things, and I spite it by doing all kinds of bad ones. They're not terribly *bad*. . . . Striking sins are out of reach. . . . But nothing comes of this except unhappiness for myself and others. The unhappiness to myself I don't mind much. The effect on others is a curse to me night and day."[46]

John Nathan, Bellow's host in Japan, noticed several "bad things" that caused others unnecessary unhappiness. When Bellow was interviewed by the Japanese novelist Kenzaburo Oe, twenty years later himself a Nobel laureate, he was withdrawn, saying little. Oe, a great fan, told Nathan that Bellow had scarcely given him "the time of day." And at least once, Bellow "ripped through" a lecture before a large audience of English professors and left without answering questions—a performance his host described as "passive/aggressive, hostile."[47]

While cordial much of the time—in Japan or elsewhere—Bellow could be arrogant or make dismissive, cutting remarks, most of which he subsequently regretted.[48] When he was awarded the Nobel Prize in Literature in 1976, Bellow was reminded, by mail from an old, no doubt bitter colleague, that this kind of verbal behavior was not so unusual. It took about six years, but Bellow turned the genuine guilt he felt over that behavior into art.

In "Him with His Foot in His Mouth" (1982), the protagonist, Professor Hershel Shawmut, aging and ill, and aware of the senselessness of modern civilization, acknowledges the "evil [he] did" years ago by making inexcusable remarks, "vile. . . . Idiotic and wicked." The story takes the form of a letter of "apology" to Miss Rose, a librarian, whom the professor thinks he hurt badly years earlier. Having come out of the stacks to get a breath of fresh air, Miss Rose sees Shawmut passing by in a baseball cap and says, in a friendly enough manner, "Oh, Dr. Shawmut, in that cap you look like an archaeologist." Before Shawmut can stop himself, he answers, "And you look like something I just dug up." Immediately he tells himself, "Awful!" Was it just "fun or psychopathology or wickedness"? No one can judge.[49]

Bellow told an interviewer that one theme of the story is "the legitimate irresponsibility of comedy. . . . It's an interesting problem; things just pop out of your mouth. They come from comic inspiration, and that is one of the prominent forms of freedom. It also sorts well with Jewishness, where there is a tradition of being able to say some things only when laughing."[50] And in this way it sorts well with Yiddish, too. "Yiddish is a hard language," Shawmut tells Miss Rose: "You may have heard charming, appealing sentimental things about Yiddish, but . . . Yiddish is severe. Yes, it is often delicate, lovely, but it can be explosive as well. 'A face like a slop jar,' 'a face like a bucket of swill.'"[51]

Although partly excusing himself, Shawmut is nonetheless apologizing sincerely. Here we laugh at the many jokes Bellow has borrowed from friends, but we recognize, too, that Shawmut is searching for spiritual content in his life and seeking forgiveness, making the story in large part a reflection of Bellow's continued quest for *menschlikhkayt*.

In the spring of 1974, soon after a trip to San Francisco with Fran Gendlin, Bellow made a brief visit to London and then spent the early months of summer at Barley Alison's villa in southern Spain working toward the completion of *Humboldt's Gift*. Here he brought Alexandra Ionescu Tulcea, partly to be "checked out" by Alison and his editor at Weidenfeld, Bellow's English publisher. Apparently, Alexandra passed the test, and she would soon become Bellow's fourth wife. They had met initially in 1969 when she was thirty-four and Bellow fifty-three. It was more than two years before they met again, but sometime in 1973, Saul and Alexandra began "seriously dating."[52]

They had met initially at a party in Hyde Park given by Mircea Eliade, a professor of comparative religion at Chicago and Bellow's colleague as a member of the Committee on Social Thought. Eliade and his wife were Romanians, as was Ionescu Tulcea, but she had only recently gotten to know the couple. She knew no one at the party and hadn't "the faintest idea of who Saul Bellow was" or why the other guests seemed to be "fawning all over him." When introduced, she told him that she hadn't read any of his books. Bellow quipped that he'd never read any of hers! She was more than surprised when Bellow's next line was a marriage proposal: "I was speechless. . . . I was very flattered but . . . also taken aback." Later she learned that it was one of Bellow's favorite opening lines with women, "a sure ice-breaker."[53]

When Alexandra told Bellow that she was moving to Boston to teach at MIT, his interest was "piqued." In the short time before she left Chicago, she and Bellow "became close." He was attracted to her for all the obvious reasons, but also because she was calm, accomplished, elegant, with a strong sense of the aesthetic, and "different." She was attracted to him partly because his literary world, about which she knew little, was totally outside of the field of higher mathematics in which she had an international reputation for her work in number theory and probability. Bellow was also "very charming, very funny, and very witty," she said, and he knew an enormous number of things, had read everything, and had a fabulous memory. Ionescu Tulcea saw in Bellow "such a contrast to the mathematicians I had known and to the life I had led before, and it really made an enormous impact."[54]

When seventeen-year-old Adam Bellow saw his father interact with Alexandra, he had the sense that Bellow "respected her and that he wanted to be the man that she saw in him. He wanted to be that guy," not merely a distinguished figure but a good man, putting bad behavior behind him. Saul came to Alexandra "like a refugee from a burning city. He told her the story of his family's 'trials and suffering'" and of his own psychological and spiritual needs. "She was very receptive," Adam said, "and provided a high-octane sympathy." She, in turn, saw Bellow as a genuinely thoughtful man, a serious man—someone she could admire like the father she had lost at the age of eleven.[55]

Bellow had a great longing to be seen in this way, making Ionescu Tulcea all the more irresistible. "If you've been through three failed marriages and a bunch of long relationships . . . knowing that you haven't been at your best," Adam ventured, "I can really understand Alexandra's appeal. . . . She brought out a side of him—courtly, indulgent, fond, paternal—I hadn't seen." And she was thoughtful, wrote thank-you notes, and made certain Bellow remembered all his sons' birthdays. The Bellow family took to Alexandra and welcomed her warmly. And she took to them, creating in the process a new family for Adam: "It was a wonderful feeling to know that I belonged to a new family. . . . They were wonderful to me." Saul and Alexandra were quietly married in November 1974.

"For a long time it worked," Adam says of the relationship: "The match was a good one, and Saul did live up to her expectations," which partly meant he remained faithful. As Adam sees it, his father was "delighted to have an opportunity to redeem himself," to become the mensch he wanted to be. As a result of having had to live the first twenty years of her life under Stalinist totalitarianism. Alexandra Ionescu Tulcea had what Bellow saw as "existential depth." He read as much as he could about the gulag and the labor camps, which intensified his resolution to meet the standards and the expectations of a woman like her, "who had lived all that."[56]

Bellow tried to incorporate those standards into his behavior as chair of the Committee on Social Thought, in relations with his family, and in expanded social and political activities. In 1973, in the manner of Elya Gruner in *Mr. Sammler's Planet,* he initiated a campaign to get his maternal cousin Mischa Ulman, electronics engineer and "refusenik," out of Latvia. With the help of his friend and lawyer Walter Pozen in Washington, Bellow made appeals on Ulman's behalf to Senator Hubert Humphrey, Henry Kissinger, Soviet ambassador Anatoly Dobrynin, Senator Jacob Javits, and President Richard Nixon. He also sent telegrams to the Soviet minister of culture and the chair of the Soviet Writers Union.

In the spring of 1973, Bellow came to New York to meet Ulman's mother, Bella, who had been allowed to emigrate to Israel, and he began a campaign to persuade the Soviet authorities to allow Ulman to do the same. Bellow's brother Sam and his wife, Nina, also campaigned on Mischa's behalf, as did several Jewish organizations. Saul Bellow wrote "Dear Cousin Mischa" to inform him that "he had made formal application to bring you to the United States. My desire is that you should live in Chicago where I will make myself responsible for you, seeing to all your needs until you are able to make your own way. . . . I speak for the entire family when I say that we shall be very happy to have you here." By December 1973, the campaign had succeeded. Ulman left Latvia for Israel, and from there after a time he moved to the United States.[57]

A year after Ulman's arrival in Israel, Bellow and Alexandra flew to Jerusalem. At small family gatherings of Bellow's maternal relatives, Saul finally met Ulman. He had found a job with Sony as an electronics engineer; his mother, Bella, "a medical worker of some sort" in Russia, was now a department-store cashier.[58]

Bellow was elated with his part in "extracting" Ulman from a brutally oppressive, antisemitic Soviet Union. And in his PEN address, he stressed the artist's obligation to defend freedom against injustice and to be on the side of the good and the true.[59] He had made the same point about an obligation to resist authoritarianism in a letter he wrote early in 1974 to the *New York Times* in defense of Alexander Solzhenitsyn. To Solzhenitsyn, as to all "the best Russian writers of this hellish century it has been perfectly clear that only the power of the truth is equal to the power of the state. . . . What Solzhenitsyn has done in revealing the unchecked brutality of Stalinism, he has done also for us. He has reminded every one of us what we owe to truth."[60]

In an earlier letter in defense of the truth, Bellow wrote to the editors of *Le Monde* on October 15, 1973, nine days after the outbreak of the Yom Kippur War. He addressed the mixed history of France in regard to Jews:

> It was France at the end of the eighteenth century that began the political liberation of the European Jews. In our own times, however, the French attitude toward the Jews has been painfully variable. The century began with the Dreyfus Case. In the Forties there was Vichy. Now there is the Pompidou government which, with a small show of neutrality and objectivity, has taken the Arab side in the present war. It associates itself politically with all of Israel's enemies, even the most bizarre of African and Asian demagogues. . . . There are two questions here. One is the question of justice to the Arabs, the other is that of the destruction of the Jews. There are also two traditions involved in this matter, those of Revolutionary France on the one hand and those of French anti-Semitism on the other.

He ends his letter by asking why France should not face the fact that Israel is democratic, while the Arab nations are xenophobic and feudal. Although he gave copies of his letter to the French playwright Eugene Ionesco, among others, to deliver to *Le Monde* directly, the letter was never acknowledged.[61]

As with his Israeli relatives, Bellow's connections to his siblings and their families were closer in this period than usual. In November 1973, he traveled to Montreal to give a lecture on James Joyce and to receive an honorary degree from McGill University. He was accompanied by his sister, Jane Bellow Kauffman, his brother Sam, and Sam's daughter, Lesha. All paid a visit to his father's extended family, the Gameroffs, in Lachine and Montreal.

Bellow also remained in contact, mostly through joint business ventures, with Maury, who by then was living in Florida. There were numerous joint investments, and although Bellow profited from many of them, in the end they generated bad feeling. It irritated Maury that Saul failed to understand the details of these deals and "didn't appreciate the business subtlety." The money was important to Bellow, but so was his relationship with Maury; when opportunities to be nearby presented themselves, Saul made several visits to his brother's Florida home. "I admired my brother," admits Herschel Shawmut in "Him with His Foot in His Mouth," "not because he was a 'creative businessman,' as they said in the family—that meant little to me—but because . . . Well, there is no 'because,' there's only the given, a lifelong feeling, a mystery."[62]

Bellow's efforts to be a good father in this period produced mixed results. Greg, who had lived with Anita and Saul for the first eight years of his life, may have felt his abandonment more keenly than Adam or Daniel. Married and a father now, Greg remained the prickliest of Saul's sons. In Greg's view, Bellow was judgmental and controlling. "By my late twenties," Greg said, he had grown "tired of judging" himself by his father's "standards."[63]

Relations were better with Adam, now a teenager and relatively happy at the Dalton School, after a rocky first year. Sasha attributed Adam's newly confident manner with his father in part to her being out of the picture. Adam and Bellow could arrange visits and meetings directly; Sasha was no longer "the referee."[64] These were the years, too, in which Sasha's own relations with Bellow began to improve. He even made some attempt to help her find editing and job opportunities in publishing.

Every Sunday and during holidays in the 1970s, Bellow was with Daniel, six years old at the start of the decade; he was the son Saul saw most often. But when, in 1972, Susan moved with Daniel from East Fifty-Fifth Street in Chicago, only minutes from Bellow's apartment and office, to Chicago's distant North Side, Saul was furious. He told Daniel (and later Susan), "I wasn't consulted about this." Her response was, "Fuck you, I'm not married to you, I can do what I want." When Daniel was asked during legal proceedings if Bellow could control himself in talks with him about Susan, he answered, "No, nor she about him. They would yell at each other," things like "'you're poisoning the child against me.'"[65]

Saul and Susan reached an initial divorce settlement in 1968, when Daniel was four, but continued to argue furiously about childcare and money and landed back in court. The battle of the Bellows went on for almost a decade and a half. In the same period, Saul Bellow produced *Mr. Sammler's Planet*, *Humboldt's Gift*, and substantial short stories, including "Zetland: By a Character Witness" and the equally affecting "A Silver Dish." He also wrote essays and a book about Israel and lectured all over the world. He chaired the Committee on Social Thought, advised foundations and grant committees, and visited the White House. He won a Nobel Prize, a Pulitzer Prize, and a third National Book Award.

All the while, Bellow was drowning in a sea of lawyers, even more so than during his first two divorce proceedings. They wore him out and nearly exhausted his money in "one of the longest, most expensive and acrimonious divorce settlements in Illinois history."[66] Bellow lost an appeal of a 1974 ruling and came out worse off in terms of the money he owed for alimony, child support, and Susan's "mental damages." The judge did not like Bellow. According to James Atlas, the judge said to one of Bellow's lawyers, "I don't like that son of a bitch, he writes pornography." Daniel thought it was "true that the judge hated him." He also thought that his father was right in thinking that "the judge was an anti-Semite . . . who thought that [Bellow] was a Jew who wrote dirty books."[67]

Susan would not give in, nor would Saul. Battles over the divorce tore at Bellow's nerves and challenged his patience. His struggles, even his own attempts to curb his stubbornness and volatility, obstructed his efforts to be the man he said he wanted to be. At his writing desk, however, these brawl-like skirmishes provided rich material, much of it dealing with his search for "higher truths" and once again demonstrating Bellow's talent for being very funny.

In *Humboldt's Gift,* as in all his mature works, Bellow performed the difficult redemptive magic of transforming his real-world suffering into art, and in this he found the truest expression of his desire to be a mensch. As we will see, in *Humboldt's Gift,* he "instructed" readers, touched them, and made them laugh even as he struggled with his own broken relationships and emotional hurt.

THIRTEEN

BELLOW'S GIFT, ISRAEL, AND THE NOBEL PRIZE

DURING AND AFTER BELLOW'S TRIALS and troubles, wrecked relationships, and emotional anguish, he gathered a rich vein of new material to draw on. His own daunting circumstances and pain, as with so much of his fiction, contributed to making *Humboldt's Gift,* Bellow's eighth novel, into an award-winning and widely praised book. The steady drollery and the tension in *Humboldt,* as in Bellow's previous novels, emerge out of the efforts of Humboldt and narrator Charlie Citrine to liberate themselves from the distractions of society in order to pursue the needs of their souls. The novel is at its heart an astonishing reflection on art and materialism.

It is a book of fiction not to be confused with anyone's "life." It is obvious, however, that the deeply distressed Delmore Schwartz was the model, deftly reimagined, for Von Humboldt Fleisher. In his own life, Bellow had tried to aid the troubled Schwartz and to provide encouragement and moral support for Isaac Rosenfeld as well as John Berryman. But he confessed to having been delinquent toward some of his cherished friends now dead. In a foreword to a posthumous collection of Isaac Rosenfeld's essays, he acknowledged, "I loved [Isaac], but we were rivals, and I was peculiarly touchy, vulnerable, hard to deal with—at times, as I can see now, insufferable, and not always a constant friend."[1]

As we have seen, Rosenfeld and Bellow grew up together as tight friends, talented and ambitious teenagers at Tuley High School in Chicago. That there was love between them, with all its reciprocity, even in the face of the competition that colored their relationship, there was no doubt. The friendly rivalry could, however, sometimes turn a little less friendly, even bitter, especially on Rosenfeld's part. When his novel *Passage from Home* (1946), despite critical admiration, was soon neglected, Rosenfeld was more than upset. He could be irritating, even hostile.[2] It didn't help that Bellow found the book overly sentimental and generally disappointing. This put a great strain on his friendship with Rosenfeld; after Bellow's *Augie March* (1953) won widespread adulation and the National Book Award, their relationship was effectively over.

Bellow also felt he was not always loyal to his friend Delmore Schwartz. As we saw in chapter 12, Bellow, with the youthful and beautiful Maggie Staats on his arm, spotted Delmore on the street in New York but hid from him; flying high, Bellow could not face Schwartz in his sickliness, mental confusion, and extreme destitution. But when Bellow read Schwartz's obituary about two months later and saw his "disastrous newspaper face staring at [him] from death's territory," he was overwhelmed with grief, and guilt continued to haunt him interminably.[3] According to Richard Stern, his friend and confidant, Bellow soon began to write a memoir about Delmore, so that the great writer "would not be . . . *Spurlos Versenkt* . . . sunk without a trace."[4] Schwartz's biographer, James Atlas, who had spoken with Bellow many times in the course of his work, said much the same thing: "Bellow, tormented by the dead, was compelled to resurrect an image of Delmore Schwartz."[5] And after eight years of imaginatively adapting his memoir, Bellow did just that, turning the manuscript into the novel *Humboldt's Gift*.

The narrator of the novel, Charlie Citrine, is the son of Jewish immigrants, a Pulitzer Prize–winning writer of biographies, plays, and historical essays. He aspires to something larger but invariably bumps up against the limits of an axiomatic American truth: The United States is indifferent if not outright hostile to its writers and poets. Still, Citrine recognizes that his own moral and spiritual shortfalls have played a part in his failure to define himself as the artist in the modern world.

Sixty years old, charming and sardonic, he blames himself for having been, in his words, "asleep on my feet, out cold. I have snoozed through many a crisis while millions died."[6] Charlie has been hankering after material rewards and obsessively chasing women while leaving the needs of his soul unattended. Chief among the women "leading him away" from his spiritual needs is the ubiquitous Renata, culturally ignorant but voluptuousness personified. With Charlie in a Mercedes showroom, Renata, "roused, florid, fragrant, large—had put her hand on the silver hood and said, 'This one—the coupe.' The touch of her palm was sensual. Even what she did to the car," Charlie says, "I felt in my own person."[7]

In trying to possess Renata, an intellectually limited and materialistic woman, and to own fancy cars and generally to live "the good life," Charlie feels he has squandered his prodigious talents. He struggles to understand this and finds himself in search of lost time, recollecting events not only in the normal Bellovian key connected to childhood but specifically wound around the person of a volcanic poet, now dead, who essentially shepherded him into the literary life as an ambitious young writer. Charlie has to come to terms with any part he may have played in the failure and untimely death of his one-time mentor and hero, the brilliant, effervescent, vastly erudite Von Humboldt Fleischer—the poet inspired by Delmore Schwartz, with Rosenfeld and Berryman in the mix.

In typical Bellow style, Citrine suffers simultaneously in both material and spiritual terms. He is enmeshed in a web of worldly problems. He suffers a weakened paddleball game, owes some $70,000 on advances for books he doesn't seem to have any plans to write, and is being battered by acrimonious divorce proceedings and cleaned out by lawyer's fees. In addition, his silver-gray Mercedes has been busted up badly with a baseball bat—the work of a petty hoodlum, Rinaldo Cantabile, whose wife is, implausibly, pursuing a PhD in English. He is a bully, a street-tough, but a very funny man, to whom Charlie has unwittingly written a bad check for an inconsequential gambling debt. A sadomasochistic relationship develops between Cantabile, the mobster, and Charlie, the intellectual—a classic example of the competitive byplay between machers or hoods on the one side and sensitive soul seekers on the other that recurs frequently in Bellow's fiction.

But all roads lead back to Humboldt. Charlie cannot fully enjoy whatever renown he has garnered because his dear friend and sometimes role model has died impoverished and in obscurity after many failures to write or publish. Manic episodes fueled by alcoholism, paranoia, shock treatments, and never-ending insomnia have brought Humboldt, for all his "radiant vividness of boundless love," to an ignominious end—early death in a fleabag hotel.[8] It disturbs Charlie greatly that his brilliant friend is gone, and he agonizes over the possibility that his own success was responsible.

If Citrine is suffering a case of survivor's guilt, it is intensified by Humboldt's accusation against him of having usurped his place as a winner in the fierce literary contest for survival. The once-venerated poet sees Citrine as having gained recognition in part by not crediting or reimbursing him for the inspiration that generated Charlie's highly acclaimed and wealth-generating Broadway play. Denying that his heavy drinking, obsessive mistrust, and endless sleeplessness had destroyed his natural talent, Humboldt blames Charlie for his decline on the cultural "Dow Jones."[9]

Humboldt had "had it all," Charlie thought. He was "an avant-garde writer, the first of a new generation, he was handsome, fair, large, serious, witty, he was learned," having read many thousands of books. Even the highest of the highbrows, the Princeton University faculty, "the fastidious goy critics on guard for the Protestant Establishment and the Genteel Tradition," welcomed this Jewish son of immigrant parents—for a time.[10]

Humboldt is quite sensitive about his Jewish identity and wants Charlie "to feel as insulted as [he] feel[s] [about antisemitism]": "Why don't you have indignation Charlie—Ah! You're not a real American. You're grateful. You're a foreigner. You have that Jewish immigrant kiss-the-ground-at-Ellis-Island gratitude. You're also a child of the Depression. You never thought you'd have a job, with an office, and a desk, and private drawers all for yourself. It's still so hilarious to you that you can't stop laughing. You're a Yiddisher mouse in these great Christian houses."[11]

One of the many reasons Bellow was attracted to Schwartz/Humboldt was that Schwartz had no hesitation in his commitment to a Jewish identity. This was complicated by his secularism and Americanness, of course; but he possessed a fundamental allegiance to an intimate, if not obsessive, self-examination of his consciousness. Deep awareness of his Jewishness fueled that exploration.[12]

Although free of the semiparanoid fears about antisemitism that plague Humboldt, Charlie thinks intermittently about the Holocaust. Speculation about the murder of the Jews is not unusual for him. He asks in one of his articles, for example, about whether Harry Houdini (b. Erik Weisz, to Jewish parents), the illusionist and stunt performer who escaped many a grave, "hadn't had an intimation of the Holocaust and was working out ways to escape from the death camps. Ah! If only European Jewry had learned what [Houdini] knew."[13]

Humboldt thought about Jews as victims, past and present, but in a nod to America as refuge, he equated poetry with "the merciful Ellis Island where a host of [Jewish] aliens began their naturalization."[14] Jews were also an important part of his ruminations and at the center of his loud, long, and humorous "speeches" about literary and political subjects. He talked about Freud's mining of the unconscious, the implications of Kafka's "The Penal Colony," and his own ideas about Trotskyism, to which he remained devoted. He also had imaginative ideas about poverty, racial injustice, fascism, and Stalinism, ideas and concepts that had so enthralled the New York Jewish intellectuals of the thirties and forties, from Philip Rahv, Paul Goodman, and Harold Rosenberg to Lionel Trilling, Sidney Hook, and Irving Howe. Among this galaxy of brilliant stars, "Humboldt was the best of them all," thinks Charlie; he "was simply the Mozart of conversation."[15] But Humboldt did not have it all, as Charlie first insisted.

Initially, he had "made it big"; he followed his initial blaze of rarefied glory with remarkable critical essays, stories, and poems in the *Partisan Review* and the *Southern Review,* but he had produced little of significance after these early brilliantly stunning triumphs. Instead, he, like Citrine, a desperate child of the Depression, had lived the good life, ferociously pursuing the trappings of material success. But he failed to attain the only symbol of achievement that matters in American culture—real wealth, money, huge money. And as Humboldt was profoundly American—crazy about Babe Ruth, the movies, and screen gossip, for example—this failure consumed him. Humboldt did not miss the mark for lack of trying. He was full of "arrangements" for making "real money," and he came very close to engineering an endowed chair at Princeton for himself.

But in the end, "all his thinking, writing, feeling, counted for nothing, all the raids behind the lines to bring back beauty had no effect except to wear him out"[16]—and bring him down. Humboldt leaves the city and finds a new abode in the back country of New Jersey, where the marginal land is good for nothing but chicken farming—done by his neighbors, old and broken people. Humboldt takes Charlie in his wreck of a Roadmaster to see the place. Approaches to the house are unpaved, and the car with its busted, incredibly loud muffler sways on huge springs through rubbishy fields. Charlie immediately realizes that poor Humboldt, who had lived in a city neighborhood surrounded by urban slums, now lives surrounded by rural slums.

Humboldt and his wife, Kathleen, ask Charlie to play football, something they do every day. It is the only time Kathleen gets out of the house. Otherwise, she spends most of her time reading—Marx, James, Proust, Wharton, and Freud—to catch up with what her husband constantly talks about. But for Humboldt, Kathleen, except for football, barely exists.

During the game, Humboldt calls out, "Look at Charlie jumping like Nijinsky." Citrine thinks, "I was as much Nijinsky" as Humboldt's deteriorated "house was Macbeth's castle." The surrounding flora—thistles, dwarf oaks, and cotton weed—are "all pauperized," and "the very bushes might have been on welfare"; the small trees seem significantly "underprivileged, dusty, orphaned-looking."[17]

But Citrine finds something lovely in the pulverized autumn leaves—"the fragrance of leaf decay"—and then, "Sunset. A red wash spreading from remote Pennsylvania, sheep bells clunking, dogs in brown barnyards. 'I was trained in Chicago to make something of such a setting. In Chicago you became a connoisseur of the near nothing.'" Bellow, if not Charlie, must have been thinking of his old Jewish neighborhood in Chicago, or more so, Napoleon Street in Montreal, where he and his older brothers prayed, where they were obligated not only to say the daily prayers but also to pray whenever seeing anything unusual—a notable person, a worthy deed, a beautiful flower, a rainbow, a stunning sunset.

Charlie actually falls in love with Humboldt's place, not because of flowers or sunsets and not because a poet lived there: "No, the influence was this: one of Humboldt's themes was the perennial human feeling that there was an original world, a home-world, which was lost. . . . But good old peculiar Humboldt," who had "the confidence of genius to commute between this patch, Nowhere, New Jersey, and the home-land world of our glorious origin," was, with his themes and schemes, essentially alone.[18]

During his lifetime, Humboldt may have at times relished being the solitary, misunderstood poet, but he clearly wanted wealth and continued acclaim as well. His failure in this regard led to his end in a flophouse in New York's West Forties, in what amounted to "suicide" on an installment plan of alcohol and drugs. Here, in the novel, Bellow avails himself of the opportunity to write a stunning paragraph on the place of poets in the mind of Americans:

> The Times was much stirred by Humboldt's death and gave him a double-column spread. The photograph was large. For after all Humboldt did what poets in crass America are supposed to do. He chased ruin and death even harder than he had chased women. He blew his talent and his health and reached home, the grave, in a dusty slide. He plowed himself under. Okay. So did Edgar Allan Poe, picked out of the Baltimore gutter. And Hart Crane over the side of a ship. And [Randall] Jarrell falling in front of a car. And poor John Berryman jumping from a bridge. For some reason this awfulness is peculiarly appreciated by business and technological America. The country . . . takes terrific satisfaction in the poets' testimony that the USA is too tough, too big, too much, too rugged, that American reality is overpowering.[19]

Bellow ends by writing, "And to be a poet is a school thing, a skirt thing, a church thing. The weakness of the spiritual powers is proved in the childishness, madness, drunkenness, and despair of these martyrs." In this eulogy for the dead poets, Bellow may very well have been thinking of his big brothers, who, using similar language, persistently mocked his sensibility, emotionalism, and flights of fancy and ridiculed his ambition to write.

The death of Humboldt increases Charlie's nearly lifelong terror of the grave, and, like Bellow, he hopes his sporadic intimations of immortality are the "real thing." He hopes that

Humboldt, whose ghost haunts him, is also the real thing—a soul with whom Charlie can be reunited in an elsewhere of forgiveness and "higher consciousness," or at the very least that Humboldt might remain a figure to be deferentially remembered in the here and now.

Bellow and Citrine draw a regretful moral warning from Humboldt's fate: Thought is not the critical component of true success. Humboldt represented the idea of poetry as a force capable of resuscitating a sick society, but he failed in pecuniary terms, American terms. Charlie Citrine, on the other hand, who has earned a modest fortune by writing, considers himself a failure in ethical terms. He, like Bellow in the 1970s, berates himself for his inability to fully understand (no less practice) his spiritual philosophy, for his failing to be good and to do good, and, at critical junctures, for neglecting friends in trouble.[20]

While he was bringing his novel to an end, Bellow, like his protagonist Charlie Citrine, was thinking again about the possibility of immortality and was still searching for a path to transcendence, back to his soul. Charlie tries, for example, to do right by his former lover Demmie Vonghel after she dies alongside her millionaire father in a plane crash in Venezuela. Canceling a pleasure trip, Charlie flies to South America and tries valiantly to locate Demmie's body; he flies from Chicago to Texas to help his brother cope with his fear of death, preceding heart surgery; and he shares with Humboldt's ancient uncle the money he has made from the bequeathed film treatment. And he has Humboldt and Humboldt's mother disinterred from "one of those necropolitan developments" in New Jersey and reburied in more dignified graves of their own.

Jewish law prescribes that the only way to obtain genuine atonement is to visit the grave of the wronged person and ask their pardon. The funeral service Citrine performs is a formal way of seeking true forgiveness from Humboldt. Acting as a pallbearer, Charlie feels how little weight the coffin holds: Of course!

"No human being's fate could be associated with such remains and superfluities!" There was nothing in there "of the charm, verve, and feverish invention, the calamity making, craziness of Humboldt." Peering into open graves was never pleasant. And now? The coffin is encased in concrete, and on top are brown clay and lumps and pebbles. "Why," Charlie thinks, "must it all be so heavy? . . . How did one get out? One didn't, didn't, didn't! You stayed, you stayed!"[21] But Charlie's own earlier reflections indeed suggested there was no "you" in there to get out. A soul would have already detached itself, leaving only memories to be carried through on Earth. Charlie may not have gained a higher consciousness through his recent experiences and Steinerian reflections, but he has recaptured his sense of responsibility and a zest for the physical quality of living.

More aware than ever of how precious his limited time on Earth is, he resolves to be an "entity," an independent person who listens to the voice of his own soul in secret, and vows to hear "the sound of truth that God puts into us" and to pay attention to a "core of the eternal in every human being."[22] He will simply no longer be an "identity," an inauthentic socially constructed self. By this choice, Citrine believes he has chosen to vanquish the "false and unnecessary comedy of history and begin simply to live."[23] Again, life is emphatically chosen over death, Bellow's predominant and ever-recurring theme. After reading *Humboldt's Gift,* Alfred Kazin, aged sixty, born in 1915 five days before Bellow, wrote in his journal, "Here I have been mooching along, more than half wishing for easeful death, waiting for the fire to blot me out completely . . . and Saul is insisting that he must continue! continue!"[24]

Actually, Bellow had his own problems "continuing." While still at work on proofs, he turned sixty. After celebrating his birthday with three dozen of his and Alexandra's friends in the apartment of Harriet Wasserman, his agent, editor, and friend, he reluctantly agreed to go to a Chinese restaurant. He was tired and upset at having had to cut short a telephone conversation with his dear friend John Cheever. On entering the restaurant, he was greeted with cries of "Surprise" and a chorus of "Happy Birthday" from a group of twenty including Philip Roth, Saul Steinberg (a renowned cartoonist), and John Cheever![25] Bellow, in his typical way, head thrown back, burst out laughing. Two months later, Saul wrote to Roth describing the birthday celebration as a "real party," although "I didn't know what I was saying or doing. . . . I do remember talking to you about the Jewish Writer but I was quite drunk and you were wasting your time. So let's try again."[26]

Soon after the party, the Bellows, now seven months married, were off to Germany to a mathematics conference where Alexandra was scheduled to give a paper. After a stop in London, where Saul met with anthroposophist Owen Barfield, the couple (accompanied by Adam) flew to southern Spain to recuperate in the Carboneras. In a long, revealing letter, Bellow told Dave Peltz, "The place is beautiful. I'm not particularly. I arrived in an exhausted state and have been sleeping, eating, swimming, reading and little else. . . . Life lays a heavy *material* on us in the States—things, cares, money. But I think that the reason . . . I feel it so much is that I let myself go here, and let myself feel six decades of trying hard and fatigue."

To Harriet Wasserman, Saul wrote that he was "oddly tired. This is Sixties fatigue, and I'm not talking about the last decade. It's only now after a week in the Carboneras, that I'm able to face a piece of paper."[27] In the letter to Peltz in which he complained about exhaustion, Bellow recognized that his attempts at becoming a better man were not yet a success. "My character," he wrote, "is like a taste in my mouth. I've tasted better tastes. . . . Life isn't kind to people who took it on themselves to do something about life. Uh-*unh*!" He went on to write what could be taken as a mixed message about himself and Adam, now twenty-one: he was "a marvelous young man, surprisingly good natured for a son of mine."[28]

After completing publicity duties for the new novel, Bellow took a much-needed three-month sabbatical, most of which he spent in Israel. Alexandra had been invited to Jerusalem to give a series of lectures on probability theory at Hebrew University; Saul had been yearning for an extended visit to the Promised Land, and here was his opportunity. Before traveling, Bellow had had no idea, certainly no plan, to write *To Jerusalem and Back* (1976), his first book of nonfiction. But the book inevitably grew out of the intense experiences and deep, wide-ranging discussions he had in Israel and the West Bank and with Arabs and Jews of all stations.

For Saul and Alexandra, adventures began early. Even as they were waiting in the departure area to board their flight from London to Tel Aviv, the couple found themselves surrounded by a crowd of Hasidim. "With their broad hats and beards and sidelocks and dangling fringes," some two hundred or more of these "black hats" were on their way from Heathrow to Israel to attend the *brit mi'lah* (circumcision ceremony) of the first-born son of their spiritual leader, the Belzer Rebbe. They were far too cheerful, too restless, to wait in any kind of line. They ran around harmlessly, "gesticulating, exclaiming." The flight attendants were furious.

None of this was unfamiliar to Bellow. In some ways, it was his "childhood revisited," a look back at his upbringing in the Jewish neighborhoods of Montreal and Chicago, which were infused, in the early twentieth century, with powerful residues of East European Jewish life. At the age of six, Bellow recalled, "I myself wore a tallit katan"—a sleeveless vest-type shirt with fringes, better known in Yiddish as tzitzit—"under my shirt." Moses was instructed by God "to speak to the children of Israel and 'bid them that they make fringes in the borders of their garments.'" So, Bellow said with amusement and a degree of admiration, "they are still wearing them four thousand years later."[29]

One young Hasid, about to be seated next to Alexandra, asked Bellow, "*Du redst Yiddish*?" ("Do you speak Yiddish?"). Encouraged by Bellow's affirmative reply, the Hasid said, "I cannot sit next to your wife; please sit between us. Be so good." This, too, ought to have been no surprise to Bellow, who knew that the "good-hearted" young man was not even permitted to look at a woman unrelated to him, let alone sit next to her or communicate with her in any way—which, Bellow thought, "probably save[d]" this unprepossessing youth "a great deal of trouble."[30]

Although he never liked the middle seat, Bellow, with no complaint, changed places with Alexandra. Indeed, in his willingness not to offend the Hasid, he asked the flight attendant for a kosher meal for himself. There were none left. Alexandra, curious, wanted to know why Saul ordered that way. "When they bring my chicken dinner this kid with the beard," Bellow said, "will be in a state." And sure enough, the young man recoiled at the sight of Saul's food: "You *are* a Jew. You must be a Jew; we are speaking Yiddish. How can you eat—*that*!"[31]

The well-meaning "kid" had with him kosher meat sandwiches packed by his "womenfolk." He offered one to Bellow and asked if his wife was Jewish. Bellow couldn't give him too many shocks at once, and so he settled for a lie of omission: "She has not had a Jewish upbringing." The sandwiches were, however, offered with a condition: "You must never eat *trephena* (unkosher) food again." This *chutzpadik* (cheeky) proposition, unsurprisingly, didn't work out, and Bellow turned to his British Airways chicken "with the chill of death upon it"; he ate guiltily, his "appetite spoiled."[32]

During the flight to Ben-Gurion Airport, Bellow learned that the Hasid had no idea what mathematics meant or who Einstein was. Even busy people with their fact-laden education in "head-culture" had heard of Einstein, even if the majority didn't know what they had heard: "These Hasidim choose not to know." Bewildered, Bellow lapsed into silence. After disembarking and before turning to the baggage area, the nattily dressed older man and the boy in black gave each other a quiet last glance. "In me," Bellow thought, "he sees what deformities the modern age can produce in the seed of Abraham. In him I see a piece of history, an antiquity." The distinction may have been experienced as striking, but Bellow himself, with a deep-seated biblical background, strongly self-defined as a Jew, was himself an offshoot of Judaism's antiquity.[33]

Not long into Bellow's stay in Israel, a "very Orthodox Professor . . . bearded and wearing a skull cap," told him that "American Jews are not Jews at all."[34] Bellow failed to respond, but he knew that many American Jews of his generation would turn the professor's remark inside out, because they saw Israelis less as Jewish and more like "*goyim*," brasher, more aggressive—and armed. He ruminated again, as he had with the Hasid on his flight, about differences in Jewish heritage—his own being very different from that of a Hasid or any other Orthodox Jew, or any indigenous Sabra ("prickly pear") Israeli. And it was different, too, from that of the Jews of London, Ankara, Morocco, Brazil, Moscow, and many other places—but Jewish nonetheless.

Although not anxious to receive VIP treatment, the Bellows were put up by Mayor Kollek in the guest house of Mishkenot Sha'aanim, southeast of the city, a seven-minute walk from the King David Hotel. The Hebrew name of the guest house and cultural center means "peaceful habitation."[35] It had not been especially peaceful in July 1946, when the house was filled with the reverberating echoes from the bombing of the King David Hotel—at the time the nerve center of British rule in Palestine. The Irgun, the Jewish national military organization opposed to Britain's continued control of Palestine, had set the explosives. During Bellow's three months in Jerusalem, no bombs went off anywhere near him. But his stay soon became anything but peaceful; fireworks of a different sort were in store for anyone asking difficult questions, even if not yet with the aim of writing a book but only in the spirit of self-education.

At the time of Bellow's visit in 1975, his fourth since 1960, the Israelis had lost the euphoria of victory in 1967 and were especially jittery about their near defeat in the 1973 Yom Kippur War. There was not yet peace with Egypt, nor had the Labor Party been vanquished by Menachem Begin's center-right Likud Party in 1977. And although there were bombings by Arab terrorists in buses and cafés and a palpable sense of siege, there was no apparent anticipation of the first violent uprising (Intifada) by the Palestinians in the occupied West Bank. Nor had the settler population yet grown exponentially to four hundred thousand or more.

Still, much in Bellow's reflections on the political convolutions in Israel, by now nearly a half-century old, remains relevant into the twenty-first century. The status of Palestinians, whom Bellow saw as having been grievously wronged over many decades, was at the top of his list. At the same time, Bellow was more than sympathetic to Israelis and intensely interested in their state of mind and general attitudes, what they said—and what they were thinking but not saying. Bellow had help in his pursuit of understanding from family, including a first cousin, and several friends living or studying in Israel. He was introduced to and interacted with scores of writers, poets, intellectuals, politicians, and "ordinary people," including his barber and his masseuse.

Before Bellow left Chicago on his way to Israel, the art critic Harold Rosenberg spoke to him "as a Jew to a Jew about Jewish powers of speech." He asked Bellow, "Going to Jerusalem? And wondering whether people will talk freely? You've got to be kidding, they'll talk your head off."[36] In Jerusalem, as he soon found out, "you fall into a gale of conversation—exposition, argument, harangue, analysis, theory, expostulation, threat, and prophecy."[37] From diplomats Bellow heard guarded explanations. Other responsible people made cautious, reticent statements, often reshaping and amending Bellow's own questions. From parents and children, he heard division, weariness, and deep sadness. "There were," after all, "few families in Israel that had not lost sons in the wars."

And from friends who occasionally let themselves go, there were ardent speeches, furious accusations and condemnations of Western Europe, of Russia, of America. Bellow listened carefully, "closely," more closely than he'd ever listened before, "utterly attentive." An Israeli relative said, "He listened not only to the story, but beyond that: he listened with all his senses, to body language, to intonation, noticing all details thoroughly and in depth." Could the artist, especially one whose powers of observation were as keen as Bellow's, get what may have been missed by those more trained in political science or international relations? Maybe. But, Saul wrote, "I often feel that I have dropped into a shoreless sea."[38]

Bellow delighted in the liveliness of Israeli life, a people on the sharp edge of history, an inch away from calamity, yet overflowing with argument—in apartments with friends and new acquaintances and in the halls of power with Yitzhak Rabin, Kissinger, Abba Eban, Teddy Kollek, scholars, diplomats, and editors. The question of survival dominated all this talk. In 1973, during the Yom Kippur War, Bellow, still in the US, told an interviewer that the "Holocaust made my generation understand that we might be annihilated, that everyone else had a right to exist" as a member of a national community, "but we might be eliminated and no one would intervene or care. This is what concerns me at present.... The attack on Israel is a test of whether Judaism and Jews will survive in the world."[39]

Is Israel the long-yearned-for safe haven for Jews—wherever in the world they are threatened—or, as one Harvard professor suggested to Bellow, "a concentration of Jews conveniently assembled for a second Holocaust."[40] No joke. A chilling idea, studied by the military chiefs and the Israeli intelligence agencies and, in the context of comedic irony, seriously entertained by Philip Roth in his novels *The Counterlife* and *Operation Shylock.*

There are constant reminders of the Holocaust in Israel, partly because it is so peopled by survivors. John Auerbach came from Caesarea to visit. Bellow had known him for only a few years, but he had become "a good friend." At sixteen Auerbach escaped from the Warsaw ghetto, leaving his parents and his sister: "They were killed. Everyone was killed."[41]

Israel, physically and spiritually, is both a garrison state and a cultivated society, and Jerusalem is both an ancient and a modern city. "You shop in a supermarket," Bellow wrote, "you say good morning to friends on the telephone, you hear symphony orchestras on the radio." But the music can stop suddenly when a terrorist bomb is reported or there is a deadly explosion outside a coffee shop on Jaffa Road: "Pained you put down your civilized drink, uneasy, you go out to your civilized dinner." During Bellow's stay in Israel, bombs were exploding all over the world. Dynamite was detonated in London. The difference is, Bellow wrote, that when there is an explosion in a West End restaurant in London, "the fundamental right of England to exist is not in dispute."[42]

A Jewish state has been established, but Jews, because they are Jews, cannot simply assume that their natural right to live is widely recognized. On the other hand, Bellow points out, many Europeans appear to believe that "the Jews with their precious and refining record of suffering, have a unique obligation to hold up the moral burdens everyone else has dumped." In the Jewish diaspora and even in Jerusalem and Tel Aviv, many believe that Israel has a duty to be a light among the nations.[43]

Bellow rightly insists, however, that even if Jews are thought, peculiarly, to be morally superior and have a duty to humanity, they also have a duty to survive. The poet David Shahar, in what started out as a relaxed discussion with Bellow over tea, ended with the poet banging on the table, shouting that the Arabs "don't want our peace proposals—they want us destroyed." Bellow realized he had irritated Shahar with his American evenhandedness and objectivity. "It's easy for outsiders," Bellow wrote, "to say there are two sides to the question. What a terrible expression. I am beginning to detest it."[44]

There appeared to be in Jerusalem no opportunity to relax, not if you were asking questions, even friendly ones and without ulterior motives. Pro-Palestinian and Israeli positions were presented as inflexible even when delineated by moderates. Mahmud Abu Zuluf, the editor of *El Kuds,* the largest Arab newspaper in Jerusalem, was hated by leftists. For his "centrism," his car had been bombed, his wife and family threatened. Still, the coffee was perfect and discussion began softly. Abu Zuluf laid out the Palestinian case in a "tone between boredom and passion." He said that "the Jews must divide authority with the Arabs. They are too reluctant to accept realities, too slow." The longer the Jews waited, he said, now beginning to shout and, like Shahar, banging the table with the flat of his hand, "the longer they wait, the worse it will be for them."[45] You lean back, Bellow wrote, with a cup of coffee to luxuriate in a conversation with an intelligent man, and "almost immediately you are involved in a tormenting discussion."[46]

In late February 1976, about a month into his visit, Bellow wrote to Steinerian Owen Barfield that though his aim had been "to wander about the Old City and sit contemplatively in gardens and churches," once he arrived, he "learned" something he likely already knew: "It is impossible in Jerusalem to detach oneself from the frightful political problems of Israel. I found myself 'doing something.' I read a great many books, talked with scores of people, and before the first month was out I was writing a small book about the endless crisis and immersed in politics. It excites me, it distresses me to be so immersed."[47] When Bellow returned to Chicago, he wrote to Barfield again, telling him he had "never seriously studied Zionism (i.e., the terrible question of the fate of the Jews) but having come to Jerusalem with my wife I 'discovered' it; I began to assume a degree of responsibility for it. A solution is beyond anyone's power, but I wanted at least to state the problem of Israel clearly to the civilized public"[48]—or, perhaps more precisely, to shape the problem in his own mind through art, the creative application of imagination.

Bellow observed, listened, and reflected; he read published lectures, newspapers, and books by historians, political scientists, and social analysts, including Elie Kedourie, Bernard Lewis, Yosephat Harkabi, Raphael Werblowsy, Raymond Aron, and Jakob Lind—a diverse international cross section of people, many of whom were not Israeli. He talked with Israeli novelists he had read, including A. B. Yehoshua and Amos Oz. He was "fascinated by the profusion and ingenuity of Jewish ideas on the future of Israel," but his vision of that future became ever cloudier and more complex. One unnamed Israeli novelist told him how "in 1948, when he was only seventeen, he lay all day feigning death among the dead" of his company—annihilated by the Jordanians. He lay there "until dark as the vultures fluttered nearby." He survived and was ready to fight again, but thirty years later he was no longer militant; he was convinced that "Israel has sinned too much . . . it has lost its *moral* compass."[49]

Yosephat Harkabi, chief of Israeli intelligence from 1955 to 1959 and considered something of a "hawk," was, in 1976, a professor of international relations at the Hebrew University. He conceded "that the Arabs have been wronged, but he insists upon the *moral* meaning of Israel's existence. Israel stands for something in Western history. The questions are not so simple as ideological partisans try to make them. The Zionists were not deliberately unjust, the Arabs were not guiltless. To rectify the evil as the Arabs would wish it rectified would mean the destruction of Israel. Arab refugees must be relieved and compensated, but Israel will not commit suicide for their sake."

Still, Harkabi added, a sweeping denial of Arab grievances is an obstacle to peace.[50] Harkabi's views on the Arab-Israeli problem, which Bellow characterizes as "rather better balanced" than those of most of his interlocuters, stayed with him well after his return to the United States.

Professor Kedourie, a British historian of the Middle East, disagreed with Harkabi. Instead, Kedourie agreed with what Bellow had heard in discussion with Prime Minister Yitzhak Rabin, that territorial concessions to the Arabs would be meaningless. "They simply want the Jews out," Kedourie said, countenancing no other point of view. He thought that at the start it would have been in Israel's best interest to have negotiated with each Arab state separately. Unfortunately, he said, "when the Jews decided through Zionism [Jewish nationalism?], to 'go political,' they didn't know what they were getting into." To historical difficulties, he said, the Jews added "the troubles of a small state facing the storms of savage hostility."[51]

Bellow tried to put it all together, to "come to clarity," as one of his professors used to say. But this issue resists illumination. There is, as Bellow would put it elsewhere, "simply too much to think about." Israeli politics, Russian ambitions, Islamic history, and American problems interject themselves, as do upheavals in the less developed countries, to say nothing of "the crisis of Western civilization." Instead of clarity, Bellow experienced a sense of "disorder." Talking to public figures he had read about in the news and in books, he said with some irony, "[did]n't always help."[52]

He read another document by Harkabi, with whose views he mostly agreed, in which the professor suggested that Israeli and Arab scholars and specialists ought to cooperate in studying and analyzing the conflict. "Perhaps," Harkabi wrote, "this bespeaks an inordinate faith in the power of rationality." The professor, Bellow thought, had recognized the flaw in his own proposal.[53] And he began to frame a hypothesis that he resisted, but it is the same one that informs his fiction: Reason is unable by itself to cut through the most important problems. Alone, or even when joined by scholarship and intelligence, reason is insufficient to overcome hopelessness in the Middle East or, so it seems, anywhere else.

Bellow's fictional protagonists, as intelligent as many of them are—Henderson, Herzog, Humboldt, and Charlie Citrine—as they ask themselves questions about identity, goals, and needs, they recognize the limits of the intellect. In *Humboldt's Gift*, when the down-to-earth Renata accuses Charlie of "trying to dope your way out of the human condition," she is reminding him that there are certain problems that no amount of intellect will solve.[54]

In *Herzog*, Moses wants to avoid evil and "do the right thing." But in the worst predicament of his life—a double betrayal by his best friend and his wife—he looks to his classical education to show him a way forward. Herzog soon discovers the limitations of his formal schooling; it gives him no clue about how to wrestle with life's true catastrophes. Bellow had come to see in his own troubled life "the inapplicability of . . . higher learning" and of intellectual training. "I began to understand," he said, "the irrelevancy" of "head-culture" and scientific rationality in solving the greatest conflicts, personal, social, and political. He had Herzog asking himself, "What are you proposing to do when your wife takes a lover?" Pull books from your shelves and look into what they say about adultery? Or about the psychology of human stubbornness?[55]

If there are "answers," or policies appropriate to bringing the problems of the Middle East closer to solution, where will they come from? It seems that Bellow, the writer, the artist, while in the holy land, was inclined to lean toward feelings, the imagination, and even the metaphysical. The light of Jerusalem had captivated him. The light was dateless, whiter and more "brilliant" than any light he had ever seen. It "ha[d] purifying power, [it] filter[ed] the blood and the thoughts." Bellow, quite strikingly, said he did not forbid himself the sense that "the reflection of that light may be the outer garment of God."[56]

The whole atmosphere of Jerusalem, he said, makes the common phrase "'out of this world' true enough to give your soul a start." And the air in the area, "the very air," that, too, is "thought-nourishing. The Sages themselves said so," and Bellow was "prepared to believe it. I know that it must have special properties." He gazed downward "toward the Dead Sea, over broken rocks," and thought, "The color of these is that of the ground itself, and on this strange deadness, the melting air presses with an almost human weight. Something intelligible, something metaphysical is communicated."[57] But what?

Although it sometimes seems that Bellow in *To Jerusalem and Back* is simply invoking apocalyptic doom, he does offer some policy choices. He generally agrees, he says, with the "balanced" views of Morris Janowitz, a Chicago friend and prominent sociologist. Born of Polish Jewish immigrants, Janowitz was a dedicated supporter of Israel and deeply involved in the Zionist issues. He proposed that the West Bank Territory, with some mutual adjustments, serve as the basis of a Palestinian state. He agreed that military force kept Israel alive but that only a political settlement would ensure its long-term survival—physically and morally. The further expansion of settlements, Janowitz also insisted, must be opposed by Israel's leadership, but at the same time he pronounced that there must be "guarantees of military security and the prevention of terrorism."[58]

Bellow, along with Irving Howe, Daniel Bell, and Lucy Dawidowicz, in an open letter to Menachem Begin declared these views as his own. Two years after the publication of *To Jerusalem and Back*, he had become a supporter of Peace Now, a group spearheaded by Amos Oz and other prominent Israelis. The open letter received front-page coverage in the *New York Times*, not in itself unusual. But agreement on the Israeli question is remarkable because the four signers had very different, sometimes conflicting opinions on various other matters. The critic Irving Howe was the editor of *Dissent*, a democratic socialist magazine;

the sociologist Daniel Bell had famously described himself as "a socialist in economics, a liberal in politics, and a conservative in culture"; and the historian Lucy Dawidowicz had moved from a left-wing position in the early thirties to one much further to the right. Bellow, having left his Trotskyism well behind him, was also moving rightward, albeit at a slower pace; and in any case, he refused to be labeled.

For his trouble in publicly suggesting that there were dangers in annexing the West Bank, Bellow said, "I have been called a sellout, a fink, a Carter-stooge and a Moscow agent." Leon Wieseltier, an American social and cultural critic and later the literary editor of the *New Republic,* was the actual organizer of the letter. He, too, was a recipient of name-calling. But Bellow reassured him: "You know what to expect from hot controversy over Jewish questions—bangs and blows on the noggin. . . . *A Dayge*!" That Yiddish phrase (meaning "a worry") is usually followed by "*hob ich*" (I have), sometimes silently but still understood; the whole phrase is perhaps best translated as "That's the least of my worries!" In other words, it is a dismissal of the issue, sometimes rude.[59]

Bellow called his book a "personal account," and his position in it is definitely pro-Israel. But *To Jerusalem and Back* is no polemic—Bellow attempted some level of objectivity. Not surprisingly, however, his "evenhandedness" infuriated hardliners from both ends of the political spectrum. The *Jerusalem Post* writer Isabella Fey thought that Bellow's essay was a "weary little collection of hedgings and evasions" and that "the careful neutrality" of his book "grates on the truth-nerve of the reader." She accused Bellow of retreating from "the real issues of Israel," by which she mostly meant Arab stubbornness. But Arab intractability—the fact that "the Arabs would not agree to the existence of Israel"—is exactly what Bellow identified as "the root of the problem."[60]

The response from the left was even more contemptuous. Noam Chomsky, once considered the father of modern linguistics, who became an activist on the radical left, charged that Bellow's book might well have been written by the Israeli Information Ministry. He took issue with almost every political claim made in *To Jerusalem and Back*, quoting countless sources and inflating his review with such expressions as "of this we hear nothing" and "he fails to mention." Bellow's "account of what he has seen and heard," Chomsky concluded, "is a disaster." Irving Howe's front-page review in the *New York Times*, which began by saying, "The best living American novelist is also a man with brains," was taken by Chomsky as an indication of the poor quality of intellectual life in America.[61]

To Jerusalem and Back, Bellow's first nonfiction book, originally appeared in abbreviated form in two consecutive issues of the *New Yorker*—a magazine that had, over four decades, accepted for publication few of his many short stories.[62] Elisabeth Sifton, esteemed editor and publisher, wrote that Bellow would "recite by heart" passages from *New Yorker* assessments of his rejected stories and from the magazine's published reviews of his books. He told Sifton that he thought the magazine's "faint praise suggested . . . anti-Semitic condescension: 'They think it's remarkable that I write as I do seeing as how [English] isn't my native language. That's the implication. Their idea of a Jewish writer is Isaac Singer—shtetls, exotic Polish ambience, magic, curious folkways. Believe me, I know whereof I speak. They never wanted stuff of mine.'" Sifton told him he was being paranoid, but privately she said, "I thought he was right."[63]

There were Jews at the *New Yorker*, of course, including William Shawn, the editor, as well as S. J. Perelman, A. J. Liebling, E. J. Kahn, and Edith Oliver, but Bellow thought they were "as assimilated as it was possible to be." Shawn never gave any clue to his ethnicity, and the initialed names of the others served as a kind of cultural smoke screen.[64] Bellow never really stopped steaming about the *New Yorker*'s treatment of his work, but other issues overwhelmed him and forced his musings about the magazine into the background. The publication of *Humboldt* in August 1975 engendered innumerable interviews and public appearances, especially after *Humboldt* was awarded the Pulitzer Prize in May 1976. The invitations multiplied when *To Jerusalem and Back* was published in October, along with Howe's rave review on the front page of the *New York Times.*

Five days later, on October 21, Bellow was named winner of the Nobel Prize in Literature. A flood of congratulations, invitations, and further honors followed. He was asked to deliver the prestigious Jefferson Lectures for the National Endowment for the Humanities and was awarded the Gold Medal for the Novel by the American Association of Arts and Letters. There were countless congratulatory phone calls, including one from Bellow's oldest son, Greg, in San Francisco, who was told by his father, "Now you know why I was after you to be quiet thirty years ago."[65]

Anita Goshkin, Greg's mother and Bellow's first wife—for nearly seventeen years—sent a telegram affirming her faith in Saul's talent. There were also calls from "a few old profs of mine," Bellow said slyly, "who are pleased with my progress." Sydney Harris, Bellow's old friend and Tuley High School classmate, a columnist for the *Chicago Daily News,* did not call, but he wrote that he remembered that Saul and he forty years earlier had "sat around our dining room table planning the books we were going to write." It was "reflected pleasure," Harris said, not "reflected glory" that he felt in Saul's prize; he was proud "that these two steads" actually came out of the same Jewish "stable."[66]

What did Bellow think of all the attention? "Nobody who writes a book likes to be ignored or neglected. There's a primitive part of me that is gratified by it. The child in me is delighted. The adult in me is skeptical." Other writers were equally worthy, Bellow noted, mentioning Andre Maurois, Ignazio Silone, and Christina Stead. And when Dave Peltz called with congratulations, Bellow said, "It should have been Isaac [Rosenfeld]." Saul's sister Jane on the phone wept over their father's lifelong resistance to Bellow's becoming a writer. Saul, with some regret, said, "Long after everyone was dead I won the fight."[67]

Well, not quite. When Maury, Saul's oldest brother, learned that "the kid" had won the Nobel Prize, he was affronted. According to Maury's grandson, his grandfather spontaneously blurted out, "How dare Saul win the Nobel Prize? When *I'm* really the smart one. *I'm* the one."[68] Competition between the two brothers had been so powerful that even at the time of his Nobel address, Bellow said that his motivation to excel was intensified by his desire to exceed his brothers, especially Maury. His oldest brother did call to congratulate him, but apparently, he could not muster whatever it would have taken to attend the Nobel ceremony. The rivalry never abated, but all who knew the brothers agreed that great love and family feeling remained even after furious arguments.[69]

Maury did not go to Stockholm, but many of Bellow's family did. In addition to Alexandra, the three Bellow sons were present. Alexandra's mother came from Bucharest with several of her relatives. Sam and Nina Bellows were there, too, with daughter Lesha and son-in-law Sam Greengus, plus three Greengus daughters. Saul's sister Jane came for her brother's speech and finagled a seat directly in front of the stage. Unfortunately, during the lecture she had to be nudged awake more than once; but she was there, as were sixteen family members in all, "an unprecedented number that made front-page news in the Stockholm papers."[70]

"This huge contingent of Bellows," as Saul called them, pretty much took over the Grand Hotel on the waterfront: "It became a kind of joke . . . A kind of family circus." Adam, the middle son, managed to have T-shirts printed up for the informal Bellow party reading "Nobel Savages." Daniel, the youngest son, escaping older brother Adam, who was supposed to be his monitor, ordered a ton of food from room service. The bill was huge. Saul was furious. "Prize officials were very amused" by the whole family scene from beginning to end, as Bellow admitted, and they "were signaling each other behind my back. That's all right," Bellow said, "they have to get something out of it, too."[71]

The ceremony was on Saturday, December 12, 1976, which meant that Sam and Nina, Orthodox Jews, and their close relatives had to walk fifteen minutes from their hotel to the concert hall for the ceremony—in the cold and snow. The family had taken a trial walk earlier and attended a Sabbath morning service at the Great Synagogue of Stockholm and a kiddush service in the community hall "in honor of all the Jewish Nobel Prize Laureates." Baruch Blumberg, sharing the prize in medicine, attended the kiddush, as did the prizewinner in economics, Milton Friedman, Bellow's neighbor and colleague on the University of Chicago's Committee on Social Thought.

Bellow never replied to the invitation from Rabbi Morton Narrowe of the Great Synagogue, sent on behalf of the city's Jewish community. Narrowe grumbles in his memoirs about Bellow's incivility, "but it is of course the Nobel Prize for Literature" that he was about to receive, "and not for manners." Sam, however, had let the rabbi know that he and several other family members were looking forward to the kiddush.[72] The more polite, civic-minded brother Sam was, however, in serious trouble.

After a prolonged trial in November, he was convicted of swindling patients in his nursing homes by selling them medicines from drug companies offering kickbacks. "I can't go into the details of this," Bellow told Norman Manea in their interview, "but it really wasn't his fault; it was somebody else in the family for whom he was covering. He was not guilty himself. He just accepted the charge." Before Sam served his sentence—sixty days in the Chicago Metropolitan Correction Center—the judge allowed him to fly to Sweden to watch his brother receive the Nobel Prize. To Bellow, Sam's attendance at Stockholm was a "last opportunity to make public his attachment to a famous brother, to lessen the sting of the fact that he was going to prison."[73]

For Alexandra, the week in Stockholm "was like a fairy tale": the ceremony itself was "absolutely gorgeous," and "everybody had a wonderful time." Alexandra "was so proud of Saul and so proud to be at his side." Greg, too, she thought (not quite correctly) was proud of his father, telling him so "just before we left for the ceremony."[74] At the press conference, asked how he felt about the prize, Bellow said, "I'm glad to get it. I could live without it." And the $160,000 award? "At this rate," Bellow said, referring to alimony and child support payments he was making, "my heirs will get the money in a day or so."[75]

But after the prize was in hand, Bellow, wearing his laurels lightly, told Richard Stern that he had had a good year. "All I started out to do," Bellow said, "was show up my brothers. I didn't have to go this far."[76] He continued with humorous quips at a formal dinner organized by Bellow's University of Chicago colleagues. In white tie and tails, Bellow rose to make a short presentation: "After years of the most arduous labor," he began, "I stand before you in the costume of a headwaiter." As Bellow said elsewhere, "there's no coming between a Jew and his jokes." An exception was made for the Nobel Lecture.[77]

Bellow's speech offered a stout defense of the novel and the individual and at the same time celebrated the "latent feeling of fellowship with all creation." He reiterated Conrad's appeal to the artist to be attentive to that part of being that is "the human capacity for delight and wonder." Attention must also be paid to "our sense of pity and pain, and to the subtle but invincible conviction of solidarity that knits together the loneliness of innumerable hearts . . . which binds together all humanity."[78]

Like Conrad, Bellow said that art was "an attempt to . . . find in [the] universe . . . what was fundamental, enduring, essential." But in the modern period, Bellow argued, what ought to have remained fundamental for artists—that is, individuals and souls—"have been wiped out." For illustration, Bellow pointed to his favorite bête noire, M. Alain Robbe-Grillet, "one of the leaders of French literature, a spokesman for 'thingism'—*choseisme*." The novel of characters, according to Robbe-Grillet, belonged entirely in the past. The Frenchman theorized that in the great contemporary works—Sartre's *Nausea,* Camus's *The Stranger,* and Kafka's *The Castle*—there are no individuals, no characters, merely entities. Could Robbe-Grillet be right, Bellow asked: "Can it be that human beings are at an end? Is individuality really so dependent on historical-cultural conditions?"

That writers "should be empowered to sign the death notice of a literary form," Bellow said, "amused" him: "A novelist should be free to drop 'character' if such a strategy stimulates him. But it is nonsense to make such a decision on the theoretical ground that the period that marked the apogee of the individual . . . is ended." Bellow did not talk about his own writing, famously filled with memorable individuals, characters, and unique characterizations; he promoted instead the value of good writing generally and the value of art. "Only art," Bellow insisted, "penetrates what pride, passion, intelligence, and habit erect on all sides—the *seeming* realities of this world."

But there is another reality, Bellow said, a genuine one that is always sending us hints. Proust and Tolstoy called these hints, these intimate glimpses, our "true impressions." These persistent intuitions, Bellow argued, are of great significance, but without art they "will be hidden from us, and we are left with nothing" but a vocabulary for achieving "practical ends which we falsely call life."

The value of literature lies in these recurrent "true impressions," Bellow said:

> A novel moves back and forth between the world of objects, of actions, of appearances and that other world, from which these "true impressions" come and which moves us to believe that *the good we hang on to so tenaciously—in the face of evil, so obstinately—is no illusion*. . . . We are reluctant to talk about this because there is nothing we can prove . . . and because few people are willing to risk the

embarrassment. They would have to say, "There is a spirit," and that is taboo. So almost everyone keeps quiet about it, although almost everyone is aware of it.

Toward the end of his address, Bellow included a positive invitation rather than a sense of grievance about the future of literature. "Writers are greatly respected," he said. And there is in "the intelligent public an immense . . . longing for a broader, more flexible . . . more comprehensive account of what we human beings are . . . and what this life is for. At the center humankind struggles . . . for its freedom; the individual struggles with dehumanization for the possession of his soul." This is an extraordinary opportunity, Bellow pointed out, for novelists, poets, and playwrights: "If the writers do not come again in the center, it will not be because the center is preempted. It is not." Writers "are free to enter. If they wish."[79]

All this Bellow had said very well, as had many of his protagonists, almost from the beginning, from *Henderson* on through *Humboldt*, surely. But would there be more to come? Five years after the Nobel ceremonies, Bellow, nearing completion of *The Dean's December*, told an interviewer from the *New York Times* that "the Nobel changes things in different ways. For one thing, you feel that you have more authority, and if the Academy was mistaken in giving you the prize, you try to make the best of it, and recover your balance and your normal poise and not feel oppressed by the weight of this honor"—an effect that winning the prize is said to have had on previous recipients: "I know people like John Steinbeck thought it was the kiss of death, but. . . . I'm treading water very successfully."[80]

At the time of the award, however, Bellow was indeed worried that the prize might cause him to lose his powers. Sinclair Lewis, in 1930, the first American to win the Nobel Prize, told his friend Lilian Gish, "This is fatal. I cannot live up to it."[81] Bellow feared the same fate. On the day of the announcement, in "a tearful phone call" to Sasha—wife number two—he confided this worry to her. At the same time, he admitted his fear of declining talent to the *New York Times*. He said he "hoped the award would not be a burden, as it was to John Steinbeck, who died in 1968. 'I knew Steinbeck quite well,' he said, 'and I remember how burdened he was by the Nobel Prize. He felt that he had to give a better account of himself than he had done.'"[82]

When Bellow's old Reichian therapist, Dr. Chester Raphael, read the article, he wrote to Bellow with genuine encouragement: "Your writings already give assurance that the trauma of the 'ultimate' recognition you have just received will not inhibit you but will spur you on to ever greater literary achievements."[83] Time would tell.

FOURTEEN

BELLOW'S DECEMBER

THE DEAN'S DECEMBER (1982), BELLOW'S ninth novel and his first after winning the Nobel Prize, was received with little enthusiasm. Some called it "mere" journalism, a long, cranky pontification on race and the "decline of civilization," similar in tone and style to *Mr. Sammler's Planet*. The reviews were not off target. Bellow had been angry and frustrated, "inwardly in chaos," when he started the book, and *The Dean's December* consequently came to be seen as a rant and not a novel at all.[1] Bellow admitted that he hadn't been "thinking 'novel'" when he began to write, and he acknowledged that *Sammler*, too, was not in fact a novel but more or less an essay, drawn from his distress over the culture of the sixties; he chose to call his new effort a "*cri de coeur*."[2]

He told D. J. Bruckner, the book review editor of the *New York Times*, that he "could no longer stand the fact that the city [of Chicago] and the country were in decay under our very eyes and people would not talk about the facts. They might talk about money to change things, but never about what was actually happening. No one levels any more. So it was a cry," Bellow said. "But I don't know whether anyone heard it."[3] Although *The Dean's December* was briefly on the bestseller list, rising as high as number six, it does not appear as if many read it; if read, no one, as Bellow guessed, seems to have "heard it."

"It makes a man unhappy," Bellow told Bruckner, but "also glad to be in Chicago. Who would not prefer the vulgarity of Chicago to the finesse of the East Coast literary establishment? You have to count your blessings you know." Bruckner did not attribute Bellow's remark to irony. But as the novelist and the editor, looking for lunch, walked a few blocks down from Bellow's apartment on Thorndale Avenue to a kosher delicatessen for corned beef and pumpernickel bagels, Bellow spied the broken base of a streetlamp stanchion filled with litter and broken bottles. He grimaced and quickly plunged into a catalog of political, cultural, and economic changes that had continued to plague Chicago in recent years.[4]

In an earlier interview, Bellow told the novelist William Kennedy that "none of the poverty programs" designed to deal with the social pathologies of the Black inner city "ever had a sense of what to do. . . . We're now in the fourth or fifth welfare generation, people who've never worked, people sealed out, set aside, and they look to me like a doomed population. And from the social organizations, educators, psychologists, bureaucrats—nothing. Just zilch."[5]

Bellow was purposely provocative in *The Dean's December.* "The idea was to hit and hit hard," he said. Well, if he was looking for a fight, he got one. Several reviewers, including Helen Dudar in the *Saturday Review,* saw Bellow's ninth novel as the beginning of the end. "Aha," she wrote, "another Nobelist bites the dust." John Updike, who once referred to himself and John Cheever as "the last non-Jewish writers in America," resented the coterie of Jewish writers of the postwar period. Out of a series of stories for the *New Yorker,* Updike had compiled *Bech: A Book* (1970) and *Bech Is Back* (1982), both about a Jewish novelist with notably unpleasant traits. He was never easy on Bellow, and his vaguely antisemitic take on *The Dean's December* was no exception. He claimed that by adding more than a "pinch of narcissism," Bellow had spoiled the flavor of the soup.[6]

When Updike's review of *Humboldt* had appeared in 1975, Bellow's friend Sam Goldberg called to ask "whether [he] had read the review in the *New Yorker* by that anti-Semitic pornographer."[7] Oddly, Updike, who had mocked the hectic pace of *Humboldt* as "a static sense of human busyness" and had dismissed Charlie Citrine as a bore, also criticized Bellow's grammar. Bellow was hurt, but he could still be playful; in a letter to Maggie Staats, he said that after reading the Updike review, "I'm actually frozen, covered with a thick ice of Jewish inhibitions. Shall I write my next book in Yiddish?" Bellow counted Updike, with good reason, among the "fastidious goy critics on guard for the Protestant establishment and the genteel tradition."[8]

Hugh Kenner, who could hardly conceal his antisemitism, argued that protagonist Albert Corde, dean of students at the University of Chicago, was "not a Jewish Dean from the Bellow Repertory Company" but a character whose WASP identity failed to camouflage the fact that he was a strange Jewish imitation of the "fox-faced" Bellow. Ten years later, Kenner, still at it, wrote that antisemitism "has no stable meaning; it can run all the way from gas ovens to a mere wish that Abe Rosenthal of the *New York Times* would moderate his frenzies." It's a term that has "no stable meaning" and is simply not a subject for "rational discussion."[9]

The Dean's December revolves largely around two cities and two actual murders—dreary, deeply oppressed Bucharest and deadly, corrupt Chicago, the cities in which the sensational murders were perpetrated. In the late seventies, a brain-addled Black man abducted a young white suburban housewife and locked her in the trunk of his car for nearly forty hours, freeing her only to rape her twice before brutally killing her. Although there were calls to the police by some good citizens of Chicago's middle-class West Side neighborhood, no one tried to stop the crime. In any case, the police never showed up. The other murder involved a white

University of Chicago graduate student who was pushed to his death through the window of his third-floor apartment by two Black people, one a prostitute, the other a street person, a member of the "underclass."

It is evident from the start of *The Dean's December* that Bellow was moving from the comic lyricism that had accompanied and helped soften (but not erase) the seriousness of *Henderson, Herzog,* and *Humboldt* to a novel bleaker even than *Sammler.* The new novel contained Bellow's first explicit portrayal of violence and sexual chaos, and the mood darkens and decadence and degeneracy deepen in this tale of two cities. Bucharest is correctly described as smothered in distrust and disloyalty and defined by Stalinist authoritarianism. Many of its "citizens" are imprisoned in labor camps or are "missing." Chicago seems hardened and accustomed to crime, but in reality, it is seething with the criminal consequences of racial injustice, unregulated capitalism, and irrepressible resentment. Many of its Black inhabitants are incarcerated or homeless.

Dean Albert Corde, a former journalist, finds himself one Christmas, with his brilliant astrophysicist wife, Minna, in the entirely cheerless and bitterly uncomfortable city of Bucharest, Rumania. The couple's stay in the communist East and their reason for coming closely resemble the adventures of Bellow and Alexandra in 1978. Minna has come to visit her dying mother, once the well-respected head of the State Division of Health, now fallen out of favor with the communist regime. The couple is frustrated by implacable and vindicative bureaucrats who refuse them visiting privileges. While Minna, anxious to see her mother, tries to break through the obstinacy of Stalinist officials, Corde rereads his recently published two-part article in *Harper's* magazine. It is a fierce polemic detailing the corruption of Chicago's political and judicial systems and the depth and scope of Black criminality in the inner city.

The dean has stirred up a considerable tempest in a deteriorating and threatened city, a city failing to respond to its many problems. Bellow includes among Chicago's problems the hypocrisy of "limousine liberals"—people, many of them well-intentioned Jews, who consider themselves progressive and who throw money at social problems and talk about "solutions" but in the end flee to the suburbs. They don't face the facts. "They don't even *see* them," Bellow explained. The good citizens of Chicago assume in a simpleminded way "that unemployment causes incoherence, sexual disorder, the abandonment of children, rape and murder."[10]

We can infer from this that while Bellow and the dean see unemployment as a factor contributing to crime and irresponsibility in the Black slums of Chicago, they also see and are irritated by a shifting of blame from the criminals to parents, schools, and the surrounding environment. They also see something independent of the immediate causal nexus, something that after a time seems to take on a life of its own. The dean is not averse to using the word *evil*.

"Look!" Bellow said of *The Dean's December*: "I was trying to display the facts. But the facts, unless the imagination perceives them" and unless they "passionately take hold," are not facts. Corde, using his imagination, passionately takes hold of Chicago and "writes his articles like an artist rather than a journalist."[11] It's hard to see what difference that makes, but at his best, Corde realizes that to see what life is like in the underclass, one must look, really *see* the world that is buried under the debris of false descriptions of life in the Black ghetto. Corde and Bellow work to unbury the truth, and they come to know more deeply that the Black men and women of Chicago have been forbidden to enter society, that Chicago's urban Black people are "doomed," a "people consigned to destruction."[12]

A non-Jew, Corde is nevertheless, like most of Bellow's Jewish protagonists, a man caught "in the middle of a spiritual crisis, overwhelmed by the sheer 'muchness' of the world," alarmed by momentous social crises, as well as by personal and existential problems: he is a recovering overly assertive pursuer of sex and is "frightened by the stubborn fact of death." He wonders if his own confusions about guilt and innocence, politics and academia, and nature and nurture are essentially his share of "the big scale insanities of the 20th century."[13]

The concern of the dean and Bellow for what Black people continue to suffer, though genuine, is compromised by the dean's unyielding insistence on prosecuting the alleged Black perpetrators, his fear of an underclass potentially out of control, his relative inattention to the connection between deprivation and social pathology, his use of terms like *savagery* and *sadism*, and the dearth of specific advice or policy proposals.[14] Our only hope, Bellow seemed to be saying, is to undertake a national moral awakening, the nature of which remains unspecified, except insofar as he and the dean promote the Bellovian trio: imagination, a new higher consciousness, and an openness to the soul. Is it wishful thinking to assume, as this novel does, that from a powerful description of American social ills, a popular clamor for justice will ensue? It's a stretch to imagine that Bellow, speaking, through the mouthpiece of Albert Corde, of "superfluous populations" and "written off" people, would get through to an inert citizenship. "It's an honorable wish," critic Diane Johnson said, "and the novel an honorable outcry." In a sense, however, as he himself said earlier, Bellow "has written a novel about how nobody will read or accept the novel he is writing."[15]

A saving grace is Bellow's portrayal of women as real and credibly detailed people. Corde's mother-in-law, Valeria, is a doctor, a loving parent, an erudite scientist, and a politically principled woman quietly distancing herself further and further from the Stalinist regime; Minna, clearly modeled on Bellow's fourth wife, mathematician Alexandra Ionescu Tulcea, is refined, sensitive, and intelligent, and a beautiful woman with an international reputation in her field. Minna and Albert offer the only complex portrait of a marriage of equals in all of Bellow's work.

The deadly, dark, nightmarish quality of *The Dean's December* should not have come as a surprise to those who followed Bellow's rightward trajectory on questions of race and the city. In the spring of 1977 in Washington, DC, Bellow delivered the first of his two Jefferson Lectures. Sponsored by the National Endowment for the Humanities, each carried an honorarium of $10,000. In both lectures Bellow talked affectionately and movingly about the Chicago of his youth.

The first lecture opened with a contrast between the tall apartment buildings of the very wealthy, who lived on Chicago's Gold Coast within sight of Lake Michigan, and the houses of the slum dwellers who passed those buildings on their way to the shore in summer. "This," Bellow said, "was how the children of immigrant laborers first came to know the smell of money and the look of luxury." He talked about the vast gap between rich and poor without real criticism or complaint, perhaps because he now lived—as did many of the Jewish buddies he had grown up with in Humboldt Park—in one of those same high-in-the-sky apartment buildings "that have risen along the shore on the north side of the city."[16]

It wasn't simply that Bellow and his Jewish immigrant friends felt they had "made it"; life in the working-class districts of their early years, Bellow insisted, wasn't so bad: "No one had money, but you needed very little."[17] Still, he never tired of sharing the miracle of his journey from the three-dollar rented rooms he lived in as a graduate student in the slums of Chicago to his high-rise apartment with all the abundance it offered. That story, according to him, was the story of the Jews in America, and in a rare moment of naivete, he argued that it was the story of America itself.

On April 2, 1977, in the august Gold Coast Room of the Drake Hotel, a Chicago landmark, Bellow delivered the second Jefferson Lecture—a much darker talk. As in Washington, the Chicago audience, including officials and guests of the city's cultural establishment, was sparkling and formally dressed. Filling the room were members of the Chicago Historical Society, the Newberry Library, Northwestern University, and the University of Chicago. Friends, colleagues, and cultural notables were joined by local philanthropists, those who funded the museums and symphony orchestras. But on this day, Bellow looked no different from them: well off, silver-haired, affluently dressed, with a red-and-lavender velvet bow tie to complement his dinner jacket.[18]

In his talk, Bellow turned to Chicago in the era of the Great Depression and to the neighborhoods populated by immigrants from Southern and Eastern Europe and Ireland. Too generously, Bellow described these neighborhoods as harmonious and industrious. But he said that thanks to the 1924 Immigration Act, things changed radically. There were far fewer immigrants and thus far fewer tailors, carpenters, printers, mechanics, and small entrepreneurs entering the country. But the immigrants who came earlier, Bellow emphasized, had improved themselves and moved upward and out.

The neighborhoods that the Jews and Poles left behind, he said,

> were repopulated by . . . internal immigration from the South and from Puerto Rico. The country people, black or white, from Kentucky or Alabama, brought with them no such urban skills and customs as the immigrants had. Assembly-line industries had no need for skilled labor. What we have taken now to calling "ethnic neighborhoods" fell into decay long ago. The slums, as a friend of mine [Harold Rosenberg] once observed, were ruined. He was not joking. The slums as we knew them in the twenties were, when they were still maintained by European immigrants, excellent places, attractive to artists and bohemians as well as to WASPs who longed for a touch of Europe. The major consequences of the devastation of these neighborhoods, invariably discussed on these occasions—the increase in crime, the narcotics addiction, the welfare problem, the whole inventory of urban anarchy—I will spare you.[19]

But there was more of this to come. Bellow pointed out that the faculty of the University of Chicago lived quietly in the apartment houses of Hyde Park. But only a few blocks away, in the Black slums, "a different sort of life . . . tears apart the [apartment houses] and leaves them looking bombed out. They are stripped of saleable metals, innards torn out, copper cable chopped to pieces and sold for scrap, windows all smashed, and finally fire and emptiness."[20]

In an attempt to discover why all this was so, Bellow had talked to civil servants—police, firemen, welfare employees, and social workers. He had visited schools in the inner city as well as courts, clinics, and the county jail; he had read scholarly articles about race and crime. "The first fact that strikes you," Bellow said of his visits to criminal court, "is that so large a part of Chicago's black population is armed—men, women, children even."[21] The inner-city slum schools were "now almost entirely black and Puerto Rican" and were far different, Bellow pointed out, from the schools he attended in his youth: "I have entered classrooms in which pupils wandered about. . . . No one heeded the teacher when she spoke."

Too many of "the kids are . . . blank, unformed." But they had "a demonic knowledge of sexual acts, guns, drugs, and [other] vices." While the density of Bellow's moral horror was not entirely inappropriate, he walked this back a bit by adding, "I am speaking, please notice, of what sociologists call the underclass, not of black Chicago as a whole, the orderly, churchgoing black working people or members of the growing middle class. These struggle to . . . protect their children from beatings in school corridors . . . from shootings in the playgrounds. No one goes out carefree for a breath of air at night."

After this bleak assessment, Bellow ended the lecture with another moment of self-correction, perhaps suggesting that he had been a little too pessimistic about the future of the slums of Chicago: "When he visited the Lower East Side, [Henry] James was alarmed by the Jewish immigrants he saw, appalled by their alien, ill-omened presence, their antics and their gabble.

There is no end to the curious ironies all this offers to an active imagination—and, in particular, to a descendant of East European Jews like myself."[22]

The muted applause at the end of the lecture was followed by a reception. Peter Carroll, attending as the cofounder of the Chicago Poetry Center, reported, "Much of the audience is missing; few who do come to sip champagne bother to shake the hand of the Nobel laureate or to congratulate him on his success."[23] There were negative reactions as well from the university community. Citing a report of the lecture in the *Chicago Sun-Times*, the University of Chicago newspaper, the *Chicago Maroon*, published an open letter of complaint titled "Bellow: False and Racist?" and signed by "The University of Chicago Committee Against Racism, accompanied by 14 signatures by members of the University community."[24] The letter writers described Bellow's remarks and categorizations as "outrageous," hoping he was misquoted. They also pointed out that Bellow failed to mention, as he had in the first lecture, the causes of social and physical disintegration in the Black slums, which were many. Nor did he mention how much more difficult the conditions were for the new migrants than for those who came before 1924.

Bellow's concern in the lecture was indeed with consequences, not causes, of discrimination. This was a conscious choice: The idea was to hit and "hit hard," especially at liberals, who turned blind eyes to the depth and scope of the pathologies of the ghetto.[25] What upset Carroll about the lecture was Bellow's claim—which either was never made or was only made obliquely—that the Black, Appalachian, and Latin slums were without culture. Bellow knew much about popular and street culture, the kind he celebrated in *The Adventures of Augie March*, culture largely unwritten, often ungrammatical, lacking the great art of Europe; a culture that not only involved Jewish tradition but included Polish, Italian, and German popular culture.

Bellow also knew something about the popular culture of Black migrants from the South from the classes he took with anthropologist Melville Herskovits at Northwestern and from his time as an undergraduate at the University of Chicago, which had a history of supporting research into "Negro-White relations." Much of Bellow's early fiction was directly concerned with racial discrimination. The unpublished novel fragment "Acatla" (1940) contains scenes in which an interracial couple are victims of prejudice; his first completed but unpublished novel, "The Very Dark Trees" (1942), concerns a white man who wakes to find that he has turned Black, a phenomenon that exposes the racism of his community.[26]

Bellow wrote about Chicago all through his adult life, but his systematic investigation of the city began only in the late 1970s when he started planning and putting together the "Chicago Book," a nonfiction essay resembling the style of *To Jerusalem and Back* or a long piece of investigative journalism in the genre of Tom Wolfe or Norman Mailer. What survives of the "Chicago Book" is an autobiographical manuscript and shorter notelike sections with such titles as "American Materialism," "A Visit to County Jail," and "Newspapers," as well as one bluntly labeled "'blacks' criminal activity."[27] Bellow also put together research files for the projected book, containing newspaper clippings on lawlessness and notes and correspondence on a variety of Chicago topics and personalities. Much of the material Bellow gathered found its way into the second Jefferson Lecture. The more gruesome items—in newspaper articles and interview accounts of monstrous murders and sexual assaults—would later find their way into *The Dean's December.*

Bellow's views on the city had grown "increasingly dystopian," according to his friend from the Steiner study group, William Hunt. Bellow himself kept away from areas where Black people congregated and always carried a twenty-dollar bill in case he was mugged.[28] He suffered great anguish and torment about Chicago, which he expressed to Hunt mostly at the Spot, a favorite local coffee shop in Evanston. Hunt thought Bellow had become obsessed about the political and judicial corruption of the city, the mayhem and nihilism of the Black slums, and the intentional blindness of liberals. Hunt told biographer James Atlas that Bellow "would be moved to tears by the bleakness of the whole damn thing. He really felt that black people were being driven into some kind of mass suicide."[29]

Brooding one afternoon about the violence and self-destructiveness that plagued the ghetto, Bellow allegedly remarked to Hunt that "black people aren't like us."[30] Was he unaware that his light-skinned friend was Black? Perhaps, but unlikely. Bellow immediately went on to express empathy for the Black and Latino populations. He resented them for having destroyed the physical neighborhood of his youth, but he commiserated with them, too; destruction, he said, may very well have been "the assertion of the other utter nothingness of their surroundings," nihilism their only recourse. "Humankind," Bellow observed, "is always involved in some kind of metaphysical enterprise."[31]

During the years Bellow worked on the "Chicago Book" and *The Dean's December,* he and Alexandra summered in Vermont. Bellow had several friends in the area, she said; "he was particularly fond of Robert Penn Warren, Bernard Malamud, and Meyer Schapiro, whom he adored." The couple would rise at about seven in the morning, have a leisurely breakfast, work in separate studios, and then take a long afternoon walk together. In a break from the daily routine, there would be afternoon trips to Brattleboro, where friends often turned up. Bellow was mostly relaxed, but at sixty-five, he was more sharply aware of aging and continued to worry about death, both the idea and the reality of losing friends and relatives, pieces of his own generation, parts of his own heart and psyche.

In a letter to Edward Shils, Bellow described his area in Vermont

> as thickly populated with writers and savants. I don't see them often but I never know when I may run into them. Last week . . . I bumped into Sidney Hook [eighty-four years old]. . . . He was spry but shaky, assisted in mid-street by his wife and calling out to numerous grandchildren who ran in and out of ice-cream parlors. . . . A few days later Meyer Schapiro [seventy-eight years old] telephoned, keenly alert but his voice quite weak. He told me how hard he was working, and he was vigorous and amusing—and doddering a little, and also a shade melancholy. I suppose that description covers all of us.[32]

In the summer of 1977, the indefatigable Susan Bellow (Glassman) and her attorneys intensified their efforts to overturn the original divorce agreement, aiming to get a share of Bellow's windfall Nobel Prize money. Susan won a big alimony boost, Saul declined to pay—his lawyer was about to enter an appeal—and Bellow was held in contempt and sentenced to ten days in jail, a sentence eventually withdrawn. In the meantime, Bellow wrote to Richard Stern on October 1, saying, "I am coming to Daniel's bar mitzvah, but I may be arrested in front of *K*[*ehilath*] *A*[*nshe*] *M*[*a'ariv*]," the oldest synagogue in Illinois. "If I'm not in County jail next weekend," Bellow ended his letter, "I shall give you a ring."[33]

Although at the bar mitzvah, Saul and Susan danced together energetically, they were back in court two days later. To help with the costs of divorce and lawyers' fees in the late seventies and into the eighties, Bellow committed to more than his usual number of guest lectures and readings. Prior to the publication of *The Dean's December*, Bellow went to Syracuse University, where for three weeks he was a visiting professor with minimal duties, an appointment for which he was paid $15,000.

Almost four years earlier, in the fall of 1977, Bellow and Alexandra took jobs as visiting professors at Brandeis University in Waltham, Massachusetts. Though teaching in Waltham, the Bellows were more visible in Cambridge, close to Harvard, where they rented an apartment and led a busy social life. They saw "quite a number of mathematicians," including the chair of the department, Shlomo Sternberg, and his wife, painter Aviva Green. On Christmas Day, the Bellows had lunch with the Sternbergs, Orthodox Jews, and their guest Graeme Segal. A visiting professor, Segal, though Jewish, fancied himself "aggressively secular." His family were outspoken anti-Zionists. When the subject of Israel came up, Bellow kept his views to himself. Segal reported that "there was also 'some sort of Jewish grace' before the meal, and Bellow asked Sternberg if he wanted him to wear a yarmulke." Whether or not Bellow put on the yarmulke goes unmentioned. Segal recalled a moment of testiness on the drive home, but there was almost "nothing but good humor on Bellow's part." About Alexandra Bellow, Segal remembered only that she was beautiful.[34]

The most important friend Bellow made in the fall of 1977 in Cambridge was Leon Wieseltier, who was at Harvard working toward a PhD in Jewish studies. "We just were crazy about each other. We used to see each other a lot," often for strolls along the Charles River or for lunch, Wieseltier said. In an interview, he described himself facetiously as having "this reputation that preceded me as the hottest thing in Jewish Studies since white bread." He remembered "bonding" with Bellow over Rudolf Steiner and Owen Barfield. Wieseltier had "a high tolerance" for such figures, but he asked Bellow, "What's a rough stringent Jew like [you] doing corresponding with Owen Barfield?" Bellow's answer included a remark that especially struck Wieseltier: "The truth, whatever it is, is strange." To Wieseltier, this statement, at once "anti-rational, but sort of reasonable to understand," became "a sort of principle about how [Bellow] operated."[35]

In the same interview, Wieseltier described Bellow as "the most brilliant dupe I ever knew," drawn to "outlandish . . . explanations . . . one doctrine after another." Yet Bellow never did fully "fall for these types"; he never made "the leap." He "deeply resented rationalism" as a singular, totalistic explanation,

Wieseltier said correctly, but he was too experienced, too intelligent, too Jewish, to oppose reason itself. This assessment rang true for Bellow from the very beginning of his career as a novelist. In *Dangling Man* (1944), Joseph asks himself what he should do in the face of the suffering and humiliation that no human escapes. "Was there no way to attain that answer except to sacrifice the mind that sought to be satisfied?" No—"What a miserable surrender that would be, born out of disheartenment and chaos." Instead, "out of my own strength it was necessary for me to return the verdict for reason, [even] in its partial inadequacy, and against the advantages of surrender."[36]

Although they may have bonded over Steiner, it was just as likely that Wieseltier and Bellow became "true, raucous, spiritually bonded friends" through their mutual saturation in Yiddish. There were *lots* of jokes.[37] Only after the Bellows left Cambridge in 1978 did Wieseltier get a true idea of Bellow's difficulties in Chicago. In a letter dated January 18, Bellow wrote, "I thought I knew corrupt Chicago, the money world, the legal and accounting professions and all their psychological types and all the political parallels—I did, of course, but it was an intelligent person's closet knowledge and fate decided that I should get a finishing course, that I should feel all the fingers on my skin and have my internal organs well squeezed"[38]—along with his wallet. Bellow told Wieseltier in another letter four months later that he had "been on the road to make money to pay taxes and legal fees as well as accountants and wives, and children's tuitions and medical expenses. . . . When insomnia permits it, I dream of monasteries or hermit's caves. But I'm a Jew, and married."[39]

Sometime toward the end of 1979, Bellow put aside the "Chicago Book" to begin work on what would become *The Dean's December.* That controversial work, which Bellow knew would bring him some significant trouble, challenged his physical condition and mood. He told Bette Howland in late January that he had outlined a plan for "a short book, altogether new, and proceeded quickly to write it. I've done more than half of it since Christmas and am subject to nightly vibrations that prevent me from sleeping." There was, he wrote, "a flood of the nerves, breathless excitement and insomniac happiness." Three weeks later, in a letter dated February 25 to Hyman Slate, Bellow was complaining that he had "overworked myself, and consequently I don't sleep well. I go around like a Zombie."[40]

Slate, by the 1970s, a retired social worker, was one of Bellow's closest friends; he, like several of the other Chicago Jewish boys linked together in the Humboldt Park and Hyde Park neighborhoods, knew Saul from the time that he was Sol. Slate was an autodidact and a reader of cerebral works such as Spinoza and William James, both of whom he could quote. Never well paid as social worker, Slate now lived in a threadbare apartment a few blocks from Bellow, with things torn, tattered, worn, or mismatched, like his furniture from the Salvation Army.

But Bellow looked forward to their "Sunday gabfests." He felt he had much to learn from such old friends. He was impressed, perhaps bewildered, too, with Slate's fidelity to his wife of forty years and the obvious pleasure they took in each other's company. As Bellow wrote in a draft of the "Chicago Book," it was "the sort of human news that doesn't get into the papers." Bellow confided in Slate, openly discussing "matters of sex, health, and neurosis," as well as finances. "My position is peculiar," he wrote Slate from Vermont in the summer of 1978, "and there are times when I have a pressing need to tell you what it's like. We are the survivors of a band of boys who were putting something of their own together in cultureless Chicago forty years ago. Now we drink tea together of a Sunday afternoon, and I feel the touch again. It would be merely sentimental if we weren't really talking. As you yourself have often observed, we talk, the subjects are real."[41]

Bellow was writing from Pasadena, at Caltech, where Alexandra Ionescu Tulcea had been invited as a Sherman Fairchild

Fellow in Mathematics. The math department arranged for Bellow to lead a series of seminars, after agreeing to certain of his conditions: "No assignments, no agenda, just literary discussions for the Caltech community." His subject was the early twentieth-century novel; the students enrolled, Bellow remembered, "were as mystified by Joseph Conrad as I was by jet propulsion." Tired and privately impatient with the basically uninterested science students, Bellow was asked one day in class one too many questions he regarded as immaterial: "Just how do you start writing every day?" His impatience no longer private, he explained "that first he checked his typewriter to see that all the letters of the alphabet were still there."[42]

At the time, Bellow's fourth marriage seemed to be working, despite occasional tensions and storms. But about the institution of marriage in general he had grown cynical. When he was thirty-two, he had told his friend Mitzi McClosky that he was a champion of monogamy as a foundation of social stability. Now he was saying that "nothing lasts more than a decade." When his Humboldt Park buddy Sam Freifeld argued that marriage would disappear as an institution, Bellow countered, "Marriage will remain as a viable institution because a man has to have something to be unfaithful to." Alexandra on this score had laid down the law: "No fucking around," as Dave Peltz put it. Bellow claimed to comply; he was "monogamous, for once," he told Rosette Lamont. She remained wary.[43]

Bellow tried to understand Alexandra's work and even hired a mathematics tutor. But he was jealous of his wife's independence and felt bitter about her mathematician colleagues; he was tired of the shop talk. And when she went missing in her study for hours—days even—or called him from her office at Northwestern and asked him to do the food shopping, he felt deserted, mortified by her ostensible indifference to the great man that he was. It bothered him, too, that Alexandra disregarded the traditional housewifely tasks and rarely cooked.[44]

By the time he wrote *To Jerusalem and Back*, despite the "love song" to her therein, he was already "getting a little frosty about Alexandra," according to Elisabeth Sifton. "Since I've never understood women anyway, I finally married one who is really a mystery," he told Dave Peltz, not quite approvingly.[45] The nature of the Bellows' marriage was reflected in the arrangement of their Chicago apartment, which was in fact two adjacent apartments with identical layouts, including kitchens, bedrooms, and bathrooms.

Bellow was lonely and frustrated at home and missed his usual share of attention elsewhere. He told Hyman Slate in 1980 that he missed their get-togethers: "Sometimes I think I have too few" people to depend on. And then a year later, he told Slate that he had "no comfortable conversations with friends my own age. I need some of your melancholy fun."[46] Fame had not changed Bellow's attachment to the past. Well into his old age, he tried to keep up with a surprising number of friends and schoolmates. The formidably gifted children of Chicago's mostly working-class Jewish immigrants from Tuley High School continued to hold an important place in Bellow's soul and psyche.

He would never forget them. The most important were Stuart Brent, Nathan Gould, Dave Peltz, Oscar Tarcov, Zita Cogan, Yetta Barshevsky, Sam Freifeld, and, for over twenty years, Isaac Rosenfeld. They had been witnesses to Bellow's early ambition, ardor, and acute intelligence, and he mourned deeply when the dying of these old friends began—Rosenfeld as early as 1956, followed by Tarcov in 1964. In a letter to Nathan Gould in 1982, with the Nobel Prize six years behind him, Bellow fell into a kind of requiem:

> I attended the Tuley reunion, and it was a depressing affair, on the whole—elderly people nostalgic for youth and the Depression years. Some came from far away . . . and some were crippled and required wheeling. . . . [One] who seemed well preserved turned out to have a hereditary disorder affecting his memory so that he was groping,

> while we talked, and his new wife was deeply uneasy. . . . But my closest friends were Oscar and Isaac, dead for many years. In every decade I try to think what they might have been like had they lived.

Bellow closed by answering an apparent question of Gould's: "A word about Jewish Life. I do my best, but I seldom write anything about Jewish Life that pleases Jewish Opinion. First thing I know there's a brawl and I come out with a shiner."[47] Manifestly Jewish—Jews talk, Jews argue, Jews take pride in their opinions, often hard-earned.

Only weeks before Bellow wrote about the reunion, John Cheever had died. His last letter to his good friend, written six months before Cheever's death on June 18, 1982, was a moving farewell:

> We didn't spend much time together but there is a significant attachment between us. I suppose it's in part because we practiced the same self-taught trade. . . . Yes, there are other, deeper sympathies but I'm too clumsy to get at them. . . . Neither of us had much use for the superficial "given" of social origins. In your origins [white, Anglo-Saxon Protestant] there were certain advantages; you were too decent to exploit them. Mine, [Jewish, immigrant] I suppose, were only to be "overcome" and I hadn't the slightest desire to molest myself that way. I was, however, in a position to observe the advantages of the advantaged (the moronic pride of Wasps, Southern traditionalists, etc.). There wasn't a trace of it in you. You were engaged, as a writer should be, in transforming yourself. When I read your collected stories I was moved to see the transformation taking place on the printed page. There's nothing that counts really except this transforming action of the soul. I loved you for this. I loved you anyway, but for this especially.[48]

Even as he and Alexandra were falling out, Bellow was working steadily toward the completion of *The Dean's December*, which, as he anticipated, was panned by most reviewers. On the very last day of 1981, he told Philip Roth (who needed no reminding after the brouhaha over *Portnoy's Complaint*) that well before writing

The Dean's December he had "discovered . . . that there was nothing to stop me from saying exactly what I thought. I expected flak, and unpleasant results are beginning to come in." A month later he told William Kennedy that, "to get away from the noise of battle," he and Alexandra planned to retreat to British Columbia, where Bellow would spend the winter term as a visiting professor at the University of Victoria. Barnett Singer, a Jewish historian at the University of Victoria who had written many fawning letters to Bellow, was one of the writer's more loquacious and ultimately irritating sycophants as well as a self-described literary neurotic. Bellow told Singer (pointedly, one supposes) that he came to Victoria "only . . . for a rest."[49]

The reviews of *Dean,* as stated, were almost consistently negative, but most failed miserably in their predictions of Bellow's demise as a writer. Was it schadenfreude that moved one critic to cheer because Bellow had written a bad book and had proved himself to be just another of those many Nobel Prize winners who had soon afterward "bit the dust"? Or was it insecurity that brought another critic to say that all Bellow's literary energies had been swallowed up in pontification and to "wonder if his earlier books could really have had the intellectual weight ascribed to them at the time."[50]

Saul Bellow quickly put to rest any doubts about the intellectual weight of his writing, past and present. He published "In the Days of Roosevelt," an essay in the form of a memoir, in *Esquire* in 1983; and between 1982 and 1984, he published three short stories, including "Cousins," which were superb pieces of fiction. In the essay, Bellow dealt with his youth in Chicago, where at seventeen, although purportedly a Trotskyist, he was intensely moved by Roosevelt's resounding victory in the 1932 presidential election. The victory brought great excitement to his circle of friends and acquaintances. Even Bellow's elderly algebra teacher, as a rule all business, interrupted her equations and sang "Happy Days Are Here Again," the theme song of the

Democratic campaign. That the teacher with white hair and blue-tinted square glasses allowed herself a show of feeling was astonishing. Bellow thought this "showed that the country had been shaken to its foundation."[51]

He wrote that though he was "fully armored in skepticism," he was "nonetheless vulnerable" to sympathy and hope. Months after the election but only days after the inauguration, done with his Sunday walk on the Chicago Midway, Bellow stopped to watch as drivers began to pull over. They parked bumper to bumper, rolled down their windows, and turned on their radios to hear Roosevelt. Bellow "felt joined to these unknown drivers, men and women smoking their cigarettes in silence, not so much considering the President's words as affirming the rightness of his tone and taking assurance from it."[52]

Whether the essay was written to indicate to howling readers and critics that he was still, along with the vast body of Chicago Jews, "some kind of liberal" is impossible to know.[53] But the stories are pure art, works that combine Proustian reminiscence with daring experiments in style. "Him with His Foot in His Mouth," a tour de force at sixty pages; "What Kind of Day Did You Have?" even longer at one hundred pages; and "Cousins," judged by many as Bellow's finest short story (alluded to in several preceding chapters), ought to have persuaded even the most skeptical that the seventy-year-old writer was still at the height of his powers.[54]

In all the stories, including "Zetland: By a Character Witness" and "The Silver Dish," both written in the seventies, and "What Kind of Day Did You Have?" and "Cousins," written in the eighties, there are light but unmistakable doses of Jewish social history and Jewish religious imagination. In "What Kind of Day," Victor, the personification of the New York Jewish intellectual, with a daughter who has dropped out of rabbinical school, is often wistful about his own Jewishness. At an airport, before boarding, Victor sees that

> on the field, in the winter light, the standing machines were paler than the air, and the entire airport stood in a frame of snow looking like a steel engraving. It reminded him of the Lower East Side in—oh, about 1912. The boys (the ancients today, those who were alive) were reading the Pentateuch. The street, the stained pavement, was also like a page of Hebrew text, something you might translate if you knew how. Jacob lay dreaming of a ladder which rose into heaven. *V'hinei malachi elohim*—behold the angels of God going up and down. This has caused Victor no surprise. What age was he, about six? It was not a dream to him. Jacob was dreaming, while Victor was awake, reading. There was no "long ago." It was all now.[55]

In "Cousins," Ijah Brodsky espouses his deep interest in his own cousins and explains that his attachments are grounded in "sympathy, not soft sentiment." And when he is asked by cousin Schana to write a letter to a judge to help cousin Tanky of the rackets, "he couldn't refuse . . . The Brodsky's had slept on cousin Schana's floor. We were hungry and she fed us. The words of . . . the prophets can never be extracted from the blood of certain people." Ijah writes the letter because "the cousins are the elect" of his memory.

To the thickness of Jewish community and hungry minds so apparent in "Cousins," Ijah adds another distinguishing layer, quintessentially Bellow: "We enter the world without prior notice, we are manifested before we can be aware of the manifestation. An original self exists, or, if you prefer, an original soul. . . . I was invoking my own fundamental perspective, that of a person who takes for granted distortion in the ordinary way of seeing but has never given up the habit of referring all truly important observations to that original self or soul."[56]

According to Cynthia Ozick, Bellow in "Cousins" had "risked mentioning—who can admit to this without literary embarrassment?—the Eye of God." At the very least, Bellow in his observations and interactions with cousins, and in the story itself, planted a splendidly detectable Jewish family feeling, or more precisely Jewish family love, though it is love characteristically "mixed with amazement and disorder." Ozick goes on to say that with the stories collected in *Him with His Foot in His Mouth*, Bellow had managed "to restore the soul in American literature."[57]

At the same time, we are meant to recognize in these stories that Ijah's spiritual expression, as with that of many Bellow characters (including Woody Selbst in "A Silver Dish," modeled in part on Dave Pelz), is a product of a secular situation—in Ijah's instance, a shameful court case involving his crooked cousin Tanky. Woody, too, is immersed in a "secret conviction that the goal set for this earth was that it should be filled with good, saturated with it." Yet the family story that stays with him as he grows older is a tale of disgraceful trickery and theft. Bellow makes us feel that the commonly used term *secular Jew* does not mean for him merely a nominal Jew, one with no obvious Jewish values. For Bellow, *secular Jew* simply gives no hint of the richly nuanced variety he sees within the category.

In February 1984, Bellow and Alexandra departed for Paris, where he was made commander of the Legion of Honor by François Mitterrand.[58] Later in the spring, Bellow received another recognition, which moved him to tears. In Lachine, the town in which Bellow was born, the mayor announced that the public library was going to be renamed the Saul Bellow Municipal Library. Bellow was invited to a naming ceremony on June 10, 1984, his sixty-ninth birthday. "He seemed genuinely moved by the gesture," the mayor recalled. On the verge of tears, Bellow said that "he had nothing named for him anywhere."[59]

Bellow returned to Lachine with Alexandra, his niece Lesha Greengus, his sister Jane, and Harriet Wasserman, his agent and sometimes editor, who had arranged for *People* magazine to cover the event. In Montreal they stayed overnight at the Ritz-Carlton Hotel on Sherbrooke Street, notably different from St. Dominique Street in the Jewish district of the city where Saul and his family had lived. In the morning, Bellow and his party drove to

Lachine, where they visited his birthplace. Later, at the library, where the group emerged from the mayor's limousine, they were greeted by what Wasserman described as "the whole town," plus a local orchestra playing "Chicago," "When the Saints Go Marching In," and "Happy Birthday."[60]

A plaque was unveiled at the library entrance, and Bellow, tearing up again, watched as a *French* mayor was about to honor an *English*-language writer who made a point of staying in touch with his local extended *Jewish* family. The mayor concluded that "Saul Bellow never forgot his roots." Bellow delivered his speech—which centered on his happy childhood in Lachine—in French and English with occasional remarks in Yiddish.[61]

The repeated assertions Bellow made that he was not an American Jewish writer seemed immaterial as he described putting on his tzitzit, the ritual vest with fringes that in Montreal was part of his youthful morning routine, or when he talked about studying the parts of Genesis that he had learned by heart in heder, which he was glad to demonstrate. It was as if he were saying, "What else but a Jew could I be?" Clearly, it was the compulsion to categorize and box him in rather than the Jewish label itself that bothered Bellow. He simply didn't fit any classification.[62]

There were celebrations and brunch over a two-day period, and more speeches, including one by Ruth Wisse, who taught Yiddish literature at McGill. On the second night, Bellow had dinner with Wisse and her husband. A hardline conservative with lots of chutzpah, Wisse shook her finger at Bellow, accusing him of "temporizing" in his support of Israel. Apparently Bellow took no offense. In fact, Wisse recalled, "he loved how passionate [she and her husband] were about Israel."

At yet another party, Wisse and Bellow, seated next to each other, conversed in Yiddish. When Wisse went to bring sweets and fruit back to the table, Bellow, playing on her name, said, "*Zi heist rut nor zi rut nisht*" ("Her name is Ruth, but she does not rest").[63] Nor did Bellow do much resting. There were more awards and readings and parties in New York, San Francisco, and Capri.

The celebration dried up for a time when Bellow was confronted once again by a series of deaths. His first wife, Anita (née Goshkin), a heavy smoker, died in March 1985 at age sixty-nine. Their son, Greg, remembered that in this circumstance, his father "was at his absolute best." As "I sobbed into the phone," Greg said, "Saul's tenderness was palpable." He said, "Come to Chicago. Your loving father will be waiting." There were, to be sure, tensions in the relationship between Bellow and his oldest son, but as Greg put it, "seeing me suffer always cut through to our fundamental emotional connection."[64]

Two months after Anita's death, Bellow's seventy-seven-year-old brother Maury, newly located in Georgia, died from colon cancer. Even as Maury had continued to make "good deals," he was struggling with prostate cancer and heart trouble. Shortly after Maury's death, Ruth Miller paid a condolence call to Bellow. He told her that at the time of his last visit with Maury, his brother knew he was dying. Balking at any discussion of death, he talked only about how lucky he was. "Life was good, was right," Maury said, and his wife was a "fine woman." He talked about his "children, and his home, and all his fine furniture," while Bellow sat in his big brother's home, "listening, grieving."[65]

The brothers knew there would be no follow-up visit, but Saul said he would return if Maury needed him. Maury did call and told Saul that, "if he meant it, if he wanted to come, now was the time. He had better come now." Before Bellow left for the airport, he received a second call, from Joyce Bellows, Maury's second wife: His brother was dead. As Bellow told Ruth Miller the story, she noticed the suit he was wearing, "a beige silk and wool suit, a very dashing well-cut suit with a vest." It had belonged to Maury, who bought it after he had lost a lot of weight. He insisted that a reluctant Bellow take the suit. As Miller puts it, "Maury was always giving Bellow a suit, and so, at the last, they reenacted the ritual between them."[66]

Within weeks of Maury's passing, Saul's middle brother, Sam Bellows, died on June 1, 1985. Contrary to his wife Nina's (b. Kahn) instructions, Sam did not want chemotherapy. His wishes were to no avail. After a time, he tried to pull out the tubes; he refused to eat. Saul was at Sam's side for much of this troubling time. He had been in New York for the operation and stayed in the same hotel as his brother's family. In Chicago, Saul "made a concerted effort to be there all the time." He also tried to get along with Nina, whom he did not like. In his life, Sam, unlike his brothers, avoided conflict—he detested it—believing in the Jewish religious ideal of *shalom bayit,* literally "peace in the home" or domestic harmony. Sam carried the injunction to be peaceful outside the home as well.[67]

Rachel Greengus, Sam's granddaughter, remembers that before he was bedridden, Sam would sit with Saul in the den, "a dark, soothing room just talking." Ruth Miller asked Bellow whether he and Sam got along. "Sam always tried," Bellow said, but "he never knew what he was to say to his brother Saul."[68] Their lives were very different. Sam was *frum,* observant, traditional, deeply rooted in the Jewish community of North Chicago. He stayed married to one woman, was a homebody, and took care of his aging father and older sister. He always made money, eventually a heap of money. Although Sam may have had a hard time knowing quite what to say to his literary younger brother, he loved him. Sam told his granddaughter Rachel that Saul was "the only sibling [he had] who [did]n't give [him] a hard time."[69]

In his final days, Sam Bellows was visited by friends, including a parade of rabbis, some of whom, Bellow told Miller, were "trying to get him to leave a large sum of money to the synagogue, the yeshiva, an old people's home, to this, to that, and he greeted them all." The funeral service took place at the Hebrew Theological College in Skokie; afterward, Bellow sat shiva with the family.

Sam, on his deathbed, had passed a kind of baton to Saul: "As we began," Sam told Saul, "so are we ending. You were there at the beginning. You're here now. It's all on you now."[70]

Bellow took the injunction seriously, as if it were a commandment that he willingly accepted, even invited. He made time for his nephews and nieces and their children, offering advice but not brashly, writing job and school references, and making phone calls when needed. He was acting out the kind of Jewish family love he so brilliantly portrayed in "Cousins" and earlier in "The Old System." Lesha, Sam's daughter, and Maury's daughter Lynn (who thought Uncle Bellow a genius) adored him, as did their children.[71]

"He was wonderful," Mark Rotblatt, Lynn's son, remembers: "I really loved Uncle Saul, because I was so grateful that he gave my mother what she needed. She needed approval. . . . And Uncle told her she was smart, she was attractive." Mark told Zachary Leader about trips to Vermont with his sister and mother. Before leaving Chicago, they would go to a North Side delicatessen,

> and my mother would get . . . five pounds of corned beef and . . . the big rugula. We'd carry it on the plane and get off in Gentile Brattleboro, and we'd lay it all out in the kitchen, and Uncle Saul was, like, in heaven. And it was nice, because he was appreciative. It was also love, what my mother was so appreciative to do. One of the things that he loved about [Lynn] was that my mother really looked to him for emotional approval. So many people who cozied up to him were looking for something else.[72]

Bellow was also close to Sam's daughter Lesha Greengus, offering her assistance and reassurance in correspondence and inviting her to go with him on trips. Prior to medical school, Rachel Greengus, Sam's granddaughter, had majored in English at Cornell. She remembers the lists of books Bellow had sent her to read. And the great-nephews and great-nieces, like the cousins (the Dworkins, Gameroffs, Gordins, et al.), mostly remember Bellow as full of family feeling, funny, appreciative, and a man who had a lot of joy in life.[73]

Keeping in touch with the extended family kept Bellow centered. It was for him, as it was for Ijah Brodsky in Bellow's story "Cousins," more than an obligation or a source of material. "I had remembered, observed, and studied the cousins," Ijah declares, "and these studies seemed to fix my own essence and to keep me as I had been."[74] With Bellow's immediate family, his sons and wives, matters were, as we have seen, a bit different.

On May 28, 1985, only days before Sam's death and within weeks of Maury's passing, Bellow had business to attend to in New York, including a dinner party at the apartment of Gerald Freund, the former director of the MacArthur Foundation. Freund was unaware, apparently, of the depth of Bellow's feelings about his brothers or his long-term obsession with aging and death; the director had planned a dinner party to celebrate the nearly simultaneous seventieth birthdays of Alfred Kazin and Saul Bellow. Clearly, Freund knew little about the current relationship between the two men, which had become quite frosty; Kazin, fifteen years earlier, had reviewed *Mr. Sammler's Planet* for the *New York Review of Books* in a manner Bellow thought hostile and churlish. It didn't seem to matter that Kazin gave high praise to *Humboldt's Gift* five years later.[75]

Oblivious to this, Freund thought that for their mutual birthdays "it would be nice to bring [Kazin and Bellow] together." Instead, after a reasonable and nostalgic start—Kazin and Bellow had shared a lifetime of experience, admiration, and mutual support—the birthday boys got into an argument about politics. While Bellow, who refused to accept the label "conservative," had moved to the right, Kazin had remained steadfastly faithful to the spirit of his youthful radicalism and his working-class origins.[76] By dessert, they were squabbling, mostly about issues directly related to Jews: Israel, particularly Menachem Begin and the Likud Party, which Kazin hated; the politics of the *New Republic*, which Bellow hated; Anthony Lewis of the *New York*

Times, whom Bellow hated even more; Leon Wieseltier's articles on Hannah Arendt—Bellow for, Kazin against.[77]

Bellow stayed for the birthday cake with two candles—"a nice touch," Adam Bellow thought—but he left early. It is unclear, however, if he walked out the door without saying goodbye. It is unclear, too, exactly what happened that entire evening. There are several contradictory or inconsistent eyewitness accounts. For sure there was pain and bewilderment for everyone. It was "an ugly scene," Kazin admitted. Although there were a small number of written exchanges between Bellow and Kazin in the early 1980s, mostly cordial, it isn't clear whether after the birthday party in June 1985 the two men ever spoke to or communicated with each other again.[78]

FIFTEEN

A WHOLE NEW LIFE

IF THERE HAD BEEN TENSION between Saul and Alexandra at the Bellow-Kazin birthday party, no guest seems to have noticed. The couple could contain themselves in public; but in December, just six months after Bellow's seventieth birthday and the death of his brothers, Alexandra sought a divorce and asked Saul to move out of their twin apartment on Sheridan Street.

Bellow claimed that the decision to divorce was Alexandra's. "I wasn't the architect," he said.[1] And in the aftermath of separation, according to William Hunt, Bellow was "pretty broken up." Eugene Kennedy, agreeing, recalled that "in the loneliness," Bellow was experiencing "something crushing."[2] Much earlier, Greg, having watched his father begin to sour on Alexandra, sensed Saul's dread: Fearful of death from early on and anxious about the indignities of aging, Bellow convinced himself that Alexandra "lacked the emotional strength" necessary to devote herself to his care as he grew older, proving, he said, that Alexandra was the responsible party in the unraveling of the marriage.[3]

In Janis Freedman, Bellow's secretary and former student, he saw something entirely different—but not immediately. A literature and philosophy student in the Committee on Social Thought program, Freedman, in Bellow's words a quiet, polite person of considerable intellectual force and independence, became his secretary in 1982. She was "fascinated by him from the first time I set foot in his class. . . . I thought he was hands down, the most intelligent person I'd ever met." But there was no "crush." He was forty-three years older and "lived in another world."[4]

Freedman interacted, even if only in passing, with Professors Edward Shils, Milton Friedman, Nathan Tarcov, Allan Bloom, and Saul Bellow, all Jewish, and at one point or another all members of the Committee on Social Thought. She called the University of Chicago "the first really Jewish place" she'd ever lived. Although her parents had been raised in an Orthodox family, Freedman had been brought up in what her sister Wendy called a secular Jewish household: there were seders, a visit to Israel, and Friday night candles and challah, but no prayers and no synagogue affiliation. Janis described the texture of Jewish life at home less as secular and more as traditional but not strictly observant. She did lean, however, more in the direction of her grandparents' rather than her parents' style of being Jewish.[5]

In any case, Freedman identified as a strongly committed Jew. She had been seriously dating Peter Ahrensdorf, a gentile political science student; but when he proposed marriage, she ultimately turned him down because he wouldn't convert to Judaism. Devoted to completing her dissertation at Chicago, Freedman decided not to follow Ahrensdorf after he took a job at Kenyon College in Ohio. The couple, by mutual agreement, ended their relationship. People tried "to fix [her] up," Freedman said. She soon grew "disgusted by all this" and had by the mid-1980s become something of a "recluse."

But in early spring of 1986, in her fourth year of working for "Professor Bellow," Freedman ran into him as she was coming out of the Regenstein Library. She was tired, had had enough of studying, and was on her way home. Bellow, without meaning injury or insult, said that Freedman looked bushed, and she admitted as much. "Why don't you come over to my house to have dinner?" he asked. When she arrived at his apartment, Bellow was "wearing an apron and holding a spatula," which she thought was "very funny." After a fish dinner, they "had a very lovely conversation . . . I ended up staying there . . . after that," she said, "we never had a night apart."[6]

At the start of her graduate education, Freedman, though fully dedicated to her studies, remembers having been intimidated by both Bellow and Bloom in her first seminar with them. "I didn't talk at all," she said, and she sat at the back of the classroom so as "not to be called on." Seminar discussions with Bloom in particular could be scary. Born in Indianapolis, the son of provincial Jewish social workers, he graduated from the University of Chicago at eighteen. He was a more charismatic figure in and out of the classroom than Bellow and by all accounts a brilliant teacher, even if more than a little pompous and not averse to rattling self-assured students with quick comebacks and witticisms. The students seemed to love it. There was a lot of laughter, Freedman recalled, beginning even as soon as Bellow and Bloom and a student or two entered the room together, already sharing a joke.

Renowned in the seminar room, Bloom became even more widely famous and fabulously wealthy with the publication of his 1987 classic, *The Closing of the American Mind*. But many of his conservative, deliberatively provocative ideas—about American mothers and teenagers and the decline of parental authority, the decline of the liberal arts and the disintegration of the university, the failures and dangers of affirmative action for African Americans, the mush of movies and popular culture generally, radical feminism's defiance of "nature," and the connections between desperation, drugs, and the failures of democracy—were relatively well known years earlier.

For Bloom, only the "Great Books," the Bible, Plato, and Socrates in particular, could fix things. These texts, along with Aristotle, Cicero, and Plutarch, were the only texts worthy of study, and only if in depth. Like Bellow, Bloom was far less elitist and antimodern in his real feelings and public statements. And both, despite their contemptuous remarks about American vulgarity and materialism, enjoyed the vitality of democratic America. But Bloom's book and his public statements were what most readers and students knew. A friendly critic, Werner J. Dannhauser, pointed out the inconsistency, quipping that it did no one any good for Bloom to write about democracy and "not mean what he says or say what he means."[7]

In the end Bloom sought intellectual support for his intuitions—principally about the soul and the afterlife. Like Bellow, who argued everywhere for the idea of an essential self or soul, Bloom in *The Closing of the American Mind* claimed the existence of an "awareness" or a "divination" that there is a human nature and that assisting in its fulfillment is the professor's task. "No real teacher," Bellow said in agreement, "can doubt that his task is to assist his pupil" in fulfilling his or her "human nature against all the deforming forces of convention and prejudice."[8] Bellow's insistence that the self should not be hemmed in by political or intellectual classification was found in all his work. And Bloom, very much like Bellow, was able to escape his ordinary origins by the power of mind. They saw themselves, not without reason, as examples of the way the self can jump the fences society builds to constrain it.[9]

Although Bloom was homosexual and fifteen years younger than Bellow, the two men had affinities that dwarfed their differences. That they had grown so close and spent so much time together was an additional factor in the unraveling of Bellow's marriage to Alexandra. Bloom was, and Bellow could be, an inexhaustible talker; between them was an endless supply of serious issues and ideas to discuss as well as an interminable treasure trove of comic anecdotes. Janis Freedman would eventually get used to the Bellow-Bloom dynamic. Alexandra Ionesco Tulcea had no patience for it.

In early January 1986, Bellow, recently bereft of his brothers, dispossessed of his apartment, and tangled again in divorce proceedings, was fearful, lonely, and seriously depressed as he boarded a plane for New York; he was headed, as a featured speaker, to the weeklong forty-eighth International PEN Congress, presided over by Norman Mailer. Among others scheduled to speak were writers Nadine Gordimer, Kurt Vonnegut, Mario Vargas Llosa, Toni Morrison, Umberto Eco, Allen Ginsberg, Amos Oz, and the exiled Soviet author Vassily Aksyonov. The audience, too, was filled with an international array of notable writers, some of whom would also make presentations, Günter Grass, Salmon Rushdie, and Susan Sontag among them.

The conference was organized around the topic of social and political disaffection. Bellow's talk, on "The State and the Alienation of the Writer," identified various types of estrangement in the literary community. Without necessarily justifying the American establishment, Bellow argued that though the US was relatively successful materially, it was a country suffering from a kind of "spiritual alienation" and therefore a place in which "the soul does not count for much." As a nation we "didn't start very high, and we didn't rise very high either."[10]

When Bellow finished speaking, Günter Grass rose from the audience immediately. Effectively ignoring the main thrust of the talk, Grass attacked Bellow, first by pointing out incorrectly that the American writer had said the US suffered no alienation, and then, in a blatant non sequitur (possibly deliberate), Grass said that he had recently visited the South Bronx, where he saw poor Black people in those streets who "would not agree that they were free and equal." The statement made little if any sense in the context of Bellow's speech, nor did it have much meaning in the general framework of the PEN conference. It did, however, indicate that Grass was unfamiliar with Bellow's novels *Mr. Sammler's Planet* and *The Dean's December*, both of which featured the horrors of urban blight.[11]

Bellow, "with patient grace" or "frigid superiority," depending on the source, said, as he had in *Sammler* and *Dean*, that "of course American cities were going to hell in a hurry; they had become monstrous." Bellow's reply did not give the German writer pause. In a session on "The Utopian Imagination," Grass, doubling down, wondered "out loud about whether capitalism is in any way better than gulag communism" and concluded with the words, "I don't think so." Vassily Aksyonov, whose own parents had served eighteen years in the gulag before being exiled and who was himself arrested and imprisoned by the NKVD, warned delegates (particularly German delegates), Grass among them, "to think twice before making parallels between the U.S. and the USSR."[12]

David Lehman, reporting for *Partisan Review*, claimed that he had heard another author speculate about the motive for Grass's persistent anti-American posture: "The burden of guilt for the Nazi past," the writer had risked saying, "supplied a secret subtext to Grass's South Bronx-equals-gulag gambit. If the South Bronx is no better than the gulag, and the gulag is not much better than the death camps, doesn't that somehow let the Germans off the hook?"[13]

No one yet knew, of course, that Grass, as soon as he had become old enough, had volunteered for submarine service with Nazi Germany's Kriegsmarine, or that after rejection for technical reasons, he was called up by the Waffen-SS and saw action in a regular Panzer division. He was captured in what is now the Czech Republic and sent to a US prisoner-of-war camp in Bavaria.[14]

In the press conference after the panel, Bellow was relatively generous in his attitude toward the Germans. He claimed to understand why Grass, his "Chief Confronter," might have taken some of the positions he did. German writers, Bellow said, were caught between East and West, in the middle of "a life and death struggle" between the two superpowers. Still, he resented the "stampeding of writers into political boxes" by the left, which included Grass, as well as by critics on the right.[15]

Although many of his views were supported, championed even, at the PEN conference, Bellow returned to Chicago in about the same state of mind he had brought to New York. The divorce from Alexandra continued to darken his mood, as did the deaths of Maury and Sam. It certainly did not help when, two months after Bellow's return, Bernard Malamud, only one year older than Saul, died suddenly on April 16, 1986, of a heart attack. Off to another PEN conference in London the very next day, Bellow's memorial for Malamud was delayed for several months. Finally, in December, after introducing his presentation with a quip about having first met Malamud at Oregon State, where he, such a "New York type," was considered an "exotic," Bellow had this to say:

> Malamud was not an exotic to me. We were cats of the same breed. The sons of Eastern European immigrant Jews, we had gone early into the streets or our respective cities, were Americanized by schools, newspapers, subways, streetcars, sandlots, Melting Pot children, we had assumed the American program to be the real thing: no barriers to the freest and fullest American choices. Of course, we understood that it was no simple civics-course matter. We knew too much about the slums, we had assimilated too much dark history in our mother's kitchens to be radiant optimists. . . . Well, we were here, first-generation Americans, our language was English and a language is a spiritual mansion from which no one can evict us. Malamud in his novels and stories discovered a sort of communicative genius in the impoverished, harsh jargon of immigrant New York. He was a myth maker, a fabulist, a writer of exquisite parables. The English novelist Anthony Burgess said of him that he "never forgets that he is an American Jew, and he is at his best when posing the situation of a Jew in urban American society." A "remarkably consistent writer," he goes on, "who has never produced a mediocre novel . . . he is devoid of either conventional piety or sentimentality . . . always profoundly convincing." Let me add on my own behalf that the accent of a hard-won and individual emotional truth is always heard in Malamud's words. He is a rich original of the first rank.[16]

While in London for the PEN conference, Bellow had a chance to see a lot of Philip Roth. Saul "was very lonely," Roth told James Atlas: "He was seventy; he had to start all over again." In the meantime, Roth tried to be supportive and accommodating. Before Bellow arrived in London, Roth and his partner, the English actress Claire Bloom, had booked tickets for a concert featuring the last string quartets of Shostakovich; but they made certain to get a seat for Bellow, too. During the cab ride to the concert hall, Bellow was quiet, staring out the window, finally saying, "Well, Schaffner is gone," an allusion to his long-standing joke about how Bellow, Malamud, and Roth were sewn together as the Hart, Schaffner, and Marx—the upscale men's clothiers—of American Jewish writing. Bellow otherwise remained silent after what Roth described as "an astonishingly beautiful" concert. He realized that in the mood Bellow was in, he "needed the last quartets . . . like a hole in the head."[17]

At dinner parties later in his stay, Bellow could be, as George Weidenfeld (his former English publisher) put it, "touchingly wonderful in his self-pity" or a guy who "kvetched" annoyingly "about this one and that one." At other times, with Roth not far from his elbow, Bellow, by another writer's waggish intervention, could be turned from a kvetch into one of a group of "American novelists matching each other with acid doses of wit."[18]

It was in May 1986, less than a month back from London, that Bellow, apparently in a better mood, asked Janis Freedman back to his apartment for dinner. From that meal forward, they were, as Janis said, inseparable. The Bellow-Freedman union was a surprise, even a shock to many, including Saul's middle son, Adam. He had known Janis in their overlapping year as students at the University of Chicago and as his father's secretary-assistant. Adam, who liked and continued to stay in touch with Alexandra Ionescu Tulcea, said he knew what his father expected in a wife: "Secretarial services, household major domo, surrogate parent."[19]

Their live-in arrangement was treated, in the words of Ruth Wisse, who knew the couple well, "as a May-December curiosity—31-year-old student . . . marries famous novelist professor." But Wisse, who, with her husband, Len, shared many a Shabbat dinner with the Bellows, saw it as "something entirely different," a homecoming for Bellow after a lifetime search. "To be sure," Wisse said, "he had found in Janis a lovely young wife, but she also gave him the unconditional love of the mother he had never ceased to mourn." Janis Freedman also had something, a package of somethings, that none of the first four wives had ever provided in full: She was a fellow Canadian, and she shared Bellow's passion for literature; his concern for Israel, which had been increasing in the decades since the 1960s; and his familiarity and comfort with being Jewish. Indeed, it was Janis who brought the traditional Jewish customs she had been raised with into the Bellow household. Not least in keeping their match strong, she also had in her a generally underestimated "amount of steel."[20]

Almost a year after they became a couple, Janis and Saul traveled to Haifa for a conference at the university devoted entirely to him. But there was to be a European holiday first, planned partly around a trip to Lugano for a filmed interview and to Turin for a visit with Primo Levi, the famed Holocaust writer-survivor, whom Bellow had met only once, in New York. There were a lot of hours spent "packing, moving, worrying," and even more hours flying, driving, and running to catch trains to and through Italy, Switzerland, France, and Israel. They were slowed down when, leaving a café in Aix, Bellow caught sight of a headline: "Primo Levi Dies." He was badly shaken. Janis had to take his arm to guide him through the crowd to the train station. After a week of rest, they were off again on April 24 for a 6 a.m. flight from Lyon through Zurich to Haifa.

Though they were "close and loving" throughout their travels, the couple was often exhausted, and Bellow depressed. "It was the difference of years," Janis Freedman said, "and of course of death." Primo Levi was sixty-eight, four years younger than Bellow. Given his nearly lifetime preoccupation with death, and with so many members of his generation gone, there approached for Bellow "a need sometimes . . . to give yourself to it." But against such darkness, Freedman said, there was always "this aching need for life."[21]

Still, the Haifa conference was not easy for him. Although the Israeli novelists A. B. Yehoshua, Aharon Appelfeld, and Amos Oz made presentations, there were also large numbers of scholars in attendance, as many as one hundred scheduled as speakers. Most were associated in one way or another with the Saul Bellow Society or the *Saul Bellow Journal*. Bellow approved of neither. He was wary of academics who presumed to "explain" his work.[22] The conference, Bellow said in an interview, resembled an autopsy, with his cadaver "dissected and laid on the table" for three days of analysis. His own talk, "The Silent Assumptions of Novelists," on the second night of the conference, drew an audience of one thousand. But Bellow seemed most impressed by the introduction delivered by Shimon Peres, former prime minister of Israel. By all accounts, he knew Bellow's works well and talked about them intelligently.[23]

Bellow also addressed a group at the conference, perhaps informally, about which the philosopher and Holocaust historian Berel Lang later wrote. He repeated this story to the author:

> That Bellow did study the Holocaust early and very personally became evident to me during my own rich conversations with him over a three-day period at Haifa University, Israel in 1987. I realized then that he had not been ignoring the subject so much as preparing for it. His grasp of barely known incidents, details, places, names, numbers, methods, personalities, and lesser-known stories, was not just the knowledge gleaned by an autodidact in his reading. Bellow had conducted his own interviews, put his own shoes on the bloody ground. As he spoke of these interviews to myself and a group of rapt listeners, we were sobered by his incisive intensity when he told

> us little known Holocaust stories gleaned from everywhere he had traveled in search of the meaning of the Shoah.[24]

Lang's report is in striking contrast to what Bellow said of himself in a long, overly self-critical letter to Cynthia Ozick on July 19, 1987 (discussed at greater length in chap. 6), less than three months after his return from Haifa.[25] In the letter, Bellow "confessed" to having been unspeakably evasive about the Holocaust, about the string of ferocious, criminal, and horrific events unfolding in Poland during the war. But he also told Ozick that for more than four decades he had been "brooding" about the Shoah and his own failure to reckon with it more fully. He had been too busy, Bellow wrote, promoting his own recognition as a writer to burden his career with the encumbering weight of Jewish history. A half century of brooding, however, counts for something, as Ozick herself pointed out. Moreover, Bellow's first two novels, *Dangling Man* (1944) and *The Victim* (1947), discussed in chapters 4 and 5, include several significant allusions to the genocide perpetrated against the Jews.

Only weeks after the Haifa conference, with Janis and Saul back in their Vermont summer home, Bellow's tenth novel, *More Die of Heartbreak,* was published. It had neither the usual Bellow style and punch nor nearly as much humor. Bellow told Martin Amis, a writer, friend, and devoted fan, that the book had emerged in an especially bleak time in his life. There were the deaths of his two brothers in 1985, only weeks apart; then Alexandra, after "twelve years of marriage, decided to divorce me, releasing me at the age of seventy to begin a new life. These events left me reeling. . . . To stave off sordid depression—if not insanity—I went back to work last June [1986] and wrote a book. . . ."[26]

It took Bellow only six months to write *More Die of Heartbreak,* a far shorter time than he took with any of his other novels. This apparent rush to escape depression may account for Bellow's less-than-sparkling performance and for the book's mixed but decidedly negative reception. In the novel, Benn Crader, one of two protagonists, is a well-known botanist, a recognized genius as a plant scientist, and an "outstanding noticer" and visionary. The narrator, Kenneth Trachtenberg, Benn's nephew and an assistant professor of Russian literature, thinks he can help his widowed uncle with his ove "yearnings," which throughout the novel bear no fruit. The problem? Benn can see through the surface details of plants to conjure their inner meaning, but he "couldn't make the psychic transfer to human relations." This is especially true, according to Kenneth, when it comes to women. And yet Benn "could not leave the women alone."[27]

Despite the nephew's annoying advice, Benn remains uncertain and confused; in the end, unlike Bellow's earlier protagonists—Augie, Henderson, and especially Herzog—who gain insight from their various journeys and resolve to begin again, Benn, leaving a fiancée behind, runs off surreptitiously to do research in "northern Scandinavia on the edge of Finland.... And beyond."[28]

For all Benn's genius and dreamy otherworldliness, he, like all males—in Bellow's view, including himself—has been infected by modernity, in particular "modernity's debasement of love into sex." In an interview days before the publication of *Heartbreak*, Bellow told Eugene Kennedy that "in sexual relationships people have become extremely literal" or specialized. We don't "view each other as persons, but only as bearers of erogenous zones.... The result is disastrous, since you cannot excise human nature and not expect people to die of heartbreak."[29]

This development, Bellow said, emerges from a loss of faith "in the ageless truths of human nature.... In the nature-nurture controversy, nurture has been regarded as *everything*. I never believed that." There is "some stable character to human nature," Bellow insisted, and he pointed out that the Bible and Shakespeare, and Homer and the Greek playwrights, also believed that. But, he argued, the idea that human nature is real has been disposed of by modernity. And that is "why the affective lives of people have changed, and why the bonds between persons have grown weaker."[30] In the novel, this idea is treated, even if tiresomely, with a good deal more complexity. But in *Heartbreak* and in his interview with Kennedy, Bellow appears to be making something of a confession.

When Janis Freedman read *Heartbreak,* she recognized "a lot of Saul" in Benn: "He, too . . . suffered from the many mistakes he'd made. He beat himself up over these things. He didn't shy away from examining all of his mistakes, big mistakes, tragic, ugly wrong-headed moves." But did Bellow make a "big mistake" in publishing *Heartbreak*? Some of his "best friends" seemed to think so.[31]

There were positive reviews from William Gaddis and Anne Tyler, but other notable critics found *Heartbreak* "dismally thin" and its talk of the soul, hollow, even "irritating."[32] Alfred Kazin in the *New York Review of Books* complained about nephew Kenneth's "exultantly sour views of modernity, sexuality, women." The depiction of women, Kazin thought, was appalling, as was the display of men's ideas about women. He was convinced that *More Die of Heartbreak* was "a book fired by misogyny."[33] Two months later in the *New Republic,* Leon Wieseltier also described the novel as "spiritually anti-American" and "a sorry tale of male self-pity . . . unrelenting in its disgust for women who are portrayed as if their reason for being is the frustration of the better selves of men."[34]

More Die of Heartbreak was listed as a bestseller for thirteen weeks but after that sold poorly. "There is nothing to complain about," Bellow wrote to his close friend the poet Karl Shapiro: "I am happy to find a few readers who would actually approve. To have even a *minyan* is ecstasy. (Do I catch myself saying, after so many decades of devotion to Anglo-American literature, that the Happy Few resemble the Jews!)."[35]

Would there be more and better work from a seventy-two-year-old Bellow? During the first three years that he and Janis were together, he published two novellas, *The Theft* and, far more important, *The Bellarosa Connection*, both in 1989, the year they were married at a very small wedding in Vermont. He followed those books with "Something to Remember Me By" (1990), one of his most critically admired short stories. Later came a small number of publications as well as work on three or more novels in progress. But post-1990, while still writing, teaching, and lecturing, Bellow was more invested in building a whole new life with Janis Freedman.[36]

Harvey Freedman, Janis's father, was not particularly receptive to Bellow in the beginning, but it didn't take long for him to see that "there was a . . . spiritual union here. They understood each other . . . emotionally, sort of kindred souls."[37] Janis Freedman-Bellow kept notes about the couple's life and their writing work, in which they were mutually interactive. In her journal she reproduced her thoughts and as often quoted Bellow's words and ideas. For example, in Janis's dissertation (1991), "Passionate Longing: Women in the Novel from Rousseau to Flaubert," she makes a compelling argument against Rousseau's idea about love. The Frenchman thought that longing in most women—more passionate, more urgent than in males—was sublimated in family, duty, and loyalty, becoming less visible, less "real." Bellow is quoted in Janis's journal as saying, "There IS such a thing as love. It isn't a manipulative product of the imagination. It's a real power. Not a winning one, no one ever said that, but real enough."[38]

The couple traveled together to every event at which Bellow was honored. In July 1988, Janis accompanied him to Washington, DC, where he was presented with a National Medal of the Arts by President Ronald Reagan. The writer was honored along with other notables in a variety of fields—the architect I. M. Pei, who, according to Pei's biographer, won "every award of any consequence in his art"; pianist Rudolf Serkin, generally regarded as one of the greatest interpreters of Beethoven in the twentieth century; and the prizewinning choreographer Jerome Robbins, who had been inducted into the American Theater Hall of Fame in 1979.

Although Bellow, who approved of Reagan's anti-Communism, was happy to meet the president, it is not clear that he voted for him. His son Adam thinks not: "For my father and I as Jews it was still very difficult to identify with Republicans socially and culturally." In any case, Bellow did not feel in any way compromised by accepting the medal from Reagan's hands.[39]

In May 1990, married now for nearly a year, Saul and Janis came to England, where Bellow delivered the Romanes Lecture at Oxford, the annual public lecture of the university. George Walden, a British politician friendly with Bellow, arranged a meeting with Prime Minister Margaret Thatcher. In answer to a question from Thatcher's office about what to talk about, Walden said that Bellow was very concerned about "the black problem" in America.[40]

The meeting did not go well. The prime minister, harried, was not at her best that day, and she hadn't read any of Bellow's novels. Her first words to him were "They can't have given you the Nobel Prize for nothing—you must have something to tell me." But then she went on to do all the talking. "They tell me," Thatcher said, "that Chicago has a bad racial problem," and she wanted to hear Bellow's views, or so she said. But before he could get past the word "Well . . ." Thatcher jumped in and proceeded to tell the Nobel Prize winner all there was to know about the issue.[41]

The "black problem" in Chicago was indeed much on Bellow's mind, not only because he thought crime in the Black slums of his city was out of control—a function of gross inequalities and political blindness or opportunism—but also because of an apparent explosion of antisemitism in Chicago's African American population, which blamed Jews for the difficulties. In 1988, Steve Cokely, an aide to Eugene Sawyer, the Black mayor of Chicago, claimed that Jews were at the head of an international conspiracy to control the world. He also accused Jewish doctors of injecting Black babies with AIDS in order to foster the epidemic, and he insisted that in November 1987, on the forty-ninth anniversary of Kristallnacht, the night of broken glass in 1938 Nazi Germany, Chicago's North Side Jewish merchants had broken their own store windows in order to gain sympathy.

It took more than a week for the mayor to fire Cokely. Even worse, only three of eighteen Black members of the city council approved of the dismissal. And the head of Chicago's Commission on Human Rights, Reverend Herbert B. Martin, said he had heard "a ring of truth" in Cokely's remarks about a worldwide Jewish conspiracy. Eugene Kennedy, writing in the *New York Times,* said that aside from the deceased Mayor Richard J. Daley's son, Richard M. Daley, Cook County state's attorney and soon to be Chicago's mayor, "hardly any Chicagoan of major influence has spoken out strongly, unambiguously, and consistently against the Anti-Semitism that has infected the city's life."[42]

As Kennedy saw it, "the Jewish people needed" more leaders who weren't Jewish to raise the issue of Black antisemitism and "to raise it as strongly as possible." Hatred of Jews had so virulently gripped Chicago's Black community, Kennedy wrote, that "nobody morally powerful enough to try to combat it, including the Rev. Jesse Jackson, who lives here, has attempted to do so." Among leaders in the non-Jewish white community, in addition to Daley, there were a select few who issued warnings: The Rev. John Egan, who for forty years had been fighting for racial and religious equality, said that the justifiable "anguish and anger of Jews" in Chicago was "real and deep." And the Rev. Andrew Greeley, a Roman Catholic priest and a writer, said that antisemitism in the city was so poisonous that "if I were Jewish, I would be terrified."[43]

In an interview, Kennedy insisted that "the Jewish people . . . had been in the vanguard of fighting for the rights of African Americans." But now there was an inexplicable hysteria among Chicago Black people. A paranoid fervor, Kennedy said, gripped the city, and "there were guys getting on television programs and talking about this. It was really bizarre." Kennedy's words upset many Chicagoans, and the *Chicago Tribune* ran an editorial denouncing him for writing about Chicago's problems in the *New York Times*. But Bellow called Kennedy and said with great appreciation, "I'll never forget you for doing this."[44]

In August 1988, two or three weeks after the *Tribune*'s editorial criticizing Kennedy, the paper published an article by Bellow defending the journalist. He accused the *Tribune* of ignoring the issues raised in Kennedy's essay by shifting attention "from Cokely's illiterate mob incitement to Kennedy himself, as if Kennedy were the guilty party." The *Tribune* argued that Kennedy was wrong to take Cokely seriously, describing the mayoral aide as "barely able to keep a grip on himself, let alone Chicago's black community," and the paper cited a poll that indicated that, unlike the city councilmen, only 8 percent of Black people opposed Cokely's firing.[45]

But Mike Royko, perhaps the paper's most widely read columnist, had warned earlier of an "inflammatory, irresponsible racial rhetoric," nearly all of it "coming from blacks."[46] In a personal letter, Bellow praised Royko as "the brainiest and the bravest of newspapermen. It takes guts to do what you are doing." The articles by Royko, Kennedy, and Bellow finally elicited a condemnation of Cokely's behavior and rhetoric from the city's most popular African American columnists, Clarence Page in the *Tribune* and Vernon Jarrett in the *Sun-Times*.

Until that time, what seems to have upset Bellow most about the whole episode was the "curious inability" of Chicago journalists and politicians "to respond to what is monstrous in a monstrous situation. Does no one remember Stalin and his 'Jewish doctors' plot? Has everyone forgotten Hitler?" This analogy is surely a stretch, but about the support Cokely received from the leaders of Black Chicago, detailed by Kennedy and repeated by Bellow, the *Tribune* said nothing.[47]

In the spring of 1988, only months before Black-Jewish tensions in Chicago erupted into explosive exchanges, Bellow was spending a good deal of time reflecting on Jewishness and the history of the Jews in the twentieth century. He was preparing to give a lengthy talk at the Jewish Publication Society in Philadelphia, the oldest publisher of Jewish books in the United States. His presentation, "A Jewish Writer in America" (discussed at some length in chap. 3 and alluded to throughout), begins like so many of Bellow's talks with some "personal history," or more precisely at a stage before personal history, a less "educated" stage, which he called "my first consciousness."

In this consciousness, Bellow said, "I was among other things a Jew. We were all Jews. We spoke Yiddish, we spoke English, we observed Jewish customs, accepted Jewish superstitions, we prayed and blessed in Hebrew, our parents spoke Russian. . . . My first consciousness was that of a cosmos, and in that cosmos I was a Jew."

Although having said more than once elsewhere that he refused to be a person determined only by his environment, Bellow never thought of turning away from or rejecting his Jewishness. Such a turn always seemed to him "an utter impossibility . . . a treason to my first consciousness, my core consciousness." He would not "unJew" himself "to go beyond the given and re-enter life at a more advantageous point."

Using illustrations drawn from his own experience, Bellow pointed to the disadvantages of Jewish identity to a young American who yearned to become a writer. But even in the face of slights and suspicions, often hurtful, he knew early on that the hostility faced by the Jewish writer in America was of a lesser order than that faced by his European counterpart. Yet even here in America, he thought, you had to "train yourself in infighting and counterpunching." He went on to quote Irving Howe: "When up against the walls of gentile politeness we would aggressively proclaim our 'difference,' as if to raise Jewishness to a higher cosmopolitan power."[48]

Reflecting on this kind of political assertiveness and its connection to the Holocaust, Bellow credited the founders of Israel and their "manliness" for removing the curse, the humiliation, of Jewish victimization and for restoring respect to Jews.[49] He knew that the rationality of Israeli politics could be "damaged by memories coming from the Jewish experiences of [the twentieth century]," but in another respect, Bellow saw the anarchic negativism inherent in the Holocaust as pointing up Jewish values that stand against "the modern world of nihilistic abysses and voids." A writer who is an American and a Jew, Bellow argued, has an obligation. He or she "has been able to explore and develop his own consciousness freely, and in this consciousness" develop a "Jewish preoccupation with the redemption of mankind from its sins and injustices. To hold to this in barbarous times without pretensions is the decent thing to attempt."[50]

In the weeks before he delivered his talk in Philadelphia and then during the entire month of May and beyond, Bellow's conversations with Janis Freedman were "about nothing but the fate of the Jews in the twentieth century." Back in Vermont, while dining at the home of their friends and neighbors Herb and Libby Hillman, Bellow introduced the question he and Janis had been mulling over for weeks: "Should the Jews feel shame over the Holocaust?" Janis was "ferociously opposed" to the notion that the Jews bore "a particular disgrace in being victimized."[51]

During the discussion, Hillman told a story about a fellow chemist he had befriended, a survivor rescued by the famous macher, producer, and organizer of extravaganzas "Broadway" Billy Rose. Somehow, Rose had helped Hillman's friend get out of a prison in Fascist Italy and then, in 1939, out of Europe entirely. Rose, however, never agreed to meet the man he had saved. Having heard the bare bones of this intriguing story, Bellow only days later began working in great energetic spurts on what became the novella *The Bellarosa Connection*.

Billy Rose, the entrepreneur, was mainly about building personal fame and fortune, but the Jewish boy from the Lower East Side of Manhattan was also an avid follower of the news from

Europe; and he determined, even as he was fighting to get ahead, to apply some of his extraordinary talents to fighting back. He reviled and spoke out against Hitler, the mass murderer of Rose's people, who was orchestrating his own theatrical extravaganzas near Nuremberg on Nazi Party rally grounds. Not so admirable in other ways, the man dubbed "beautiful rose" by Bellow was morally flawed, petty, even greedy, and occasionally brutal. But Broadway Billy's refreshingly proactive response to the desperation of European Jews compared favorably to the avoidance behavior of too many other Americans, Gentiles and Jews alike.[52]

We never learn if Rose was running a covert operation or if the rescue of Bellow's fictive Harry Fonstein was a singular case. Nor do we discover why Rose refused to acknowledge his mitzvah, his good deed, or to meet Fonstein. Bellow was centered on another question altogether: how to understand the significance of his unnamed narrator's long-standing neglect of Fonstein, to whom he was a distant cousin. The narrator is a mnemonic master, a successful teacher of techniques for improving memory, but he wants no memory of the Holocaust. He is not a denier but "didn't want to hear this," the specifics of the humiliation, torture, and murder of the Jews in concentration camps.[53]

Bellow, for the first time in his fiction writing, is substantively explicit about these horrors. Although he had been making thematic use of the Holocaust in his novels as early as 1944 and mentioned Nazi barbarities several times in *Mr. Sammler's Planet* (1970), it was not until the 1989 publication of *The Bellarosa Connection* that he seemed to seek a kind of redemption, not so much from his overstated self-condemnation for ignoring the Holocaust—which he clearly did not do—but from the self-leveled charge that he had not properly represented the Holocaust, the "central event" of his time.[54]

The narrator of *The Bellarosa Connection* hadn't wanted to hear about the horrors of the Holocaust: "It suffocated me. . . . I didn't want to think of the history and psychology of these abominations, these death chambers and furnaces." But Fonstein's formidable American-born wife Sorella is well up on the subject and had at one time overcome the narrator's resistance to hearing. After all, he said, "You couldn't say no to Jewish history after what had happened in Nazi Germany."[55]

Ultimately, however, he had come to feel that thinking about and remembering the Holocaust was "utterly beyond me, a pointless exercise." Even Billy Rose, like the narrator, finally sees things this way. But Sorella, an unusually large woman, who may have been "trying to incorporate in fatty tissue what [her husband] had lost—members of his family," is as formidable as she is outsized.[56] And she is indefatigable in her attempt to convince the impresario to remember Fonstein as a person, not just as an object of rescue, and to meet with him personally if only for fifteen minutes. "I can't believe you don't remember," she says. Broadway Billy comes back with, "Remember, forget—what's the difference to me?"[57] Sorella relays this exchange to the narrator and asks how he sees "the whole Billy business." Not satisfied with his answer, she supplies her own: "If you want my basic view, here it is: The Jews could survive everything that Europe threw at them. I mean the lucky remnant. But now comes the next test—America. Can they hold their ground, or will the U.S.A. be too much for them?"[58]

Years later, the narrator, who has managed to flush Sorella and Harry out of his memory, is suddenly reminded of the Fonsteins by a caller from Israel looking for Harry on behalf of another survivor. The narrator, recognizing a deep need of his own, welcomes the chance to reconnect with the Fonsteins. But they are impossible to find. The other relatives have lost touch, about which they appear to have no regrets. Finally getting through to a home number, our narrator learns from a house-sitter friend of Fonstein's son, Gilbert, that Harry and Sorella have been killed in an auto accident. The house-sitter seems indifferent to the entire situation. Indeed, he appears to mock the narrator for his attachment to Old World values and feelings.

"He was taunting me—for my Jewish sentiments," the narrator concludes, and thinks, "What a young moron!"[59] Should he call the moron back? "Suppose I were to talk with him about the roots of memory in feeling—about the themes that collect and hold memory; if I were to tell him what retention of the past really means. Things like: 'If sleep is forgetting, forgetting is also sleep, and sleep is to consciousness what death is to life.' So that Jews ask even God to remember, '*Yiskor Elohim*.'"[60]

But how, he wonders, is he "to make an impression on a kid like that?"—an obviously assimilated Jew, whose historical obliviousness represents the post-Holocaust generation in America. Sorella's question seems to have been answered. The US *has* proved too hard for the Jews. Instead of calling back, the narrator reminds himself that "God doesn't forget, but your prayer requests him particularly to remember your dead," your beloved dead, of whom Bellow, nearing seventy-five, had many, most notably his mother. The first mention of God, the first use of Hebrew on the very last page of the novella, signifies that it is not too late for the Bellovian narrator. He acknowledges his need to incorporate Harry's story into Jewish traditional forms of memory and so offers a midrash, an interpretation, of the *Yiskor* prayer for remembrance of souls: "I chose to record everything I could remember of the Bellarosa Connection, and set it all down with a Mnemosyne flourish."[61]

The Bellarosa Connection helped fulfill Bellow's desire to properly represent the Holocaust and at the same time served his apparent need to properly mourn the millions of Jewish victims. "Something to Remember Me By," a short story published in 1990 only months after *The Bellarosa Connection* appeared, similarly helped serve his enduring and haunting need to properly mourn the mother he lost when just a boy. Bellow's dying mother is central to this new story in the same way that her death was at the heart of *Herzog*.

The short story is cast in the form of a letter, a memoir really, written by Louie, now an elderly man, to his son. The father reveals a shameful incident he had undergone is his youth, which represented a kind of adolescent rite of passage. At the age of eighteen, Louie was tricked by a prostitute who robbed him of his clothes, forcing him to make his way home in the Chicago winter in a flimsy woman's dress. The tale he tells in his letter has classic dreamlike elements, including the appearance of a naked woman seemingly out of nowhere, Louie's embarrassment over his own nakedness, and his being dressed in women's clothing in public. There is a nightmarish dimension to his experience, too, full of complex events, some hysterically funny, some frightening, all entangled with thoughts about sex and death and guilt, all confusing, all challenging to a young man's understanding of the world and himself, all delaying a return to home.

At home, his mother, a tender, nurturing woman, is dying of cancer. Louie feels shame from the various predicaments he has found himself in and suffers guilt for neglecting his mother. "I knew she was dying," he writes, "and didn't allow myself to think about it. . . . The truth is I didn't want to talk about my mother." But in Louie's unconscious attempt to extinguish his sexual urge in the face of the prostitute's nakedness, his "mother's chest, mutilated by cancer surgery, passed through [his] mind."[62]

When he finally makes it home (hours late), his father, up waiting for him, swiftly hits him on the head. This blow, however, comes as a relief; had his mother already died, Louie knows he would have been embraced instead, and he thinks of his father's "blind Old Testament rage" not "as cruelty but as archaic right everlasting."[63] Chicago is modern, American; but life at home for several Bellow figures, like Louie, and particularly Moses Herzog, and Max in "Zetland: By a Character Witness" (1974), is traditional, "archaic," respectably Jewish, with memories and customs of life in the Old World.

"I had no sympathy for myself," Louie claims. "I confessed that I had this coming, a high-minded Jewish school-boy, too high and mighty to be Orthodox and with his eye on a special destiny. . . . The facts of life were having their turn. Their effect was ridicule."[64] Bellow's heroes often represent his own self-confessed weaknesses. They can be vain, stubborn men who think they are a breed apart—unique, beyond the common fate. Lofty protagonists like Henderson, Herzog, or Charlie Citrine are brought face-to-face, typically through some kind of comic scourge and humiliation, with the fact that they are no better than the ordinary schlemiel—men mostly led astray by lust. Louie is no exception.

Nor is Bellow an exception. He was unfaithful to his wives and his girlfriends and for many years found himself in embarrassing situations—psychologically and morally challenging situations. It is not insignificant that the Yiddish word for "male genitals" and "fool" is the same: *schmuck*. But now that Bellow and Janis were soulmates in a marriage filled with mutual love, his new story may also have been written, like Louie's letter, as a form of repentance.

After living together for three years, Bellow (seventy-four) and Janis (thirty-one) were married near their summer home in Vermont in August 1989. They celebrated the event with a small wedding party at the home of their neighbors, Herb and Libby Hillman. Champagne was followed by the Jewish traditional challah and honey. Shortly afterward, the Bellows left to teach a semester at Boston University. In the meantime, Bellow had written "The Theft," a story that was turned down by the *New Yorker* and *Vanity Fair* as too long. He decided to have it published as a stand-alone paperback novella. Not among his stronger works, *The Theft* was mostly overlooked. The reviews were lukewarm at best, and sales were poor, 100,000 copies of 250,000 printed.[65]

Bellow was outwardly stoic. "I've lived long enough not to be edgy about my reputation," he told a British journalist. But he was very unhappy about the reviews. The critics were "a *pritchek* on my *tuches*," he said to Stuart Brent—"a prick on my ass."[66]

But Bellow bounced back from disappointment, publishing *The Bellarosa Connection*, which was well received critically, and giving talks and readings from earlier works to packed audiences of hundreds.

In May 1990, Janis invited one hundred people to a surprise seventy-fifth birthday party for Saul. She singlehandedly organized the entire celebration at Le Petit Chef in Wilmington, Vermont, where the Bellows often dined. When they entered the restaurant, there were "great screams and cheers" from some seventy-five well-wishers.[67] There were large contingents from Chicago and New York. Saul Steinberg flew in from the Hamptons by helicopter. Bellow's cousins from Riga made a toast in Yiddish. Other Russian cousins, only recently arrived from a crumbling Soviet Union, joined in the general tumult. John Auerbach, to whom Bellow had dedicated *The Bellarosa Connection*, came from Israel with his wife.

There were nieces and nephews, too, along with sons Adam and Daniel and their families. Greg was absent. He had just returned home to California after touring colleges in the East with his daughter Juliet. But his son, Andrew, came with his mother to represent the family. To Philip Roth the party was "Chekhovian . . . with people popping up suddenly to make speeches and to break into tears, to tell you how much they love you. Chekhov and no one else would have thrust forward the Russian cousin to announce, 'I *chav* a song.'" There were enough kisses and tears "to keep the Moscow Art Theater busy for many seasons."[68]

Bellow told Roth, "In you I had a witness of my own kind and a point of balance. Without your support the energy waves would have dashed me on the stern and rockbound Jewish coast. . . . Anyway, you are a great comfort to me—representing what it was essential to represent"—art, writing, and gemütlichkeit (warm, homey feeling).[69]

There was a second birthday party in Chicago in October—a grand celebration organized by Mayor Richard M. Daley, who said that Bellow had brought "vitality" to Chicago and that he personally had been inspired by Bellow's books "to become a better man." Allan Bloom flew in from Paris to make a toast, saying that "Bellow was to Chicago what Balzac was to Paris." Richard Stern was amazed enough about the literary event to describe it as "downright Unamerican."[70]

Soon after the party, it was determined that Bloom was suffering from Guillain-Barré syndrome, a debilitating neurological disorder that could lead to paralysis and atrophy. He was bedridden for months. Never fully returned to health, Bloom resumed some activities including teaching. But in late 1991, it became evident that he had had a setback, and the Bellows put off a holiday planned for Paris to help attend to Bloom—daily. He died in October 1992, nursed throughout at home by his partner and helpmate, Michael Z. Wu.

Bloom faced the end squarely and, like Bellow, was deeply thoughtful about the nature of death and about the possibility that there was immortality after the physical death of the body, instead of mere oblivion. Much of this is discussed in *Ravelstein* (2000), Bellow's last published novel, a thinly fictionalized biography of Bloom and a salute to his courage and his pronounced Jewish values.

During one of Bloom's remissions, Bellow and Janis flew to Florence, Italy, where Saul gave a talk to mark Mozart's biennial. Thinking of Bloom, Bellow said that Mozart's genius "forces" one to speculate about transcendence and to see that "there is a dimension to music that prohibits final comprehension." He argued that against Mozart's earthly record, full of distractions and harassments, endless travels, and disappointments in love, is Mozart's "understanding that work must be transformed into play"—perhaps as it is written in the book of Proverbs: "The Lord possessed me in the beginning of his ways. . . . I was set up from eternity and of old before the earth was made. . . . I was with him forming all things and was delighted every day, playing before

Him at all times; playing in the world. And my delights were to be with the children of men.'"[71] Whatever Bellow intended, the thrust of his remarks fit well with his own efforts to recapture his original soul, or at the very least the innocence of childhood, and to fend off the absolutism of reason and materialism—a continuous theme in Bellow's life and writing.

Despite fatigue from the rigors of travel in Italy, the Bellows left Florence for a trip to Israel from mid-December until January 3, 1992. He and Janis visited some of Saul's old friends and several relatives as well as numerous notables including Teddy Kollek, with whom Saul had developed a strong friendship, and Nathan Sharansky, mayor of Bethlehem and director of the Jerusalem Museum. On his return to Chicago, Bellow wrote to John Auerbach, saying, "I took to my bed for some weeks . . . with accumulated fatigue," followed by "weeks of tests [and] examinations." From these Bellow emerged "relatively clean." Only half joking, he said, "The doctors say, 'You're in good condition' and they add 'for a man your age.'"[72]

Feeling much better, Bellow and Janis, too, took up François Furet's invitation to come to Paris to give several lectures at the Raymond Aron Institute. A French historian and a member of the Committee on Social Thought since 1985, Furet had gotten to know Bellow fairly well and was excited to have him as a guest lecturer in Paris.[73] Bellow worked at home every morning, as did Janis. She was writing a review for *Bostonia* magazine of Philip Roth's novel *Operation Shylock* (1993), which she and Bellow thought had been treated unfairly by the press.[74]

Janis also explored just about every quartier in the city, often walking them again with Bellow in the afternoon. Most dinners were taken quietly at home or at a local brasserie. The couple also enjoyed meals with friends, including Bellow's old Chicago pal Harold "Kappy" Kaplan and Julian Behrstock, a classmate and friend from Northwestern days, now working for UNESCO in Paris. Bellow and Janis also spent some time with Roger Kaplan,

Kappy's writer son. Roger's impression, confirmed by Janis, was that simple pleasures mattered most to the Bellows. Even though Janis and Saul were lavishly accommodated in Paris and also in Budapest and Lisbon when Bellow lectured there, what they enjoyed best was strolling arm in arm and walking home after dinner without fear—which had become impossible in Chicago's Hyde Park.

The perceived and very real dangers of Hyde Park influenced the decision the Bellows made to leave Chicago. After being invited by Boston University more than once in recent years, Bellow finally accepted a generous offer to become a university professor there. Looking for a teaching position for Janis, Bellow wrote to John Silber, the president of the university. He sang Janis's praises without having to exaggerate, emphasizing her ability to teach political theory and literature, and pointed out the value of her dissertation. Janis, too, would be at BU.[75]

The president of the University of Chicago, Hannah Gray, was sorry to see Bellow leave and tried to match BU's offer. David Grene, who occasionally cotaught with Bloom and Bellow, expressed "great sorrow" that Bellow had decided on Boston and assured him that their thirty-year friendship "won't dissolve." Stuart Brent, Bellow's bookseller friend, not knowing that Ruth Wisse had recently been appointed professor of Yiddish at Harvard, asked Bellow, "Who will you have to talk Yiddish with? Not those *farshtinker* Goyim."[76] But in 1993, even after he viewed the public unveiling of a bust of himself at the main Chicago library, Bellow could no longer "cope with life in Chicago."[77]

It was not only the issue of safety in a crime-ridden city that influenced his decision to leave. Looking back in 1999, at the age of eighty-four, Bellow, who had thought and wrote about the question of death for many decades, told Norman Manea that he left Chicago because he couldn't "walk the street anymore without thinking of my Dead, and it was time. I had a girlfriend here or went to a party there or attended a meeting there and so forth.

Most of the people whom I had known so well and loved so well were gone, and I didn't want to be occupying a cemetery. . . . That was how it was beginning to feel."[78]

In addition to his Chicago dead, Bloom having been the most difficult loss, Bellow from 1988 to 1994 was affected by the deaths of nine people, some of whom he loved dearly, including Paolo Milano, Robert Penn Warren, and Edith Tarcov, Oscar's widow. Other deaths with some impact on Bellow's sense of himself and his place among the living included Alberto Moravia, Isaac Bashevis Singer, and George Sarant, son of Isaac and Vasiliki Rosenfeld. There would be many more losses in the final decade of Bellow's life.

When he settled in at Boston University at the beginning of 1994, Bellow taught a course called "An Idiosyncratic Survey of Modern Literature." It featured living writers he found "especially interesting," including Denis Johnson, Cormack McCarthy, Martin Amis, and Philip Roth. Bellow was described by students as friendly, accessible, open to questions and welcoming differing opinions, and relaxed.[79] But just around the corner, in the academy and in the media, a truckload of trouble was about to be unloaded on Bellow, trouble that in one way or another would trail him for the rest of his life.

SIXTEEN

BELLOW BANISHED AND BRUISED

BY 1994, SAUL BELLOW'S NOVELS *Mr. Sammler's Planet* (1970) and *The Dean's December* (1982), together with his public statements about student radicalism and Black nationalism in the sixties and feminism in the seventies, seriously tarnished his reputation as "some kind of liberal." That reputation would soon be in tatters, especially among academics and the media.[1]

Bellow had effectively finished reframing his political identity in 1987 by writing a preface to Allan Bloom's provocatively conservative *The Closing of the American Mind*.[2] Indeed, Bellow had given Bloom the idea for the book and helped arrange its publication. A wildfire success, *The Closing of the American Mind* held that the openness and relativism of American culture, especially on campuses, foreclosed critical thinking and narrowed the mind. The intolerant dogmatism of contemporary liberalism, Bloom argued, dismisses any attempt to provide a rational basis for moral judgments, whether by Plato, the Bible, or Enlightenment thinkers, and leaves the university in all its diversity incoherent and its students purposeless. Without a longing for truth that transcends society, Bloom predicted presciently that students would descend into parochial loyalties, admixed with the worst of identity politics and the extremes of "political correctness."

In 1988, Bellow was asked on a phone call from James Atlas about Bloom's rejection of multiculturalism. Bloom was against the concept and its implementation, Bellow said, because he thought it led, at least indirectly, to such things as student demands for ending courses on Western civilization. Bloom pointed to Stanford University, where in 1987 some five hundred undergraduates demonstrated against having to take a freshman course that they claimed focused on the writings of white men from Plato and the Bible to Freud and Marx and was filled with sexist and racist stereotypes. The chant of the day was, "Hey hey, ho ho, Western Culture's got to go!"[3]

In defense of Bloom and implicitly of Western civilization, Bellow ostensibly said, "Where is the Tolstoy of the Zulus? The Proust of the Papuans?" If these remarks, pregnant with racist implication, were Bellow's actual words, they were carelessly delivered. But Atlas, who effectively admitted in his memoir that he had invented the statements, called them "wildly offensive," which was precisely what they became after many reiterations and misquotations over the years.[4] Odd, then, that Atlas included Bellow's flippant comment—in parentheses and unnecessarily—in his *New York Times Magazine* profile of Bloom. Odder still that Atlas, hot to write a biography of Bellow, would include the "offensive" words spoken in a telephone interview but neither written anywhere by Bellow nor ever uttered by Bloom.

Atlas had already become an irritating presence in Bellow's life by the late 1980s. Over a period of several years, the biographer made several phone calls and wrote some half-dozen letters to Bellow. Almost none were answered. "On an impulse," Atlas in 1989 flew to Chicago to see the man himself, perhaps in part to apologize for publicizing Bellow's "Zulus and Papuans" remark. But it looked more like an attempt to wheedle permission from Bellow to look at his letters and papers and to interview his friends and relatives.[5]

Bellow, sometimes inscrutable about whether or not he wanted a biography, was mostly annoyed by Atlas's requests for entrée into his personal world. He had been "burned," he said, by Ruth Miller's manuscript for *Saul Bellow: A Biography of the Imagination.* He was angry enough at Miller, his lifelong friend and former pupil, to withdraw his authorization to quote from his letters even after she had her book already in typescript. Bellow told Atlas, "I'm not ready to be memorialized. I don't have all the answers, I'm still trying to figure things out." In the future, Bellow said, he might "simmer down" and be more accommodating. Atlas had been forewarned by Richard Stern that there would be not be a yes or no from Bellow. Atlas himself ought to have known to lower his expectations; he had, after all, seen the way Bellow dealt with Mark Harris, another obsessive wannabe biographer who had gone on to write a book, not about Bellow but about the difficulties involved in trying to write a biography of the Nobel Prize winner.[6]

In 1988, after Atlas published Bellow's alleged remark about Zulus and Papuans, there had been some fleeting criticism; but indignation at Bellow's purported comment intensified in 1994 when an extract from Alfred Kazin's forthcoming memoir, *New York Jew,* was published in the *New Yorker.* It included Bellow's supposed impolitic remark made six years earlier as part of Kazin's argument that Bellow was "moving right . . . like many Jewish intellectuals from the immigrant working class." With echoes of *Sammler* and *The Dean's December* still in the literary air, Kazin's article inadvertently reactivated criticism of Bellow exponentially.[7]

Bellow made a lame defense, claiming that he didn't remember everything he had said in the six-year-old interview; but in such a dialogue, he argued, he would have been speaking of the general differences between oral and literate cultures, not about a hierarchy of superior-inferior cultures. "My critics, many of whom could not locate Papua New Guinea on the map," Bellow wrote, "want to convict me of contempt for multiculturalism and defamation of the third world. I am an elderly white male—a Jew, to boot. Ideal for their purposes."[8] These remarks taste of arrogance and exaggeration. But it is good to remember that Jews, socially and academically, were mostly omitted from the multicultural rainbow coalition which by the 1990s had been growing for decades.[9]

Bellow's unsubstantiated remark eliciting charges of racism needs also to be measured against his recollection, three days after the Kazin article appeared, that "there was a Zulu novel after all: 'Chaka' by Thomas Mofolo, published in the 1930s."[10] He had read it in translation in his student days as a budding anthropologist under the supervision of the famous Africanist M. J. Herskovits. Bellow was not completely off the hook, but the accusation of racism needs also to be measured against his jokey but positive description of Africa thirty years earlier in *Henderson the Rain King* (1959) and even against racist remarks in *Mr. Sammler's Planet* (1970).[11] The Black pickpocket depicted in *Sammler* has no name or any lines of dialogue, but he is described more than once, and far from facetiously, as "princely"; and by the end of the novel, Mr. Sammler has an intuitive grasp of something essential, and a kind of spiritual bond is created between Jewish victimization and the victimization of Black people.

Nonetheless, the words supposedly uttered by Bellow about Zulus and Papuans did more than any others "to alienate liberal and academic opinion" and to banish Bellow's fiction from college syllabi. Much of the episode might have been seen as fairly innocuous had there not been, only a month before Kazin's article in the *New Yorker*, an extract in the *New York Times Magazine* from *Parallel Time: Growing Up in Black and White*, a memoir by African American writer Brent Staples. A member of the *Times* editorial board, Staples had been a graduate student at the University of Chicago a quarter-century earlier, where he had become—and still was—a great fan of Bellow's fiction, which he read voraciously, to the point of being able to recite whole passages from memory.[12]

But Staples took great offense at the wannabe mafioso Rinaldo Cantabile's characterization of Black people in *Humboldt's Gift* as "pork chops" and "crazy buffaloes"—the kinds of expressions used by some white street people, in this case, Italians, out of whose fictional mouths the terms *Negro* or *African American* would be unrealistic, even jarring. More understandable was Staples's disgust at the shockingly loathsome and ill-fated phrase "sexual niggerhood" in *Mr. Sammler's Planet.* Understandably, it made no real difference to Staples or to very many others, Black and white, that Bellow's unfortunate choice of words, while head-snappingly ugly, was used to criticize white people who romanticized the "oceanic, boundless, primitive" outlaw status they associated with Blackness.[13]

On his early evening strolls in Chicago's Hyde Park neighborhood, Staples made it a point to pass Bellow's high-rise apartment building on Dorchester Avenue. After playing with the idea of confronting the Nobel Prize winner about his racism, he spotted his prey as evening fell and gave chase, hoping to catch Bellow in the dark, "lift him bodily . . . pin him against a wall," and "trophy his fear." Bellow caught sight of Staples on the move, picked up his pace, and made a nimble getaway through the protective gates of his building. Bellow was annoyed by the excerpt from Staples's book, which depicted him not only as a star hawker of racial stereotypes but also as a frightened old man.[14]

His annoyance turned to anger stoked by a sense of betrayal—the editor who selected the excerpt from Staples's memoir was none other than the ubiquitous and unreliable James Atlas. The prospective biographer tried to placate Bellow about the selection: "It was beautifully written; it was about Bellow; it was news." Bellow was having none of it and asked Atlas sensibly why Staples hadn't simply come to visit and talk. Atlas later admitted in his own memoir, *The Shadow in the Garden,* that he'd thought the passage he chose would be good for his planned book on Bellow. The biographer found himself in a very awkward situation. He "had become accustomed to thinking of Bellow not only as a father figure, but as a father, whose unconditional love—or at least forgiveness—I could count on no matter what I did." That didn't turn out to be the case, and getting further into what was a tangled web of his own making, Atlas recognized the darker side of father-son relationships: "Could I have been making [Staples's] aggression a stand in for my own?"[15]

Bellow and Atlas would meet again, but from this point on, Bellow invariably belittled Atlas in correspondence and discouraged his friends from talking to him, telling some, truthfully, that Atlas was not "writing this book of his with my blessing." It was not "authorized. Nothing of the sort."[16]

The dimension of irritation in Bellow's impulsive remark about Zulus and Papuans in the interview with Atlas in 1988, if actually uttered, was most likely meant to be humorous as well as provocative and may have derived from his growing contempt for unnamed critics he likened to "thought police." In a 1994 op-ed, although he makes no clear-cut answer to allegations of racism in his fiction, Bellow, perhaps with Brent Staples in mind, said that "the ground rules of the art of fiction are not widely understood. No writer can take for granted that the views of his characters will not be attributed to him personally." Nothing controversial is permitted today, nor anything jokey, Bellow wrote; "all is righteousness and rage."[17]

Bellow's impatience may have had roots, too, in his anger at the Black antisemitism so evident in Chicago in the 1980s. Novelist Richard Stern told James Atlas that Bellow was "obsessed with black-Jewish relations" and was deeply troubled by the apparent popularity of the Chicago-based Black Nationalist and head of the Nation of Islam, Louis Farrakhan. Bellow "couldn't leave it alone," Stern said.[18] David Remnick, a young journalist with the *New Yorker,* discovered something similar when he interviewed

Bellow in May 1994 in New York preceding a talk that the Nobel Prize winner would give as part of a panel on antisemitism at the Ninety-Second Street Y. When Remnick asked Bellow about "today's racial politics [Saul] had winced," hoping to find an "un-dangerous way" to talk about it.[19]

Bellow had no trouble, he said, talking with African American writer Stanley Crouch, who, after having seen Brent Staples go "after [Bellow] in the Times . . . advised [him] to pick up [his] bat and step forward."[20] There were other Black men, including sociologist William Julius Wilson and the poet and social worker William Hunt, with whom Bellow could have quiet dialogue. And, of course, there was his very good friend Ralph Ellison, who died in April 1994, just as the fireworks about Bellow and race were growing more intense.

Bellow still considered himself a liberal of sorts, he said, but he didn't like where liberalism and the necessary struggle for racial justice and equality were going: "It's becoming mindless medallion wearing and placard-bearing. . . . I have very little use for . . . these terrible outbursts from people whose principles are affronted when you disagree with them." There is a taboo on discussing these issues openly; no habits or vocabulary have developed for nuanced discourse. This refusal to discuss differences in a society that values free speech, Bellow said, is "poisonous stuff." It has created a "tangible, palpable fear of putting your foot" in any controversial issue, including antisemitism among Black people.

He told Remnick he didn't know how deep the antisemitism went among Black people, but referring to Farrakhan and other hateful rhetoricians, he said, "it certainly is conspicuous." There is "this sort of attitude" among some Black people: "Whatever else we may be, whatever handicaps we may labor under, we are nevertheless not Jews," who, like other immigrant groups, step "on the black in order to rise higher." This might have had some kind of "foundation," Bellow said, but there was no "Jewish conspiracy" against Blacks.[21] Bellow had concluded years earlier that one of the fondest hopes of the democratic left, which he shared—for a Black-Jewish alliance—had become a thing of the past.

Remnick, near the end of his piece, quoted from Bellow's op-ed "Papuans and Zulus": "The rage of rappers and rioters takes as its premise the majority's admission of guilt for past and present injustices, and counts on the admiration of the repressed for the emotional power of the uninhibited and 'justly' angry. Rage can also be manipulative; It can be an instrument of censorship and despotism. . . . We can't open our mouths without being denounced as racists, misogynists, supremacists, imperialists or fascists."[22]

Does that mean, Remnick asked, that Bellow would censor himself "for fear of attack?" No, he said: "I write as I write." Bellow had always been daring, and in the case of his Papuans and Zulus statement, he remained bold, perhaps impetuous, but seemingly indifferent to the cost to his reputation and the fortunes of his fiction. Bold as he was, however, he did not want to drown in what he considered the muck of these issues. When a member of the audience at the panel discussion at the Ninety-Second Street Y raised the issue of Black antisemitism, Bellow was distinctly reluctant about "putting [a] foot" in: "With lights shining in my eyes I don't think I should actually tell you what I think of these things."[23]

By the end of June 1994, Saul and Janis were more than ready to withdraw from the battles over cultural relativism, antisemitism, and multiculturalism. At the same time, Bellow, who had not had a novel or novella published since 1989, had been hoping to finish "All Marbles Accounted For," a book he had been working on for years. The central story explores "the ruminations of an octogenarian" about questions involving mortality, the soul, and goodness, "which never stop gnawing the heart of humanity." The final section of "Marbles" was to be set in New Guinea, and Bellow planned to complete it in a tropical setting similar to the area he had been writing about. Finally, in November, the Bellows chose Saint Martin in the Caribbean and took an apartment in Grand Case, a small fishing village on the French side of the island.[24]

At first, their new temporary residence seemed idyllic—a beachfront apartment with no phones or forwarded mail and with a view of the bluest sea, in which Saul and Janis swam twice a day. After writing, he and Janis read Shakespeare together on the beach. The apartment itself, however, was in Janis's words "unpleasant," airless, with a narrow bedroom and trails of insects. But they had a little terrace at the front with hovering butterflies and the shade of a lime tree, where Bellow worked surrounded by the anthropology texts and gruesome books about cannibalism he had lugged from Boston.[25]

At dusk, relaxation on the terrace with wine and olives was followed by walks along the beach in search of dinner. On one fateful evening, they tried a restaurant in town. Bellow couldn't finish what he had ordered—red snapper served cold with mayonnaise. Raw at the center, it was tainted, they later learned, with ciguatera, a toxin found in hundreds of species of coral reef fish. Within a week Bellow would be in the hospital in a coma, close to death.

That night, back at the apartment, Bellow fell violently ill. Within hours, Janis managed to get Saul on a plane to Boston, where Boston University president John Silber arranged for his admission to the ICU of BU Medical Center. At first it was thought that Bellow was infected with dengue, a mosquito-borne fever. By the time he was brought to the hospital on Thanksgiving Day, Bellow was suffering from double pneumonia and potential heart failure.

Dr. John Barnardo, a pulmonary specialist, thought Bellow would not survive without a ventilator. Everyone agreed except Bellow; he stubbornly resisted but finally surrendered. His room and entryway were filled with doctors (some on the phone with other doctors) quietly disagreeing on diagnosis and prognosis, treatments and tests, and medications and bills; and Janis, the most tension-ridden, was the responsible party in charge. Janis's relatives were there, as were Bellow's sons Greg and Adam. Daniel's arrival was unavoidably delayed. Discussions occasionally became intemperate arguments. The doctors calmed down; everyone else remained overwrought, especially Janis, who did not leave the hospital or change clothes during the first week. Opinions clashed, resentments built, apologies were made. Some complicated resentments among the sons and between them and their father and Janis lingered and endured.

Saul, in and out of lucidity and before lapsing into a coma, was enraged at his sons, thinking they wanted him dead in order to inherit the estate. Greg did say later that a man who had left three sons in custody of their mothers could not expect them to care for his day-to-day welfare. But there is no indication that any sort of greed was operative here. Greg, and perhaps Dan and Adam, too, thought that Janis, who took copious notes throughout Saul's illness, was the source of the inheritance fairytale. These hospital episodes could have been drawn faithfully from Shakespeare's plays or Balzac's *Père Goriot,* but Greg put it best: Even thinking about "filial greed and patricidal wishes," he said, "provoked the most powerful of forces in the Bellow family—the specter of the Hebraic Abraham and his long-lasting threats to disown his children, along with chilling images of King Lear."[26]

After more than a month on a ventilator; innumerable spinal taps, MRIs, and CAT scans; and "interminable medications" for the clouded lungs, a bladder infection, and heart stabilization, Bellow's pneumonia was finally defeated, sedation was reduced, and delusions receded. Dr. Barnardo described Janis as "a very strong factor in Bellow's recovery." And Bellow said later that his "divided consciousness recognized at all times that [Janis] was present and that she determined that I should live."[27]

After intubation was removed, the doctors could tell that Bellow was "pushing himself to get back." Dr. Barnardo remembered "vividly" seeing Saul sitting there with a pile of books at his bedside, reading. Surprised and a little worried, Barnardo asked, "What are you doing?" Bellow said, "I'm writing." He also could have reiterated something he had repeated several times in years past—now with even more meaning: "What else could I have done? I'm not fully myself unless I'm writing something. If I stop writing, I might as well stop breathing." But he did say he had "had several hallucinations, so great that what I was writing dwindled in contrast."[28]

Out of the hospital, the drama around Saul continued for several more months. Daniel was invited to Vermont by his father for one of their favorite lunches, kosher salami on rye, with pickles. All was going well, Daniel told Zachary Leader, until Saul brought up the alleged inheritance discussion his sons were having "in my hospital room while I was unconscious." Daniel was furious and felt that his father "was forcing me to enact the first scene of King Lear. And [Janis] was telling lies to set him against me." Daniel had read "enough Russian novels," he said, "to know things were to go very badly for me and my brothers." Finally, when pressed, Bellow said he didn't believe the story about Daniel's purported greed, but it was almost too late. Daniel left, slamming the door behind him. He, very much like his brothers, who continued to have fierce friction with their father, insisted that he still loved him, but "in a way," Daniel said, "I never forgave him for it, never trusted him again."[29] Daniel, however, turned out to be the son with whom Bellow spent the most time and whose attitude toward his father matured most and softened over time.

When Daniel was working on a story of his own with literary agent Andrew Wylie, he told the agent something revealing about his relationship with his father: "My father . . . is a brilliantly talented writer and thinker who should never have been allowed around small children. . . . My attitude towards him has mellowed in recent years as I realize that while he never took me sledding, he made sure I had read Dickens, Twain, Conrad, London and

Kipling before I was 12. What I took for neglect and cruelty I now recognize as the standard Russian Jewish child rearing method, seldom seen in this country anymore."[30]

Bellow's hospital experience surely strengthened his lifelong preoccupation with aging and death. But it also reinforced his determination to live, to choose life. This is not to say that the fight against the darker side was easy. Bellow had more than one round in his middle and later years when death seemed to come in bunches. Then Ralph Ellison died in the spring of 1994. "I loved Ralph," and news of his death "came as a blow," Bellow said: "When you get to be [my] age death comes to you with the regularity of a drum tattoo."[31]

Edward Shils, who had been a great friend of Bellow's for decades but was angry with him by the 1970s and broke from him altogether in the 1980s, refused Bellow's attempts at reconciliation and near the end barred him from a hospital visit (just as Isaac Braun's estranged sister did to him in "The Old System"), before he died in 1995.[32] His demise was followed over the next two years by the deaths of Yetta Barshevsky Shachtman, the Tuley High School class orator and Bellow's first crush, whose subtle mysteriousness and "Jewish beauty" he passionately admired[33]; Zita Cogan, another Tuley classmate, an erstwhile girlfriend, and an accomplished pianist who taught at the University of Chicago during Bellow's years there; and Stanley Elkin, novelist, essayist, and friend, who corresponded with Bellow frequently and died of a heart attack at sixty-five after years of struggling with multiple sclerosis.

In 1996, Bellow suffered four losses: Eleanor Clark, a widow of Bellow's former colleague and friend Robert Penn Warren and the mother of Rosanna Warren, a well-known poet and essayist with whom Bellow had a deep rapport; Susan Bellow, Saul's third wife, who died suddenly of an aneurysm at age sixty-three after years of heavy smoking; Meyer Schapiro, renowned art critic and Bellow's good friend; and Hyman Slate, one of Saul's fondest, most beloved, and longest personal connections to Hyde Park, with whom Bellow got together when they were in their sixties "every Thursday to drink tea and consider the question of immortality." Slate believed that "a sense of humor should be part of every conversation," especially "about the existence of God." Laughing, according to Slate, "was proof that there was a God."[34] In his last letter to Slate, Bellow wrote, "One has to be much younger to have any real gift for relationships. Those we had when we were young remain the best. One of the things that . . . grieved me about living in Hyde Park was to pass the houses where my late friends once lived. . . . The daily melancholy of passing those places were among the things that drove me East. Here I have no melancholy past to bug me. But we did have an agreeable group of pals and rivals, didn't we?"[35]

Bellow experienced these losses as subtractions from his life. Even Susan's death hit him hard. She was no longer in Bellow's life directly, but when thirty-two-year-old son Daniel told his father of her death, Saul "burst into tears." When he, though still frail, offered to make the trip from Boston to the funeral in Chicago, Daniel told his father not to try that—"I didn't want to lose both parents in the same weekend." After Daniel said, "Pop, you're a great guy. I really admire you," Bellow, in another of the honest self-assessments he had begun making in the 1970s, said, "I'd like it if you were a better man than me."[36]

The string of deaths among his familiars made Bellow even more determined to survive, just as he had consciously determined to hold on to life as a child in a Montreal hospital. "The choice I made at eight," Bellow told James Atlas, "remained effective seventy years later."[37] Still relatively active, writing, and lecturing during the second half of 1995, Bellow sat for an interview in May with the London *Sunday Times*. He talked about having survived a near-fatal illness and the role of religion in his life, telling Bryan Appleyard of the *Times* that in "truly serious moments . . . I really do feel a turning toward God in some way. I'm gullible about spirituality; I have a weakness for it."[38]

About God and religion, Bellow added in a letter to Cynthia Ozick, "As might be expected of a man my age, I think a lot about the life to come, but for me it always begins with a reunion. I see my parents again and my dead brothers and cousins and friends. Since my life has not been as virtuous as I would have liked it to be, I expect to be reproached by those I have injured and punished."[39] For a man who was at the very least open to the idea of an afterlife and who expressed a strong interest in seeing "[his] dead" in the next world, Bellow continued to reaffirm most powerfully the life he had in the here and now. He not only chose life; he devoted himself to writing again. In January 1995, shortly after he got out ("crawled out," he said) of the Boston hospital, Bellow began work on a new story, which may already have begun to gestate in semiconsciousness and hallucination. He said that writing "By the St. Lawrence," his last published short story, "would be a test to see whether there was a charge left in the batteries."[40]

Published in *Esquire* in July 1995, "By the St. Lawrence" draws on characters who appear in earlier works, particularly in *Herzog* and "The Old System." Unsurprisingly, it draws, too, from Bellow's own childhood experiences in Jewish immigrant Canada and dips deeply into his treasure chest of memories of family and neighborhood. The protagonist, Rob Rexler, "crippled in adolescence by infantile paralysis," is an aging, erudite, and internationally renowned historian and political philosopher who, though weary and cynical about academic achievement and tired of Marx and Brecht, is scheduled to speak in Montreal at McGill University. While in Canada, he feels the need, after a harrowing experience with a near-fatal illness, to return to nearby Lachine, Quebec, where he was born. A driver in a Mercedes limousine supplied by McGill gets him there.

With some difficulty Rexler goes "limping" through town and then "trampling" along the banks of the St. Lawrence River, whose power he loved as a boy. Countless things have changed, even disappeared. So many landmarks are gone. The tiny synagogue has become a furniture warehouse. He remembers the locations of everything but thinks he is through with "nostalgia, subjectivism, inwardness." His recollections, however, are solid, detailed, "nothing dreamlike about them."

Rexler ruminates about his older cousin Ezra (almost an uncle, really), an insurance adjuster and dealer in real estate who was entertaining company for him as a boy. But when having "business thoughts," Ezra would grow silent, and "all laughing was shut down. No Yiddish jokes then, or Hebrew double meanings." In isolated Lachine, "a few thousand years of archaic gravity [could] settle on him" and allow him to "freely improvise from the Old Testament."[41] Rexler's memories are thorough. He thinks he must have been coming back to them repeatedly over the years.

Two memories reemerge more sharply than the others. Rexler recalls riding with his cousin Albert, a lawyer and local political figure; they were stuck at a railroad crossing where there had been an awful accident. Rexler, standing on the running board of the Model T, could see the body parts of the victim clearly: "How finite they looked."[42] Only a month after the story was published, Bellow wrote elsewhere that in "part the story had to do with anatomy." But the soul, the spirit, Bellow and Rexler seem to be asking—can it be so vulnerable, so fragile? "The vital organs scattered on the tracks—all the absurd looking parts on which the spiritual life rest."[43]

A more recent memory centers on Rexler's visit to his then much older cousin Albert, who was dying, years after he himself had been deformed by a crippling disease. Rexler thinks there may be some connection between Albert's warped body and the "bald" body parts they saw strewn at the railroad crossing. He resists the thought that "everything," the soul, too, "depends on these random-looking parts"—those "spongy soft swelled ovals patched pink and red."[44] The story is unwavering in its focus on the vulnerability and dissolution of the body. Are the vital organs, which are so necessary for keeping the body together, also essential to keeping the soul whole?

Rexler, standing at the river, turns his thoughts again to death, which he himself has so recently dodged. Death, he thinks, is like "a magnetic field that every living thing must enter." It is sublime in its power but is unfeeling, much like the St. Lawrence itself, its roaring rapids and steely speed notwithstanding. When, in the final line of the story, the limo comes to the canal to fetch Rexler, he gets in, reluctantly "turning his thoughts to the afternoon lecture he didn't particularly want to give."[45]

Bellow himself was not so reluctant about lecturing. In December, two weeks before a scheduled gall-bladder operation, Bellow returned to Chicago to give a talk ambitiously titled "Literature in a Democracy: From Tocqueville to the Present." His lecture was full of references to Nietzsche and Dostoyevsky, and although he was not featured until the second half of the talk, Tocqueville was favorably and optimistically quoted as saying that in democratic America "each man sees all his fellows when he surveys himself" and that "in the end democracy diverts imagination from all that is external"—social status, wealth—"and fixes on man alone. . . . Here and here alone, the rude sources of poetry among such nations are to be found." This took some of the sting out of what Bellow had said many times in the past, that even if democracy is the safest form of government, it tends to have a leveling effect on the arts: "We didn't start very high, and we didn't rise very high either."[46]

Bellow, however, did not dismiss out of hand the idea that great art could exist within a democracy. Indeed, he thought liberal democracy at its best was a great and necessary protection of the freedom to generate such art. But he worried over democracy's propensity to recruit art for its own ends, and he called for artists themselves to resist it. Bellow had made it clear at the PEN Congress in 1986 that he thought once writers get directly involved in power politics that they are writers no longer. Bellow also seconded Nadine Gordimer's view that the writer's imagination ought to remain his or her own and not become an instrument of the state.[47]

Richard Stern was at the Chicago lecture in December and said that Bellow tired toward the end; he lost his place a time or two, until the speech "tottered and fell." Stern pronounced his old friend "about 75% of what he was a dozen years ago, maybe a little less."[48] Bellow's frailty was evident to the audience of one thousand, and when he ended with an amused but plaintive, "That's all I've got," there was thunderous applause. The text of the talk was difficult, complex in places. "Not everyone absorbed every word," according to the *Chicago Tribune*: "To some it was enough to be in Bellow's presence, to welcome him back to the place where his career took off."[49]

His career had taken off in Chicago, but now he was at home (as much as Bellow could be at home) in Brookline, Massachusetts. The suburb of Boston, especially its markets and shops, reminded him of "Montreal when I was a kid."[50] Now, twenty years later as a full-time resident, living on Crowninshield Road off Commonwealth Avenue, he ate nearby at Rubin's Kosher Deli, got his fish at Wulf's, and shopped and browsed at other stores at Coolidge Corners, a North Brookline neighborhood much frequented by Russian Jewish immigrants, including several Gordin cousins. Bellow was reminded of his youth in Montreal, but Janis added that "Coolidge Corners replicated all the little shops . . . of Chicago," too. And "you could hear Yiddish spoken there."[51]

In the spring of 1996, a year after his two hospitalizations, Bellow was fully recovered. He and Janis flew to Miami for Daniel's wedding; the bride, Heather Hershman, the daughter of a Miami physician, was a graduate student in criminal justice at American University. The match and the wedding buoyed Bellow, but travel sapped his energy. Only weeks later, however, he flew to New York by himself to give a talk at Queens College. He told Al Glotzer that he regretted leaving Janis behind: "I am like you in my boyish rejection of elderliness (antiquity: why not come right out with it?). You pack a snowball on a winter day and imagine taking a belly-flop on your sled as we all used to do back in the beautiful twenties—I was ten years old in 1925. All that remains is the freshness of the impulse."[52]

Childhood memories were, as always, a tonic for Bellow. But clearly, he was feeling his age—eighty-one—and questioned how much he had left in the tank. By the summer, still lacking stamina, he gave up on the "Marbles" novel. The more surprising thing is that, early in 1996, Bellow began writing an entirely new piece of fiction.

The Actual, originally titled "Changing Places," published as a novella in April 1997, was described by many reviewers as "thin" or "slight," missing the weight of Bellow's important works. But several critics, even those who used these descriptions, including Alfred Kazin, found Bellow's writing as "sharp as ever." James Wood pointed out that Bellow was writing about our never-ending struggle to separate the essential from the trivial, the great theme of Bellow's fiction.[53]

More than one character in the novella is in search of the authentic, "the actual," those things smothered or lost in the detritus of materialism or drowned in untapped emotional reservoirs. Sigmund Adletsky, a super-rich entrepreneur in his nineties, is at the cusp of realizing that his single-minded chase after money and power has kept him from the "real" world, kept him from even sensing what happiness or moral satisfaction might be. Harry Trellman is a "sixty something" businessman "with a gift for putting together . . . deals" that are "sufficiently legal."[54] He is in "spiritual exile" in the Far East and hides his feelings from everyone, including himself; and he has pined for decades over a love lost by his own mistake—his reluctance to declare. He returns to Chicago from Asia after many years to find Amy Wustrin, the warm, intelligent, and sexually alluring high-school sweetheart he had failed to pursue and compete for hard enough forty years earlier. He tells Amy, after they reacquaint, that she is his "actual," not only in his adolescent longings or even in his maturing and enduring imagination, but here now, older, in the flesh. He always loved her, he says, and now he, "an elderly gent," is even more convinced that there is nothing stronger, more essential, than love.

This direct declaration is in good part a product of Bellow's relationship with Janis. But it is very much also a realization, conscious or otherwise, that he ought never to have left Anita Goshkin, his first wife, something he had actually confessed to his son Greg much earlier. A half-dozen years before the publication of *The Actual*, Janis, after discussing Rousseau's idea of love with Saul, quoted him in her journal: "There IS such a thing as love. It isn't a manipulative product of the imagination. It's a real power."[55] If there's anything new in *The Actual*, it's Bellow's focus on sweetness and simplicity. Not all love in the modern world need be profane, he seems to say; and love, even in aging, is a reality. It's almost as if Bellow, after too many loveless relationships with women, is finally openly declaring himself.[56]

Despite the negative reaction among liberals and academics to his displays of chauvinism and his increasingly visible movement to the right, Bellow's reputation as a writer continued to be strong. The *Sunday Times* of London published the results of a poll it had undertaken among Britain's leading critics and writers, who answered the question, "Who is the greatest living novelist writing in English?" Bellow came out ahead with ten mentions, followed by Updike—no doubt amusing both of them for different reasons—and then Muriel Spark. Among those placing Bellow in the number-one position was Salmon Rushdie, who maintained that if any book deserved to be called the Great American Novel, it was *Augie March*.[57] Four years later, in 1998, the Modern Library put together a board of scholars and writers to select the one hundred greatest novels of the twentieth century. *Henderson the Rain King* sat at twenty-one, *The Adventures of Augie March* at eighty-eight.[58]

But Bellow, having had only two novels published between 1985 and 1999, was troubled by the suspicion that he was becoming irrelevant to readers. The members of his literary generation who had helped bring the Jewish American experience into the mainstream were a diminished force in numbers and influence. "I had a cheering section once," Bellow told Atlas—"no longer." Philip Roth, more than twenty years Bellow's junior, remained among the best-selling novelists of the 1990s, but other younger writers from different backgrounds and ethnic groups were now making their names known.[59] Isabel Allende, Don DeLillo, Toni Morrison, Thomas Pynchon, and Mary Gordon wrote some of their most ambitious work in this period, and there were also many talented emergent writers, including Sherman Alexie, Chang-Rae Lee, E. Annie Proulx, David Foster Wallace, and Claire Messud.

Still, between 1995 and 2000, Bellow regained a substantial number of readers with *The Actual* and even more with the critically acclaimed novel *Ravelstein*. The manager of 57th Street Books in Chicago said that *Ravelstein* "is flying off the table. People are talking about it everywhere." More copies were sold in its initial week of release than any other hardback work of fiction in the store's history.[60]

In the same years, Bellow stayed active teaching and lecturing. Though still a bit sluggish and lacking full strength, he also made public appearances. On June 12, 1997, two days after his eighty-second birthday, Bellow attended a ceremony at the National Portrait Gallery in Washington, DC, for the unveiling of his painted likeness. He grumbled some about all the fuss, especially about the birthday cake and song, but he was gentle. A reporter from the *Washington Post* felt moved to write, "Life has a certain sweetness, so does Bellow."[61]

The speakers at the unveiling "tried to turn [Bellow] into a marble statue while he sat in front of them," recalled Richard Stern. He described his old friend as "a bit fragile and osteopathic, but Jesus, when he got up and spoke for five minutes the marble dissolved and there [stood] a unique mensch."[62] Bellow deflected the notion that he was a media star; instead, he said, quoting Hebrew scripture, "See the man who is diligent in his work, he shall stand before kings." Gesturing toward his portrait, Bellow said, "We don't have kings in a democracy, but this will do for me."[63]

In addition to personal appearances, Bellow sat for uncountable interviews, from a long chat with *Playboy* magazine to an ongoing exchange with Philip Roth that took more than a year. Roth was trying to write about Bellow's novels as a kind of protection against the shallow or negative interpretations they were expecting from James Atlas, whose book on Bellow was scheduled for publication in 2000. Norman Manea, Saul's good friend and a regular visitor to the Bellows' Vermont retreat, also interviewed him over an extended period at the end of 1999.[64]

Bellow continued to write essays, more literary than political, for newspapers and journals, including the *New York Times* and the *Chicago Tribune*. Many of these pieces were published in *There Is Simply Too Much to Think About* (2015), an updated and extended version of *It All Adds Up* (1994). The 2015 collection repeated "A Matter of the Soul" and "Israel: The Six-Day War," as well as memoirs on Isaac Rosenfeld and Allan Bloom, and it added, among other essays, "A Jewish Writer in America," "Laughter in the Ghetto," "Up from the Pushcart: Abraham Cahan," "On Jewish Storytelling," and "Americans Who Are Also Jews." These Jewish-centered pieces, about 35 percent of the collection, stood alongside the other pieces, many if not most of which contained important thought and material about Jews.[65]

Occasional short commentaries by Bellow on individual contributions were included in several issues of *News from the Republic of Letters* (a successor to his earlier coedited periodicals, including the *Noble Savage*). His response to "The Nihilist and the Inventor," a 1998 short story contributed by Jack Miles, is telling insofar as it points up Bellow's continued emphasis on "choosing life." Miles had written what might be called a "parable," featuring a rock musician who, after thorough self-examination, decides that life has no meaning and withdraws into the California woods. Bellow, for whom the soul and the possibility of immortality were more than abstract concepts, was disturbed by the non-Jewish, bourgeois, and potentially deadly nihilism in Miles's hero.

It is true that Bellow occasionally quoted Socrates's claim that "the unexamined life was not worth living," but, aware that his own life had hardly been a model of virtue, he often added that "sometimes the examined life makes you wish you were dead." Still, neither nihilism nor death was ever appealing to Bellow; he was far less fond of citing Socrates than of invoking the doomed Claudio in Shakespeare's *Measure for Measure*:

> The weariest and most loathed worldly life
> That age, ache, penury and imprisonment
> Can lay on nature is a paradise
> To what we fear death.[66]

And death, as far as Bellow was concerned, would have to wait.

SEVENTEEN

LIFE AND DEATH

SAUL BELLOW KNEW, OF COURSE, that death was inevitable, but he was more curious about it than fearful. When he was in Jerusalem in 1976, for example, he spoke twice at some length with Amos Oz. The Israeli writer didn't remember how the subject of death came up, but he recalled "vividly" what Bellow had to say on the subject. When Oz mentioned that he was hoping to die in his sleep, "Saul responded by saying that, on the contrary, he would like to die wide awake and fully conscious, because death is such a crucial experience, he wouldn't want to miss it."[1]

In an apparent preparation for his own demise, Bellow traveled to his Canadian birthplace in 1999, visiting old favorite watering holes and haunts. He showed Janis the Montreal streets of the Jewish Quarter where he had lived eighty years earlier. Dapper in a bowtie and pink striped shirt, he ordered a "smoked meat sandwich" at Schwartz's Kosher Deli after doing a reading at a Montreal synagogue. When asked after his talk how he preserved so great a memory, Bellow apparently brought the house down, saying, "I forget."

At the Saul Bellow Library in Lachine, he told relatives, friends, and fans that the best way to fend off death was to have unfinished business you feel compelled to complete. Many in the audience were surprised when Bellow announced that he was about to finish a new book. It was obvious that there was also another work in progress: Janis, now forty, after suffering four miscarriages, was visibly pregnant. An older man at the library wondered aloud, "How did Bellow do it?" Having overheard, Bellow responded, "Practice, Practice, Practice."[2]

Janis desperately wanted a child. Bellow, still low on energy and in his mid-eighties, was resistant. His record as a father, as he himself knew well, had not been good. But after more than a decade together, Saul loved Janis, needed her, indeed owed his life to her. He also knew how much she desired a child. Out of love for Janis, Bellow encouraged her to try one more time. The fifth and final attempt was successful, and Naomi Rose, "Rosie," was born on December 12, 1999.

Bellow was eighty-four when his daughter arrived. Four months later, his final novel, *Ravelstein*, which he'd been working on since 1996, was published to both critical acclaim and a firestorm of controversy. In an unusual break with his tradition, Bellow admitted that his protagonist, Abe Ravelstein, was based on his close friendship with Allan Bloom, and that Chick, Abe's friend and protégé, was Bellow's own refashioned alter ego. Indeed, nearly all the characters in the novel are thinly disguised versions of real people, including Janis Freedman and Alexandra Ionescu Tulcea, Bellow's fourth wife.

Despite their differences, Ravelstein, a genius on the order of Bloom, and gay like him, often travels with Chick. The two of them also live in adjacent apartment buildings, debate literature and life interminably, and cement their extraordinary relationship around their Jewishness. No matter what they talk about, Ravelstein inevitably asks, "And what about the Jewish side of the thing?"[3] As Gary Shteyngart writes in his introduction, "At bottom, the digressive, meandering, largely plotless [novel] boils down to . . . Hebraic men kibitzing on the edge of eternity . . .

something like relatives—the nearest thing to family available. Their obsession—Jews, death, the death of Jews."[4]

A lot of the story and most of its meaning appeared to be lost in the frenzy of criticism in the media and in academia accusing Bellow of "outing" Bloom as a homosexual.[5] But Bloom's sexual orientation, despite his sovereign stature as a defender of traditional values and norms, was no secret among his friends and followers and the University of Chicago community generally.[6] Moreover, Bellow told all who inquired (and even those who hadn't) that Bloom had asked him, just as Ravelstein asks Chick, to write a kind of "fictional memoir" of him. "I trust you to write this," Bloom told Bellow, and "without softeners and sweeteners."[7]

More vexing to some of Bloom's admirers than Bellow's alleged outing of his friend was that in early drafts and manuscripts (seen by many editors, reviewers, and journalists), Bloom's death was attributed to AIDS, which carries not only a clinical diagnosis but, for conservatives, a moral stigma. Bellow underestimated, he said, "the sensitivity over HIV and AIDS." It seems "people carry over attitudes more appropriate to the Middle Ages." Still, Bellow told D. T. Max of the *New York Times*, he "didn't like the feeling" that his alleged outing of Bloom "brought with it, and the sense of recklessness on my part." Max went on to write an article titled, "With Friends Like Saul Bellow." It was accompanied by a photographic composite: the left half of Bloom's face, the right half of Bellow's, and between them a typewriter with a sheet of paper bearing a sketch of a stiletto.[8]

Ultimately, Bellow removed the word *AIDS* in the published book and wrote instead that Ravelstein confessed to being "HIV positive" and that "he was dying of complications from it." Bellow went so far as to apologize: "I don't know if [Bloom] died of AIDS really," he admitted. "It was just an impression that he may have . . . in which case I think it was irresponsible to say he did by saying so of Ravelstein."[9] Bellow also took out the phrase alluding to Ravelstein's dalliances with "barely legal boys of African

American provenance," but he left in the suggestion that Bloom, like Ravelstein, "relished *louche* encounters" and thought "a lot about those pretty boys in Paris."[10]

In late December 1999, only months before the publication of *Ravelstein* in October 2000, with the manuscript finished or very close, Bellow, in a long interview over a two-day period, made a stunningly honest and deeply reflective statement: "I suppose you might say that insofar as it is true that there is some sort of religion working in me—in daily life I don't ask myself often what is honorable, but I do when I am writing: I ask myself if it would be dishonorable to put a thing this way. That is, would it discredit my religious faith . . . or my artist's faith? But then there is some connection between the two."[11]

Not only does Bellow make the crucial point here that his religious faith is linked to his writing; he also seems to be thinking—in terms of "honorable" or "dishonorable"—about his forthcoming novel. He knew, of course, about the conflagration of criticism over *Ravelstein* and had already expurgated some words and terms critics thought offensive. Still, he infuriated lots of people, including critic Sam Tanenhaus, who had read only excerpts and feared that Bloom's "iconic status" among conservatives, already slipping, would be undermined further by the confirmation of his homosexuality.[12] Bellow also upset several friends, including Nathan Tarcov and Werner Dannhauser, and he distressed his wife, Janis.

More important to Janis than the "details about Bloom's private life" was Bellow's mistake, even before the publication of the novel, of revealing "the truth" of those details to a reporter. Bloom was "a great man," Bellow said to D. T. Max, and he admitted that "he wanted to get him down on paper."[13] Saul spoke only this "handful of words," Janis wrote in a retrospective essay, "and instead of protecting himself, his friend, and his book . . . threw his own stick of dynamite," demolishing the wall "separating novel from memoir."[14] Ravelstein is turned from a character into a person—a famous person, with "dirty secrets" on which the vultures were ready to pounce.

The charge of betrayal was serious, but the furor over it might have been defused, as Janis Bellow implies, by an unwavering insistence on a different "handful of words": *Ravelstein* is fiction, not a biography. Many early enthusiastic reviewers assumed just that. *Ravelstein* was a novel, a brilliant one about Bloom, and not a "memoir." James Wood, for example, argued that *Ravelstein* is full of Bellow's "old, cascading power . . . an overflowing quality that dissolves the book's biographical powders, and insists on its own autonomy."[15]

The search for Allan Bloom in the text often overshadowed the significance, substance, and implications of the novel itself, which, to repeat Gary Shteyngart's words, boils down to "Hebraic men kibitzing . . . about their obsession—Jews, death, and the death of Jews." Abe Ravelstein, like Bloom, is an atheist-materialist or thinks he is. He (and Bloom, too) is better described as a deep-thinking Jew who revels in physical and philosophic flamboyance and in an expensively maintained hyperconsumerism, made possible by the millions earned from a surprising bestseller.

Ravelstein treasures Chinese furniture, fine porcelain, Lalique crystal, expensive cars with luxuriously customized interiors, Lanvin leather jackets, and Zegna ties.[16] But it isn't clothing or possessions that make Ravelstein the man. More characteristically, he loves to talk and think while walking, his ideas overflowing, examined, debated, and celebrated, all along using his fluent Greek with his stammering, roaring, and rushing translation, embroidered with Jewish jokes.

He tries to rescue Chick, his friend and colleague at the University of Chicago, "from my pernicious habits. He thought I was stuck in privacy and should be restored to community. . . . 'Too many years in inwardness,'" he would say. Chick is struggling to accept some of Ravelstein's ideas, including his view that antisemitism, behind a veil of gentility, is a tangible undercurrent of life at the university. Chick is finally convinced that their Romanian colleague, the influential Radu Grielescu (a thinly disguised Mircea Eliade, international scholar of mythology and religion), was a fascist. Ravelstein never exaggerates such things. So, when he tells Chick that Grielescu was often alluded to by scholars of religious philosophy as a member, or certainly a close associate, of the Romanian Iron Guard, Chick believes his younger but wiser mentor. The Iron Guard was connected to the Romanian prewar fascist government, and Grielescu, Chick discovers, was in fact a foreign service agent of the Nazi regime in Bucharest.

Ravelstein disparages myth, Griselescu's great subject, not so much from the perspective of his own expertise as a Platonist but as a Jew: "The Jews had better understand their status with respect to myth." Why, Ravelstein wants to know, "should they have any truck with myth?" It was myth, after all, that demonized Jews, "connected them with conspiracy theory"—the Protocols of Zion, for instance, and world domination. Ravelstein tells Chick that Grielescu is just making use of him and his Romanian non-Jewish wife in order to live down his Hitlerism. Have you "no memory," he asks Chick, "of the massacre in Bucharest," when they hanged Jews "alive on meat hooks in the slaughterhouse, and butchered them—skinned them alive?"[17]

Here, in his most Jewish book, Bellow has returned to a scene he described in *Dangling Man* (1944), his first novel, arguably his least Jewish book, and one in which the word *Jew* never appears. But the following sentence, part of protagonist Joseph's fervid dream, does appear: "It was . . . in Bucharest that those slain by the Iron Guard were hung from hooks in a slaughterhouse. I have seen the pictures."[18]

Chick, with his first wife, Vela, a Romanian—clearly modeled on Alexandra Ionesco Tulcea, Bellow's fourth wife—has been socializing with the Grielescus, prompting Ravelstein's warnings about Radu's Iron Guard connections. After Chick's divorce, he is free to marry Rosamund, Jewish and a stand-in for Janis, although without one of her best characteristics: a warm, shrewd, and limitless quality of strength and patience.

In conversation about Abe Ravelstein, Chick talks with Rosamund about "what it means to the Jews that so many others, millions of others, willed their death." World War II made it clear that the Jews in the eyes of the rest of the world simply had "no right live." Insofar "as this relates to Grielescu," Chick tells Rosamund, "I don't think he was a malevolent Jew-hater, but when he was called to declare himself," he did—on the side of evil.[19]

As Ravelstein saw it, Chick had been refusing to do the "unpleasant work of thinking it all through." And in the first section of the novel, Chick, in order to maintain a peaceful, relatively high-status American life, ignores or doesn't quite "see" antisemitism. "Well," Chick admits, "I had a Jewish life to lead in the American language, and that's not a language helpful with dark thoughts."[20] But Ravelstein thinks Chick had been trying to make his Jewishness less noticeable, something Abe thinks neither possible nor desirable. Moreover, Ravelstein believes that the world, despite itself, needs the Jews, who all through history, time after time, were witness to the presence of evil and the absence of redemption in the world. Jews "had been used to give the entire species a measure of"—a way of measuring—"human viciousness."[21]

Although he knew that "not every problem can be solved," Ravelstein, as he approached his own death, concluded that "a Jew should take deep interest in the history of the Jews—in their principles of Justice, for instance."[22] Here, Bellow was repeating his own earlier argument that a writer who is an American and a Jew has an obligation. He or she "has been able to explore and develop [their] own consciousness freely, and in this consciousness," develop a "Jewish preoccupation with the redemption of mankind from its sins and injustices. To hold to this in barbarous times without pretensions is the decent thing to attempt."[23]

Ravelstein is brave and uncomplaining about the pain he suffers in his illness, now terminal; and he reflects on the human wastefulness of suicide. "If you dislike existence, then death is your release . . . You can call this nihilism," he says. "But the Jews feel that the world was created for each and every one of us and when you destroy a human life you destroy an entire world—the world as it existed for that person."[24]

Like Bloom, Ravelstein had been a student of the German Jewish American political philosopher and classicist Leo Strauss at the University of Chicago, where Strauss spent much of his career. Strauss is noted for his new understanding and illumination of Plato and Aristotle, retracing their analyses through medieval Islamic and Jewish philosophy and encouraging application of these ideas to contemporary political theory. For Strauss and his students, many of whom were fervent devotees, there were two ways of facing modernity, reduced to two symbols—Jerusalem (faith) and Athens (reason)—with biblical wisdom and Greek wisdom serving as bookends of feeling and thought. The Hebrew scriptures explicitly emphasize faith as the beginning of wisdom, which is rooted in "fear of the Lord" (Proverbs 1:7): "All that God has spoken we will do [*na,aseh*] and we will hear [*v'nishma*]" (Exodus 24:7–8).

Many modern Jews, however, by saying that they wish to hear first before they decide or act, seem to have already chosen Athens over Jerusalem. Ravelstein, "choosing" between "the twin sources of civilization," has most often done the same. But as he comes closer to his own demise, Abe demonstrates a perceptible shift in his intellectual allegiances. Chick can see that his friend is "following a trail of Jewish ideas or Jewish essences." And in his final days, he is no longer talking about Plato or Thucydides. Ravelstein is "full of scripture now," Chick announces; he "talk[s] about religion and the difficult project of being man in the fullest sense."[25]

Bellow is suggesting that Jerusalem and Athens are not as diametrically opposed as Strauss's teaching would have it. He agreed with Columbia University's professor of Jewish history, Yosef Hayim Yerushalmi, that "the blandly generic term secular Jew gives no indication of the rich variety within the species."[26] Jewish spirituality risked being diluted in such an intermingling of belief and reason. But in his writing, Bellow successfully melded strong echoes of Judaism and Yiddishkeit with rational philosophy, even if not always in perfect comfort.[27]

Abe Ravelstein, presented at first as a materialist-atheist, feels his own brand of Jewishness grow to include a critical religious spirit and a belief that Judaism could help him understand his impending death. When Chick, with a polite but doubtful smile, comments on this change and on Abe's constant talking about Jews, Ravelstein is annoyed: "Why not talk about them. . . . We mustn't turn our backs on them."[28] In any case, as Abe tells Chick more than once, it is neither possible nor desirable to "unJew" oneself—a phrase used and repeated persistently by Bellow throughout his writing and speaking career. His unwavering position about his Jewish identity, and the vast Jewish content Bellow used in what he must have known was his last novel, make inconsequential Bellow's repeated declarations that he was not an "American Jewish writer." "What else but a Jew could I be?" was an answer Bellow characteristically made in class to queries about his identity as a Jewish writer.[29] What bothered Bellow was not so much the Jewish label as the narrowness of that label and the pressure to lock him into a reductive category that others, especially scholars and journalists, had made for him.

When James Atlas's *Bellow: A Biography* (2000) was published almost simultaneously with *Ravelstein*, Bellow thought the tumult over the novel might be repeated. Saul and Janis talked about moving to France—or to Yemen, they joked. Ruth Wisse knew they weren't serious, but the couple were sure they would be pulverized.[30] Philip Roth, who thought that Atlas would be remiss in his interpretation of Bellow's work and willful in his critique of Bellow's personal life, said he wanted to beat the biographer to the punch and write everything that Atlas "isn't going to do or won't say." Beginning in the summer of 1998 and running into 2000, Roth had Bellow sit for a number of long interviews to discuss his novels, all of them.[31] The project went uncompleted, but when Atlas's book was published in October, it appeared a week after Roth had published an article based on his interviews with Bellow in the *New Yorker*.[32] Whether Roth's article tempered any commotion over Atlas's book is impossible to measure, but Atlas did take a beating from several prominent reviewers, including James Wood and Lee Siegel.[33]

Although Bellow had wearied of Roth's project, he was entertaining the idea of writing yet another novel. At eighty-five, he turned again to "Marbles" and hired Will Lautzenheiser, a young summa cum laude graduate of the University of Chicago, to be his assistant. But Will soon noticed that Bellow could write only paragraphs before he tired. His attention span was much more attenuated than it had been, and there were lapses of memory, too.

In 2001, tests showed a "probability of dementia." Bellow suffered occasional confusion, but he retained what Janis called "huge poetic energy," and up until a year before he died, he exhibited his old wit and sense of humor, with songs, anecdotes, and jokes "bubbling up" all the time.[34] In the classroom, however, Bellow suffered occasional moments of silence, confusion, and repetition. In spring 2002, Janis asked James Wood (now living with his wife, writer Claire Messud, in Northampton, about one hundred miles from Brookline) to coteach a course with Bellow. Wood was helpful, respectful, and sensitive, but at the end of the semester he thought it would be a good idea for his friend and mentor to retire.[35]

There would be little more teaching—his last course was in spring 2003. But family matters continued to roil. Bellow fully intended in September 2002 to go to Brooklyn for the wedding of Juliet Bellow, Gregory's daughter, but his doctor advised against the trip. Nevertheless, the assumption that some "unresolved conflict" between Greg and Saul was the real reason that Bellow stayed away was widespread. Adam was suspicious, but Greg and Juliet were furious. Daniel said his father was "very dependent on Janis. . . . And she didn't want to go because she hates Greg."[36]

Although Saul sent a lovely note and a generous gift, Greg did not speak to his father for at least eighteen months. He thought, as he wrote in a confusing letter in January 2003 (quoted in full in his memoir), that Saul was incapable of putting anything "beyond [his] own needs," thereby rending "the fragile fabric that holds this family together." Greg had "no desire for contact" with his father—no visits, no phone calls—but he ended the letter with, "In any case I remain your son—even in absentia." Three months later, Greg wrote again, accusing his father of having "become less tolerant of differences between yourself and others. . . . So here we are. As a child you are my pop and I love you. . . . But when it becomes a choice between my values and hurting someone—even you—my values will prevail."[37] That there is love in Greg's heart is difficult to deny. Present, too, in many of the clashes among the Bellows was Jewish family feeling, Jewish family love; but as in Bellow's most important stories including "Cousins" and "The Old System," it is love characteristically mixed with confusion and disorder.

Despite it all, Greg did visit in fall 2004 when his father was bedridden and not expected to survive. It did not go well. In Will Lautzenhauser's words, Greg had experienced some kind of "meltdown" and was screaming at his father about missing Juliet's wedding. Maria, the housekeeper, told Janis, who had been out, that she was alarmed enough to consider calling the police.[38] Apparently, what Bellow called "the Jewish immigrant family opera" continued into the second generation. Greg remained bitter, but he confesses that, "shouting over the phone," the "last thing I ever said to my father" was "'I love you sweetheart.'"[39]

Although he had to be told repeatedly that people in his life had died, including his sister Jane in 2003, Sam Freifeld in 1990, and David Grene in 2004, there were short periods of recovered strength and decreased confusion. When Bellow received an honorary degree from Boston University in June 2004, he knew exactly what was going on and climbed the few steps to the stage unassisted. And Rosie was a great solace to him. He dandled her on his knee and delighted in watching her play. Saul was much more involved with his daughter than anyone expected him to be. He even played the recorder for Rosie and sang songs to her in Yiddish. Bellow's last known letter, written on February 19, 2004, to Eugene Kennedy, gives a sense of how exhilarating Rosie was for eighty-nine-year-old Saul:

> I don't do anything these days and I spend much of my time indoors. By far my pleasantest diversion is to play with Rosie, now four years old. It now seems to me that my parents wanted me to grow up in a hurry and that I resisted, dragging my feet. They (my parents, not my feet) needed all the help they could get. They were forever asking. "What does the man say?" and I would translate for them in heavy-footed English. That didn't help much either. The old people were as ignorant of English as they were of Canadian French. We often stopped before a display of children's shoes. My mother coveted for me a pair of patent-leather sandals with an elegantissimo strap. I finally got them—I rubbed them with butter to preserve the leather. That is when I was six or seven years old, a little older than Rosie is now. It is amazing how it all boils down to a pair of patent-leather shoes.[40]

Cynthia Ozick, as she does so often with any kind of text, captures the sense, mood, and meaning of this letter. It is not only a "dying old man's sentimental nostalgia, but a fruitlessly self-indulgent yearning for a mother . . . lost too soon," and it is just as much an elegy on the passage of time. In a mere nine sentences, Ozick said, we have "an annotated history of an immigrant family, where it settled, how it struggled, how it aspired; and a hint of the future novelist's moral aesthetic, the determination to preserve."[41]

Bellow was not likely to notice, but at two-and-a-half, Rosie had become an extremely willful child and refused to follow anyone's instructions. She was diagnosed as suffering from autism spectrum disorder. Fortunately, her acute symptoms softened considerably as she matured, but in the meantime, Janis, caring for a declining husband and a nearly uncontrollable child and at the same time keeping up with her teaching job, was exhausted. No one knew how she managed it all.

She did have help from Will and Maria and from occasional visitors, most often Ruth and Len Wisse, Eugene Goodheart, Walter Pozen (Bellow's friend and lawyer), and the writers Martin Amis and Philip Roth, whom Janis called Saul's "twin pillars." James Wood served as another important source of strength, making it a trio of writers who treated Saul Bellow as if he were their father.[42]

In his last months, Bellow was gentle, grateful, and, to whatever degree he could manage, gregarious. Daniel remembers that in the final days, Saul "just loved me. . . . It was sweet at the end." Middle brother, Adam, characterized his father during this time as "calmed down. . . . Sweet and childlike." Will, who saw more of Saul than his sons did, said, that "yes, there were silences," but in the best sense "Saul was still Saul."[43]

It was rumored that in his last hours, in and out of consciousness, Bellow asked Goodheart a stunning question: "Was I a man or a jerk?" Janis, however, said that "Gene and Saul had had that kind of exchange more than once, but never at Saul's bedside, and certainly not as a final parting question about the quality of Bellow's life." The two men would sometimes joke around with that question when either had doubts about personal decision-making, but it wasn't in any way a plea for absolution on Saul's part. Nor was a small copy of the New Testament spotted by James Wood on Saul's bedside table "used by him as a way of coming to terms with his death." The Christian Bible and books of Hebrew scripture were often within Bellow's reach and were mostly perused for literary purposes.[44]

At his bedside, when Bellow's breathing slowed, everyone witnessed Janis whispering in his ear. It was, she said, a Russian phrase, something tender his mother had said to him in stressful times. He opened his eyes for a moment, looked at Janis, and, as Will put it, "was in awe, he was, like OK."[45]

The funeral was held at the Jewish section of Morningside Cemetery in Brattleboro, Vermont, with more than one hundred family members and friends attending. There had been some tension in the family about where Bellow should be buried—in Chicago, next to his parents, or in Vermont adjacent to Janis's future burial site. Janis won that battle, as she did almost all the others. Several people, family and friends, spoke at the event, including Greg, who surprised some people with words of praise for Janis. Martin Amis—who, according to Ruth Wisse, looked deeply bereft, "as though he were experiencing the death of his own father again"—reviewed Bellow's achievement as a writer. Roth, who looked dazed, "old and hollowed out," according to James Wood, seemed too overcome to say anything.

Wisse spoke about Bellow's Jewishness, saying among other things that Saul had wanted a plain, traditional Jewish burial and gravestone, which he got. She also reminded family and friends that, according to tradition, they had "to bury the deceased themselves without leaving it to strangers."[46] Wisse later explained why she thought she was asked to speak: "Janis might have worried that Saul's soul would never have been brought to rest" if there were no one to put some focus on his rich Jewish identity and values.[47]

Greg remembered "that Saul's thin wooden casket was so light that I had to remind myself that I was carrying my father, who often seemed larger than life." Greg's memory is similar to what Bellow had written in *Humboldt's Gift*, twenty-five years earlier. Acting as a pallbearer at Humboldt's reburial, Charlie Citrine is surprised by how "very little weight" is in the coffin. Of course! he thinks. There is nothing in there "of the charm, verve, and feverish invention, the calamity making craziness of Humboldt."[48] Just as Bellow's casket held only "remains and superfluities," there was nothing in there of the writer's energy, imagination, spirit, humor, and memory, his acute ability to "notice" or observe, or his disciplined dedication to work.

At the gravesite, a black cloth with its white Star of David was removed from the casket, and Saul Bellow was lowered into the ground. Greg took a handful of sand, kissed it, and threw it onto the top of the coffin. Daniel and Adam, who wept openly, took turns with shovels, followed by many others who fulfilled "the required task of filling the grave level to the ground." James Wood remembers the three middle-aged sons "hugging each other" when that job was done. Roth asked Andrew Wylie, "I wonder if the earth knows what it just received."[49]

After the funeral, Greg's family and the family of Sam Bellows's daughter, Lesha, gathered at the home of Daniel and his wife, Heather, where they "shared family stories over dinner." A different shiva at the Bellows' apartment on Crowninshield Road was attended by Janis's family, Bellow's Boston friends and neighbors, and two other Bellow "sons," Martin Amis and James Wood. Amis came every day for the whole week of sitting. Mourners recited passages from Bellow's books, Wood and Amis often from memory.

Though Bellow would never use the term himself, he was, among other things, a secular humanist; but like the labels "liberal" or "conservative" or "American Jewish writer," it was too narrow and too vague, too simple, and too misleading for him to adopt. Whatever he might think to call it, his humanism was rooted in great part in the accumulated wisdom of Jewish experience. It provided in vision and value an alternative to the commonly felt postwar pessimism and despair among many writers and intellectuals and parts of the American community left behind in the prosperous late forties and fifties. But Bellow, life affirming and never without hope, was far from naive; he followed his larky and overly optimistic Augie March with the desolate and clumsy Tommy Wilhelm, a victim of the smashing and crashing nature of capitalism and the protagonist's own lack of spunk and self-confidence. But even *Seize the Day* ends on an ambiguous note of possible self-recognition, truth-facing, and recommitment—as do *Henderson the Rain King*, *Herzog*, and *Humboldt's Gift*.

Bellow's most celebrated books, his biggest, most boisterous, and bodacious books—featuring Henderson, Herzog, and Humboldt, despite Humboldt's tragic denouement, give us affirmative characters trying to define what it means to be a "good man" and what it takes to live as one. The chief protagonists, like Bellow himself, attempt to separate the essential from the trivial, the soul or self from the constructed personality, the imaginative from the conventional, growth and learning from what passes as higher education.

The darker novels—*Mr. Sammler's Planet* and *The Dean's December*—came out of the disheartening disappointments and discontents of the late sixties and seventies: the culture clashes, the neglect of urban poverty and blight, and bitter racial politics. Even these books, however, featured central characters who refused in the end to surrender to despair and nihilism. But neither Bellow nor his characters could say exactly what the essential was, what it meant to be a good man, or how to describe the nature of God. Mr. Sammler could say at the completion of his journey back to the human community, "We know, we know," over and over again; but the hunger for knowing, for separating the essential from the unimportant, and for becoming a good man, a mensch, continued in Bellow's post-Sammler life and fiction.

At least two obstacles stood in the way: the imperfection or disfigurement of the world and the imperfection or impurity of the self. These obstacles are rarely overcome in life or in fiction. This is not a case of irresolution in Bellow's novels and stories or in his behavior. It is a commitment to keep seeking.

The failures in his characters and their clumsy attempts to break through the metaphysical fog provide much of the hilarity and pathos in Bellow's writing. As importantly, they give us the rich variety of Bellow's self-reflective fictional worlds: the rough, noisy, and sometimes fatally destructive world of competitive jostling and striving, along with the vital world of pleasure and temptation in American materialism. We also get, powerfully presented, the world of authentic if quixotic seeking for the spiritual and the world in which true love is discovered. In his late years, with the resourceful and resilient Janis at his side, Bellow appreciated that love is real, not to be doubted or mocked but to be appreciated as authentic and lived as essential.

Bellow, the "great observer," recognized his own powerful feeling for family and for right conduct. Although he did not, as he repeatedly acknowledged, act on these feelings often enough, he did experience long periods of regret and remorse. Back on October 22, 1963, Bellow wrote to Nathan Tarcov, who had days earlier lost his father, Oscar. The elder Tarcov, along with Isaac Rosenfeld and Bellow, had been part of an ambitious triumvirate at Tuley High School aspiring to become writers. Rosenfeld, who died at thirty-eight, had written many articles and one novel. Tarcov, too, had written only one novel before he died at forty-eight. By that age, Bellow had written five novels and was about to publish a sixth—the blockbuster *Herzog*.[50]

Bellow told Nathan Tarcov that although his father may not have had a successful life as a writer, he'd had a truly successful life as a man. Oscar, Bellow said, was a rare human being. He had "invested his life in relationships. In making such a choice a man sooner or later realizes that to love others is his answer to inevitable death."[51] Bellow tried to be a good man, a mensch, and his enduring struggle should not be lightly dismissed. Finally, however, whether he made the "right choices" or was "honorable" or "dishonorable" as a man, it was Bellow's shimmering fiction, his extraordinary gift to us, that will remain his legacy.

APPENDIX

SAUL BELLOW'S FIRST PUBLISHED PIECE

Long after completing *Saul Bellow: "I Was a Jew and an American and a Writer,"* I had the pleasure of finding what looked to be fourteen-year-old Sol's first "published" piece. It was posted in a blog by Yannay Spitzer, an economist at the Hebrew University of Jerusalem on June 9, 2015, one day before what would have been Saul Bellow's one hundredth birthday. Printed originally in Sol's junior high school yearbook in 1929, the autobiographical sketch carries the mark of a budding writer.[1] Indeed, by the time he was ten, Bellow was already writing stories, sometimes in creative imitation of Jack London and O. Henry.[2]

Those stories don't survive, but "My Life Thus Far" does, and in it we have a demonstration of Bellow's extraordinary memory and examples of what would become his characteristically long but lively sentences. There is humor here, too, and irony, both of which would mark so much of his later work.

My Life Thus Far
By Sol [Saul] Bellow

I doubt if many children of my age have had as varied experiences as I have had. I was born in the little town of Lachine Quebec, a suburb of Montreal, on June 10, 1915, the youngest of four children, there being my two brothers, and my sister. In Europe my father had been a wealthy man, but in Canada he became a bakery driver.

My mother tells me that as a child I liked to try to eat paper and coal. We had a family of kittens, and my favorite pastime was to put them into the bath, and let the water run. At the age of two I put my left foot into the stove. This foot still bears a mark. I remember the time when at the age of three I was allowed to hold the reins of my father's horse. When I was four the family moved to Montreal. I remember the house also. It was large and roomy, and ancient.

At the age of five I entered Strathorn School Kindergarten. The teacher was a French girl and made us repeat the morning prayer after her. The first lines went like this, "Our fathers fought in heaven, what shall be our name." When I came home I asked my brother if my father fought in heaven over my name, and he said he did not know.

Montreal is a wonderful place for a boy to live in. Everything a boy can wish for is there. There is nutting in the fall, skiing, skating, sleigh riding, hockey, la crosse for winter sports, and in the spring there were the mountains to climb. In the summer I would go to Lachine for a vacation. There were no mountains to climb in Lachine but, oh my! there were woods, and rapids, and Indian reservations, a rocky beach, roads to hike, berries to pick, and many other things to do. You may rest assured that I had a good time. Every summer the Fair would come to Fletcher's Field and I would go home to see it, there I would eat popcorn and pink lemonade and gaze in wonder at Wah Wall the Indian snake charmer or at the sword swallower. In the big tent there would be clowns, and a lion drinking out of a saucer, all these things impressed me.

When I entered the Devonshire School, I was put into third grade. Then we began a study of French. I regret that I never had an opportunity to learn French thoroughly. I only remember a smattering of words. At the age of eight I underwent an operation for appendicitis. The operation was not successful, and I received a blood infection. I believe now that if I hadn't had my early training in Canada, I would never have had enough resistance to pull through. The doctors told my mother that I must be in the open air constantly. In this way I was cured, but I missed a half grade of school. During my illness my father's business failed. And seeing there was no work to be found, my father decided to move to Chicago, where he would be sure to find work.[3] My father went ahead of the family and found a job as Manager of the Imperial Baking Co. This was about five and one-half years ago. The family followed soon afterwards, and before we went I visited my birthplace and all the other places that I knew, loved so well and still remember. When we came to Chicago we moved to Augusta Street, and the rooms. They would crowd around I entered the LaFayette School.

Here I found many friends, who were proud to have a Canadian member in me and ask me questions which astonished me such as, "Did you live with the Indians," or "Did you live with the Eskimos," etc. In school I was no shining star either, but I soon picked up. We then moved to Cortez Street, and I entered the Columbus School. From then on school was easy. I entered Sabin with one hundred twenty on the intelligence test, a row of E's, and a lot of high hopes. I entered 206; Miss Maher was sick and we had a young substitute Miss Nelson. The first month I walked around in a daze and came out with two D's in minors. But I came back with interest. To make up a half year that I missed, I went to summer school and made up. I am now in 8A.

In my early age I wanted to be a street car conductor. Later I wanted to be a mountaineer. At the present I have better and higher ambitions, like being a professional man.

ABBREVIATIONS

ABBREVIATIONS FOUND IN NOTES SECTION

Atlas, *Bellow*	James Atlas, *Bellow: A Biography* (New York: Random House, 2000)
Conversations with SB	Gloria L. Cronin and Ben Siegel, eds., *Conversations with Saul Bellow* (Jackson: University of Mississippi Press, 1994)
Koch, "Interview"	Sigmund Koch, "Interview of Saul Bellow" (Geddes Language Center at Boston University, Boston, 1987), in Zachary Leader, *The Life of Saul Bellow: To Fame and Fortune, 1915–1964* (New York: Alfred A. Knopf, 2015)
Leader, *To Fame and Fortune*	Zachary Leader, *The Life of Saul Bellow: To Fame and Fortune 1915–1964* (New York: Alfred Knopf, 2015)

Leader, *Love and Strife*	Zachary Leader, *The Life of Saul Bellow: Love and Strife, 1965–2005* (New York: Alfred Knopf, 2018)
NYRB	*New York Review of Books*
NYT	*New York Times*
NYTBR	*New York Times Book Review*
NYTM	*New York Times Magazine*
SB, *Settling My Accounts*	SB, *Settling My Accounts before I Go Away: A Words and Images Interview by Norman Manea* (Rhinebeck, NY: Sheep Meadow Press, 1999)
SB	Saul Bellow
SB, *IAAU*	Saul Bellow, *It All Adds Up: From the Dim Past to an Uncertain Future* (New York: Viking, 1994)
SB, *STM*	SB, *There Is Simply Too Much to Think About* (New York: Viking, 2015)
SB, *TJAB*	SB, *To Jerusalem and Back: A Personal Account* (New York: Viking, 1976)
SB, *With his Foot*	SB, *Him With His Foot in His Mouth in his Mouth and Other Stories* (New York: Harper and Row, 1984)

NOTES

INTRODUCTION

1. Judith Shulevitz, "Mr. Bellow's Planet," *Atlantic*, May 2015.

2. The Atlas biography is well worth reading, but its value is reduced by the author's apparent inability to forego tainting with sarcasm many of the positive things he says about Bellow. The biography is also scarred by Atlas's contentious, unnecessary, and occasionally wrongheaded assessments of Bellow's work; his disparaging references to Bellow's intellectual pretentions; and his ironic, often snide moral judgments when writing about Bellow and his wives, girlfriends, and children. Atlas admits to having made somewhere between six and twelve slips (there are more) that he labels "neurotic," "small-minded," "judgmental," and "ungenerous." James Atlas, *Bellow: A Biography* (New York: Random House, 2000), 596; James Atlas, *The Shadow in the Garden: A Biographer's Tale* (New York: Vintage, 2017), 314–15.

3. Jewishness, Bellow said, is a "fact" of his life and part of his creative power: "It simply comes from the fact that at a most susceptible time of my life I was wholly Jewish. That's a gift, a piece of good fortune with which one doesn't quarrel." Chiranton Kulshrestha, "A Conversation with Saul Bellow," in *Conversations with Saul Bellow*, ed. Gloria L. Cronin and Ben Siegel (Jackson: University Press of Mississippi, 1994), 92. Originally published in *Chicago Review* 23, no. 4.1 (1972), 7–15. See also SB, "A Jewish Writer in America," *NYRB*, October 27, 2011; SB, "A Jewish Writer in America—II," *NYRB*, November 10, 2011, http://www.nybooks.com/contributors/saul-bellow/.

4. Zachary Leader, *The Life of Saul Bellow: To Fame and Fortune, 1915–1964* (New York: Knopf, 2015), 731n46.

5. Janis Freedman Bellow, "Preface," *Saul Bellow: Collected Stories,* with an introduction by James Wood (New York: Viking, 2001), ix.

6. Cynthia Ozick, "Throwing Away the Clef," *New Republic,* May 22, 2000, 27–31.

7. David Mikics, *Bellow's People: How Saul Bellow Made Life into Art* (New York: W. W. Norton, 2016).

8. Roth quoted in Cynthia Ozick, "A Narrative Masterpiece," *NYTBR,* April 1, 2021. Malamud quoted in Morris Dickstein, "The Complex Fate of the Jewish-American Writer," *Nation,* October 4, 2001; Ozick in "Judaism and Harold Bloom," *Commentary,* January 1979; Also see Sanford Pinsker, "The Tortoise and the Hare; or, Philip Roth, Cynthia Ozick, and the Vagaries of Writing Fiction," *Virginia Quarterly Review* 81, no. 3 (2005). https://www.vqronline.org/essay/tortoise-and-hare-or-philip-roth-cynthia-ozick-and-vagaries-fiction-writing.

9. Kulshrestha, "Conversation with Saul Bellow," 89.

10. Steven Zipperstein, *Rosenfeld's Lives: Fame, Oblivion, and the Furies of Writing* (New Haven, CT: Yale University Press, 2009), 154–59.

11. Philip Roth, *Reading Myself and Others* (New York: Penguin, 1985).

12. Bellow's quote is from Nina Steers, "Successor to Faulkner?" in *Conversations with Saul Bellow,* 34. Originally published in *Show,* September 1964, 36–38; Bellow's position is made even clearer in Kulshrestha, "Conversation with Saul Bellow," 90.

13. Giles Harvey, "Cynthia Ozick's Long Crusade," *NYTM,* June 23, 2016.

14. Kulshrestha, "Conversation with Saul Bellow," 92.

15. Michiko Kakutani, "A Talk with Saul Bellow: On His Work and Himself," *NYTBR,* December 13, 1981, 28–29.

16. Quote from "Bletlach" (leaflet or essay in Yiddish), published in *Shtrom,* no. 1, 1922.

17. Steers, "Successor to Faulkner," 34.

18. Alfred Kazin, "The Earthly City of the Jews: From Bellow to Singer," in *Bright Book of Life: American Novelists and Storytellers from Hemingway to Mailer* (Boston: Little, Brown, 1973), 127–28.

19. Ben Siegel, "Bellow as Jew and Jewish Writer," in *A Political Companion to Saul Bellow,* eds. Gloria L. Cronin and Lee Trepanier (Lexington: University Press of Kentucky, 2013), 49.

20. Bellow was the first American to be awarded this coveted prize, said to be the French equivalent of the Nobel Prize in Literature. Earlier winners included Samuel Beckett and Jorge Luis Borges.

21. Gordon Lloyd Harper, "Saul Bellow: The Art of Fiction," in *The Paris Review Interviews*, vol. 1, with an introduction by Philip Gourevich (New York: Picador, 2006), 97. Originally published in *Paris Review*, Issue 1966, 36. In 2005, *Time* magazine named *Herzog* one of the one hundred best novels in the English language since *Time*'s founding in 1923.

22. Steers, "Successor to Faulkner," 29.

23. SB, "Prologue: Starting Out in Chicago," in *There Is Simply Too Much to Think About*, ed. Benjamin Taylor (New York: Viking, 2015), 2.

24. SB, "Jewish Writer in America"; SB, "Jewish Writer in America—II."

25. Frank McConnell, "The Terms of Our Contract," in *Saul Bellow*, ed. Harold Bloom (New York: Chelsea House, 1986), 101–14. Originally published in *Four Post-war American Novelists* (Chicago: University of Chicago Press, 1977).

26. Ibid.

27. Philip Roth, "Influences? Saul Bellow and Augie March," Web of Stories, accessed April 4, 2016. https://www.webofstories.com/play/philip.roth/68.

28. James Wood, "The Jewish King James Version: Saul Bellow—Not Exactly English but Biblically English," *Times Literary Supplement*, August 5, 2005, 12–13, 32.

29. Irving Howe, *World of Our Fathers: The Journey of the East European Jews to America and the World They Found and Made* (New York: Harcourt Brace Jovanovich, 1976), 594.

30. SB, *Mr. Sammler's Planet*, with an introduction by Stanley Crouch (New York: Penguin Classics, 2004), 196. Originally published 1970 by Viking (New York).

31. Bruce Cook, "Saul Bellow: A Mood of Protest," in *Conversations with Saul Bellow*, 17–18. Emphasis mine. Originally published in *Perspectives on Ideas and the Arts*, February 12, 1963, 46–50.

32. SB, *Herzog*, with an introduction by Philip Roth (New York: Penguin Classics, 2001), 14.

33. Steers, "Successor to Faulkner," 32–33.

34. SB, "Recent American Fiction: A Lecture" (Washington, DC: Library of Congress Speech, 1963), 6.

35. Harper, "Art of Fiction," 86–110; Steers, "Successor to Faulkner," 28–36; Rockwell Gray et al., "Interview with Saul Bellow," in *Conversations with Saul Bellow*, 199–222. Originally published in *TriQuarterly* 60 (1984). Michael Ignatieff and Martin Amis, "Our Valuation of Human Life Has Become Thinner," in *Conversations with Saul Bellow*, 228. Originally published in *Listener*, March 13, 1986.

36. Gray et al., "Interview with Saul Bellow," 203. See also Robert Siegel, "Interview of Zachary Leader," *Moment Magazine,* (winter 2019), and Maggie Simmons, "Free to Feel," in *Conversations with Saul Bellow,* 170, originally published in *Quest,* February 1979, 31–35.

37. SB, *Herzog,* 226, 82.

38. Cook, "Mood of Protest," 17–18.

39. SB, *Mr. Sammler's Planet,* 196.

40. Alfred Kazin, "Midtown and the Village," *Harper's,* January 1971, 82–91.

1. IN THE BEGINNING

1. SB, *Settling My Accounts before I Go Away: A Words and Images Interview by Norman Manea* (Rhinebeck, NY: Sheep Meadow Press, 1999), 37.

2. Ibid., 28.

3. James Atlas, *Bellow: A Biography* (New York: Random House, 2000), 6.

4. SB, *Herzog,* with an introduction by Philip Roth (New York: Penguin Classics, 2001), 151. First published 1964 by Viking (New York).

5. SB, *Settling My Accounts,* 32.

6. Ibid., 35.

7. SB, *Settling My Accounts,* 32.

8. Zachary Leader, *The Life of Saul Bellow: To Fame and Fortune, 1915–1964* (New York: Alfred A. Knopf, 2015), 35. See also SB, *Settling My Accounts,* 32.

9. SB, *Settling My Accounts,* 32.

10. Leader, *Fame and Fortune,* 33–34.

11. Sigmund Koch, "Interview of Saul Bellow" (Geddes Language Center at Boston University, Boston, 1987), in Leader, *Fame and Fortune,* 58.

12. SB, "Cousins," in *Him with His Foot in His Mouth and Other Stories* (New York: Harper and Row, 1984), 240.

13. Cathleen Medwick, "A Cry of Strength: The Unfashionably Uncynical Saul Bellow," *Vogue,* March 1982, 368–69, 426–27.

14. Matthew C. Roudané and Saul Bellow, "An Interview with Saul Bellow," *Contemporary Literature* 25, no. 3 (1984): 265–80.

15. Koch, "Interview," in Leader, *Fame and Fortune,* 57. See also Atlas, *Bellow,* 11.

16. Koch, "Interview," in Leader, *Fame and Fortune,* 57. See also Ann Weinstein, "Bellow's Reflections on His Most Recent Sentimental Journey to His Birthplace," *Saul Bellow Journal* 4, no. 1 (1985): 62–71.

17. Leader, *Fame and Fortune*, 57. The "Chicago Book" is located in the Regenstein Library at the University of Chicago. Wordworth's poem "Ode: Intimations of Immortality," st. 2, lines 2–4.

18. SB, "I Believe in God but I Don't Bug Him," in Antonio Monda, *Do You Believe? Conversations on God and Religion*, trans. Ann Goldstein (New York: Vintage Books, 2007), 28–29 (emphasis mine).

19. SB, *Seize the Day*, with an introduction by Alfred Kazin (New York: Fawcett, 1968), 30; SB, *Herzog*, 152; SB, *Humboldt's Gift*, with an introduction by Jeffrey Eugenides (New York: Penguin Classics, 2008), 303. First published 1975 by Viking (New York).

20. Koch, "Interview," in Leader, *Fame and Fortune*, 58.

21. SB, *Humboldt's Gift*, 303.

22. SB, "A Jewish Writer in America," *NYRB*, October 27, 2011; SB, "A Jewish Writer in America—II," *NYRB*, November 10, 2011.

23. Genesis 2:27.

24. SB, *Herzog*, 153–54.

25. SB, *Settling My Accounts*, 56.

26. Leader, *Fame and Fortune*, 64. See also Atlas, *Bellow*, 10.

27. SB, *Settling My Accounts*, 32.

28. Ibid., 90–91.

29. Ibid., 91.

30. Roudané and Bellow, "Interview with Saul Bellow," 267.

31. Aline Gubbay, *A Street Called the Main: The Story of Montreal's Boulevard St. Lauren* (Montreal: Meridan, 1989), 107. Quoted in Leader, *Fame and Fortune*, 67.

32. Leader, *Fame and Fortune*, 68. Bellow told *Playboy*, "I was abused when I was a child by a stranger in an alley. Playboy: Sexually? Bellow: Yeah. Playboy: How old were you? Bellow: Seven, six. Playboy: Did he make you cry? Bellow: He threatened me. Playboy: How far did it go? Bellow: It went pretty far. I don't want to go into detail on that." "Saul Bellow," in *50 Years of Playboy Interviews: Men of Letters* (New York: Playboy Enterprises, 1997), loc. 6769 of 8075, Kindle.

33. Leader, *Fame and Fortune*, 68; SB, *To Jerusalem and Back: A Personal Account* (New York: Viking, 1976), 2. The fringes are attached to a *tallit katan*, a lightweight vestlike garment worn under a shirt.

34. Nina Steers, "Successor to Faulkner?," in *Conversations with Saul Bellow*, ed. Gloria Cronin and Ben Siegel (Jackson: University Press of Mississippi, 1994), 29, 36; SB, *Settling My Accounts*, 23.

35. SB, *Settling My Accounts*, 22–23.

36. Ibid., 25, 32.

37. Interview with Bette Howland, in Leader, *Fame and Fortune*, 76.

38. SB, letter to Eugene Kennedy, February 19, 2004, in *Saul Bellow: Letters*, ed. Benjamin Taylor (New York: Viking, 2010), 552. This is part of the last known letter Bellow wrote.

39. See Michael Greenstein, "Bellow's Canadian Beginnings," *Saul Bellow Journal* 7, no. 1 (1988): 3.

40. SB, "Laughter in the Ghetto: On Sholom Aleichem," in *There Is Simply Too Much to Think About* (New York: Viking, 2015), 47.

41. SB, "Introduction," in *Great Jewish Short Stories*, ed. Saul Bellow (New York: Dell, 1988), 12; "*Carta Blanca* Interviews Saul Bellow," YouTube, https://video.search.yahoo.com/search/video?fr=mcafee&ei=UTF-8&p=%E2%80%9CCarta+Blanca+Interviews+Saul+Bellow%2C%E2%80%9D+YouTube%2C&type=D214US662G0#id=1&vid=b800f632bfd270179a9a92e5ced6f354&action=click. Mendele Mokher Seforim, literally "Mendel the Book Seller," is the pen name of Sholem Yankev Abramovitsh.

42. SB, *Settling My Accounts*, 96.

43. Ibid.

44. SB, "Introduction," 11.

45. Weinstein, "Bellow's Reflections," 70–71.

46. Atlas, *Bellow*, 13.

47. Ibid., 60.

48. Leader, *Fame and Fortune*, 21.

49. Atlas, *Bellow*, 516; Leader, *Fame and Fortune*, 44.

50. SB, "A Second Half Life," in *It All Adds Up: From the Dim Past to an Uncertain Future* (New York: Viking, 1994), 321.

51. SB, *Herzog*, 161.

52. SB, "Something to Remember Me By," in *Something to Remember Me By* (New York: Viking, 1991), 207.

53. "Saul Bellow," in *50 Years of Playboy Interviews*, loc. 6707.

54. SB, letter to Stephen Mitchell, June 22, 1991, in *Saul Bellow: Letters*, 483–85.

55. SB, *Settling My Accounts*, 44. See also Weinstein, "Bellow's Reflections."

56. "Saul Bellow," in *50 Years of Playboy Interviews*, loc. 6714.

57. SB, *Settling My Accounts*, 44.

58. "Saul Bellow," in *50 Years of Playboy Interviews*, loc. 6717.

59. SB, letter to Stephen Mitchell, June 22, 1991, in *Saul Bellow: Letters*, 483–85.

60. SB, *Settling My Accounts*, 44.

61. "Saul Bellow," in *50 Years of Playboy Interviews,* loc. 6748.

62. SB, *Henderson the Rain King* (New York: Viking, 1959), loc. 276 of 342, Kindle; SB, *Humboldt's Gift,* 142.

63. SB, "The Old System," in *Mosby's Memoirs and Other Stories* (New York: Viking, 1996), 82–83. Originally in *Playboy,* January 1968.

64. SB, *Ravelstein* (New York: Viking, 2000), 210.

65. SB, *Settling My Accounts,* 28–29.

66. Ibid., 34.

67. Ibid., 45, 30.

68. Ibid., 30–31.

69. SB, "A Half Life," in *IAAU,* 289; SB, *Settling My Accounts,* 34.

70. SB, *Settling My Accounts,* 45.

71. "Saul Bellow," in *50 Years of Playboy Interviews,* loc. 6732. In an earlier interview, Bellow said the book was a New Testament for children. SB, "A Half Life," in *IAAU,* 288.

72. SB, *Settling My Accounts,* 45; "Saul Bellow," in *50 Years of Playboy Interviews,* loc. 6732.

73. SB, letter to Stephen Mitchell, June 22, 1991, in *Saul Bellow: Letters,* 483–85.

74. Ibid.

75. Ibid.

76. SB, *Settling My Accounts,* 46.

77. Ibid., 45.

78. SB, "A Half Life," in *IAAU,* 287.

2. ADAPTING TO AMERICA

1. SB, *Herzog,* with an introduction by Philip Roth (New York: Penguin, 2003), 144. First published 1964 by Viking (New York).

2. Zachary Leader, *The Life of Saul Bellow: To Fame and Fortune, 1915–1964* (New York: Alfred A. Knopf, 2015), 84.

3. Cathleen Medwick, "A Cry of Strength: the Unfashionably Uncynical Saul Bellow," *Vogue,* March 1982, 368–69, 426–27.

4. Ann Weinstein, "Bellow's Reflections on His Most Recent Sentimental Journey to His Birthplace," *Saul Bellow Journal* 4, no. 1 (1985): 70–71.

5. SB, "Starting Out in Chicago," in *There Is Simply Too Much to Think About,* ed. Benjamin Taylor (New York: Viking, 2015), 6.

6. SB, "Cousins," in *Him with His Foot in His Mouth and Other Stories* (New York: Harper and Row, 1984), 282.

7. SB, "Starting Out in Chicago," 6.

8. SB, "Memoirs of a Bootlegger's Son," excerpt in *Granta*, November 5, 1992, accessed October 23, 2019, https://granta.com/memoirs-of-a-bootleggers-son. Bellow appended a note to the excerpt: "About forty years ago I tried my hand at novel called Memoirs of a Bootlegger's son. . . . I put it aside. A few of these recollections are to be found in *Herzog*, but when I wrote that novel, I had virtually forgotten *The Bootlegger's Son* and was reminded of it only recently by Mr. James Atlas who exhumed it from a midden of discarded manuscripts. The editors of *Granta* evidently believe that the vanished world of its setting may interest contemporary readers."

9. SB, *Herzog*, 162.

10. SB, *Settling My Accounts Before I Go Away: An Interview with Norman Manea* (Rhinebeck, NY: Sheep Meadow Press, 1999), 56.

11. SB, "In the Days of Mr. Roosevelt," in *It All Adds Up: From the Dim Past to an Uncertain Future* (New York: Viking, 1994), 20–22.

12. Ibid.

13. SB, "A Matter of the Soul," in *IAAU*, 73–74.

14. "Saul Bellow: Made in America," interview with Keith Botsford in *Conversations with Saul Bellow*, ed. Gloria Cronin and Ben Siegel (Jackson: University Press of Mississippi, 1994), 243 (emphasis mine).

15. SB, "A Matter of the Soul," in *IAAU*, 73–74.

16. Leader, *Fame and Fortune*, 84.

17. SB, "Memoirs of a Bootlegger's Son."

18. SB, *Settling My Accounts*, 37.

19. Ibid., 38.

20. Leader, *Fame and Fortune*, 120.

21. SB, *Settling My Accounts*, 38.

22. Philip Gillon, "Bellow's Credo," *Jerusalem Post Weekly*, December 24, 1974, 13.

23. Leader, *Fame and Fortune*, 92.

24. Medwick, "Cry of Strength," 369.

25. SB, "Americans Who Are Also Jews," in *STM*, 302; James Atlas, *Bellow: A Biography* (New York: Random House, 2000), 26; SB, "I Said That I Was an American, a Jew, a Writer by Trade," *NYT*, December 14, 1976. The phrase "reverence for the source of one's being" was borrowed by Bellow from George Santayana.

26. "Some People Come Back Like Hecuba," *Time*, February 8, 1970, 82.
27. Leader, *Fame and Fortune*, 88.
28. SB, "A Half Life," in *IAAU*, 297.
29. Atlas, *Bellow*, 26.
30. SB, *Saul Bellow: Letters*, ed. Benjamin Taylor (New York: Viking, 2010), xviii.
31. Atlas, *Bellow*, 26.
32. Cynthia Ozick, "The Lasting Man," *New Republic*, February 10, 2011.
33. "Some People Come Back Like Hecuba," *Time*, February 8, 1970, 82. Bellow said, "As an adolescent I read an unusual number of Russian novels," and "the children of immigrants in my Chicago high school believed they were also somehow Russian." Letter to Stanley Elkin, March 12, 1992, in *Saul Bellow: Letters*, 492–93.
34. Jack Miles, "Saul Bellow's Life Is an Open Book," *Los Angeles Times*, March 30, 1989.
35. SB, "Isaac Rosenfeld," *Partisan Review* 23 (1956): 565 (emphasis mine).
36. Steven Zipperstein, *Rosenfeld's Lives: Fame, Oblivion, and the Furies of Writing* (New Haven, CT: Yale University Press, 2009), 28.
37. Ibid., 14.
38. Ibid., 29.
39. The Tate quote is part of a dust-jacket blurb on *Bravo, My Monster* (Chicago: Henry Regency, 1953).
40. Bellow quoted in Leader, *To Fame and Fortune*, 146.
41. Marx, according to several students of Marxism, considered Jews to be the incarnation of capitalism and the best illustration of all its evils. He argued that the modern commercialized world was the accomplishment of Judaism, a false religion whose god is money. "On the Jewish Question," an example of Marx's early Jew-hatred, became one of the classics of antisemitic propaganda. In later years, because of strong public identification of him with antisemitism by his political enemies on both the right and the left, Marx limited what he considered to be antipathy toward Jews to private letters and conversations.
42. Leader, *Fame and Fortune*, 175.
43. SB, *Humboldt's Gift*, with an introduction by Jeffrey Eugenides (New York: Penguin Classics, 2008), 39–40. First published 1975 by Viking (New York).
44. Leader, *Fame and Fortune*, 173–74.
45. SB, "Mozart: An Overture," in *IAAU*, 2.

46. Atlas, *Bellow*, 34n.

47. SB, *Humboldt's Gift*, 302–3.

48. SB, "In Memory of Yetta Barshevsky," in *Saul Bellow: Letters*, 527.

49. Ibid., 528.

50. Ibid.; Atlas, *Bellow*, 33.

51. Joshua Rubenstein, *Trotsky: A Revolutionary's Life* (New Haven, CT: Yale University Press, 2011); Al Glotzer, *Trotsky: Memoir and Critique* (Buffalo: Prometheus, 1989), 310.

52. *Saul Bellow: Letters*, xix.

53. Atlas, *Bellow*, 40–41.

54. SB, *Settling My Accounts*, 38–39.

55. SB, "Zetland: By a Character Witness," in *Him with His Foot in His Mouth and Other Stories* (New York: Harper and Row, 1984), 187. Originally published in *Modern Occasions* (Port Washington, NY: Kennikat, 1978).

56. SB, *Dangling Man* (New York: Vanguard, 1944), 23.

57. SB, *Settling My Accounts*, 81.

58. Ibid., 35.

59. Ibid.

60. Irving Kristol, "Memoirs of a Trotskyist," *NYTM*, January 23, 1977.

61. Trotsky, quoted in Irving Howe, *A World More Attractive* (New York: Horizon, 1963), xi–xii.

62. SB, "Writers, Intellectuals, Politics: Mainly Reminiscences," in *IAAU*, 100.

63. Theodore Dreiser, *Jennie Gerhardt*, ed. James L. W. West III (Philadelphia: University of Pennsylvania Press, 1994), 125–26 (emphasis mine). See also Rockwell Gray, Harry White, and Gerald Nemanic, "Interview with Saul Bellow," in *Conversations with Saul Bellow*, 205, where Bellow speaks of how deeply Dreiser "feels the power of the great city—the purposeful energy of the crowds. . . . Factories, horsecars, hotel lobbies . . . luxury shops, fast women, plausible salesmen." From *TriQuarterly* 60 (1984): 12–34.

64. SB, *Humboldt's Gift*, 157.

65. SB, "The Distracted Public," in *IAAU*, 153.

66. Sigmund Koch, "Interview of Saul Bellow" (Geddes Language Center at Boston University, Boston, 1987), in Leader, *Fame and Fortune*, 177.

67. Atlas, *Bellow*, 405; Nina Steers, "Successor to Faulkner?," in *Conversations with Saul Bellow*, 37.

68. SB, *Settling My Accounts*, 35.

69. Ibid., 36.

70. Several quotations unless otherwise indicated are by Lescha Greengus, Maury's niece, in Leader, *Fame and Fortune,* 107; SB, with Philip Roth, "I've Got a Scheme," in *STM,* 467–94.

71. SB, with Philip Roth, "I've Got a Scheme," in *STM,* 481.

72. SB, *Him with His Foot in His Mouth,* 42.

73. SB, *Humboldt's Gift,* 246–47.

74. Ibid., 395.

75. Ibid.; SB, letter to Herman Wouk, May 21, 2000, quoted in Leader, *Fame and Fortune,* 127.

76. Lesha Greengus, email to Zachary Leader, in Leader, *Fame and Fortune,* 126n17.

77. SB, *Settling My Accounts,* 36–37, 31–32.

78. Ibid., 37.

79. SB, "The Civilized Barbarian," *NYT,* March 6, 1987.

80. SB, "Something to Remember Me By," in *Something to Remember Me By* (New York: Viking, 1991), 202–3. First published in *Esquire Magazine,* July 1, 1990.

81. SB, with Philip Roth, "I've Got a Scheme," in *STM,* 485, 484.

82. SB, "The Old System," in *Mosby's Memoirs and Other Stories* (New York: Penguin, 1996), 58–59. First published 1969 by Fawcett Crest.

83. Leader, *Fame and Fortune,* 115.

84. SB, *Settling My Accounts,* 52.

85. Michiko Kakutani, "A Talk with Saul Bellow: On His Work and Himself," *NYTBR,* December 13, 1981.

86. Peltz, quoted in Leader, *Fame and Fortune,* 690n89.

87. SB, *Herzog,* 253–55.

88. Glotzer, quoted in Leader, *Fame and Fortune,* 165.

89. Atlas, *Bellow,* 35–37. See also Leader, *Fame and Fortune,* 152.

3. THE EDUCATION OF SAUL BELLOW

1. Sigmund Koch, "Interview of Saul Bellow" (Geddes Language Center at Boston University, Boston, 1987), in Zachary Leader, *The Life of Saul Bellow: To Fame and Fortune, 1915–1964* (New York: Alfred A. Knopf, 2015), 177.

2. Leader, *Fame and Fortune,* 178.

3. SB, *Settling My Accounts before I Go Away: An Interview with Norman Manea* (Rhinebeck, NY: Sheep Meadow Press, 1999), 85, 52.

4. SB, "A Half Life," in *It All Adds Up: From the Dim Past to an Uncertain Future* (New York: Viking, 1994), 305.

5. "Some People Come Back Like Hecuba," *Time*, February 8, 1970, 82.

6. Both schools were awash in antisemitism, of which Minnesota was known as the capital; Northwestern had quotas on Jewish admissions until 1964.

7. Other Jewish pioneers in modern anthropology include Edward Sapir, Robert Lowie, Lucien Levy-Bruhl, Ellen Hellman, Ruth Landes, and Marcel Mauss.

8. SB, "A Half Life," in *IAAU*, 299.

9. *Saul Bellow: Letters*, ed. Benjamin Taylor (New York: Viking, 2010), xix.

10. SB, *Settling My Accounts*, 45, 30.

11. *Saul Bellow: Letters*, xix.

12. SB, "Cousins," in *Him with His Foot in His Mouth and Other Stories* (New York: Harper and Row, 1984), 255.

13. Ibid., 268 (emphasis in original).

14. SB, "A Half Life: An Autobiography in Ideas," in *Conversations with Saul Bellow*, ed. Gloria Cronin and Ben Siegel (Jackson: University Press of Mississippi, 1994), 266.

15. See Eusebio L. Rodrigues, "Bellow's Africa," *American Literature* 43, no. 2 (1971): 242–56.

16. SB, *Dangling Man* (New York: Signet, 1965), 56.

17. Koch, "Interview," 196.

18. James Atlas, *Bellow: A Biography* (New York: Random House, 2000), 49; Koch, "Interview," 196.

19. Koch, "Interview," 196. For accounts of antisemitism in English departments before World War II, see Diana Trilling, "Lionel Trilling: A Jew at Columbia," in *Speaking of Literature and Society* (New York: Harcourt Brace Jovanovich, 1989). The story ended well, however, when Trilling's protest against the department's rejection resulted in his retention and promotion to assistant professor and eventually tenure in 1936, which made him the first Jewish member of the permanent faculty.

20. Steven Zipperstein, *Rosenfeld's Lives: Fame, Oblivion, and the Furies of Writing* (New Haven, CT: Yale University Press, 2009), 106.

21. SB, letter to Tarcov, October 2, 1937, in *Saul Bellow: Letters*, 7–8.

22. SB, letter to Tarcov, October 13, 1937, in *Saul Bellow: Letters*, 9–10.

23. SB, "Isaac Rosenfeld," *Partisan Review*, fall 1956, 566.

24. Zipperstein, *Rosenfeld's Lives*, 42–43. Prufrock is also linked by Zipperstein to a well-established Yiddish convention of translating English

classics, including Shakespeare (most memorably *King Lear*), that announced themselves as "translated and improved."

25. Ibid.

26. Ruth Wisse, *The Modern Jewish Canon* (New York: Simon and Schuster, 2000), 289.

27. It was not until the 1963 edition of Eliot's work that "jew" was changed to "Jew." T. S. Eliot, "Sweeney among the Nightingales," Poets.org, accessed November 17, 2017, https://poets.org/poem/sweeney-among-nightingales; T. S. Eliot, "Burbank with a Baedeker: Bleistein with a Cigar," Genius, accessed November 17, 2017, https://genius.com/ts-eliot-burbank-with-a-baedeker-bleistein-with-a-cigar-annotated; T. S. Eliot, "Gerontion," Poetry, accessed November 17, 2017, https://www.poetry.com/poem/54141/gerontion.

28. See Russel Kirk, "On T.S. Eliot's After Strange Gods," *Touchstone* 10, no. 4 (1997), accessed August 20, 2023, https://search.yahoo.com/search?fr=mcafee&type=D214US662G0&p=Russel+Kirk%2C+%E2%80%9COn+T.S.+Eliot%E2%80%99s+After+Strange+Gods%2C%E2%80%9D.

29. Rockwell Gray, Harry White, and Gerald Nemanic, "Interview with Saul Bellow," in *Conversations with Saul Bellow*, 220–22.

30. SB, "A Jewish Writer in America," *NYRB*, October 27, 2011; SB, "A Jewish Writer in America—II," *NYRB*, November 10, 2011.

31. Ibid.

32. Gray, White, and Neumanic, "Interview with Saul Bellow," 220–21.

33. Ibid.; Irving Howe, "The Range of the New York Intellectuals," in *Creators and Disturbers: Reminiscences by Jewish Intellectuals of New York*, ed. Bernard Rosenberg (New York: Columbia University Press, 1982), 281.

34. SB, *Herzog*, with an introduction by Philip Roth (New York: Penguin Classics, 2001), 138.

35. SB, *Dangling Man*, 126.

36. Bruce Cook, "Saul Bellow: A Mood of Protest," in *Conversations with Saul Bellow*, 6–18. For Bellow's alleged need for obeisance to a higher power, see especially Edward Mendelson, "The Obedient Bellow," *NYRB*, April 28, 2011; Edward Mendelsohn, *Moral Agents: Eight Twentieth Century American Writers* (New York: NYRB Books, 2005), 101–26; Pankaj Mishra, "The Sound of Cracking," *London Review of Books*, August 16, 2015.

37. Joseph Dorman, *Arguing the World* (New York: Free Press, 2000), 51.

38. SB, *Herzog*, 138–39.

39. Leader, *Fame and Fortune*, 211.

40. SB, "Starting Out in Chicago," in *There Is Simply Too Much to Think About* (New York: Viking, 2015), 3.

41. Dara Horn, "Requiem for a Luftmentsh," *Jewish Review of Books*, spring 2010. *Kestler* comes from *kest*: room and board, or more particularly, food and shelter for a young married couple paid for by the bride's parents to enable the son-in-law, for a specified period of time, to carry on his studies in Torah and Talmud. Solon Beinfeld and Harry Bochner, eds., *Comprehensive Yiddish-English Dictionary* (Bloomington: Indiana University Press, 2013), 628.

42. James Atlas, "Starting Out in Chicago," *Granta*, November 5, 1992.

43. SB, "Starting Out in Chicago," 3–4.

44. Edward Shils, letter to James Atlas, March 20, 1994, in Atlas, *Bellow*, 6.

45. SB, *Dangling Man*, 13.

46. SB, "A Half Life," in *IAAU*, 306.

47. Atlas, *Bellow*, 41.

48. SB, letter to Tarcov, in *Saul Bellow: Letters*, 14–15.

49. Ibid.

50. Greg Bellow, *A Son's Heart* (New York: Bloomsbury, 2013), 189.

51. The correspondent is addressed only as "Mr. Levinson." Letter cited in Leader, *Fame and Fortune*, 41, 678n66.

52. SB, with Philip Roth, "I've Got a Scheme," in *STM*, 476.

53. Quoted in Leader, *Fame and Fortune*, 44.

54. Ibid.

55. SB, with Philip Roth, "I've Got a Scheme," 476–77.

56. Ibid.

57. Ibid.

58. SB, "Summations," in *Saul Bellow: A Mosaic*, eds. L. H. Goldman, Gloria L. Cronin, and Ada Aharoni (New York: Peter Lang, 1992), 35–47.

59. SB, with Philip Roth, "I've Got a Scheme," 477.

60. Stephen J. Whitfield, "Commercial Passions: The Southern Jew as Businessman," *American Jewish History* 71 (1982): 342–57. See also Irving Howe and Kenneth Libo, *We Lived There Too* (New York: St. Martin's/Marek, 1984), 327–28.

61. Northern Jews took pride in their support for racial justice, but most did so from the comfort of their living rooms, where they read newspaper articles about direct-action protests or watched them on television. Marc Dollinger, *Black Power, Jewish Politics: Reinventing the Alliance in the 1960s* (Waltham, MA: Brandeis University Press, 2018).

62. Atlas, "Starting Out in Chicago."
63. Ibid.
64. SB, *The Adventures of Augie March* (New York: Library of America, 2003), 811; Bellow, *IAAU*, 101.
65. SB, with Philip Roth, "I've Got a Scheme," 477; Atlas, *Bellow*, 68.

4. DANGLING MEN

1. Greg Bellow, *Saul Bellow's Heart: A Son's Memoir* (New York: Bloomsbury, 2013), 55.
2. SB, letter to Oscar Tarcov, February 8, 1941, in *Saul Bellow: Letters*, ed. Benjamin Taylor (New York: Viking, 2010), 17–18.
3. Among many other ethnic novels, two need special mention because they reached for something beyond the parochial: Michael Gold, *Jews without Money* (1930), and Daniel Fuchs, *Homage to Blenholt* (1934).
4. The journal moved its offices to the campus of Rutgers University in 1963 and then to the campus of Boston University in 1978, gradually losing its cultural relevance. The final issue of the publication appeared in April 2003.
5. Michiko Kakutani, "A Talk with Saul Bellow: On His Work and Himself," *NYTBR*, December 13, 1981.
6. Irving Howe, *A Margin of Hope: An Intellectual Autobiography* (New York: Harcourt Brace Jovanovich, 1982), 140.
7. Ibid.; Alan L. Berger, "Blinded by Ideology: Saul Bellow, the *Partisan Review*, and the Impact of the Holocaust," *Saul Bellow Journal* 23, no. 1-2 (2007): 7-22.
8. Sanford Pinsker, *Jewish American Fiction, 1917–1987* (New York: Twayne, 1992), 46.
9. Irving Howe, "Foreword," in *In Dreams Begin Responsibilities and Other Stories*, by Delmore Schwartz, ed. James Atlas (New York: New Directions Books, 1978), ix.
10. Leslie Fiedler, "Partisan Review: Phoenix or Dodo?," in *To the Gentiles* (New York: Stein and Day, 1972), 41.
11. SB, "Foreword," in *Sixty Years of Great Fiction from the Partisan Review*, ed. William Phillips (New York: Partisan Review, 1997), viii.
12. Irving Howe, *World of Our Fathers: The Journey of the East European Jews to America and the World They Found and Made* (New York: Harcourt Brace Jovanovich, 1976), 646.
13. SB, *Saul Bellow: Letters*, xxiv–xxv.

14. SB, "A Jewish Writer in America," *NYRB*, October 27, 2011; SB, "A Jewish Writer in America—II," *NYRB*, November 10, 2011.

15. James Atlas, "The Changing World of New York Intellectuals," *NYTM*, August 25, 1985, 70; William Barrett, *The Truants: Adventures among the Intellectuals* (Garden City, NY: Anchor/Doubleday, 1983), 24.

16. Lionel Trilling, quoted in "Under Forty: A Symposium on American Literature and the Younger Generation of American Jews," *Contemporary Jewish Record*, February 1944, 16–17. Only two of the eleven other respondents in the symposium explicitly recognized any affinity for "American Jewish Culture." Alfred Kazin, who thought differently before and would do so afterward, went so far as to deny the existence of anything that could be called American Jewish culture. Kazin praised the work of the great Yiddish writers Sholem Aleichem, Peretz, and I. J. Singer but traced his own literary influences to Blake, Melville, and Emerson. See "Under Forty," 18–35.

17. SB, "Jewish Writer in America."

18. Howe, *Margin of Hope*, 137.

19. Anton Chekhov, "Chekhov's Politics and Religion," Scribd, accessed September 1, 2021, https://www.scribd.com/doc/49331373/Anton-Chekov-Religion-and-Politics. Bellow used this Chekhov aphorism or variations on it often through at least 1993. SB, "Writers, Intellectuals, Politics: Mainly Reminiscence," in *There Is Simply Too Much to Think About* (New York: Viking, 2015), 399. Originally published in *National Interest*, spring 1993.

20. SB, letter to Kazin, n.d., the Berg Collection, New York Public Library.

21. Gertrude Himmelfarb, quoted in James Atlas, *Bellow: A Biography* (New York: Random House, 2000), 84.

22. William Phillips, *A Partisan View: Five Decades of the Literary Life* (New York: Stein and Day, 1981), 118, 119.

23. SB, letter to Tumin, cited in Zachary Leader, *The Life of Saul Bellow: To Fame and Fortune, 1915–1964* (New York: Alfred A. Knopf, 2015), 257.

24. SB, "I've Got a Scheme," in *STM*, 469.

25. Phillips, *Partisan View*, 119.

26. John Leonard, "Novelist Deals with Jews in America," *NYT*, October 22, 1976, 1.

27. Atlas, *Bellow*, 76.

28. Ibid., 76–79.

29. Sigmund Koch, "Interview of Saul Bellow" (Geddes Language Center at Boston University, Boston, 1987), in Leader, *Fame and Fortune*, 240.

30. Ibid., 241.

31. Atlas, "Changing World"; *Saul Bellow: Letters*, xxi.

32. SB, "Foreword," in *Preserving the Hunger*, by Isaac Rosenfeld, ed. and introduced by Mark Shechner (Detroit: Wayne State University Press, 1988), 15.

33. Alfred Kazin, *On Native Grounds: An Interpretation of Modern American Prose Literature* (New York: Harcourt Brace Jovanovich, 1982). Originally published 1942 by Reynal and Hitchcock (New York).

34. Irving Howe, although under the radar, wrote critical studies of Sherwood Anderson (1951) and William Faulkner (1952), which were also proof enough that the sons of immigrants could take on American literature.

35. The quotes in this paragraph and the three subsequent ones are in Alfred Kazin, *New York Jew* (New York: Knopf, 1978), 40–42; D. H. Lawrence, preface to *All Things Are Possible*, by Lev Shestov (Union City, CA: Facsimile Press, 1920).

36. James Atlas, "Starting Out in Chicago," *Granta*, November 5, 1992, https://granta.com/starting-out-in-chicago/.

37. Quoted in Pankaj Mishra, "The Sound of Cracking," *London Review of Books*, August 27, 2015, 13–15.

38. Other important examples in this regard were Randall Jarrell's *Losses* (1948) and William Styron's *Lie Down in Darkness* (1951).

39. SB, *Herzog*, with an introduction by Philip Roth (New York: Penguin Classics, 2003), 82. First published 1964 by Viking (New York).

40. SB, letter to David Bazelon, March 20, 1944, in *Saul Bellow: Letters*, 36.

41. SB, letter to Alfred Kazin, March 25, 1944, in *Saul Bellow: Letters*, 37.

42. SB, "A Mood of Protest: A Conversation with Bruce Cook," in *Conversations with Saul Bellow*, ed. Gloria Cronin and Ben Siegel (Jackson: University Press of Mississippi, 1994), 18. From *Perspectives on Ideas and the Arts*, February 12, 1963, 46–50. Letter to Mel Tumin, undated (but likely in the early months of 1963), cited in Leader, *Fame and Fortune*, 247.

43. SB, *Dangling Man* (New York: Vanguard, 1944), 13, 52, 98.

44. Ibid., 97.

45. Ibid., 27.

46. Ibid., 61; Dave D. Galloway, "An Interview with Saul Bellow," in *Conversations with Saul Bellow*, 23. From *Audit-Poetry* 3 (1963): 19–23.

47. SB, *Dangling Man*, 61.

48. Ibid., 109.

49. Ibid., 57.

50. Ibid., 10, 63.

51. Ibid., 52.

52. See especially John 8:44, 5:16–18. The phrase *the Jews* is used seventy-one times in John, almost always negatively.

53. SB, *Dangling Man*, 80. The Iron Guard was an ultranationalist, anti-semitic, far-right movement and political party in Romania in the period from 1927 into the early part of World War II.

54. Ibid., 55.

55. Ibid., 40.

56. Ibid., 18, 46.

57. P. Shiv Kumar, "The Hero as Prophet: A Study of Saul Bellow's Fiction," in *Saul Bellow: A Symposium on the Jewish Heritage*, ed. Vinda and Shiv Kumar (Hyderabad, India: Nachson, 1983), 137–49.

58. Ibid.; Genesis 1:9–31.

59. SB, *Dangling Man*, 126.

60. SB, letter to David Bazelon, March 25,1944, in *Saul Bellow: Letters*, 36.

61. SB, letter to Mel Tumin, n.d., 1942, in *Saul Bellow: Letters*, 28.

62. SB, *Dangling Man*, 32, 91.

5. IN THE SHADOW OF THE HOLOCAUST

1. SB, letter to Dwight Macdonald, n.d., 1943, in *Saul Bellow: Letters*, ed. Benjamin Taylor (New York: Viking, 2010), 34.

2. SB, letter to Mel Tumin, n.d., 1942, in *Saul Bellow: Letters*, 26; SB, letter to James Henle, October 1944, cited in James Atlas, "Starting Out in Chicago," *Granta*, November 5, 1992.

3. SB, *Dangling Man* (New York: Vanguard, 1944), 24.

4. SB, "Half Life," in *It All Adds Up: From the Dim Past to an Uncertain Future* (New York: Viking, 1994), 309–10. Originally published in *Bostonia*, November/December 1990.

5. Alfred Kazin, *New York Jew* (New York: Knopf, 1978), 41–42; SB, "Half Life," 309–10.

6. Kazin, *New York Jew*, 26–27; Lionel Abel, *Intellectual Follies* (New York: W. W. Norton, 1984), 270–71.

7. Alfred Kazin, "In Every Voice, in Every Ban," *New Republic*, January 10, 1944, 45–46.

8. SB, letter to Kazin, March 25, 1944, in *Saul Bellow: Letters*, 37.

9. SB, "The Jefferson Lectures," in *IAAU*, 127.

10. Zachary Leader, *The Life of Saul Bellow: To Fame and Fortune, 1915–1964* (New York: Alfred A. Knopf, 2015), 214.

11. Diana Trilling, "Reviews in Fiction," *Nation*, April 15, 1944. Trilling couldn't have been more wrong. Delmore Schwartz had it right: "Here are the typical objects of a generation's sensibility: phonograph records, the studio couch . . . the cafeteria; and the typical relationships: the small intellectual circle which gradually breaks up, the easy and meaningless love affairs . . . hysterical outbreaks of sickness of heart, the gulf separating this generation from the previous one and the family life from which it came." Schwartz, "A Man in His Time," *Partisan Review*, summer 1944, 348–49.

12. SB, *Dangling Man*, 97.

13. Leader, *Fame and Fortune*, 249; James Atlas, *Bellow: A Biography* (New York: Random House, 2000), 102.

14. James Atlas, "Starting Out in Chicago," November 5, 1992, https://granta.com/Starting-Out-in-Chicago/ November 5, 1992.

15. SB, "Half Life," in *IAAU*, 309.

16. Michael Ignatieff, "Our Valuation of Human Life Has Become Thinner," in *Conversations with Saul Bellow*, ed. Gloria L. Cronin and Ben Siegel (Jackson: University Press of Mississippi, 1994), 228.

17. Ann Birstein (Alfred Kazin's third wife), *What I Saw at the Fair: An Autobiography* (New York: Welcome Rain, 2003), 121; Atlas, *Bellow*, 101.

18. Nina Steers, "Successor to Faulkner?," in *Conversations with Saul Bellow*, 37. Originally published in *Show*, September 1964, 36–38.

19. Atlas, *Bellow*, 101–2 (capitals in original).

20. Wilson's essay, "Hull House in 1932," originally appeared in the *New Republic* and was reprinted in *Travels in Two Democracies* in 1936, which was republished by Hesperides Press in 2008. See also Atlas, "Starting Out in Chicago."

21. SB, letter to Freifeld, n.d., 1945, in *Saul Bellow: Letters*, 39–40.

22. Ibid.

23. Kazin, *New York Jew*, 150.

24. Ibid.

25. SB, letter to Steve Hare, October 5, 1998, in Leader, *Fame and Fortune*, 378n21.

26. Atlas, *Bellow*, 109.

27. Ibid.

28. Leader, *Fame and Fortune*, 289.

29. Ibid., 298.

30. Isaac Rosenfeld, *Passage from Home*, with an introduction by Marc Shechner (Princeton, NJ: Markus Wiener, 2009). Daniel Bell wrote a

major essay centered on *Passage*, arguing that Rosenfeld's novel was "the fullest articulation [yet] of . . . generational conflict between Jewish fathers and sons." Bell, "A Parable of Alienation," in *Jewish Frontier Anthology, 1945–1967*, ed. Marie Sirkin (New York: Jewish Frontier Association, 1967), 52.

31. Rosenfeld, *Passage from Home*, 272.

32. Irving Howe, "Of Fathers and Sons," *Commentary*, August 1946, 190–92.

33. Irving Howe, "The Lost Young Intellectual: Marginal Man, Twice Alienated," *Commentary*, October 1946, 361–67.

34. Kafka, letter to Max Brod, June 1921, quoted in Reiner Stach, *Kafka: The Years of Insight* (Princeton, NJ: Princeton University Press, 2013), 484; Howe, "Lost Young Intellectual," 367.

35. Atlas, *Bellow*, 114–16.

36. Leader, *Fame and Fortune*, 300.

37. Carey McWilliams, *A Mask for Privilege: Anti-Semitism in America* (New Brunswick, NJ: Transaction, 1999). For more on McWilliams and antisemitism, see Max Kampelman, *Entering New Worlds: The Memoir of a Private Man in Public Life* (New York: HarperCollins, 1991).

38. "Anti-Semitism in Minneapolis History," *MPR News*, October 18, 2017.

39. Leader, *Fame and Fortune*, 299–301.

40. SB, letter to Warren, November 17, 1947, in *Saul Bellow: Letters*, 45.

41. Atlas, *Bellow*, 115.

42. SB, letter to Warren, November 17, 1947, in *Saul Bellow: Letters*, 45; SB, letter to Bazelon, autumn 1948, cited in Leader, *Fame and Fortune*, 301.

43. Leader, *Fame and Fortune*, 302.

44. Sarah Blacher Cohen, "*The Victim*: The Grim Comedy of Pride and Prejudice," in *Saul Bellow: A Symposium on the Jewish Heritage*, ed. Vinda and Shiv Kumar (Hyderabad, India: Nachson, 1983), 76.

45. Atlas, "Starting Out in Chicago."

46. SB, *The Victim* (New York: Signet, 1965), 43–44.

47. Ibid., 111.

48. Jean Paul Sartre, *Anti-Semite and Jew*, trans. George J. Becker (New York: Schocken Books, 1965), 6.

49. SB, *Victim*, 102.

50. Ibid., 13.

51. Allbee says "you people" six times. The phrase "universe of moral obligation" is borrowed from Helen Fein, *Accounting for Genocide* (New York: Free Press, 1979). It refers to that circle of people who feel reciprocal

obligations to protect each other, whose bonds arise from a relationship to a sacred source of authority, or from felt roots of a former relationship to a sacred source of authority.

52. SB, *Victim*, 70.

53. Ibid., 131–32.

54. Ibid., 107.

55. "When [the merchant] had ended eating the dates he threw away the stones with force and lo! An Ifrit appeared, huge of stature and brandishing a sword, wherewith he approached the merchant and said, 'Stand up that I may slay thee even as thou slewest my son!' Asked the merchant, 'how have I slain thy son?' and he answered. 'When though atest dates and threwest away the stones, they struck my son full in the breast as he was walking by so that he died forthwith.'" From "The Tale of the Merchant and the Jinni."

56. SB, *Victim*, 139.

57. Ibid., 121.

58. Atlas, "Starting Out in Chicago."

59. SB, *Victim*, 77.

60. Ibid., 26.

61. Ibid., 132–33.

62. SB, *Dangling Man*, 18; SB, *Victim*, 151.

63. The phrase "unwitting but not unwilling" comes from Victoria Aarons, "'Not Enough Air to Breathe': *The Victim* in Saul Bellow's Post-Holocaust America," *Saul Bellow Journal*, nos. 1 and 2 (2008): 23–36; "The Longest Hatred" is part of the title of Robert Wistrich's book *Antisemitism: The Longest Hatred* (New York: Pantheon, 1992).

64. SB, *Victim*, 231.

65. Ibid., 145.

66. Ibid., 36, 89, 96, 150–51, 163–64.

6. IN THE LAND OF THE HOLOCAUST

1. Zachary Leader, *The Life of Saul Bellow: To Fame and Fortune, 1915–1964* (New York: Alfred A. Knopf, 2015), 310.

2. Bellow, undated letter to Bazelon, in Leader, *Fame and Fortune*, 310. In a letter to an editor at Vanguard Press, Anita said the vacation in Wisconsin "wasn't as bad as I thought it would be." Leader, *Fame and Fortune*, 311.

3. Leader, *Fame and Fortune*, 319.

4. Mitzi McClosky, quoted in James Atlas, *Bellow: A Biography* (New York: Random House, 200), 120.

5. SB, *Settling My Accounts before I Go Away: A Words and Images Interview by Norman Manea* (Rhinebeck, NY: Sheep Meadow Press, 1999), 44.

6. SB, "A Half Life," in *It All Adds Up: From the Dim Past to an Uncertain Future* (New York: Viking, 1994), 311. Originally published in *Bostonia*, November/December 1990.

7. SB, quoted in Atlas, *Bellow*, 121.

8. SB, "Spanish Letter (1948)," in *IAAU*, 181–95. Originally published in *Partisan Review* 15, no. 2 (1948) 15.

9. Ibid.; SB, "Half Life," 311.

10. Leader, *Fame and Fortune*, 314; Atlas, *Bellow*, 121.

11. SB, "Half Life," 311.

12. Atlas, *Bellow*, 123.

13. SB, letter to Mel Tumin, April 21, 1948, in *Saul Bellow: Letters*, ed. Benjamin Taylor (New York: Viking, 2010), 55–57.

14. Ibid.

15. Atlas, *Bellow*, 123.

16. James Atlas, *The Shadow in the Garden: A Biographer's Tale* (New York: Vintage, 2017), 338–39. The quote, taken from her "memoir," is attributed to Bobby Markel, but there is no accessible document cited by Atlas. SB, *Herzog* (New York: Viking, 1964), 90.

17. Leader, *Fame and Fortune*, 318–20.

18. Ibid., 731n46.

19. SB, *Settling My Accounts*, 75.

20. "Suffering for Nothing," *Time*, December 1, 1947.

21. *Partisan Review* 15, no. 2 (1948) 2–8.

22. Martin Greenberg, "Modern Man as Jew," *Commentary*, January 1, 1948.

23. Chiranton Kulshrestha, "A Conversation with Saul Bellow," in *Conversations with Saul Bellow*, ed. Gloria Cronin and Ben Siegel (Jackson: University Press of Mississippi, 1994), 92. From *Chicago Review* 23.4–24.1 (1972): 7–15. See also SB, "Americans Who Are Also Jews," in *There Is Simply Too Much to Think About*, ed. Benjamin Taylor (New York: Viking, 2015), 302–3.

24. Atlas, *Bellow*, 128.

25. SB, with Philip Roth, "'I've Got a Scheme'" in *STM*, 46.

26. SB, *Settling My Accounts*, 99.

27. SB, letter to Bazelon, December 1, 1947, in *Saul Bellow: Letters*, 49.

28. SB, letter to Tumin, April 21, 1948, in *Saul Bellow: Letters,* 55.
29. James Atlas, "Starting Out in Chicago," *Granta,* November 5, 1992.
30. SB, letter to Tumin, April 21, 1948, in *Saul Bellow: Letters,* 55.
31. Ibid.; SB, letter to Bazelon, January 5, 1948, in *Saul Bellow: Letters,* 51.
32. SB, letter to Tumin, n.d., in *Saul Bellow: Letters,* 52–53.
33. SB, letter to Bazelon, January 5, 1948, in *Saul Bellow: Letters,* 51.
34. SB, "I've Got a Scheme: With Philip Roth," in *STM,* 469.
35. SB, "My Paris," in *IAAU,* 231. Originally published as "The Sophisticated Traveler," *NYTM,* pt. 2, March 13, 1983.
36. SB, "I've Got a Scheme," 470.
37. Speech by French president Francois Hollande to commemorate the seventieth anniversary of the *Rafle,* reprinted and translated in *NYRB,* September 27, 2012. The number of Jews deported is in dispute, ranging from forty thousand to seventy-five thousand, but about the survival rate there is no argument. Three-quarters of the Jews of France had survived the war, meaning France had one of the highest Jewish survival rates in Western Europe. Much of this result was a consequence of France's sacrifice (deportation to extermination camps) of its resident foreign Jews. At liberation, with its Jewish population of 180,000 to 200,000 individuals, France became the home to the largest Jewish community in western continental Europe. See several excellent essays in *Post-Holocaust France and the Jews,* ed. Sean Hand and Steven T. Katz (New York: New York University Press, 2015). For France's ahistorical claim to equal victimhood, see Daniella Doron, "Lost Children and Lost Childhoods: Memory in Post-Holocaust France," in Hand and Katz, *Post-Holocaust France,* 85–117.
38. Anita Bellow, letter to Herb and Mitzi McClosky, undated, cited in Leader, *Fame and Fortune,* 739n71.
39. SB, "My Paris," 237.
40. SB, letter to Tarcov, December 5, 1949, in *Saul Bellow: Letters,* 89.
41. SB, "My Paris," 237.
42. SB, *Settling My Accounts,* 42. In the Israeli newspaper *Haaretz* under the headline "Antisemitic Author's Manuscripts, Worth Millions, Are Setting France's Literary Scene on Fire," the following story appeared: "Currently inflaming the French literary world are 6,000 pages in the handwriting of Louis-Ferdinand Céline. This literary treasure . . . appeared suddenly, as though from another world, in June 2020 and is continuing to raise controversy. The trove includes three unknown novels and extensive correspondence between Céline and various well-known personages. The value of the manuscripts is estimated at tens of millions of euros. It is not

surprising that their unexpected discovery has roiled both his admirers and those who hate him." Gaby Levin, *Haaretz*, September 13, 2021.

43. SB, "My Paris," 235–36 (emphasis in original).

44. Ibid.; Rockwell Gray et al., "Interview with Saul Bellow," in *Conversations with Saul Bellow*, 217. From *TriQuarterly* 60 (1984): 12–34.

45. SB, letter to Ozick, July 19, 1987, in *Saul Bellow: Letters*, 437–40.

46. Jonathan Rosen, "The Uncomfortable Question of Anti-Semitism," *NYTM*, November 4, 2001; Jonathan Rosen, "Saul Bellow's Seven Layers," *Forward*, November 16, 1990.

47. SB, *Settling My Accounts*, 43.

48. SB, letter to Gold, December 16, 1997, quoted in Leader, *Fame and Fortune*, 369.

49. Bruce Cook, "Saul Bellow: A Mood of Protest," in *Conversations with Saul Bellow*, 17–18. Originally published in *46-50*.

50. Leader, *Fame and Fortune*, 363.

51. Herbert Gold, *Still Alive! A Temporary Condition: A Memoir* (New York: Arcade, 2008), 204–6.

52. SB, letter to Tarcov, December 5, 1949, in *Saul Bellow: Letters*, 90; SB, "My Paris," 233.

53. *La Storia* (*The History*) is Morante's most famous and controversial work. Published in 1974, it tells the story of a Jewish woman and her two sons in Rome, during and immediately after the Second World War. Morante and her husband were part of Italy's postwar generation of stellar writers—Cesare Pavese, Carlo Levi, Giorgio Bassani, and Natalia Ginzburg. Levi, Bassani, and Ginzburg were Jewish. All were actively anti-Fascist.

54. SB, "I've Got a Scheme," 481.

55. Ibid., 471.

56. Anne Goldman, "In Praise of Saul Bellow," *Michigan Quarterly Review* 47, no. 1 (2008), accessed August 21, 2023, http://hdl.handle.net/2027/spo.act2080.0047.101. Leader, *Fame and Fortune*, 370–71.

57. SB, "I've Got a Scheme," 471–72; SB, "A Second Half Life," in *IAAU*, 318. Originally published in *Bostonia*, January/February 1991. See also Atlas, *Bellow*, 147.

58. SB, "Second Half Life," 318.

59. Leslie Fiedler, "What Can We Do about Fagin?," *Commentary*, May 1, 1949.

60. James Grossman, "The Jewish Writer and the English Literary Tradition: A Symposium—Part II," *Commentary*, October 1, 1949.

61. SB, letter to Oliver Schmidt, June 7, 1996, in Leader, *Fame and Fortune*, 376; Alfred Kazin, *New York Jew* (New York: Alfred A. Knopf, 1978), 168.

62. Bellow wrote in a letter to Robert Hivner, who had been a friend and colleague at the University of Minnesota, saying, "This time I *saw* Rome, Paolo Milano, leading," but he was weary of touring, and "the kid [Greg]," he told Henry Volkening, his literary agent, "has put his ban on churches and won't enter another one. He's now seen St. Peter's, the biggest of them all, and feels he understands the principle." Quoted in Leader, *Fame and Fortune*, 377.

63. The schools contacted included the New School, Queens College, Harvard, Princeton, and Bard. For NYU, see Leader, *Fame and Fortune*, 388.

64. Atlas, *Bellow*, 379.

65. Greg Bellow, *Saul Bellow's Heart: A Son's Memoir* (New York: Bloomsbury, 2013), 67–68; Greg Bellow, "Biographic Sketch," 6–7, quoted in Leader, *Fame and Fortune*, 380.

7. THE ADVENTURES OF SAUL BELLOW

1. Zachary Leader, *The Life of Saul Bellow: To Fame and Fortune, 1915–1964* (New York: Knopf, 2015), 320–21.

2. Wilhelm Reich, *Selected Writings: An Introduction to Orgonomy* (New York: Farrar, Straus and Giroux, 1973), 337 and passim.

3. SB, *Settling My Accounts before I Go Away: A Words and Images Interview by Norman Manea* (Rhinebeck, NY: Sheep Meadow Press, 1999), 82.

4. Alfred Kazin, *New York Jew* (New York: Alfred A. Knopf, 1978), 150.

5. In talking with James Atlas, Bellow tried to play down the seriousness of his participation in Reichianism by calling the therapy a "game." James Atlas, *Bellow: A Biography* (New York: Random House, 2000), 165.

6. Ibid.; SB, "I've Got a Scheme: With Philip Roth," in *There Is Simply Too Much to Think About*, ed. Benjamin Taylor (New York: Viking, 2015), 491; SB, *Settling My Accounts*, 82. For the increasingly problematic relationship between Bellow and Isaac Rosenfeld, see Bellow's letter to Tarcov, June 26, 1950, in *Saul Bellow: Letters*, ed. Benjamin Taylor (New York: Viking, 2010), 104–5; Leader, 388; SB to Tarcov, March 20, 1953, Tarcov Papers, private collection, quoted in Steven J. Zipperstein, *Rosenfeld's Lives* (New Haven, CT: Yale University Press, 2009), 193. Bellow told Tarcov

that he was "tired of being envied or grudged every bit of success" and was annoyed about Isaac's "not too well-hidden hope that I fall on my face." Later, Bellow felt "guilty" over his success with *Augie March*, while Rosenfeld voiced dissatisfaction with the novel. But in the 1950s, Rosenfeld had predicted, "Someday Saul or I will win the Nobel Prize." When Bellow actually won, twenty years after Rosenfeld's death in 1956, he told David Peltz, "It should have been Isaac." David Mikics, *Bellow's People* (New York: W. W. Norton, 2016), 95–106; Zipperstein, *Rosenfeld's Lives*, 2, 225.

7. Leader, *Fame and Fortune*, 319.

8. Ibid., 319–20.

9. SB, handwritten notes for Brandeis commencement speech, 1974, cited in Leader, *Fame and Fortune*, 214, 710n13. Bellow's impression of Anita's rigidity doesn't quite square with her permissive child-raising. Greg was apparently allowed by both parents, in restaurants and at the tables of friends, to do messy tricks with his spaghetti, eat chocolate pudding with his fingers, and at age seven to undress fully and remain in the orgone box for hours on end. Greg Bellow, *Saul Bellow's Heart: A Son's Memoir* (New York: Bloomsbury, 2013), 69.

10. G. Bellow, *Saul Bellow's Heart*, 67–71.

11. Ibid., 72–73.

12. Leader, *Fame and Fortune*, 369–70; Atlas, *Bellow*, 166.

13. Gordon Lloyd Harper, "Saul Bellow: The Art of Fiction," in *The Paris Review Interviews*, vol. 1, with an introduction by Philip Gourevich (New York: Picador, 2006), 93.

14. SB, *Settling My Accounts*, 81–82.

15. Leader, *Fame and Fortune*, 320.

16. Harper, "Art of Fiction," 104.

17. G. Bellow, *Saul Bellow's Heart*, 73.

18. Harper, "Art of Fiction," 93.

19. Ibid.

20. SB, "Man Underground," *Commentary*, June 1952, 608–10.

21. Ibid.

22. Ralph Ellison, *Invisible Man* (New York: Random House, 1952), Kindle loc. 62.

23. Ibid., loc. 9408.

24. SB, "Man Underground," 608.

25. Ibid., 609. Emerson wrote, "Voices which we hear in solitude . . . grow faint and inaudible as we enter into the world. Society everywhere is in a conspiracy against the manhood of every one of its members," in "Self-Reliance" (1841).

26. Irving Howe, "Ralph Ellison's *Invisible Man*," *Nation*, May 10, 1952. Howe thought this assertion of absolute individuality vapid and naively ignorant of the social barriers to freedom, especially for a person born Black in America. See Gerald Sorin, *Irving Howe: A Life of Passionate Dissent* (New York: New York University Press, 2002), 191–94.

27. SB, "Man Underground," 609.

28. G. Bellow, *Saul Bellow's Heart*, 69.

29. In an essay written in 1963, Ellison said, "Speaking personally both as a writer and as a Negro American, I would like to see the more positive distinctions between whites and Jewish Americans maintained." The essay, "The World and the Jug," appears in Ralph Ellison, *Shadow and Act* (New York: Vintage 1972), 109–141.

30. Mikics, *Bellow's People*, 79; wcd2, "Housemates: Ralph Ellison, Saul Bellow, John Hersey," American Literature in the World, September 11, 2013, http://amlitintheworld.yale.edu/2013/09/11/housemates-ralph-ellison-saul-bellow-john-hersey/.

31. SB, "Ralph Ellison in Tivoli," in SB, *STM*, 417.

32. Ralph Ellison, "The World and the Jug," in *The Collected Essays of Ralph Ellison: Revised and Updated*, ed. John Callahan, preface by Saul Bellow (New York: Modern Library, 2003), 155. Originally published 1994 by Random House (New York).

33. SB, "Looking for Mr. Green," in *Mosby's Memoirs and Other Stories* (New York: Penguin Books, 1996), 85. Originally published in *Commentary*, March 1951.

34. Ralph Ellison, "Twentieth Century Fiction and the Black Mask of Humanity," in *Collected Essays*, 97.

35. Ralph Ellison, "Introduction," in *Collected Essays*, 56; Mikics, *Bellow's People*, 89.

36. SB, *Humboldt's Gift*, with an introduction by Jeffrey Eugenides (New York: Penguin Books. 1975), 10.

37. Ibid., 125.

38. Leader, *Fame and Fortune*, 402.

39. SB's eulogy for Malamud, read by Howard Nemerov in Bellow's absence, reprinted in *Saul Bellow: Letters*, 435.

40. SB, "A Second Half Life," in *It All Adds Up: From the Dim Past to an Uncertain Future* (New York: Viking, 1994), 315. Originally published in *Bostonia*, January/February 1991.

41. Leader, *Fame and Fortune*, 748n60.

42. Baker, quoted in Atlas, *Bellow*, 179.

43. SB, "Second Half Life," 316.

44. Irving Howe, *A Margin of Hope: An Intellectual Autobiography* (New York: Harcourt Brace Jovanovich, 1982), 164.

45. Ibid.

46. Eileen Simpson, *Poets in Their Youth* (New York: Vintage, 1983), 219–22.

47. Stanley Burnshaw, quoted in Atlas, *Bellow*, 175; the remark about "sex appeal" is from p. 139 of an unfinished memoir by Lillian Blumberg McCall found by Zachary Leader among Bellow's papers at the Regenstein Library. Leader, *Fame and Fortune*, 420–21.

48. Sondra Tschacbasov, "What's in a Name?," unpublished memoir, cited in Leader, *Fame and Fortune*, 418–23, 750n95 (manuscript in possession of Zachary Leader).

49. Ibid.

50. Ibid.

51. SB, "A Jewish Writer in America," *NYRB*, October 27, 2011. At the turn of the century, Henry James worried about the appalling impact that the abrasive, urban tenors of immigrant voices would have on American speech. E. A. Ross, in his nativist attack on immigration, *The Old World in the New*, wrote specifically of "the Jewish invader": "What is disliked in the Jews," Ross argued, is not their religion but "certain ways and manners." As a result of a "tribal spirit intensified by social isolation" in Europe, "they use their old-world shove and wile and lie in a society like ours. . . . They rapidly push up into a position of prosperous parasitism, leaving scorn and curses in their wake." E. A. Ross, *The Old World in the New: The Significance of Past and Present Immigration to the American People* (New York: Century, 1914), 164, 154.

52. Harper, "Art of Fiction," 93.

53. SB, *The Adventures of Augie March*, in *Saul Bellow's Novels, 1944–53* (New York: Library of America, 2003), 876, 918, 995.

54. SB, "Jewish Writer in America."

55. SB, *Augie March*, 393.

56. Karl Shapiro, *The Younger Son* (Chapel Hill, NC: Algonquin Books, 1988).

57. SB, *Augie March*, 750, 587, 682. That Bellow had been nurturing this new language was evident in several short pieces of fiction in 1949. After the publication of *The Victim* (1947), his stories are marked by juxtapositions of the ascendant and the down and dirty, as well as by sentences containing high and low images—hamburgers and Hippocrates, for example. See "Dora," *Harper's Bazaar*, November 1949; "A Sermon by Dr. Pep," *Partisan Review*, May 1949.

58. Atlas, *Bellow*, 192; SB, *Augie March*, 634.

59. Mikics, *Bellow's People*, 49–50.

60. Irving Howe, "Strangers," *Dissent*, June 1, 1977. Originally published in *A Voice Still Heard: Selected Essays of Irving Howe*, ed. Nina Howe (New Haven, CT: Yale University Press, 1977).

61. Rosenfeld, Bellow's high school friend and writing partner, wrote, among many other things, the novel *Passage from Home* (1946), which, according to literary critic Mark Shechner, "helped fashion a uniquely American voice by marrying the incisiveness of Mark Twain to the Russian melancholy of Dostoevsky." Schechner, *Haaretz*, May 17, 2009. Tarcov, for all kinds of reasons, got around to writing only one novel, *Bravo, My Monster* (1953)—with a Kafkaesque theme and mood.

62. SB, *Augie March*, 447.

63. Ibid., 632.

64. Ibid., 383.

65. Howe, *Margin of Hope*, 261–65; Sorin, *Irving Howe*, 131–32.

66. Mikics, *Bellow's People*, 29. Bellow later explained what he thought he might have contributed to the work and what he learned from it: "What was perhaps lacking in my own work back in the early 50s was a full and satisfactory immersion in Eastern European subject matter; what was necessary in translating Gimpel was a rich and complex English style. Singer had the one and I had the other." Letter to Janet Hadda, July 12, 1995, cited in Leader, *Fame and Fortune*, 446.

67. SB, "Laughter in the Ghetto," *Saturday Review of Literature*, May 1953, 30.

68. Ibid.; SB, *Augie March*, 689.

69. SB, "Laughter in the Ghetto."

70. Ibid.

71. SB, *Augie March*, 759–60. Nearly all of Bellow's protagonists say something contemptuous about Rousseau, Romanticism, and the love of "nothingness"—contrary to principles of Judaism.

72. Steven M. Gerson, "The New American Adam in 'The Adventures of Augie March,'" *Modern Fiction Studies* 25, no. 1 (1979): 117–28. The term *Reality Instructor* is used in *Herzog* by the eponymous protagonist to describe those who seek "to teach" and "to punish" Moses Herzog with "lessons of the Real," but it also applies to the cynics in *The Adventures of Augie March* who want to rid Augie of his implacable optimism.

73. SB, *Augie March*, 439, 390.

74. Ibid., 390.

75. Ibid., 423.

76. Ibid., 411–12.

77. In a lengthy appreciation of the book, novelist Martin Amis said that *Augie March* often "resembles a surrealist catalogue of apprenticeships. During the course of the novel, Augie becomes (in order) a handbill distributor, a paper boy, a dime-store packer, a news vendor, a Christmas extra in a toy department, a flower deliverer, a butler, a shoe salesman, a saddle shop floor walker, a hawker of rubberized paint, a dog washer, a book swiper, a coal-yard helper, a housing surveyor, a union organizer, an animal trainer, a gambler, a literary researcher, a salesman of business machines, a sailor, and middleman for a war profiteer. As late as a third of the way into the novel, Augie is still poring over magazines in search of vocational hints." Martin Amis, "A Chicago of a Novel," *Atlantic Monthly,* October 1995, 114–27.

78. SB, *Augie March,* 592.

79. Ibid., 515.

80. Ibid., 430.

81. Ibid.

82. Ibid., 657.

83. Ibid., 622.

84. Ibid., 516.

85. Ibid., 622.

86. Ibid., 710.

87. SB, letter to Edith Tarcov, n.d., in *Saul Bellow: Letters,* 126–27.

88. SB, letter to Bernard Malamud, 1953, in *Saul Bellow: Letters,* 128–29.

89. SB, *Augie March,* 929.

90. Ibid., 937.

91. Ibid.

92. Ibid., 843.

93. Ibid., 903.

94. Ibid., 905.

95. *Animal ridens* (Latin) means literally "animal laugh or spirit." Here Augie and Bellow are using the phrase to define someone who "will refuse to lead a disappointed life." *Augie March,* 994–95.

96. SB, *Augie March,* 995.

97. Unsigned essay last page of *New Yorker,* October 6, 2003.

8. FATHERS AND SONS

1. Ralph Ellison, *Invisible Man* (New York: Random House, 1962), 572, loc. 62, Kindle; Ralph Ellison, *The Collected Essays of Ralph Ellison,* ed.

John F. Callahan, with an introduction by Saul Bellow (New York: Random House, 1995), 710–14.

2. Daniel Bell, Irving Howe, Norman Mailer, et al, "Our Country and Our Culture," *Partisan Review*, May/June 1952, 287–310; C. Wright Mills, Delmore Schwartz, Richard Chase, et al, *Partisan Review*, September/October 1952, 576–80. *Partisan* editors William Phillips and Philip Rahv solicited written responses from a large number of New York intellectuals to several questions like "To what extent have American intellectuals . . . changed their attitude toward America and its institutions?" The questions and the very pronouns of the title of the symposium suggested that affirmations of America were in order—as did the editorial statement that "the American artist and intellectual no longer feels 'disinherited'. . . . Most writers no longer accept alienation as the artist's fate in America." As expected, the answers were mostly positive, though with some demurrers; and there were strenuous protests by Irving Howe and Norman Mailer. It appears that Saul Bellow, not yet having published *Augie March*, had not been invited to participate. The phrase "Marxist deconversion" is borrowed from Mark Shechner, who coined it in *After the Revolution*.

3. Rockwell Gray, "Interview with Saul Bellow," *TriQuarterly* 63 (1985): 647.

4. SB, *The Adventures of Augie March* (New York: Library of America, 2002), 414; Matthew C. Roudane, "An Interview with Saul Bellow," *Contemporary Literature* 25, no. 3 (1984): 265–80.

5. SB, letter to Lionel Trilling, October 11, 1953, in *Saul Bellow: Letters*, ed. Benjamin Taylor (New York: Viking, 2010), 121–23.

6. SB, letter to Edith Tarcov, n.d., in *Saul Bellow: Letters*, 126–27.

7. SB, letter to Sam Freifeld, November 30, 1953, in *Saul Bellow: Letters*, 127.

8. SB, letter to Edith Tarcov, n.d., in *Saul Bellow: Letters*, 126–27.

9. Judd L. Teller, "From Yiddish to Neo-Brahmin," *Strangers and Natives: The Evolution of the American Jew from 1921 to the Present* (New York: Delacorte, 1968), 266.

10. SB, *Augie March*, 441; SB, *Dangling Man* (New York: Signet, 1965), 97. After Mel Tumin's qualified praise of the page proofs, the close relationship between him and Bellow grew chilly. The friendship became warmer in the 1960s but never regained the intimacy of their earlier connection.

11. "Saul Bellow/Philip Roth Interview," typescript, quoted in Zachary Leader, *The Life of Saul Bellow: To Fame and Fortune, 1915–1964* (New York: Alfred A. Knopf, 2015), 115. Roth's claim about a "new voice . . . exclusively Bellow's" needs some qualification. Bellow had no "anxiety of influence"—a

phrase coined by Henry James—and named Balzac, Dickens, Dos Passos, Farrell, Dreiser, James Joyce, and a host of others who had in one way or another "influenced" him. One could add the Jewish writers Daniel Fuchs, Meyer Levin, Samuel Ornitz, Nathaniel West, Henry Roth, and others who since the 1930s had made the patterns of Jewish speech, childhood and adolescence, and the aromas and tastes of the Jewish kitchen familiar to readers of American novels These writers used partly conscious Yiddish idiom and gave readers echoes of the American patois of the street. Bellow sharpened the discourse with a clearer immigrant syntax and a new ironic boisterousness.

12. Philip Roth, "Influences? Saul Bellow and Augie March," Web of Stories, accessed March 16, 2016, https://www.webofstories.com/play/philip.roth/68.

13. Christopher Hitchens, "Introduction," in *The Adventures of Augie March*, by SB (New York: Penguin Books, 2001), viii.

14. Lionel Trilling in "Under Forty: A Symposium on American Literature and the Younger Generation of American Jews," *Contemporary Jewish Record*, February 1944, 16–17.

15. Irving Howe, letter to Edward Alexander, June 2, 1983, quoted in Alexander, *Irving Howe and Secular Jewishness* (Cincinnati: University of Cincinnati, 1995), 2.

16. Trilling in "Under Forty," 16–17.

17. "I've Got a Scheme! The Words of Saul Bellow," *New Yorker*, April 25, 2005; "Saul Bellow/Philip Roth Interview," quoted in Leader, *Fame and Fortune*, 116–18, 154, 225, 227, 230, 336, 413, 431, 679n1. In contexts other than face-to-face with Roth, Bellow had mostly positive things to say about Malamud. And in his eulogy for him, Bellow said, "Malamud in his novels and stories discovered a sort of communicative genius in the impoverished, harsh jargon of immigrant New York. He was a myth maker, a fabulist, a writer of exquisite parables. . . . He is a rich original of the first rank." Reprinted in *Saul Bellow: Letters*, 435–36.

18. SB, *Humboldt's Gift* (New York: Penguin Books, 1984), 360; "Saul Bellow/Philip Roth Interview." Bellow's fascination with Maury can be measured by how many times his eldest brother's type figures as an important character in his fiction, notwithstanding differences in each portrayal—Simon in *Augie*, Shura in *Herzog*, Philip in "Him with His Foot in His Mouth," and Julius in *Humboldt's Gift*.

19. "Saul Bellow/Philip Roth Interview.'"

20. SB, *Settling My Accounts before I Go Away: A Words and Images Interview by Norman Manea* (Rhinebeck, NY: Sheep Meadow Press, 1999),

36–37; "Saul Bellow/Philip Roth Interview"; SB, "A Half Life: An Interview with Keith Botsford, in SB, *It All Adds Up: From the Dim Past to an Uncertain Future* (New York: Penguin Group, 1994), 293. Later, toward his own family, including his wife and children, Maury was heartless and ruthless, ultimately cutting everyone off completely.

21. "Saul Bellow," in *50 Years of Playboy Interviews: Men of Letters* (New York: Playboy Enterprises, 1997), locs. 6908–11 of 8907, Kindle.

22. SB, "I've Got a Scheme," in *There Is Simply Too Much to Think About*, ed. Benjamin Taylor (New York: Viking, 2015), 469.

23. Ibid.

24. Philip Roth, "Introduction" to *Herzog*, by SB (New York: Penguin Classics, 2001), xi–xii.

25. "Saul Bellow," in *50 Years of Playboy Interviews*, loc. 6911; Roth, "Introduction," xi.

26. SB, *Augie March*, 995; Roth, "Introduction," xii–xiii.

27. The more than a dozen others included Irwin Shaw, Meyer Levin, Budd Schulberg, Stanley Elkins, and Bruce Jay Friedman. Norman Mailer's *The Naked and the Dead* (1948) included two prominent Jewish characters preceding Bellow's *Augie March* (1953).

28. Pearl K. Bell, "New Jewish Voices," *Commentary*, June 1981, 62.

29. Leslie Fiedler, *To the Gentiles* (New York: Stein and Day, 1972), 103–10.

30. SB, *Saul Bellow: Letters*, xxiv.

31. SB, letter to Sam Freifeld, October 19, 1953, in *Saul Bellow: Letters*, 123.

32. Leader, *Fame and Fortune*, 50.

33. SB, "A Second Half Life," in *IAAU*, 320.

34. Draft version of Botsford's memoir, *Fragments*, 2–3, in Leader, *Fame and Fortune*, 459, 758n7.

35. Ibid.; Leader, *Fame and Fortune*, 468–69.

36. SB, letter to John Berryman, n.d., 1954, in *Saul Bellow: Letters*, 112; SB, letter to Freifeld, April 25, 1954, in *Letters*, 132–33; SB, letter to Oscar Tarcov, *Saul Bellow: Letters*, 131.

37. SB, letter to Freifeld, April 25, 1954, in *Saul Bellow: Letters*, 132–33.

38. Gregory Bellow, *Saul Bellow's Heart* (New York: Bloomsbury, 2013), 73; Gordon Lloyd Harper, "Saul Bellow: The Art of Fiction," in *The Paris Review Interviews*, vol. 1, with an introduction by Philip Gourevich (New York: Picador, 2006), 93. Originally published in *Paris Review*, 1966, 36.

39. SB, letter to Herb McClosky, 1954, quoted in Leader, *Fame and Fortune*, 475; SB, letter to Ted Weiss, n.d., 1954, in *Saul Bellow: Letters*, 133–34.

40. G. Bellow, *Saul Bellow's Heart*, 72.

41. SB, *Herzog*, with an introduction by Philip Roth (New York: Penguin Classics, 2001), 265.

42. SB, letter to Mark Harris, n.d., in *Saul Bellow: Letters*, 205.

43. Ruth Miller, *Saul Bellow: A Biography of the Imagination* (New York: St. Martin's, 1991), 296–97.

44. SB, *Settling My Accounts*, 33.

45. SB, *Herzog*, 305.

46. SB, letter to Martin Amis, March 16, 1996, in *Saul Bellow: Letters*, 516–17 (emphasis in original).

47. SB, quoted in James Atlas, *Bellow: A Biography* (New York: Random House, 2000), 220.

48. Atlas, *Bellow*, 43–44.

49. SB, "I've Got a Scheme," 489.

50. SB, letter to John Berryman, quoted in Leader, *Fame and Fortune*, 506.

51. Henry Roth's *Call It Sleep* (1934), Isaac Rosenfeld's *Passage from Home* (1946)—hailed by Diana Trilling as "the fullest articulation of generational conflict between Jewish fathers and sons"—and Philip Roth's *Letting Go* (1962) are other good examples of novels centered on difficulties between generations. And for a vivid exploration of a troubled relationship between father and daughter, Anzia Yezierska's classic novel *The Breadwinners* (1925) is essential.

52. Donald Weber, "Manners and Morals, Civility and Barbarism: The Cultural Contexts of *Seize the Day*," in *New Essays on Seize the Day*, ed. Michael P. Kramer (Cambridge: Cambridge University Press, 1998), 43–70.

53. SB, *Seize the Day*, with an introduction by Alfred Kazin (New York: Fawcett Books, 1956), 33, 15.

54. Ibid., 27.

55. Ibid., 55.

56. Ibid., 55–56.

57. Ibid., 30.

58. Ibid., 18.

59. SB, "The Distracted Public," in *IAAU*, 168.

60. SB, *Seize the Day*, 118–20.

61. Ibid., 36.

62. Ibid., 92.

63. Ibid., 92–93.

64. Irving Howe, "Introduction to *Seize the Day*," in *Classics of Modern Fiction*, ed. Irving Howe (New York: Harcourt Brace, 1968), 516.

65. Ibid., 70.
66. Ibid., 8.
67. SB, "The Writer as Moralist," *Atlantic Monthly*, March 1963, 62.
68. SB, *Seize the Day*, 79.
69. Ibid.
70. Leon Wieseltier, "Saul Bellow's Ferocious Beliefs," *New Republic*, June 10, 2014.
71. Teller, "From Yiddish to Neo-Brahmin," 266. The Yiddish writers included Sholem Aleichem, I. L. Peretz, and Isaac Bashevis Singer. The American Jewish novelists included Herbert Gold, Grace Paley, and Bruce Jay Friedman.
72. Clifford Geertz, "'Thick Description': Toward an Interpretive Theory of Culture," in *Interpretation of Cultures: Selected Essays* (New York: Basic Books, 1973).
73. SB, *Seize the Day*, 94.
74. Ibid., 88, 94.
75. "Father, why hast thou forsaken me?" Nine syllables in each aphorism. The phrase may also reflect Job's questions of God.
76. Michael P. Kramer, "The Vanishing Jew: On Teaching Seize the Day as Ethnic Fiction," in *New Essays on Seize the Day*, ed. Michael P. Kramer (Oxford: Cambridge University Press, 1998), 1–24. Beginning with the 1974 edition of *Seize*, the Star of David doesn't appear in the book again until 2007 in the Library of America edition.
77. Miller, *Saul Bellow*, 39–43.
78. Alfred Kazin, "Introduction" to SB, *Seize the Day*, xviii.
79. Brendan Gill, "Long and Short," *New Yorker*, January 5, 1957, 66, 69–70; Leader, *Fame and Fortune*, 512, 767n63.
80. Daniel and Pearl Bell, quite close with Bellow at the time that he was writing *Seize*, believed that the last pages of the novel were rewritten with Rosenfeld's tragedy in mind. Interview with Daniel and Pearl Bell, October 30, 1998. Several decades later, Bellow wrote to George Sarant, Rosenfeld's son, saying that Isaac was "an extraordinarily gifted man" but that life in Greenwich Village, as Rosenfeld "interpreted it, was his undoing. . . . His liberation degenerated into personal anarchy." SB, letter to George Sarant, September 9, 1990, in *Saul Bellow: Letters*, 472–73. But see Steven Zipperstein, *Rosenfeld's Lives: Fame, Oblivion, and the Furies of Writing* (New Haven, CT: Yale University Press, 2009), especially 206, 234, for a more optimistic interpretation of Rosenfeld. When he died of a heart attack at the age of thirty-eight, Isaac was not down and out or living in squalor but writing, teaching, and living with a girlfriend in a "new, airy, Chicago apartment."

81. SB, letter to Ralph Ellison, May 27, 1957, in *Saul Bellow: Letters,* 160. "I congratulated myself with being able to deal with New York," Bellow told Philip Roth near the end of his life, "but I never won any of my struggles there, and I never responded with full human warmth to anything that happened there." SB, "I've Got a Scheme," 490.

82. SB, *Seize the Day,* 62.

83. Ibid.

84. SB, letter to Berryman, November 26, 1956, quoted in Leader, *Fame and Fortune,* 506.

85. Ibid.

86. SB, *Seize the Day,* 94.

9. HUSBANDS AND WIVES

1. SB, "I've Got a Scheme: With Philip Roth," in *There Is Simply Too Much to Think About,* ed. Benjamin Taylor (New York: Viking, 2015), 490.

2. SB, letter to Pat Covici, November 1, 1955, in *Saul Bellow: Letters,* ed. Benjamin Taylor (New York: Viking, 2010), 140.

3. Sondra Tschacbasov, "What's in a Name?," unpublished memoir, cited in Zachary Leader, *The Life of Saul Bellow: To Fame and Fortune, 1915–1964* (New York: Knopf, 2015), 418–23, 750n95. All of Tschacbasov's quotations and paraphrased statements are from "What's in a Name?" unless otherwise indicated.

4. SB, letter to Ruth Miller, n.d., 1956, in *Saul Bellow: Letters,* 145–46.

5. SB, *To Jerusalem and Back: A Personal Account* (New York: Viking, 1976), 71–72.

6. James Atlas, *Bellow: A Biography* (New York: Random House, 2000), 242; Leader, *Fame and Fortune,* 495. Sasha says nothing of Maury's recent problems, which had made the news. Maury and his wife, Marge, now owned and managed the Shoreland Hotel, in which the head of the Teamsters Union, Jimmy Hoffa, had an interest. Whenever Hoffa or his enforcers were in Chicago, they stayed at the hotel. In November 1956, Maury confronted a Teamster enforcer, Robert "Barney" Baker, to complain that his unpaid bill was too high (it included cash advances of $1,200). A brutal wrestling match followed, which was reported in the press.

7. SB, *Herzog,* with an introduction by Philip Roth (New York: Penguin Classics, 2001), 132.

8. Ibid., 132.

9. Leader, *Fame and Fortune,* 501–2.

10. SB, letter to Faulkner, January 7, 1957, in *Saul Bellow: Letters,* 144. Bellow's opinion on Pound's incarceration was the same as his friend Karl Shapiro's in an earlier Pound controversy. Shapiro, the only Jew on the 1949 Bollingen Prize Jury, was the one judge who voted against awarding the prize to Pound for *Pisan Cantos.* When he began writing in the late 1930s, a friend advised Shapiro to choose a non-Jewish pen name because, as he put it, no prestigious poetry magazine would publish somebody with the name Shapiro. No surprise here. The 1948 edition of "The Literary History of the United States"—more than a thousand pages long—did not include any Jewish American names. Shapiro helped change that.

11. Leader, *Fame and Fortune,* 513.

12. SB, letter to Ellison, May 27, 1957, in *Saul Bellow: Letters,* 169.

13. SB, "Literature," in *The Great Ideas Today,* ed. W. Benton (Chicago: Encyclopedia Britannica, 1963), 164–71.

14. SB, *Settling My Accounts before I Go Away: A Words and Images Interview by Norman Manea* (Rhinebeck, NY: Sheep Meadow Press, 1999), 96. The interview was taped at Boston University, December 22–23, 1999.

15. SB, ed., *Great Jewish Short Stories* (New York: Laurel, 1963), 12 (emphasis in original).

16. Sigmund Koch, "Interview of Saul Bellow" (Geddes Language Center at Boston University, Boston, 1987), in Leader, *Fame and Fortune,* 58.

17. SB, *Herzog,* 66. Tikhon Zadonsky was a Russian Orthodox bishop and spiritual writer who was glorified (canonized) in the eighteenth century as saint of the Orthodox Church. Vladimir the Great was grand prince of Kiev (Kyiv) and ruler of Kievan Rus' from 980 to 1015.

18. Ibid., 47 (emphasis in original). See also SB, *Settling My Accounts,* 96.

19. Tschacbasov, "What's in a Name?," 100.

20. Weiss, quoted in Atlas, *Bellow,* 258.

21. Gregory Bellow, *Saul Bellow's Heart* (New York: Bloomsbury, 2013), 93–109.

22. SB, "I've Got a Scheme," 494.

23. SB, "Ralph Ellison in Tivoli," in *STM,* 417.

24. Ralph Ross, quoted in Atlas, *Bellow,* 263.

25. SB, letter to Josephine Herbst, February 19, 1959, quoted in Leader, *Fame and Fortune,* 553.

26. In April, Bellow wrote to Covici about sales: "You said it wouldn't sell a hundred and fifty thousand copies. Of course not. But forty? Thirty? Even thirty would be very good. It would pay the mortgage at Tivoli." SB, letter to Covici, April 6, 1959, in *Saul Bellow: Letters,* 172. But *Henderson* failed even to earn back Bellow's advance of $15,000. It lasted only three

weeks on the bestseller list, achieving respectable sales, perhaps twenty thousand copies, "but hardly a commercial triumph." Atlas, *Bellow,* 268, 276.

27. "Henderson is not a Jew," Bellow protests, "but he has been accused by some of being a sort of convert. But that's false, that's simply not the case." Chiranton Kulshrestha, "A Conversation with Saul Bellow," in *Conversations with Saul Bellow,* ed. Gloria Cronin and Ben Siegel (Jackson: University Press of Mississippi, 1984), 90. Originally published in *Chicago Review,* spring/summer 1972.

28. SB, "I've Got a Scheme," 493. Elizabeth Hardwick agreed that the subject was America; in a hostile review, she said that Henderson "is not a 'character' . . . he is an 'American.'" She also argued that the novel "cannot be understood except symbolically," and then only thinly. *Partisan Review,* spring 1959, 300. Even Philip Roth called Henderson an allegory, but uninterpretable.

29. SB, *Henderson the Rain King,* with an introduction by Adam Kirsch (New York: Penguin Classics, 2012), 120, 82. Originally published 1959 by Viking (New York).

30. Nina Steers, "Successor to Faulkner?," in *Conversations with Saul Bellow,* 34. Originally published in *Show,* September 1964, 36–38. See also Ruth Miller, *Saul Bellow: A Biography of the Imagination* (New York: St Martin's, 1991), 122.

31. SB, *Henderson,* 22.

32. Steers, "Successor to Faulkner?," 34; Miller, *Saul Bellow,* 122. "I want, I want," is from William Blake's book of engravings, *For Children: The Gates of Paradise* (1793), and expresses a need for a reawakening into spiritual well-being.

33. Alfred Kazin, "The Earthly City of the Jews: From Bellow to Singer," in *Bright Book of Life: American Novelists and Storytellers from Hemingway to Mailer* (Boston: Little, Brown, 1973), 127–28.

34. Steers, "Successor to Faulkner?," 34; SB, letter to Richard Stern, in Atlas, *Bellow,* 314.

35. Adam Kirsch, "Introduction" to SB, *Henderson,* xi.

36. SB, *Henderson,* 1. The model for Henderson, it is generally agreed, was Chanler Chapman, who owned the garage apartment Bellow rented when he was teaching at Bard. Chapman was a big, gruff, and (according to his cousin and neighbor, Wint Aldrich) extremely "difficult man . . . albeit cultivated." Although Bellow could be characterized in the same way, the two shared "an unhappy landlord/tenant relationship." In any case,

Chapman denied that he was the inspiration for Henderson. But when the *Rain King* was singled out by the Nobel Committee, Chapman, according to his cousin, "was heard to say, 'the S.O.B. could not have won the Nobel without him.'" Letter, Wint Aldrich to author, October 7, 2020.

37. SB, *Henderson*, 28.

38. Ibid., 76.

39. Ibid., 45.

40. Ibid., 44.

41. Bellow was open about his sources: "During the Depression I wasn't having much luck with sorority girls, so I spent two years in library stacks reading missionary accounts of life in Africa. After a while it all melted into a growing lump and became *Henderson the Rain King*. Herskovits . . . had his nose put out of joint by it. . . . He claimed it was a serious subject that I was making light of, but other specialists have told me it was an accurate account." Eusebio L. Rodrigues in "Bellow's Africa," a study of *Henderson*'s sources, tries with some success to demonstrate the inventiveness of *Henderson* as well as its indebtedness to anthropology by providing significant evidence of "Bellow's genius for transmuting bare facts into vivid dramatic event." *American Literature* 43, no. 2 (1971): 242–56. See also Sheila Fischman, "Saul Wanders the Streets of Montreal," *Montreal Star*, May 3, 1976.

42. Catherine Fitzpatrick, "John Berryman and Saul Bellow: Literary Friendship and Mutual Influence" (PhD diss., University of Sheffield, 2011), 47, quoted in Leader, *Fame and Fortune*, 520. Bellow used a language he developed together with John Berryman, his colleague and officemate at the University of Minnesota. Berryman used the language in "Mr. Bones" in *The Dream Songs* (1964). The controversial language continues to be subject to debate. See Francine Prose, "What's It Like Reading Saul Bellow's 'Henderson the Rain King' Today?," *NYT*, April 28, 2015.

43. SB, *Henderson*, 46.

44. Ibid., 132.

45. At Northwestern, Bellow was immersed in reading and study under Melville J. Herskovits, the author of important studies of the cattle cultures of Africa and the kingdom of Dahomey. "The Cattle Complex in East Africa," PhD diss., Columbia University, 1923 (published as a book in 1926).

46. SB, *Henderson*, 56.

47. Ibid.

48. Ibid., 58.

49. Ibid., 77.

50. Ibid., 30.

51. SB, *Settling My Accounts,* 72; SB, *Humboldt's Gift,* with an introduction by Jeffery Eugenides (New York: Penguin Classics, 1975), 266.

52. "Saul Bellow," in *50 Years of Playboy Interviews: Men of Letters* (New York: Playboy Enterprises, 1997), loc. 7045 of 8095, Kindle.

53. SB, *Settling My Accounts,* 94.

54. SB, *Henderson,* 96.

55. Matthew C. Roudané and Saul Bellow, "An Interview with Saul Bellow," *Contemporary Literature* 25, no. 3 (1984): 265–80.

56. Ibid.

57. SB, *Henderson,* 262.

58. SB, *The Adventures of Augie March,* in *Saul Bellow's Novels, 1944–53* (New York: Library of America, 2003), 876, 918, 937; SB, *Henderson,* 275.

59. SB, *Henderson.,* 251.

60. On the eve of the publication of *Henderson,* Bellow wrote a piece titled "Deep Readers, Beware" for the *New York Times,* which argued that the search for symbols in literature misses all the fun and fact of the story. Bellow was wary of "serious" interpretations of books that concentrated on what this or that meant and failed to connect in any way with creatures of flesh and bone.

61. SB, *Settling My Accounts,* 81–82.

62. SB, *Henderson,* 297, 220.

63. Ibid., 168, 244.

64. William Deresiewicz, "The Whole Human Mess: On Saul Bellow," *Nation,* November 23, 2010.

65. SB, *Henderson,* 160.

66. SB, letter to John Berryman, February 19, 1958, in *Saul Bellow: Letters,* 163.

67. SB, *Saul Bellow: Letters,* 180–83.

68. SB, letter to Richard Stern, November 3, 1959, in *Saul Bellow: Letters,* 182.

69. SB, letter to Harvey Swados, February 13, 1960, cited in Leader, *Fame and Fortune,* 570.

70. SB, letter to Tarcov, January 13, 1960, cited in Leader, *Fame and Fortune,* 571.

71. SB, letter to Mimi Sheraton, August 18, 1993, cited in Leader, *Fame and Fortune,* 572.

72. SB, *Settling My Accounts,* 62.

73. Atlas, *Bellow,* 287.

74. SB, *TJAB*, 129; Leader, *Fame and Fortune*, 574.

75. SB, "Introduction" to *Great Jewish Short Stories*, 14–16. See also SB, "A Jewish Writer in America," *NYRB*, October 27, 2011.

76. SB, "Introduction" to *Great Jewish Short Stories*, 14–16.

77. Leslie Fiedler, "On the Road: Or the Adventures of Karl Shapiro," *Poetry* 96 (1960), 171–182; SB, letter to Fiedler, June 4, 1960, in *Saul Bellow: Letters*, 197.

78. SB, letter to Covici, March 4, 1960, in *Saul Bellow: Letters*, 192; Leader, *Fame and Fortune*, 573.

79. SB, letter to Marshall Best, March 16, 1960, in *Saul Bellow: Letters*, 193.

80. SB, "Introduction" to *Great Jewish Short Stories*, 16.

81. George Weidenfeld, quoted in Leader, *Fame and Fortune*, 574.

82. Ibid., 575–76.

10. FRIENDSHIPS AND BETRAYALS

1. SB, letter to Ross, October [?], 1960, quoted in Zachary Leader, *The Life of Saul Bellow: To Fame and Fortune, 1915–1964* (New York: Knopf, 2015), 578.

2. James Atlas, *Bellow: A Biography* (New York: Random House, 2000), 296.

3. SB, "Ralph Ellison in Tivoli," in *There Is Simply Too Much to Think About*, ed. Benjamin Taylor (New York: Viking, 2015), 417.

4. Ibid., 418.

5. Ibid.

6. SB, *Settling My Accounts before I Go Away: A Words and Images Interview by Norman Manea* (Rhinebeck, NY: Sheep Meadow Press, 1999), 96.

7. SB, "Ralph Ellison in Tivoli," 419.

8. Ibid.

9. SB, "Preface," in *The Collected Essays of Ralph Ellison: Revised and Updated*, ed. John F. Callahan (New York: Modern Library, 2003). All the quotations concerning Ellison that follow in this Tivoli section are from the above source.

10. Atlas, *Bellow*, on Roth, 254. Leo Rosten, writing in *The Joys of Yiddish*, points out that the singular of *tsuris* is *tsorah* or *tsureh*. But those words are rarely if ever used by Jews. Rabbi Sharon Kleinbaum, a longtime student of Yiddish and a former assistant director of the National Yiddish Book Center, agrees. What is interesting, she says, is that *tsuris*, the

Yiddish word for "troubles," simply has no singular; "Jews don't do trouble in the singular. It has to be in the plural." Eileen Lavine, "Nobody Knows the Tsuris I've Seen . . . ," *Moment*, December 31, 2012, https://momentmag.com/jewish-word-tsuris/.

11. Atlas, *Bellow*, 305; Leader, *Fame and Fortune*, 586.

12. Contributors to the magazine included many accomplished and admired writers—for example, Ralph Ellison, Arthur Miller, John Berryman, Cynthia Ozick, Jules Feiffer, Thomas Berger, and Thomas Pynchon.

13. SB, letter to Jack Ludwig, February [?] 1961, in *Saul Bellow: Letters*, ed. Benjamin Taylor (New York: Viking, 2010), 210–12.

14. Leader, *Fame and Fortune*, 586.

15. SB, letter to Ralph Ross, March 22, 1977, in *Saul Bellow: Letters*, 347–48.

16. SB, letter to Jack Ludwig, in *Saul Bellow: Letters*, 210–12.

17. Atlas, *Bellow*, 548.

18. David Laskin, *Partisans: Marriage, Politics and Betrayal among the New York Intellectuals* (New York: Simon and Schuster, 2000).

19. SB, letter to Richard Stern, in *Saul Bellow: Letters*, 212.

20. Many students wrote to Bellow and petitioned the school with a copy of the letter. They said they were "active Bellowites all. We read your books and follow your articles and have put you at the center of our intellectual life. We sincerely hope that you will be with us again in Minnesota"—all to no avail. The quote appears in Atlas, *Bellow*, 310.

21. Atlas, *Bellow*, 306.

22. Leader, *Fame and Fortune*, 602–3. Although there is no direct citation or quote from Susan's unpublished essay "Mugging the Muse," Susan's son, Daniel Bellow, provided Zachary Leader with access to the essay.

23. Ibid., 592.

24. Ibid., 607. Both Atlas and Leader based their accounts of Bellow's time at Wagner on Susan Dworkin, "The 'Great Men' Syndrome: Saul Bellow and Me" (unpublished manuscript, March 1, 1977).

25. Neil Genzlinger, "Bette Howland," *NYT*, December 17, 2017.

26. Leader, *Fame and Fortune*, 607–8.

27. SB, "Where Do We Go from Here: The Future of Fiction," in *STM*, 121–30. Originally delivered as the Hopwood Lecture at the University of Michigan, reprinted in *Michigan Quarterly Review* 1, no. 1 (1962), 27–33.

28. Gordon Lloyd Harper, "Saul Bellow: The Art of Fiction," in *The Paris Review Interviews*, vol. 1, with an introduction by Philip Gourevich (New York: Picador, 2006), 108.

29. SB, "Herzog: In Which the Troubles of Job Are Inflicted on the Uncomforted Wisdom of a Modern Moses," *Esquire*, July 1961.

30. Hardwick to SB, January 13, 1962, in Leader, *Fame and Fortune*, 605–6.

31. Nothing about the decision to marry, or any description of the wedding, is in the couple's correspondence or in any of the numerous interviews conducted by Bellow's biographer Zachary Leader.

32. SB, letter to Susan Glassman, January 9, 1962, in *Saul Bellow: Letters*, 230–31. There were other reasons, too, for Maury to be upset. The *Chicago Daily Tribune* reported on February 10 that he and his wife Marge had divorced. She claimed he had physically abused her a good many times. Marge settled for many of Maury's assets, including their Florida home and over $300,000.

33. Leader, *Fame and Fortune*, 616.

34. Joseph Epstein, "My Friend Edward," in *Portraits: A Gallery of Intellectuals*, by Edward Shils, ed. and with an introduction by Joseph Epstein (Chicago: University of Chicago Press, 1997), 15.

35. Atlas, *Bellow*, 321.

36. Ibid., 320.

37. Ibid., 321.

38. SB, letter to Albert Glotzer, August 5, 1990, in *Saul Bellow: Letters*, 471–72.

39. Ibid.

40. Tumin, "Tribute to Saul Bellow," delivered at one of the many award ceremonies for Saul. Quoted in Atlas, *Bellow*, 403.

41. Leader, *Fame and Fortune*, 25.

42. Atlas, *Bellow*, 321.

43. Susan Bellow, letters to Margaret Schafer (the wife of the Bard chaplain and a close friend in Tivoli), cited in Atlas, *Bellow*, 321.

44. Ibid., December 24, 1963, in Atlas, *Bellow*, 326.

45. SB, letter to John Berryman, October 19, 1963, in *Saul Bellow: Letters*, 245.

46. Atlas, *Bellow*, 327.

47. SB, letter to Nathan Tarcov, October 22, 1963, in *Saul Bellow: Letters*, 245–46.

48. Barbara Hanson's journal, quoted in Atlas, *Bellow*, 347. All quotes by Hanson are from her journal.

49. Susan Bellow, letter to Margaret Schafer, August 1964, quoted in Atlas, *Bellow*, 348.

50. Barbara Hanson's journal, quoted in Atlas, *Bellow,* 348.
51. Atlas, *Bellow,* 348.
52. Ibid.
53. SB, *Herzog,* with an introduction by Philip Roth (New York: Penguin, 2003), 3.
54. Ibid., 55. Italics are used throughout *Herzog* when his actual unsent letters are quoted.
55. Ibid., 345, 83.
56. According to SB, his uncle Aron Gordin, Lescha's brother, was forced to dig his own grave and then murdered by his Latvian neighbors. Abram's three sisters were named Borchka, Hassya, and Pesse. Janis Bellow, email to Zachary Leader, July 4, 2009.
57. SB, "A Second Half Life," in *Conversations with Saul Bellow,* ed. Gloria Cronin and Ben Siegel (Jackson: University Press of Mississippi, 1994), 286–87. Originally published in *Bostonia,* January/February 1991, 35–39.
58. Matthew C. Roudané and Saul Bellow, "An Interview with Saul Bellow," *Contemporary Literature* 25, no. 3 (1984): 265–80.
59. Saul Bellow, "The Civilized Barbarian," *NYTBR,* March 8, 1987, l.
60. David Mikics, *Bellow's People* (New York: W. W. Norton, 2016), 116–22, 127–39.
61. SB, *Settling My Accounts,* 57.
62. See Bellow's letters to friends and associates in SB, *Letters,* 202-250, 317, 352, 540.
63. Cronin and Siegel, *Conversations with Saul Bellow,* viii-ix.
64. SB, *Settling My Accounts,* 83.
65. Irving Howe, "Odysseus Flat on His Back," *New Republic,* September 19, 1964; Stanley Edgar Hyman, "Saul Bellow's 'Glittering Eye,'" *New Leader,* September 28, 1964; SB, *Herzog,* 47.
66. SB, *Herzog,* 5.
67. Ibid., 7.
68. Ibid., 182.
69. Ibid., 153.
70. Ibid., 29, 19.
71. Ibid., 154.
72. Ibid.
73. Nina Steers, "Successor to Faulkner?," in *Conversations with Saul Bellow,* 32–34. Originally published in *Show,* September 1964, 36–38.
74. SB, *Herzog,* 226.
75. Ibid., 219. In part a respectful parody of "Ode to the West Wind," a poem by Percy Bysshe Shelley.

76. Ibid., 281.
77. Ibid., 90.
78. Ibid., 82.
79. Ibid., 315.
80. Ibid., 82–83.
81. SB, "Literature," in *The Great Ideas Today*, ed. Mortimer Adler and Robert M. Hutchins (Chicago: Encyclopaedia Britannica, 1963), 134.
82. SB, "Some Notes on Recent American Fiction," in *The American Novel Since World War II*, ed. Marcus Klein (New York: Fawcett, 1969), 171.
83. Shiv Kumar, "The Hero as Prophet: A Study of Saul Bellow's Fiction," in *Saul Bellow: A Symposium on the Jewish Heritage*, ed. Vinda and Shiv Kumar (Hyderabad, India: Nachson, 1983), 137–49.
84. SB, *Herzog*, 254.
85. SB, *Herzog*, 44. Emphasis mine.
86. Steers, "Successor to Faulkner?," 32–34.
87. SB, *Herzog*, 258–61.
88. John Clayton, *In Defense of Man*, 2nd ed. (Bloomington: Indiana University Press, 1979), 50, 53.
89. Robert Alter, "Sentimentalizing the Jews," in *After the Tradition: Essays on Modern Jewish Writing* (New York: E. P. Dutton, 1969), 39. See also Alter's *Necessary Angels: Tradition and Modernity in Kafka, Benjamin, and Scholem* (Cambridge, MA: Harvard University Press, 1991) and *Pleasures of Reading in an Ideological Age* (New York: W. W. Norton, 1990).
90. SB, *Herzog*, 344–45.
91. Daniel Majdiak, "The Romantic Self and *Henderson the Rain King*," *Bucknell Review* 19 (1971): 125–46.
92. SB, *Herzog*, 344–45.
93. The presentation of suffering in Bellow's work may also have been influenced by Dostoevsky's fiction, especially in its portrayal of the acute mental turmoil of sensitive actors when they are faced with cruel suffering of the innocent, and their subsequent attempts to avoid playing down, getting around, or glorifying suffering. See Allan Chavkin, "The Problem of Suffering in the Fiction of Saul Bellow," *Comparative Literature Studies* 21, no. 2 (1984): 161–74.
94. SB, *Herzog*, 221. The curses are most likely derived from Psalms 109 and 31.
95. Ibid., 280.
96. Ibid., 51.
97. Ibid., 265.
98. Ibid., 281.

99. Ibid., 296. Derived from William Blake and/or Deuteronomy 29:10–15.

100. SB, *Herzog*, 116, 181, 350.

101. Bellow had learned much from Freud but essentially opposed his fundamental determinism. The novelist recognizes the reality of *an* unconscious, but not *the* unconscious. Though fully aware of the forces that oppose autonomy, Bellow insists on its reality, arguing that there is always a margin of self-definition. The repression of the desire to murder was for Freud the beginning of civilization, the source of religion. For Bellow, while the origins of civilization and religion depend to some extent on forms of repression, there is also positive aspiration. Daniel Fuchs, "Bellow and Freud," *Studies in the Literary Imagination* 17, no. 2 (1984): 59. Bellow knew that Freud wanted to preserve human nature from cultural determinism, but he firmly resisted Freud's biological determinism.

About eight days after *Herzog* was published, Bellow's play *The Last Analysis* opened. A comedy, in the main a farcical takedown of the reductive claims of psychoanalysis, it was about an aging comedian on his way down and out, partly because he feels he has a responsibility to tell people things. It was a bust. "I wanted to bring rhetoric back to the theater," Bellow said, "and I did but I brought too much. About eight hours too much." Robert Gutwillig, "Talk with Saul Bellow," in *Conversations with Saul Bellow*, 25. Originally published in *NYTBR*, September 20, 1964.

102. SB, *Herzog*, 315–16.

103. Ibid., 354.

104. Ibid., 250.

105. Ibid., 330.

106. Harper, "Art of Fiction," 86–110.

107. Ibid., 357.

108. SB, *Herzog*, 358.

109. Ibid., 345.

110. SB, *Herzog*, 337. More than merely a naïve expression of being physically in a particular location, the word "Hineni" is really more of "an existential expression. I'm not only here, but I'm *here*. Spiritually, I'm all in. I'm prepared to reflect on who I am, what's important to me, and how I can effect change for others." Cantor Matt Axelrod, "Hineni: A Prayer for the Ability to Pray," accessed August 24, 2023, https://www.myjewishlearning.com/article/hineni-a-prayer-for-the-ability-to-pray/. Interview with Rabbi William Strongin, August 24, 2023: "I would interpret the word 'Hineni' (somewhat tongue in cheek) as Yo! or Hey! It is often translated

as 'I am here,' which I like, but the feeling of the term is very much comparable to "Behold, I am here and now, ready!"

111. SB, *Herzog*, 219.
112. Ibid., 198
113. Ibid., 199, 350 (emphasis in original).

11. WEALTH, FAME, AND JEWISH IDENTITY IN 1960S AMERICA

1. Gordon Lloyd Harper, "Saul Bellow: The Art of Fiction," in *The Paris Review Interviews*, vol. 1, with an introduction by Philip Gourevich (New York: Picador, 2006), 107. Originally published in *Paris Review*, 1966, 36.
2. Sanford Pinsker, "Saul Bellow in the Class Room," *College English* 34 (1973): 977. See also Jo Brans, "Common Needs, Common Preoccupations: An Interview with Saul Bellow," in *Conversations with Saul Bellow*, ed. Gloria L. Cronin and Ben Siegel (Jackson: University Press of Mississippi, 1994), 142–43. Originally published in *Southwest Review* 62 (1977): 1–19. Also see Keith Michael Opdahl, *The Novels of Saul Bellow: An Introduction* (University Park: Pennsylvania State University Press, 1967), 169n7. Opdahl argues that Bellow's imagination is essentially "metaphysical and religious, passing from the historic fact to the larger universal issue."
3. Brans, "Common Needs," 142–43.
4. Ibid.
5. Fawcett bought the paperback rights for $371,000.
6. Bellow was the first American to be awarded this coveted prize, said to be the French equivalent of the Nobel Prize in Literature. Earlier winners included Samuel Beckett and Jorge Luis Borges.
7. Harper, "Art of Fiction," 98.
8. Julian Moynihan, "The Way Up from Rock Bottom," *NYT*, September 20, 1964.
9. Harper, "Art of Fiction," 97.
10. Ibid. In 2005, *Time* magazine named *Herzog* one of the one hundred best novels in the English language since *Time*'s founding in 1923.
11. SB, letter to Stanley Burnshaw, February 19, 1965, in *Saul Bellow: Letters*, ed. Benjamin Taylor (New York: Viking, 2010), 251–52.
12. Zachary Leader, *The Life of Saul Bellow: Love and Strife, 1965–2005* (New York: Alfred A. Knopf, 2018), 667n32. Rosten was a poet and playwright.

13. Robert Gutwillig, "Talk with Saul Bellow," in *Conversations with Saul Bellow*, 25. Originally published in *NYTBR*, September 20, 1964. *The Last Analysis* did better the second time around; there were other plays, some of which received only middling reviews.

14. Quoted in James Atlas, *Bellow: A Biography* (New York: Random House, 2000), 339.

15. Rachel Cooke, "Saul Bellow's Widow on His Life and Letters: 'His Gift Was to Love and Be Loved,'" *Guardian*, October 9, 2010.

16. Atlas, *Bellow*, 348–49.

17. Leader, *Love and Strife*, 25.

18. SB, *Humboldt's Gift*, with an introduction by Philip Roth (New York: Penguin Classics, 2008), 43. Originally published 1975 by Viking (New York).

19. In later years, Bellow angered feminists who were justifiably offended by the way he represented women in his fiction. The wives range from the bitter Ivy in *Dangling Man* to the emasculating Madeleine in *Herzog*. The mistresses—and they are legion—are usually buxom or particularly sensual in some other way. Most exhibit a combination of the sexy and the maternal. Vivian Gornick, "Radiant Poison: Saul Bellow, Philip Roth, and the End of the Jew as Metaphor," *Harper's Magazine*, September 2008, https://harpers.org/archive/2008/09/radiant-poison.

20. "Gloria Steinem Spends a Day in Chicago with Saul Bellow," *Glamour*, July 1965, 98, 122, 125, 128; Antonio Monda, *Do You Believe: Conversations on God and Religion*, trans. Ann Goldstein (New York: Vintage Books, 2007), 32; Harper, "Art of Fiction"; Jack Miles, "Saul Bellow's Life Is an Open Book," *Los Angeles Times*, March 30, 1989.

21. "Gloria Steinem," 125.

22. Richard Poirier, "Bellows to Herzog," *Partisan Review*, Spring 1965.

23. "Gloria Steinem," 128.

24. Irving Howe, quoted in SB, "A Jewish Writer in America," *NYRB*, October 27, 2011.

25. Sigmund Koch, "Interview of Saul Bellow" (Geddes Language Center at Boston University, Boston, 1987), in Leader, *Love and Strife*, 196.

26. Eric Norden, "Playboy Interview," in *Truman Capote: Conversations*, ed. M. Thomas Inge (Jackson: University Press of Mississippi, 1987), 158. Originally published in *Playboy*, March 15, 1968, 51–53, 56, 58–62, 160–62, 164–70. The Jewish writer Josh Lambert thinks that Jewish literary success is a function of a "suspect" power that becomes a tool of exclusion. He overstates his case and fails to make it credible. *The Literary Mafia: Jews,*

Publishing and Postwar American Literature (New Haven, CT: Yale University Press, 2022), 26.

27. Norden, "Playboy Interview."

28. "Saul Bellow," in *50 Years of Playboy Interviews: Men of Letters* (New York: Playboy Enterprises, 1997), loc. 7077 of 8095, Kindle.

29. Michiko Kakutani, "A Talk with Saul Bellow: On His Work and Himself," *NYTBR*, December 13, 1981, 28–29.

30. Katherine Anne Porter, *Conversations*, ed. Joan Givner (Jackson: University Press of Mississippi, 1987), 120, 134. Originally published in *Harper's*, September 1965, 58, 68.

31. Ibid. Resentment may have played a role in Porter's bitter statements. During the 1930s, 1940s, and 1950s, she achieved a prominent reputation as one of America's most distinguished writers, but her limited production and equally limited sales forced her to live on grants and advances for most of the postwar period. "Obituary: Katherine Anne Porter," *Variety*, September 24, 1980.

32. Gore Vidal, "Literary Gangsters," *Commentary*, March 1970, 62. Mentioned were John Simon (father Jewish); Richard Gilman; Robert Brustein, "a notorious hood," who "like Cosa Nostra . . . will infiltrate anything"; and Susan Sontag.

33. Kakutani, "Talk with Saul Bellow," 28–29.

34. Atlas, *Bellow*, 359.

35. SB, letters to Maggie Staats, in *Saul Bellow: Letters*, dating from May 29, 1966, to January 4, 1994, the most important of which are found on pages 258–76.

36. Ibid., 362. The French is conversational.

37. Atlas, *Bellow*, 363.

38. "The Old System" first appeared in print in January 1968 in *Playboy*, after being rejected by the *New Yorker* because they thought it too long. ("*The New Yorker* wanted deletions," Bellow wrote to Meyer Schapiro on March 18, 1968, "so I gave it to *Playboy* in protest—lucrative protest. . . . Hugh Hefner [editor of *Playboy*] has pleasanter vices than Wm. Phillips [editor of *Partisan Review*]." SB, letter to Meyer Schapiro, in *Saul Bellow: Letters*, 273–74.)

39. SB, "The Old System," in *Mosby's Memoirs and Other Stories* (New York: Penguin, 1996), 60–61. Originally published in *Playboy*, January 1968.

40. Ibid., 70, 82.

41. Koch, "Interview," 58.

42. Adam Bellow, quoted in David Mikics, *Bellow's People: How Saul Bellow Made Life into Art* (New York: W. W. Norton, 2016), 143.

43. Atlas, *Bellow*, 369. Bellow also signed a letter to the *NYT* in the spring of 1967 demanding that the USSR be more responsive to "Jewish Cultural Institutions."

44. SB, letter to Ruth Miller, May 31, 1967, quoted in Atlas, *Bellow*, 369.

45. Bellow's dispatches from the Six-Day War: *Newsday*, "After the Battle: Troops, Sightseers," June 9, 1967; "In Israel's Eyes, It's a Crazy World," June 12, 1967; "Sinai's Savage Sun Fits Its Scenery," June 13, 1967; "A Look O'er Jordan," June 16, 1967. Some of these reports were later incorporated into the text of SB, *To Jerusalem and Back: A Personal Account* (New York: Viking, 1976). Bellow's last three reports are reprinted in *It All Adds Up: From the Dim Past to an Uncertain Future* (New York: Viking, 1994) under the general title "Israel: The Six-Day War."

46. Ibid., 214–15.

47. SB, *TJAB*, 26.

48. Greg Bellow, *Saul Bellow's Heart: A Son's Memoir* (New York: Bloomsbury, 2013), 132.

49. At the invitation of CORE, Bellow drafted the preface of *We Shall Overcome*, a book about Schwerner, Goodman, and Chaney, the three Mississippi Freedom Summer volunteers who were murdered for their civil rights activism in 1964. Bellow confirmed their courage and his belief in the movement for which they died. The unpublished book is in the University of Chicago library. In a letter to the *Chicago Sun-Times*, Bellow defended the teach-ins and rallies that had emerged all over America. Atlas, *Bellow*, 344. Bellow did attend the Festival of the Arts at the White House, even though there was pressure from antiwar left liberals not to. He replied to a particularly pointed objection from Harvey Swados, who said going to the White House in June 1965 was "an act of solidarity with those who will be bombing and shelling even as you read from your works to the assembled culture bureaucrats." Bellow replied in an angry letter rejecting the "implied responsibility for death in Vietnam. Let me make it clear that the glamour of power means little to me. . . . I don't like what J[ohnson] is doing in Vietnam and S. Domingo. But I don't see how holding these positions requires me to treat Johnson like a Hitler. He's not that. . . . Intellectuals, and esp. former Marxists, will have to decide in the end what they think government *is*." SB, *Saul Bellow: Letters*, 253.

50. David Remnick, "Mr. Bellow's Planet," *New Yorker*, May 23, 1994; Edward Shils, "Totalitarians and Antinomians," in *Political Passages*, ed. John Bunzell (New York: Free Press, 1988).

51. SB, *Humboldt's Gift*, 111.

52. Atlas, *Bellow*, 384–85; Arlette Landes, quoted in Atlas, *Bellow*, 405.

53. Pirke Avot, 2:15–16. Pirke Avot is a subsection of Mishnah, the first major written work of Jewish oral tradition and part of the Talmud. Herbert Marcuse in his seminal work, *One-Dimensional Man* (1964), introduced the concept of "repressive desublimation," which by offering instantaneous rather than facilitated gratifications had the power to erase energies otherwise available for social critique and meaningful social action. Although reductionist in its failure to see the sincerity and authenticity of student movements for real change beyond sexual freedom, repressive desublimation was something, according to Marcuse, that could operate as a conservative force under the semblance of liberation. Marcuse's idea was used by the Old Left to "explain" how dreams of escape through sex and drugs were commodified as part of the growing commercialization of leisure in later stages of capitalism.

54. Students were particularly active at the University of Chicago in the late 1960s; Bellow was not shy about stating his position publicly in newspapers. For example, see his article "The Young Lack Faith in Leaders," *Chicago Sun-Times*, November 30, 1967.

55. Quoted in Mark Harris, *Drumlin Woodchuck* (Athens: University of Georgia Press, 1980), 119.

56. The material about the talk at SFUS is as accurate a composite as I could put together from the following accounts: Andrew Gordon, "*Mr. Sammler's Planet*: Saul Bellow's Speech at San Francisco State University," in *A Political Companion to Saul Bellow*, ed. Gloria Cronin and Lee Trepanier (Lexington: University Press of Kentucky, 2013), 153–66; Harris, *Drumlin Woodchuck*, 119–20; Atlas, *Bellow*, 374, 644 (Atlas relies on a letter from Leo Litwak, a faculty member who attended Bellow's talk; a clipping from the *San Francisco Chronicle*; and a transcript of the confrontation); Leader, *Love and Strife*, 49–51, which cites an avalanche of sources, 665–66.

57. Atlas, *Bellow*, 374, 644; Leader, *Love and Strife*, 49–51.

58. Gordon, "*Mr. Sammler's Planet*."

59. SB, letter to Harris, October 22, 1968, in *Saul Bellow: Letters*, 283.

60. Bellow's reputation as a conservative has masked the significance of his early enthusiasm for Trotskyism in his life and writings. The first letter in *Saul Bellow: Letters* (published in 2010), written when Saul was seventeen, is to Yetta Barshevsky, a fellow high school student who introduced him to Trotskyism and for whom he wrote a eulogy more than six decades later. SB, "In Memory of Yetta Barshevsky," in *Saul Bellow: Letters*, 527. That Bellow was still thinking about Trotsky in the 1990s is indicated

by his correspondence with Albert Glotzer, his enduring friend (and once Trotsky's secretary). *Saul Bellow: Letters*, 373–74, 470–72, 511–12, 518–19, 538, 542. See also Julie Newman, "Bellow and Trotsky," *Berfrois*, June 2011, https://www.berfrois.com/2011/06/judie-newman-bellow-and-trotsky/.

61. Joseph F. McCadden, *The Flight from Women in the Fiction of Saul Bellow* (Washington, DC: University Press of America, 1981), 171.

62. Leader, *Love and Strife*, 69.

63. SB, *The Victim* (New York: Signet, 1965), 134.

64. SB, *Herzog*, with an introduction by Philip Roth (New York: Penguin Classics, 1992), 258–61. Originally published 1964 by Viking (New York).

65. SB, *Mr. Sammler's Planet*, with an introduction by Stanley Crouch (New York: Penguin Classis, 2004), 3. Originally published 1970 by Viking (New York).

66. SB, *Victim*, 48.

67. SB, *Mr. Sammler's Planet*, 28–29. Sammler's views are traditional—"Women had once been brought up to chastity." But his insistent repugnance toward females and their "grossness" seems to call for some kind of explanation. In the novel none is made; therefore, some readers assumed the repugnance was Bellow's. As Bellow's biographer Zachery Leader explains, however, nothing in Bellow's sexual history suggests either authorial prurience or repression: "Nor is there anything like Sammler's language in Bellow's letters at this time. . . . On the evidence of his writing any feelings of disgust Bellow had about female physicality were more than matched by feelings of attraction." Leader, *Love and Strife*, 100–101. This is not to say that Bellow was free of misogyny. Artur Schopenhauer, for whom Artur Sammler is named, had very similar attitudes about women. In his 1851 essay "On Women," Schopenhauer expressed opposition to what he called the "stupidity" of "reflexive, unexamined reverence for the female." Women, he wrote, are "childish, frivolous and short-sighted." They "are deficient in artistic faculties and sense of justice," he said, and he made clear his opposition to monogamy.

68. Atlas, *Bellow*, 386.

69. SB, *Mr. Sammler's Planet*, 28–29.

70. Ibid., 132–33. Both the Black man's potency and Sammler's impotence are being displayed in this scene, which could be taken as a graphic demonstration of the attraction-repugnance of Jewish males toward what they feared and envied of Black male sturdiness, street smarts, and sheer studliness. But neither Sammler nor Bellow, unlike Norman Mailer,

promoted any of the outlaw worship or intellectual primitivism fashionable among some in the sixties. Mailer endorsed both of these phenomena in "The White Negro" (*Dissent*, Fall 1957), running the risk, consciously or otherwise, of distorting the actuality of race in America. The hipster or White Negro in Mailer's essay looks for what Bellow in his *Commentary* review of Ellison's *Invisible Man* calls the "instinct cellar" of the Black man, and the hipster does so, as Mailer puts it, at "no matter what price in individual violence." The hipster, with what appears to be Mailer's approval or encouragement, seeks the elimination of "every social restraint" and behaves like a "psychopath." One can come away from this essay wrongly thinking that "psychopathology is most prevalent with the Negro." When Mailer writes of noxious Black hoodlums "daring the unknown," he gives them élan, precisely the élan Sammler and Bellow execrate. Irving Howe, the editor of *Dissent*, forever afterward regretted publishing Mailer's piece.

71. Ralph Ellison, *Invisible Man* (New York: Random House, 1952), 62.

72. Adam Kirsch, "Flower Children," *Tablet*, March 14, 2012.

73. SB, *Mr. Sammler's Planet*, 3.

74. Ibid., 252.

75. Ibid., 115.

76. Ibid.

77. One kabbalistic theory attests that the light of ten vessels, created with the universe, was unstable, combining good and evil in an explosive mix that blew up. This idea contends that the first release of the divine light was a way for God to purify himself of the evil that was mixed in with the good. Seven of the ten vessels were completely shattered. Clinging to the broken shards are sparks of the light left over from inside the vessels. These precious sparks are to be assembled and restored to their original place, higher in the heavens. A broken world that must be repaired, or tikkun olam, is a kabbalistic theme that has resounded throughout the centuries, probably beginning with the sixteenth; it is especially prevalent in the contemporary Jewish world and is invoked by different groups across a spectrum of religious and political groups.

78. Bellow thought that Arendt lacked "human understanding" and that her empathetic faculties were "stunted"; in bondage to theory, she was blind to "simple facts," by which Bellow implied the facts of Jewish death and suffering. Letter to Leon Wieseltier, March 12, 1982, in *Saul Bellow: Letters*, 392. The publication of *Eichmann in Jerusalem* was a searing event for the New York Jewish intellectuals, among whom Bellow had friends and associates. Arendt was saying that the Jewish leadership

in Nazi-occupied Europe was passive and inept and that they were even collaborators with the bureaucratic machinery of the Final Solution; therefore, they were responsible for the deaths of millions of Jews. The aloof tone of Arendt, a German Jew, cast the murdered Jews of Europe in a very unfavorable light and seemed to reduce one of the most tragic human dramas in history to an abstract philosophical debate. Arendt, *Eichmann in Jerusalem: The Banality of Evil* (New York: Viking, 1963). The book originally appeared as a two-part series of articles in the *New Yorker* beginning February 9, 1963. To get a better sense of the heat generated in the intellectual community and the Jewish community generally, and for the various perspectives, see *Partisan Review*, summer 1963, fall 1963, winter 1964; *Commentary*, September 1963, October 1963, February 1964.

79. SB, *Mr. Sammler's Planet*, 14.

80. SB, "Old System," 44.

81. Ibid., 1.

82. "Literature and Culture: An Interview with Saul Bellow," *Salmagundi*, spring 1975, 17, 23. A public interview conducted at Skidmore College on November 8, 1973. Interviewing Saul Bellow were Robert Boyers, Robert Orrill, Ralph Ciancio, and Edwin Moseley, all members of the Skidmore faculty.

83. Ibid., 16.

84. SB, "Mr. Sammler and Hannah Arendt's Banality," in *Saul Bellow: A Mosaic*, ed. L. H. Goldman, Gloria L. Cronin, and Ada Aharoni (New York: Peter Lang, 1992), 22–25.

85. SB, *Herzog*, 258–61.

86. "Literature and Culture," 16.

87. SB, *Mr. Sammler's Planet*, 237.

88. Ibid., 238–39.

89. Ibid., 240 (emphasis mine).

90. Ibid., 241.

91. Ibid.

92. Ibid., 242–44.

93. Ibid., 242.

94. Stanley Crouch, "Introduction," in *Mr. Sammler's Planet*, xiii.

95. Gloria Cronin, "Our Father's Politics: Gregory, Adam, and Daniel Bellow," in *Political Companion*, 216–17, 192.

96. Crouch, "Introduction," xiii.

97. SB, *Mr. Sammler's Planet*, 254.

98. Ibid., 69.

99. Ibid., 252. Elya's name is equivalent to Elijah, a major prophet in the ninth century BCE. Perhaps Bellow in choosing this name assures us that Gruner was a responsible man, morally accountable, dependable—a man who gave thought to others. Also, in the Bible, Elijah doesn't really die but is carried up to heaven in a fiery chariot. And he will return at the end of days, which at points in the novel Sammler thinks is coming soon.

100. Ibid., 61.

101. Leader, *Love and Strife*, 35; SB, *Settling My Accounts before I Go Away: A Words and Images Interview by Norman Manea* (Rhinebeck, NY: Sheep Meadow Press, 1999), 32.

102. SB, *Mr. Sammler's Planet*, 193.

103. Ibid., 260.

104. Ibid. In Joyce's *Ulysses*, Molly declares, "yes and his heart was going like mad and yes I said yes I will Yes."

105. Hannah Wirth-Nesher and Andrea Cohen Malamut, "Jewish and Human Survival on Bellow's Planet," *Modern Fiction Studies* 25, no. 1 (1979): 59–74; Earl Rovit, "Saul Bellow and Norman Mailer: The Secret Sharers," in *Saul Bellow: A Collection of Critical Essays* (Englewood Cliffs, NJ: Prentice-Hall, 1975), 167–70.

106. SB, *Mr. Sammler's Planet*, 155.

107. David C. Dougherty, "Finding before Seeking: Theme in *Henderson the Rain King* and *Humboldt's Gift*," *Modern Fiction Studies* 25, no. 1 (1979): 93–101.

108. SB, *Herzog*, 199.

109. As early as 1963, in his "Recent American Fiction" lecture at the Library of Congress, Bellow decried "the theme of alienation of the Self," naming as especially guilty Céline, Robbe-Grillet, Eliot, Sartre, D. H. Lawrence, and Andre Gide. "Recent American Fiction" (speech given at the Library of Congress, Washington, DC, 1963), 6.

12. LOVE AND DEATH

1. SB, quoted in Zachary Leader, *The Life of Saul Bellow: Love and Strife, 1965–2005* (New York: Alfred A. Knopf, 2018), 54.

2. Ibid., 92.

3. Ibid., 87–89.

4. Ibid., 672n64.

5. Ibid., 370.

6. SB, letter to Herbst, in SB, *Letters*, September 5, 1959, 179.

7. SB, quoted in Elinor Langer, *Josephine Herbst: The Story She Could Never Tell* (Boston: Little, Brown, 1984), 309–10.

8. Elinor Langer, *Josephine Herbst: The Story She Could Never Tell* (Boston: Little, Brown, 1984), 309–10.

9. SB, *Humboldt's Gift*, with an introduction by Jeffrey Eugenides (New York: Penguin Classics, 2008), 156. First published 1975 by Viking (New York).

10. SB, letter to James Laughlin, October 22, 1957, in *Saul Bellow: Letters*, ed. Benjamin Taylor (New York: Viking, 2010), 161.

11. Ibid.

12. James Atlas, *Delmore Schwartz: The Life of an American Poet* (New York: Farrar, Straus and Giroux, 1977), 315.

13. SB wrote to Meyer Schapiro telling him that Schwartz's best bet for a teaching job was Syracuse University: "I hope he's well enough to function. Teaching makes him more stable, but Syracuse is a small town where he would be continually observed by people who had heard of his troubles. . . . But then I haven't seen Delmore since '57 or '58, the year of the crisis, and I've no idea what he's like. But I wish him well." Letter cited in Leader, *Love and Strife*, 666n10.

14. Diane Wood Middlebrook, *Anne Sexton: A Biography* (New York: Vintage, 1992); Lee Siegel, "Seize the Job," *Harper's Magazine*, August 2001; SB, letter to Anne Sexton, n.d., 1962, in *Saul Bellow: Letters*, 233. "'Monster of Despair' could be *Henderson's* subtitle. I think you coined the expression. . . . At this particular point we seem to have entered each other's minds. A marriage of true minds, or meeting arranged by Agape′ [a term that is usually defined as God's immeasurable, incomparable love for humankind]. . . . Your poem ["Old Dwarf Heart"] is genuinely Hendersonian—'breathing in loops like a green hen' is absolutely IT! Yours in true-minded friendship." *Saul Bellow: Letters*, 233.

15. SB, letter to Ralph Ross, August 14, 1973, in *Saul Bellow: Letters*, 314–15.

16. SB, letter to Howland, Summer 1968, quoted in "Bette Howland, Author and Protegee of Bellow's, Dies at 80," *NYT*, December 17, 2017. Letter in possession of Jacob Howland, Bette's son. Bette Howland, letter to Bellow, January 21, 1970 (when Saul was planning to go to Africa with Dave Peltz and without her), quoted in Leader, *Love and Strife*, 141. See also Carrie Golus, "Rediscovering Bette Howland," *University of Chicago Magazine*, fall 2019, accessed July 19, 2023, https://mag.uchicago.edu/arts-humanities

/rediscovering-bette-howland#. After recovery, Bette published several books, including *W-3* (New York: Public Space Books, 1974), a memoir narrative about people in a psychiatric ward, in which she never names herself or the reasons for trying to end her life. In 1972 she studied at University of Chicago's Committee of Social Thought, of which Bellow was the chair. She also wrote a number of articles for *Commentary* in the seventies.

17. Irving Howe, *A Margin of Hope: An Intellectual Autobiography* (New York: Harcourt Brace Jovanovich, 1982), 164.

18. Leon Wieseltier, "Saul Bellow's Quest for the Vernacular Sublime," *NYTBR*, November 18, 2010; SB, letter to Meyer Schapiro, March 18, 1968, in *Saul Bellow: Letters*, 273.

19. SB, *Humboldt's Gift*, 142.

20. Leader, *Love and Strife*, 93.

21. Maggie Staats, interviewed by Leader three times between 2008 and 2014, quoted in Leader, *Love and Strife*, 655.

22. Jane Howard, "Mr. Bellow Considers His Planet," in *Conversations with Saul Bellow*, ed. Gloria Cronin and Ben Siegel (Jackson: University Press of Mississippi, 1994), 77–79. Originally published in *Life Magazine*, April 3, 1970.

23. Ibid., 80.

24. Ibid., 79; Adam Bellow, email to Zachary Leader, January 24, 2018, in Leader, *Love and Strife*, 674n4.

25. Howard, "Mr. Bellow Considers His Planet," 79.

26. SB, "Saul Bellow on America and American Jewish Writers," *Congress Bi-Weekly*, pt. 1, October 23, 1970; pt. 2, December 4, 1970.

27. Transcript of panel discussion at US Cultural Center in Tel Aviv, June 28, 1970, quoted in Ruth Miller, *Saul Bellow: A Biography of the Imagination* (New York: St. Martin's, 1991), 43.

28. Ibid.

29. SB, quoted in David Remnick, "When He Was Good: A Life of Philip Roth," *New Yorker*, March 29, 2021. The internecine Jewish pandemonium that accompanied the publication of *Portnoy's Complaint* was serious enough, but for many non-Orthodox, nonestablishment Jewish groups, the book was a source of insight into the urban world of American-born, secularizing Jewish sons and daughters. And it was hilarious. It could be hoped that the comedy cauterized any tendency on the part of readers to adopt the despondency of the victim. The best book on the subject is Alan Cooper, *Philip Roth and the Jews* (New York: SUNY Press,

1996). Also useful is Bernard Avishai, *Promiscuous: "Portnoy's Complaint" and Our Doomed Pursuit of Happiness* (New Haven, CT: Yale University Press, 2012).

30. Alfred Kazin, *New York Jew* (New York: Knopf, 1978), 285.

31. James Atlas, *Bellow: A Biography* (New York: Random House, 2000), 384. Leader, *Love and Strife*, 173–74.

32. SB, "What Kind of Day Did You Have?," *Vanity Fair*, February 1984.

33. Atlas, *Bellow*, 511; Nathaniel Rich, "Swiveling Man," *NYRB*, March 21, 2019.

34. SB, letter to William Maxwell, March 14, 1970, in Leader, *Love and Strife*, 119; SB, letter to Daniel Fuchs, April 10, 1974, in *Saul Bellow: Letters*, 318.

35. *Mr. Sammler's Planet*, Kazin wrote, is "a brilliantly austere set of opinions, more than usually impressive because of the decisive intellectual elegance that by now Bellow has turned into a language of his own. But Sammler's opinions are set in a context so uncharitable, morally arrogant toward every other character in the book but one, and therefore lacking in dramatic satisfaction." *NYRB*, December 3, 1970.

36. Leader, *Love and Strife*, 105, 156, 157, 164.

37. Hans Kohut, *How Does Analysis Cure?* (Chicago: University of Chicago Press, 1984); Atlas, *Bellow*, 384–85.

38. Leader, *Love and Strife*, 95.

39. Ibid., 116.

40. Joseph Epstein, "Saul Bellow of Chicago," *NYTBR*, May 9, 1971.

41. Landes, quoted in Atlas, *Bellow*, 405.

42. SB, letter to Edward Shils, February 27, 1972, in Leader, *Love and Strife*, 156.

43. Fran Gendlin, email to Zachary Leader, June 19, 2015, in Leader, *Love and Strife*, 165–66.

44. SB, "John Berryman, Friend," *NYT*, May 27, 1973.

45. Clive Barnes, "Bellow's Psychology of 'The Last Analysis,'" *NYT*, June 24, 1971; SB, letter to Constance Perrin, June 25, 1971, in Leader, *Love and Strife*, 156; SB, letter to the cast of the Circle in the Square production of *The Last Analysis*, in *Saul Bellow: Letters*, 304.

46. SB, letter to Fran Gendlin, May [?], 1972, in *Saul Bellow: Letters*, 307–8.

47. Atlas, *Bellow*, 417.

48. One of Bellow's Japanese hosts who was witness to and victim of Bellow's occasionally wounding expletives saw his behavior as "a kind of Tourette's." Leader, *Love* and *Strife*, 163.

49. Ted Hoffman, Bellow's old friend from the Salzburg Seminars and Bard College, was probably into his cups when he wrote a heavily ironic letter reminding Bellow of his exchange with Ada Green, the actual librarian. Bellow used his own "bad behavior" and the words Hoffman remembered in *Him with His Foot in His Mouth and Other Stories* (New York: Harper and Row, 1984). Bellow's title story originally appeared in the *Atlantic*, November 1982. It can now be found in several story collections including *Saul Bellow: Collected Stories*, with an introduction by James Wood and a preface by Janis Bellow (New York: Viking, 2001). Hoffman's letter is quoted in Leader, *Love and Strife*, 205.

50. D. J. Bruckner, "A Candid Talk with Saul Bellow," *NYTBR*, April 14, 1984.

51. SB, "Him with His Foot in His Mouth'" in *Collected Stories*, 383.

52. All quotations of and information about Alexandra Bellow are drawn from interviews done by Zachary Leader in Chicago on February 5 and April 1 and 3, 2008, and from Alexandra Bellow, "A Mathematical Life." See full citations of all sources in Leader, *Love and Strife*, 681–82.

53. Ibid.

54. Ibid. Ionescu Tulcea studied with Shizuo Kakutani, famous for his work in five-point theorems. In Euclidean and projective geometry, just as two points determine a line, five points determine a conic. Wikipedia, s.v. "Shizuo Kakutani," accessed September 6, 2019, https://en.wikipedia.org/wiki/Shizuo_Kakutani.

55. All of Adam Bellow's quotations are drawn from interviews by Zachary Leader in Chicago on March 23 and 27 and April 3, 2008. Leader, *Love and Strife*, 197–98, 683n69.

56. Ibid.

57. SB, letter to Mischa Ullman, May 1, 1973, quoted in Leader, *Love and Strife*, 193–94. Mischa later returned to make a permanent home in Israel.

58. SB, *To Jerusalem and Back* (New York: Viking, 1976), 129.

59. The acronym PEN stands for "Poets, Playwrights, Essayists, Novelists." The organization, though primarily devoted to literature, was active in social justice issues as well.

60. SB, letter to the *NYT*, January 7, 1974.

61. SB, *TJAB*, 9. In the beginning of the book, Bellow points to *Le Monde*'s pro-Arab bias: France "supports terrorists. It is friendlier to [Idi] Amin," president of Uganda, "than to Rabin," prime minster of Israel.

62. SB, *Foot in His Mouth*, 32.

63. Greg Bellow, *Saul Bellow's Heart: A Son's Memoir* (New York: Bloomsbury, 2013), 136.

64. Adam was so unhappy in that first year that he himself suggested psychiatric therapy. Although Saul resisted, Sasha thought the therapy was exceptionally helpful to Adam. Sondra "Sasha" Bellow, "What's in a Name?" (unpublished memoir), 118, quoted in Leader, *Love and Strife,* 197–98.

65. All of Daniel Bellow's quotations are drawn from interviews by Zachary Leader on May 11 and 15, 2008, and May 31, 2017 (Great Barrington, MA, by telephone). Leader, *Love and Strife,* 197–98, 653. In 2015, Daniel Bellow "boxed up his mother's papers relating to the divorce and shipped them to [Leader] . . . to look through and then deposit 'in the midden heap of the Regenstein [Library] to gross out future historians.'" Leader, *Love and Strife,* 228.

66. Leader, *Love and Strife,* 198–99.

67. Atlas, *Bellow,* 467; Leader, *Love and Strife,* 229.

13. BELLOW'S GIFT, ISRAEL, AND THE NOBEL PRIZE

1. Isaac Rosenfeld, *An Age of Enormity: Life and Writing in the Forties and Fifties,* ed. and with an introduction by Theodore Solataroff, with a foreword by Saul Bellow (New York: World, 1962).

2. When Bellow applied for a job at NYU, where Rosenfeld was teaching, he wrote to his old friend, as a courtesy, about the possible opening at the school. Apparently, Rosenfeld replied with a "frosty note." Bellow then wrote to Monroe Engel, another old friend: "Is Isaac's nose out of joint about NYU?. . . . Mine is a little. He makes me feel that I've undermined him there. I can still drop out if he's affected. How can I know whether he is? I have no way of telling what's at stake for him. For me there's nothing. I simply don't want to get in his way. Not from friendly feeling—there's not much lost between us now. He'd like to become strangers, and I'm not so opposed to that as I formerly was—but because I'd prefer, if I have to struggle with someone for survival, it be a person I never struggled with before." Quoted in James Atlas, *Bellow: A Biography* (New York: Random House, 2000), 160.

3. SB, *Humboldt's Gift,* with an introduction by Jeffrey Eugenides (New York: Penguin Books, 1975), 54. Atlas suggests that Bellow in *Humboldt's Gift,* in the guise of a tribute to Schwartz, was actually attacking him. But this is a questionable judgment. Would Bellow have taken revenge on Schwartz by writing, "Ah Humboldt had been great—handsome, high-spirited, buoyant, ingenious, electrical, noble. To be with him made you feel the sweetness of life"? *Humboldt's Gift,* 164.

4. Richard Stern, "Bellow's Gift," *NYTM*, November 21, 1976, 46.

5. James Atlas, *Delmore Schwartz: The Life of an American Poet* (New York: Farrar, Straus and Giroux, 1977), 378.

6. SB, *Humboldt's Gift*, 109.

7. Ibid., 44.

8. Samuel Beckett read *Humboldt's Gift* in 1978 and was interested in meeting its author. James Wood complains that Atlas's biography of Bellow mentions a meeting between Bellow and Beckett for a drink in Paris in 1981 but leaves it at that. Wood points to James Knowlson's biography of Samuel Beckett, where we read that Beckett was excited by the novel and asked, "through intermediaries, to meet Bellow." They did meet in the bar of the Hotel Point Royal, St. Germain-des-Pres. "It might have been interesting to discover what Bellow thought about Beckett's writing. It might have been revealing to compare their achievements, since Bellow and Beckett were the major postwar English-language writers. It is, after all, one of the significances of Bellow's career that, in the age of Beckett, the age of late modernism, he had retained the soul-pungency of the nineteenth-century novelists and the metaphysical leanings of the great Russians. He was like an earlier generation of writers in his determination to deliver his characters from the inessential. He once wrote that when we read the best nineteenth and twentieth century novelists, we soon realize that they are trying in a variety of ways to establish a definition of human nature." The meeting was apparently awkward. These literary giants do not seem to have expressed an interest in meeting again. James Wood, "Give All," in *New Republic*, November 13, 2000; James Knowlson, *Damned to Fame: The Life of Samuel Beckett* (New York: Grove Press, 1996).

9. SB, *Humboldt's Gift*, 10, 121.

10. Ibid., 6, 1, 4, 10, 11.

11. Ibid., 115–26.

12. Alan Ward, "A Tale of Two Delmore's: Marxism and the Modern Poet," *Against the Current*, May/June 2021, 17–24; David Zucker, "'Alien to Myself': Jewishness in the Poetry of Delmore Schwartz," *Studies in American Jewish Literature* 9, no. 2 (1990): 1; Morris Dickstein, "Writer Delmore Schwartz: Forgotten Genius," *Tablet Magazine*, August 11, 2011. In the *Nation*, June 22–29, 2015, Vivian Gornick makes the case for the revival of Delmore as a major Jewish poet.

13. SB, *Humboldt's Gift*, 442.

14. Ibid., 12–14.

15. Ibid., 12.

16. Ibid., 5.

17. Ibid., 24.
18. Ibid., 22–24.
19. Ibid., 119.
20. Ibid., 15, 3.
21. Ibid., 493–94.
22. Ibid., 484, 455.
23. Ibid., 356, 483.
24. Alfred Kazin, *Alfred Kazin's Journals,* ed. Richard Cook (New Haven, CT: Yale University Press, 2012), 435.
25. Steinberg is best known for his work for the *New Yorker,* most famously for "View of the World from 9th Avenue" (March 29, 1976). He described himself as "a writer who draws."
26. SB, letter to Roth, August 8, 1975, in *Saul Bellow: Letters,* ed. Benjamin Taylor (New York: Viking, 2010), 330.
27. SB, letter to Wasserman, July 1, 1975, in *Saul Bellow: Letters,* 327.
28. SB, letter to Peltz, July 2, 1975, in *Saul Bellow: Letters,* 327–28.
29. SB, *To Jerusalem and Back: A Personal Essay* (New York: Vintage, 1976), 2–3; the injunction to make fringes is in Numbers 15:38.
30. SB, *TJAB,* 3.
31. Ibid. (emphasis in original).
32. Ibid., 3–4.
33. Ibid., 5.
34. Ibid., 70.
35. "My people will dwell in a peaceful habitation, and in sure dwellings, and in quiet places." Isaiah 32:18.
36. SB, *TJAB,* 25.
37. Nathaniel Rich, "Swiveling Man," *NYRB,* March 21, 2019.
38. SB, *TJAB,* 25.
39. Philip Gillon, "Bellow's Credo," *Jerusalem Post Weekly,* December 24, 1974.
40. SB, *TJAB,* 15.
41. Ibid., 22–23.
42. Ibid., 25.
43. Ibid., 136.
44. Ibid., 36.
45. Ibid.
46. Ibid.
47. SB, letter to Owen Barfield, February 26, 1976, in *Saul Bellow: Letters,* 334–35.

48. SB, letter to Owen Barfield, August 13, 1976, in *Saul Bellow: Letters,* 339–340.

49. SB, *TJAB,* 59–60.

50. Ibid., 157–58.

51. Ibid., 145.

52. Ibid., 175.

53. Ibid., 92.

54. SB, *Humboldt's Gift,* 437.

55. SB, "A Second Half Life," in *Conversations with Saul Bellow,* ed. Gloria Cronin and Ben Siegel (Jackson: University Press of Mississippi, 1994), 286–87. Originally published in *Bostonia,* January/February 1991.

56. SB, *TJAB,* 93. "The Lord wraps himself in light as with a garment, he stretches out he heavens as a tent." Psalms 104:2. In regard to Bellow's leaning metaphysical, he was still reading Steiner in Jerusalem, and wrote to Owen Barfield mentioning Lucifer and Ahriman, both considered forces of darkness and evil, the first in Judeo/Christian tradition and the second in Zoroastrianism.

57. Ibid., 10, 93.

58. Ibid., 167.

59. Dubbed the "Letter of 37," it was published in full in *Moment Magazine* in 1978. The letter urged Prime Minister Begin to continue talks with President Sadat of Egypt and advocated a negotiated settlement to the Israeli-Palestinian problem that would include a two-state solution. SB, letter to Ladislas Farago, May 7, 1978, in *Saul Bellow: Letters,* 360. Farago was the author of many books on World War II, including *Aftermath: Martin Borman and the Fourth Reich* (New York: Simon and Schuster, 1974).

60. Isabella Fey, "Strategic Withdrawal," *Jerusalem Post,* November 16, 1976; SB, *TJAB,* 167.

61. Noam Chomsky, "Bellow's Israel," *New York Arts Journal,* spring 1977, repr. in *Toward a New Cold War* (New York: Pantheon, 1982), 299–307; Irving Howe, "People on the Edge of History—Saul Bellow's Vivid Report on Israel," *NYTBR,* October 16, 1976.

62. *New Yorker,* July 12 and 19, 1976.

63. Elisabeth Sifton, "The Novelist Was a Wizard with a Dark Side," *Slate,* April 8, 2005. Bellow told Sifton that the *New Yorker* had "never taken any of his stories." Oddly, Sifton let this pass or did not know that the magazine had published an excerpt from *Augie* in 1952 and the stories "A Father to Be" in 1955, "Mosby's Memoir" in 1968, and "A Silver Dish" in 1978.

64. Ben Yagoda, *About Town: The New Yorker and the World It Made* (New York: Scribner, 2000), 297.

65. SB, quoted in Atlas, *Bellow,* 457.

66. Ibid.; Greg Bellow, *Saul Bellow's Heart: A Son's Memoir* (New York: Bloomsbury, 2013), 139; Sydney Harris, "One of Us Won the Nobel Prize," *Chicago Daily News,* November 15, 1976.

67. SB, quoted in Atlas, *Bellow,* 457.

68. Zachary Leader, *The Life of Saul Bellow: To Fame and Fortune, 1915–1964* (New York: Alfred A. Knopf, 2015), 115 (emphasis in original).

69. G. Bellow, *Saul Bellow's Heart,* 138. In the summer of 1976, a business deal involving Saul, Maury, and Jane seemed to go sour. An absence of returns raised suspicions in Saul and Joel, Maury's son, who served as his accountant. There was bad blood only months before the winner of the Nobel Prize was announced, which may be part of an explanation for Maury's absence in Stockholm.

70. Harriet Wasserman, *Handsome Is: Adventures with Saul Bellow* (New York: Fromm International, 1997), 54.

71. SB, *Settling My Accounts before I Go Away: A Words and Images Interview by Norman Manea* (Rhinebeck, NY: Sheep Meadow Press, 1999), 79–80.

72. Rabbi Narrowe's memoir, quoted in Leader, *Fame and Fortune,* 209.

73. SB, *Settling My Accounts,* 79.

74. G. Bellow, *Saul Bellow's Heart,* 139. Greg told James Atlas years later that he had had a bad time during the Nobel festivities. "My feeling was," Greg said, "Fuck that. I'm not going to put up with that shit." The mood changed publicly the day after the speech. Bellow's Swedish publisher, Gerald Bonnier, gave a luncheon in Bellow's honor. The whole Bellow clan plus a host of American and European publishers attended. At the end of the luncheon, Bonnier gave a short speech, offered a toast, and sat down. Harriet Wasserman describes the scene: "Daniel clinked his glass with his fork. When he had gotten everyone's attention, he said: 'I'd just like to say my father has been so busy, but he still had time for me. Thanks, Pop.' Up stood Greg, who was at his father's table. 'My young brother has given me the courage to say something I've always wanted to say.' Greg's voice was cracking. Alexandra put her elbows on the table and her face in her hands. . . . 'I never thought you loved me [Greg said], and I never understood what the creative process was. You were behind a closed door all the time, writing, listening to Mozart.' He was looking straight at his father. . . . 'I didn't understand the creative process.' All the

European publishers . . . were sitting very stiff and upright. . . . Looks of total shock—horror almost—on their faces. . . . 'And then I had my own child. I witnessed the birth of my own child and I understood what the creative process was, and I understood then that you really did love me.' No one moved . . . Greg sat down and after a stunned silence people began to leave their tables. Saul . . . stood up quickly and went straight over to his middle child, put out his hand, and shook Adam's. 'Thanks, kid, for not saying anything.' And off he went, in a stretch limo, entourage at his side." Wasserman, *Handsome Is*, 67–68. See also James Atlas, *The Shadow in the Garden* (New York: Vintage Books, 2018), 332; Leader, *Fame and Fortune*, 685n33.

75. "A Laureate for Saul Bellow," *Time*, November 1, 1976.

76. Atlas, *Bellow*, 462.

77. SB, *Settling My Accounts*, 96.

78. Conrad, preface to *The Nigger of the "Narcissus"* (New York: W. W. Norton, 1979). Originally published as *The Children of the Sea: A Tale of the Forecastle* (New York: Dodd, Mead, 1897).

79. SB, "Nobel Lecture," delivered in Stockholm, December 12, 1976. Published in *The Nobel Lecture* (New York: Targ, 1979). The full speech can also be found in SB, *It All Adds Up: From the Dim Past to an Uncertain Future* (New York: Viking, 1994), 88–97; SB, *There Is Simply Too Much to Think About* (New York: Viking, 2015), 291–300.

80. Michiko Kakutani, "A Talk with Saul Bellow: On His Work and Himself," *NYTBR*, December 13, 1981.

81. Robert Gottlieb, "Main Street," *NYTBR*, January 2, 2022.

82. "Saul Bellow, Laureate," *NYT*, October 23, 1976.

83. Raphael, quoted in Leader, *Fame and Fortune*, 213.

14. BELLOW'S DECEMBER

1. Katha Pollitt panned the book with so much apparent anger that one wonders if Bellow's book was her only issue. She said that *The Dean's December* is "a novel as flat as the paper on which it is printed, for all Bellow's literary energies have been swallowed up in pontification. This is a book so bitter, so self-infatuated, so boring, as to make one wonder if his earlier books could really have had the intellectual weight ascribed to them at the time." "Bellow Blows Hot and Cold," *Mother Jones*, February–March 1982, 66–67. See also David Evanier, "Bare Bones," *National Review*, April 2, 1982, 364–

66. The daily and Sunday editions of the *New York Times* were exceptions. Christopher Lehmann-Haupt's review was mixed but mostly positive; Robert Tower ended his Sunday review by writing, "Sentence by sentence, page by page, Saul Bellow is simply the best writer that we have." Robert Tower, "A Novel Of Politics, Wit And Sorrow," *NYT*, January 11, 1982.

2. Matthew C. Roudané and Saul Bellow, "An Interview with Saul Bellow," *Contemporary Literature* 25, no. 3 (1984): 274.

3. D. J. Bruckner, "A Candid Talk with Saul Bellow," *NYTBR*, April 14, 1984.

4. Ibid.

5. William Kennedy, "If Saul Bellow Doesn't Have a True Word to Say, He Keeps His Mouth Shut," *Esquire*, February 1, 1982.

6. The reviews were almost uniformly negative. The hardest hitting by a major reviewer was John Updike, "Toppling Towers Seen by a Whirling Soul," *New Yorker*, February 22, 1982. See also Helen Dudar, "The Graying of Saul Bellow," *Saturday Review of Literature*, January 1982. For Updike as non-Jew, see Adam Begley, *Updike* (New York: Harper-Collins, 2014), 267. There would be a third Bech book by Updike in 1998: *Bech at Bay*.

7. SB, letter to Maggie Staats, September 15, 1975, in *Saul Bellow: Letters*, ed. Benjamin Taylor (New York: Viking, 2010), 330–31.

8. SB, *Humboldt's Gift*, with an introduction by Jeffrey Eugenides (New York: Penguin Books. 1975), 10. Updike is the author of *Bech: A Book* (1965) and *Bech Is Back* (1970). In both volumes, Henry Bech is a Jewish American writer, almost certainly a caricature of Saul Bellow. Bech writes much, travels the world over, and beds a variety of mistresses. The books are humorous and clever but demonstrate the author's resentment in regard to the success of Jewish American writers, and they hint of antisemitism. Suffering from a loss of religious faith, Updike immersed himself in Kierkegaard and theologian Karl Barth. His "reborn" Christianity stayed with him for the rest of his life Whether this was the root of his antisemitism is hard to tell, but his religious faith served him well in many of his short stories.

9. Hugh Kenner, "From Lower Bellowvia," *Harper's*, February 1982, 62–65. Kenner referred to Bellow as a "sardonic connoisseur of Old Testament motifs." He possesses a "tribal penchant for arguing," Kenner said, and that Albert Corde, the non-Jewish narrator of the novel is but a biblical Jonah hooked to his whale by "a Hebrew safety pin." In response Bellow wrote, "Kenner was openly anti-Semitic. He won't set off a wave of Jew-hatred but it's curious that he should decide to come out openly in his Eliot-Pound anti-Semitic regalia." SB, letter to Robert Boyers, March 12, 1982, in *Saul Bellow: Letters*, 393.

10. Roudané and Bellow, "Interview with Saul Bellow," 272.

11. Ibid.

12. SB, *The Dean's December* (New York: Harper and Row, 1982), 204.

13. Michiko Kakutani, "A Talk with Saul Bellow: On His Work and Himself," *NYT*, December 13, 1981.

14. SB, *Dean's December*, 196.

15. Diane Johnson, "Point of Departure," *NYRB*, March 4, 1982, 6, 8.

16. SB, "The Jefferson Lectures," in *It All Adds Up: From the Dim Past to an Uncertain Future* (New York: Viking, 1994), 117.

17. Ibid., 119.

18. Zachary Leader, *The Life of Saul Bellow: Love and Strife, 1965–2005* (New York: Alfred A. Knopf, 201), 252.

19. SB, "Jefferson Lectures," 145.

20. Ibid., 148.

21. Ibid. The following Bellow quotes are on pages 148–52.

22. Ibid., 152.

23. Paul Carroll, "Bellow's Culture Shock," *Chicago*, September 1977.

24. Leader, *Love and Strife*, 255.

25. Ibid., 255, 259. William Kennedy, "If Saul Bellow Doesn't Have a True Word to Say, He Keeps His Mouth Shut," *Esquire*, February 1, 1982. When the lectures were published in *It All Adds Up: From the Dim Past to the Uncertain Future* (1994), the sentence, "In the slums today comes a savage fury directed at the middle class," was stricken, perhaps because the preponderance of Black crime in the slums was lower-class Black-on-Black crime.

26. Both "Acatla" and "Very Dark Trees" are discussed in chap. 3.

27. Leader, *Love and Strife*, 256; James Atlas, *Bellow: A Biography* (New York: Random House, 2000), 474.

28. Leader, *Love and Strife*, 259; Atlas, *Bellow*, 473.

29. Atlas, *Bellow*, 474.

30. Ibid., 473–74. This is likely another example of an invention by Atlas.

31. Ibid.

32. SB, letter to Edward Shils, August 22, 1980, quoted in Leader, *Love and Strife*, 291–92.

33. SB, letter to Richard Stern, October 1, 1977, in *Saul Bellow: Letters*, 351–52.

34. Leader, *Love and Strife*, 291–92. What Aviva Green wished foremost to say about Bellow about the day (they had met before in Jerusalem, where the Sternbergs had a house) was how confirming he was to her as an artist. Bellow not only bought one of her paintings; he gave her two

pieces of extremely good advice: first, to go to her studio every day, since "nothing can happen in the studio unless you are in the studio"; second, to put aside "the business of art . . . just don't think about it." "He recognized I was very ambitious and was saying, don't let the business of art intrude."

35. Leon Wieseltier, "Saul Bellow's Ferocious Beliefs," *New Republic*, June 10, 2014.

36. SB, *Dangling Man* (New York: New American Library, 1944), 46.

37. Leader, *Love and Strife*, 295.

38. SB, letter to Leon Wieseltier, January 18, 1978, in *Saul Bellow: Letters*, 353–55. In 1978, Wieseltier, while still a graduate student at Harvard, had organized an open letter to protest the Begin government's foot-dragging in responding to the peace initiatives of Egyptian president Anwar Sadat. Signed by prominent American Jews including Bellow, Irving Howe, Jacob Neusner, Seymour Martin Lipstadt, and Lucy Dawidowicz, the letter received front-page treatment from the *New York Times*.

39. SB, letter to Leon Wieseltier, May 19, 1978, in *Saul Bellow: Letters*, 358–60. In a letter dated October 9, 1978, to his old friend Julian Behrstock, Bellow complained that the IRS had "presented its bill and cleaned me out. . . . I had a sudden and unhappy need for dollars, so I went on the road, and every time I gave a talk Washington took away 50% of the fee." *Saul Bellow: Letters*, 363. Julian Behrstock (1915–97), a classmate from Northwestern days, had after the war moved permanently to Paris, where he worked at UNESCO.

40. SB, letter to Hyman Slate, July 22, 1980, in *Saul Bellow: Letters*, 377.

41. SB, letter to Hyman Slate, summer 1978, quoted in Atlas, *Bellow*, 475.

42. SB, quoted in Leader, *Love and Strife*, 297.

43. Atlas, *Bellow*, 471.

44. Ibid., 518–21.

45. Ibid., 472.

46. SB, letters to Hyman Slate, July 22, 1980, and August 21, 1981, in *Saul Bellow: Letters*, 377, 385–86.

47. SB, letter to Nathan Gould, August 4, 1982, in *Saul Bellow: Letters*, 398–99.

48. SB, letter to John Cheever, December 9, 1981, in *Saul Bellow: Letters*, 386–87.

49. SB, letter to Philip Roth, December 31, 1981, in *Saul Bellow: Letters*, 389; SB, letter to William Kennedy, February 4, 1982, in *Saul Bellow: Letters*, 389–90; Barnett Singer, "Looking for Mr. Bellow," *Jewish Dialog*, Hannukah 1982; Leader, *Love and Strife*, 315; Atlas, *Bellow*, 500.

50. Pollitt, "Bellow Blows Hot and Cold,"66–67; Dudar, "Graying of Saul Bellow."

51. SB, "In the Days of Roosevelt," in *IAAU*, 17–31. Originally published in *Esquire*, February 1983.

52. Ibid., 31.

53. David Remnick, "Mr. Bellow's Planet," *New Yorker*, May 23, 1994.

54. See, in particular, acclamatory reviews by Cynthia Ozick, "Farcical Combat in a Busy World," *NYTBR*, May 20, 1984; Robert M. Adams, "Winter's Tale," *NYRB*, July 19, 1984; Eugene Goodheart, "Parables of the Artist," *Partisan Review* 52, no. 2 (1985).

55. SB, *Him with His Foot in His Mouth and Other Stories* (New York: Harper and Row, 1984), 117. Originally published in *Atlantic Monthly*, February 1984.

56. SB, "Cousins," in *Foot in His Mouth*, 267.

57. Ibid., 245, 241–42; Ozick, "Farcical Combat."

58. As Mitterrand tied the decoration around his neck, Bellow quietly told him in French, "'Better to be decorated than hanged!' I hope he didn't hear me. . . . At a solemn moment, you know, when a man puts his arms around you and he's fastening a knot around your neck." Interview with Curt Suplee, "Getting It Right," *Washington Post*, May 20, 1984, quoted in Leader, *Love and Strife*, 334.

59. Leader, *Love and Strife*, 334.

60. Harriet Wasserman, *Handsome Is: Adventures with Saul Bellow* (New York: Fromm International, 1997), 109, 110.

61. Ruth Wisse, "Bellow's Gift—a Memoir," *Commentary*, December 1, 2001.

62. Ibid.

63. Ibid. Wisse would go on to become a professor of Yiddish at Harvard in 1993.

64. Greg Bellow, *Saul Bellow's Heart* (New York: Bloomsbury, 2013), 159.

65. Ruth Miller, *Saul Bellow: A Biography of the Imagination* (New York: St. Martin's, 1991), 303.

66. Ibid., 302–3.

67. "Samuel Bellows, 74, Jewish Leader," *Chicago Tribune*, June 4, 1985.

68. Leader, *Love and Strife*, 343; Miller, *Saul Bellow*, 304.

69. Miller, *Saul Bellow*, 304.

70. Ibid., 303–4.

71. Leader, *Love and Strife*, 343–44.

72. Ibid.

73. Ibid.

74. SB, "Cousins," 294.

75. Alfred Kazin, "Though He Slay Me," *NYRB*, December 3, 1970; Alfred Kazin, *Alfred Kazin's Journals*, ed. Richard Cook (New Haven, CT: Yale University Press, 2012), 435.

76. Alfred Kazin, interview by author, May 15, 1997, a year before he died in 1998 on June 5, his eighty-fourth birthday. Kazin assured me that he had "always been on the left. I saw the same problems Irving [Howe] did. I still do," he said—"the poverty, the greed, the materialism, the complacency of intellectuals, the racism."

77. Wieseltier's two-part essay on Arendt concluded, "There are not anti-Semites because there are Jews, and there are not Jews because there are anti-Semites. There are peoples and a longing for paradise. The Jews are there for when the longing goes bad, when it ends in tumbrils or in boxcars. But now they have Israel, an America, and the night vision that has always sustained them, that has helped them to believe in the best even when they knew the worst, and kept them steady, and on their course in the dark." Leon Wieseltier, "Hannah Arendt and the Jews," *New Republic*, October 7 and 14, 1981.

78. At the dinner were Alexandra; Adam Bellow and his girlfriend, Rachel Newton (soon to be his wife); Kazin and his third wife, Judith Dunford; and Freund and his wife, Peregrine. Atlas, *Bellow*, 518; Kazin, entries of May 29, 1985, and June 1, 1985, in *Alfred Kazin's Journal*, 522, 523. Bellow and Kazin were corresponding cordially through at least June 1983. In June 1982, Bellow sent these lines: "A happy birthday to you and admiration and love and a long life—everything. Never mind this and that, this and that don't matter much in the summing up. Love from your junior by five days." *Saul Bellow: Letters*, 397. See also p. 412. A little more than three years after the birthday party, Bellow may have softened toward Kazin. Asked to serve with Eudora Welty and Kazin on a panel to recommend candidates for the Gold Medal in Fiction, Bellow wrote, "I don't mind chatting with Eudora Welty. Alfred Kazin and I, who have known each other from the beginning of time, always found it difficult to agree. I like to think, though, that while he has grown more rigid I have grown more flexible. . . . I see no reason why we shouldn't produce a good list." SB, letter to Margaret Mills, October 26, 1988, quoted in Leader, *Love and Strife*, 705.

15. A WHOLE NEW LIFE

1. James Atlas, *Bellow: A Biography* (New York, Random House, 2000), 474.

2. Zachary Leader, *The Life of Saul Bellow: Love and Strife, 1965–2005* (New York: Alfred A. Knopf, 2018), 375, 706n140.

3. Greg Bellow, *Saul Bellow's Heart* (New York: Bloomsbury, 2013), 162.

4. Leader, *Love and Strife,* 355. All of Janis Freedman's quotations, unless otherwise indicated, are from interviews done by Zachary Leader on August 5, 6, and 7, 2010, and February 23, 2017.

5. Janis Bellow, interview by author, November 14, 2021.

6. Leader, *Love and Strife,* 386.

7. Werner J. Dannhauser, "Allan Bloom and His Critics," *American Spectator,* October 1988. Perhaps even more important was the attack on Bloom's scholarship. The philosopher Martha Nussbaum was in the lead on this front, taking Bloom to task for failing to point out the enormous difficulty of the classical texts he promoted. There was a troubling silence, too, Nussbaum wrote, between Bloom's official allegiance to Socrates and Socrates's own view of himself as the "idiot questioner." "Undemocratic Vistas," *NYRB,* November 5, 1987.

8. SB, preface to *The Closing of the American Mind,* by Allan Bloom (New York: Simon and Schuster, 1987), 20.

9. Ibid.

10. SB, "Writers, Intellectuals, Politics: Mainly Reminiscences," in *It All Adds Up: From the Dim Past to an Uncertain Future* (New York: Viking, 1994), 111–12; Daniel Fuchs, "Literature and Politics: The Bellow/Grass Confrontation," in *Writers and Thinkers: Selected Literary Criticism* (Piscataway, NJ: Transaction, 2015), 144–45. In 1984, two years before the PEN Congress, Bellow in an interview had already laid out that position, and not for the first time: "After something like half a century in Chicago I think I may claim to have well-founded views on American commercial democracy. I know that art is not one of the stronger interests of American communities. That's not what the enterprise is about. The main enterprise was not to produce a 'higher life' but stable prosperity, a middling condition, personal liberties guaranteed, a reasonable facsimile of justice. A state of decent dullness. That hasn't worked either. The decay of the city makes that clear to everybody." Matthew C. Roudané and Saul Bellow, "An Interview with Saul Bellow," *Contemporary Literature* 25, no. 3 (1994): 266.

11. David Lehman, "When Pens Collide," *Partisan Review* 53, no. 2 (1986), 190. Some things did not go as planned or fit with Norman Mailer's opening statement: "The purpose of the Congress will be to embrace relations rather than smash them. We are not going to seek for invidious comparisons. . . . Writers speak across national boundaries. . . . One may hope that new solutions, even surprisingly creative solutions, can be found."

12. SB, *IAAU*, 111; R. Z. Sheppard, "Independent States of Mind," *Time*, January 27, 1986; Rhoda Koenig, "At Play in the Fields of the Word: Alienation, Imagination, Feminism and the Foolishness of PEN," *New York*, February 3, 1986.

13. Lehman, "When Pens Collide," 197.

14. S. Taberner, ed., *The Cambridge Companion to Günter Grass* (Cambridge: Cambridge University Press, 2009), xiv–xviii. Panzer divisions were part of the Wehrmacht of Nazi Germany and were a key element of German success in the blitzkrieg operations of the early years of the war.

15. Richard Stern, "Some Members of the Congress," *Critical Inquiry* 14, no. 4 (1988): 885; Lehman, "When Pens Collide," 198–99. In any case, Bellow largely agreed with writers like Mario Vargas Llosa, another delegate to the congress, who said that once a writer "becomes an instrument of power he isn't a writer anymore." Nadine Gordimer seconded Llosa's view and supported Bellow's position in his answer to an inane question by Salman Rushdie about the "task" of the writer: "We don't have any tasks," Bellow said, "we just have inspirations." In Gordimer's view, the writer's imagination "must be private not collective . . . The state thinks of the imagination of the writer as merely something that can be put into service." Fuchs, "Literature and Politics," 144–45, 150.

16. SB, "In Memory of Bernard Malamud," in *Saul Bellow: Letters*, ed. Benjamin Taylor (New York: Viking, 2010), 435–36. The memorial was delivered in Bellow's absence by Harold Nemerov at the annual luncheon of the American Academy and Institute of Arts and Letters, New York, December 5, 1986.

17. Atlas, *Bellow*, 522.

18. Timothy Garton Ash, email to Zachary Leader, April 15, 2010. Writer Edna O'Brien was one of the "interveners."

19. Leader, *Love and Strife*, 397.

20. Ruth R. Wisse, "The Novelist," *Tablet Magazine*, March 7, 2011; Janis Bellow, interview by author, November 14, 2021.

21. Leader, *Love and Strife*, 418.

22. Bellow's attitude about overanalyzed literature is most accessible in SB, "A Matter of the Soul," in *IAAU*, 73–79. Originally published in *Opera News*, January 11, 1975. "There must be 25,000,000 college graduates in the U.S., but one of the problems of this country is the silliness, instability, and philistinism of its educated people. I often think there is more hope for the young worker who picks up a paperback copy of Faulkner or Melville or Tolstoy from the rack in the drugstore than there is for the B.A. who has

had the same writers 'interpreted' for him by his teacher and can tell you, or thinks he can, what Ahab's harpoon symbolizes or what great Christian symbols there are in *Light in August*." SB, "Matter of the Soul," 76.

23. Leila H. Goldman and Ada Aharoni, "A Talk with Saul Bellow," *Israel Scene*, April 1988, quoted in Leader, *Love and Strife*, 420, 422.

24. Berel Lang, telephone conversation with author, July 2, 2021; SB, letter to Ozick, July 19, 1987, in *Saul Bellow: Letters*, 437–40; SB, "My Paris," in *IAAU*, 231–39.

25. SB, "My Paris" in SB, *STM*, ed. Benjamin Taylor (New York: Viking, 2015), 338–46. Originally published as "The Sophisticated Traveler," *NYTM*, pt. 2, March 13, 1983.

26. SB, letter to Martin Amis, January 7, 1987, quoted in Leader, *Love and Strife*, 713n87.

27. SB, *More Die of Heartbreak* (New York: William and Morrow, 1987), 98, 190

28. Ibid., 326.

29. Eugene Kennedy, "Saul Bellow Teaches an 'Object' Lesson," *Chicago Tribune*, May 31, 1987.

30. Ibid.

31. Leader, *Love and Strife*, 413; Janis Bellow, interview by author, November 14, 2021.

32. Bellow was taken to task by Terrence Rafferty in "Hearts and Minds," *New Yorker*, July 20, 1987; Craig Raine, usually a reliable admirer of Bellow's work, was equally tough in "Soul Bellow," *London Review of Books*, November 12, 1987. More positive were William Gaddis, "An Instinct for the Dangerous Wife," *NYTBR*, May 24, 1987; Anne Tyler, "Saul Bellow's Magic," *Chicago Sun-Times*, May 31, 1987.

33. Alfred Kazin, "Trachtenberg the Rain King," *NYRB*, June 26, 1987.

34. Wieseltier's review damaged his relationship with Bellow for some time. "I missed him," Wieseltier said over the course of their estrangement: "He was one of the most charismatic persons I ever met . . . He was a magical Jew." Whatever he meant by "magical Jew," it did not stop Wieseltier from including in his assessment, "The novel is in a sense spiritually anti- American." It presents the United States as a "commotion of deceits and distractions . . . a tawdry shrine to money and power." Leon Wieseltier, interview by Zachary Leader, in Leader, *Love and Strife*, 715n103; Leon Wieseltier, "Soul and Form," *New Republic*, August 31, 1987.

35. SB, letter to Karl Shapiro, July 31, 1987, in *Saul Bellow: Letters*, 440–41.

36. Bellow had been working on three novels, a novella, and a short story and continued some of that work until at least the mid to late 1990s. The two longest unfinished manuscripts were "A Case of Love" (207 typed pages) and "All Marbles Accounted For" (279 typed pages). See Leader, *Love and Strife*, 427–28. In April 1992, Bellow served on a panel at Rutgers University with Ralph Ellison, Czeslaw Milosz, and Joseph Brodsky titled "Intellectual and Social Change in Central and Eastern Europe." Bellow said that the collapse of Communism was something to celebrate, but now the West was forced to confront the emptiness of its own values.

37. Leader, *Love and Strife*, 427.

38. Ibid., 34, 432.

39. Gloria L. Cronin, "Our Father's Politics: Gregory, Adam, and Daniel Bellow," in *A Political Companion to Saul Bellow*, ed. Gloria L. Cronin and Lee Trepanier (Lexington: University Press of Kentucky, 2014), 201.

40. Walden, quoted in Leader, *Love and Strife*, 438.

41. George Walden, *Lucky George: Memoirs of an Anti-politician* (London: Penguin, 2000), 272–76.

42. Eugene Kennedy, "Anti-Semitism in Chicago: A Stunning Silence," *NYT*, July 26, 1988.

43. Ibid.

44. Leader, *Love and Strife*, 441.

45. SB, "Voice of the People: Face the Truth of Racial Turmoil," *Chicago Tribune*, August 14, 1988.

46. Mike Royko, "Put Up or Shut Up Time in Chicago," *Chicago Tribune*, May 18, 1988.

47. SB, "Voice of the People."

48. Irving Howe, *A Margin of Hope: An Intellectual Autobiography* (New York: Harcourt Brace Jovanovich, 1982), 137–38.

49. Bellow quotes from Lionel Abel's memoir, *The Intellectual Follies* (1984). Abel had only heard vague reports of mass killing in the concentration camps in Eastern Europe. But in newsreels that accompanied a motion picture to which he had taken his mother, he witnessed the discovery at Buchenwald of "mounds of dead bodies, the emaciated, wasted, but still living prisoners." He saw the gallows and the gas chambers, which were employed to kill Jews en masse. "It was an unforgettable sight on the screen," but as remarkable, Abel wrote, was what his mother said when they left the theater: "I don't think the Jews can get over the disgrace of this." *Intellectual Follies*, 17.

50. SB, "A Jewish Writer in America," *NYRB*, October 27, 2011; SB, "A Jewish Writer in America—II," *NYRB*, November 10, 2011.

51. Janis Freedman Bellow, preface to *Saul Bellow: Collected Stories,* with an introduction by James Wood (New York: Viking, 2001), v–ix.

52. See Mark Cohen, *Not Bad for Delancey Street: The Rise of Billy Rose, America's Greatest Jewish Impresario* (Waltham, MA: Brandeis University Press, 2018).

53. SB, *The Bellarosa Connection* (New York: Penguin Group, 1989), 28–29.

54. The word *Holocaust* appears only once in *Sammler.* A scene in which Sammler crawls out of a mass grave is described a number of times with variations. He also loses an eye as a result of a whack with the butt of a Nazi's rifle, and there is a paragraph that reads, "In their peculiar transformation: a people changed into uniform, massed in military cloth and helmets, and coming with machinery for the purpose of murdering boys, girls, men, women, making blood run, burying, and finally exhuming and burning rotten corpses." SB, *Mr. Sammler's Planet* (New York: Viking, 1970), 200.

55. SB, *Bellarosa Connection,* 28–29.

56. Ibid., 48.

57. Ibid., 53.

58. Ibid., 85.

59. Ibid., 101–2.

60. Ibid. The prayer recited during Yom Kippur services begins "*Yiskor elohim nishmat* . . ." ("May God remember the soul of . . .").

61. SB, *Bellarosa Connection,* 102.

62. SB, "Something to Remember Me By," in *Something to Remember Me By* (New York: Viking, 1991), 187, 188. Originally published in *Esquire,* July 1990.

63. Ibid., 207.

64. Ibid., 213.

65. Atlas, *Bellow,* 543.

66. Ibid.

67. Ibid., 544.

68. Philip Roth, letter to SB, June 11, 1990, quoted in Leader, *Love and Strife,* 476.

69. SB, letter to Philip Roth, June 24, 1990, in *Saul Bellow: Letters,* 467.

70. Leader, *Love and Strife,* 479. See also Gerald Nemanic, "Politicians Sing of Bellow's Gift to Fiction, City," *Chicago Tribune,* October 9, 1990; Mary A. Johnson, "Bellow Marks His 75th," *Chicago Sun-Times,* October 8, 1990.

71. Proverbs 8:22–23, 30–31; SB, "Mozart: An Overture," in *IAAU,* 1–14. Originally published in *Bostonia,* spring 1992. Delivered at the Mozart Bicentennial, December 5, 1991, in Florence, Italy.

72. SB, letter to John Auerbach, March 2, 1992, in *Saul Bellow: Letters,* 494–92.

73. Furet was president of the Saint-Simon Foundation and best known for his books on the French Revolution.

74. Janis Freedman Bellow, "Double Trouble in the Promised Land," *Bostonia,* winter 1993.

75. Leader, *Love and Strife,* 492–93, 497.

76. Atlas, *Bellow,* 566.

77. SB, letter to Jonathan Kleinbard, April 25, 1993, in *Saul Bellow: Letters,* 493.

78. SB, *Settling My Accounts before I Go Away: A Words and Images Interview by Norman Manea* (Rhinebeck, NY: Sheep Meadow Press, 1999), 53.

79. Leader, *Love and Strife,* 501–2.

16. BELLOW BANISHED AND BRUISED

1. David Remnick, "Mr. Bellow's Planet," *New Yorker,* May 23, 1994.

2. SB, preface to *The Closing of the American Mind,* by Allan Bloom (New York: Simon and Schuster, 1987). Bellow's take, however, was not political; it was much more about the powers of the self to overcome obstacles to its own definition.

3. James Atlas, "Chicago's Grumpy Guru," *NYTM,* January 3, 1988; James Atlas, *The Shadow in the Garden* (New York: Vintage Books, 2018), 267–69; Robert Curry, "'Hey, Hey, Ho, Ho, Western Civ Has Got to Go,'" *Charlemagne Institute Chronicles Magazine,* June 11, 2019, https://www.intellectualtakeout.org/article/hey-hey-ho-ho-western-civ-has-got-go/.

4. Zachary Leader, *The Life of Saul Bellow: Love and Strife, 1965–2005* (New York: Alfred A. Knopf, 2018), 726n33; Atlas, *Shadow in the Garden,* 178n.

5. Leader, *Love and Strife,* 401.

6. James Atlas, *Bellow: A Biography* (New York: Random House, 2000), xii–xiv; James Atlas, "The Shadow in the Garden," *New Yorker,* July 3, 1995. See also his memoir with the same title (New York: Vintage Press, 2018); Mark Harris, *Drumlin Woodchuck* (Athens: University of Georgia Press, 1980).

7. Alfred Kazin, "Jew," *New Yorker,* March 7, 1994.

8. SB, "Op-Ed: Papuans and Zulus," *NYT,* March 10, 1994.

9. See Peter F. Langman, "Including Jews in Multiculturalism," *Journal of Multiculturalism Counseling and Development* 23, no. 4 (1995): 222–36;

Dan Ian Rubin, "Still Wandering: The Exclusion of Jews from Issues of Social Justice and Multicultural Thought," *Multicultural Perspectives* 15, no. 4 (2013): 213–19.

10. SB, "Papuans and Zulus." Bellow actually misidentifies Thomas Mofolo's *Chaka* as a "Zulu novel." It is about a Zulu king, but it was written in Sesotho around 1909 and translated into English in the 1930s.

11. Rhoda Koenig, a journalist covering the 1986 PEN Conference, told Zachary Leader that Bellow had made a similar remark about Zulus and Papuans at the conference. She was more than surprised that when Bellow said these words there had been "no protest or even indignation." Leader, *Love and Strife*, 726n39; Rhoda Koenig, "At Play in the Fields of the Word: Alienation, Imagination, Feminism and the Foolishness of PEN," *New York*, February 3, 1986.

12. Leader, *Love and Strife*, 507; Brent Staples, "Into the Ivory Tower," *NYTM*, February 6, 1994; Staples, *Parallel Time: Growing Up in Black and White* (New York: Pantheon Books, 1994), 191–243.

13. See chap. 11, note 70.

14. Staples, *Parallel Time*, 238.

15. Atlas, *Shadow in the Garden*, 267–69.

16. SB, letter to Paul Hollander (political sociologist), September 7, 1995; James Atlas, quoted in Leader, *Love and Strife*, 728n55.

17. SB, "Papuans and Zulus."

18. Atlas, *Bellow*, 573.

19. Remnick, "Mr. Bellow's Planet."

20. SB, letter to Milton Hindus, May 31, 1994, quoted in Leader, *Love and Strife*, 511.

21. Remnick, "Mr. Bellow's Planet."

22. SB, "Papuans and Zulus."

23. "Symposium: Is There a Cure for Anti-Semitism?," *Partisan Review* 61, no. 3 (1994). Bellow was the first speaker, but he was joined by Cynthia Ozick, historian Eugene Genovese, writer-critic Stanley Crouch, culture critic and editor Norman Podhoretz, and several editors and journalists including Martin Peretz and Jim Sleeper. About the word *anti-Semitism* in the title of the symposium, *Partisan Review* had not yet dropped the hyphen. Holocaust historian Yehuda Bauer wrote in 1994, "Anti-Semitism is altogether an absurd construction, since there is no such thing as 'Semitism' to which it might be opposed." Bauer quoted in https://www.jewishvirtuallibrary.org/anti-semitism-or-antisemitism. Today, the hyphen is eliminated by scholars in the field and in the titles of journals—e.g., *Antisemitism Studies* (University of Indiana Press). ADL has also

adopted the spelling of *antisemitism* instead of *anti-Semitism*. Shira Hanau, "The New York Times Updates Style Guide to 'antisemitism,' Losing the Hyphen," December 8, 2021.

24. Atlas, *Bellow*, 576.

25. SB, letter to Eugene Kennedy, November 10, 1994, in *Saul Bellow: Letters*, ed. Benjamin Taylor (New York: Viking, 2010), 504.

26. Greg Bellow, *Saul Bellow's Heart* (New York: Bloomsbury, 2013), 195.

27. SB, "View from Intensive Care," in *Editors: The Best from Five Decades*, by SB and Keith Botsford (London: Toby, 2001), 73–82.

28. SB, *Settling My Accounts before I Go Away: A Words and Images Interview by Norman Manea* (Rhinebeck, NY: Sheep Meadow Press, 1999), 99; SB, "View from Intensive Care." Bellow wrote to the chair of the Promotions Committee at the BU Department of Medicine, telling him that "to say that [Barnardo] saved my life would not be an overstatement," and the letter was punctuated with words of great praise, including, "As an attending physician he is undoubtedly brilliant, energetic, devoted, but perhaps his qualities as a human being are even more rare and worthy of recognition." SB, letter to Jay D. Hoffman, August 1, 2000, quoted in Leader, *Love and Strife*, 730n9.

29. Daniel Bellow, email to Zachary Leader, March 24, 2017. Other quotes attributed to Daniel Bellow are, if not otherwise indicated, from interviews done by Zachary Leader on May 11 and 15, 2008, and May 31, 2017.

30. Daniel Bellow's point about "the standard Russian Jewish child rearing method" is either an exaggeration or too optimistic an assessment. It is true, however, that Saul's father, Abraham, was a reader and read aloud to his children. Abraham Bellow did not want his youngest son to become a writer, but he unwittingly contributed to Saul's motivation to become one. See Daniel Bellow, "Our Father's Politics," in *A Political Companion to Saul Bellow*, ed. Gloria L. Cronin and Lee Trapanier (Lexington: University Press of Kentucky, 2013).

31. SB, quoted in Atlas, *Bellow*, 581.

32. Shils thought, probably correctly, that he was a model for Mr. Sammler, who through most of *Mr. Sammler's Planet* (1970) was drawn in a distinctly unflattering way. He also refused to let Bellow get jobs at the Committee for Social Thought for his undeserving girlfriends, or as Shils called them, *nafkas* (Yiddish for "whores").

33. SB, "In Memory of Yetta Barshevsky Shachtman," printed in the program for Yetta Schachtman's memorial service in New York City, September 22, 1996, repr. in *Saul Bellow: Letters*, 527–28.

34. SB, letter to Werner Dannhauser, September 1, 1997, in *Saul Bellow: Letters*, 535.

35. SB, letter to Hyman Slate, November 25, 1996, in *Saul Bellow: Letters*, 527–28. Slate died only weeks later. He believed laughter was proof of God. "But," Bellow said, "God in the end laid two kinds of cancer on him and took him away very quickly." SB, letter to Werner Dannhauser, September 1, 1997, in *Saul Bellow: Letters*, 535.

36. Atlas, *Bellow*, 587. As late as 2011, Daniel told an interviewer that he had had a political argument with his father in the late 1980s. Bellow seemed to lump his son's liberalism together with the left and "its insincerity, its hypocrisy." But he soon saw the mistake he had made and issued a genuine apology. "Pop was the best," Daniel said; "I'm so proud to be his son." D. Bellow, "Our Father's Politics," 215.

37. Atlas, *Bellow*, 587.

38. Bryan Appleyard, "Angry Old Man," *Sunday Times* (London), May 21, 1995. In 1982, Bellow gave a more direct "Yes" about his belief in God. But he prefaced that by saying, "The first thing you have to do is to locate your soul and find out what it has to suggest. . . . The farther you get away from the promptings of your soul, the more trouble you are in." Melvyn Bragg, *South Bank Show*, BBC-TV, March 28, 1982; Atlas, *Bellow*, 580. Asked in 1989 by Jack Miles, author of *God: A Biography* (1996), whether he prayed, Bellow said, "It's a casual checking in at universe headquarters at night, as I pull up the covers." Jack Miles, "Saul Bellow's Life Is an Open Book," *Los Angeles Times*, March 30, 1989.

39. SB, letter to Cynthia Ozick, October 17, 1997, quoted in Leader, *Love and Strife*, 250.

40. Appleyard, "Angry Old Man."

41. SB, "By the St. Lawrence," in *Collected Stories*, with an introduction by James Wood and a preface by Janis Bellow (New York: Viking, 2001), 1–5. Originally published in *Esquire*, July 1995, 1.

42. Ibid., 11.

43. SB, letter to Werner Dannhauser, August 25, 1995, quoted in Leader, *Love and Strife*, 547.

44. SB, "By the St. Lawrence," 8.

45. Ibid., 11.

46. Daniel Fuchs, "Literature and Politics: The Bellow/Grass Confrontation," in *Writers and Thinkers: Selected Literary Criticism* (Piscataway, NJ: Transaction, 2015), 144–45.

47. Ibid., 144–45, 150.

48. Richard Stern, letter to James Atlas, quoted in Atlas, *Bellow*, 582.

49. Sabrina L. Miller, "Bellow's Return: It All Adds Up," *Chicago Tribune*, December 7, 1995.

50. SB, letter to Alan Lelchuck, March 22, 1976, in Leader, *Love and Strife*, 615.

51. Leader, *Love and Strife*, 615–16.

52. SB, letter to Glotzer, April 19, 1996, in *Saul Bellow: Letters*, 518–19.

53. David Gates, "The Heavy Hitters Are Up," *Newsweek*, April 8, 1997; Alfred Kazin, "Struggles of a Prophet," *NYRB*, June 26, 1997; James Wood, "Essences Rising," *New Republic*, June 16, 1997.

54. SB, *The Actual* (New York: Viking, 1997), 3, 9.

55. Leader, *Love and Strife*, 34, 432.

56. See Louis Begley, "Old Flames and Trillionaires," *NYTBR*, May 25, 1997; Martin Amis. "Hitting His Stride," *Los Angeles Times Book Review*, June 8, 1997.

57. Nicolette Jones, "The Order of Merit," *Sunday Times* (London), March 13, 1994.

58. Atlas, *Bellow*, 570n.

59. None of this is to say that Jewish Americans weren't writing fiction in the 1990s and on through to the first decades of the twenty-first century. Cynthia Ozick is a special case. She wrote her first novel, *Trust*, in 1966, and then, at the age of ninety-three, *Antiquities* in 2021. An arbitrary but alphabetical list of Jewish American writers who were writing from the 1990s onward follows: Paul Auster, David Bezmozgis, Joshua Cohen, Rebecca Goldstein, Eli Gottlieb, Allegra Goodman, Joshua Henkin, Rachel Kadish, Rachel Kushner, Jonathan Lethem, Tova Mirvis, Steve Stern, Gary Shteyngart, Lara Vapnyar, Adam Wilson, and Jonathan Wilson.

60. Julia Keller, "Between the Covers, Bellow Sparks Firestorm," *Chicago Tribune*, April 30, 2000.

61. David Streitfeld, "A Jolly Good Fellow: The Author, in Person and Paint, at Portrait Gallery," *Washington Post*, June 12, 1997.

62. Richard Stern, letter to James Atlas, in Atlas, *Bellow*, 590.

63. Proverbs 22:29; SB, quoted in Atlas, *Bellow*, 590.

64. "Saul Bellow," in *50 Years of Playboy Interviews: Men of Letters* (New York: Playboy Enterprises, 1997), loc. 7045 of 8095, Kindle; SB, "I've Got a Scheme: With Philip Roth," in *There Is Simply Too Much to Think About*, ed. Benjamin Taylor (New York: Viking, 2015), 467–93; SB, *Settling My Accounts*. This interview with Manea was conducted over a two-day period, December 22 and 23. Bellow told *New York Times* interviewer Mel Gussow

that "if you asked me if I believed in life after death, I would say I was an agnostic. There are more things between heaven and earth, Horatio, etc." Mel Gussow, "For Saul Bellow, Seeing the Earth with Fresh Eyes," *NYT*, May 26, 1997. See also Hillel Italie, "The New Adventures of Saul Bellow," *Chicago Sun-Times*, May 4, 1997.

65. SB, *It All Adds Up: From the Dim Past to an Uncertain Future* (New York: Viking, 1994); SB, *STM*.

66. Atlas, *Bellow*, 592.

17. LIFE AND DEATH

1. Zachary Leader, *The Life of Saul Bellow: Love and Strife, 1965–2005* (New York: Alfred A. Knopf, 2018), 221.

2. James Atlas, *Bellow: A Biography* (New York: Random House, 2000), 593.

3. SB, *Ravelstein*, with an introduction by Gary Shteyngart (New York: Viking, 2015), xi. Originally published 2000 without introduction.

4. Gary Shteyngart, introduction to *Ravelstein*, xiv.

5. The *Washington Post* and the *Toronto Star* assumed early on that the novel was actually a biography and that Bellow had revealed "for the first time that Bloom was a homosexual." The British and American press followed suit. Within days the equation Ravelstein = Bloom was firmly established. Journalists all over the United States were announcing, as the *New York Daily News* put it, that Bellow had "outed" Bloom. See D. T. Max, "With Friends Like Saul Bellow," *NYTM*, April 16, 2000. Many who made the connection were praiseworthy and failed to accuse Bellow of anything much. See Robert Fulford, "Saul Bellow, Allan Bloom, and Abe Ravelstein," *Globe and Mail*, November 2, 1999; Stephen Moss, "*Ravelstein* by Saul Bellow," *Guardian*, May 11, 2000; Dinitia Smith, "A Bellow Novel Eulogizes a Friend," *NYT*, January 27, 2000. David Cohen, who knew Bloom and Bellow well, wrote enthusiastically that "the central figure, Abe Ravelstein, is more than simply modeled on Allan Bloom, he *is* Bloom." Cohen, "Notes on Ravelstein" (unpublished manuscript, 2008), http://editorialnote.net/files/ravelstein.pdf.

6. In *Bound and Gagged: Pornography and the Politics of Fantasy in America* (New York: Grove, 1998), Laura Kipnis writes that "it was fairly common knowledge around the University of Chicago campus . . . that Bloom was gay. . . . Given that his public pronouncements and political

affiliations seemed in conflict with his personal life, this was of some local interest." Ibid., 222n19.

7. SB, *Ravelstein*, 115. Of course, as Andrew Patner, a Chicago cultural icon and a student of Bloom's, wrote in the *Chicago Sun-Times Book Week*, "Only two people know what promise Bloom extracted from Bellow, and one of them is dead." See Atlas, *Bellow*, 597–98.

8. Max, "With Friends Like Saul Bellow."

9. Ibid.

10. SB, *Ravelstein*, 27, 118.

11. SB, *Settling My Accounts before I Go Away: A Words and Images Interview by Norman Manea* (Rhinebeck, NY: Sheep Meadow Press, 1999), 48.

12. Sam Tanenhaus, "Bellow, Bloom, and Betrayal," *Wall Street Journal*, February 2, 2000.

13. Max, "With Friends Like Saul Bellow."

14. Janis Bellow, "Rosamund and *Ravelstein*: The Discandying of a Creator's Confection," in *On Life Writing*, ed. Zachary Leader (Oxford: Oxford University Press, 2015), 113.

15. James Wood, "The Worldly Mystic's Late Bloom," *Guardian*, April 15, 2000. Sir Malcolm Bradbury said, "Just when we didn't expect it, there now wonderfully comes a large new novel from the master. . . . Via print, Ravelstein survives; and Bellow survives." Notice no mention of Bloom. Bradbury, quoted in Stephen Moss, "*Ravelstein* by Saul Bellow." The Guardian, May 11, 2000; Andrew Sullivan says simply that Ravelstein is "a rumination on Allan Bloom. . . . It is written by a friend and imbued with the honest distance that true friendship confers." Andrew Sullivan, "Longing: Remembering Allan Bloom," *The New Republic*, April 17, 2000.

16. Is Bellow illustrating here in cartoon fashion America's ultramaterialism, or is his admiration for Ravelstein's possessions another example of his competitive relationship with his more affluent brothers? Is it a demonstration of his public but honest repulsion of "things," living alongside his also honest yearning for the trappings of the affluent life?

17. SB, *Ravelstein*, 107, 109–10.

18. SB, *Dangling Man* (New York: Vanguard, 1944), 80. The Iron Guard was an ultranationalist, antisemitic, far-right movement and political party in Romania in the period from 1927 into the early part of World War II.

19. SB, *Ravelstein*, 145.

20. Ibid.

21. Ibid., 154–55, 151.

22. Ibid., 155.

23. SB, "A Jewish Writer in America," *NYRB*, October 27, 2011; SB, "A Jewish Writer in America—II," *NYRB*, November 10, 2011.

24. SB, *Ravelstein*, 133–34.

25. Ibid., 155. One can hear, in Ravelstein, an echo of Martin Buber, the great Jewish theologian who wrote that "the uniqueness of man proves himself in his life with others. For the more unique a man really is, so much more can he give to the other"; or "When two people relate to each other authentically and humanly, God is the electricity that surges between them." Martin Buber, *I and Thou* (New York: Free Press, 1958).

26. Yosef Hayim Yerushalmi, *Freud's Moses: Judaism Terminable and Interminable* (New Haven, CT: Yale University Press, 1993), 9.

27. Steven Jaron, "Saul Bellow: Athens and Jerusalem," in *Makers of Jewish Modernity*," ed. Jacques Picard, Jacques Revel, Michael P. Steinberg, and Idith Zertal (Princeton, NJ: Princeton University Press, 2016), 507–18.

28. SB, *Ravelstein*, 151.

29. Ruth Wisse, "Bellow's Gift—a Memoir," *Commentary*, December 1, 2001.

30. James Atlas, *The Shadow in the Garden* (New York: Vintage Books, 2018), 313–15. Ruth Wisse told Leader that Janis and Saul were "terrified." Leader, *Love and Strife*, 606.

31. Philip Roth, "I've Got a Scheme: The Words of Saul Bellow," *New Yorker*, April 25, 2015; SB, "I've Got a Scheme: With Philip Roth," in *There Is Simply Too Much to Think About*, ed. Benjamin Taylor (New York: Viking, 2015), 467–94; both excerpted from the interviews from 1998–2000.

32. Philip Roth, "Re-reading Saul Bellow," *New Yorker*, October 9, 2000.

33. James Wood, "Give All," *New Republic*, November 2000; Lee Siegal, "Seize the Job: Sacrificing Saul Bellow on the Altar of One's Career," *Harper's Magazine*, March 20, 2001.

34. Leader, *Love and Strife*, 619.

35. Ibid., 621–22.

36. Ibid., 624–25; Janis Bellow, interview by author, November 14, 2021.

37. Greg Bellow, letters to Saul Bellow, January and May 2003, in Greg Bellow, *Saul Bellow's Heart* (New York: Bloomsbury, 2013), 205–7.

38. Leader, *Love and Strife*, 630.

39. G. Bellow, *Saul Bellow's Heart*, 212.

40. SB, letter to Eugene Kennedy, February 19, 2004, in *Saul Bellow: Letters*, ed. Benjamin Taylor (New York: Viking, 2010), 552.

41. Cynthia Ozick, "The Lasting Man," *New Republic*, February 10, 2011.

42. Janis Bellow, interview by author, November 14, 2021.

43. Leader, *Love and Strife*, 632–33.

44. Janis Bellow, interview by author, November 14, 2021. Janis is still "really upset" that the words "Was I a man or a jerk?" were misused and cited in too many places as Saul's dying words.

45. Ibid. Much of the information in this paragraph and several that follow is gathered from Zachary Leader's interviews with witnesses, including family and friends. Peripheral vascular disease includes diseases that affect the delivery of blood to the extremities. Chronic venous insufficiency is when valves within the veins fail, allowing blood to pool in the legs.

46. Ruth Wisse, email to Zachary Leader, June 16, 2017, quoted in Leader, *Love and Strife*, 640, 742n44.

47. Ibid. Later, the gravestone in Battleboro, Vermont, was carved with the name *BELLOW* in large caps, above which sat an engraving of two books. The Hebrew names *Lescha* and *Abram*, Saul's parents, hover over his full name in caps, followed by his dates of birth and death; the single word *WRITER* carved in large block letters sits at the center of the stone, followed appropriately by Hebrew initials, which stand for "may he be bound into the book of life."

48. SB, *Humboldt's Gift*, with an introduction by Jeffry Eugenides (New York: Penguin Classics, 1975), 491–92.

49. Leader, *Love and Strife*, 641–42.

50. Isaac Rosenfeld's *Passage from Home* (1946), according to literary critic Mark Shechner, "helped fashion a uniquely American voice by marrying the incisiveness of [Mark] Twain to the Russian melancholy of Dostoevsky." Oscar Tarcov's *Bravo, My Monster* (1953) was Kafkaesque in theme and mood.

51. SB, letter to Nathan Tarcov, October 22, 1963, in *Saul Bellow: Letters*, 245–46. According to Miriam Tarcov (Oscar's daughter), her father, perilously ill with a family to support, quit a steady job at the Anti-Defamation League and devoted himself to writing. But as Zachary Leader reveals, Tarcov found lucrative part-time work as an editor at Collier Books, eventually making more money than he had earned with the ADL.

APPENDIX

1. Sabin Junior High School, *Junior Sabinite* (n.p., 1929), 22; "U.S. School Yearbooks, 1880–2012," Ancestry.com, accessed June 14, 2023,

http://www.ancestry.com. A former student of mine, Miriam Strouse, who knew I was writing about Bellow, suggested that I look at Spitzer's website.

2. Ruth Miller, *Saul Bellow: A Biography of the Imagination* (New York: St. Martin's, 1991), 7.

3. Abraham Bellow suffered a string of business failures, including a risky period of bootlegging. During one cross-border run with alcohol, Abraham's truck was hijacked, and he was beaten badly. This particular reason for leaving Montreal for Chicago is omitted from Sol's essay for obvious reasons.

SOURCES AND SELECTED BIBLIOGRAPHY

Zachary Leader's two-volume biography, *The Life of Saul Bellow* (2015 and 2018), is indispensable for Bellow studies. David Mikics's *Bellow's People* (2015) was also especially valuable and a joy to read. A long telephone interview (November 14, 2021) with Janis Freedman Bellow was fruitful. A substantial email correspondence, from January 4 through February 24, 2023, with Daniel Bellow was also useful.

WORKS BY SAUL BELLOW

Novels and Longer Fiction

Dangling Man. New York: Vanguard, 1944.
The Victim. New York: Vanguard, 1947.
The Adventures of Augie March. New York: Viking, 1953.
Seize the Day. New York: Viking, 1956.
Henderson the Rain King. New York: Viking, 1959.
Herzog. New York: Viking, 1964.
Mr. Sammler's Planet. New York: Viking, 1970.
Humboldt's Gift. New York: Viking, 1975.
The Dean's December. New York: Harper and Row, 1982.
More Die of Heartbreak. New York: William and Morrow, 1987.
The Bellarosa Connection. New York: Penguin, 1989.
A Theft. New York: Penguin, 1989.
The Actual. New York: Viking, 1997.
Ravelstein. New York: Viking, 2000.

Story Collections

Mosby's Memoirs and Other Stories. New York: Viking, 1968.

Him with His Foot in His Mouth and Other Stories. New York: Harper and Row, 1984.

Something to Remember Me By. New York: Viking, 1991.

Saul Bellow: Collected Stories. With an introduction by James Wood and a preface by Janis Freedman Bellow. New York: Viking, 2001.

Nonfiction

Great Jewish Short Stories. Edited and introduced by Saul Bellow. New York: Dell, 1963.

To Jerusalem and Back: A Personal Account. New York: Viking, 1976.

It All Adds Up: From the Dim Past to an Uncertain Future. New York: Viking, 1994.

Saul Bellow: Letters. Edited by Benjamin Taylor. New York: Viking, 2010.

"A Jewish Writer in America." *New York Review of Books*, October 27, 2011.

"A Jewish Writer in America—II." *New York Review of Books*, November 10, 2011.

There Is Simply Too Much to Think About: Collected Nonfiction. Edited by Benjamin Taylor. New York: Viking, 2015.

INTERVIEWS AND CONVERSATIONS

Bellow, Saul. "I Believe in God but I Don't Bug Him." In Monda, *Do You Believe?*

———. *Settling My Accounts before I Go Away: A Words and Images Interview by Norman Manea*. Rhinebeck, NY: Sheep Meadow Press, 1999.

Cronin, Gloria L., and Ben Siegel, eds. *Conversations with Saul Bellow*. Jackson: University Press of Mississippi, 1994.

Harper, Gordon Lloyd. "Saul Bellow: The Art of Fiction." In *The Paris Review Interviews*, vol. 1, with an introduction by Philip Gourevich, 86–110. New York: Picador, 2006. Originally published in *Paris Review*, 1966, 36.

"Literature and Culture: An Interview with Saul Bellow." *Salmagundi*, spring 1975, 6–23.

Monda, Antonio. *Do You Believe? Conversations on God and Religion*. Translated by Ann Goldstein. New York: Vintage Books, 2007.

SECONDARY MATERIAL

Articles

There are hundreds of scholarly articles about Bellow in the *Saul Bellow Journal*, which ran from 1982 to 2013. They are of uneven quality. The best of them, along with other journal articles about Bellow, have been published in edited collections.

The Cambridge Companion to Saul Bellow. Edited by Victoria Aarons. Cambridge: Cambridge University Press, 2017.

The Critical Response to Saul Bellow. Edited by Gerhard Bach. Westport, CT: Greenwood, 1995.

New Essays on Seize the Day. Edited by Michael Kramer. Cambridge: Cambridge University Press, 1998.

A Political Companion to Saul Bellow. Edited by Gloria L. Cronin and Lee Trepanier. Lexington: University Press of Kentucky, 2013.

Saul Bellow. Edited by Harold Bloom. New York: Chelsea House, 1986.

Saul Bellow: A Collection of Critical Essays. Edited by Earl Rovit. Englewood Cliffs, NJ: Prentice-Hall, 1975.

Saul Bellow: A Mosaic. Edited by L. H. Goldman, Gloria L. Cronin, and Ada Aharoni. New York: Peter Lang, 1992.

Books

Atlas, James. *Bellow: A Biography*. New York: Random House, 2000.

———. *Delmore Schwartz: The Life of an American Poet*. New York: Farrar, Straus and Giroux, 1977.

———. *The Shadow in the Garden*. New York: Vintage Books, 2018.

Bellow, Greg. *Saul Bellow's Heart: A Son's Memoir*. New York: Bloomsbury, 2013.

Bloom, Allan. *The Closing of the American Mind*. With a preface by Saul Bellow. New York: Simon and Schuster, 1987.

Clayton, John. *In Defense of Man*. 2nd ed. Bloomington: Indiana University Press, 1979.

Cook, Richard. *Alfred Kazin: A Biography*. New Haven, CT: Yale University Press, 2007.

———. *Alfred Kazin's Journals*. New Haven, CT: Yale University Press, 2012.

Cooper, Alan. *Philip Roth and the Jews*. New York: SUNY Press, 1996.

Fein, Helen. *Accounting for Genocide*. New York: Free Press, 1979.

Hand, Sean, and Steven T. Katz, eds. *Post-Holocaust France and the Jews.* New York: New York University Press, 2015.

Howe, Irving. *A Margin of Hope: An Intellectual Autobiography.* New York: Harcourt Brace Jovanovich, 1982.

———. *A World More Attractive.* New York: Horizon, 1963.

———. *World of Our Fathers: The Journey of the East European Jews to America and the World They Found and Made.* New York: Harcourt Brace Jovanovich, 1976.

Kazin, Alfred. *The Bright Book of Life: American Novelists and Storytellers from Hemingway to Mailer.* Boston: Little, Brown, 1973.

———. *New York Jew.* New York: Knopf, 1978.

———. *On Native Grounds: An Interpretation of Modern American Prose Literature.* With a new preface. New York: Harcourt Brace Jovanovich, 1982.

Langer, Elinor. *Josephine Herbst: The Story She Could Never Tell.* Boston: Little, Brown, 1984.

Leader, Zachary. *The Life of Saul Bellow: To Fame and Fortune, 1915–1964.* New York: Alfred A. Knopf, 2015.

———. *The Life of Saul Bellow: Love and Strife, 1965–2005.* New York: Alfred A. Knopf, 2018.

McCadden, Joseph F. *The Flight from Women in the Fiction of Saul Bellow.* Washington, DC: University Press of America, 1981.

Mendelsohn, Edward. *Moral Agents: Eight Twentieth Century American Writers.* New York: New York Review of Books, 2005.

Middlebrook, Diane Wood. *Anne Sexton: A Biography.* New York: Vintage, 1992.

Mikics, David. *Bellow's People: How Saul Bellow Made Life into Art.* New York: W. W. Norton, 2016.

Miller, Ruth. *Saul Bellow: A Biography of the Imagination.* New York: St. Martin's, 1991.

Opdahl, Keith Michael. *The Novels of Saul Bellow: An Introduction.* University Park: Pennsylvania State University Press, 1967.

Phillips, William. *A Partisan View: Five Decades of the Literary Life.* New York: Stein and Day, 1981.

Pinsker, Sandford. *Jewish American Fiction, 1917–1987.* New York: Twayne, 1992.

Rosenberg, Bernard, ed. *Creators and Disturbers: Reminiscences by Jewish Intellectuals of New York.* New York: Columbia University Press, 1982.

Rosenfeld, Isaac. *An Age of Enormity: Life and Writing in the Forties and Fifties*. Edited and introduced by Theodore Solotaroff. With a foreword by Saul Bellow. New York: World, 1962.

———. *Passage from Home*. With an introduction by Marc Shechner. Princeton, NJ: Markus Wiener, 2009.

———. *Preserving the Hunger*. Edited and introduced by Mark Shechner. Detroit: Wayne State University Press, 1988.

Roth, Philip. *Reading Myself and Others*. New York: Penguin, 1985.

Rubenstein, Joshua. *Trotsky: A Revolutionary's Life*. New Haven, CT: Yale University Press, 2011.

Sartre, Jean Paul. *Anti-Semite and Jew*. Translated by George J. Becker. New York: Schocken Books, 1965.

Schwartz, Delmore. *In Dreams Begin Responsibilities and Other Stories*. Edited by James Atlas. New York: New Directions Books, 1978.

Sorin, Gerald. *Irving Howe: A Life of Passionate Dissent*. New York: New York University Press, 2002.

Staples, Brent. *Parallel Time: Growing Up in Black and White*. New York: Pantheon Books, 1994.

Teller, Judd L. *Strangers and Natives: The Evolution of the American Jew from 1921 to the Present*. New York: Delacorte, 1968.

Wasserman, Harriet. *Handsome Is: Adventures with Saul Bellow*. New York: Fromm International, 1997.

Yerushalmi, Yosef Hayim. *Freud's Moses: Judaism Terminable and Interminable*. New Haven, CT: Yale University Press, 1993.

Zipperstein, Steven. *Rosenfeld's Lives: Fame, Oblivion, and the Furies of Writing*. New Haven, CT: Yale University Press, 2009.

INDEX

GERALD SORIN is Distinguished Professor of American and Jewish Studies at the State University of New York at New Paltz. He is author of *Irving Howe: A Life of Passionate Dissent* (winner of the National Jewish Book Award in History, 2002) and *Howard Fast: Life and Literature in the Left Lane* (winner of the National Jewish Book Award in Biography, 2013).

For Indiana University Press

Brian Carroll, Rights Manager
Gary Dunham, Acquisitions Editor and Director
Anna Francis, Assistant Acquisitions Editor
Brenna Hosman, Production Coordinator
Katie Huggins, Production Manager
David Miller, Lead Project Manager/Editor
Dan Pyle, Online Publishing Manager
Stephen Williams, Marketing and Publicity Manager
Jennifer Witzke, Senior Artist and Book Designer